"Old Hoodoo"
The Battleship Texas
America's First Battleship
1895-1911

Mark D. Cowan & Alan K. Sumrall

Copyright © 2011 Mark D. Cowan & Alan K. Sumrall

LCCN: 2011915229

All rights reserved.

ISBN-10: 1466248947
ISBN-13: 978-1466248946

FOREWORD

One of the more overlooked eras in U.S. naval history is the latter half of the 19th century. Because of the Barbary Wars, War of 1812, and Civil War, historians have written much on the earlier half of the century due to the personalities that emerged (Decatur, Bainbridge, Oliver T and Matthew Perry, Dahlgren, Farragut, Porter, and so on) as well as the quality and technology used in our ships. With the Bicentennial of the War of 1812 and the Sesquicentennial of the Civil War, it is only natural that the earlier part of the 19th century will get even more attention.

Fortunately, there are some historians doing excellent work on period following the American Civil War. At a recent McMullen Naval History Symposium at the Naval Academy, Captain Henry J. Hendrix gave an outstanding presentation about the industrial base during this period, arguing that Navy support helped push this nation into the industrial age which contributed to the United States becoming a world power.

The dawn of the new steel navy began with the commissioning of the ABCD ships (protected cruisers *Atlanta*, *Boston*, *Chicago* and dispatch ship *Dolphin*) in the mid-1880s. Fully rigged with sail, these warships marked a first step in a modernization process that still had the United States not only lagging the navies of Europe, but also many of the navies of South America. As part of the protected cruiser building program, the Navy would eventually turn to Union Shipbuilding in San Francisco to build the *Olympia*. This ship remains as the sole example of the Navy's entry into the industrial revolution and the age of steel.

Recognizing the need to build capital ships, the United States purchased a design from abroad and used a domestic design to construct *Texas* and *Maine*. As discussed in the following narrative, these two warships were not sisters. Because of *Maine's* eventual fate in Havana (Remember the *Maine*!), she would become the more famous of the two ships.

Indeed, despite the *Texas* being placed in service as America's first battleship, very little is written about her. A search of the extensive Navy Department book catalog reveals that the books written on *Texas* are about that OTHER ship that resides as a memorial ship at San Jacinto. Commissioned before World War I and served this nation with distinction through the Second World War THAT ship not only claimed more historical interest, but it also claimed the name of the first battleship, as the long obsolete USS *Texas* finished her days in the Navy as USS *San Marcos* to be used as a target ship in the Chesapeake Bay.

This is not to say that the acclaim given to BB 35 is not well-deserved. However, in stripping the name and memory of the first *Texas*, the Navy did a disservice to history. Fortunately, Mark D. Cowen and Al Sumrall have stepped up to compile an impressive amount of material about the building and service of America's first battleship. Rich with images, drawings, and original documents, the following narrative fills a void in naval history. Cowan and Sumrall place the construction of this ship within the context of the era. Noting the ship was already obsolete when she was commissioned, Cowan and Sumrall stress how the ship laid a path for improving the national industrial base. They also provide a perspective of the Spanish-American War from the deck plates of this pioneering warship. "Old Hoodoo" The Battleship *Texas*, will be a "go-to" resource for future historians of this era.

While the only way to visit this ship today is to don a diving suit and swim around her rusting remains in the Chesapeake, it is still possible to visit a ship of this vintage – for now! Thus I join with the authors in urging readers to support the National Trust for Historic Preservation and other efforts to save the USS *Olympia*. By preserving this ship, we help keep alive an era where the *Texas* reigned supreme.

- David F. Winkler, Ph. D.
Naval Historical Foundation

Cover Illustrations: The *Texas* in her "war paint", from a period hand-tinted photograph.

Flags shown indicate (from l. to r.):

"250" (The Enemy is coming out) in contemporary U.S. Navy signal flag code. This was the signal hoisted by all U.S. warships when the Spanish squadron appeared at the mouth of Santiago Bay on July 3, 1898.

"RNQTHGBQKJ" (Remember the *Maine*) in contemporary international maritime code. RNQ was a standard abbreviation for "remember". TH was "the", as there were no vowels in the code at that time. G indicated that the following name was a warship, rather than the name of a state. BQKJ were the USS *Maine's* call letters. This signal was to be flown by U.S. warships when Spanish vessels were in sight.

"GRLC" (USS *Texas*) in contemporary international maritime code.

The striped pennant with four stars shown on the cover as well as on the title page was flown by vessels that had seen service in the Spanish-American War.

CONTENTS

	Acknowledgments	
1	Precedents	1
2	The Competition	17
3	Building the Battleship	27
4	Machinery & Controls	50
5	Main Battery	76
6	Secondary Battery	93
7	Equipment & Small Arms	114
8	USS Texas & USS Maine	129
9	Troublesome Torpedo Boats	140
10	Early Service	147
11	"Old Hoodoo" in the New Navy	155
12	Preparing for War	168
13	The Spanish Fleet	181
14	Seek the Enemy	206
15	Invasion	233
16	Battle of Santiago	251
17	After the Battle	272
18	Victorious Return	297
19	Later Career	312
20	A Fitting End	330
	Appendixes	346
	Bibliography	400
	About the Illustrations	405

ACKNOWLEDGMENTS

A number of people and organizations have lent their support or assistance in the creation of this book including: Gregg Biggs, Gordon Calhoun (Command Historian/Editor, Hampton Roads Naval Museum, Norfolk, VA.), Ana Clark, Germa Coenders, Ned Coleman, Carolina DeLaRosa, Dale Farmer, Elizabeth Howe, Doug Howser, Charles W. Johnson, Lee Johnson, Rebecca Livingston, Billy McCaskill, Patrick McSherry, Brian Marten, Charles Moore (USS *Texas* / BB35 historian), Rick Peuser, Julio Pillet, Trevor Plante, Dariush Rad, Cmdr. Juan Escrigas Rodriguez, William Shuey, David L. Smith, Shirley Snider, Carrie Sumrall, Phillip Vasquez, Matt Weeks, Dr. David Winkler, Biblioteca Nacional de España, Hampton Roads Naval Museum, Institute of Naval Architects, National Archives and Records Administration, New York Public Library, Portsmouth Naval Shipyard Museum, Yonge Library at the University of Florida, Texas Historical Commission, US Army, US Library of Congress, US Marine Corps, US Navy, US Naval Academy, and the Dept. of Naval Architecture & Marine Engineering at the University of Glasgow and Strathclyde.

The authors wish to convey a special word of thanks to Commander Juan Escrigas Rodriguez of the Spanish Navy who provided assistance and encouragement towards the creation of this book in memory of his great-grandfather Condestable de 2a Rosendo Escrigas Marco of the Spanish Navy's warship *Reina Mercedes*, who died in Santiago, Cuba on August 13, 1898 as result of wounds sustained in the defense of the Spanish trenches encircling the besieged city.
- Mark D. Cowan & Alan K. Sumrall

I would also acknowledge the tireless efforts of my parents Burnice and Sylvia Cowan as well as the guidance of a score of educators in helping to instill in me an appreciation of history which was fundamental to my taking up this project. I would especially like to thank my wife, Joy, for her unfailing support and encouragement without which I would not have been able to contribute to this book's creation and I am also indebted to the incessant efforts on the part of my sons, William and James, to motivate me to action.
– Mark D. Cowan

I dedicate my efforts in memory of my mother, Mattie L. Sumrall, an educator who taught me to appreciate the value of a good book.
- Alan K. Sumrall

1 PRECEDENTS

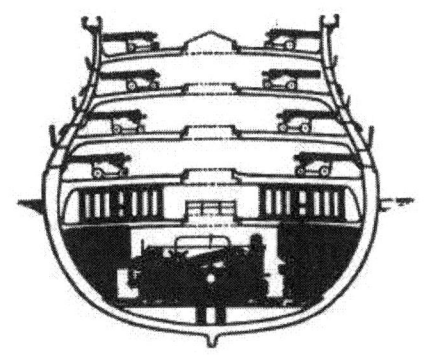

Section of Ship-of-the-Line, converted (1850) into Screw Steamer.

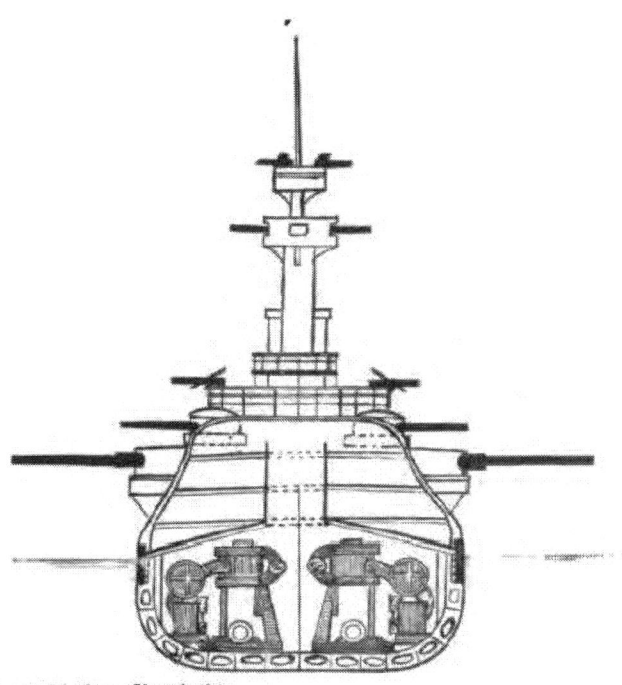

Section of Modern Battleship

The USS *Texas* was designed in an era when navies around the world were dominated by cycles of advancement and retrenchment. Naval powers and would-be upstarts alike designed and built new classes of warships that sought to outdo previous vessels, giving the world a bewildering variety of warships. This period encompassed the end of the age of the sail and wood warship and the beginning of the age of steam and steel. It was in this environment that the design philosophy leading to the *Texas* matured.

The *Texas* was a curious product of both advanced thinking and retrenchment. Her foreign-born design was secured to help propel the US Navy from its post-Civil War technological malaise, towards an anticipated future as the dominant naval power in the Western Hemisphere. At the same time her British designer, working within a very strict US Congress-imposed design specification, created a ship which drew upon British precedent, not pressing the technological envelop except in the effort to fit the required features into an abnormally small displacement. The USS *Texas* refined previous naval developments without bringing anything appreciably new into the equation, yet her construction still tested the limits of American manufacturing, resulting in a much-delayed construction period and virtual obsolescence before she was even launched.

The conservative design did mean that she was built to proven principles though, and in a war that gave full play to her virtues, she found for herself an important niche in naval history. The following pages illustrate the design concepts that led to the USS *Texas*, a ship that marked a new beginning as the first battleship in the New Navy and a turning point in a fascinating era of US naval development.

The USS *Fulton* was the first steam powered vessel in the United States Navy, but saw only one day of active service before being made into a floating barracks at the Brooklyn Navy Yard. Designed by Robert Fulton as the *Demologos*, this innovative vessel was constructed in New York City during the War of 1812 to aid in the defense of the harbor against vastly superior numbers of conventional British warships.

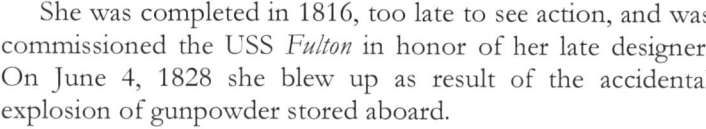

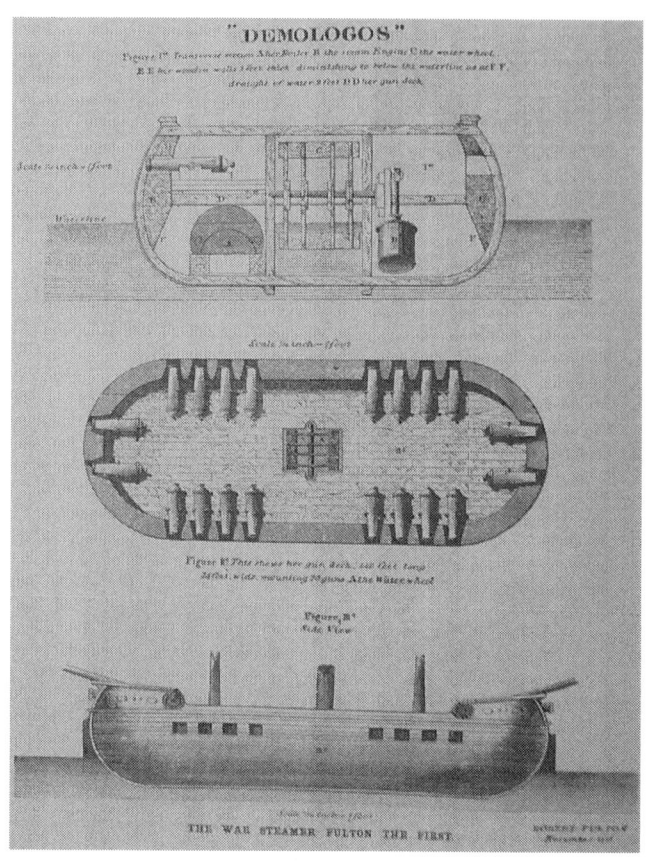

She was completed in 1816, too late to see action, and was commissioned the USS *Fulton* in honor of her late designer. On June 4, 1828 she blew up as result of the accidental explosion of gunpowder stored aboard.

In 1850s the French Navy and British Navy developed ironclad floating batteries. French examples, including the Lave (1855), saw service that year against Russian fortifications in the Crimean War and again in 1859 against Italy in the Adriatic. These vessels combined steam and armor, but were much too ponderous to participate in more conventional naval engagements.

Inspired by the ironclad floating batteries successfully utilized during the Crimean War, the French armored warship *La Gloire* (right), launched in 1859, effectively laid down the gauntlet to cross-channel rival Great Britain. *La Gloire* was a first attempt at an ocean going steam-powered armored warship, having iron plate armor affixed to a wooden hull.

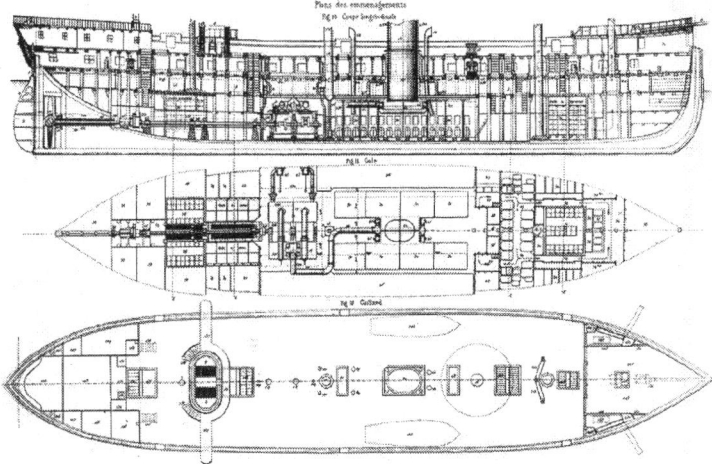

Drawing on the industrial might of her world-leading shipbuilding industry, the British responded with the *HMS Warrior* of 1860 (left), an outstanding synthesis of modern technological design and construction possessing an iron framed hull and mounting 4.5 inch thick iron plate armor affixed to a shock-absorbing 18 inch thick teak backing.

Entering service before the French could complete *La Gloire*, France's attempt to leapfrog British naval power through the introduction of new technology was effectively circumvented.

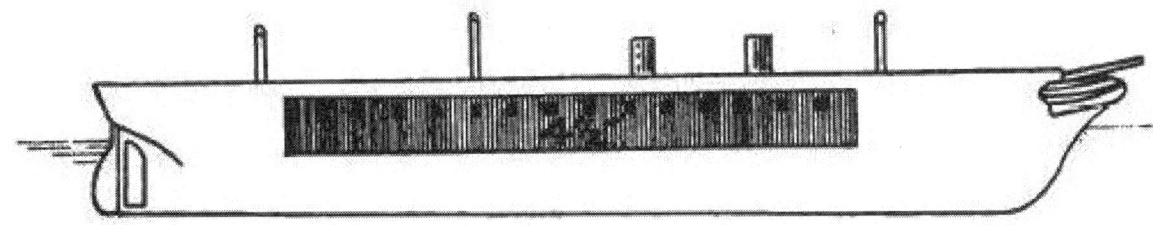

H. M. S. Warrior, 1860

Throughout the dynamically evolving period of the Victorian Navy, the British would continue to remain at the forefront of "battleship" design, balancing the introduction of new designs and materials against the risk these technological revelations posed of rendering her powerful existing navy obsolete.

During the American Civil War Swedish engineer John Ericsson designed the armored USS *Monitor*, a 987-ton gunboat that introduced the gun turret and was the forerunner of a class of warships known around the world as "Monitors." The *Monitor* was constructed in response to reports that the Confederate Navy was building a fleet of ironclad warships intended to break the Union's blockade by technologically leapfrogging the numerically superior US Navy.

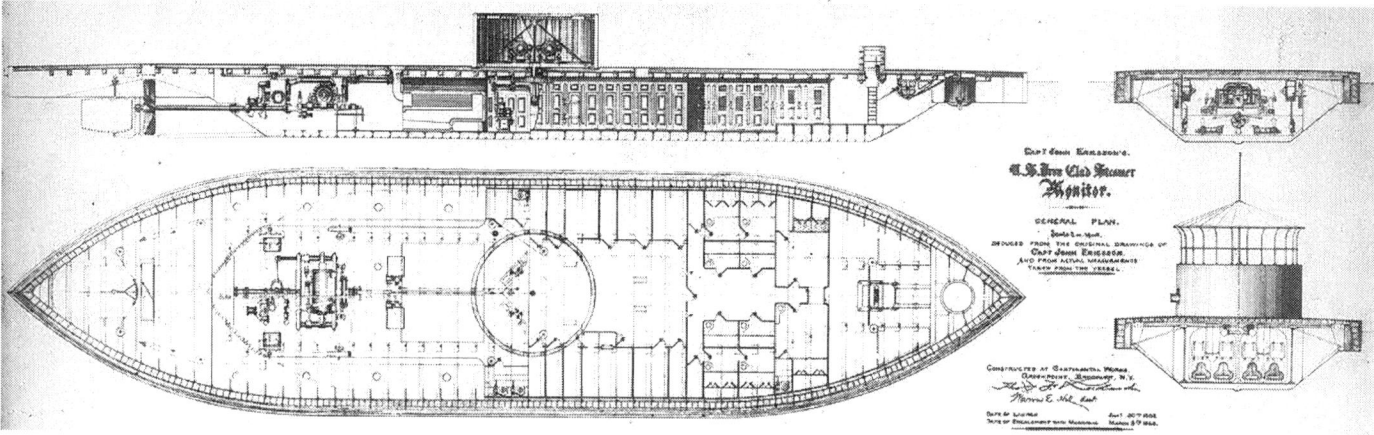

Monitor was constructed in great haste in New York. She was commissioned on February 25, 1862 and dispatched to Hampton Roads, Virginia for a showdown with the Confederate ironclad, the *CSS Virginia*. The *Virginia* made her appearance in dramatic fashion on March 8, 1862, sinking two US Navy ships and scattering the rest of the blockading squadron. *Monitor* arrived late on the scene and saw battle with the *Virginia* the next day. The resulting engagement, the first between armored steamships, ended in a draw. The *Monitor* however turned the naval balance of power in the region back in favor of the US Navy and preserved the Federal blockade.

After supporting the Union Army's abortive Peninsular Campaign, the *Monitor* moved south only to reveal a critical lack of seaworthiness that would haunt early turreted warships. On December 31, 1862 she foundered in a storm off Cape Hatteras.

THE WRECK OF THE IRON-CLAD "MONITOR."

The USS *New Ironsides*, launched on May 10, 1862, was an ironclad carrying masts and sailing rig for use on long passages but powered by steam in action. The vessel, though cutting edge technology, retained the traditional broadside arrangement of her armament. Her heavy armor made her effective in shore bombardment duties and allowed her to survive an attack by the spar torpedo-armed *CSS David* on October 5, 1863. Laid up at the end of hostilities, she burned at her moorings at League Island on December 16, 1866.

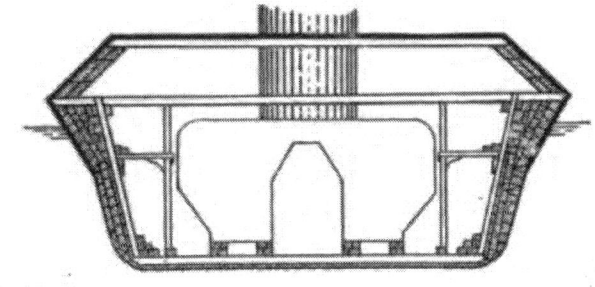

Midship Section

The USS *Dunderberg* was laid down in 1862 as a sea-going ironclad intended to counter the potential threat of a Confederate-British naval alliance. Designed along the lines of the *CSS Virginia* this vessel had a wooden hull over 370 feet in length with iron armor and featured both sail and steam power. Wood backing behind the iron armor served to absorb the shock of shells striking the armored plates. This practice was continued in many armored ships, including the *Texas*, well into the 20th century.

Completed too late to see service in the Civil War, she was sold to France in 1867, becoming the *Rochambeau*.

Section through Battery

U. S. S. DUNDERBERG, 1862

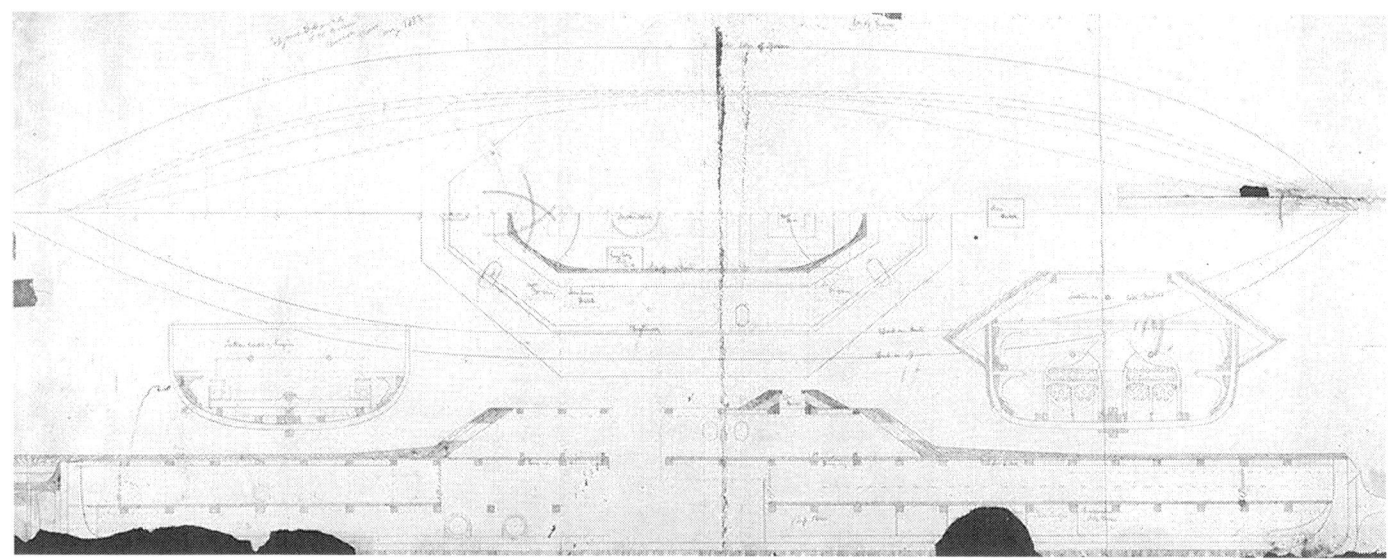

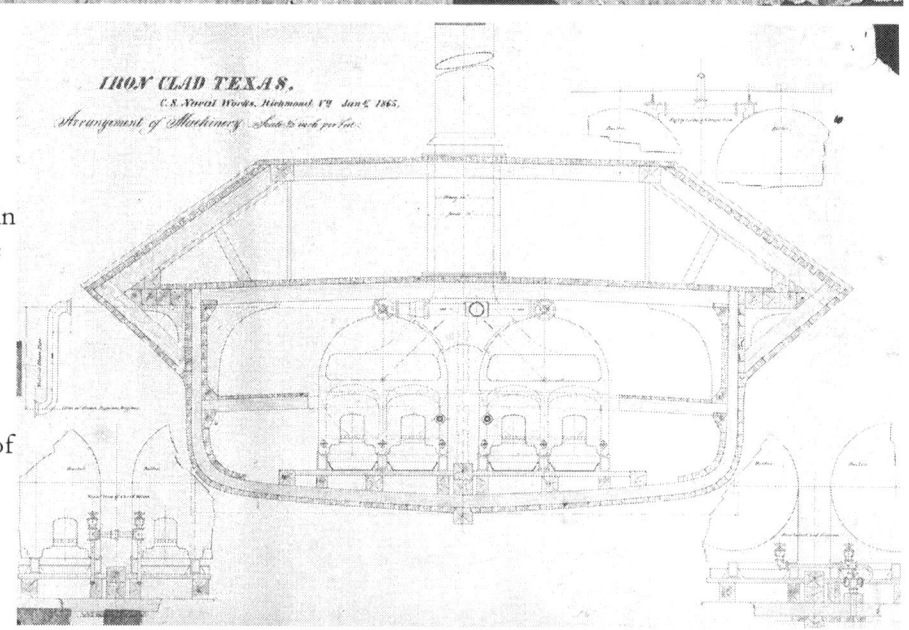

Civil War era plans for the Confederate "ironclad" *CSS Texas*. This 217 foot armored warship was launched in Richmond, Virginia in January 1865. She was captured by Federal forces while fitting out and taken by the US Navy to the Norfolk Navy Yard to be completed.

Still incomplete when the war drew to a close, the vessel was sold in October 1867. The *CSS Texas* marked the zenith of Southern-built armored warships.

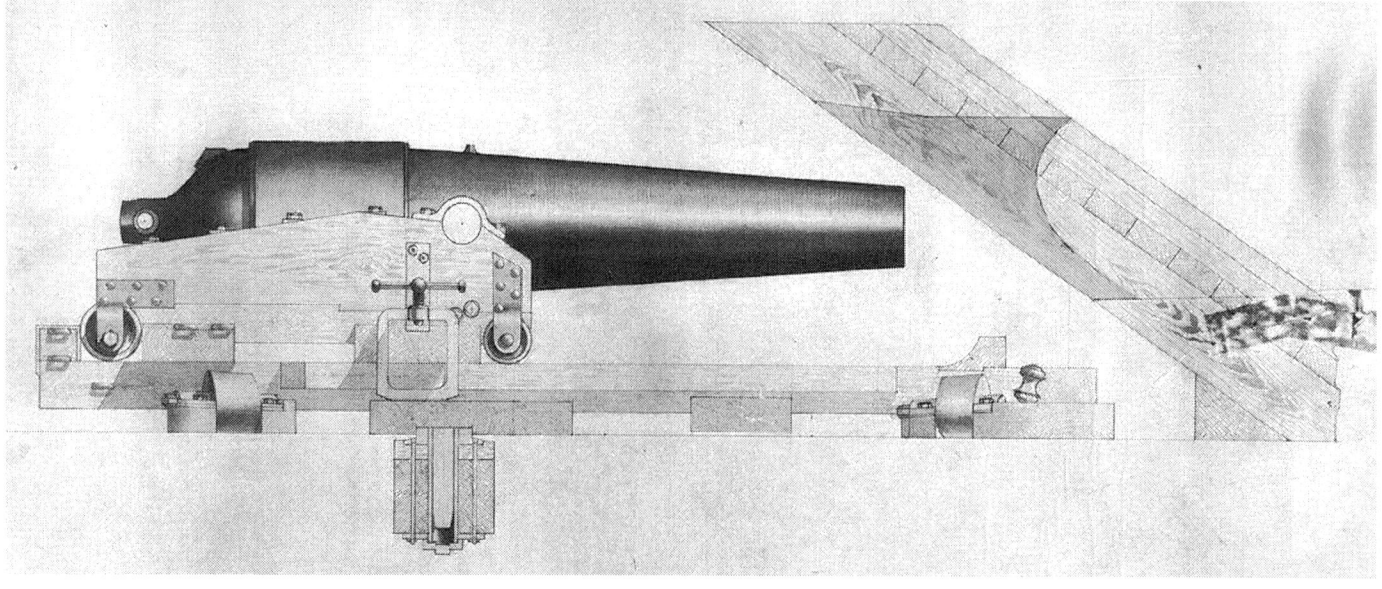

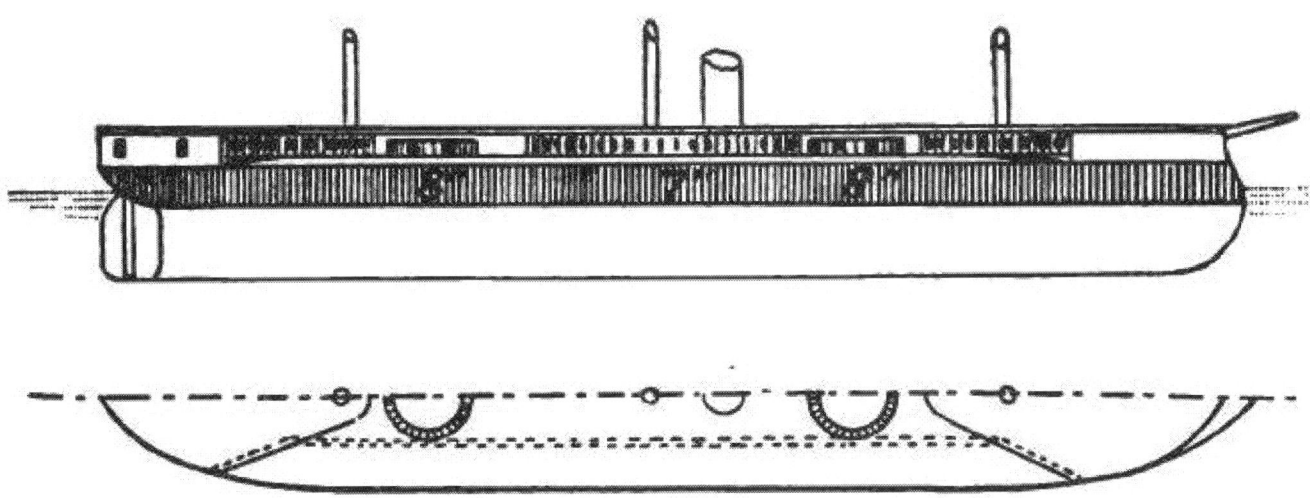

The British warship *HMS Captain*, completed as result of intense political pressure and without direct Admiralty oversight in 1870, was intended to be a "pure" embodiment of innovative British Captain Cowper Phipps Coles' concept for the ideal ocean-going turret ship. The inefficient and unreliable nature of steam propulsion at the time required the retention of a full sailing rig, the influence of which, not properly appreciated by Coles and the ship's builders, resulted in a vessel of dangerously low stability.

Before the year was out the *HMS Captain* capsized and sank in a sudden gale while under sail, confirming the dire predictions of the Admiralty's Chief Constructor Edward Reed and his mathematically-minded subordinates the talented young constructors William White (himself a future Chief Constructor of the Admiralty) and William John (the future designer of the USS *Texas*.)

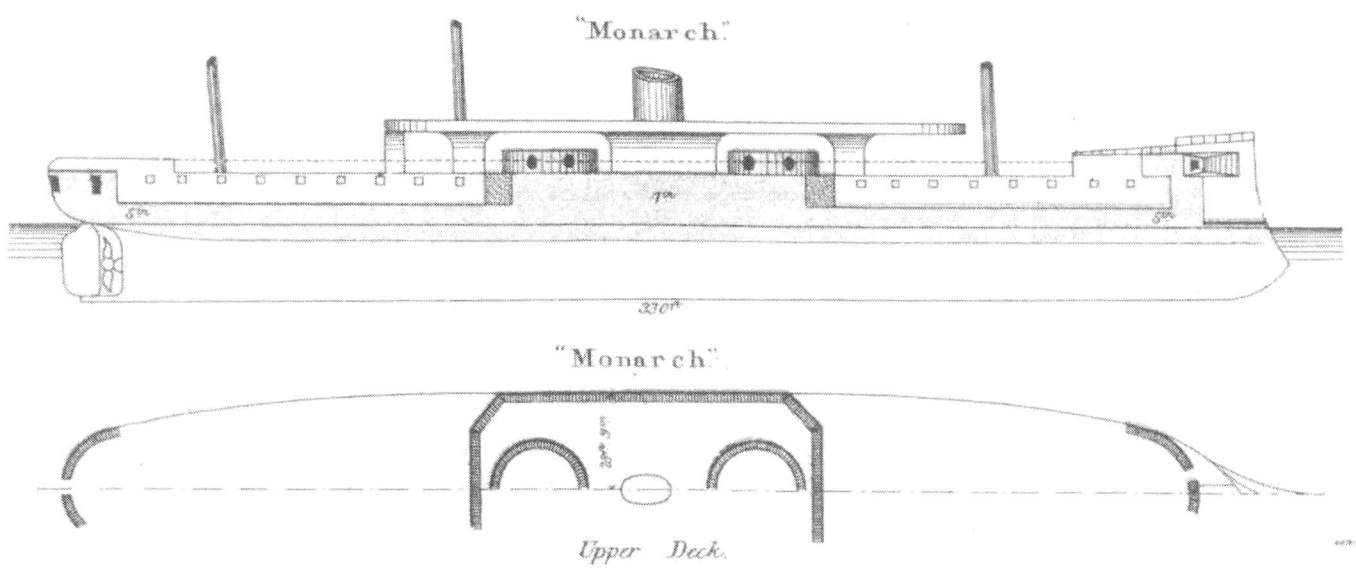

The *HMS Monarch* (1869), designed by Admiralty Chief Constructor Edward Reed and a direct competitor to the *HMS Captain*, introduced the turret to ocean-going warships and represented a scientific approach to design. While featuring armored turrets similar to Capt. Coles' *HMS Captain*, the *Monarch* was mathematically designed by Reed and his expert staff and, as result, had many times the resistance to capsize when compared to the Captain.

The *Monarch* successfully rode out the same gale that claimed the *Captain*. Chief Constructor Reed, however resigned his post at the Admiralty in the wake of the disaster.

The *Monarch* would be the apogee of Reed's designs, the echoes of which would still be apparent in the plans for a new US battleship he later submitted to the US Navy.

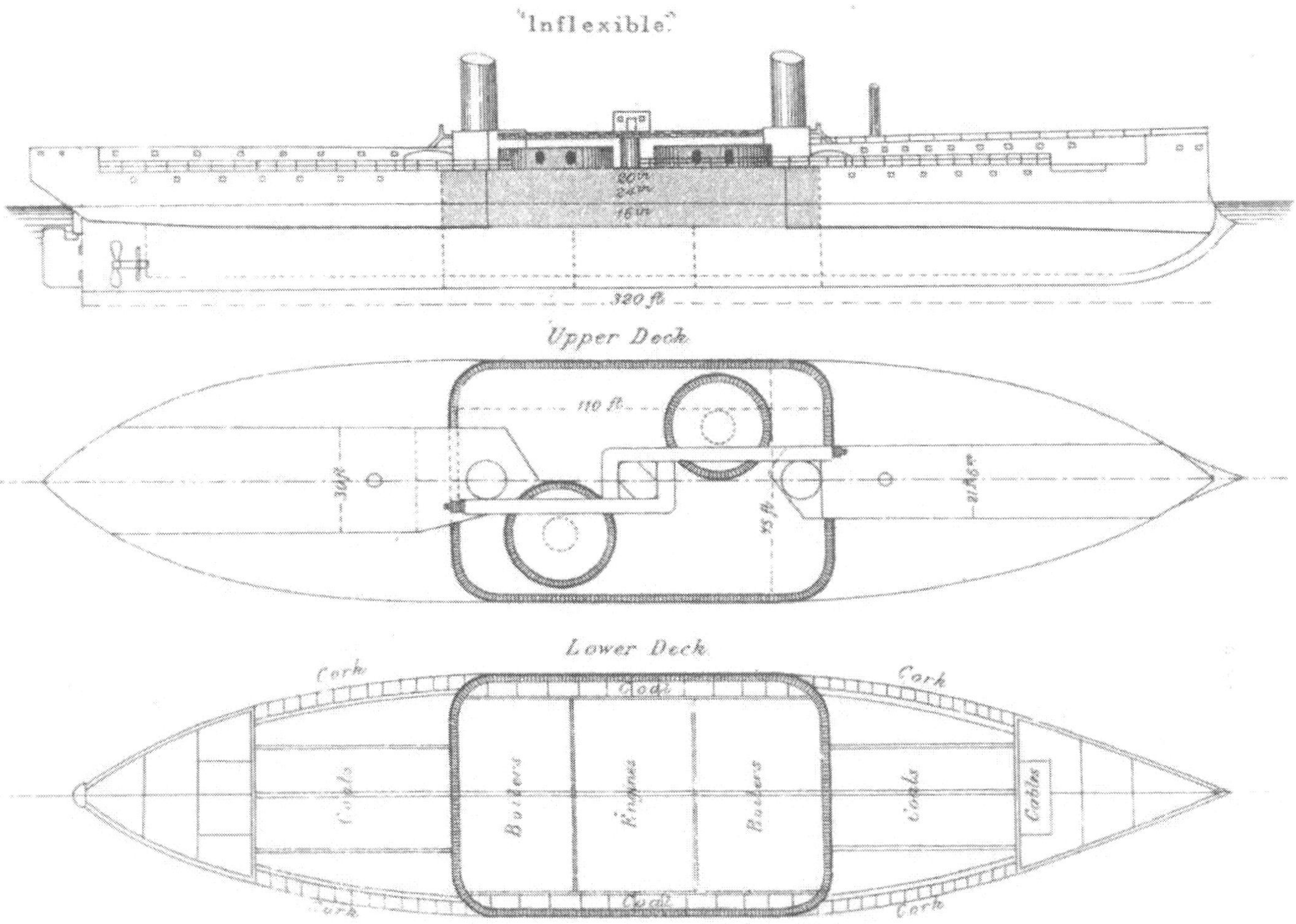

The *HMS Inflexible* of 1876 retained the sail and steam mixed propulsion of earlier battleships. In her armor and armament, however, she was innovative. The *Inflexible* featured a heavily-armored central citadel incorporating the thickest armor ever installed on a British warship. Her continued buoyancy in battle was assured through the use of a waterline armored deck running the length of the ship, protecting her vital machinery. The remainder of the vessel's upper works were considered to be largely expendable in battle. Her turrets were placed offset "en echelon" on the theory that this allowed both turrets to fire ahead, astern as well as to either beam

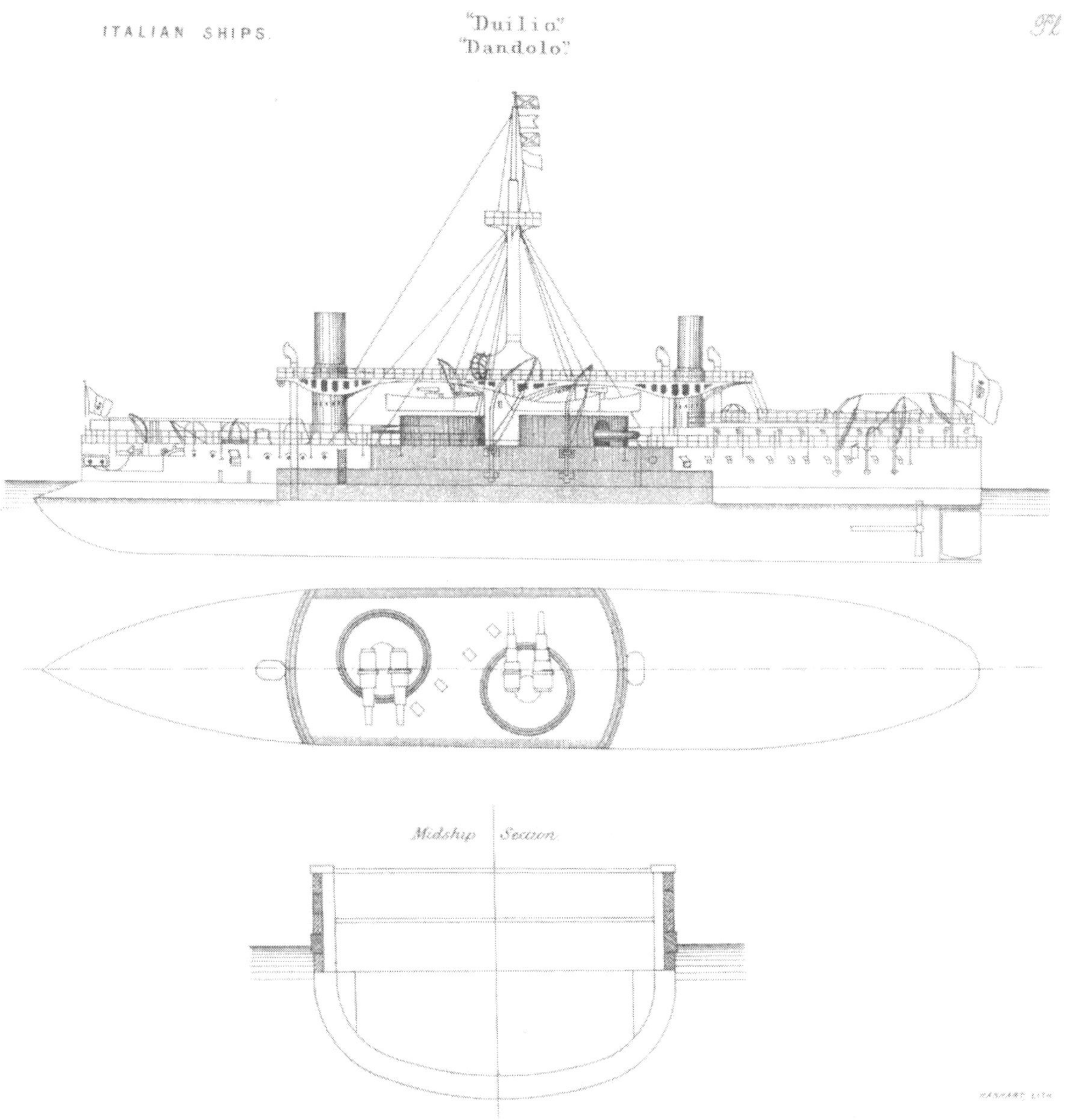

ITALIAN SHIPS.   "Duilio."
               "Dandolo."

Midship Section

The Italian vessels *RN Caio Dandulo* and *RN Duilio*, completed in 1880, were widely recognized in their day as the most powerful warships afloat. Their design derived from a philosophy centered upon the primacy of the big gun. They were therefore equipped with the largest available: four of Armstrongs' 450mm rifled muzzle loaders mounted in two turrets placed en echelon.

This massive armament came at the cost of armor and cruising range. The armor was limited to an amidships belt at the waterline and an armored citadel enclosing the base of the turrets. Extensive water-tight compartmentalization was intended to mitigate damage to the lightly protected remainder of the ship. Sailing rig was vestigial and coal supplies small.

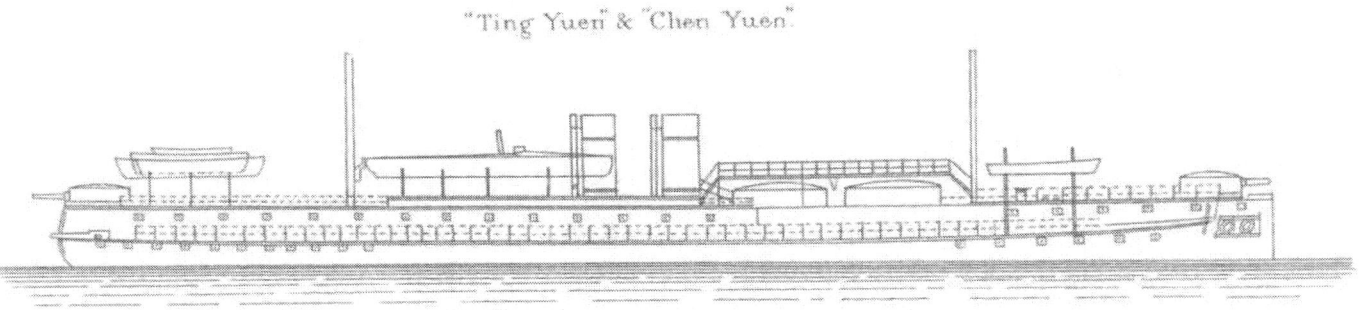
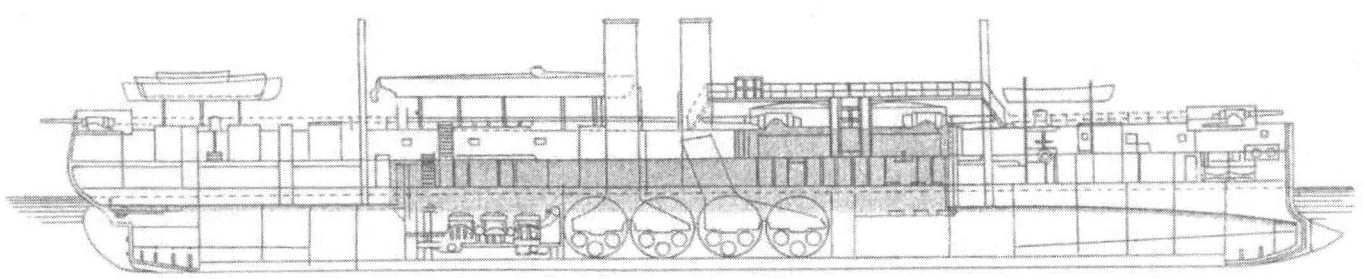

The battleships *Ting Yuen* and *Chen Yuen* were constructed in Germany for the Chinese Empire, entering service in 1883 and 1884 respectively. The 12" guns of these vessels were located in barbette, armored tubs depressed into the deck, rather than in true turrets. Light shields over the guns gave them the appearance of fully enclosed turrets. These barbettes were placed en echelon to maximize all-around fire. An armored citadel amidships protected the engineering spaces as well as the bases of the barbettes.

During the Sino-Japanese War, at the 1894 Battle of the Yalu, both ships survived the Japanese onslaught to continue the fight, even though the *Ting Yuen* had received hundreds of hits from Japanese shells. *Ting Yuen* later succumbed to a torpedo strike and was beached, a total wreck, while *Chen Yuen* survived the war to be surrendered to the victorious Japanese, who subsequently incorporated her into their own fleet.

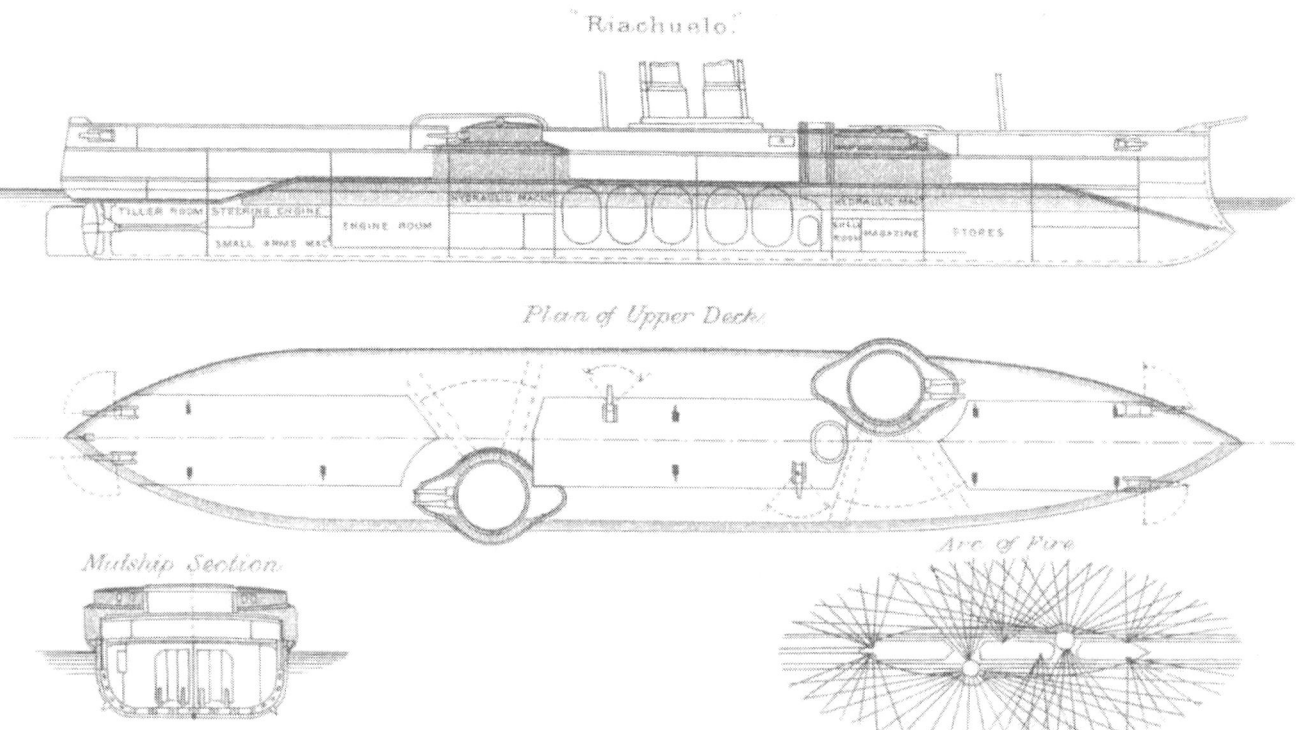

Recognizing Britain's position in the forefront of warship design, Brazil commissioned British shipbuilders to design and construct the *Riachuelo*, a combination sail and steam powered battleship, far eclipsing anything in the arsenal of the US Navy at the date of her commissioning in 1883. The *Riachuelo*, like the *HMS Inflexible*, utilized the en-echelon arrangement of turrets to maximize her theoretical weight of firepower from any angle.

Public awareness in the US gradually dawned that other nations in the Western Hemisphere were acquiring the might necessary to dominate not only US warships and commercial vessels on the high seas, but potentially American seaboard cities as well. The *Riachuelo* and her sister the *Aquidaba* (seen below) motivated the US Navy and Congress to institute new naval construction, resulting in the issue of a specification for the *Texas* and the *Maine*, ships whose designs significantly overmatched the *Riachuelo* and *Aquidaba* while maintaining a hull size consistent with the US strategy of coastal defense.

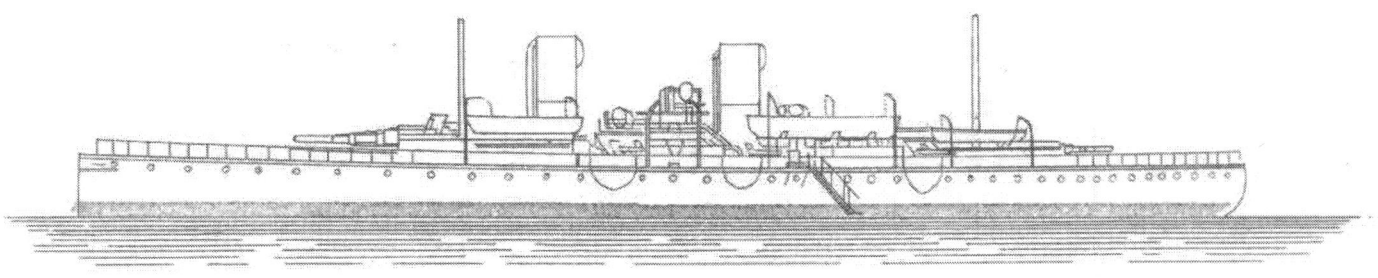

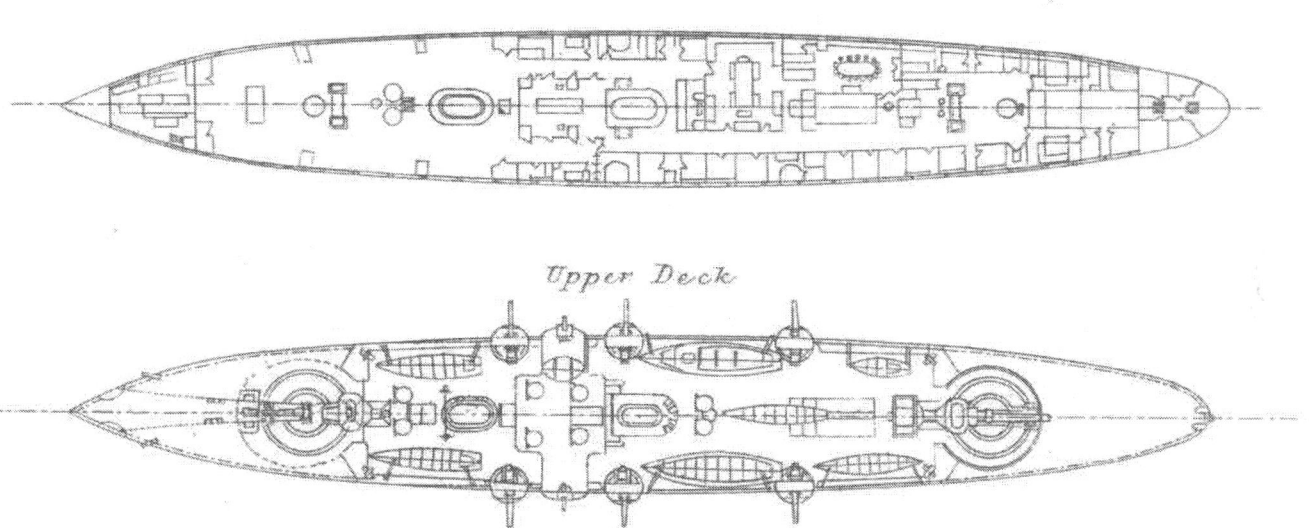

The Chilean *CHL Esmeralda* (1883), like the contemporary Brazilian battleship *Riachuelo*, was built in Britain. This vessel was notable as being the first realization of a design incorporating a complete protective deck together with protection for the ships' guns in barbette and good speed. This came to be known as the "protected cruiser" class of warship design.

The protective deck of the *Esmeralda* gave her a shield providing protection to the ship's vital engines and magazines from shells hitting her upper decks. American cruisers of the time could not face such a ship with confidence. The design of the *Texas* would incorporate this concept of armored protection as well, but added a strong main battery outmatching ships of the *Esmeralda*'s class.

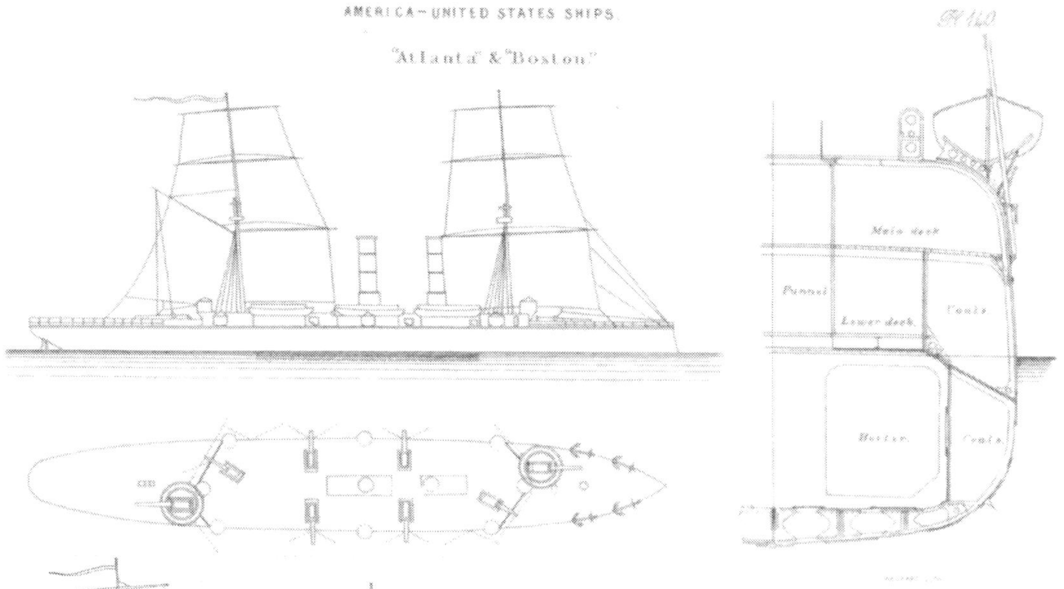

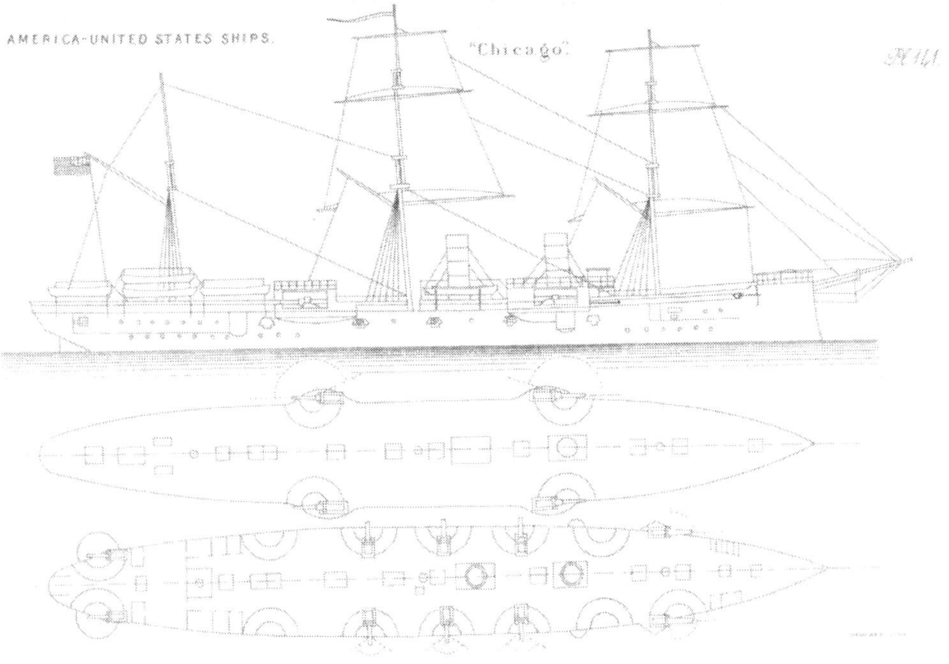

The "ABCD" ships USS *Atlanta*, *Boston*, *Charleston*, and *Dolphin*, were authorized and funded by Congress in 1883 as result of the increasingly apparent need to modernize the U.S. Navy after years of decline and neglect following the Civil War. These ships represented the birth of the "New Navy", equipped with steel hulls, steam propulsion (in these vessels augmented by sail), and mounting modern breach-loading guns they set the course subsequent vessels would follow.

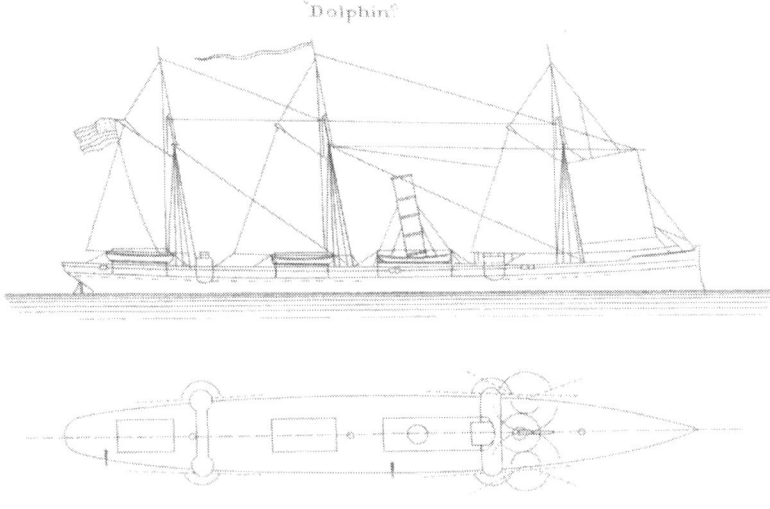

Technologically, they were conservative when compared to contemporary European warships, yet they served as test beds for the design and construction capabilities of the United States shipbuilding and steel industries.

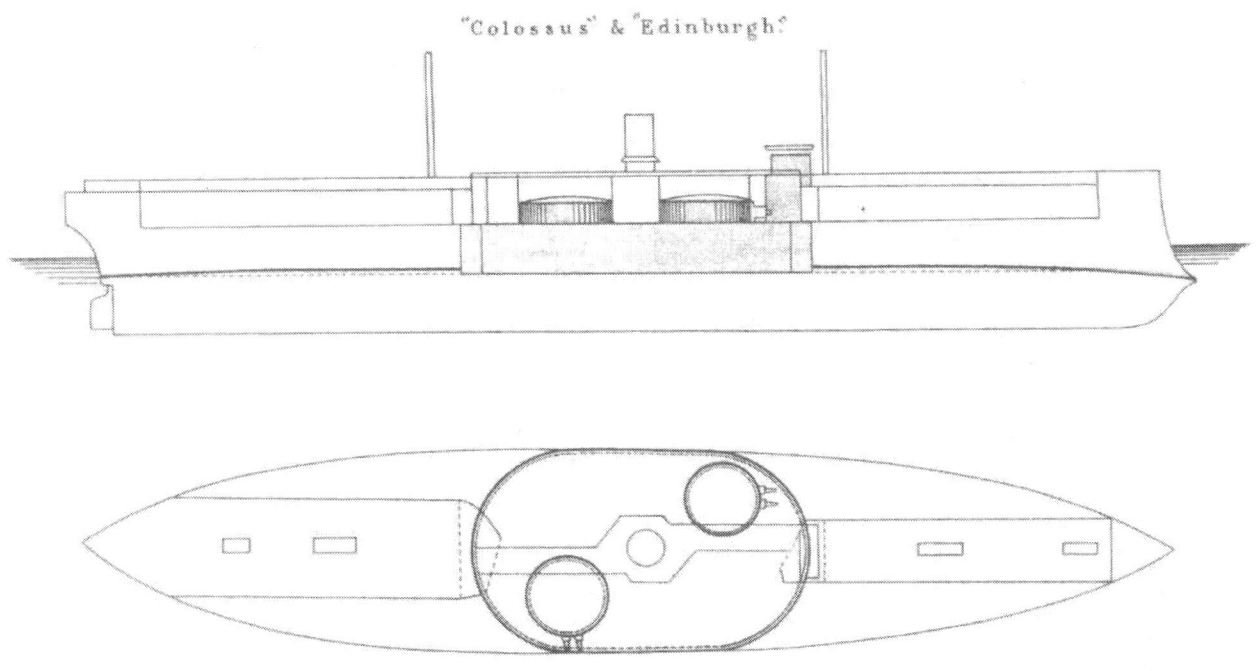

The *Colossus* class of British battleships, entering service in the mid-1880s, reintroduced the breech-loading gun to British capital ships. (Vessels constructed after the *HMS Warrior* of 1860 had reverted to muzzle-loading ordinance following difficulties experienced with the *Warrior's* 110 pounder breech-loading guns.) This class of vessels featured steam propulsion, steel hulls, and an en-echelon arrangement of turrets. Like many vessels so designed, cross deck firing of the main guns was found to be damaging to the ships decks and superstructures.

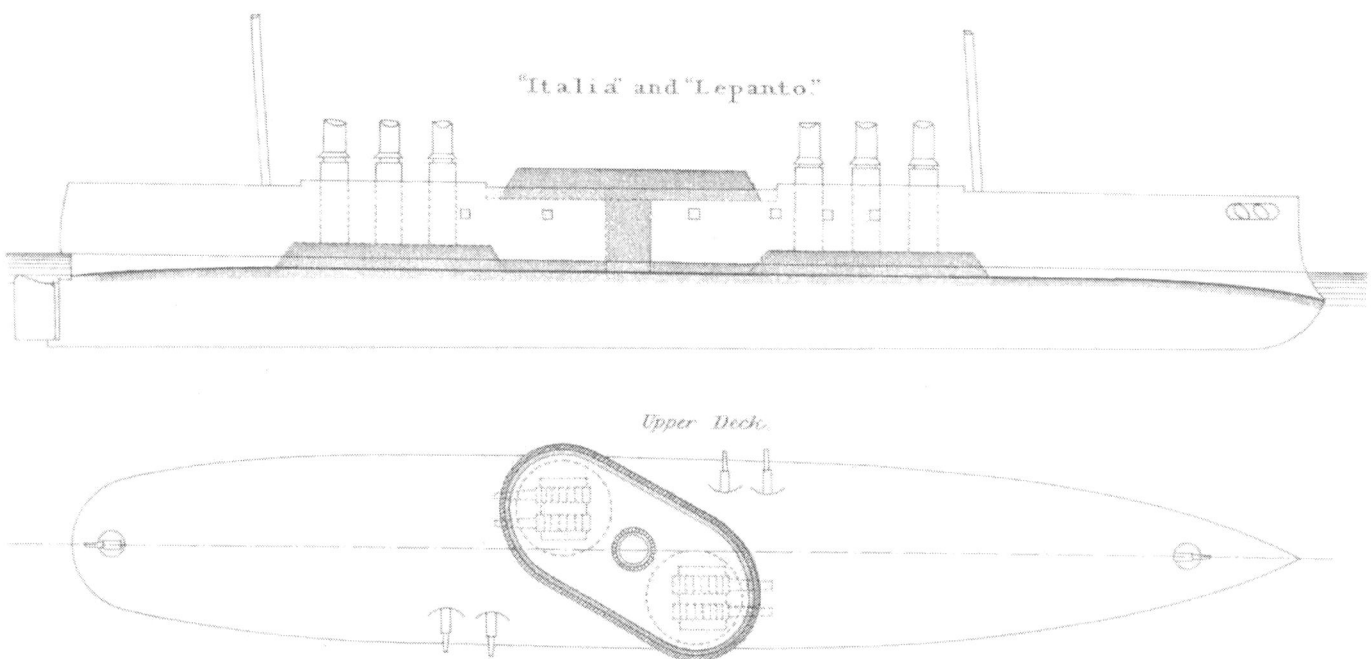

In the *RN Italia* and *RN Lepanto* the Italian Navy took a different approach to design, focusing on speed rather than armor. Forsaking almost all vertical armor, these warships, completed in the late 1880s, possessed armor relying primarily of an armored deck running from bow to stern but could claim a speed of almost 18 knots. These vessels are seen as the forerunners of the battle cruiser class of vessels developed in the 20th Century.

"LEPANTO".
ITALIAN BATTLE SHIP.

2 THE COMPETITION

June 9, 1886 Scientific American cover story described the design of what was to become the first battleship in the "New" US Navy. Of note in this early depiction of the *Texas* are the dual smoke stacks, the presence of two torpedo boats, and the continuous boat deck.

To develop its first battleship and armored cruiser designs, the US Navy solicited plans through a public competition open to anyone world-wide. This circular, reproduced from the Institute of Naval Architects' *Proceedings*, detailed the terms of the competition and the requirements for the warship's design, was authorized on August 21, 1886. The armored cruiser would become the USS *Maine* while the battleship would be the USS *Texas*. Based on their displacement of less than 10,000 tons, both vessels were later re-designated as second class battleships, a distinction necessitated by the dramatically larger battleships that were soon to follow.

CIRCULAR, EMBODYING THE CONDITIONS THAT MUST BE CONFORMED TO BY THOSE WHO SUBMIT DESIGNS TO THE UNITED STATES NAVY DEPARTMENT IN PURSUANCE OF THE FOLLOWING ADVERTISEMENT.

"*Notice to Naval Architects and others concerning Designs of Steel Armoured Vessels for the United States Navy:*

"The United States Navy Department, having in view the construction, in pursuance of the authority conferred by Act of Congress approved August 3, 1886, of two armoured vessels of different types, of about 6,000 tons displacement each, invites the submission of designs from naval or marine architects, from engineers or mechanics of established reputation, all reputable manufacturers of vessels, steam engines, boilers and ordnance; and especially from all naval constructors, steam engineers, and ordnance officers of the Navy having experience in such work.

"One of the proposed vessels is to be an armoured cruiser, and the other as powerful an armoured battle-ship as can be obtained on the above displacement.

"The requirements of the Department are laid down in a Circular, which will be furnished to those interested on application to the Department, or to Commander F. E. Chadwick, U.S.N., Naval Attaché U.S. Legation, London, England, or to Lieutenant B. H. Buckingham, U.S.N., Naval Attaché U.S. Legation, Paris, France.

"The designs submitted will be carefully examined, and one of each type will be selected for purchase, provided it can be obtained at the price mentioned in the Circular, and otherwise conforms to its terms.

"After purchase the Department will be at liberty to make such modifications in the design as it may desire. It will then order working drawings. These must embody the modifications, and must conform in price and otherwise to the terms of the Circular.

"Designers are at liberty to offer any design deemed by them most desirable, whether conforming to the data prepared by the Department or not. The designs must, however, conform to the conditions named in the Law of Congress, or they will not be considered. These are as follow :—

"'Two sea-going double-bottomed armour vessels of about 6,000 tons displacement, designed for a speed of at least sixteen knots an hour, with engines having all necessary appliances for working under forced draught, to have a complete torpedo outfit, and be armed in the most effective manner.'

"Designs not accepted will be returned, and no copies taken or retained by the Department.
"WILLIAM C. WHITNEY,
"*Secretary of the Navy.*
"Navy Department, Washington, D.C., August 21, 1886."

The receipt of this Circular must be formally acknowledged to the Department by those who submit designs.

In order that a design should be selected for purchase it must, in the opinion of the Department be thoroughly adapted to the purposes in view, as generally set forth herein, and must be a substantial improvement on existing designs of the same type.

Unimproved copies of well-known designs will not be considered.

The decision of the Department will be final on all questions that may arise concerning the designs, drawings, conditions, and other matters herein referred to.

A design must be sufficiently in detail to enable the Department to clearly ascertain its value. The location and disposition of the battery, armour, motive power, coal, stores, and all important features of the ship must be shown; and it must include all matters essential to the design of a modern first-class fighting-vessel, although they may not be specifically mentioned in this paper.

It must be accompanied by a detailed statement of weights, which are to be separated into groups as hereinafter laid down; and full particulars must be given concerning the kind, power, and economy of the engines, boilers, and screws.

It must be clearly shown that the displacement and stability are sufficient, and that the balance of qualities is such that everything will be carried properly and safely at sea; and such further information must be given as will enable the Department to readily determine the correctness of the calculations upon which the design is based.

The following are some of the principal points which must be shown in the design, or established to the satisfaction of the Department by data furnished by the designer:—

WEIGHTS.

Hull and fittings, masts and spars, including the tops and their barbettes, rigging, blocks, sails, awnings, ground tackle, galley, boats, furniture; motive machinery complete, including water in the boilers and condensers; stores, spare parts, auxiliary engines and boilers, coal; ordnance and equipments complete, including ammunition and stores; torpedo apparatus, torpedo defence nets complete, electric lighting plant, provisions, general stores, clothing, water, officers and crew and their effects, armoured deck separate from hull, other armour separate from hull.

CALCULATIONS.

The results of all calculations as to the strength and nautical qualities of the ship must be satisfactorily given: and among these particular attention is called to the following :—

Displacement, draught of water, centre of buoyancy, transverse and longitudinal metacentre, moment to change trim one inch, centre of gravity when fully equipped for sea, both with and without water in the boilers, and with and without coal; co-efficient of displacement of load water-line and of midship section; curves of displacement, curves of stability, metacentric diagram, curves of stress when vessel is in still water, and when at sea in hollow of or on crest of waves.

Attention must be given to the preservation of safe conditions when any spaces that may exist below the water-line and above the armoured deck are flooded.

All the calculations must be given in full on the design of the motive engines, boilers and appendages, with full particulars of their peculiarities.

Among other things give pressure of steam to be used, diameter of cylinders, length of stroke, piston-speed, diameter and length of boilers, area of grate-surface and of heating-surface; consumption of coal per indicated horse-power per hour; a graphic exhibit of the steam-pressure in the cylinders at maximum power, in the form of an indicator diagram, and satisfactory data regarding the sufficiency of the motive machinery and of all boilers, and the sufficiency of all auxiliary engines and pumps.

Also state the maximum maintained speed to be attained on the measured mile (both with and without the reserve coal), all the other weights being on board; and the coal endurance at the maximum, and at other speeds.

In order to have a uniform standard of comparison, Nixon's navigation coal is supposed to be used in all cases.

It must be remembered, however, that this coal has from 10 to 15 per cent. more evaporative power than the American bituminous coals used for steaming purposes, and this fact must be kept carefully in view while designing the boilers, which will, of course, be used chiefly with American coal.

All designs must be submitted on or before March 7, 1887.

For each design accepted $15,000 will be paid.

WORKING DRAWINGS.

In case a design is accepted, the Department will indicate the modifications it desires. These will be made by the designer without additional charge, after which an order will be given him to make the working drawings accordingly.

The drawings of the hull and fittings must be executed to a scale of $\frac{1}{4}$ inch = 1 foot, except midships cross-section, and details of stem and stern, which are to be $\frac{1}{2}$ inch = 1 foot. Those of the machinery are to be $1\frac{1}{2}$ inch = 1 foot.

They must be full and complete to the satisfaction of the Department, showing all details, with scantlings, and weight per foot of all materials marked on drawings; and must be so clearly set forth that from them the vessel could be properly constructed and equipped in every respect.

The working drawings must be delivered with sufficient rapidity to enable the work to proceed at once, and must be completed and delivered within eight months of the date of the order.

Each bidder must specify in his bid the price of working drawings in each case.

Designs, drawings, and all information and data to be furnished under this Circular will be sent addressed to "Hon. Wm. C. Whitney, Secretary of the Navy, Washington, D.C., United States of America." Receipt will be acknowledged, and those not accepted will be returned at the expense of the Department.

It may be distinctly understood that the Department both desires and intends to purchase a set of designs and working drawings of each type aforesaid, in case such are offered as fulfil the conditions, &c., herein set forth.

The following is a statement of the general features to be embodied in the designs of each type of ship. It is only a partial exhibit, and the designer is purposely left free on most of the important points.

ARMOURED CRUISER.

Hull of steel (not sheathed with wood), with double bottom, and divided into numerous water-tight compartments, fitted with a complete and powerful pumping system, and with drainage and ventilation throughout.

A ram bow, and a steel armoured deck running the whole length of ship, the boilers, engines, and ammunition rooms being underneath.

Two-thirds of full sail power to be carried on two or three masts, each with a protected top, with one or more machine guns mounted thereon.

MAIN BATTERY.

Four 10-in. guns, each weighing $26\frac{1}{2}$ tons.
Space occupied by the gun, 29 ft. 4in.
Space occupied by the plug, 24 in.
Space occupied by the projectile, 40 in.
Space occupied by the cartridge, 39 in.
Centre of gravity of gun from breech, 108 in.
Six 6-in. guns, each weighing 5 tons.
Space occupied by the gun, 16 ft. $2\frac{1}{2}$ in.
Space occupied by the plug, $16\frac{1}{4}$ in.
Space occupied by the projectile, 24 in.
Space occupied by the cartridge, 38 in.
Centre of gravity of gun from breech, $69\frac{1}{4}$ in.

AMMUNITION FOR MAIN BATTERY.

150 rounds for each 10-in. gun. Weight of one round, 800 pounds. 150 rounds, $53\frac{1}{2}$ tons, including powder tanks.

100 rounds for each 6-in. gun. Weight of one round, 165 pounds. 100 rounds, 7·4 tons, including powder tanks.

Mounts and shields not included above. A mount and circles of the ordinary type for a 6-in. gun (exclusive of shield) weigh about two-thirds as much as the gun.

SECONDARY BATTERY.

Four 6-pounder Hotchkiss rapid-fire guns, with mounts; total, 3·5 tons.
Four 3-pounder Hotchkiss rapid-fire guns, with mounts; total, 3 tons.
Two 1-pounder Hotchkiss rapid-fire guns, with mounts; total, 0·5 ton.
Four 47-mm. Hotchkiss revolving cannon, with mounts; total, 4 tons.
Four 37-mm. Hotchkiss revolving cannon, with mounts; total, 2·50 tons.
(Some of the 37's for tops.)
Four Gatling guns (one or more for top), with mounts; total, 0·2 ton.
Shields are not included in the foregoing. The guns must be shielded or placed in towers or other shelter.

200 rifle muskets.
100 revolvers.
150 swords.
Aggregate weight of the above, 1 ton.

AMMUNITION FOR SECONDARY BATTERY.

19,600 rounds Hotchkiss (boxed).
80,000 rounds, Gatling (boxed).
100,000 rounds, musket, (boxed).
10,000 rounds, revolver (boxed).
Aggregate weight of the above, 68·0 tons.
Ordnance equipments and stores, 10 tons.

TORPEDO OUTFIT.

Six torpedo-tubes—one bow, one stern, and two on each side; at least one on each side forward should be under water. Approximate weight each, 4,000 pounds.

Fourteen torpedoes, 16 ft. long. Approximate weight each, 600 pounds.

Two air-compressors. Approximate weight each, 1,500 pounds.

NOTE.—The bow and stern tubes need not necessarily be put through the stem and stern posts, but the fire from them must be parallel to the keel, and safe for the ships.

SEARCH-LIGHT OUTFIT.

Four electric search-lights (ship's).
Two electric search-lights (boat's).
Dynamos and engines (for ship and boats).
Aggregate weight of the above, 11½ tons.
Electric lighting circuit with dynamo and engines.
Aggregate weight, 5 tons.

The guns are to be so arranged as to obtain the greatest command, both horizontal and vertical, consistent with other essential conditions, and must afford a heavy bow and stern fire.

The 10-in. guns must load in at least two positions, and are to be loaded and worked by power, and protected by at least 10½ in. of steel armour, properly backed, while the 6-in. guns are to be efficiently shielded.

Any vertical armoured protection at the water-line must be at least 11 in. thick in the heaviest part, and thicker if practicable.

There must be one conning tower forward, and ammunition tubes to the 10-in. guns, all heavily armoured.

The motive machinery is to be below the armoured deck, and well covered from hostile fire; and the ship must be driven by twin-screws.

When fully equipped, and with all her weights on board, not including the reserve coal, she must be able to maintain a rate of speed of 17 knots per hour on the measured mile.

The coal endurance must be large, the consumption economical, and the distance to be covered at moderate speed as great as practicable.

The furnaces must be arranged to work with forced draught when desired, air for combustion being furnished independently of the ventilating system.

Quarters must be provided for 270 officers and men, with provisions for three months and water for one month.

The ship must be capable of being steered either by power or by hand, from several positions.

A suitable distilling apparatus is to be provided for.

A sufficient number of boats to carry all the *personnel* must be allowed, two being second-class torpedo-boats and two others steamboats; each of the latter mounting one of the 3-pdrs. shielded.

The anchors and torpedo-boats must be purchased by power.

If the designer can show that any decided and very valuable results will be obtained, the following reduction of weight will be allowed:—

The ammunition for the 10-in. guns may be reduced 100 rounds each, accomplishing a reduction of 71 tons.

The foregoing conditions are to be fulfilled at a maximum draught of 22 ft., and on a displacement of about 6,000 tons.

ARMOURED BATTLE SHIP.

Hull of steel (not sheathed with wood), with double bottom, and divided into numerous watertight compartments, fitted with complete and powerful pumping system, and with drainage and ventilation throughout.

A ram bow, and a steel armoured deck running the whole length of ship, the boilers, engines, and ammunition rooms being underneath.

One or two military masts, each with a projected top, with one or more machine guns mounted therein.

MAIN BATTERY.

Two 12-in. guns, each weighing 46½ tons.
Space occupied by the gun, 35 ft. 3 in.
Space occupied by the plug, 31 in.
Space occupied by the projectile, 48 in.
Space occupied by the cartridge, 75 in.
Centre of gravity of gun from breech, 129 in.
Six 6-in. guns, each weighing 5 tons.
Space occupied by the gun, 16 ft. 2½ in.
Space occupied by the plug, 16¼ in.
Space occupied by the projectile, 24 in.
Space occupied by the cartridge, 38 in.
Centre of gravity of gun from breech, 69½ in.

AMMUNITION FOR MAIN BATTERY.

150 rounds for each 12-in. gun. Weight of one round, 1,375 pounds. 150 rounds, 92 tons. This includes powder tanks.

100 rounds for each 6-in. gun. Weight of one round, 165 pounds. 100 rounds, 7·4 tons. This includes powder tanks.

Mounts and shields not included above. A mount and circles of the ordinary type for a 6-in. gun (exclusive of shield) weigh about two-thirds as much as the gun.

SECONDARY BATTERY.

Four 6-pdr. Hotchkiss rapid-fire guns, with mounts, total, 3·5 tons.
Six 3-pdr. Hotchkiss rapid-fire guns, with mounts, total, 5 tons.
Two 1-pdr. Hotchkiss rapid-fire guns, with mounts, total, 0·5 ton.
Four 47 mm. Hotchkiss revolving cannon, with mounts, total, 4 tons.
Four 37 mm. Hotchkiss revolving cannon, with mounts, total, 2·50 tons.
(Some of these 37's for tops.)
Four Gatling guns, with mounts, total, 0·2 ton.
(One or more for tops.)
Shields are not included in the foregoing. The guns must be shielded or placed in towers or other shelter.

200 rifle muskets.
100 revolvers.
150 swords.
Aggregate weight, 1 ton.

AMMUNITION FOR SECONDARY BATTERY.

21,600 rounds, Hotchkiss (boxed).
80,000 rounds, Gatling (boxed).
100,000 rounds, musket (boxed).
10,000 rounds, revolver (boxed).
Aggregate weight, 72·0 tons.
Ordnance equipment and stores, 10 tons.

TORPEDO OUTFIT.

Six torpedo tubes, one bow, one stern, and two on each side; at least one on each side forward should be under water. Approximate weight each, 4,000 pounds.

Fourteen torpedoes, 16 feet long. Approximate weight each, 600 pounds.

Two air compressors. Approximate weight each, 1,500 pounds.

NOTE.—The bow and stern tubes need not necessarily be put through the stem and stern posts, but the fire from them must be parallel to the keel, and safe for the ship.

SEARCH LIGHT OUTFIT.

Four electric search lights (ship's).
Two electric search lights (boat's).
Dynamos and engines (for ship and boats).
Aggregate weight, 11½ tons.
Electric lighting circuit with dynamo and engines.
Aggregate weight, 5 tons.

The guns are to be so arranged as to obtain the greatest command, both horizontal and vertical, consistent with other essential conditions, and must afford a heavy bow and stern fire.

The 12-in. guns are to load in at least two positions, and to be loaded and worked by power, and protected by at least 12 inches of steel armour, properly backed, while the 6-in. guns are to be efficiently shielded.

Any vertical armoured protection at the water-line must be at least 12 inches thick in the heaviest part, and thicker if practicable.

There must be one conning tower forward, and ammunition tubes to the 12-in. guns, all heavily armoured.

The motive machinery is to be below the armoured deck, well covered from hostile fire, and the ship is to be driven by twin screws.

When fully equipped, and with all her weights on board, not including the reserve coal, she must be able to maintain a rate of speed of at least 17 knots per hour on the measured mile.

The coal endurance must be large, the consumption economical, and the distance to be covered at moderate speed as great as practicable.

The furnaces must be arranged to work with forced draught when desired, air for combustion being furnished independently of the ventilating system.

Quarters must be provided for 270 officers and men, with provisions for three months and water for one month.

The ship must be capable of being steered either by power or by hand, from several positions.

A suitable distilling apparatus is to be provided for.

A sufficient number of boats to carry all the *personnel* must be allowed, two being second-class torpedo boats and two others steamboats; each of the latter mounting one of the 3-pdrs. shielded.

The anchors and torpedo boats must be purchased by power.

If the designer can show that any decided and very valuable results will be obtained, the following reductions of weight will be allowed:—

The ammunition for the 12-inch guns may be reduced to 100 rounds each, accomplishing a reduction of 61 tons.

The foregoing conditions are to be fulfilled at a maximum draught of 23 feet, and on a displacement of about 6,000 tons.

NAVY DEPARTMENT,
WASHINGTON, *August* 21, 1886.

WILLIAM C. WHITNEY,
Secretary of the Navy.

In response to this circular, a number of proposals were received from renowned naval constructors, ship's builders, naval officers, and rank amateurs, as well as a "back-up" entry submitted by the Navy's own Bureau of Construction and Repair. From these entries the proposal of William G. John of Barrow-in-Furness, England was selected to become the US Navy's first battleship. The Bureau of Construction's design for the armored cruiser was selected and became the USS *Maine*. The cruiser's design, though quite conservative and in some ways inferior to some proposals, received special consideration due to the desire to have at least one of the new warships be of American design.

From 1867 until 1870 William G. John (1845-1890), the British designer of the *Texas*, had worked as a draftsman for Sir Edward Reed, Chief Constructor for the Admiralty from 1863-1870. There he had assisted in Reed's design for the breastwork monitor type of vessel that was to evolve into the "Centre Battery" ship. John was also the first to calculate the curves of stability for a ship in 1868. These calculations were a critical step in the advancement of scientific ship design, allowing for the first time a quantifiable and accurate assessment of the stability of a particular ship before it was constructed. This theory was embraced by the Admiralty. However, through a series of political maneuvers, Parliament was convinced to authorize construction of the *HMS Captain* - without the direct oversight of the Admiralty design staff. William John warned of the risk of capsizing due to fundamental defects in the *Captain*'s design but the ship was never-the-less completed - and soon lost.

Upon leaving the Admiralty in 1872 John entered employment with Lloyd's Register of British and Foreign Shipping, rising quickly to Assistant Chief Surveyor. There John authored several well-received scientific papers on quantitative nautical design and stability.

In 1881, at the age of 36, William John left Lloyd's to become the General Manager of Barrow Ship Building and Engineering Company (subsequently reorganized into Naval Construction & Armament Works – Vickers). At Barrow he was responsible for designs such as the high-speed passenger ships *City of Rome* (1881, below left) and *La Normandie* (1882, below right).

Prior to the design for the *Texas* and Barrow's reorganization, the only navy vessels the shipyard had built were the torpedo boat destroyer, *HMS Fearless* (1886) and a small number of gunboats.

The following pages are a reprint of paper delivered by USS *Texas* designer William John to the prestigious British Institution of Naval Architects on March 21, 1888 describing, in his own words, the design competition for the USS *Texas* and his winning concept.

ON AMERICAN WAR-SHIP DESIGN.
By W. John, Esq., Member of Council.

[Read at the Twenty-ninth Session of the Institution of Naval Architects, March 21st, 1888; the Right Hon. the Earl of Ravensworth, President, in the Chair.]

I have had the honour upon several occasions to read Papers before this Institution on matters relating to the Mercantile Marine or the Royal Navy of this country, but the present Paper has reference to the Navy of another Power, as its title indicates. I hope, however, it may not on that account be without interest to the Members and Associates of this Institution, or without some value as a record in our Transactions.

It is well known that the United States Government have not, since their great war, gone to any great length in building up an ironclad fleet such as is possessed by this country, France, Italy, and Germany, but there have been signs within the last few years of their wishing to make an effectual start in this direction.

It is well known that they have bought designs from private firms in this country, and in August, 1886, they made a fresh and somewhat novel departure.

The present Secretary of the United States Navy, Mr. W. C. Whitney, issued an advertisement with a "Notice to Naval Architects and others, concerning designs of Steel Armoured Vessels for the United States Navy," with a Circular "embodying the conditions that must be conformed to by those who submit designs to the United States Navy Department."

This advertisement was in effect asking in the open market for competitive designs for two types of ship, one to be called a battle-ship and the other an armoured cruiser.

I have appended a copy of the Circular to this paper for record in the Transactions, and it will be found that it lays down very definitely the conditions the ships had to fulfil as to speed and armament, although the type was left in the hands of the designers.

The terms of the Circular were quite fair, although it was freely conjectured here that no one outside the States would be awarded the prize—for there was a prize of 15,000 dollars offered for each successful design. I need not say I did not share this feeling, or I should not have risked my name, and whatever reputation I may have as a naval architect, in such a competition.

I was at the time General Manager of the Barrow Shipbuilding Company, which has since been succeeded by the Naval Construction and Armaments Company, and towards the end of 1886, our draughtsmen being then only partially employed on current work, I determined upon the types and dimensions of the ships, and started on the competition. The designs had to be in by the 7th March, and it speaks volumes for the efficiency of the draughting and calculating staff that the two complete designs, with full calculations of strength, weight, buoyancy, and stability, were finished in six weeks, and one of them, the battle-ship, was awarded the 15,000 dollar prize by a committee of experts, and recommended to be built in America for the United States Government. There is also a contract entered into for the making of the working drawings, which will be done by the Naval Construction and Armaments Company under my supervision.

One reason why I have thought that a general description of this design might be of interest to the Meeting is that I have been asked for particulars by professional gentlemen from several countries, who could not quite make out the design from the meagre and imperfect accounts that have appeared in the Press.

That the American Government will not object to a general description I feel sure, because many particulars were published in the American Press before I got any intimation that the design had been accepted.

I should here say that during the preparation of the working drawings some alterations may be made in her armour and armament, and there certainly will be in her speed, for there has been a distinct advance in the use of forced draught since the engine designs were prepared, which will be taken full advantage of by the combined engineering talent possessed by the Naval Construction and Armaments Company.

The dimensions of the battle-ship are as follows:—

	Ft.	in.
Length between perpendiculars	290	0
Breadth (extreme)	64	1
Depth (moulded to upper deck)	39	8
Mean draught of water	22	6
	Tons.	
Displacement at 22 ft. 6 in. draught, when fully equipped and with 500 tons of coal on board	6,300	

We were limited at first by the Circular to a maximum draught of water of 23 feet and a displacement of about 6,000 tons, but we were afterwards allowed to go up to 6,300 tons.

I may here mention that the cruiser I proposed differed entirely from the battle-ship in almost every feature of the design, the problem to solve being an entirely different one. In the cruiser there were four heavy guns, 10-in., each weighing 26¼ tons, while in the battle-ship there were to be two heavy guns only, viz., 12-in., each weighing 46¼ tons. In both cases heavy bow and stern fire was required, and in both vessels a number of 6-in. guns had to be provided, as well as a powerful secondary battery of quick-firing guns, and torpedo tubes, all specified, had to be provided for, and the cruiser had to be furnished with sails to the extent of a two-thirds full rig.

Having in the cruiser four 10-in. guns to dispose of, as well as six 6-in. guns and the secondary battery, I determined on a broadside arrangement, with fore and aft and broadside fire from the corners of the battery for the heavy guns; but in the battle-ship, where I had only two 12-in. guns, with six 6-in. and the secondary battery, I determined to put each 12-in. gun in a turret, and to échelon them. The designer was left more or less free as to water-line protection, but if vertical armoured protection was adopted, it had to be at least 12 in. thick.

Now, I am one of those who believe in a water-line belt in preference to the internal sloping protection, and I believe in its being carried sufficiently far forward and aft to give the ship a moderate degree of metacentric height, however much the unarmoured ends are riddled or blown away by shot and shell; and this view I tried to embody in the design of the battle-ship which you will see on the wall.

A very interesting discussion took place in this Hall last year on a valuable paper read by Mr. Biles, in which this question of water-line protection received much prominence. I did not take any part in it, because I had then despatched the Competitive Designs to America, and was awaiting the result. I felt then as I feel now, that, given a certain depth of belt from so much above the water to so much below, I would prefer the vertical armour to the internal sloping armour, both for broadside fighting and especially for a running fight, where in the one case the shot and shell would probably glance from the vertical armour, while the internal armour would give you a background for bursting shell against, that might tear out yards of your thin side in the region of the water-line, rip it off in fact, which must not only affect your stability, but also your speed.

The depth of the belt is, of course, an important element; but where you are limited to the displacement of your ship, as well as to the thickness of your armour, you have to make your belt more shallow than you perhaps otherwise would. At any rate, that was my case; but without being allowed more displacement, I do not know that I would now, after more mature reflection, seriously alter the arrangement.

The actual depth of the belt amidships is 2 ft. above water and 4 ft. 6 in. below the water at the Constructor's Load Water line, that is, with 500 tons of coal and all stores and equipment on board. I need scarcely go into the vexed question of how much deeper she would be in the water with all her spare bunkers full, because the American Government were furnished with full detailed calculations as to her weights, tons per inch of immersion, and detailed conditions of her stability, and were therefore in as good a position to judge of the coal supply as I was. With an additional 450 tons of coal in the bunkers between decks, the draught would be 14 in. deeper, leaving the top of the belt still 10 in. above water.

Before describing the plans of the battle-ship, I had better perhaps read out to you what the secondary battery was to be composed of. I have already mentioned that there were to be two 12-in. and six 6-in. breachloaders forming the main battery.

The secondary battery was—

Four 6-pr. Hotchkiss rapid fire guns, with mounts.
Six 3-pr. do. do. do.
Two 1-pr. do. do. do.
Four 47 mm. Hotchkiss revolving cannons, with mounts.
Four 37 mm. do. do. do.
Some of these 37 mm.'s for tops.
Four Gatling guns with mounts, one or more for tops.

The number of rounds of ammunition for the secondary battery was also provided, as also for the main battery, and these are given in detail in the printed Circular which is appended.

Six torpedo tubes were also stipulated for—one in the bow, one in the stern, and two on each side; and four electric search lights for the ship were stipulated for, in addition to two others for the boats.

Fig. 1 (Plate XVIII.) represents the midship section of the vessel, which, as will be seen, is to be built on the cellular double-bottom principle. This double bottom extends under the engines, boilers, and magazines for a length of 158 ft., and is divided both longitudinally and transversely into numerous water-tight compartments fitted for water ballast, so that the vessel may be trimmed when coal, ammunition, or stores are partly consumed. Forward and aft a continuation of the double-bottom is formed by the flats of the provision and store rooms, the extreme ends of the vessel being arranged as trimming tanks.

There is a protective deck 3 in. thick extending over the top of the armour belt, and then sloping down forward and aft at the forward end to the point of the ram, 10 ft. below the water, and at the after end sufficiently down to protect the steering gear. This protective deck was stipulated for in the Circular as follows: "A ram bow and a steel armoured deck running the whole length of the ship, the boilers, engines, and ammunition rooms being underneath."

Below this protective deck there are wing compartments arranged for, so as to lessen the extent of possible damage of ram or torpedo attack.

The hull of the vessel is, of course, to be built of mild steel throughout, and to have twin-screws; and the design provides for a steel-faced armour belt 12 in. thick, extending beyond the engines, boilers, and all magazines, and ending in an armoured bulkhead—not one going straight across the ship, but pointed at the middle line outwards towards the bow and stern of the ship, as shown on Fig. 2 (Plate XIX.).

Above the top of the belt and the protective deck there are two continuous decks, and the turrets, with the 12-in. guns, are above the upper of these, as seen in the profile, Fig. 3 (Plate XIX.).

These bulkheads are of 6-in. steel-faced armour. In end-on firing they have, of course, the additional protection of the protective sloping deck, and are, therefore, partly sheltered; and in broadside fighting they must necessarily, from their position, be struck at an oblique angle, if at all. The armour belt is backed up with 6-in. teak, two thicknesses of 25-lb. plating, rigid framing, and girders.

Between the protective deck and the one next above, which may we call the main deck, there is no armour, except round the communications for working and fighting the ship, but the space is divided into water-tight compartments, forming additional coal bunkers, store rooms, accommodation for crew, &c. These additional coal bunkers are further subdivided by water-tight girders longitudinally, at a height of 5 ft. above the water-line, and coffer-dams are fitted round the engine and boiler hatches. This main-deck carries an armoured redoubt, surrounding the lower part of the turrets and the hydraulic machinery for moving and loading the guns. The redoubt and turrets are of 12-in. steel-faced armour, with 6-in. teak backing, well supported; and the top plating, which forms part of the upper or weather deck, is 1 in. thick. The arrangement of the armour on the redoubt is shown on the main-deck plan, Fig. 4 (Plate XIX.). On this plan also is shown the arrangement of four of the 6-in. guns, and most of the secondary battery.

On the upper-deck plan, Fig. 5 (Plate XIX.), is shown the arrangement of the turrets, two of the 6-in. guns, and the conning tower. The conning tower is protected by 12-in. steel-faced armour, and extends above the top of the turrets and the flying deck.

The space between the upper and main decks not appropriated by the redoubt and the secondary battery is taken up by the quarters of the officers and crew, which are well lighted and ventilated. Access to the redoubt and turrets is obtained from the protective deck.

Steam and hand-steering gear is fitted below the protective deck, and steering connections are made with them from the conning tower, after-wheelhouse, and flying bridge.

The communications from the conning tower for navigating the vessel are protected by an armoured tube 3 in. thick. The hoists from the magazines are also heavily protected with 6-in. steel-faced armour.

I will now describe more in detail the range of fire obtained from the particular distribution of the armament. It was important to my mind that the two heavy turret guns should be high out of the water, and under the immediate command of the officer fighting the ship, who obviously must be in the conning tower or near the conning tower, and therefore above the upper deck and capable of seeing all round. The secondary battery of quick-firing guns, or the bulk of them, are better placed, in my opinion, under cover in the 'tween-decks below, because they would be, as I take it, largely employed firing at the unprotected parts of the enemy's load-line in order to cripple her speed and stability, and in keeping off torpedo boats, and they are still high enough for that purpose, and to avoid being interfered with by the ordinary waves that a battle would be fought amongst.

The 12-in. guns are so placed that both command a fore and aft fire, and each gun has a complete broadside range on one side, and a range on the opposite side of 40 degrees for the forward gun and of 70 degrees for the after one. Two loading positions are provided for these guns, and for each gun the ammunition is lifted by hydraulic power direct from the magazines in one of these positions.

Two 6-in. guns are arranged as bow and stern chasers on central pivot mountings on the weather deck, one forward and one aft, with a range of 120 degrees. These guns are protected by steel shields, but some care would have to be exercised in fighting them when the heavy turret guns are being fired fore and aft.

Four 6-in. guns are arranged on sponsons on the main deck, two commanding a range from right forward to 25 degrees abaft the beam, and two a range from right aft to 25 degrees forward of the beam.

Four 6-pr. and four 3-pr. rapid-firing guns, and four 47 mm. revolving cannons are fought on the main deck, the whole of the guns on this deck being protected by side plating 1½ in. thick, and the guns dispersed to secure a heavy bow and stern fire and a good defence against torpedo boat attack.

Two Gatling guns, and two 37 mm. revolving cannon are placed on the bridge; two 1-pr. rapid-firing guns are placed on the flying bridge, and two Gatling guns, with two 37 mm. revolving cannons are fought in the mast tops, and two 3-pr. rapid-firing guns are fitted in the steam cutters.

The ammunition for the secondary battery is stowed in magazines placed forward and aft, the ammunition being passed up to the main deck through an armoured tube 3 in. thick, and thence through hand-up scuttles to the guns.

Communication between the forward and after magazines below the protective deck is established through the central passage.

Means are provided for ejecting torpedoes through tubes in six positions, as required by the Circular, one forward through the bow and one aft through the stern, two through the sides aft above water, and two through the sides forward below water.

Air compressors are to be fitted forward and aft, and stowage room is provided for fourteen torpedoes. Stowage room is also arranged for submarine mines.

The engines are placed in two compartments, and the boilers in four compartments, communication being established between these, and between the ends of the vessel, through a central passage above the main magazines, and below the protective deck.

The coal which may be carried on the 22 ft. 6 in. draught, viz., 500 tons, is stowed in the lower bunkers, and the additional coal proposed to be carried is so arranged as to afford as much protection as possible to that unarmoured part of the vessel.

The ventilation of magazines and crew spaces is provided for.

The distilling condensers for fresh water are carried in the engine-room.

Two military masts are to be fitted as shown on the profile, carrying, as before stated, four machine guns in their tops.

Two second-class torpedo boats are provided for, and a sufficient number of other boats to carry the crew, including one steam pinnace, and one steam cutter, each mounting a 3-pr. Hotchkiss rapid-firing gun.

The boats are stowed, as will be seen by the profile, on the flying deck, which is large enough to afford a clear space for navigating the vessel and for mounting a few machine guns and search lights. There is also a chart house with a flying bridge above, carrying two 1-pr. rapid-firing guns, and two search lights.

Such is briefly a description of the battle-ship selected by the committee of experts including naval officers, engineers, and civilians, and accepted by the United States Naval Department out of the competitive designs submitted to them; and I hope it will fulfil their expectations. I have the stability calculations, and also schedules of all the weights, which I hope to have permission from the Navy Department to record in the Transactions.

In conclusion, I will briefly sum up what the fighting qualities of the ship are. She is to have a speed in fighting trim of 17 knots. If she is cruising alone and meets with an enemy of about her own size, but without her armour protection, and with, say, a knot or more greater speed, and that enemy chooses to run away, starting from a safe distance, this vessel could not capture her, bar accidents to the retreating ship's machinery or a lucky shot from her pursuer. But if the vessels, after sighting each other, approach and mean fighting, then this vessel has, as long as they are bow on, her full battery of heavy guns available, as well as three out of her six 6-in. guns and a large proportion of her secondary battery bearing, and with her sloping protective deck, and her armoured bulkheads at the end of the water-line belt behind it, she is practically free from destruction until they come within torpedo or ram striking distance, when the coolness of the heads on board, rather than any particular or possible merits in the ships, will decide the action. In the event of a swifter enemy coming astern to engage her until a fleet arrives, while she is steaming ahead to join her consorts, her power of fighting astern is practically the same. But bear in mind, if the enemy in either of these cases is one of the internally protected cruisers, she—the enemy—will be liable to be raked fore and aft by shot, and more especially by highly explosive shells, that will bring back to our minds the old days of unprotected wooden ships and the havoc produced by raking fire,—in a greatly, I would say, most seriously intensified form.

In the next place, suppose both ships avoid the ram and torpedo, as they probably will, and it becomes a matter of artillery. The action, then, as I conceive it, would first develop into one of oblique firing—in which case the belt would have the best of the internal protection, unquestionably in my mind, with shell-fire—and eventually the vessels would move in circles, after the manner of the *Kearsage* and *Alabama*, until the artillery fire crippled one or other of them. In this case the battle-ship I am describing would have full play on her broadside with both her 12-in. guns, four out of the six of her 6-in. guns, and a large proportion of her secondary battery. This view of the possible fighting of future single actions gives, to my mind, the advantage to the main guns being echeloned and placed so high that their fire fore and aft cannot be interfered with by forecastles or poops, such as we have seen in vessels like the *Captain* and *Huascar*, and others; but I think it is almost equally important that you should be able to maintain your heavy broadside concentration.

If your heaviest guns are masked either forward or aft, a faster ship, even if lighter armed or armoured, has the better of you. If you are masked on the broadside, a ship of equal speed and turning power can keep you working broadside to broadside, or compel you to close and take the chances of the ram and torpedo.

Even in fleet fighting I believe there is an advantage in the heaviest guns being placed unsymmetrically, but I do not think I would put the échelon in all cases the same way. A ship such as I am describing would have certain advantages on the port side over those she has on the starboard, and *vice versâ*, and it would depend upon her consorts and the dispositions of the admiral in command, and the rival fleet, whether he would place her in the left or right wing, or how he would order her to be fought.

I know in this matter I am going beyond the legitimate bounds of the Naval Architect, and am presuming upon the forbearance of Naval Officers; but when a naval architect has to design a fighting ship, he should, I think, place himself in mind and imagination as nearly as he can in the position of the man who has to fight the ship, and I do not think an effort of that kind—amateur sailor situation though it may be—is likely to detract from the merits of the design.

I must apologise for trespassing into the domain embraced by the latter part of my paper, but trust the interest always evoked by many of the admitted uncertainties of future naval battles will secure the indulgence of the meeting for my temerity.

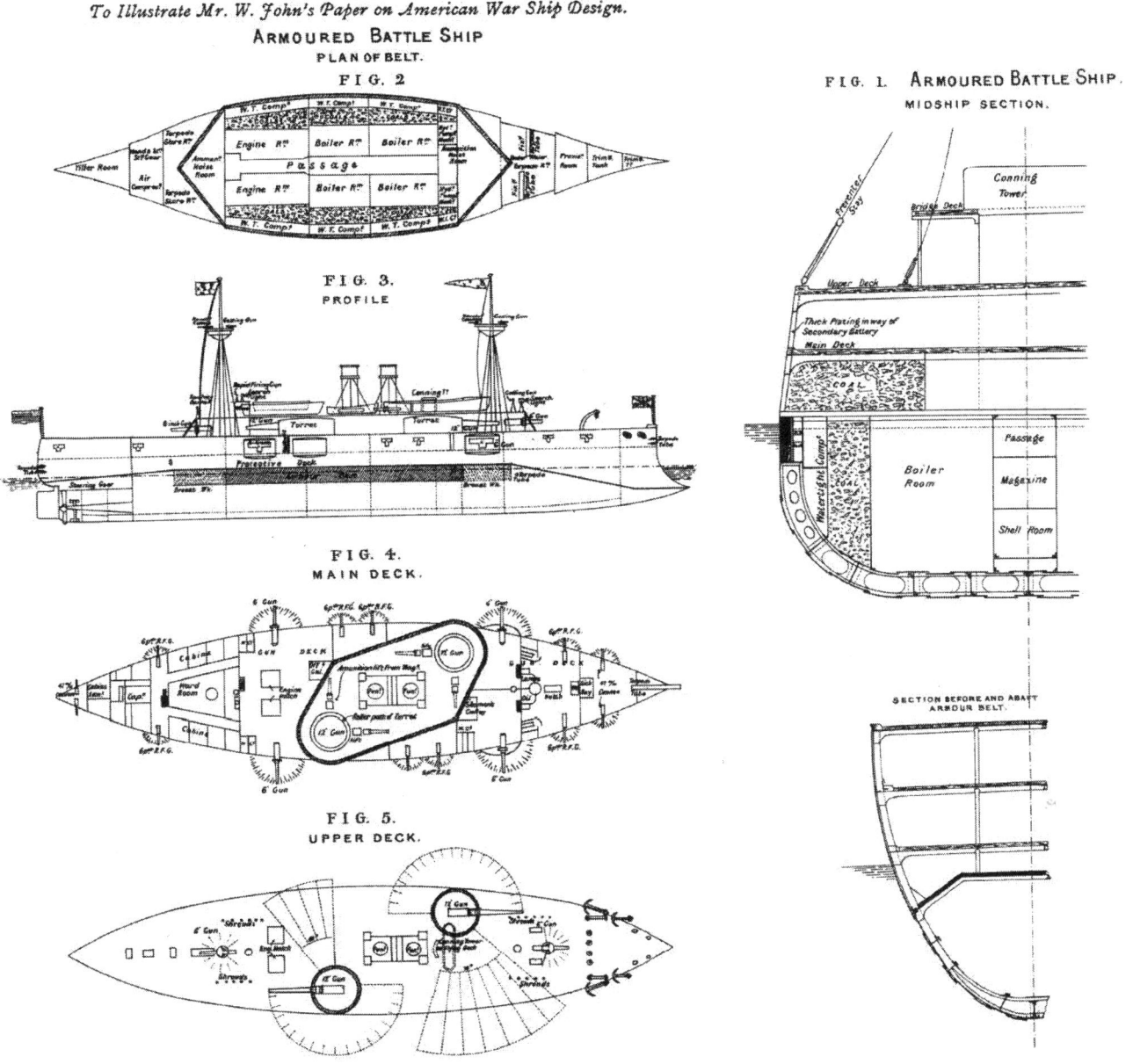

William John's plans presented to the Institution depict a vessel of compact design with twin stacks and torpedo boats that could be lowered into the water to attack independently. A ram graces her bow and an armored deck in combination with a waterline armored belt, protects her vitals and ensures her buoyancy in action. An en echelon arrangement of turrets, pushed outward in sponsons, allowed her 12" main guns arcs of fire ahead and astern as well as to either beam.

This arrangement was in keeping with her intended operational use. She was not primarily conceived of as a traditional line-of-battle ship, slogging it out with other battleships while steaming along a parallel course. Instead, her design favored single combat and direct engagement, where strong forward fire would be critical on the attack and strong rearward fire would be needed should superior forces come on scene.

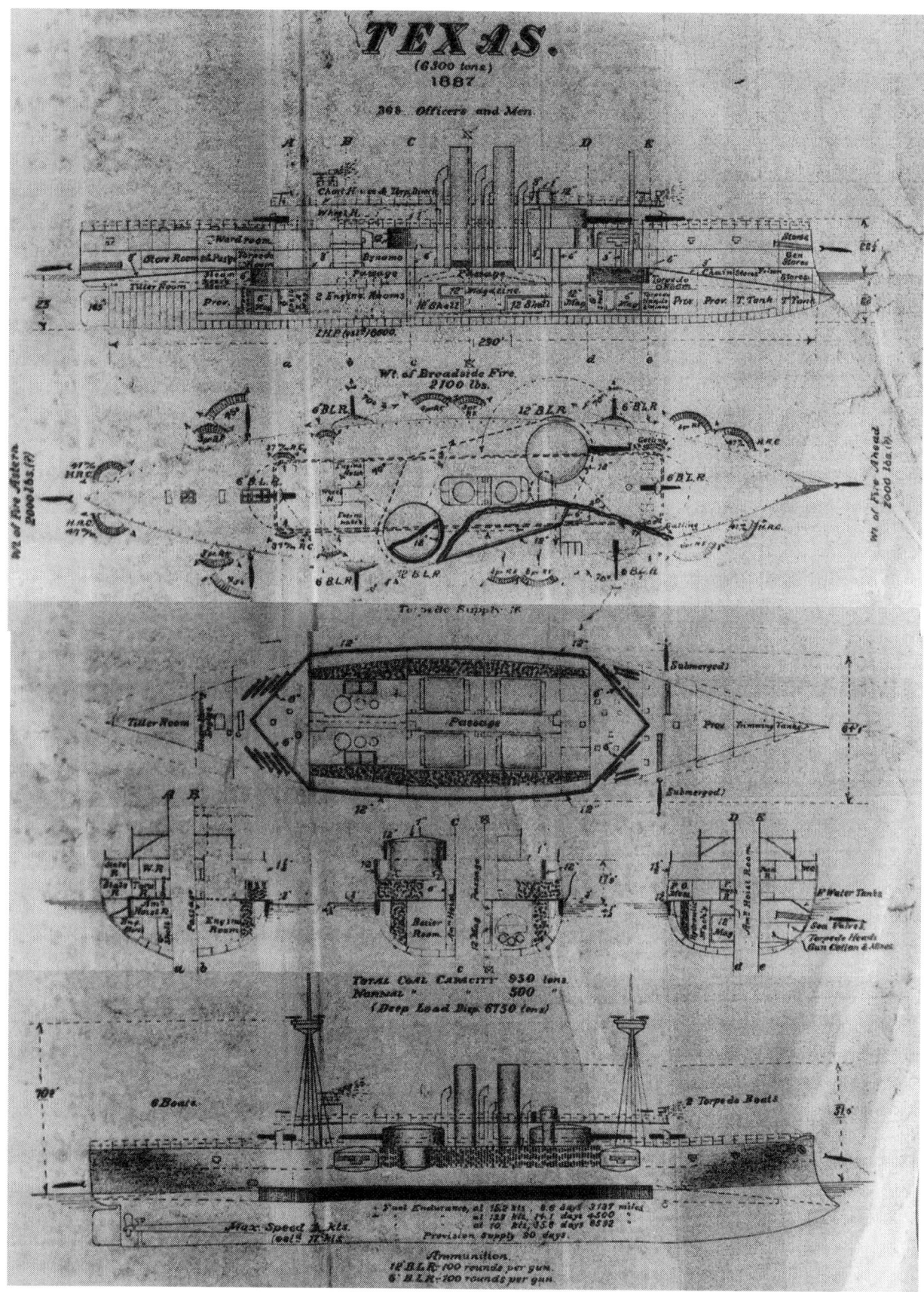

Strategically placed coal bunkers and the slope of her armored deck contributed to her protection, as did armored bulkheads closing either end of her belts. Her competition plans reveal additional detail of her arrangement and armament.

While the Navy Department was careful to return the non-winning design proposals to their owners, the plans on this page illustrate several schemes which remained in the Navy's possession.

Former Chief Constructor of the British Admiralty Edward Reed submitted a plan reminiscent of his *HMS Monarch*, the ship that had proven its superiority to its contemporary the *HMS Captain* many years before. Naval design, however, had passed beyond this type of warship.

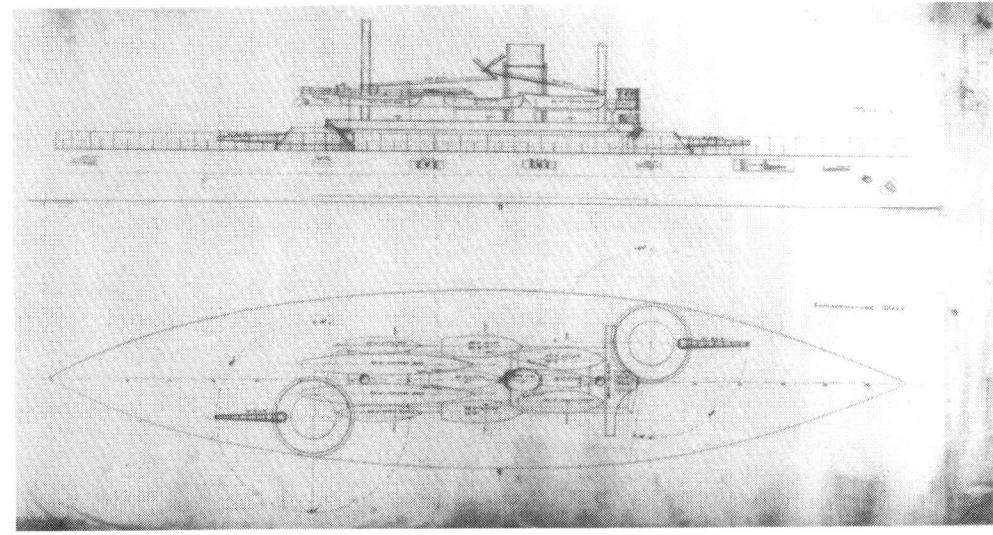

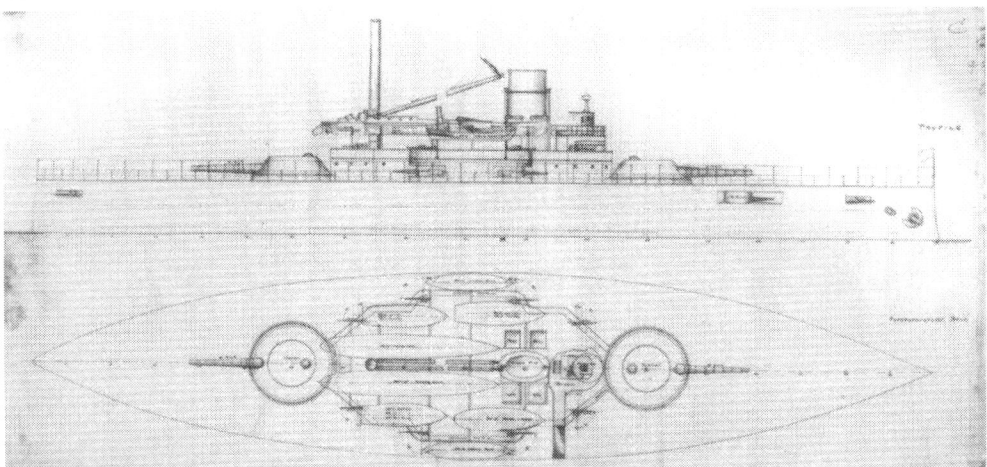

The Bureau of Construction and Repair examined a number of configurations for the battleship, including one very similar to that proposed by William John. The Bureau was awarded the design of the armored cruiser but, perhaps with an eye towards gaining new insight into modern British practice, the proposal of William John of Barrow-in-Furness was settled upon for the battleship. Note the pair of torpedo boats carried on deck in each of these proposals.

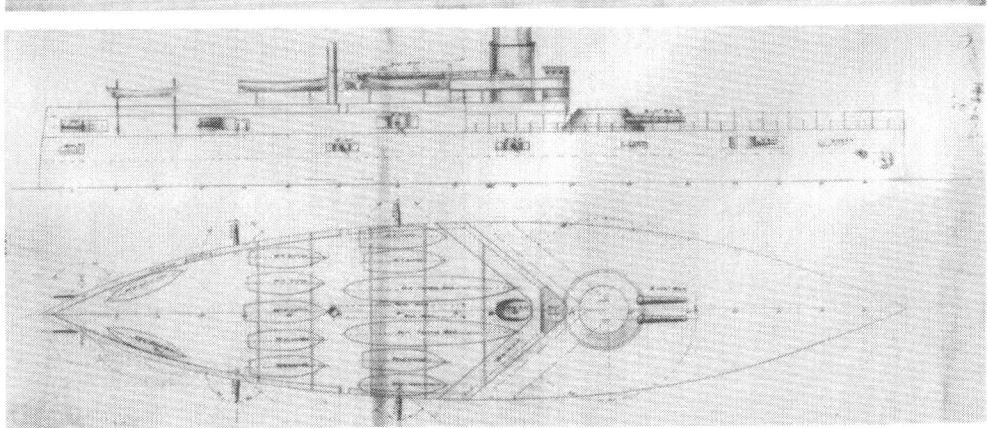

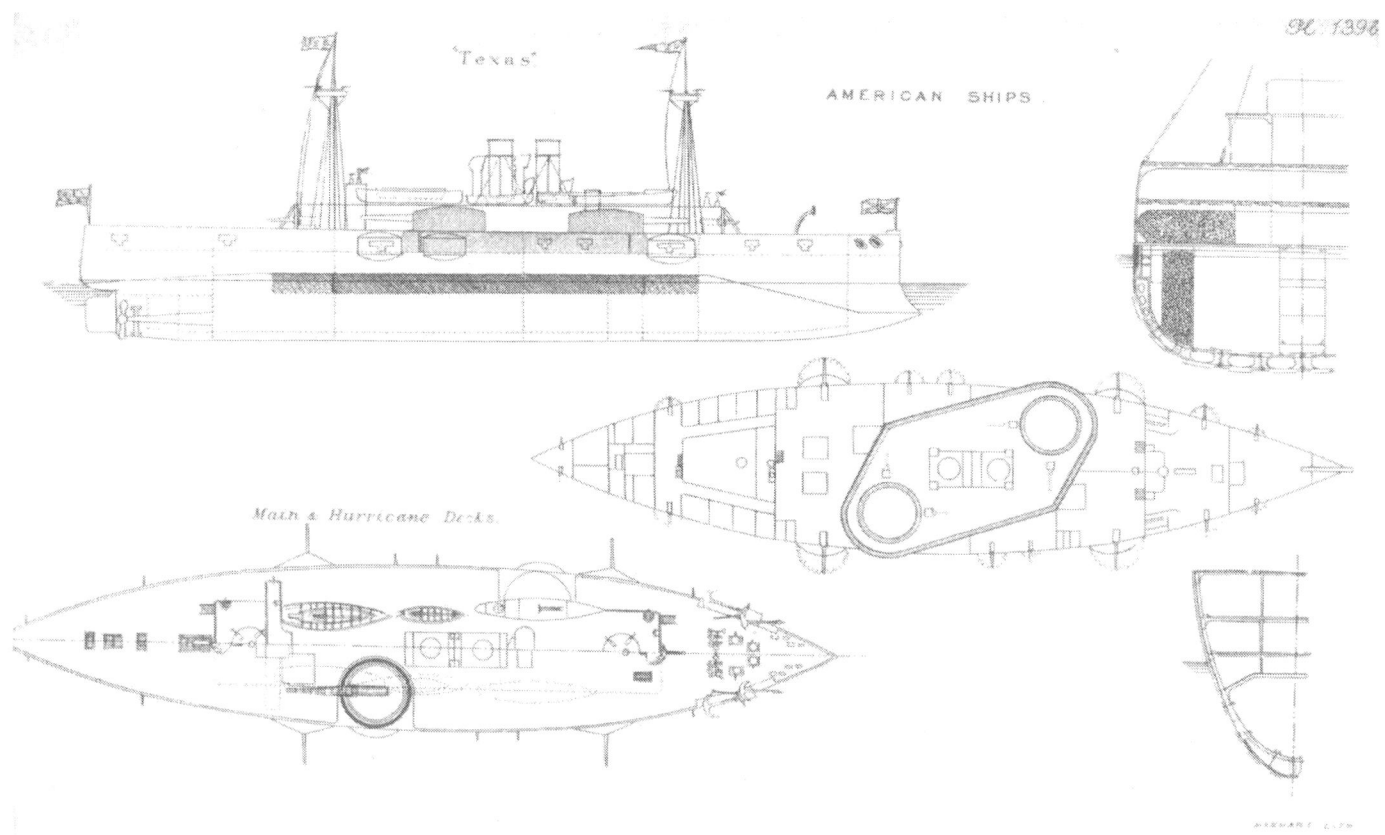

In laying the foundations for the development of the "New Navy", United States Navy warships once again began to achieve an international significance not seen since the close of the Civil War, when the government had sold off of her once world-leading ironclad fleet. Foreign governments took notice of this rising power.

Rear Admiral French Ensor Chadwick
Naval Attaché to Great Britain during the *Texas'* competition and design phase

REAR-ADMIRAL PHILIP HICHBORN
Chief of the Bureau of Construction and Repairs during the war

REAR-ADMIRAL FRANCIS TIFFANY BOWLES
Secretary of the Second Naval Advisory Board, recently Chief Constructor of the Navy

3 BUILDING THE BATTLESHIP 1889-1895

Once the selection process was complete, the battleship project immediately ran into trouble. Months were lost in contract negotiations, mainly concerning whether William John, the individual, or Naval Armaments Ltd. (formerly Barrow), his employer, would receive the $15,000.00 award for the design. At one point the Secretary of the Navy became so exasperated that he considered dropping the design. However, in a last minute agreement, John was permitted to retain the prize. After this incident, however, John's influence on the project waned and Naval Armaments undertook the task of "Americanizing" the design, as it was discovered that manufacturers in the United States were not able to directly produce many of the parts called for in the British plans. Revised boilers were substituted, as were some structural components, and this may have led to subsequent problems. However part of the intent in building the *Texas*, while she was very conventional and almost outdated by European standards, was to stretch American industry and force improvement. Lessons learned from the construction of the *Texas* helped the United States' steel industry fulfill later obligations more expeditiously, so that ships laid down after the *Texas* were completed more rapidly.

The construction of the *Texas* was placed in the hands of Naval Constructor Francis Tiffany Bowles at the Norfolk Navy Yard in Virginia, the very same yard that had seen the construction of the *CSS Virginia* during the Civil War and where the captured ironclad *CSS Texas* had been taken to be fitted out by the US Navy in 1865. Despite its history of armored vessel construction, this project required the yard to expand its tooling and capabilities, leading to further delays.

Even before the keel was laid, a major challenge occurred which showed how delicate was the balance of cooperation between Naval Armaments Ltd. and the Bureau of Construction and Repairs. Arguments arose after rumors came to light that the design of the *Texas* was overweight. Naval Armaments, while denying the problem, asserted that any weight issue that might exist could be resolved by making the *Texas* ten feet longer in the middle of the ship, which would not only give her greater displacement, but would increase internal coal capacity and add a bit of extra speed to the design. This was seen by some as a concession by Naval Armaments that an error had been made in the weight calculations of the vessel. Constructor Francis Tiffany Bowles, however, insisted the *Texas* be built as-is, with no major "improvements" to the basic design. Had he anticipated the subsequent troubles and delays regarding the delivery of suitable steel and armor for the *Texas*, perhaps he would not have been so insistent, but to him the priority was getting the *Texas* built and launched. The US Navy was under great pressure to catch up with the world, and it was far behind. It needed hulls in the water rather than optimized ships gracing the stocks in its shipyards. However this would not be the last attempt to materially change the design.

Having cleared these hurdles, the keel of the *Texas* was laid in June of 1889 and the laborious process of building the warship began. The delays had cost the *Texas* at least eight months and her construction was lagging behind that of the USS *Maine*, but the problems that would continue to dog the *Texas* also affected the *Maine*. The many challenges facing Constructor Bowles had to be addressed as they came up, pushing the resources of the Norfolk Navy Yard to the limit. Fortunately, the problems faced by Constructor Bowles were appreciated by the Navy, and he did not face criticism for the many delays associated with the construction, as the all-American USS *Maine* also became mired in snail-like progress. A long and dolorous seven year construction period ensued for both ships, a time period that sentenced their designs to near obsolescence.

Following the lengthy contract negotiations, construction documents for the new battleship began to arrive at the Navy Department in mid 1888. A series of modifications to the design were necessary to bring the ship into line with US construction practices and these, together with the long distance relationship between designers and shipyard, were another source of delay, as were the growing pains of the fledgling domestic steel industry. The keel was not laid until June 1, 1889, almost eight months after that of the *Maine* in the Brooklyn Navy Yard.

Among the changes incorporated into the design was the consolidation of the flues into a single stack. The ship's compact arrangement of boilers allowed this modification, which opened up more space within the armored citadel between the turrets but may have cost the ship some efficiency and speed when compared to dual funnels. 1901 modifications would seek to redress this and improve the exhaust flow by raising the height of the stack. The flying bridge, formerly to have been solid-decked from before the foremast to aft of the mainmast, was made skeletal without decking amidships in an effort to reduce the damaging effects of the 12" guns' muzzle blast when fired across the deck. The results of this change, however, later proved to be far from adequate.

Other changes were made related to the working of the guns. Most notable was the enlargement of the turret diameter by three feet. This alteration unfortunately would lead to increased operational difficulties when docking or when coaling at sea due to the overhanging turret-supporting sponsons bulging from her sides.

February 1890: The full length of the keel is in place and framing for the sloped armored deck is underway.

November 1889: Keel framing is progressing and ribs are being carried up above the bottom of the hull. Note the use of rough timber poles for scaffolding and the lack of heavy equipment associated with the building of steel vessels today.

February 1890: Interior plating for the double bottom is being installed in this view facing aft. Note the lightening holes visible in the ribs. The framing of the *Texas*' hull was considered to be light-weight in its day, leading the press to publicly question the strength of the vessel. This light-weight construction was in fact a result of its scientific design, in which the designer sought to achieve the maximum strength on the lowest displacement. The Congressional limit on the ship's final displacement also factored into the decisions being made as details of the construction were worked out.

In the end the Congress would get what it paid for, a small, light battleship of unusual power and speed for its size.

July 1890: Framing for the armored deck continues. In the distance unarmored decking has begun. The *Texas* was originally to have been equipped with compound armor made by joining together with molten steel a wrought iron plate with a heat-hardened mild steel plate. This results in an armor approximately four times the density of wrought iron. In 1890, however, the Navy Department shifted its preference to the newly developed American "Harveyized" nickel-steel (also known as face-hardened or "cemented" nickel-steel.) While this decision would result in ships whose armor protection pound-for-pound and inch-for-inch exceeded even that of the British Navy, it would delay the completion of both the *Texas* and the *Maine* by almost two years while domestic steel manufacturers tooled up for its production.

May 1891: The hull of the *Texas* begins to take form. Framing for the diagonal central redoubt is under way, angling from the forward/port turret position (whose sponson is here outlined in white) across the deck to the aft/starboard turret position.

The hull of the *Texas* was of all steel "cellular construction" made up of 129 water-tight compartments interconnected by steam and hand pumps. She had a double hull below the lower deck level as well as fore and aft trimming tanks within the hull. Spaces fore and aft above the armored deck were each divided by a water-tight bulkhead. The boiler and engine spaces below the armored deck were divided into six watertight compartments, three on each side. Ammunition magazines were located below the passageway between the boiler room compartments, separated from the ship's coal bunkers which were notoriously prone to spontaneous combustion, a design consideration not found in the *Maine*.

Many of the steel plates that had been delivered for the *Texas* were rejected as they did not meet the quality standards required. On several occasions manufacturers complained that the Navy's requirements were too rigorous. However the Navy remained adamant about the quality of steel it wanted.

The *Texas'* problems with suppliers were not limited to the steel industry. Bowles rejected out of hand the pine material that had been delivered as decking. After a sharp rebuke, and over the suppliers protestations, Bowles found enough suitable wood among the stores already on hand at the yard to deck the *Texas*.

June 1892: The timber scaffolding is being removed, exposing the newly painted hull. The light colored lower hull is likely coated in a white lead primer.

May 1891: Framing and plating for the bow has reached the main deck. Visible through the scaffolding is the ram bow. In the *Texas* the structure of the forward portion of the protected deck was brought down to reinforce the ram bow. During a ramming attack, the strength of the ram and its supporting structure would be critical to ensuring that the *Texas* would not suffer the same fate as the vessel being rammed.

From September 1890 through November 1891 the US Navy conducted a series of tests demonstrating the relative resistance to shellfire of the various types of armor then in existence. These tests were watched with interest, not merely by naval constructors in the United States, but by naval experts throughout the world.

Both 6 inch and 8 inch guns were used. A 10 ½ inch thick armor plate of each type was mounted to a shock absorbing wood backing, as was typically done in warship construction. Each plate received four 6 inch shots near the corners, followed by a single 8 inch shot in the center. The plates were then carefully examined for penetration, cracking, spalling, bulging, or other signs of failure. High carbon nickel steel Harveyized plate was found to be the best for American warships, although the tests showed room for improvement in production techniques to ensure uniformity throughout the plate.

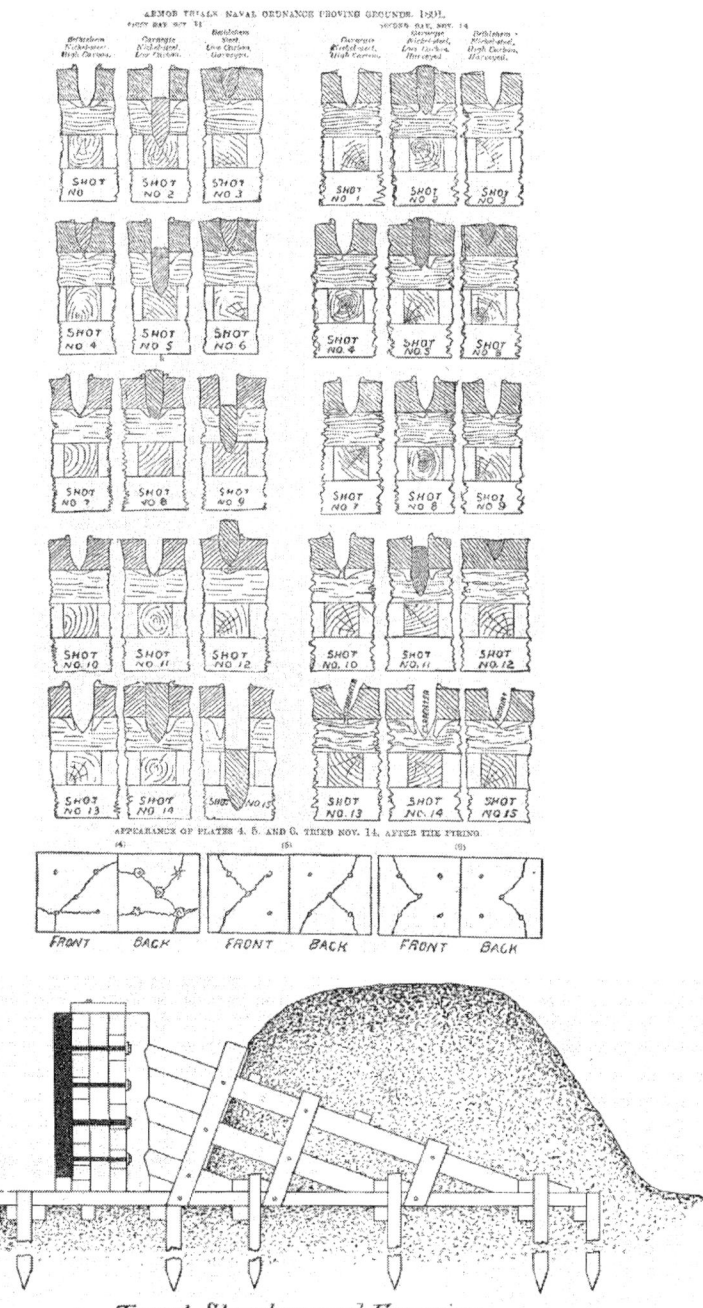

The Navy had determined which armor was the best, it was now up to the developing United States steel industry to work out how to make it in the quantities necessary to equip a growing fleet.

June 24 1892: Preparations for launch are being made. Note the bracing timbers and wooden speed brake temporarily mounted to the rudder and the sliding cradle supporting the hull. Also note that the armor for the turrets and waterline belt have not been installed.

June 24, 1892: The men behind the ship. (l. to r.) Steel fitter R.E. Glover, Naval Constructor F.T. Bowles, rigger Wm. Hoffman, Verg. Powers, Assistant Naval Constructor Wm. J. Baxter, and master fitter J. H. Hazler.

June 28, 1892: USS *Texas* shortly before launch as seen in an illustration commemorating the event which carried the statement: "The first battle ship ever launched in America." The USS *Maine* though launched on November 18, 1889, well before the *Texas*, , was still classified at that time as an armored cruiser.

Excerpts from F. T. Bowles' blocking and ground ways plans for the USS *Texas*, dated September 1888, help to illustrate the level of complexity of the hull support and launching structure. At left can be seen the forest of pilings extending well out into the channel that were necessary to bear the weight of the hull as the vessel slipped into the water. Without the support of such ground ways, a long ship risked breaking her keel during the launching process as the weight of the hull transferred from the blocking to the water.

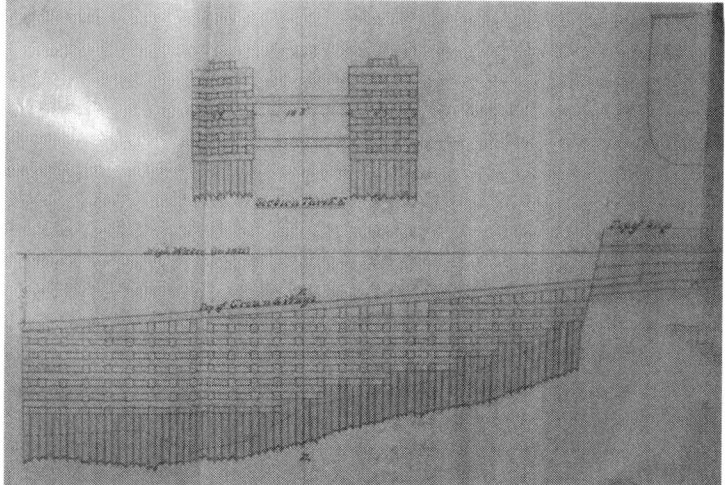
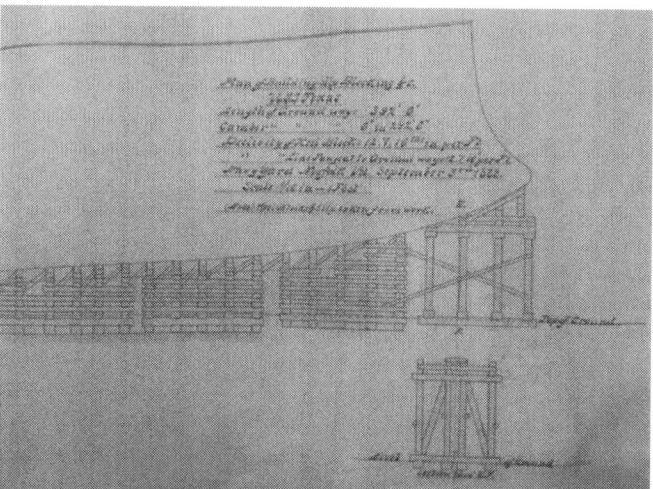

June 28, 1892: "At 11:17 o'clock this morning Miss Madge Houston Williams of Texas at a signal from Naval Constructor Francis T. Bowels broke the bottle of wine on the bow of the finest armored battle ship ever launched in the United States, and in a clear, firm voice cried: 'I christen thee *Texas.*'

Immediately the hurrahs from thousands of throats and the screeching of steam whistles announced the fact that the new ship had started for the plunge in her native element.

The weather was very bad, but, notwithstanding this, about 15,000 braved it, and the sight was well worth their effort. It was conceded to be one of the prettiest launching ever witnessed. Not a hitch or flaw occurred, and as the massive structure of iron and steel rode the waves of the Elizabeth like a swan and was moored to the dock a lusty hurrah again arose…

The *Texas* is by 2,600 tons the largest ship ever launched in this country, and her successful launch demonstrates the ability of the heads which have planed and directed her building. Constructor Bowles is a proud man today, even more so than at the Raleigh's launch, for he has had a perfect triumph." - *New York Times* 6-29-1892

Bethlehem Steel had to design and build a new plant for the construction of armored plates. *American Engineer and Railroad Journal* described the creation of the armor in detail: "The steel is melted in open hearth furnaces, and drawn out into ladles having capacities of from 40,000 to 90,000 lbs. each. These ladles are mounted upon trucks that travel over rails laid along each side of the casting pit. The ingot molds are set up in this pit, and in casting the larger ingots, the contents of several ladles, each consisting of the charge of one furnace, are poured into the mold...After an ingot has been allowed to cool in its mold for several days it is taken, while still hot, to the great 125-ton hammer or 14,000-ton press and forged down to the proper thickness, that portion of the ingot which was cast at the bottom forming the body of the plate...When the plate is forged to the required thickness, and somewhat full of width, a large amount of metal from the top of the ingot and a small amount from the bottom is cut off at the hammer or press. The plates are then annealed... Machining consists in trimming the plates on their longer edges to somewhat full of their finished width, and in beveling or rounding the edges if required. This work is done with cold saws, planers and milling machines...After the first machining the plates are sent to the 7,000-ton bending press to be bent or curved as per templates...The operation of tempering requires a powerful crane, large heating furnaces and a great tank of oil. Its object is to toughen the steel and give to it the proper hardness, and it calls for much experience and skill...The plates are ready for ballistic test...If the ballistic test is successful, the lot or group which it represents is ready for finishing. The finishing process consists in 'rectifying' - that is, slightly bending at the press to bring the plates as nearly as possible to the shape of the templates, and in accurately machining all the edges to required dimensions. The last operation is drilling and tapping of the bolt holes...From the above description, it will be seen that the whole manufacture is one requiring great care and a thorough knowledge of conditions both chemical and physical at every step, and the wonderful results of the ballistic tests already referred to, where several 8-in shots striking with the energy of nearly 7,000 foot-tons fail to develop any cracks, indicate to what perfection the production of this material has been brought."

March 3, 1893: Norfolk Navy Yard. The *Texas* pays the first of a series of visits to dry dock as her shafts and propellers are fitted. The *Texas* had two four-bladed manganese bronze propellers 14 foot 6 inch in diameter with a 15 foot 7 inch pitch.

March 22, 1893 Reading Pennsylvania: Test-plates of redoubt and turret armor for the *Texas* demonstrated their "proof" against an 8" breech-loading rifle at the Bethlehem Iron Company. Impressively, while creating craters in the surface of the armor, the 8" shells failed to penetrate or crack the plates. Each plate was tested with multiple shots to verify that an individual hit could not compromise the plate's protection versus subsequent shells. Fragments of the test shells litter the ground before the turret plate.

TEST PLATE OF REDOUBT ARMOR UNITED STATES BATTLESHIP "TEXAS."

Normally, warships were armored on the principle that the equivalent of the warship's own armament should not be able to penetrate it's vitals at long battle ranges. Battleships were not intended to close the range with other individual battleships, unless they had superiority of numbers or position. A rule of thumb generally followed for battleships was 1" of armor for every 1" of diameter of shell. The *Texas* with her twelve inch guns had twelve inch armor. Most of the testing done on armor was at close range with smaller shells. At the time the *Texas* was built, long range firing was considered more art than science so armor was primarily constructed to resist shells impacting on nearly horizontal trajectories. At these trajectories the water surrounding the ship provided significant protection to spaces below the waterline, therefore the thickness of a warship's armor tapered thinner below this level.

TEST PLATE OF TURRET ARMOR UNITED STATES BATTLESHIP "TEXAS."

Only one half a decade later it was found during the Spanish-American War that battle ranges had increased beyond what had previously been anticipated, reflecting in part a desire to maintain a healthy distance from enemy warships due to the increasingly effective automotive torpedo. Many a shell failed to hit its target during that war due to gunners underestimating the range when firing over open sights. Battle ranges would grow geometrically over the following years, dramatically affecting the design of future battleships, influencing the selection and operation of the armament, the placement of the armor, and the sighting of targets.

1892-1893 Norfolk Navy Yard: The "new" monitor USS *Amphtrite* awaits the arrival of her armor with the also delayed *Texas* moored beyond.

Amphtrite had been laid down in 1874, launched in 1883, and would not be commissioned until 1895. Once installed, the weight of her armor would lower her upper deck to the point that it would nearly be awash. Even more so than the *Texas*, by the time *Amphtrite* entered service she would be an antiquated design - equipped though with the latest armor, armaments, and fittings.

July 1893 – July 1894: The construction schedule continued to slip due to the unavailability of new armor. Further delays resulted from a major fire at the factory building her machinery. Each of these setbacks lead in a snowball effect to further delays in fitting out the warship. The *Texas* rides high without her armor and armaments.

July 14, 1894 Norfolk Navy Yard: The incomplete *Texas* sits dripping superficial rust, waiting for her belt armor. The turrets, however have been installed as have her 6" guns on the main deck. Awnings affixed above the upper deck hint at activity stirring within as they provide shade from the intense summer sun in an attempt to moderate the temperature inside the hull. The ship's boat cranes serve to lift and set machinery and materials.

June 29, 1895 Norfolk: The USS *Texas* rapidly approaches completion. The warship has received her 12" main battery and has been freshly painted. Note that her lower hull now sports a dark red oxide paint where previously it was painted a light color below the waterline. Work continues on deck as preparations are made for her upcoming commissioning.

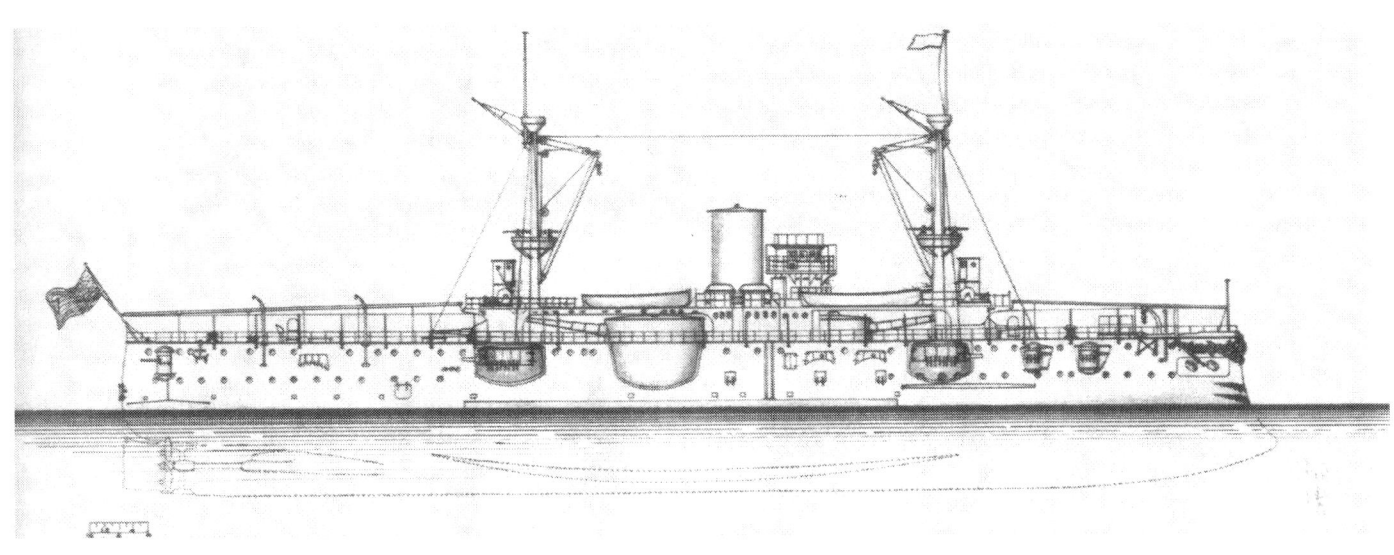

Circa 1895 drawings showing the USS *Texas* as originally completed.

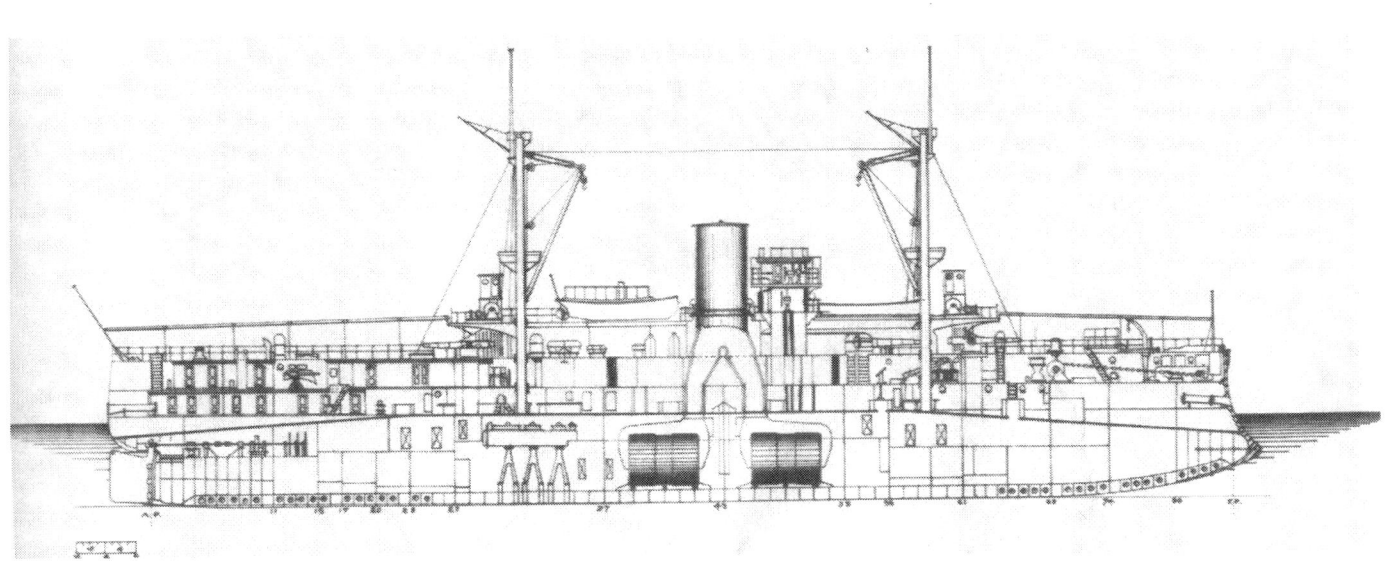

The torpedo boats that were to be carried on deck were now nowhere to be seen in these as-built drawings.

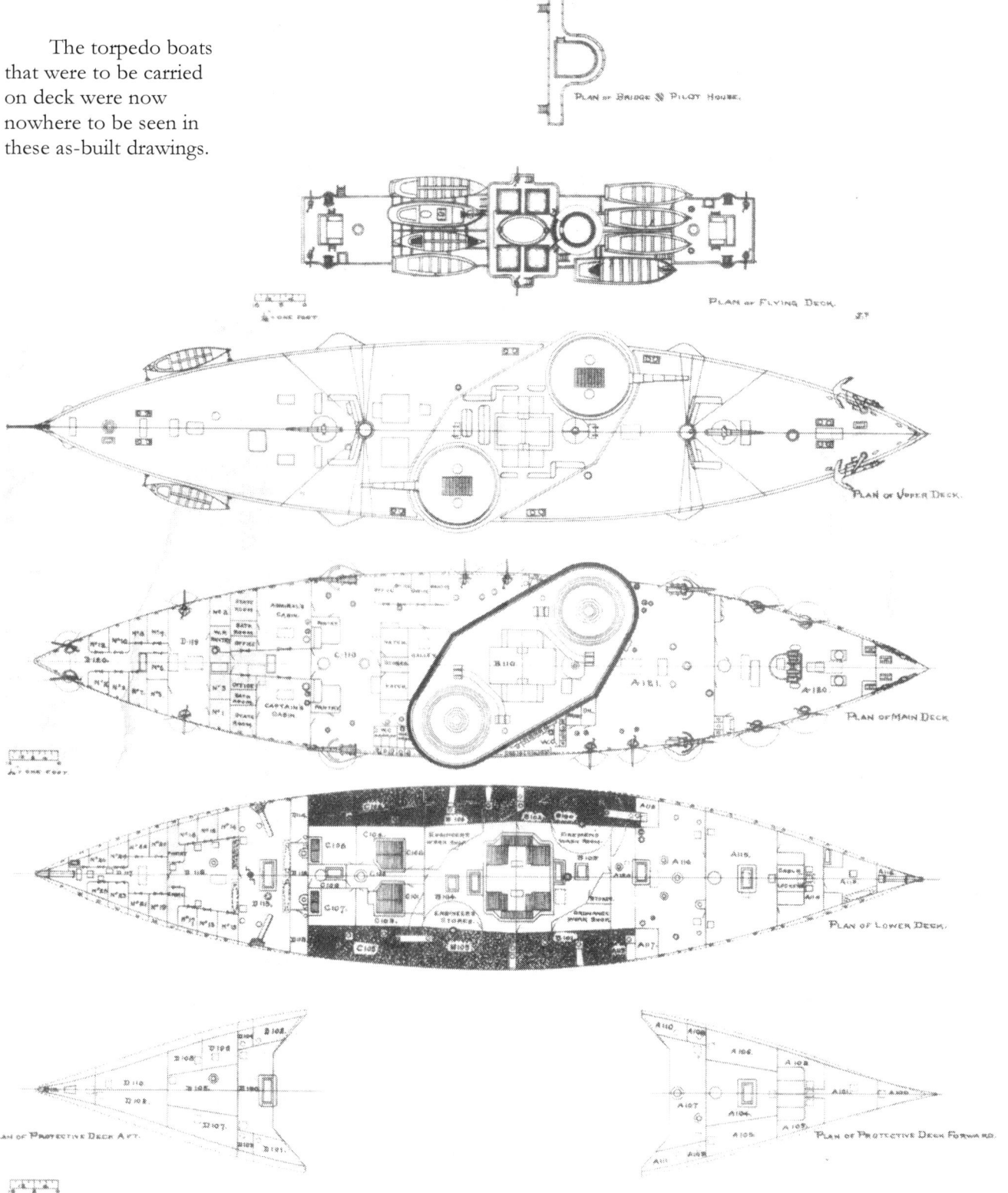

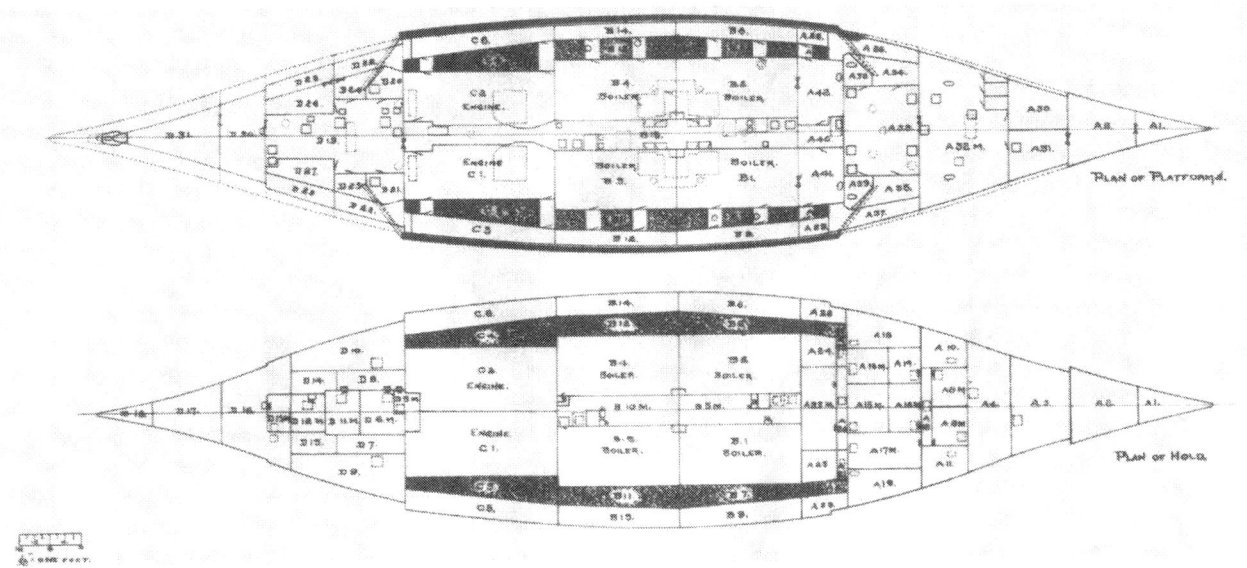

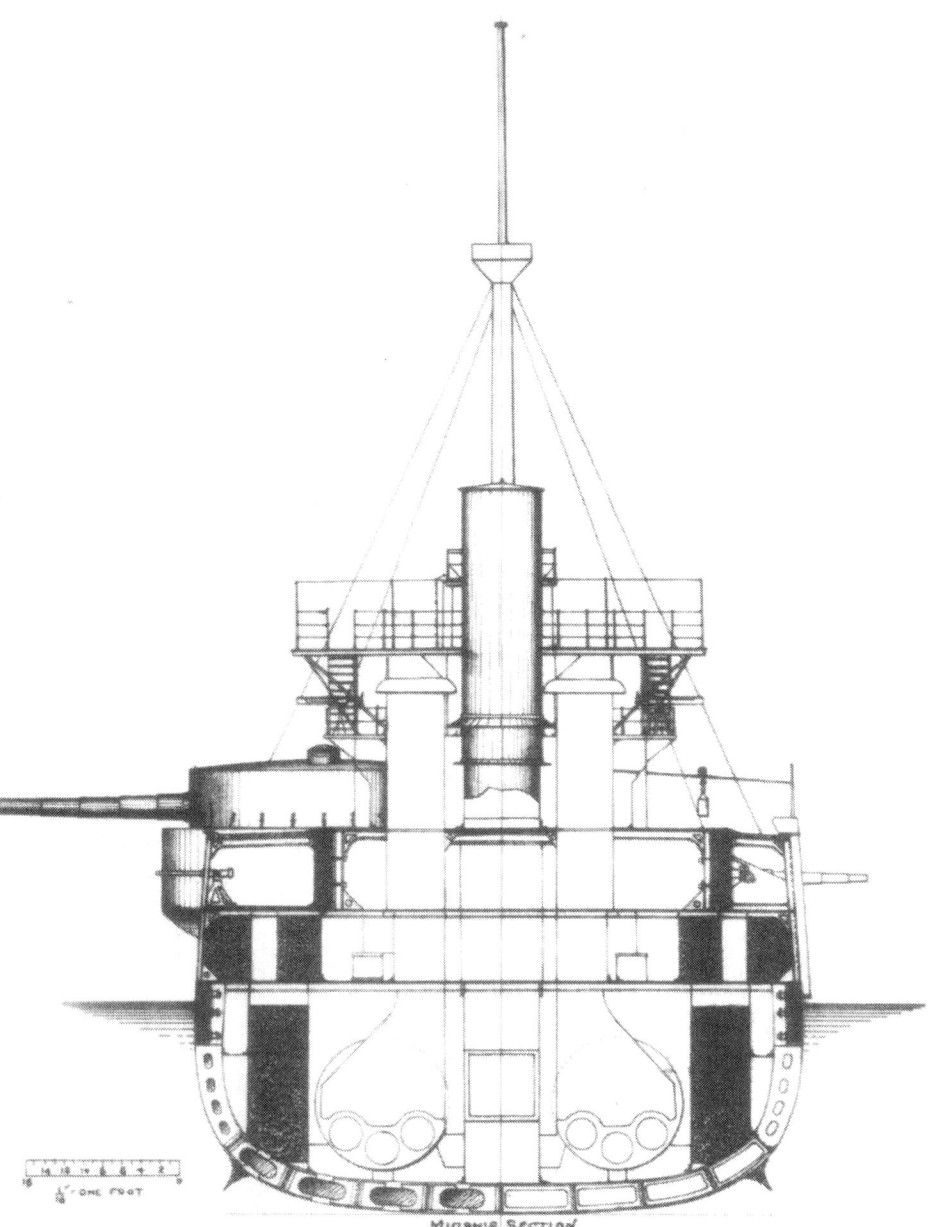

In this amidships section (left) the ventilating and exhaust flues for the boiler room are visible. The *Texas* featured a forced draft system in which the boiler's air intakes could be pressurized to increase the rate of combustion in the boilers' fireboxes, thereby raising the steam pressure and increasing the power and speed of the engines. A blower driven by a vertical engine and a 4 foot 6 inch diameter exhaust fan was provided for each of the four fire rooms.

The forward section (below left) shows the ship's capstan and donkey engine. The anchor chains and cables could be manipulated by steam power or by traditional manual means, if necessary.

Visible in both the forward and aft sections (below right) is the sloped armored deck protecting the ships vital machinery, and her buoyancy, during battle.

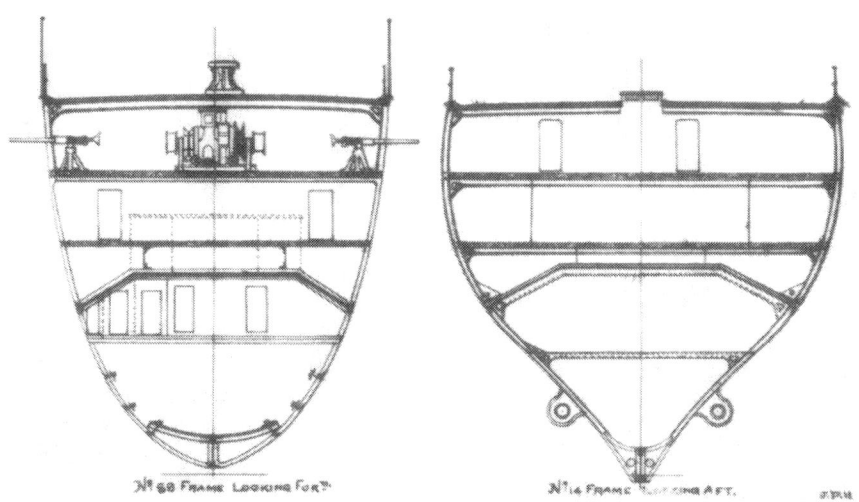

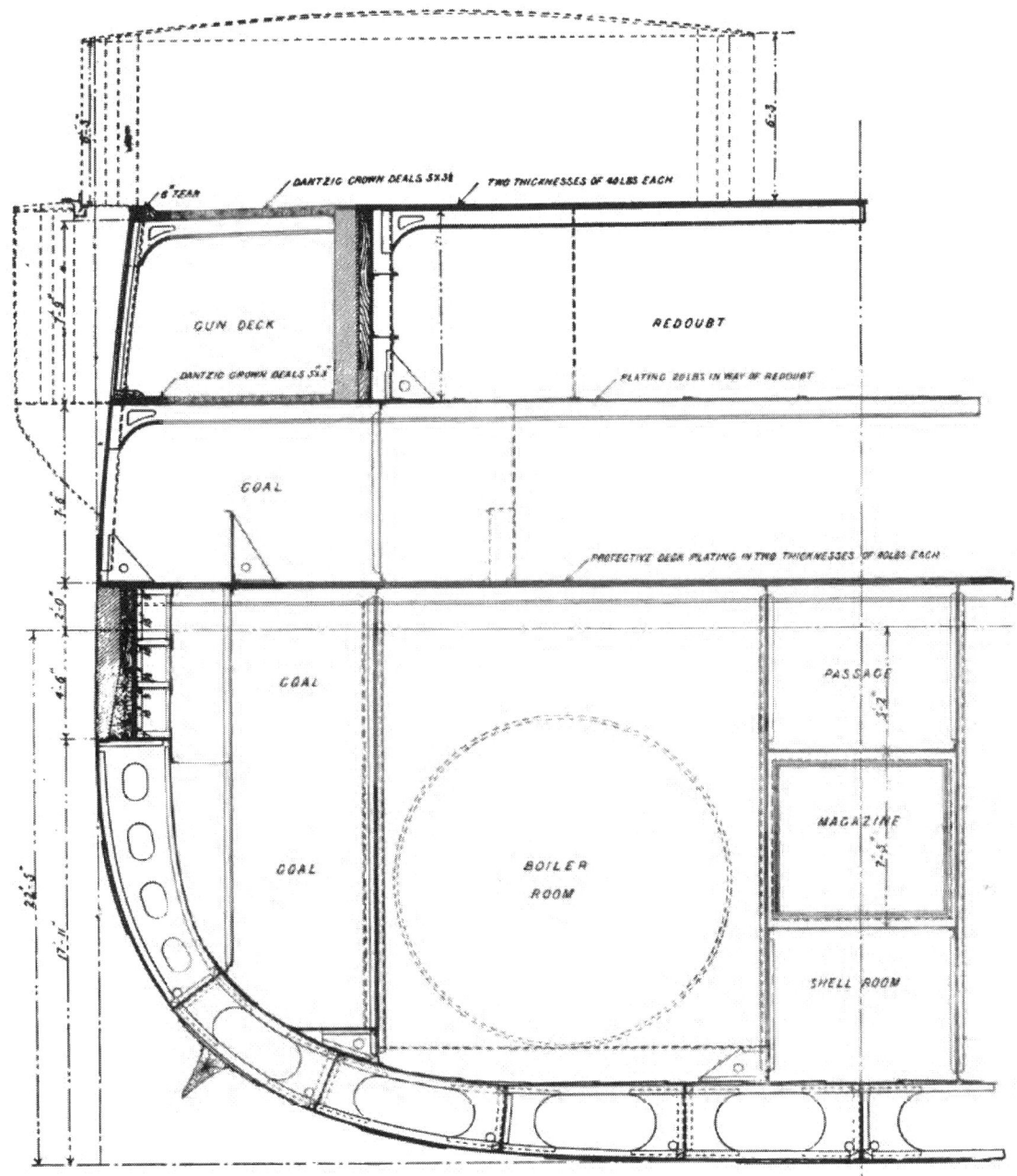

HALF CROSS-SECTION OF THE UNITED STATES BATTLESHIP TEXAS.

Half section through the boiler room of the *Texas* showing the arrangement of armor and compartments. The coal bunkers were purposefully arranged above the juncture of the protective deck and the belt armor. Additional bunkers were placed within the armored spaces, directly adjacent to the boiler room. This both ensured a ready fuel supply during combat and provided an additional measure of protection to the vital boilers. The magazines were located along the centerline of the ship, ensuring maximum protection from enemy shells but also placing the explosive powder adjacent to the hottest spaces in the ship. The *Maine's* magazines in contrast were surrounded by coal bunkers, a design solution with other, now-apparent risks.

Also visible in this plan is the typical manner in which the belt and redoubt armor was emplaced over wood. Along its belt the *Texas* had 6" of pine backing to its 12" of Harveyized nickel-steel armor. The pine backing not only helped absorb shock but also worked through a system of bolts with rubber washers, screwed into the back of the armor, to pull tight and hold the armor in place. It could be quite embarrassing having your armor fall into the sea after being hit a few times - as happened to the Russians at Tsushima in 1904.

As with the production of new armor, American industry was forced to expand it's factories to accommodate ever-larger guns in a race to keep pace with rapidly advancing ordnance technology. A domestic factory for modern naval guns was authorized by Congress in 1886 to be built at the Washington Naval Yard and was in production by 1889. Here the stages of "hydraulic" gun casting are revealed to the public through the illustrations of a period magazine.

Fig. 2.—HYDRAULIC GUN CASTING.

Fig. 3.—HYDRAULIC GUN FORGING.

Fig. 4.—A ROW OF FOURTEEN SIX INCH GUNS.

At the Washington Navy Yard the forged barrels were received and machined into guns in a range of standardized sizes. Increasing bore and length, improvements in powders, and a variety of new breech designs required ever-greater machining precision than in preceding years using increasingly larger tooling.

New guns required new gun-mounts. Technology was rapidly advancing in the science of gun-mount design as well. The guns of the *Texas* featured sliding returns and hydraulic power for many operations - cutting edge innovations in the early 1890's US Navy.

United States naval gun factory, Washington, D. C. North gun shop.

United States naval gun factory, Washington, D. C. Rifling machine.

A completed heavy gun on turret mount assembled at the Washington Navy Yard, ready for delivery to the Navy's range for testing.

4 MACHINERY AND CONTROLS

An engine of the USS *Texas* set up in the workshops of the manufacturer, Richmond Locomotive and Machine Works of Richmond, Virginia (left) and an 1890 ad for the company (below).

Post-Civil War Southern pride led more than one newspaper to refer to the ship as "The *Texas*: a Southern built battleship."

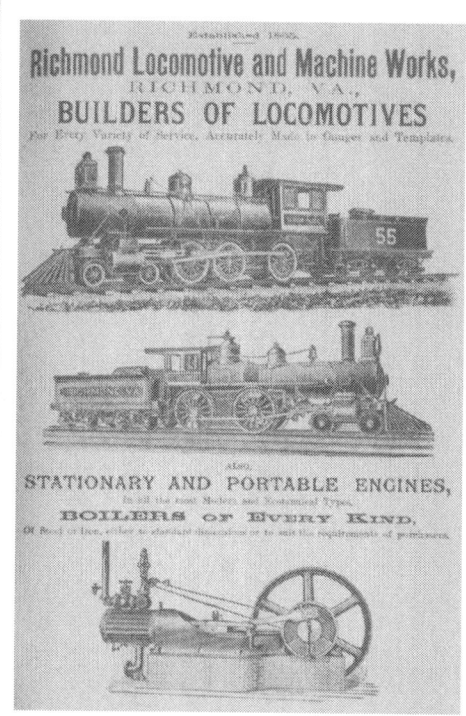

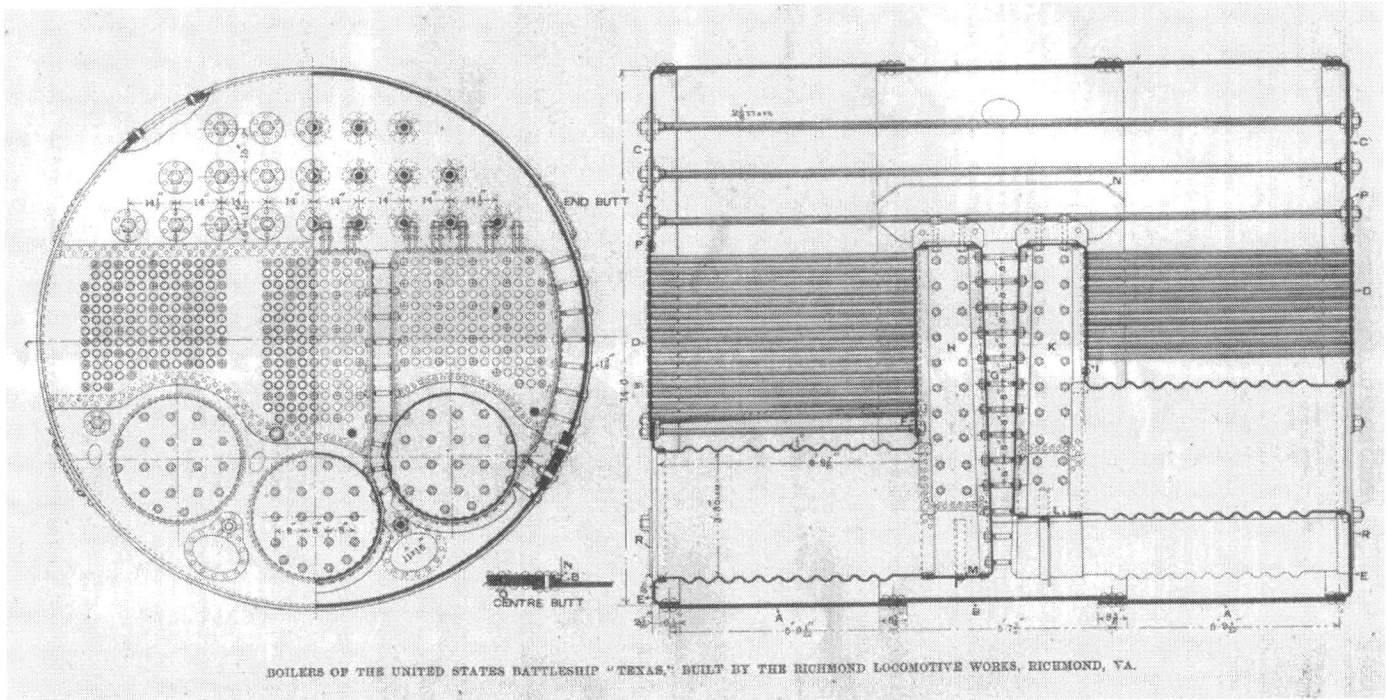

BOILERS OF THE UNITED STATES BATTLESHIP "TEXAS," BUILT BY THE RICHMOND LOCOMOTIVE WORKS, RICHMOND, VA.

The *Texas* was fitted with four, double-ended cylindrical "Bureau Express" boilers 14 feet in diameter and approximately 17 feet in length. These featured horizontal return, fire tubes, and corrugated "Fox" furnace flues. A total of 810-2 ½" diameter tubes were incorporated into each boiler, 168 stay-tubes and 642 ordinary tubes, each of 6 feet 9 inches in length. There were three furnaces on each end of the boiler, six per boiler, for a total of twenty-four. The total heating surface for the *Texas'* boilers was 16,918 square feet, with a total grate surface of about 532 square feet. The boiler's working pressure was 150 pounds per square inch.

Coal was supplied entirely by hand. There was bunkerage provided on board for a typical loading of 500 tons, with additional capacity allowing a maximum total load of 850 tons of coal. With 500 tons, the ship's endurance was 1110 nm at 17 knots, 2050 nm at 15 knots, or 3179 nm at 12 knots. With 850 tons this was extended to 2180 nm at 16.5 knots, 3900 nm at 14.75 knots, or 6000 nm at 11.8 knots.

The boiler flues produced for the *Texas* at the Continental Iron Works in Brooklyn, demonstrated that no one state or region could claim exclusive bragging rights to the *Texas*.

CORRUGATED FLUES FOR BATTLESHIP "TEXAS," MADE BY THE CONTINENTAL IRON WORKS BROOKLYN N.Y.

Two boilers for the *Texas* await barge shipment to Norfolk. The boilers were too big to pass through the Church Hill Tunnel on the Chesapeake and Ohio Railroad, so they were instead loaded at the shops onto a special rail carriage and taken to the James River to be placed on board a barge for transport to the navy yard.

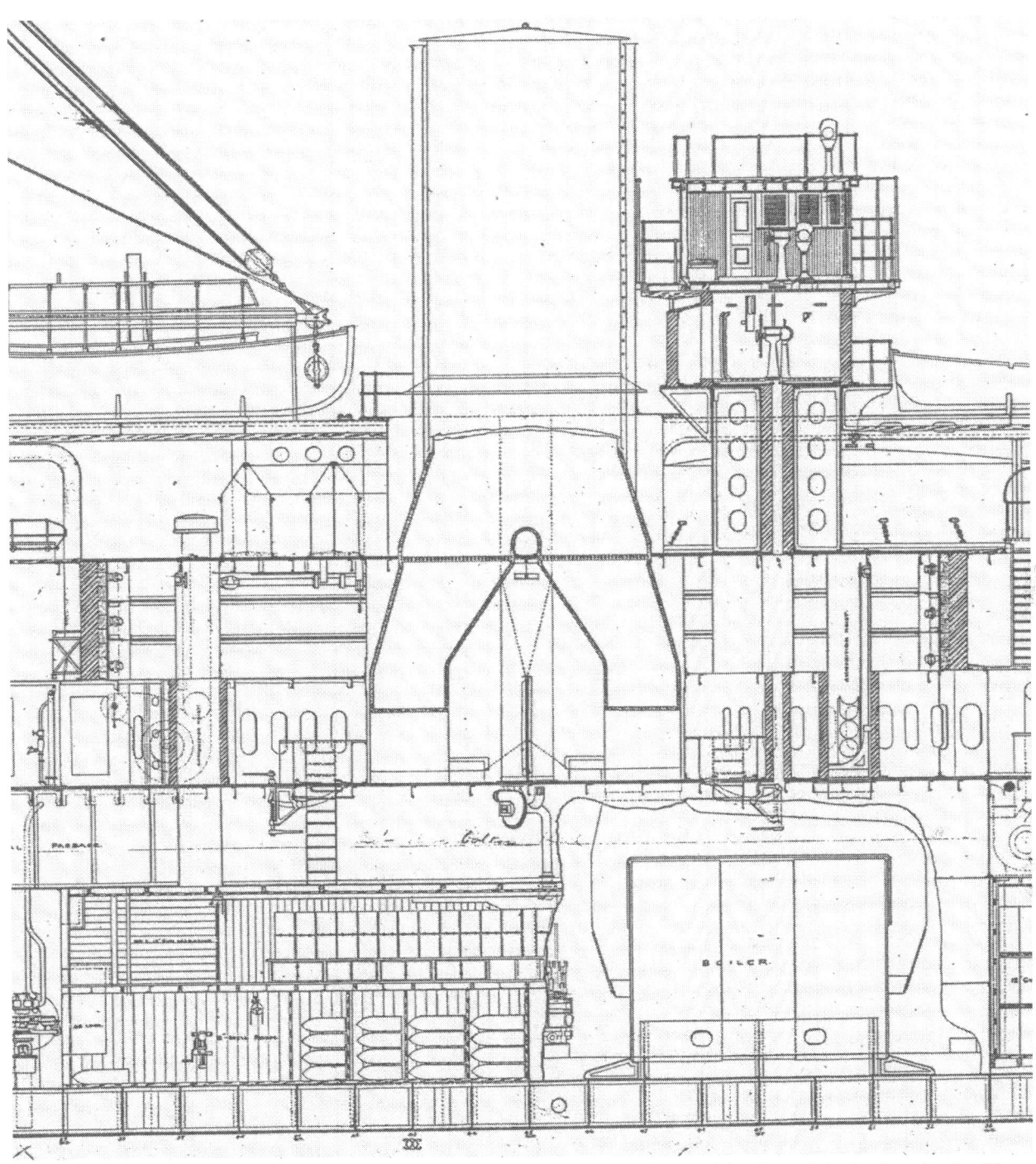

The boiler room, uptakes, and funnel of the *Texas*. The close-together positioning of the boilers in the *Texas* allowed the design to be modified during construction so that a single funnel could be used. The change from two slender funnels to a single, proportionally squat funnel may have reduced the draft in the stack and slightly lowered her speed. Modifications made after the Spanish-American War would seek to redress this.

Note the convoluted configuration of the armor revealed in this section drawing. Beneath the wooden pilot house, the *Texas* had an armored conning tower, above a vertically unarmored main deck, above an armored "redoubt", above a vertically unarmored berth deck, all on top of an armored horizontal "protective" deck. Due to this alternating arrangement, critical systems passing vertically through this portion of the ship had to pass in and out of armored scuttles and shafts. The limited extent of armored protection was due to the constraints Congress had placed upon the ship's displacement. Some protection at the level of the otherwise unarmored berth deck was afforded, however, by the strategic placement of coal storage compartments along the ship's sides.

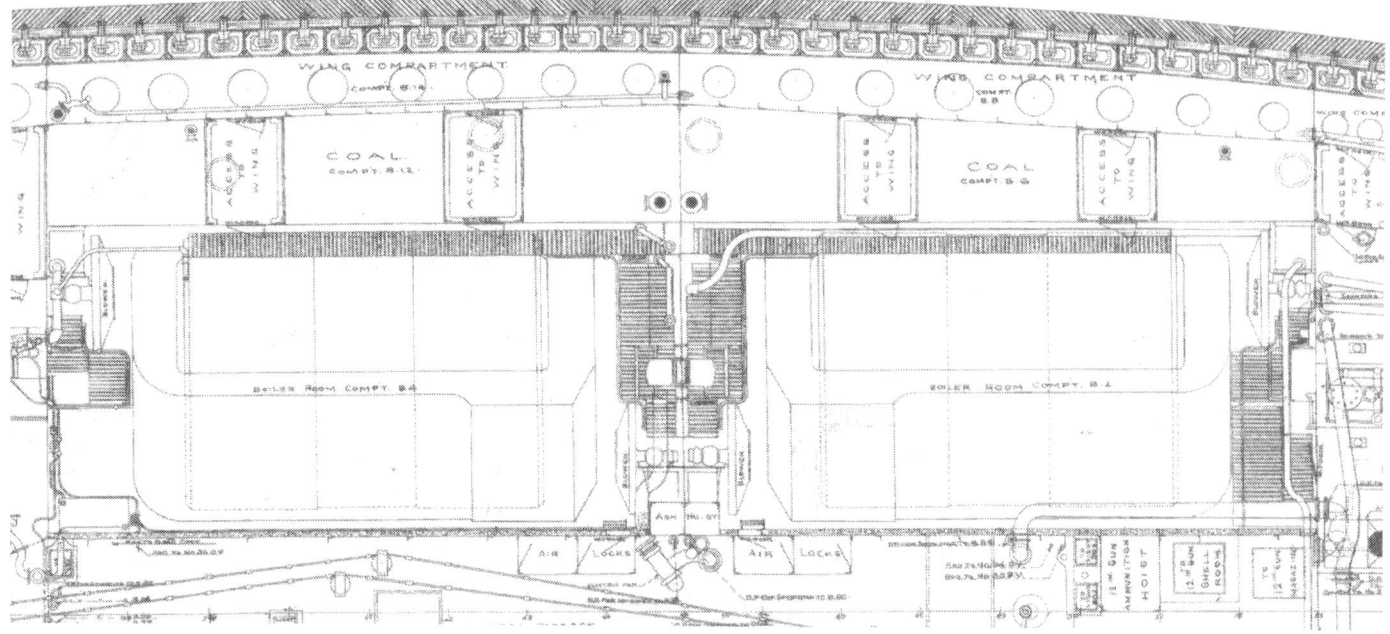

The upper (platform deck level) boiler rooms on the port side of the *Texas*. Each boiler occupied a separate compartment. Coal was delivered down from storage compartments located above on the berth deck as well as from compartments located outboard of each boiler room. The ship's armored belt can be seen in section across the top of this plan.

The lower (hold deck level) boiler rooms or "fire rooms" on the port side of the *Texas*. From this level the fire boxes at the bottom of the boilers were stoked by hand and shovel, in a hellish environment of oppressive heat, oily dust, and naked flame. Only a short distance away, separated by an insulated bulkhead, lay the magazines for the 12" guns' powder and ammunition. Heat prostration of officers and men in the engineering spaces, as well as elevated temperatures in the magazine, would be a chronic concern.

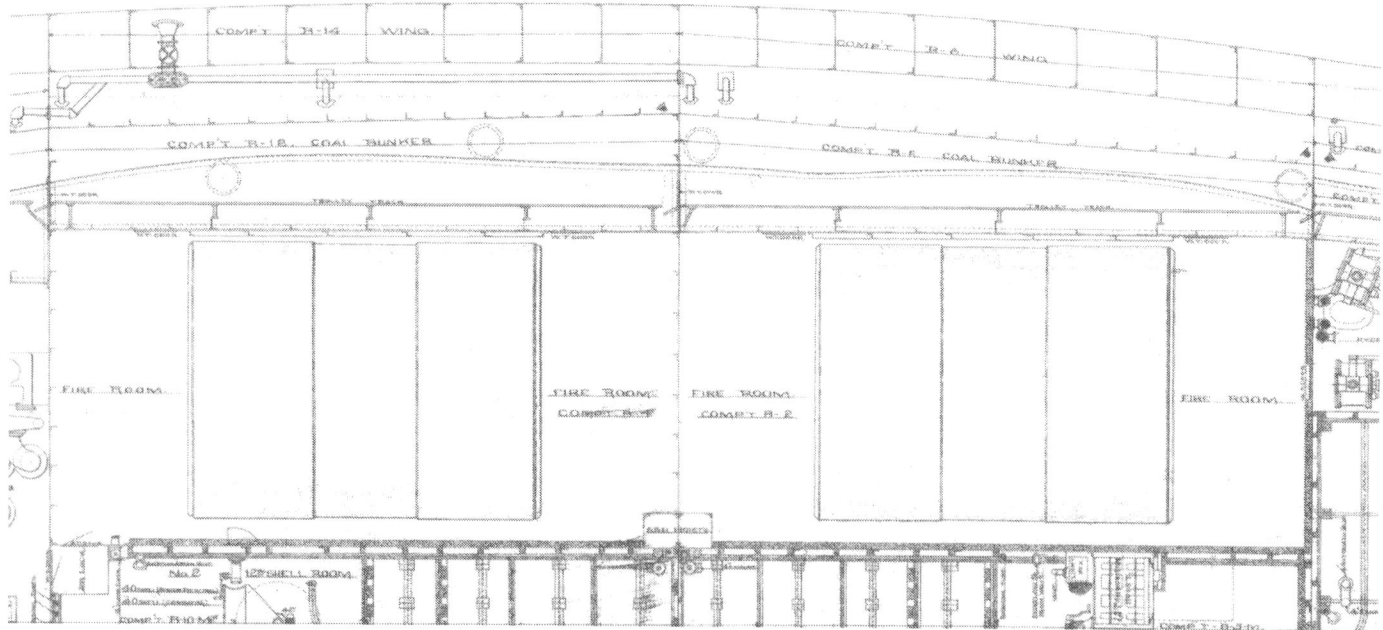

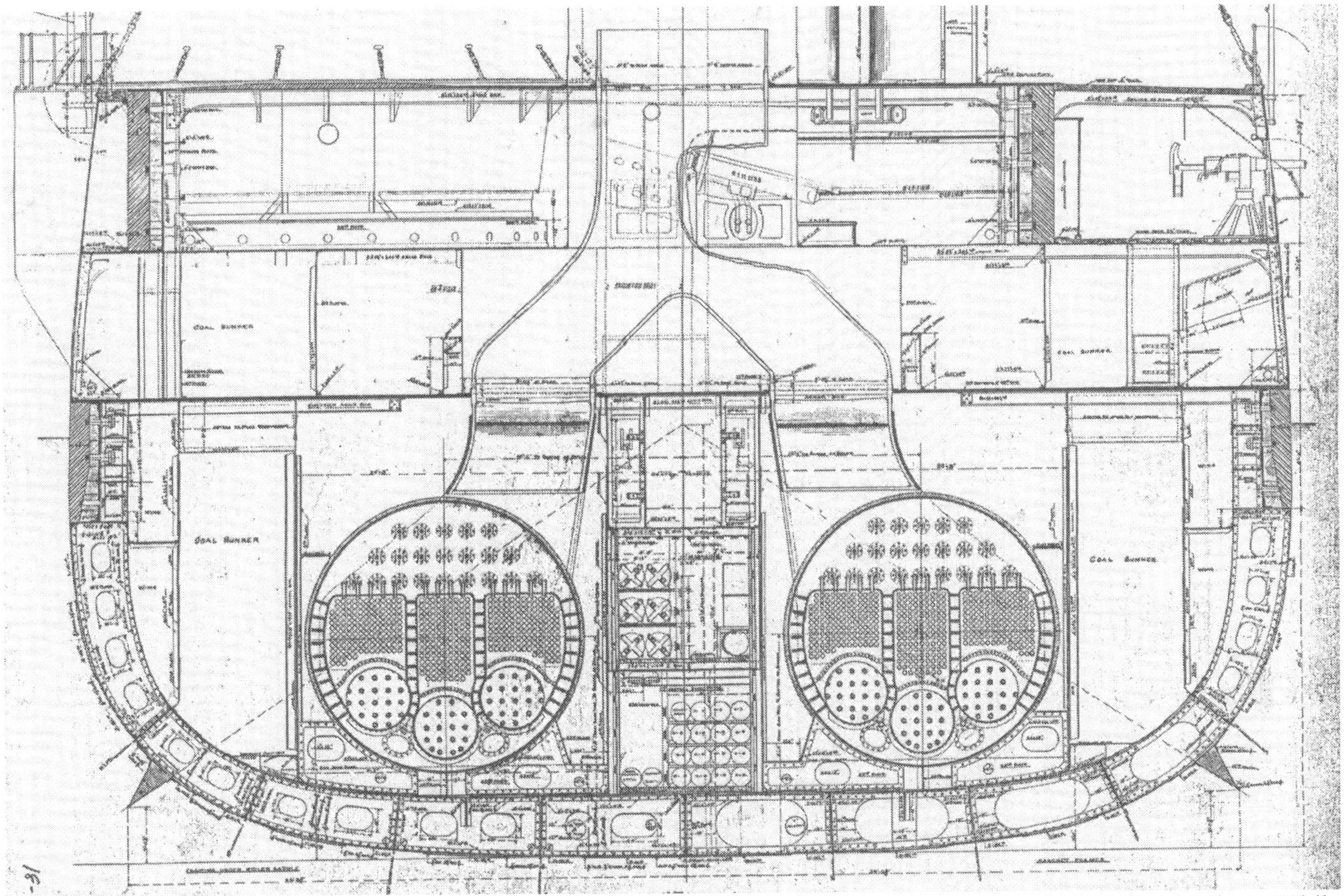

Midships section of the *Texas* showing the arrangement of the boiler room, uptakes, and central magazine. While the magazine was certainly in the most protected space when in battle and well isolated from the coal bunkers, which were prone to spontaneously ignite, the proximity of the boilers and their fire boxes to the magazine is striking.

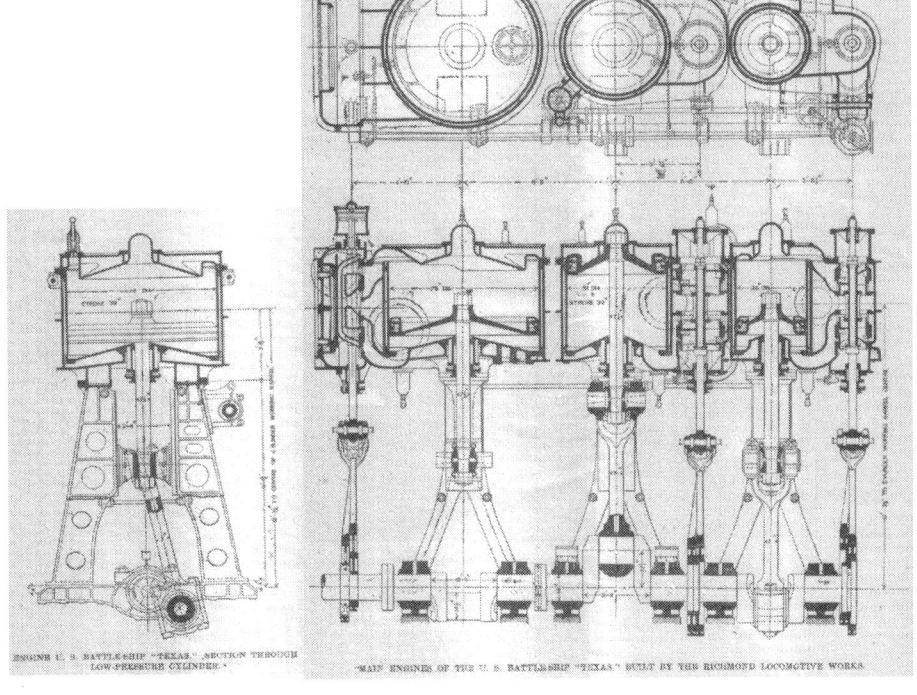

Plan and section of the engines of the USS *Texas*. The *Texas* was equipped with a pair of vertical inverted direct acting triple expansion engines. Each engine had three cylinders with a piston stroke of 39 inches. Power was transmitted via 19'-8" long 13 ½" diameter line shafts connected to the engines. Propeller shafts were 25'-3" and 30'-4 ½" long and 14 3/8" and 14" diameter, respectively.

ENGINES U. S. BATTLE-SHIP "TEXAS," BUILT BY RICHMOND LOCOMOTIVE WORKS, RICHMOND, VA.

An engine of the USS *Texas* assembled in the shops of the Richmond Locomotive and Machine Works. The engines were of British design which can be visually differentiated from American by the use of columns (frames) in the form of an inverted "Y" rather than straight columns, as was the normal practice in America at that time.

In operation steam was fed first into the 36" diameter high-pressure piston, then to the larger 51" diameter intermediate-pressure piston, and finally into the largest 78" diameter low-pressure cylinder. When tested at 90 rpm, the high-pressure cylinder produced 478.52 horsepower, the intermediated-pressure cylinder produced 606.58 horsepower, and the low-pressure cylinder produced 711.54 horsepower for a total of 3,591.49 horsepower from a single engine.

Both engines of the *Texas* in the shops of the Richmond Locomotive and Machine Works being erected side-by-side to lay out controls and connections.

The engines of the *Texas* occupied spaces on the platform and hold decks, beneath the protective deck that formed the floor of the berth deck. A central passage crossed fore and aft at the platform deck level and a central bulkhead separated the engine rooms at the level of the hold deck. Hatches in the decks above allowed large components to be raised or lowered from the engine rooms during major overhauls.

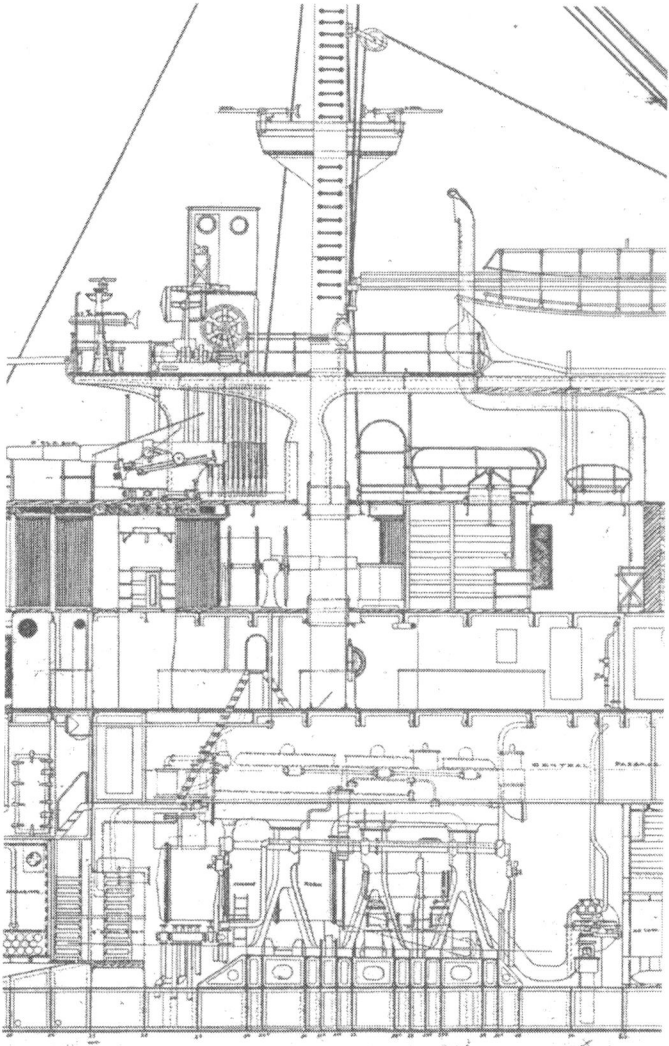

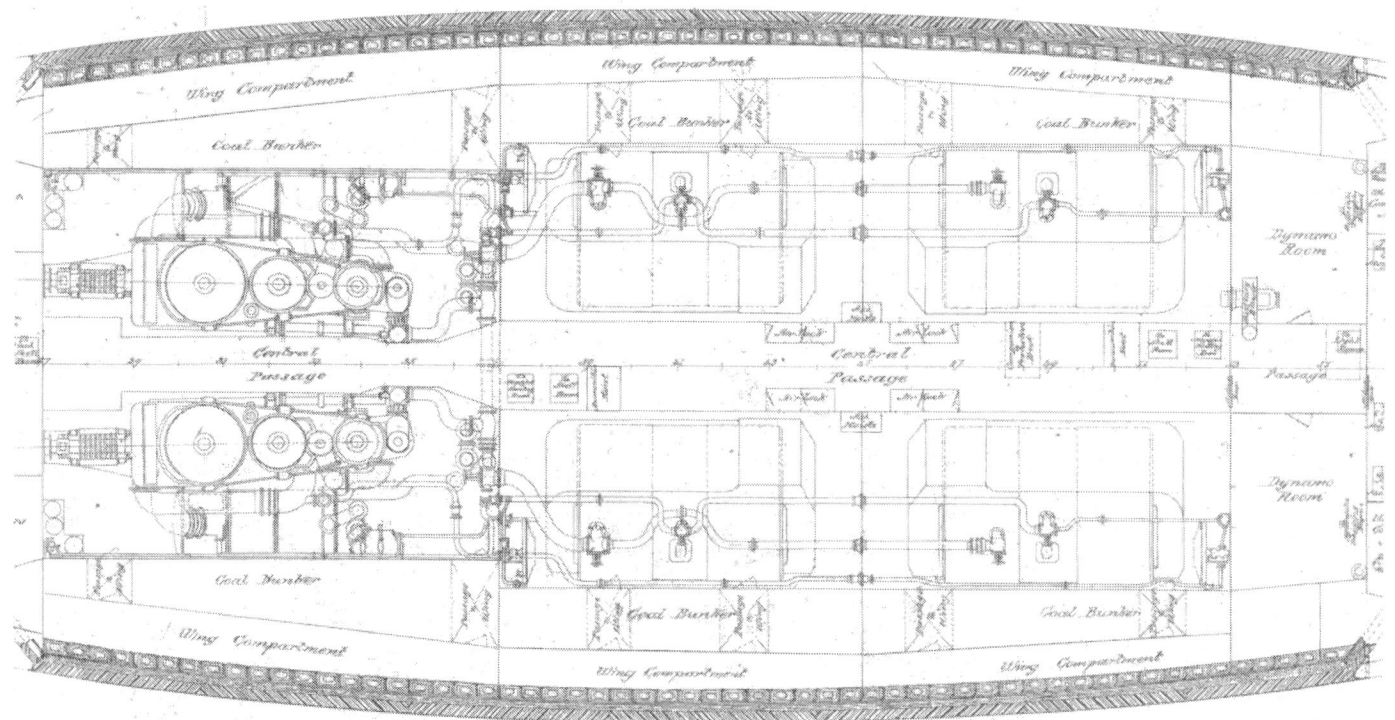

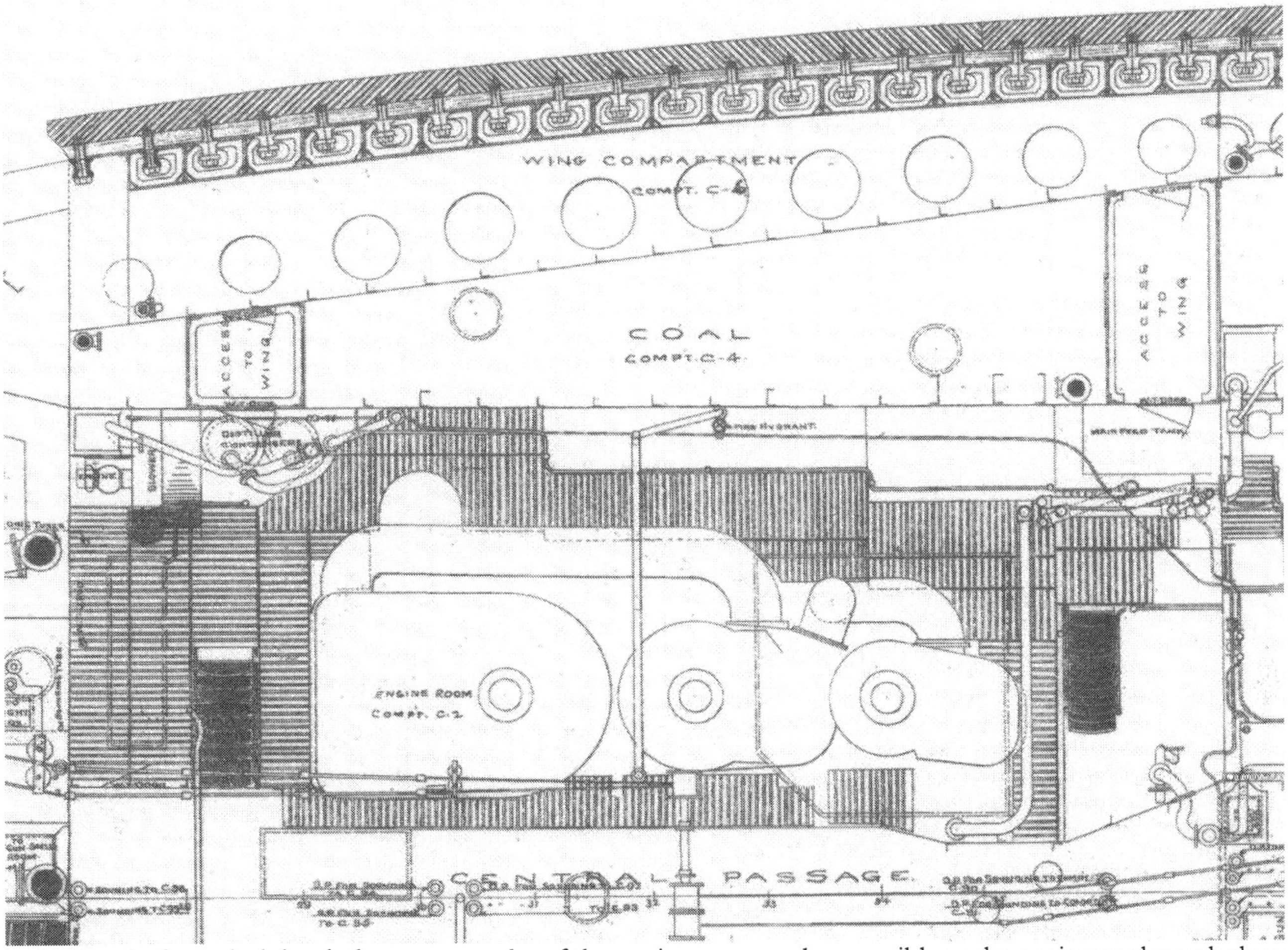

At the platform deck level, the upper works of the engine were made accessible to the engineers through the use of gratings and ladders. The ship's armored belt is seen at the top of this plan.

At the level of the hold deck, the massive drive-shafts emerged from the engine, passed through a decoupling, and traveled aft beneath the steering and tiller rooms before transitioning outside of the hull to the propellers. A condenser in each engine room recaptured the precious fresh water from the spent steam for reuse.

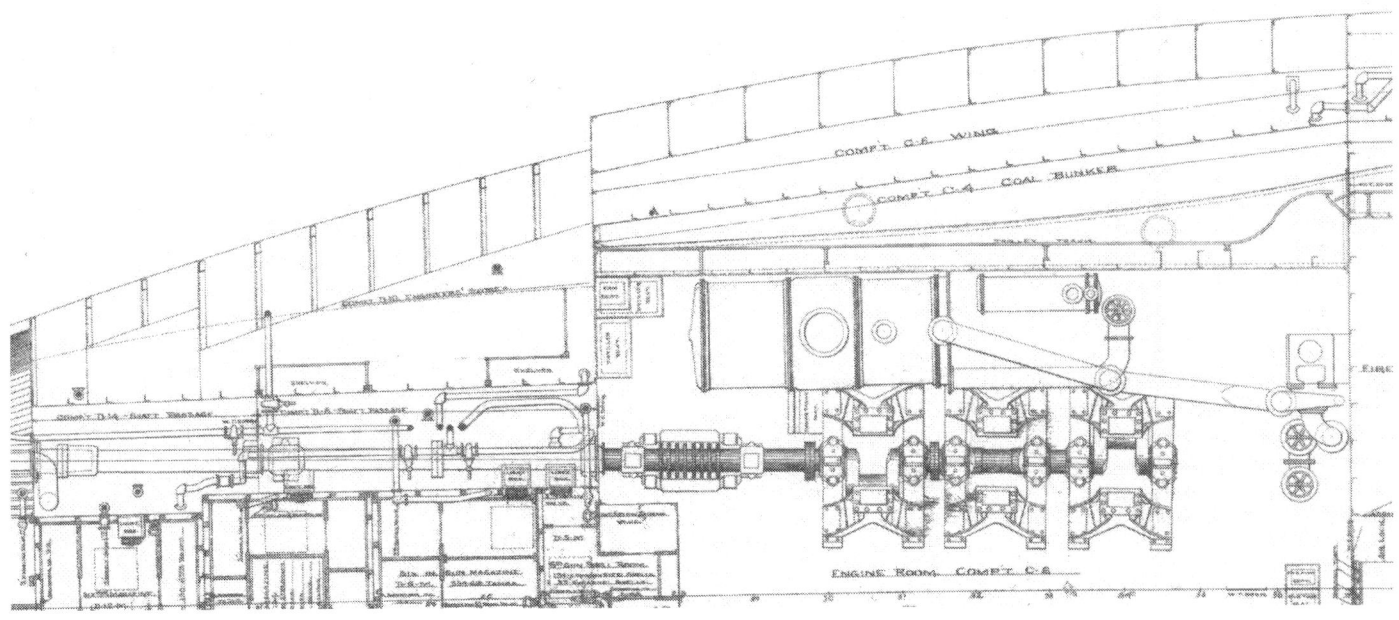

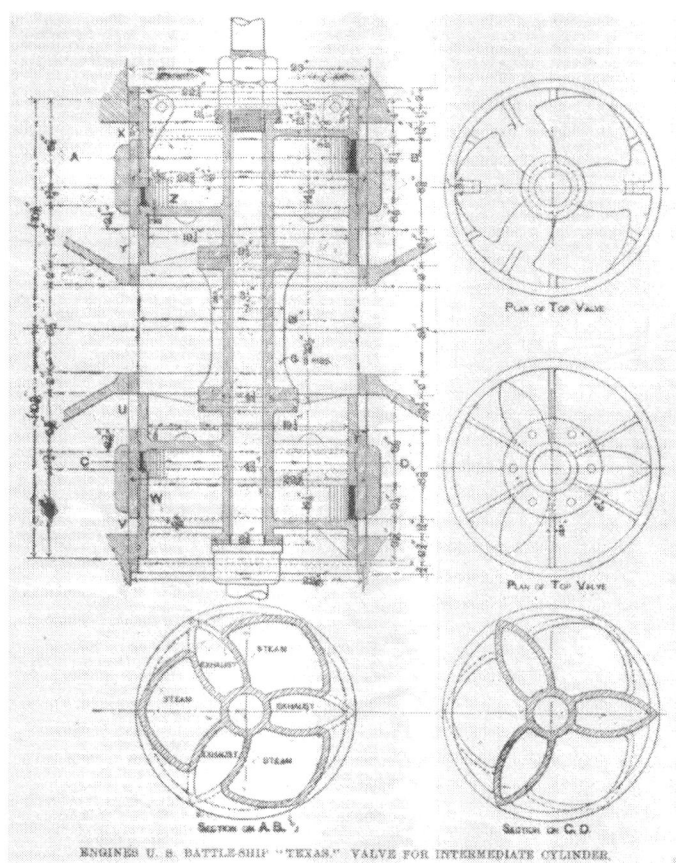

Valve plans for the intermediate and low-pressure cylinders on the engines of the *Texas*. The valve design for the high-pressure cylinder was "exactly similar in design" to that of the intermediate-pressure cylinder shown here. Speed and power control was a function of boiler pressure, valve timing, and resistance of the hull through the water.

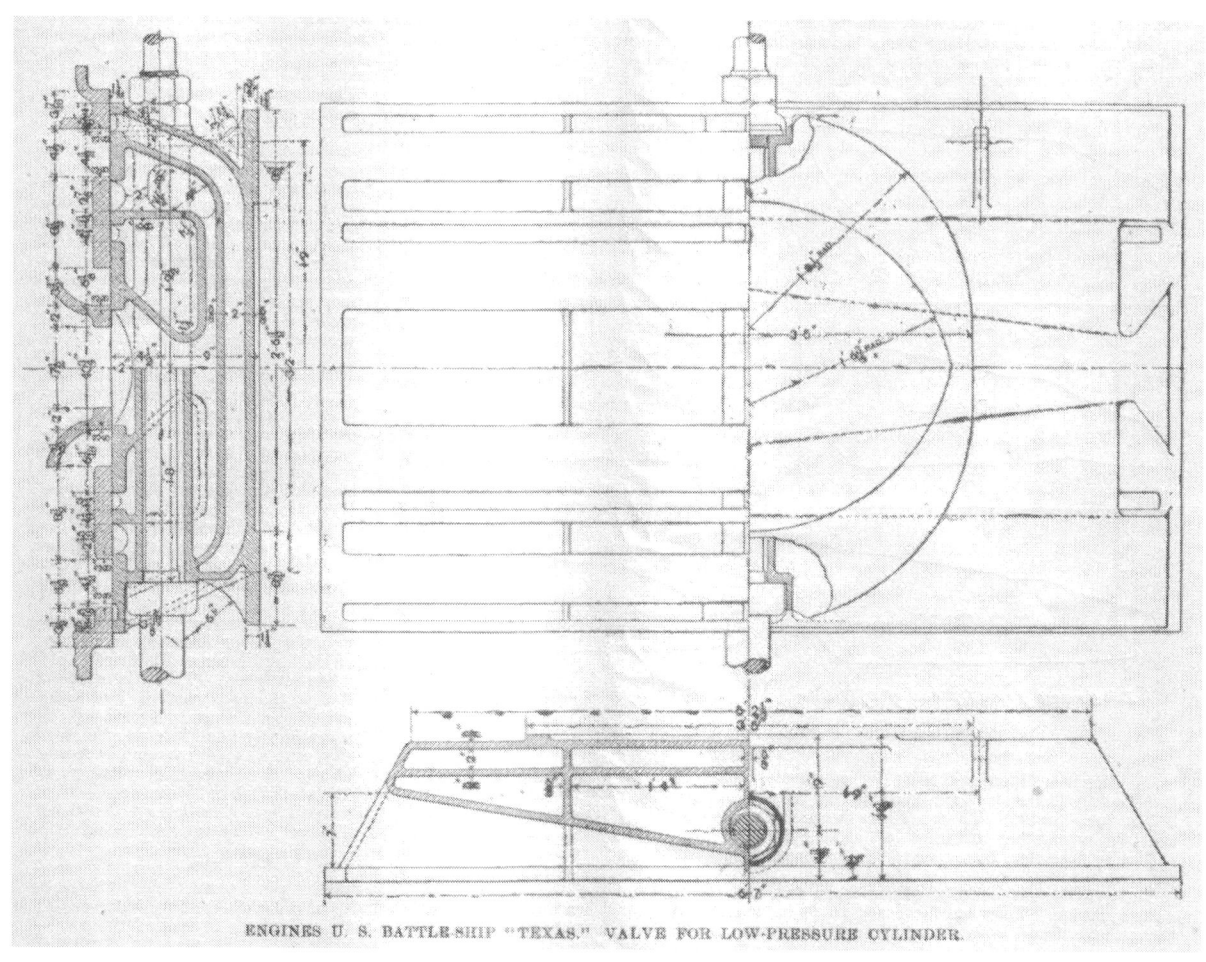

![The partially assembled condenser for the *Texas* in the Richmond Locomotive and Machine Works shops.]

The partially assembled condenser for the *Texas* in the Richmond Locomotive and Machine Works shops.

Indicator cards showing the results of the 90 rpm engine tests for the *Texas*, in which the engines registered a total of 7,183 horsepower. The engines were designed to produce a total of 5,800 horsepower naturally drafted or 8,000 horsepower at 2" pressure. The theoretical maximum of 8,600 horsepower was achieved at 123 rpm.

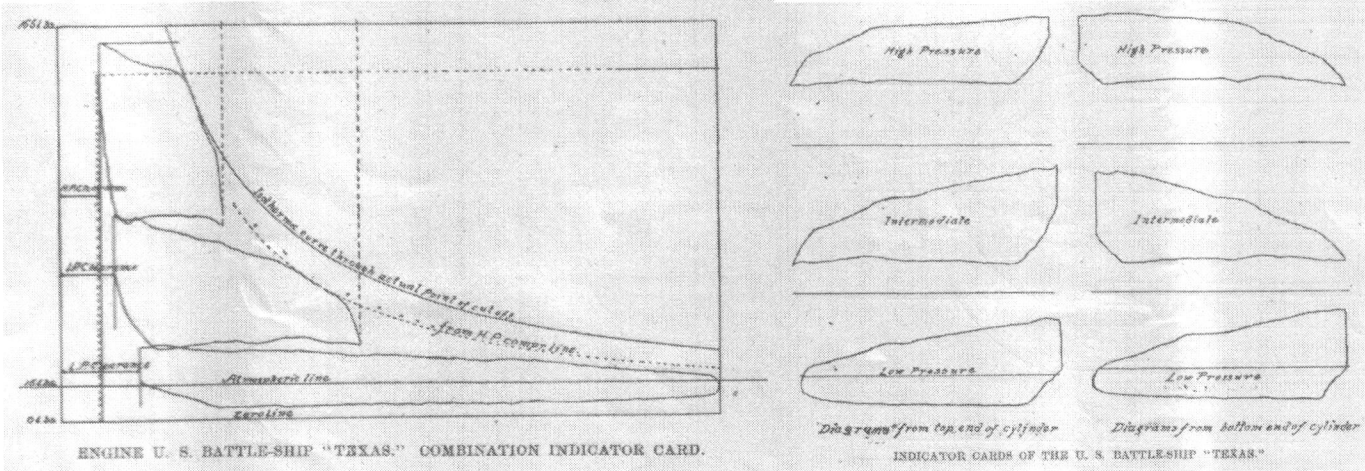

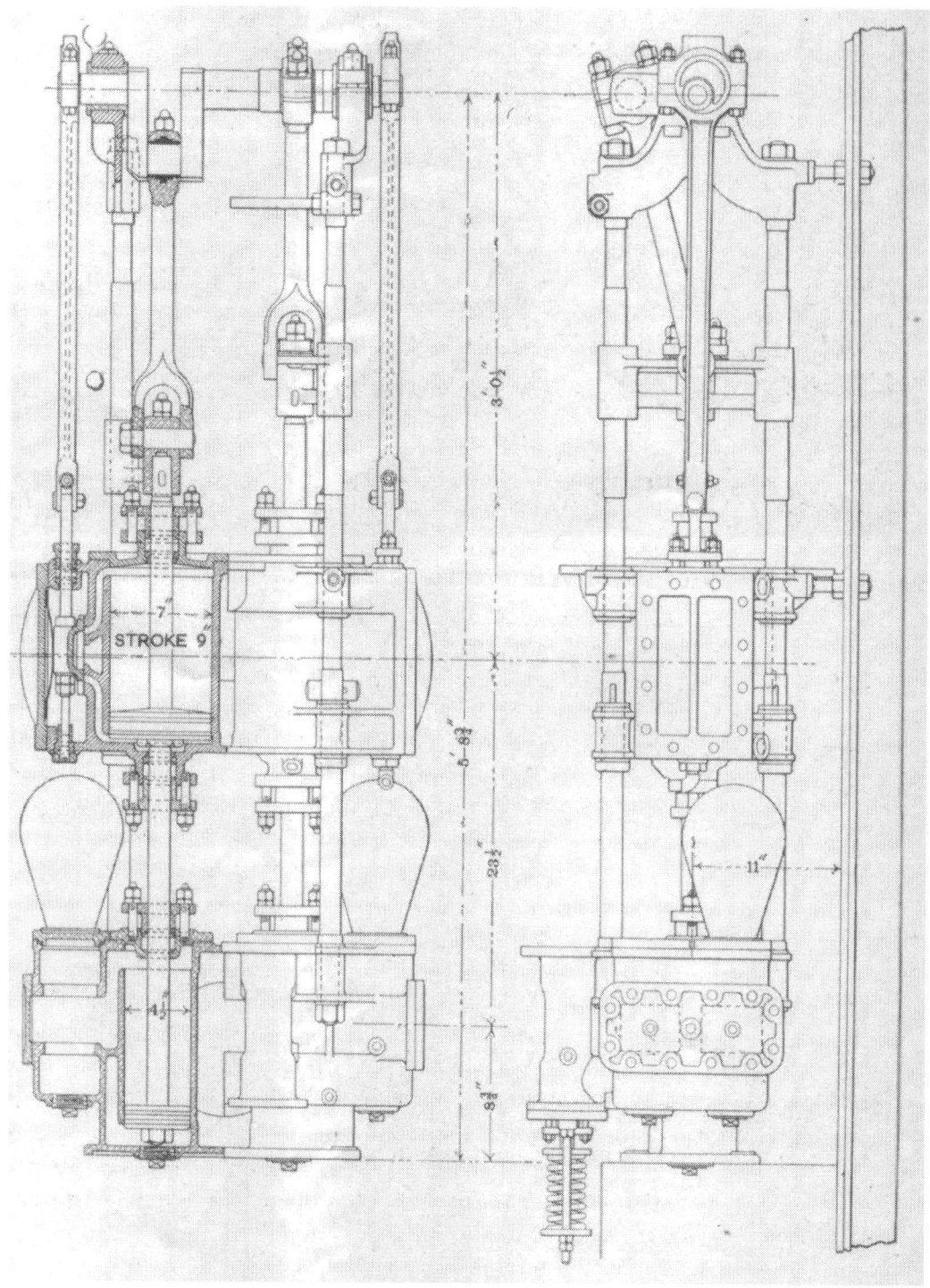

A plan of the fire, bilge, and feed pumps of the *Texas*. The *Texas* extensively utilized steam and hydraulics to do much of the work formerly done by hand in previous vessels. Pumps of the type depicted here were used to move water throughout the ship. Each engine room was equipped with such a pump, capable of throwing 300 gallons per minute, for use in fighting fires.

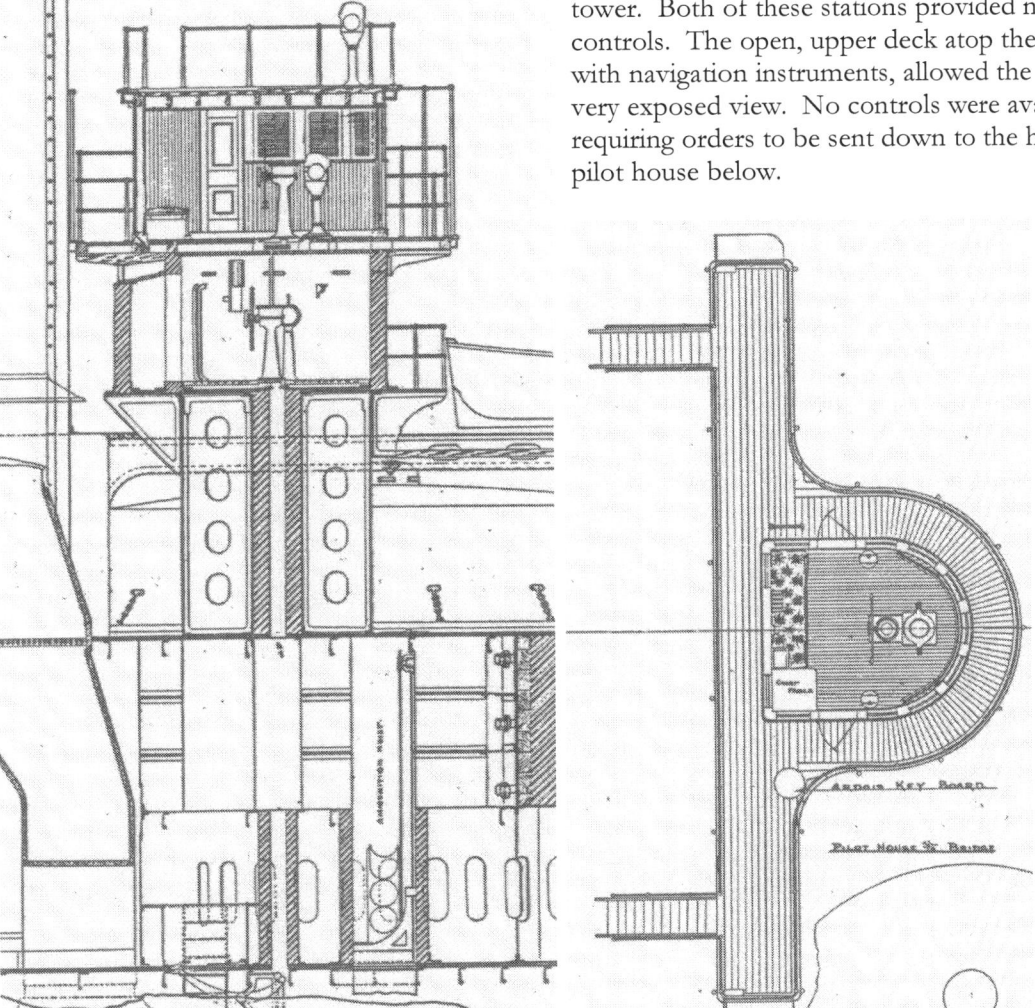

On the *Texas*, the pilot house stood atop the armored conning tower. Both of these stations provided navigation instruments and controls. The open, upper deck atop the pilot house, also equipped with navigation instruments, allowed the officers an unobstructed but very exposed view. No controls were available at this level, however, requiring orders to be sent down to the helmsman stationed in the pilot house below.

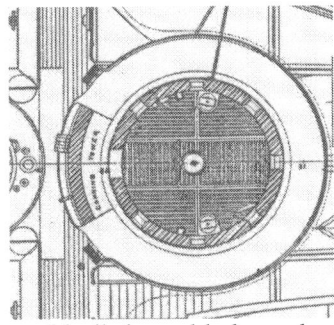

All-weather command and navigation took place in the pilot house. In addition to a ship's wheel, navigation instruments, and engine telegraphs, the pilot house accommodated a chart table and built-in padded couch. Ship-to-ship communications were provided via the Ardois "key board" located just outside on the open bridge.

The conning tower, located below the pilot house, afforded armored protection for the captain and command staff during battle. Almost 360 degree visibility was provided via narrow vision slits. Note the use of a curved, armored shield in lieu of an armored hatch, allowing officers to quickly duck in and out when under fire. (Photo of similar tower being fabricated for the USS *Massachusetts*.)

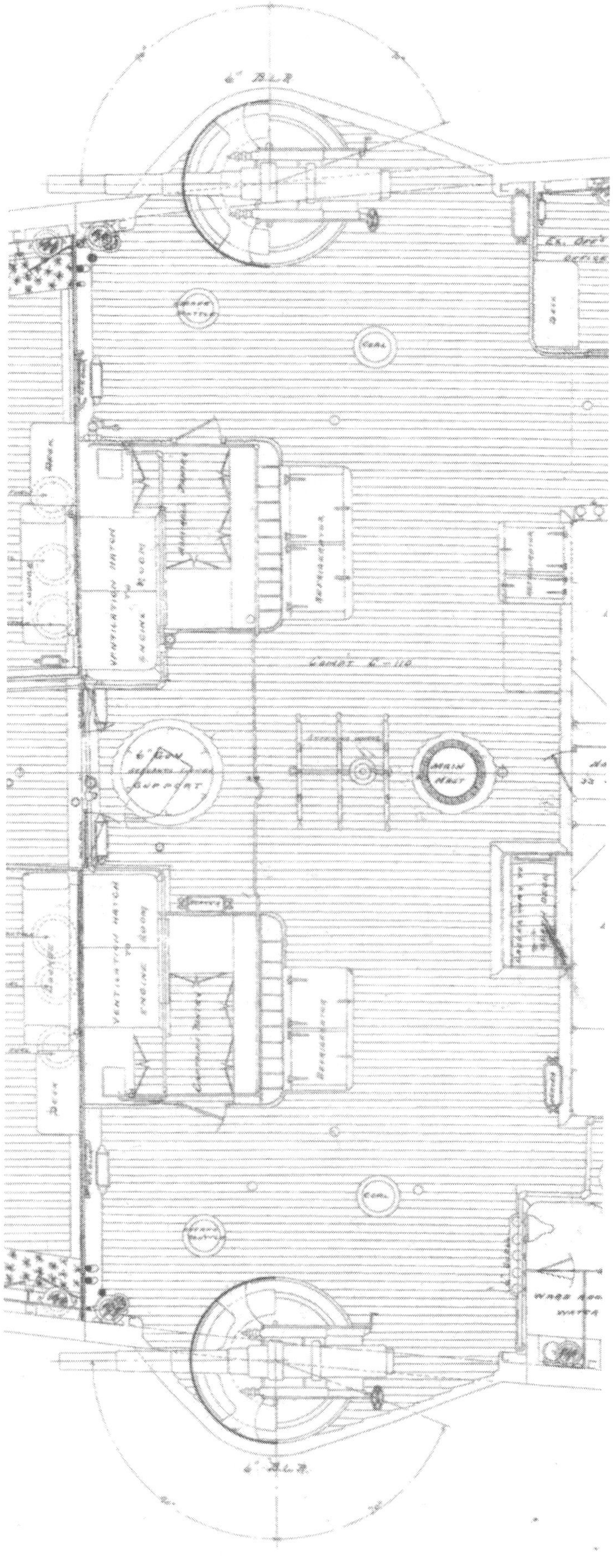

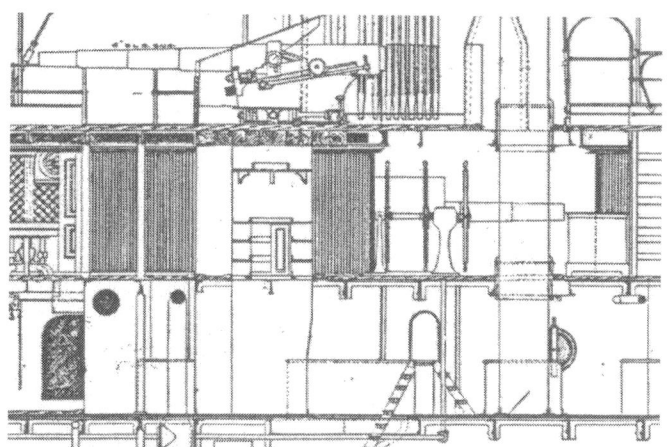

An auxiliary steering position was provided on the gun deck immediately aft of the main mast. Steering from this station was hand-powered via shafts, necessitating the use of the triple wheel which allowed multiple sailors to work in concert to change the angle of the massive rudder The steering cables passed down through the berth deck to the ceiling of the platform deck, from whence they translated aft to the steering and tiller rooms near the stern. Visibility from this position was very limited, even when the armored shutters at the 6" gun sponsons on either side of the ship were open.

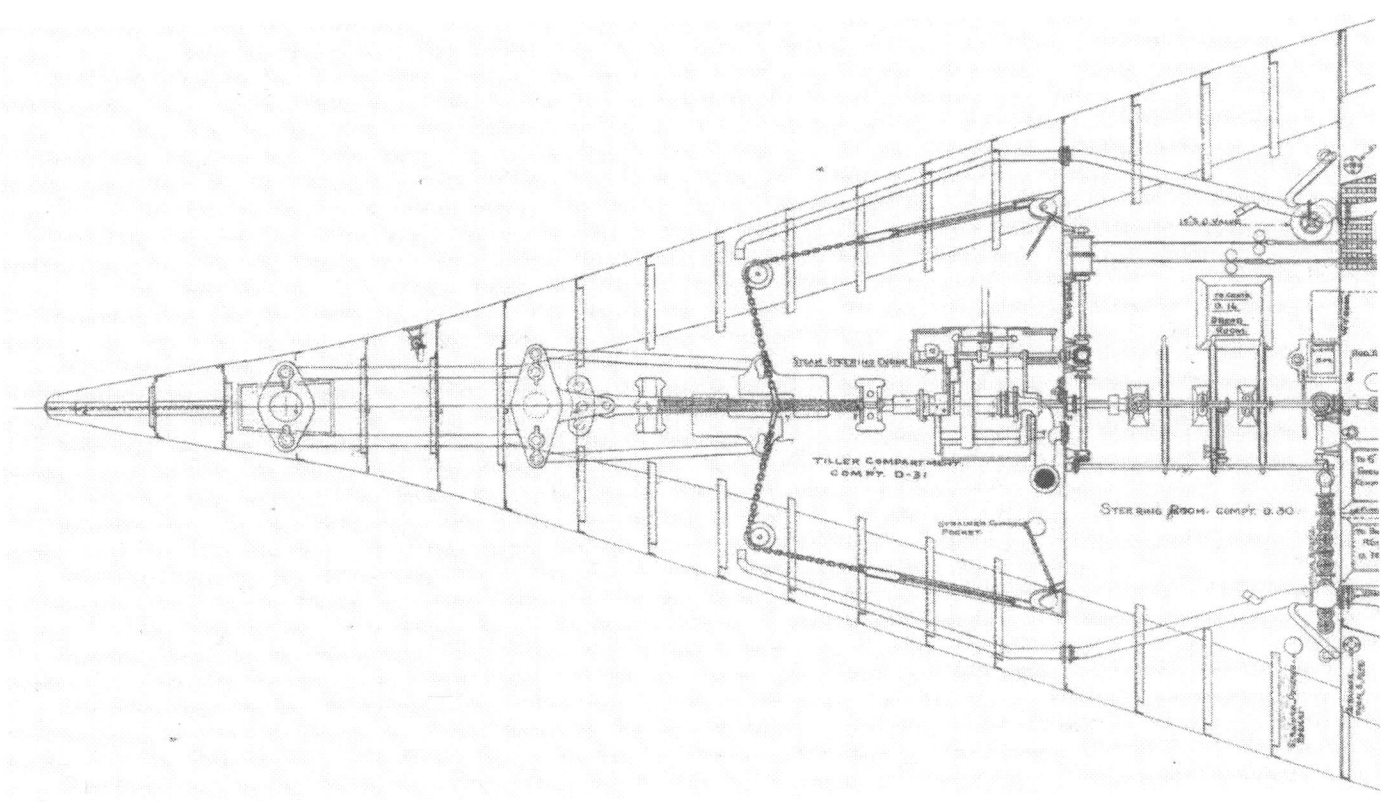

The steering room on the platform deck was also equipped as an auxiliary steering position with large triple wheels similar to those on gun deck in addition to a smaller wheel linked to the steering engine. The tiller compartment, aft of the steering room, housed a steam-powered steering engine which took its input from the ship's wheels in the pilot house, conning tower, and/or steering room and correspondingly moved the rudder. If the primary steering was inoperative, this engine could be disengaged and the tiller moved using block and tackle connected via chains, cables, and shafts to the manually-operated auxiliary steering positions.

Section through the steering room and tiller compartment on the platform deck of the *Texas*. Note the ceiling-mounted shafts coming in from the auxiliary steering position located further forward up on the gun deck. Also note the wood-filled rudder.

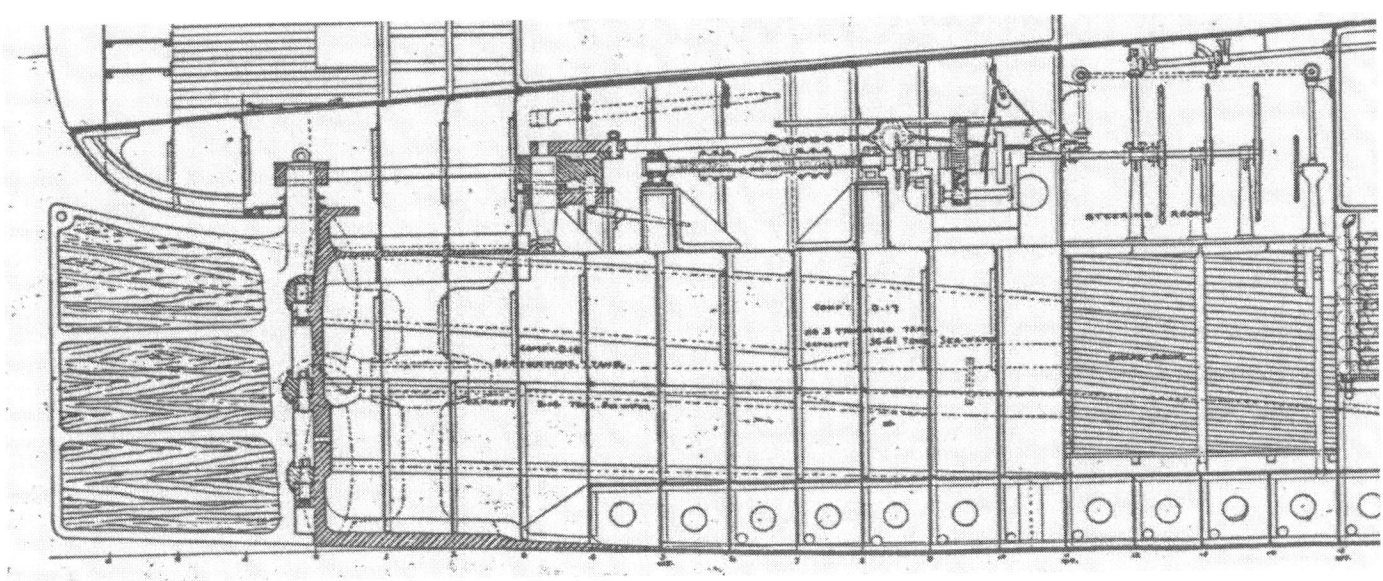

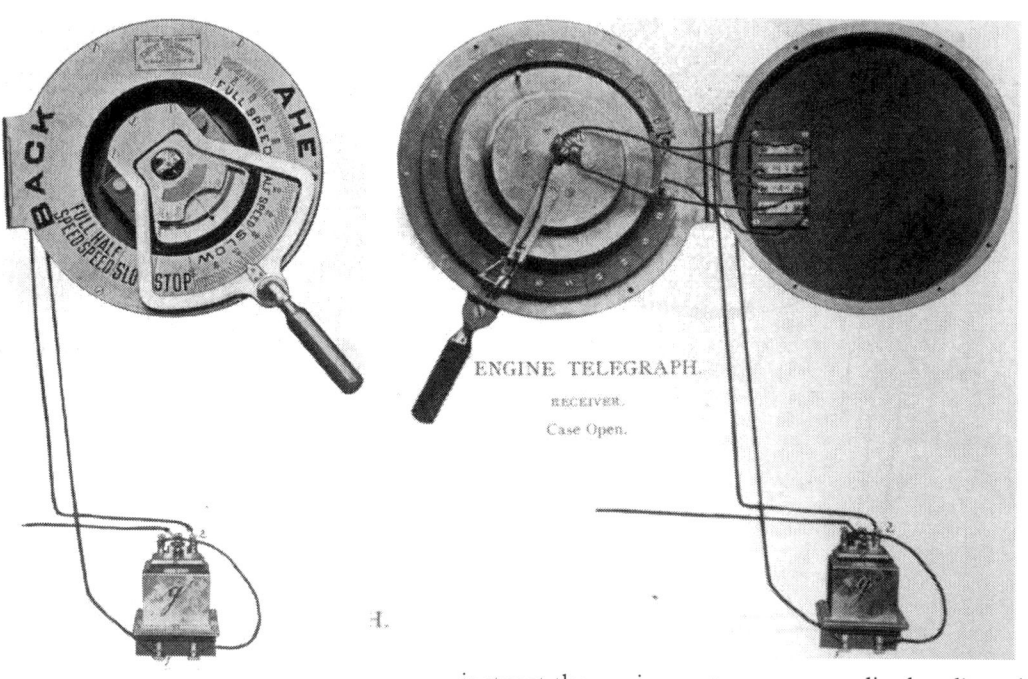

Controls and internal communications were evolving rapidly in the period preceding the Spanish American War. Many new controls were developed by United States naval officer and prolific inventor Bradley A. Fiske

The engine telegraph shown here used electricity to communicate orders from the navigation bridge to the engine room. By simply sliding the port or starboard lever to the desired speed, either forward or reverse, the bridge officers could instruct the engineers to correspondingly adjust the engines, a much improved technique over passing the word down open hatches.

Enlargement (below) from the plans of the hold deck engine room showing the internal communications panel mounted to the forward bulkhead on the *Texas*.

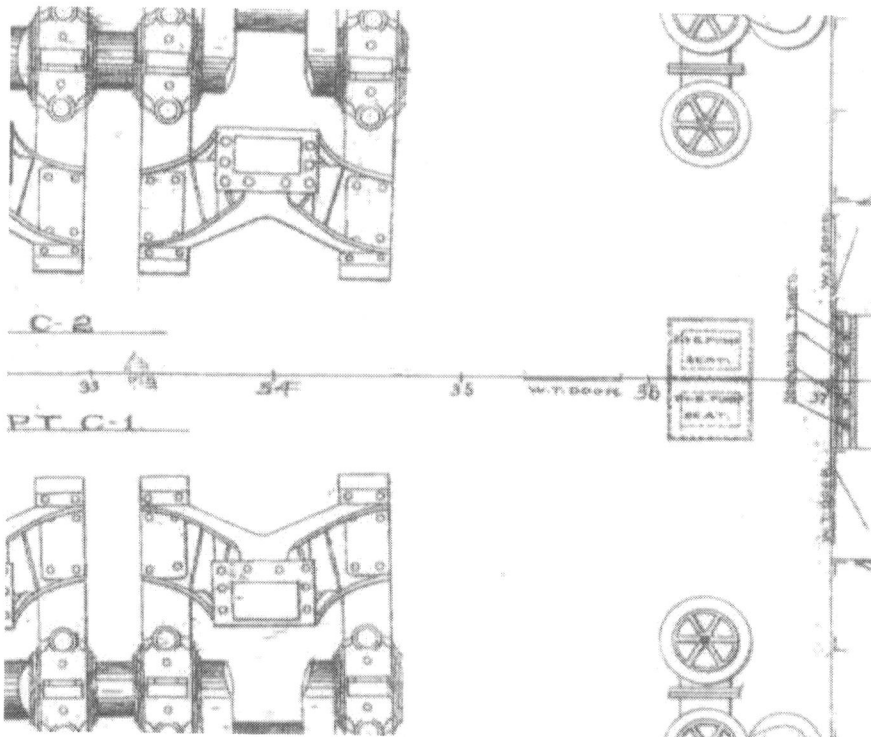

TRANSMITTER HANDLE
—ENGINE TELEGRAPH—

ENGINE TELEGRAPH
— DIAGRAM OF —
ELECTRICAL CONNECTIONS

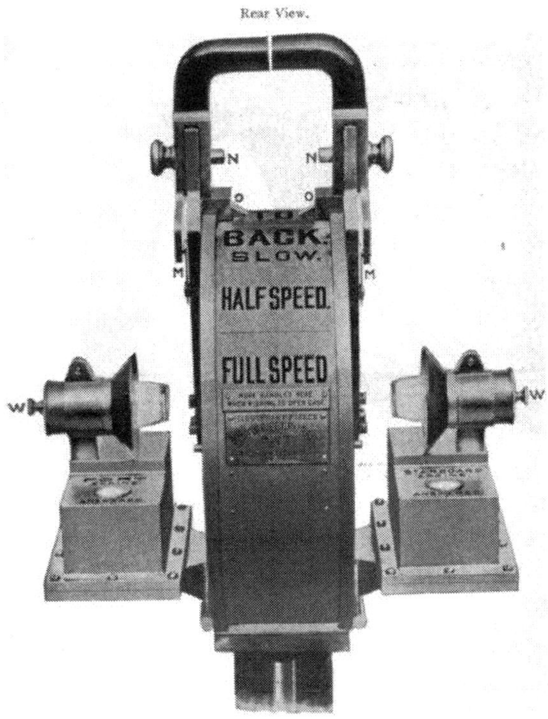

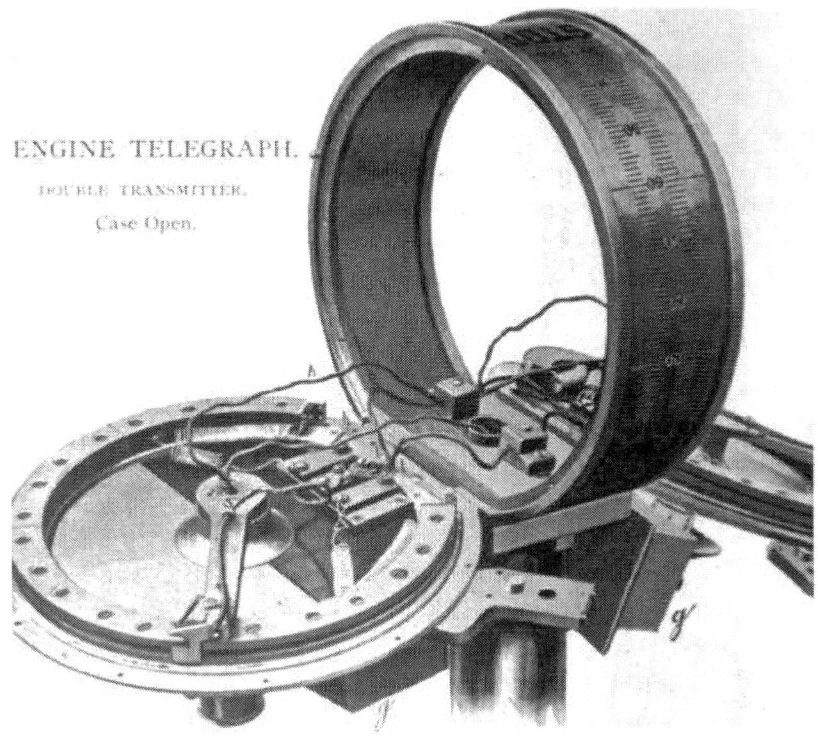

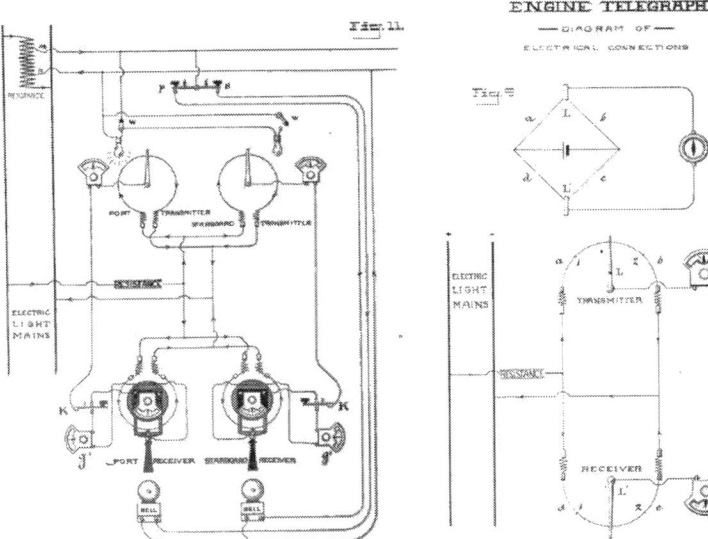

External and internal views of the engine telegraph along with detail plans. Wiring diagrams illustrate the arrangement and connections between the controls and readouts.

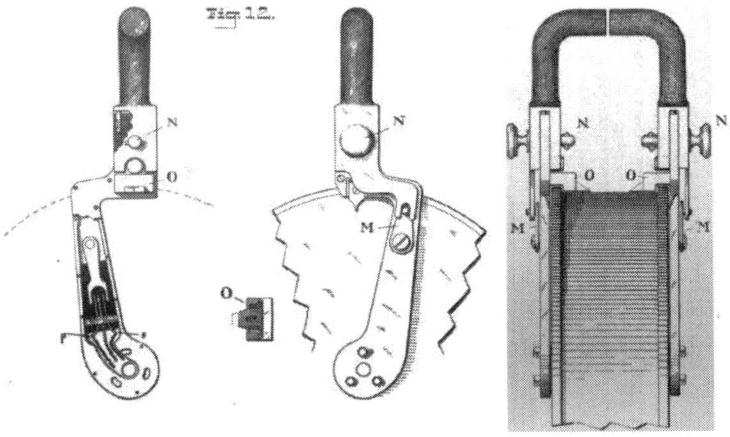

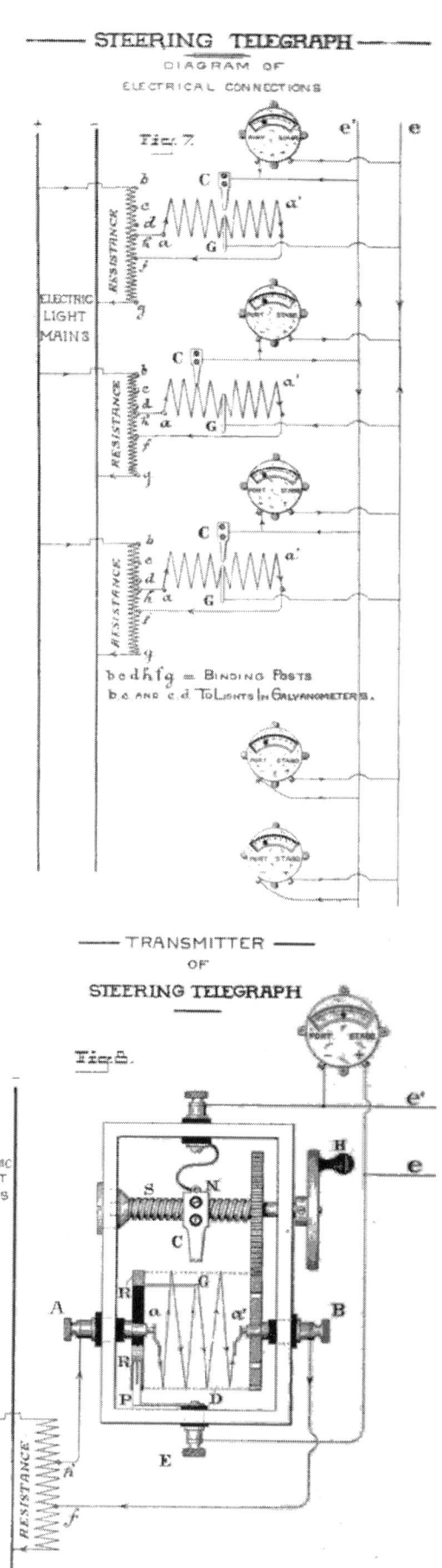

Steering telegraphs and helm indicators were also newly developed technologies for the US Navy.

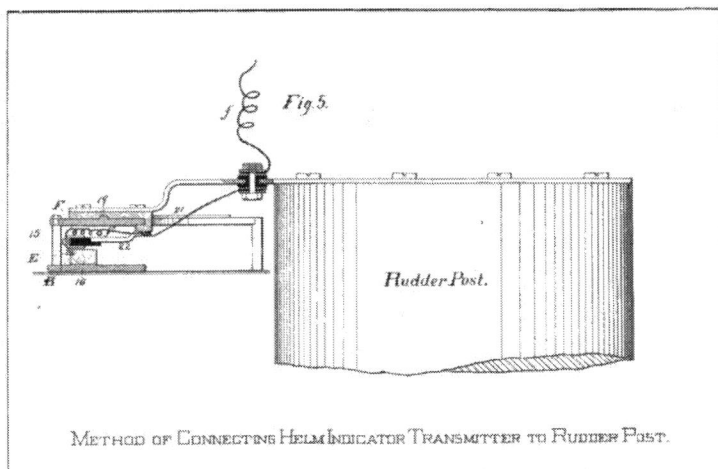

The helm indicator electrically transmitted helm and rudder position information.

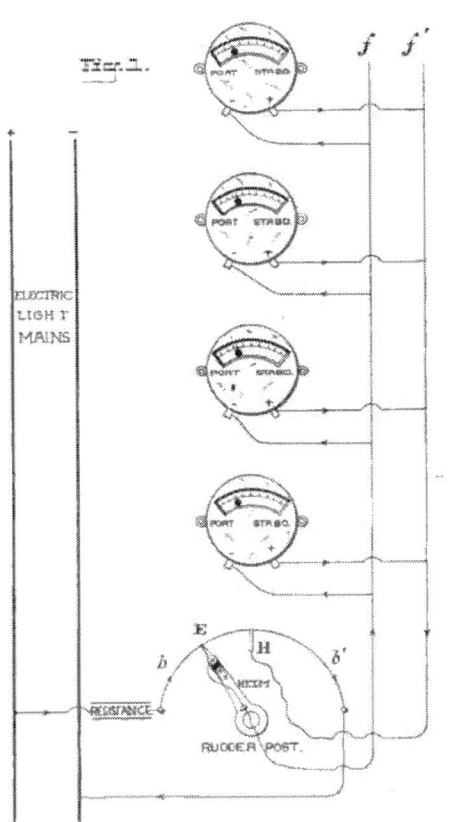

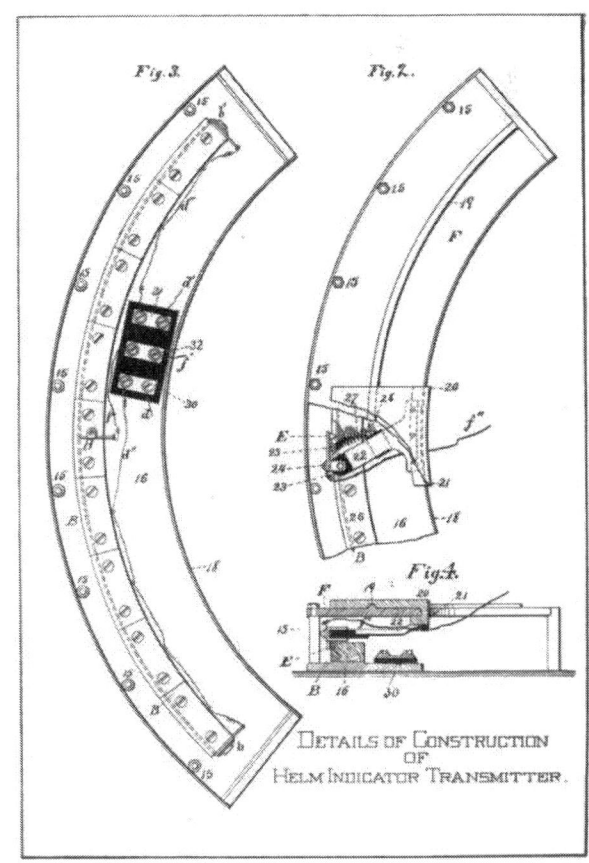

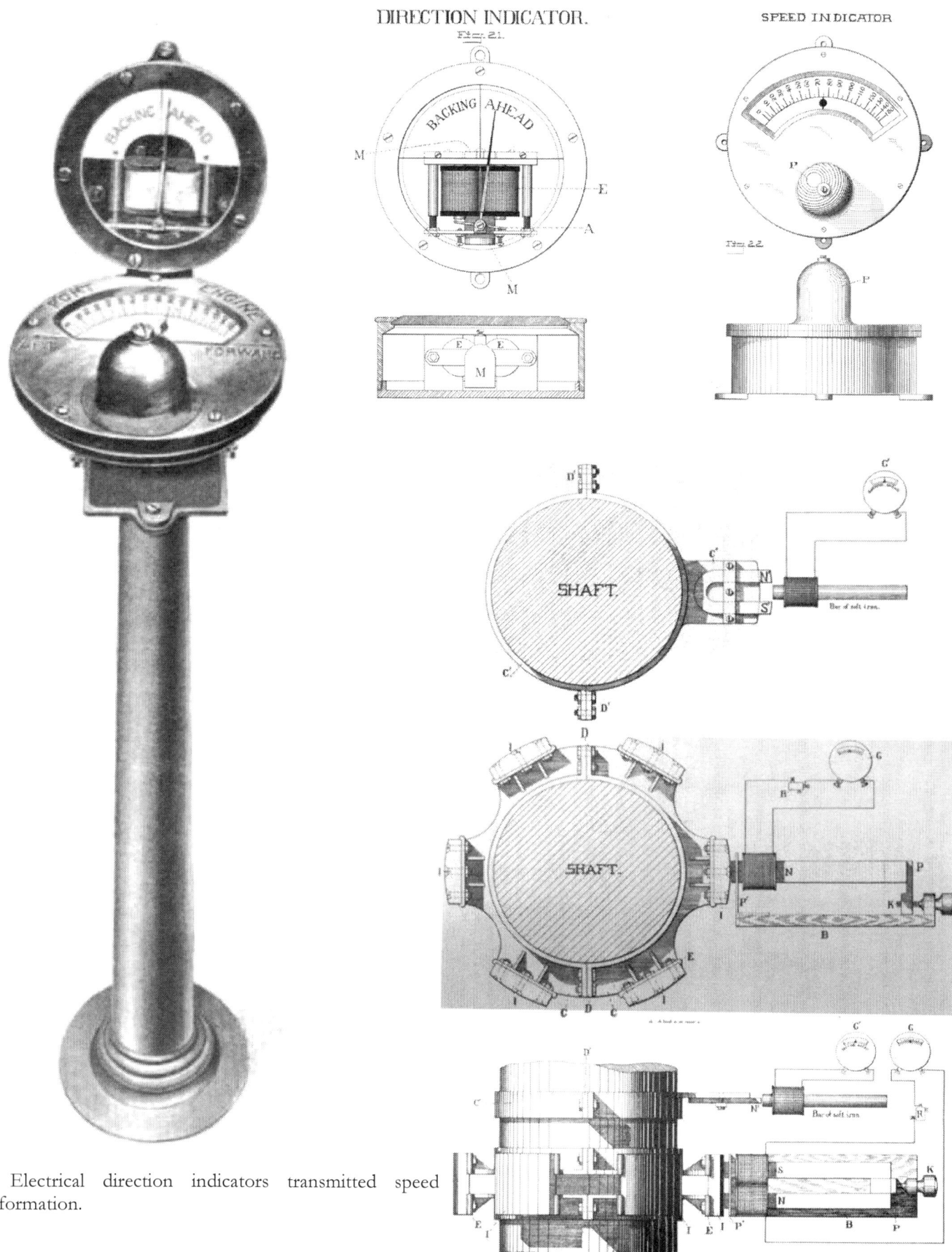

Electrical direction indicators transmitted speed information.

Desk Light.

Portable.

Single Signal Lantern.

Battle Lantern.

Ceiling Fixture.

Cargo Reflector.

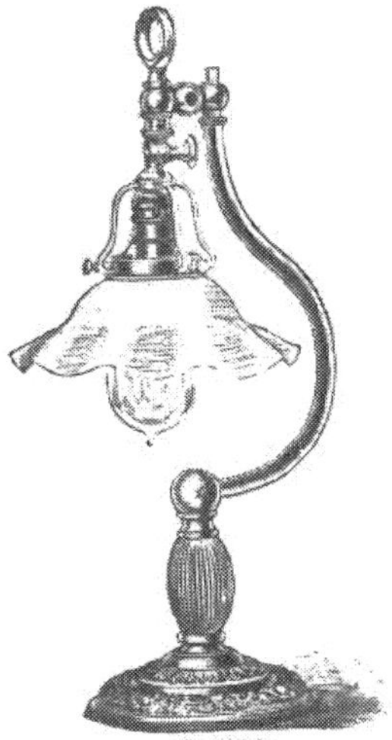

Standard electrical fixtures of the US Navy. Electricity had been introduced to United States naval vessels by the "Edison Company for Isolated Lighting" in 1883 on board the USS *Trenton.* The *Atlanta* and *Boston* were subsequently equipped with similar lighting systems, leading to the Navy's recommendation of this mode of lighting over previous types in 1886. The *Texas* was fitted with 62,641 feet of wiring and 550 electric lights, in addition to its powerful searchlights.

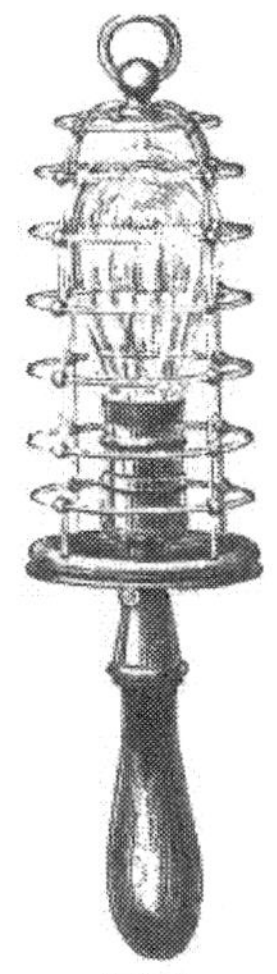

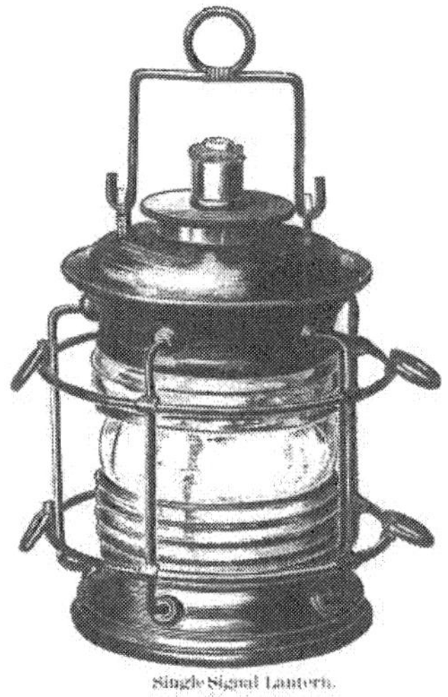

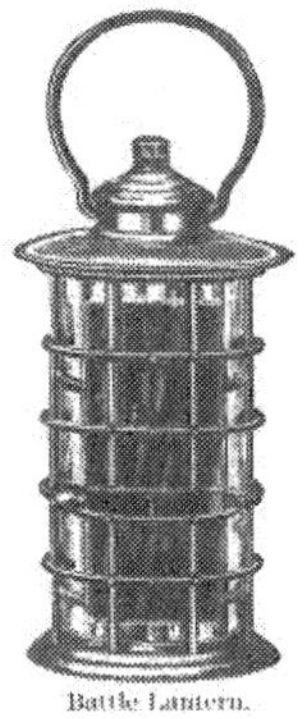

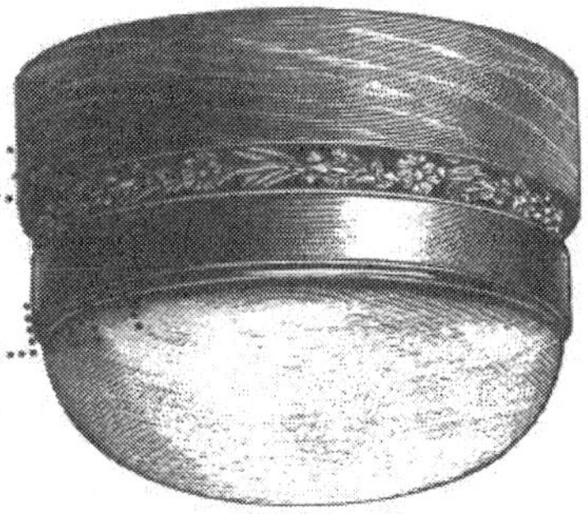

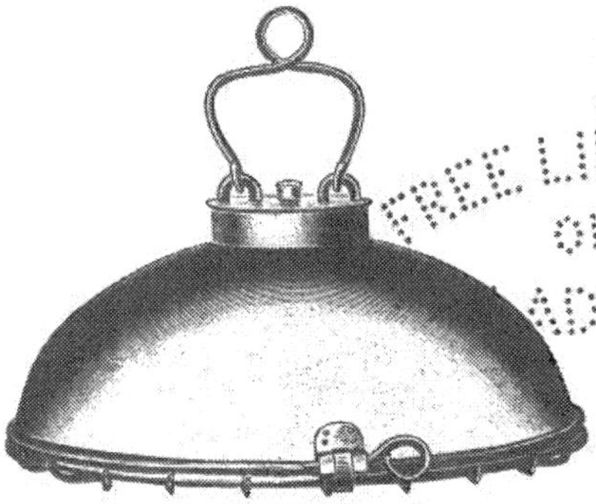

The *Texas* was also equipped with telephones, although their utility in the din of battle was questionable. Captain Philip, commander of the *Texas* during the 1898 Naval Battle of Santiago, reportedly stated his preference for ship's messengers over telephones or speaking tubes during battle.

Steam-tight Globe Fixture.

Steam-tight Globe. With Guard.

Bulkhead Fixture.

KEY AND KEYLESS SOCKETS, NAVY STANDARD.

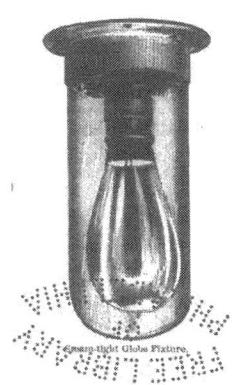

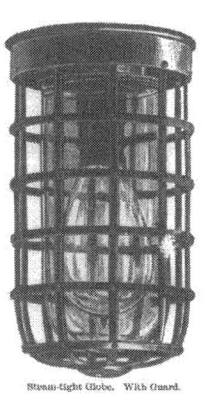

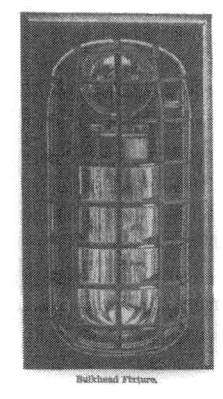

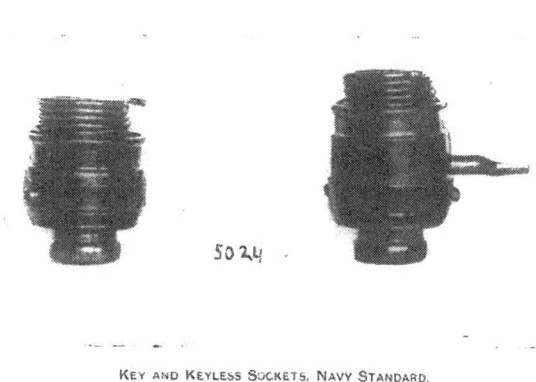

The *Texas* was equipped with four 20,000 candlepower electric searchlights mounted fore and aft on the bridge deck. Searchlights were used not only to provide illumination for nocturnal activities, but also for communication, especially at night. During the Spanish American War ship-to-ship searchlight signals were successfully transmitted over distances of up to 30 miles. These communications were sent in a binary code of dots and dashes called Myers code, in a system similar to civilian Morse code.

Along the coast of the United States, the Navy utilized shore mounted searchlights of up to 200 million candlepower to pass messages to warships operating up to 100 miles out to sea.

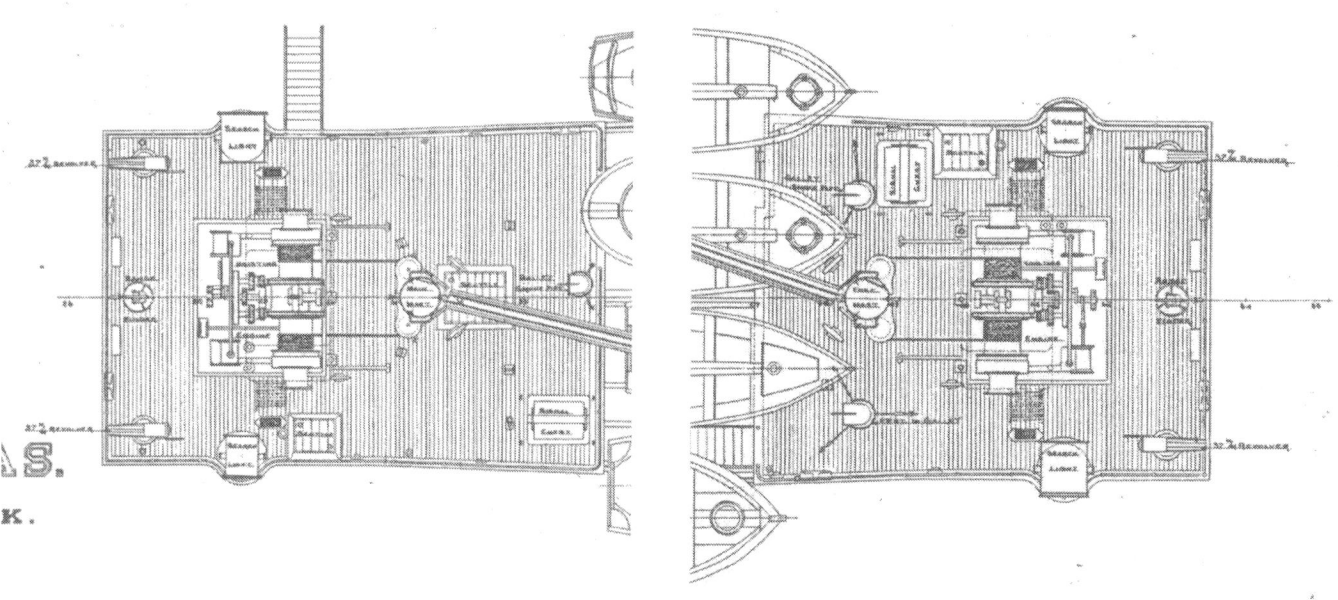

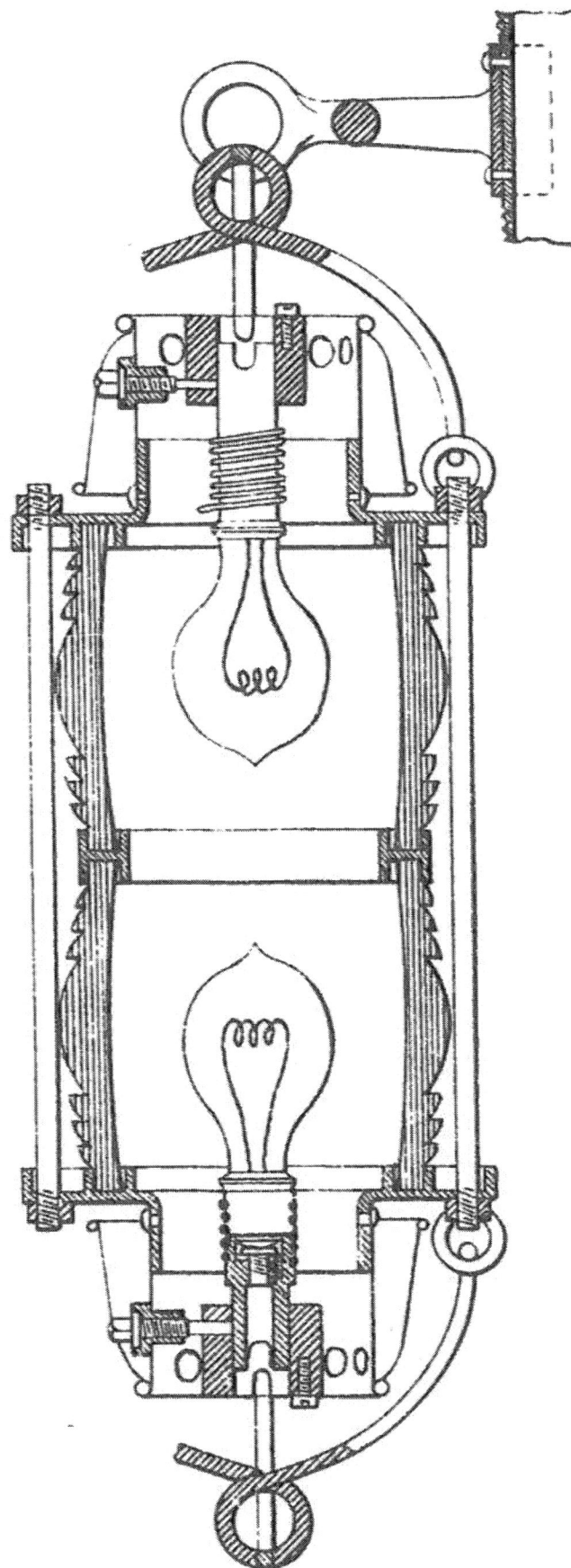

Ship to ship communications were achieved using the Ardois System of signal lamps. Five electrically powered lamps were suspended on a cable running to the ship's mast. Each lamp held a white and a red bulb. By lighting these fixtures in specific combinations, predetermined signals could be rapidly transmitted at night. Note the special prismatic lenses, similar to those used in lighthouses, utilized to horizontally direct the maximum amount of light.

Circa 1897: Androis system affixed to the forward mast of the *Texas*.

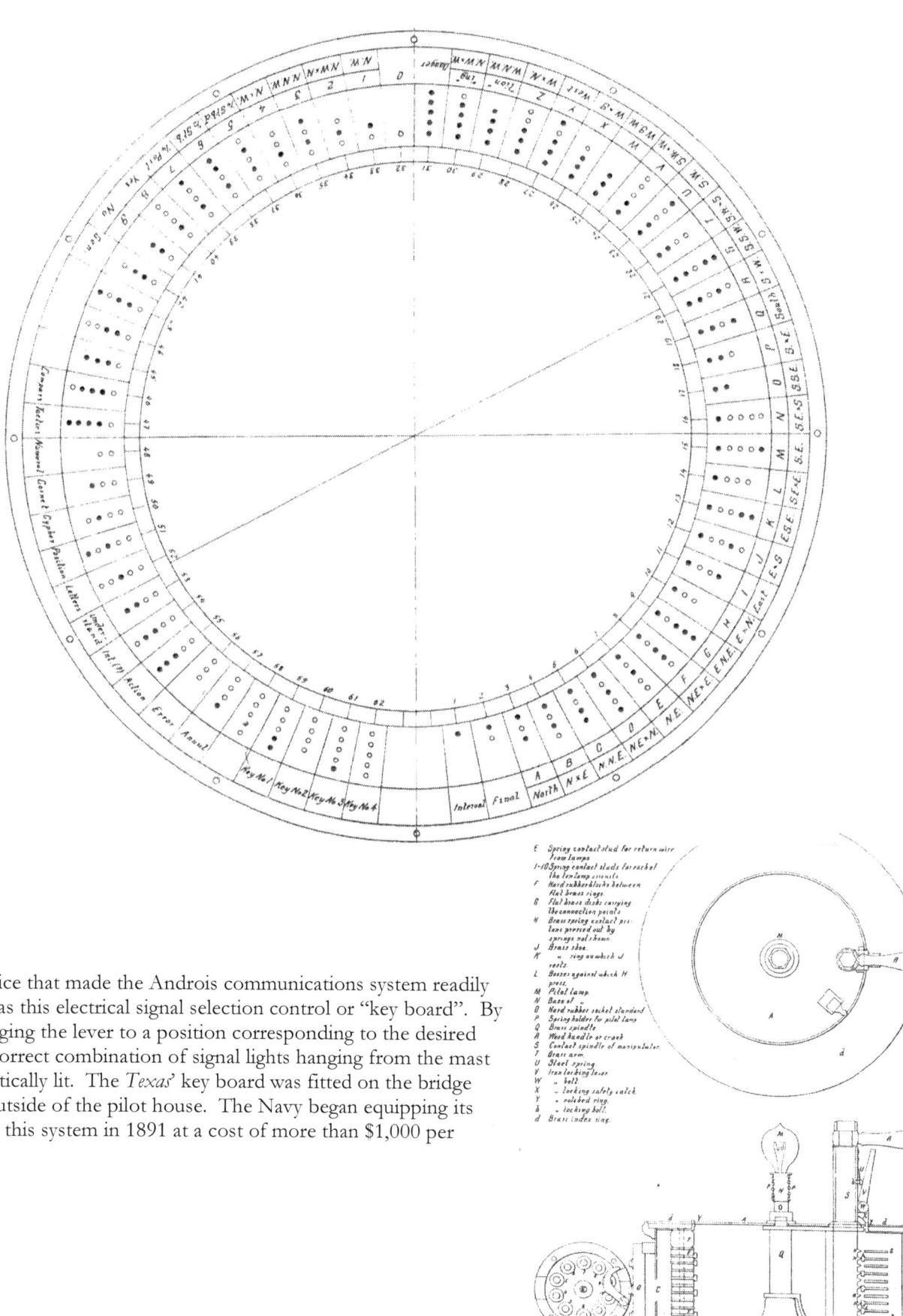

The device that made the Androis communications system readily workable was this electrical signal selection control or "key board". By simply swinging the lever to a position corresponding to the desired signal, the correct combination of signal lights hanging from the mast was automatically lit. The *Texas'* key board was fitted on the bridge deck, just outside of the pilot house. The Navy began equipping its vessels with this system in 1891 at a cost of more than $1,000 per installation.

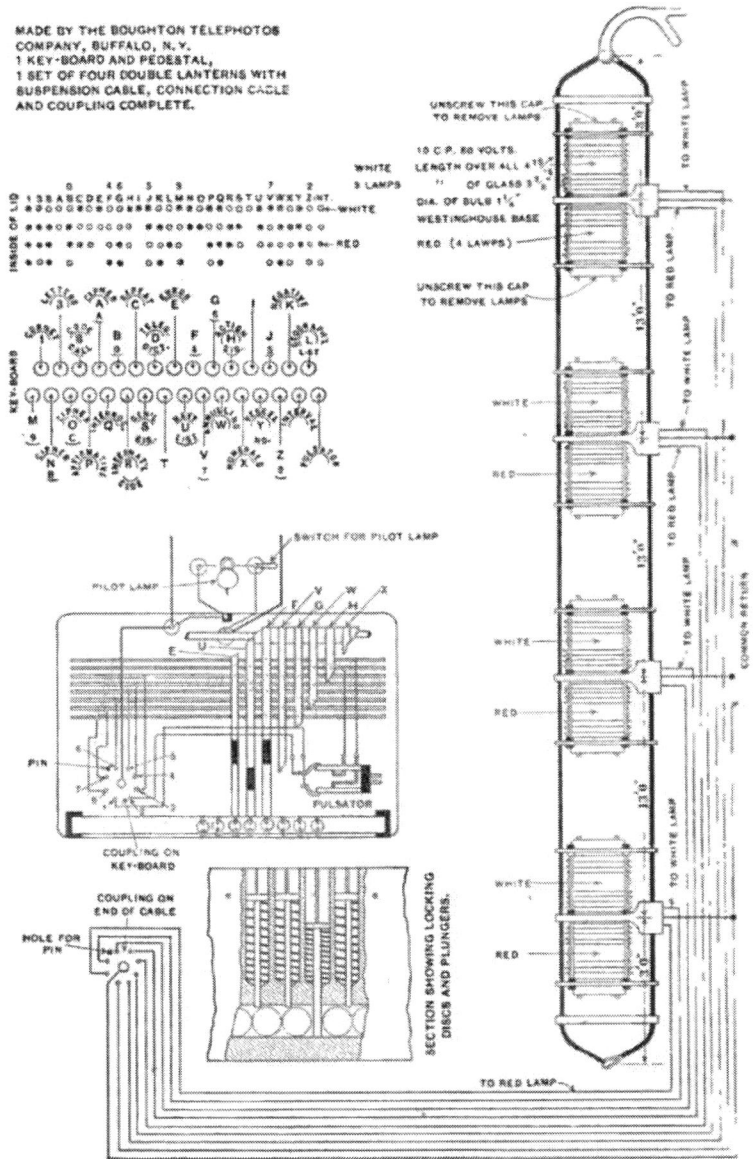

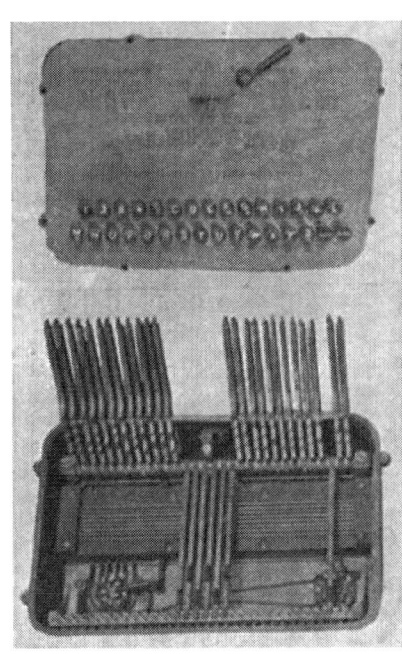

In 1897 the Navy began to install the improved Telephotos keyboards on warships to supplement the Androis system. The *Texas* is recorded as having one of each type of keyboard in 1905.

5 MAIN BATTERY

The main battery of the *Texas* consisted of two 12"/35 cal Mk I breech loading guns, weighing 46 ½ tons apiece (not including breech). Although capable of firing about 12,000 yards, practical range was limited by aiming practices of the day to less than about 2,000. Raised, round-topped aiming copulas sprout from the roof of the turret. Supplementing this was a battery of four 6"/30 Mk III guns mounted in sponsons on the main deck behind drop-down shields. Two more 6"/35 Mk III guns were mounted to the upper deck, on centerline, protected by small turret-like shields, to act as bow and stern chasers.

Theoretically each 12" gun could fire through a 170 degree arc on the near side and a 36 degree arc across the deck on the opposite beam. In practice, full charge cross-deck firing was operationally limited to combat situations, as the muzzle blast would cause damage to the decks and superstructure. The fact that deck structures were within the training arc of the turrets resulted from the basic design requirement calling for the accommodation of 12" guns within a very limited displacement. This weight limit necessitated placing the turrets as closely together as possible to minimize the weight of armor, leading to the en echelon arrangement of the turrets and, through the design compromises this entailed, to the placement of the 6" chasers behind shields.

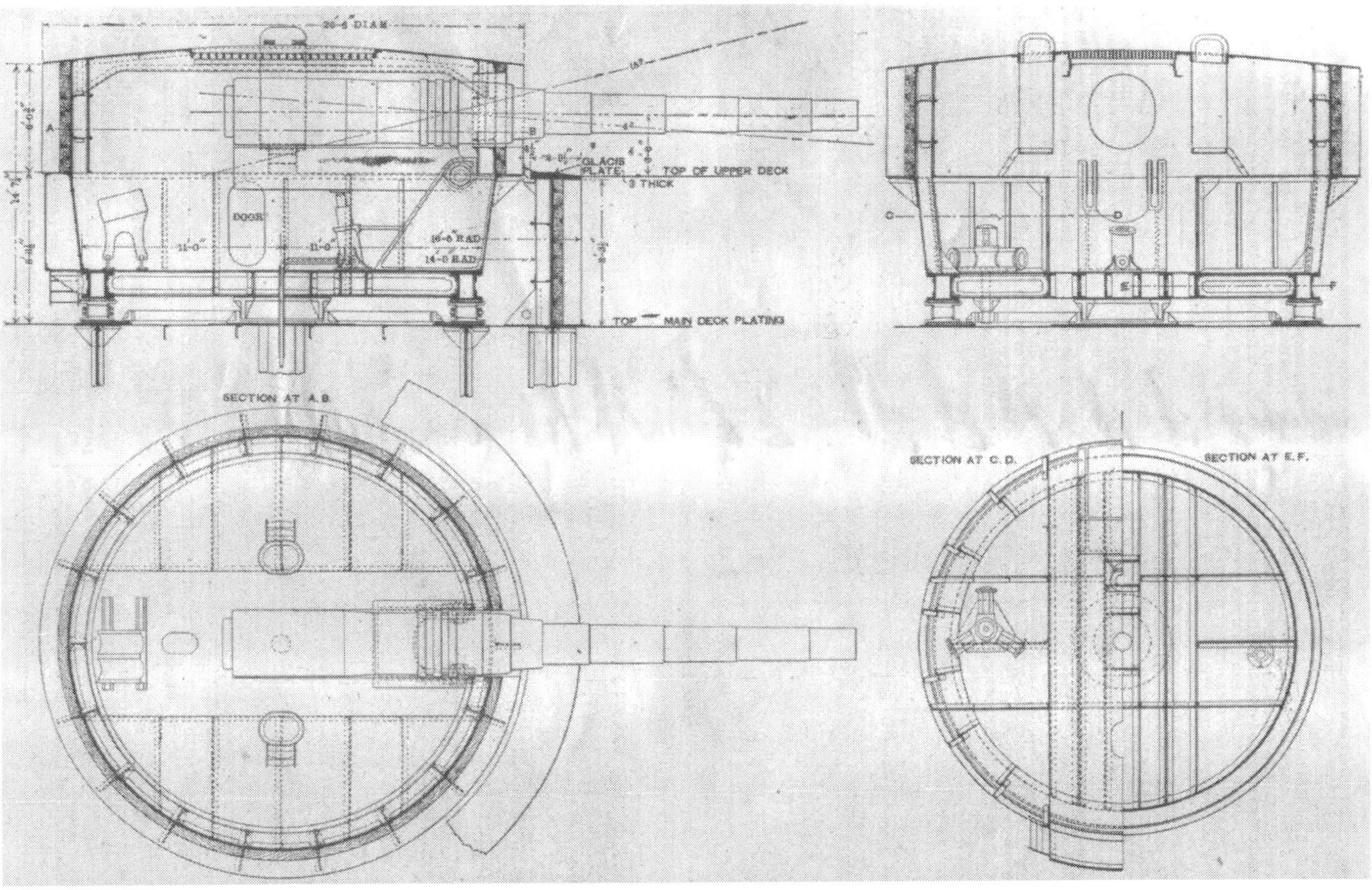

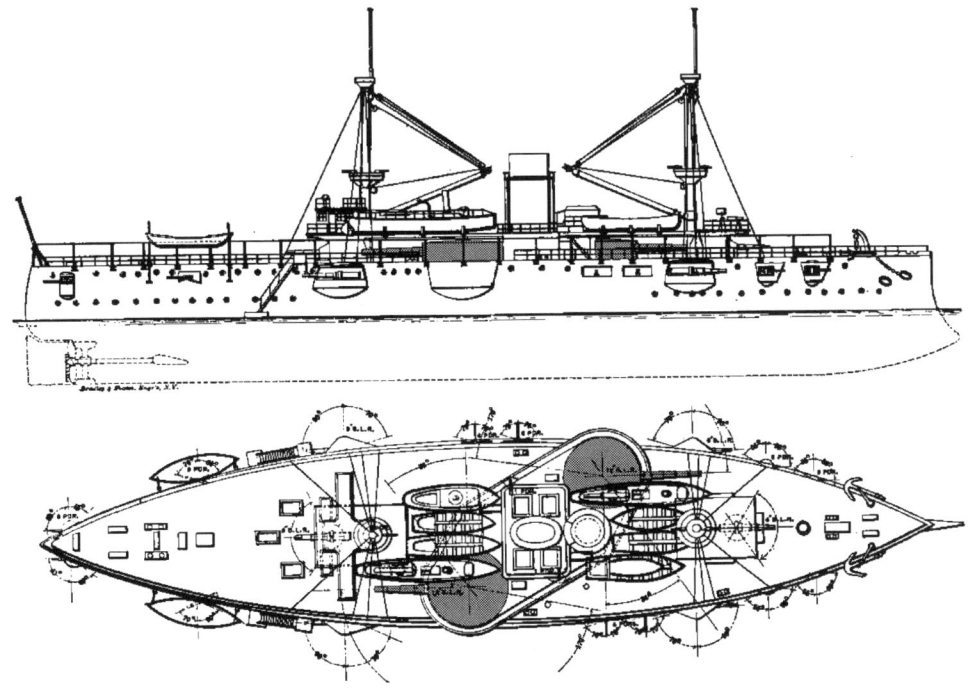

A hydraulic ram was fitted in the turret below the breech of each gun to raise and lower the barrel through a range of -4 degrees to +15 degrees. Above the level of the upper deck the turret was armored with 12 inches of nickel-steel backed with 6 inches of wood. Like in the USS *Monitor* of an earlier generation, a grating in the turret top provided light and ventilation. Combat was still expected to occur at relatively close ranges where the low trajectory of shells and the slightly rounded turret top would prevent hits to the grating.

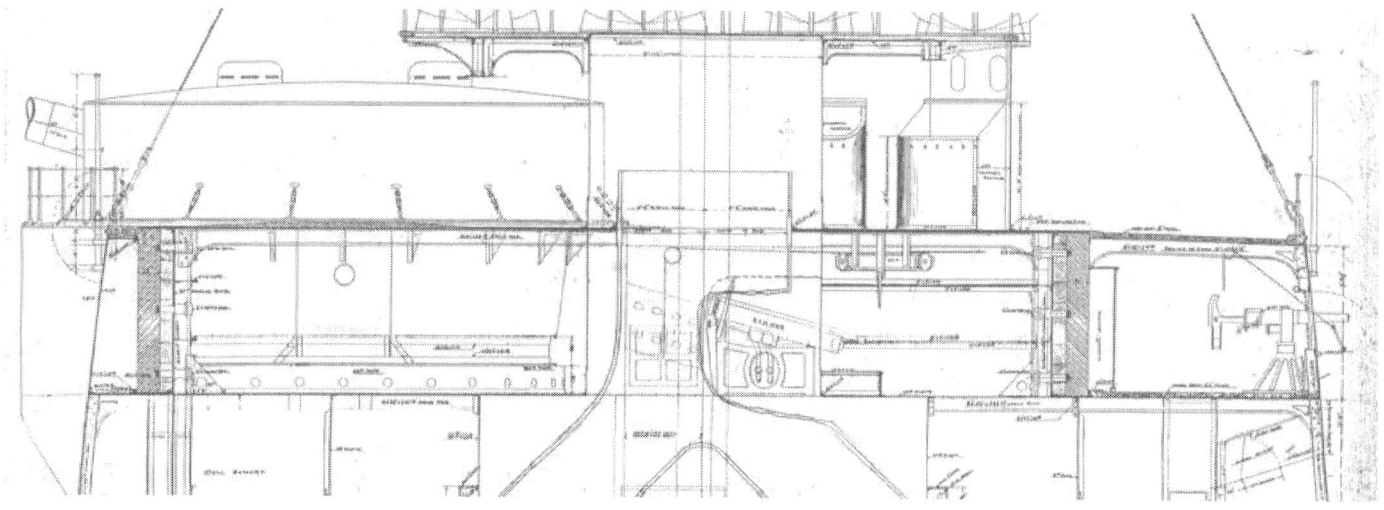

As originally constructed, each 12" gun was loaded using one of a pair of hydraulic rams located in fixed positions, 90 degrees apart, on the gun deck. This required the turret to be traversed and elevated to 9.5 degrees to align with a rammer for reloading between each shot. This system, though similar to that used on European battleships at the time of her design, was considered slow and archaic by the time the *Texas* joined the fleet, and was subsequently replaced in 1898. With their original external rammers, the firing interval for each 12" gun between shots was approximately seven minutes. Given the slow rate of fire, the need for relatively rapid-to-work 6" guns as part of the main battery is apparent.

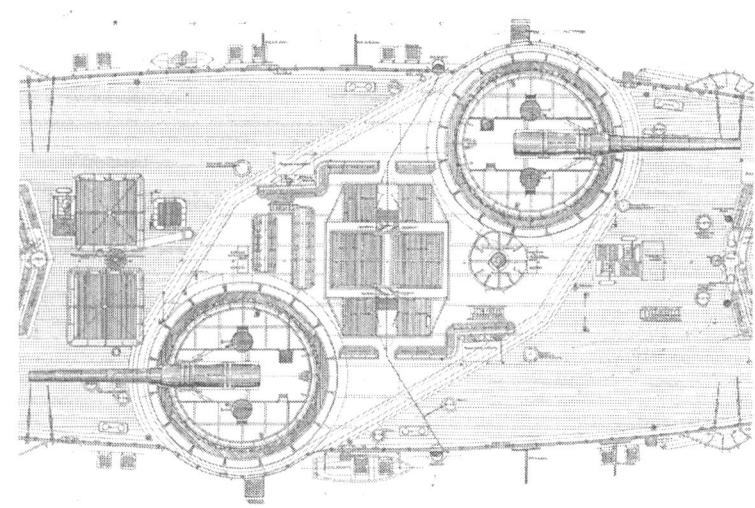

The turrets revolved on rollers placed in a track. Protection for the lower portion of the turret at this level was provided by an armored redoubt composed of 12 inches of nickel-steel backed with 6 inches of wood. Crew access to the redoubt and gun turrets was via ladder from the berth deck below.

Note that the redoubt prevented access at this level from the forward parts of the ship to the stern. Forward of the redoubt were crew spaces while aft of the redoubt was "Officer's country."

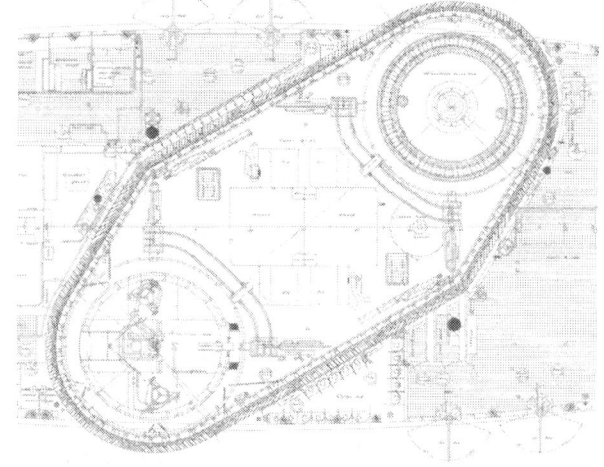

The gun deck redoubt was capped, at main deck level, with thin armored plating intended to deflect shells traveling along the nearly horizontal trajectories expected in naval engagements of the period. Surrounding the base of the turret itself was an angled glacis plate set into the main deck to protect the gap between the revolving turret and the armored deck. To minimize the number of hatches in the armor, there was no access into either the turrets or the redoubt from the main deck level.

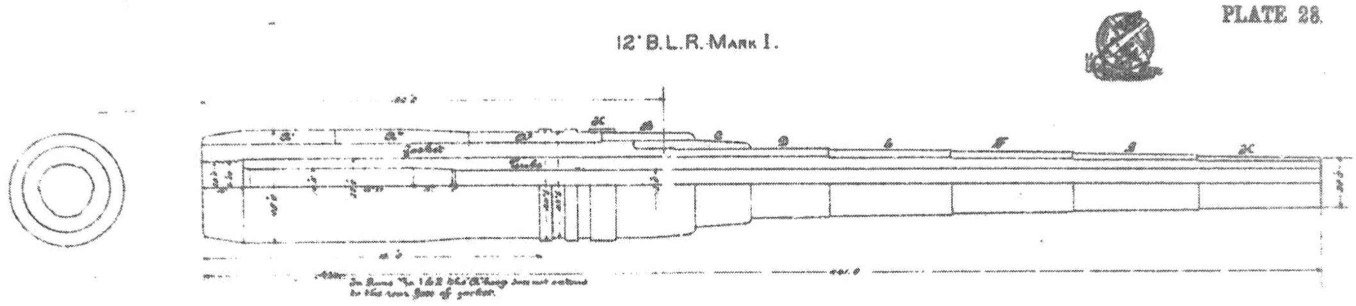

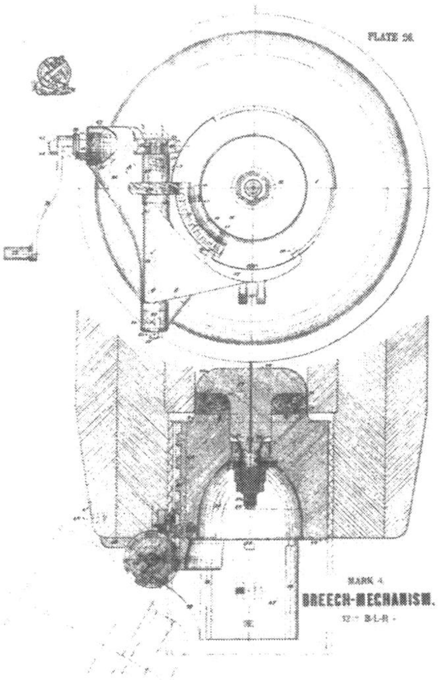

The breech mechanisms of the 12 inch guns were of the interrupted screw type and were opened and closed by hand.

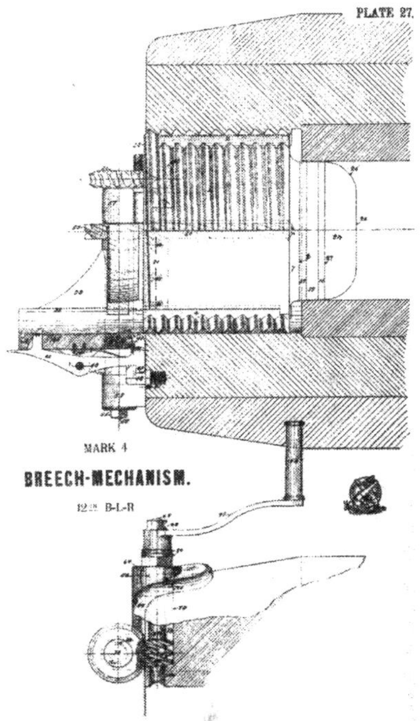

12 inch gun being fired on the Navy's test range.

12-inch breech-loading rifle.

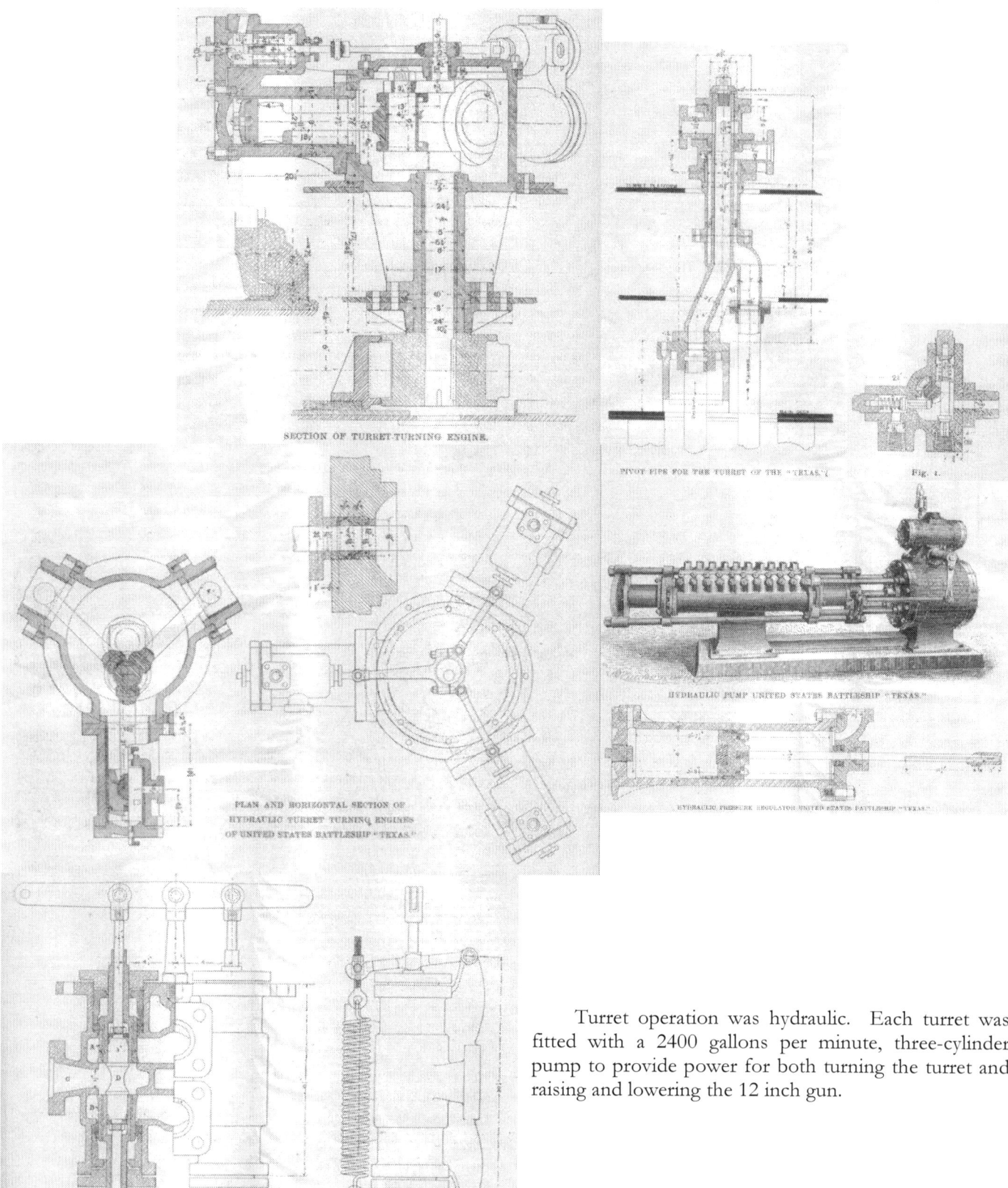

Turret operation was hydraulic. Each turret was fitted with a 2400 gallons per minute, three-cylinder pump to provide power for both turning the turret and raising and lowering the 12 inch gun.

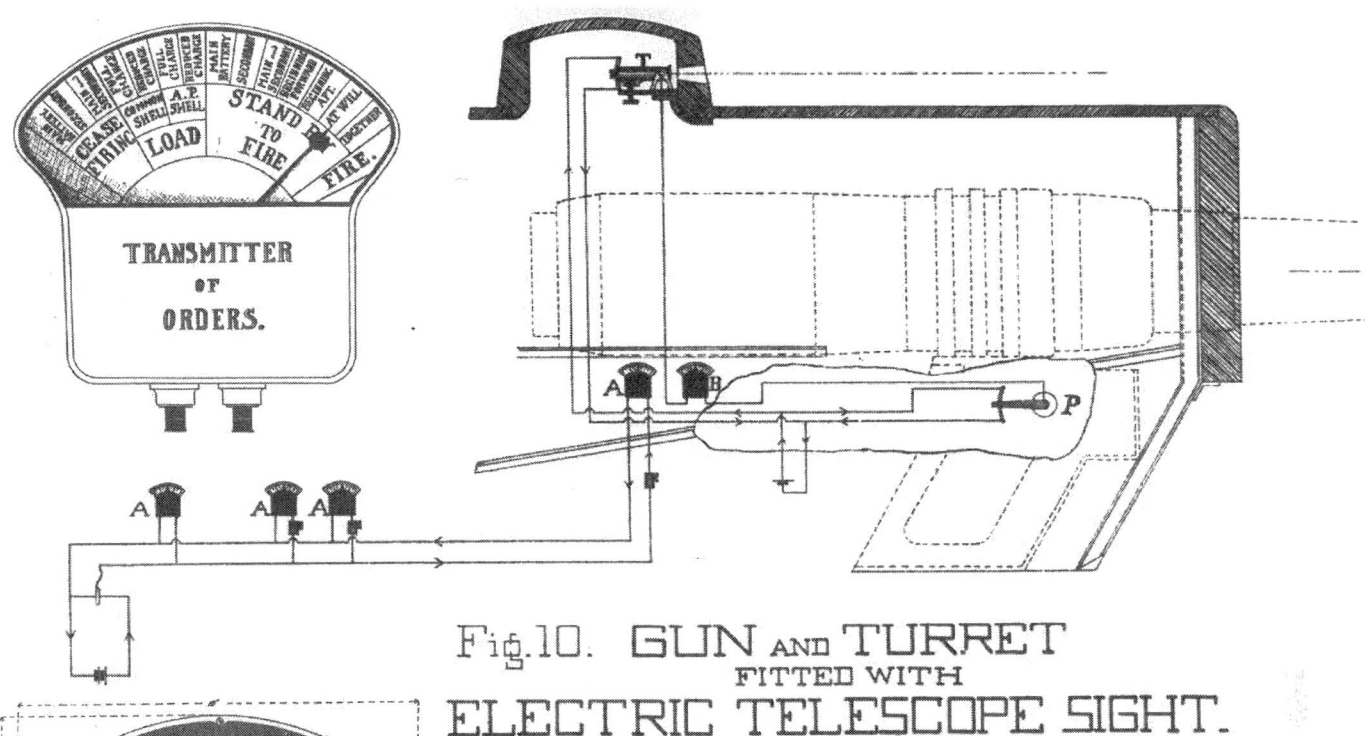

Fig. 10. GUN AND TURRET FITTED WITH ELECTRIC TELESCOPE SIGHT.

Following successful testing on board the USS *San Francisco* in 1893, the *Texas* was the first battleship in the US Navy to be equipped with the new electric range finder, electric range transmitter, range indicators and telescopic sights for its main guns. This system was developed by naval officer and inventor Bradley A. Fiske. These innovations helped to increase effective gunnery ranges out to about 2000 yards, a great improvement when compared to firing over open sights, paving the way for the high-precision mechanical and electrical targeting computers developed less than two decades later.

A similar system is shown (below right) in use in the sighting hood of the USS *Indiana*. The *Texas*, with her single-gun turrets, had only one optical sight in each of her turret hoods.

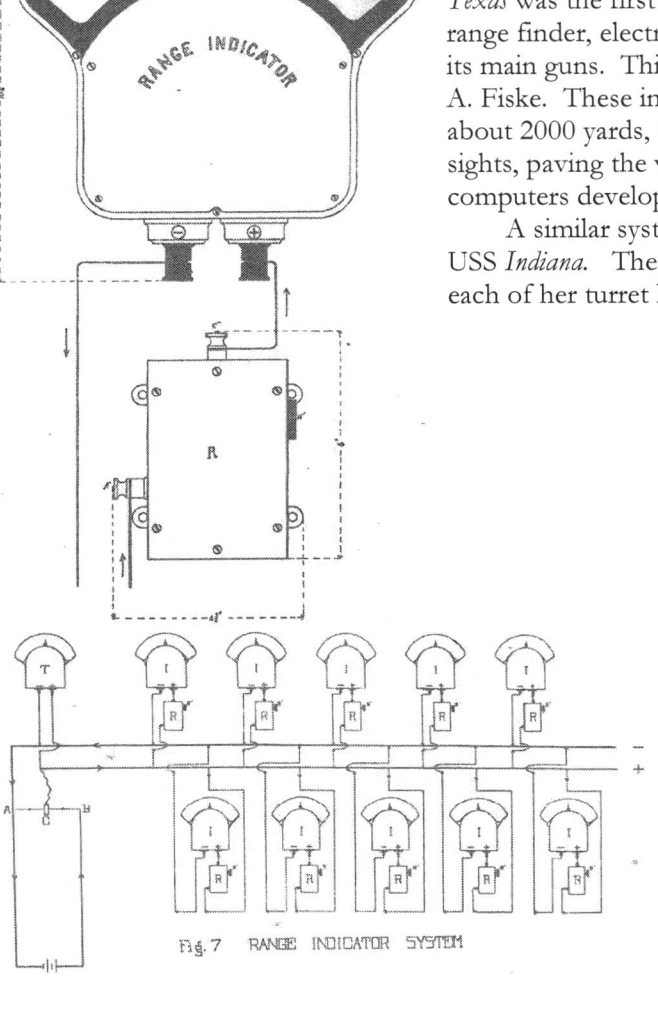

Fig. 7 RANGE INDICATOR SYSTEM

"INDIANA" - SIGHTING THE GUNS IN THE SIGHTING HOOD OF 13-INCH GUN TURRETS.

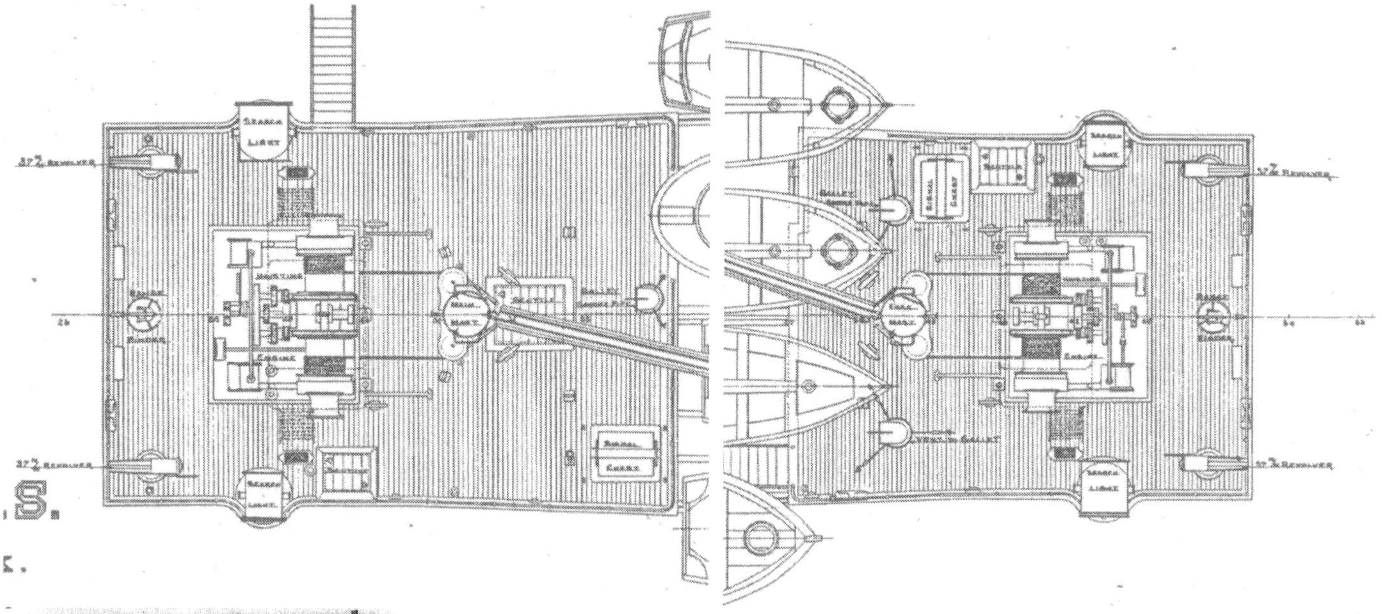

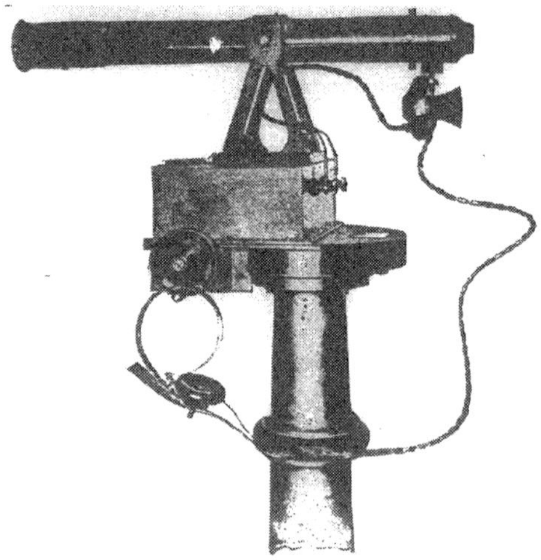

Deck plan showing the positions of the range finders at extreme opposite ends of the fore and aft bridge decks, along the centerline of the ship.

These devices were connected electrically and, using trigonometry and the known distance between the two fixed range finders, computed the distance to any object simultaneously viewed through both telescopes. This equipment was most accurate when targeting objects broadside on. Accuracy dropped off as target angles approached the bow or stern. Range finding triangulation directly ahead or astern was blocked by the ship's own superstructure.

Figs. 3, 4, and 5. Range finder.

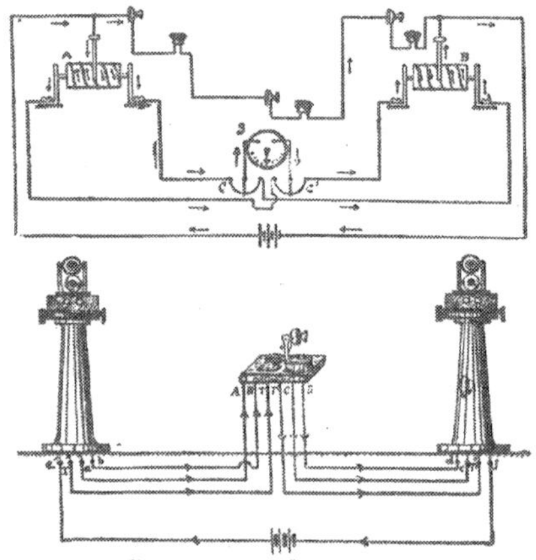

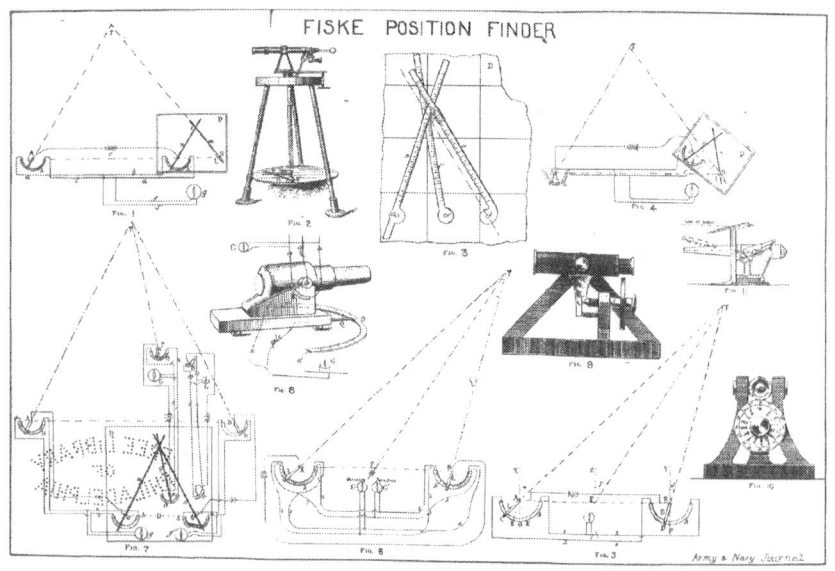

The Fiske position finder took the range-finding process one step further and directly determined and electrically transmitted gun-laying solutions based on the triangulation of the target's position relative to the ship. This system was well on the way to the gun laying computers in use in the following decades.

Fig. 6.—STADIMETER.

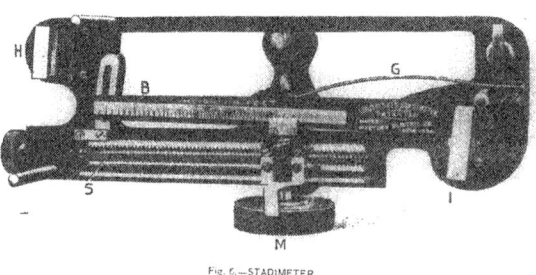

The issue of the placement of the 6" bow and stern chasers was a natural target of criticism regarding the design of the *Texas*. Their location within the arc of the 12" guns did greatly limit their utility and posed an increased risk to the 6" gun crews.

The *Texas*' designer, William John, considered the 6" guns to be an important part of the main battery, not as merely a secondary battery subservient in all situations to the demands of the 12" guns. In the days before plotting computers and long-range fire control, the effective range for accurate fire of the 12" and 6" guns was essentially similar, being dependant on the eye and ability of the individual gunner. In a long-range chase scenario, success depended on landing a fortunate shot on the adversary which would reduce their speed, allowing the *Texas* to either seek close engagement with a fleeing inferior vessel or to elude a superior warship. For this purpose a more rapidly worked 6" gun would answer better than a slower, and therefore less likely to achieve a hit, but more powerful 12" piece. William John had foreseen the need to have bow and stern chasers of a size that could be handily managed and located as high as practical above the water, so that they could fire at long range during a chase. In choosing the location for these guns, William John selected a spot that would be in the firing "shadow" of the masts and structural supports for the flying deck, obstructions which had been required by the Navy.

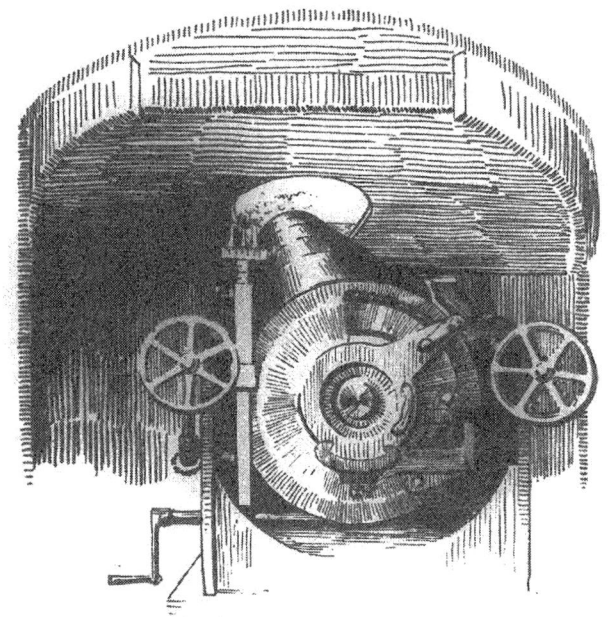

Fig. 11.—A BATTLE SHIP 300 FEET LONG, MASTS 150 FEET HIGH, SEEN OVER ORDINARY GUN SIGHT AND THROUGH PORT IN GUN SHIELD.
Horizontal field in gun port 9.5°. Vertical field 3°. Eye of gun captain being 60 inches behind rear sight. Ship is 2,000 yards distant.

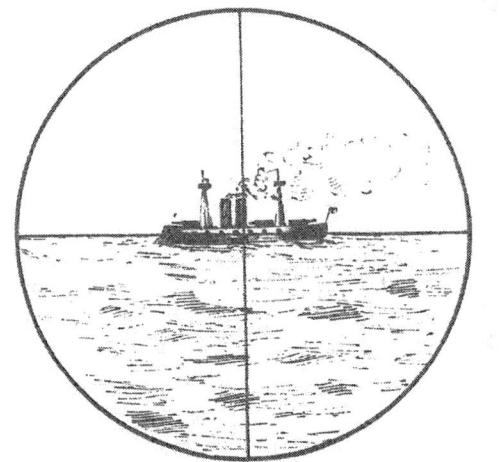

Fig. 12.—SAME SHIP SEEN, AT SAME DISTANCE, THROUGH TELESCOPIC GUN SIGHT.
Horizontal field 8°. Vertical field 8°. Magnification, 4 diameters.

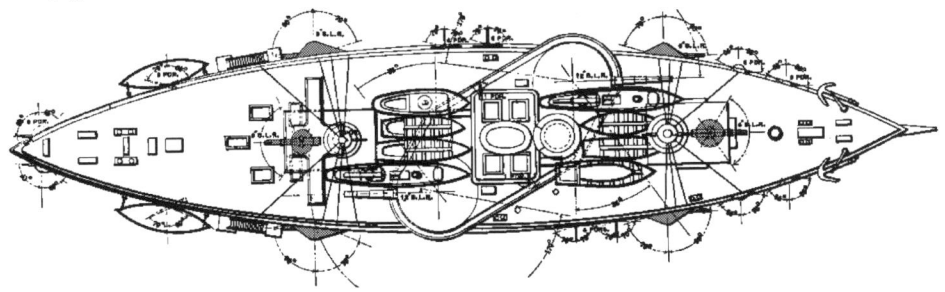

The aft 6"/35 caliber (below left) MK III gun position on the main deck of the *Texas*. These guns were fitted with a small turret-like shield that protected little more than the gun carriage but were worked by crew standing otherwise exposed on the deck. A blast shield incorporating hammock berthing was fitted forward this position to provide some measure of protection from the muzzle blast of the ship's aft 12" gun. The en echelon arrangement of the turrets left this position within the turning arc of the main gun. An accidental discharge at an inopportune moment while the 12" gun was swinging from its loading position past the blast shield could have caused extensive damage and loss of life.

An accidental discharge of the 12" gun did in fact occur on June 4th 1898 during the *Texas*' wartime service off of Cuba. Fortunately, the gun was trained outboard and the shell passed harmlessly out to sea.

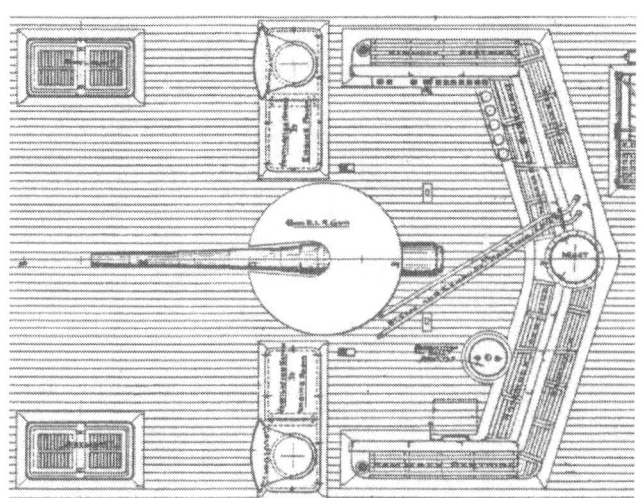 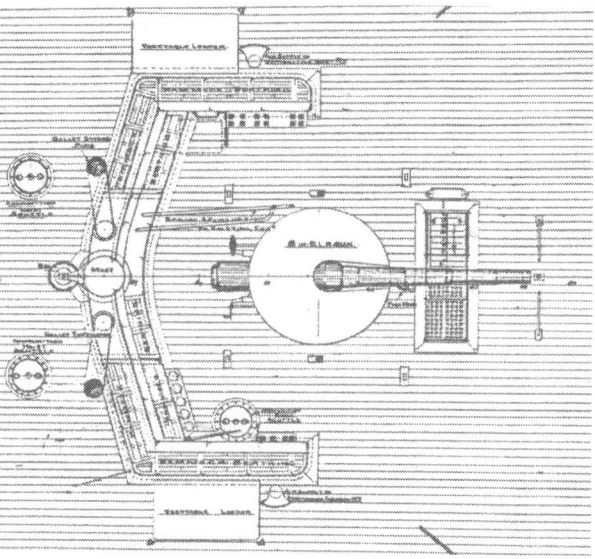

The forward 6"/35 caliber MK III gun position on the main deck of the *Texas* (above right), similarly fitted out and shielded from the blast of the forward 12" gun.

February 1897: Galveston, Texas. Crewmen pose leaning against the forward 6 inch gun. Note the storage of shells against the bulkhead.

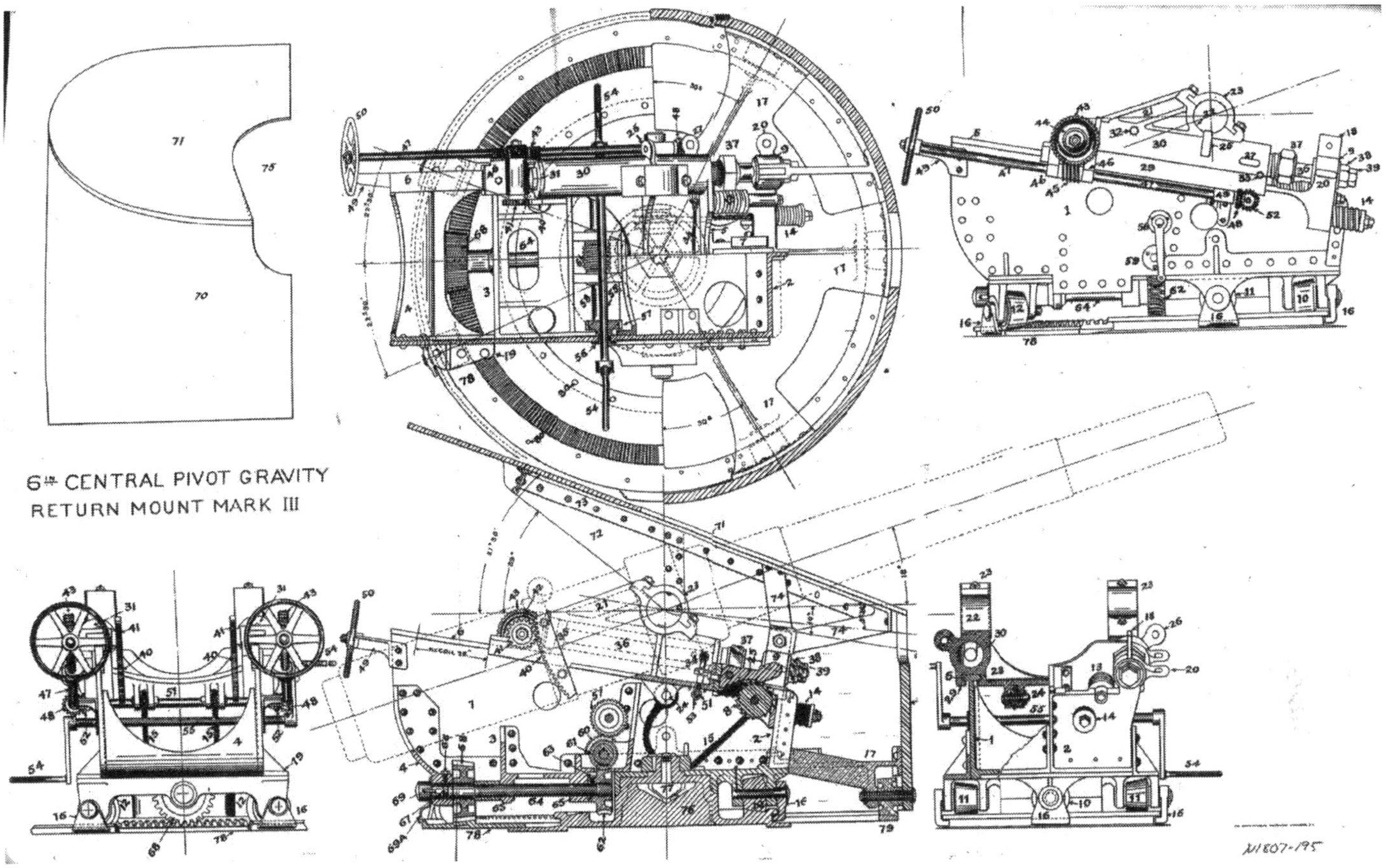

6 inch gun mount and shield of the type fitted on the main deck of the *Texas*. Note that the carriage mechanism checks the recoil of the gun but relies on gravity acting through an inclined plane to return the gun to firing position. Training of the 6 inch guns was done by hand.

1898 Captain Phillip stands at a hatch railing in front of the aft 6 inch gun.

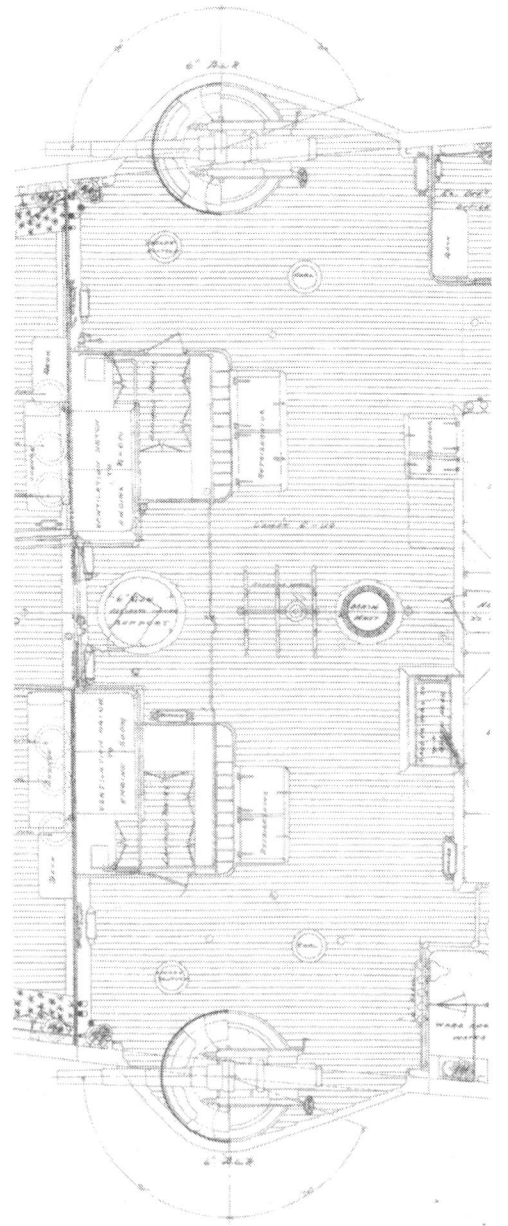 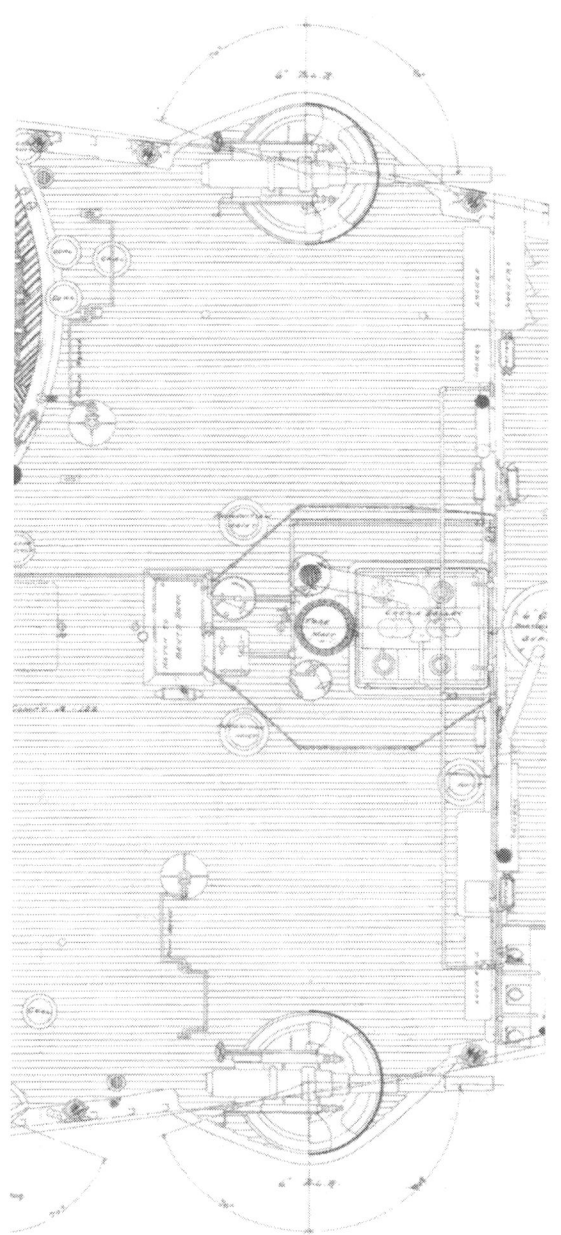

Forward (right) and aft (left) 6"/30 caliber gun positions on the gun deck of the *Texas*. These guns were mounted in small sponsons projecting from the sides of the ship in order to provide them with an increased firing arc. Gun carriages were Mk III similar to those on the main deck but lacking the turret-like shields fixed to the gun. Instead, armored panels fitted to the sponsons could be individually dropped down or raised to allow the guns to be trained while still providing some measure of protection to the gun crew.

Profile views of starboard 6"/30 caliber sponsons: forward (right) and aft (left).

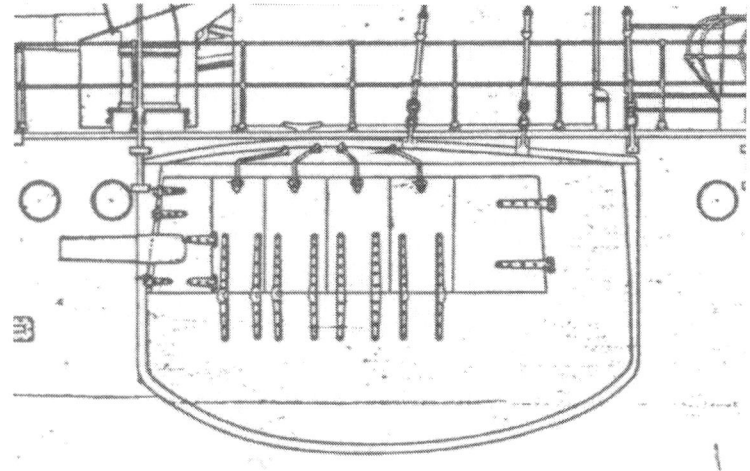 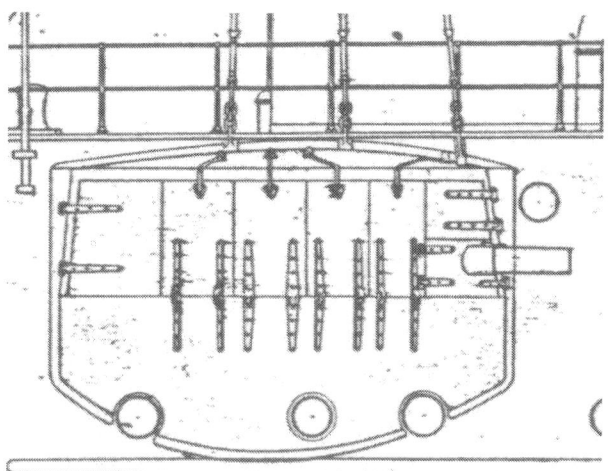

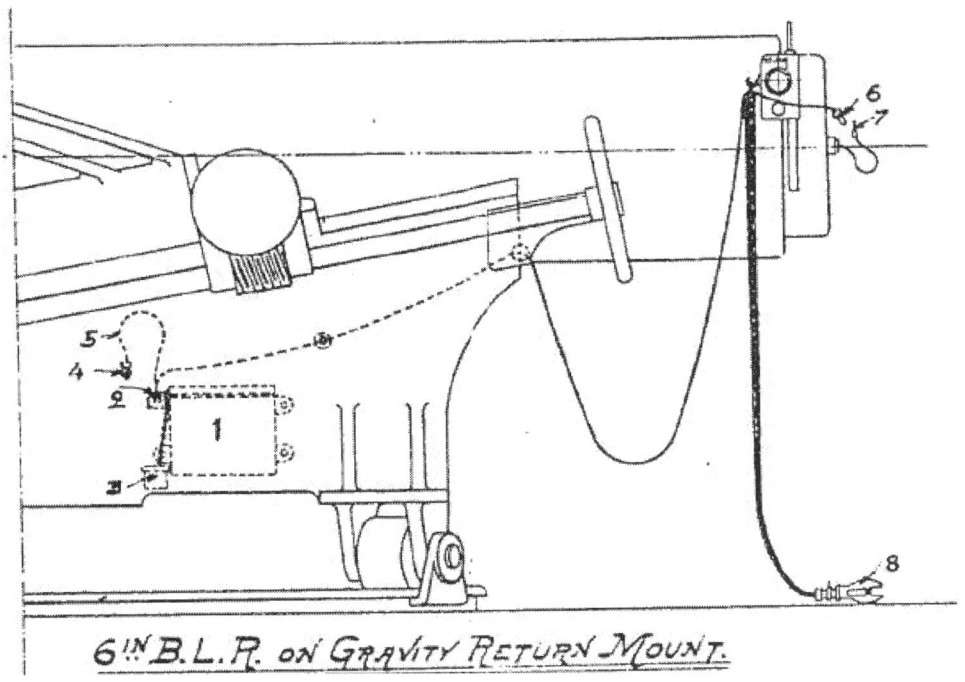

6 IN. B.L.R. ON GRAVITY RETURN MOUNT.

1911: Chesapeake Bay. Main deck 6"/30 caliber guns photographed during the last days of the ship. Note the removable shields in place in the sponson through which the barrel of the guns protrude, even when not in action. For testing purposes dummies were hung around the guns at simulated action stations. "Herbie" is presumed to have given his last full measure in action soon thereafter.

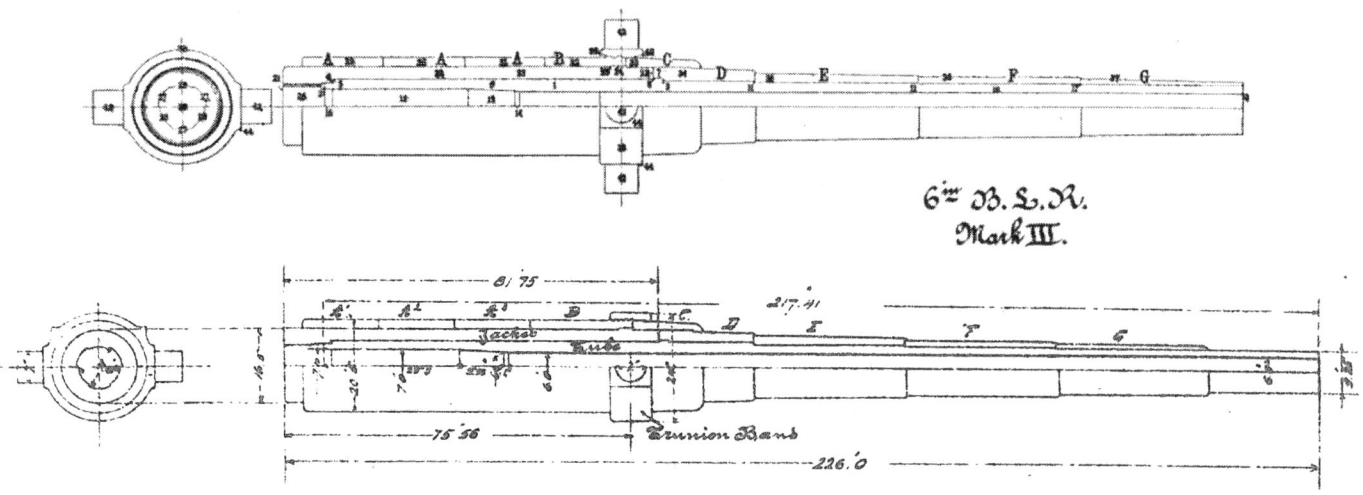

Plans showing the construction of the 6"/30 (top) and 6"/35 caliber (bottom) MK III guns. Note in the section drawings how the guns are built up in bands that sleeve into one another.

6 inch gun being fired on the Navy's test range

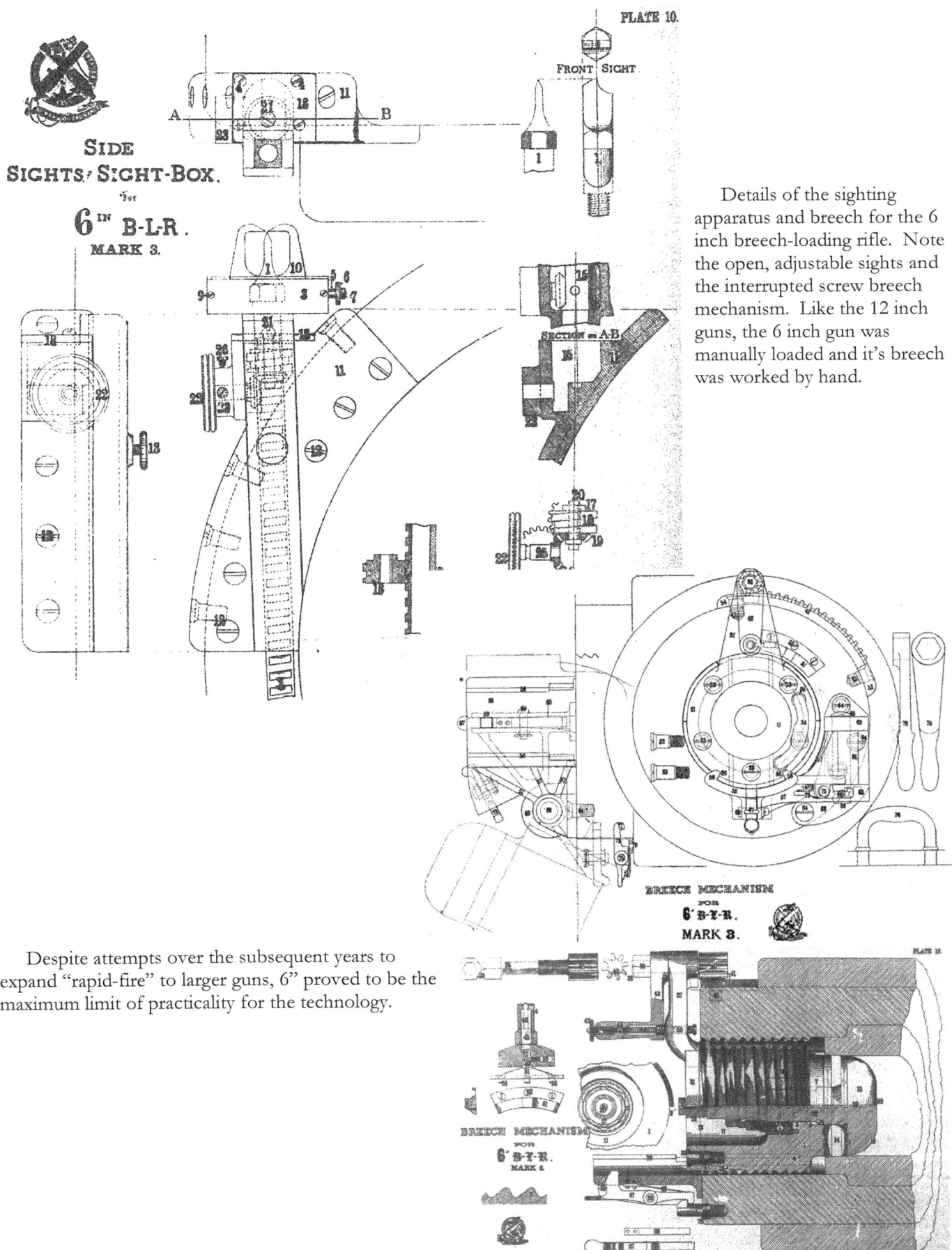

Details of the sighting apparatus and breech for the 6 inch breech-loading rifle. Note the open, adjustable sights and the interrupted screw breech mechanism. Like the 12 inch guns, the 6 inch gun was manually loaded and it's breech was worked by hand.

Despite attempts over the subsequent years to expand "rapid-fire" to larger guns, 6" proved to be the maximum limit of practicality for the technology.

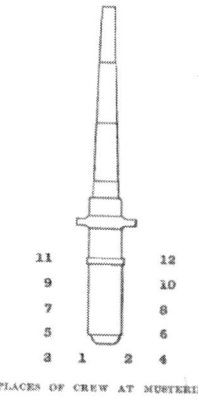

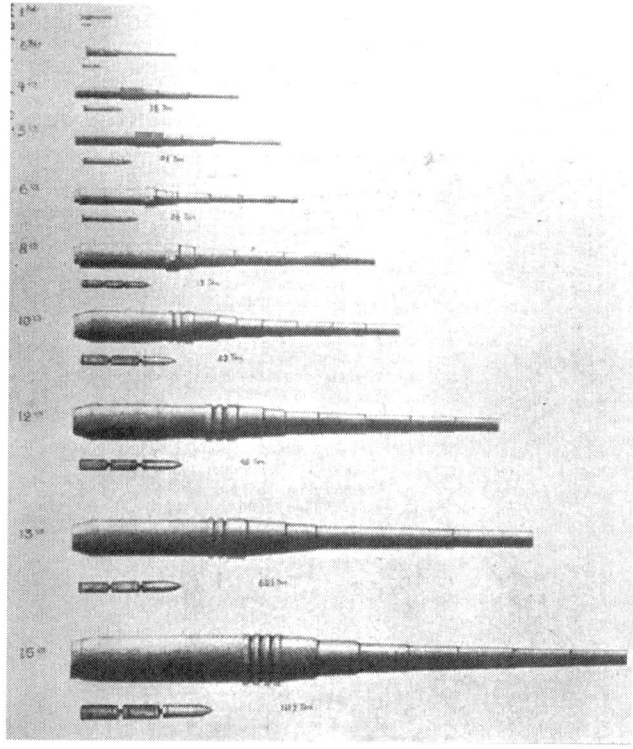

The illustration above describes the positions and functions of each member of the crew for the 6" gun.

Comparison of the relative sizes of shells, powder charges, and guns in use in the United States Navy.

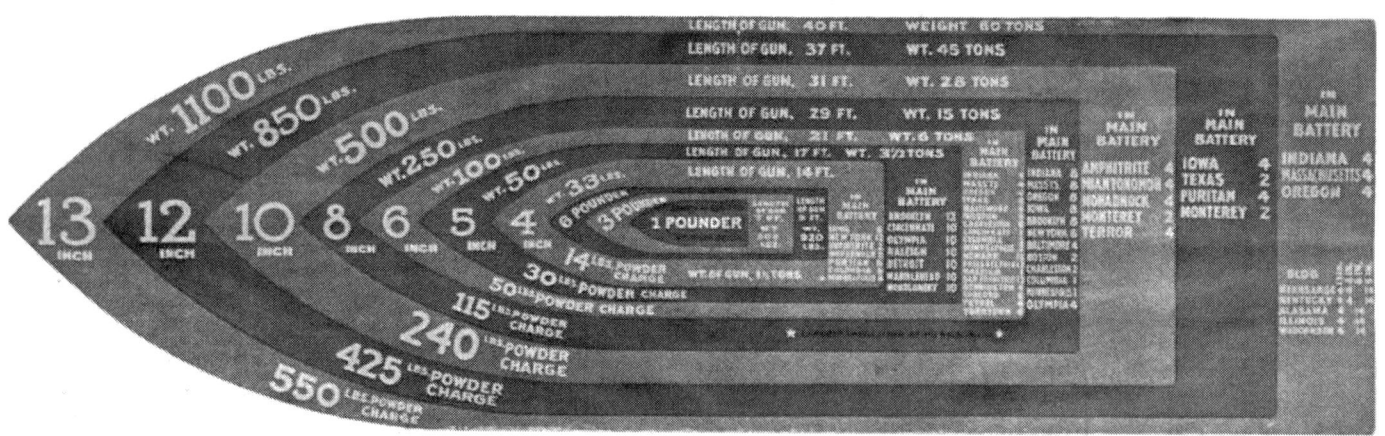

1898: Probably Brooklyn, New York. Twelve inch shells on the deck of the *Texas*. Each 12 inch shell weighed 850 pounds. 425 pounds of brown powder were used for each full-charge armor piercing shot, producing a working pressure of 15.5 tons per square inch and giving a muzzle velocity of approximately 2,100 feet per second. This was sufficient to penetrate 24.16 inches of steel at the muzzle, decreasing to 19.10 inches of steel at 2,500 yards. Steel or iron common shells utilized a reduced charge of 315 pounds of brown powder, resulting in a muzzle velocity of 1,700 feet per second. The *Texas* typically stored 80 rounds per gun.

1898 (below): Probably Brooklyn, New York. Six inch shells on the deck of the *Texas*. Note the rope harnesses used to help carry the shells. Each 6 inch armor piercing shell weighed 100 pounds. 47 pounds of brown powder were used for each armor piercing shot producing a working pressure (for the 30 cal guns) of 13.3 tons per square inch, and giving a muzzle velocity of 1,950 feet per second. This was sufficient to penetrate 10 inches of steel at the muzzle, decreasing to about 6 inches of steel at 2,500 yards. 35 caliber guns produced a muzzle velocity of 2,075 feet per second. This was sufficient to penetrate about 10.5 inches of steel at the muzzle, decreasing to about 7 inches of steel at 2,500 yards. Steel common shells utilized a charge of 35 pounds of brown powder. Rate of fire was about 1 round every 90 seconds. The *Texas* typically stored 100 rounds per gun.

One of the main deck 6 inch guns is partially visible to the left and a 12 inch gun turret can be seen in the distance behind a crowd of visitors.

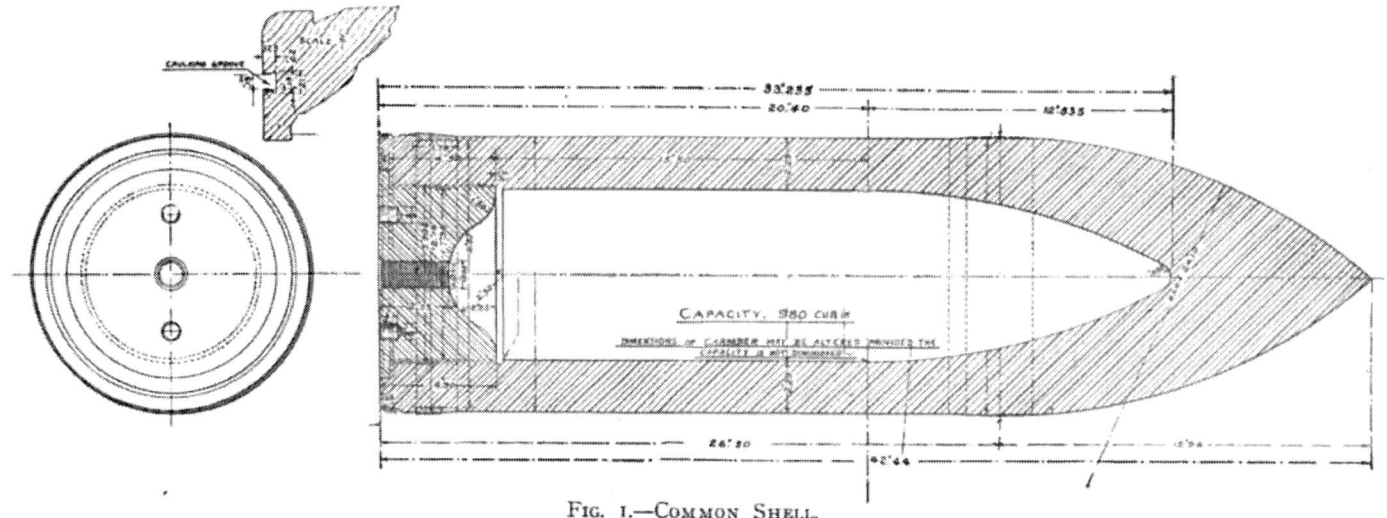

Fig. 1.—Common Shell.

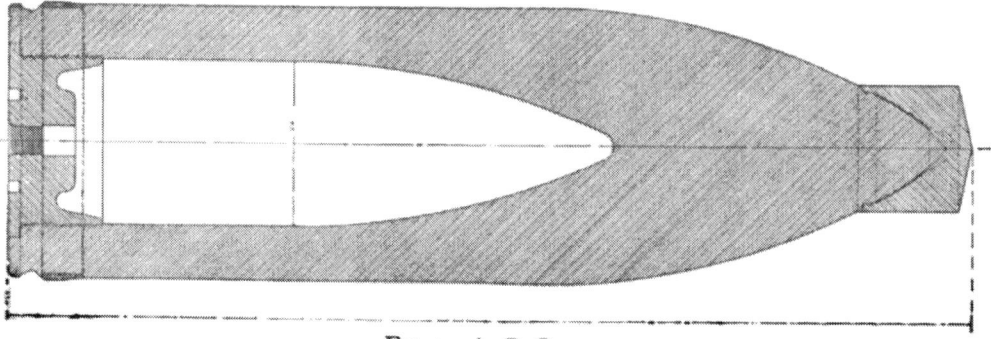

Fig. 2.—A. P. Shell.
12-INCH PROJECTILES.

"A new shell that has lately come into use, and which did good service during the late war [the Spanish American War], is known as a "semi" shell. It is a combination of the other two, of the same weight, has a hard steel head designed to penetrate light armor, and carries in addition a bursting charge of about 50 pounds. This shell is especially designed for use against armored cruisers or vessels of light protection, and is very effective. The igniting fuse for this shell is a base fuse, instead of the old nose fuse used in common shells. Common shells are intended to be used against forts, earthworks, and unprotected vessels, and were used almost entirely against the batteries before Santiago." – *Scientific American*, 1898

"Formerly, for these 12-inch guns, there were but two kinds of shells, common and armor-piercing, as shrapnel are not used in the larger guns. Common shells are rather long, weigh 850 pounds, and carry a bursting charge of about 60 pounds of powder. Armor-piercing shells are the same weight, but are somewhat shorter, carrying no explosive charge. They are made of the hardest steel, with toughened point, intended, as the name indicates, to penetrate armor. The new armor-piercing shells have soft steel caps on the points, supposed to give them a greater penetrating effect." – *Scientific American*, 1898

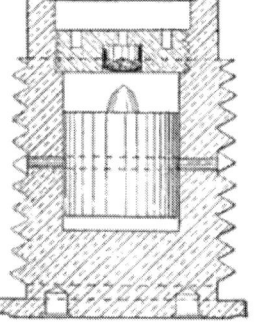 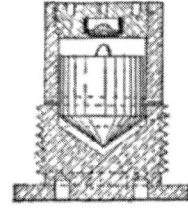

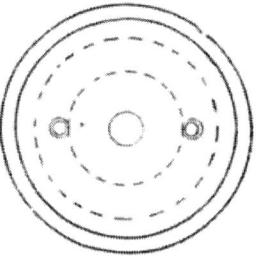 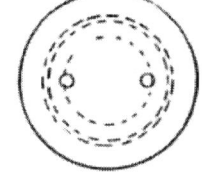

Fig. 1.　　　　　　　　　Fig. 2.

NAVY BASE-PERCUSSION FUSES.

6 SECONDARY BATTERY

According to several contemporary sources, as initially fitted out, the standard secondary battery of the Texas consisted of:

12 – 6 pdr. 10 Driggs-Schroeder and 2 Hotchkiss guns on cage stands.

6 – 1 pdr. Driggs-Schroeder "heavy" guns. 3 cage stands for boats and 4 ship's cage stands were carried as well as 5 boat "circles" and 2 ship "circles". 4 mounts for ship's tops were also available.

4 – 37mm Hotchkiss Revolving Cannon on cage stands.

2 – "Short" machine guns

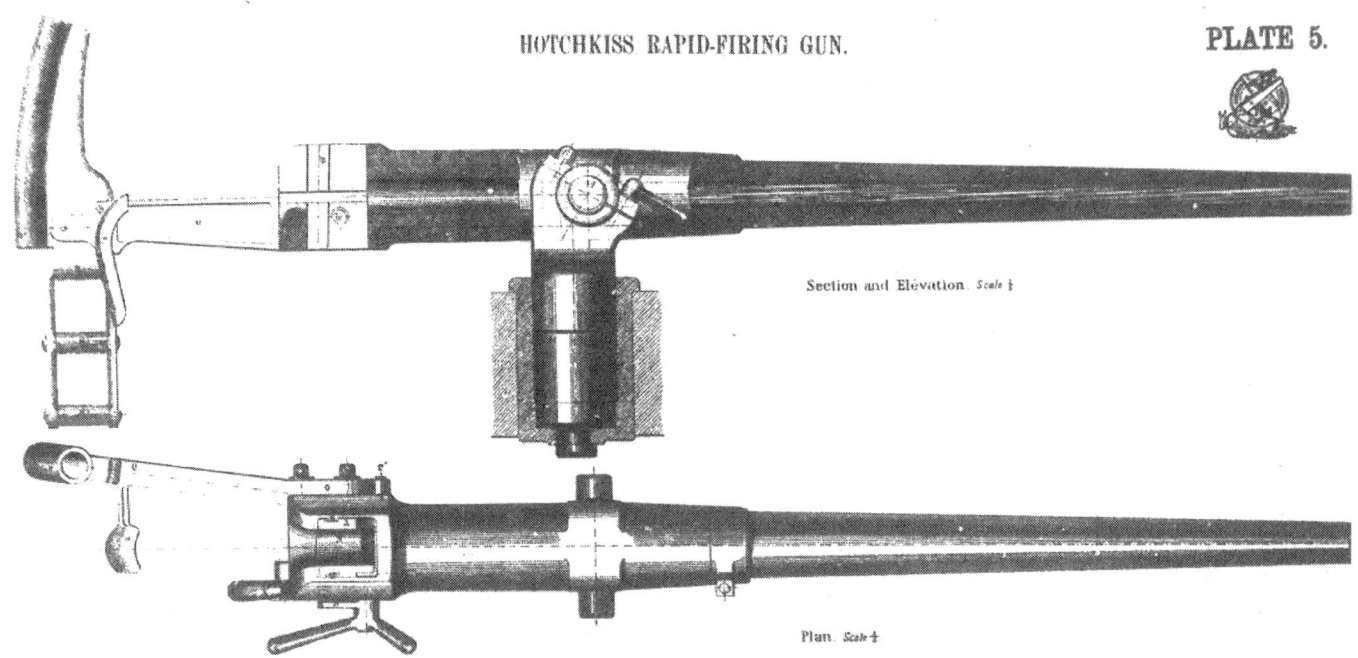

The *Texas* carried ten 6 Pounder (Pdr.) 57mm Driggs-Schroeder and two 6 Pdr./40 caliber 57mm Hotchkiss Mk1 rapid fire guns (firing the same ammunition) on the gun deck. These single shot weapons were called "rapid fire" as they fired a fixed cartridge case and shell and could lay down a curtain of fire in a broadside, each gun firing at about 20 rounds a minute. They were primarily intended as anti-torpedo boat defense as they could engage torpedo boats well outside the 400 yard optimum range of the then current torpedoes. However, they could also be utilized against any target on the water or land in relatively close range work (as the *Texas* would find during her wartime service). The "six pounder" ammunition came in both armor piercing and shell variety. The guns were turned by a "rudder" that the gunner held against his shoulder.

The Driggs-Schroeder was a US Navy-developed gun while the Hotchkiss was imported from Europe. The Hotchkiss was later produced under license in the United States. By 1898 the number of Hotchkiss and Driggs-Schroeders guns in the US Navy was about equal. The two Hotchkiss guns on the *Texas* were at the No. 5 position port and starboard.

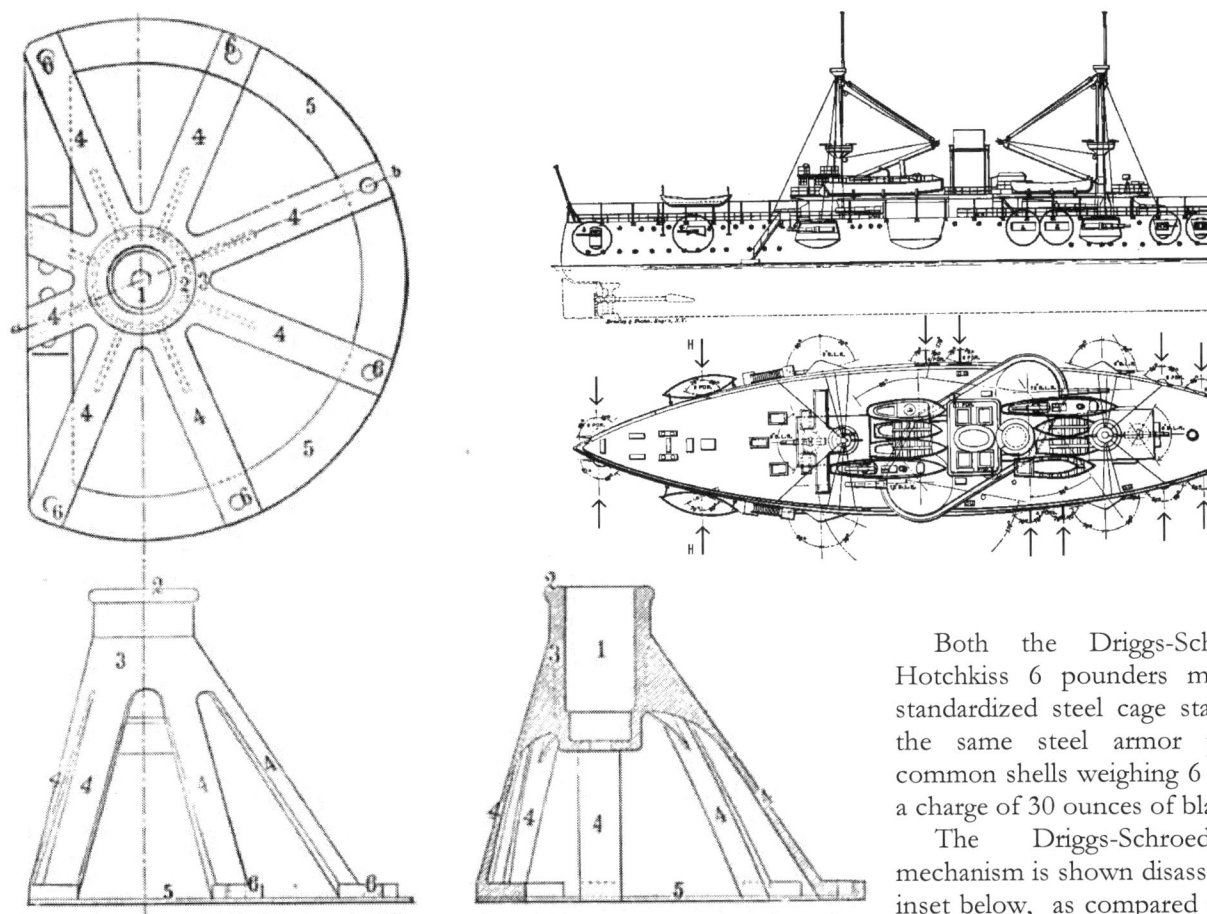

STEEL CAGE-STAND FOR 3-POUNDER AND 6-POUNDER RAPID-FIRING GUNS.
Nomenclature.
1. Pivot-Socket. 2. Cage-Head. 3. Cage-Body. 4. Cage-Legs. 5. Cage Deck-Plate. 6. Cage Deck-Fastenings.

Both the Driggs-Schroeder and Hotchkiss 6 pounders mounted to a standardized steel cage stand and fired the same steel armor piercing and common shells weighing 6 pounds using a charge of 30 ounces of black powder.

The Driggs-Schroeder breech mechanism is shown disassembled in the inset below, as compared to that of the Hotchkiss.

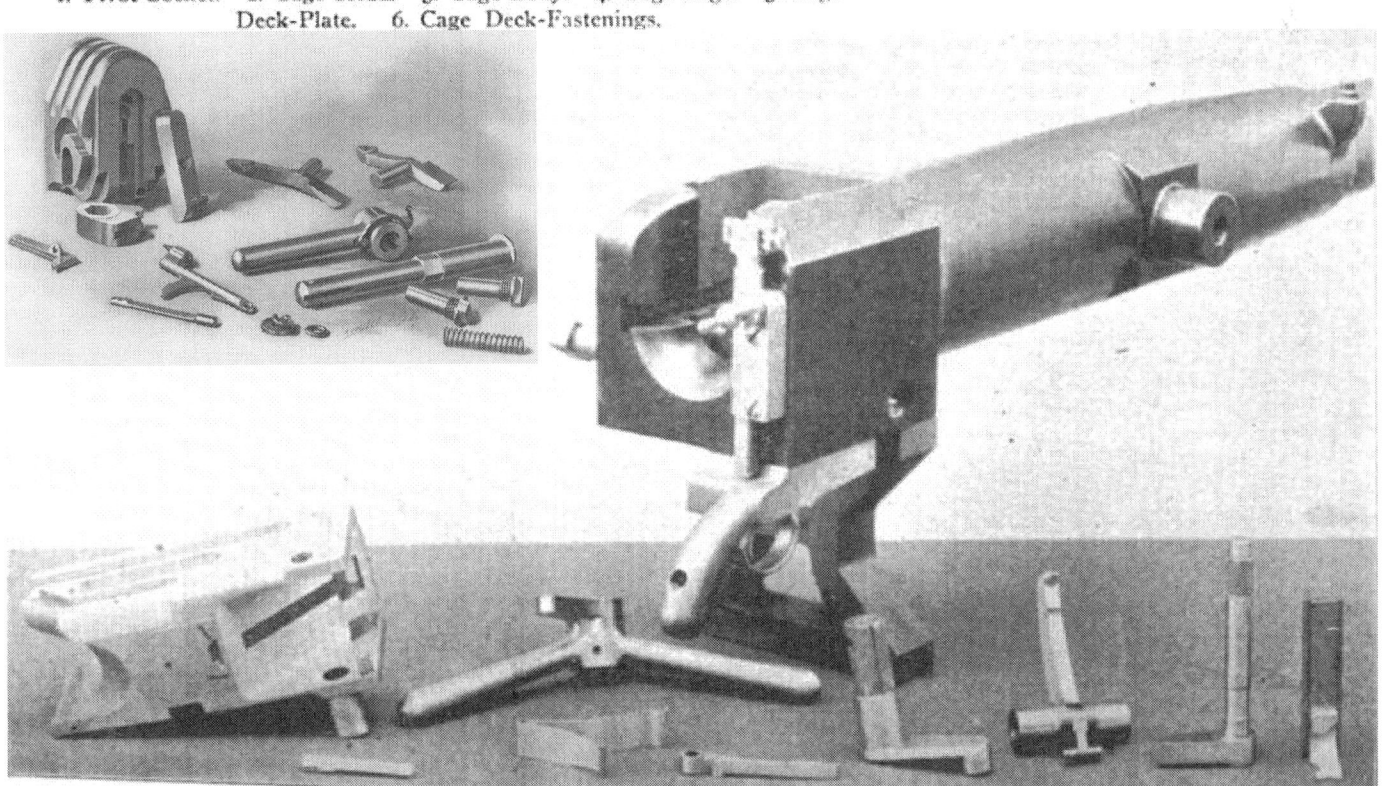

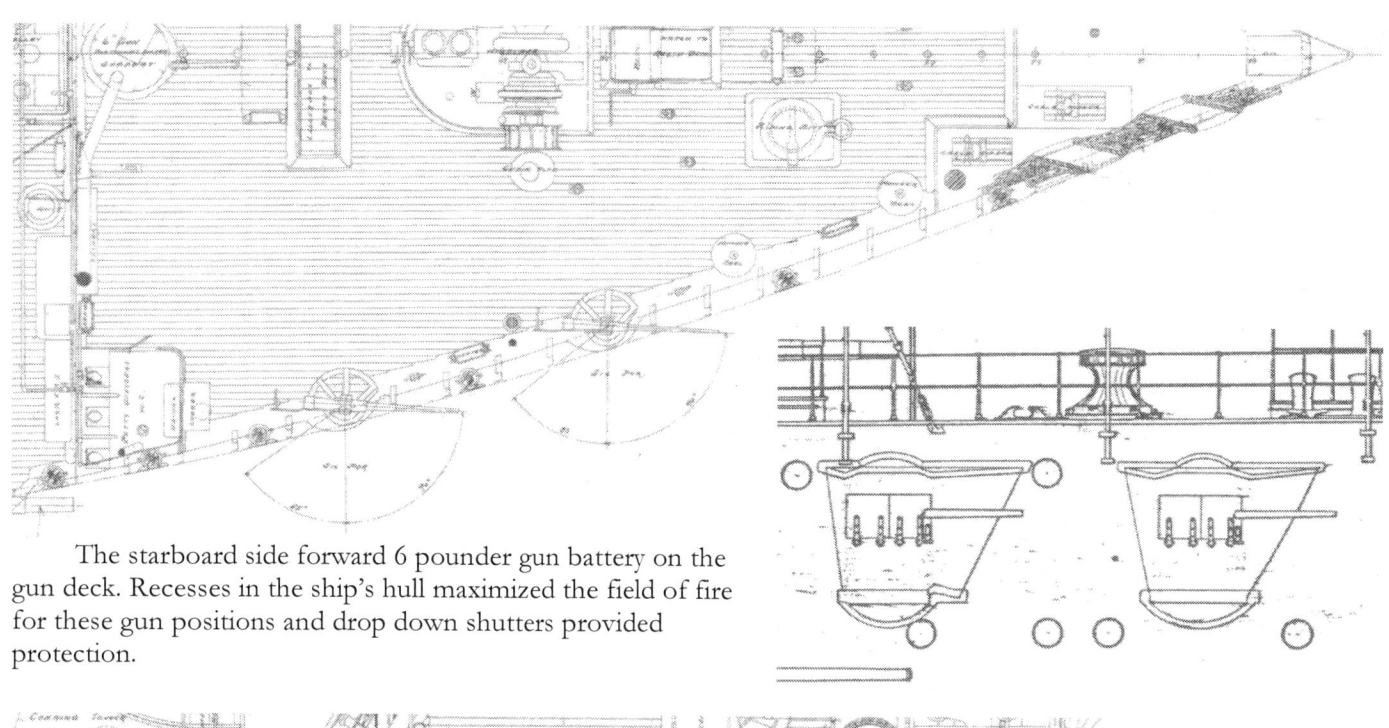

The starboard side forward 6 pounder gun battery on the gun deck. Recesses in the ship's hull maximized the field of fire for these gun positions and drop down shutters provided protection.

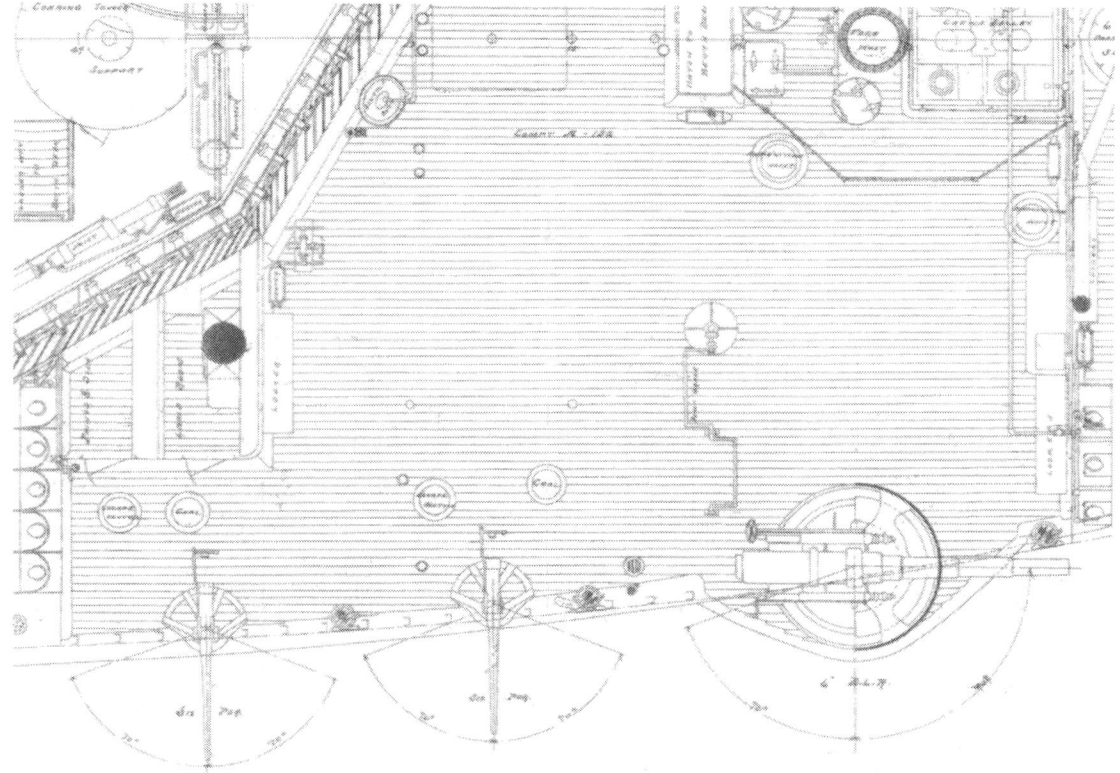

The starboard side amidships 1 pounder battery located just forward of the armored redoubt on the gun deck. These guns shared the compartment with the forward starboard 6"/30 cal gun. The port 6 pounders were placed relatively closer to the redoubt and were separated from the aft port 6"/30 cal gun by the ship's offices.

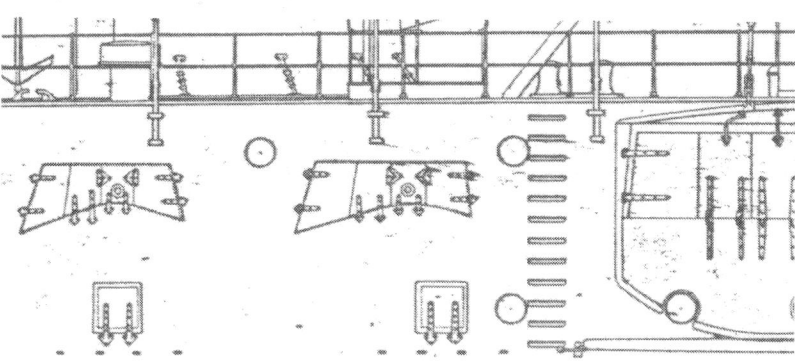

Hinged plates provided some measure of protection from weather and, to a lesser extent, hostile fire.

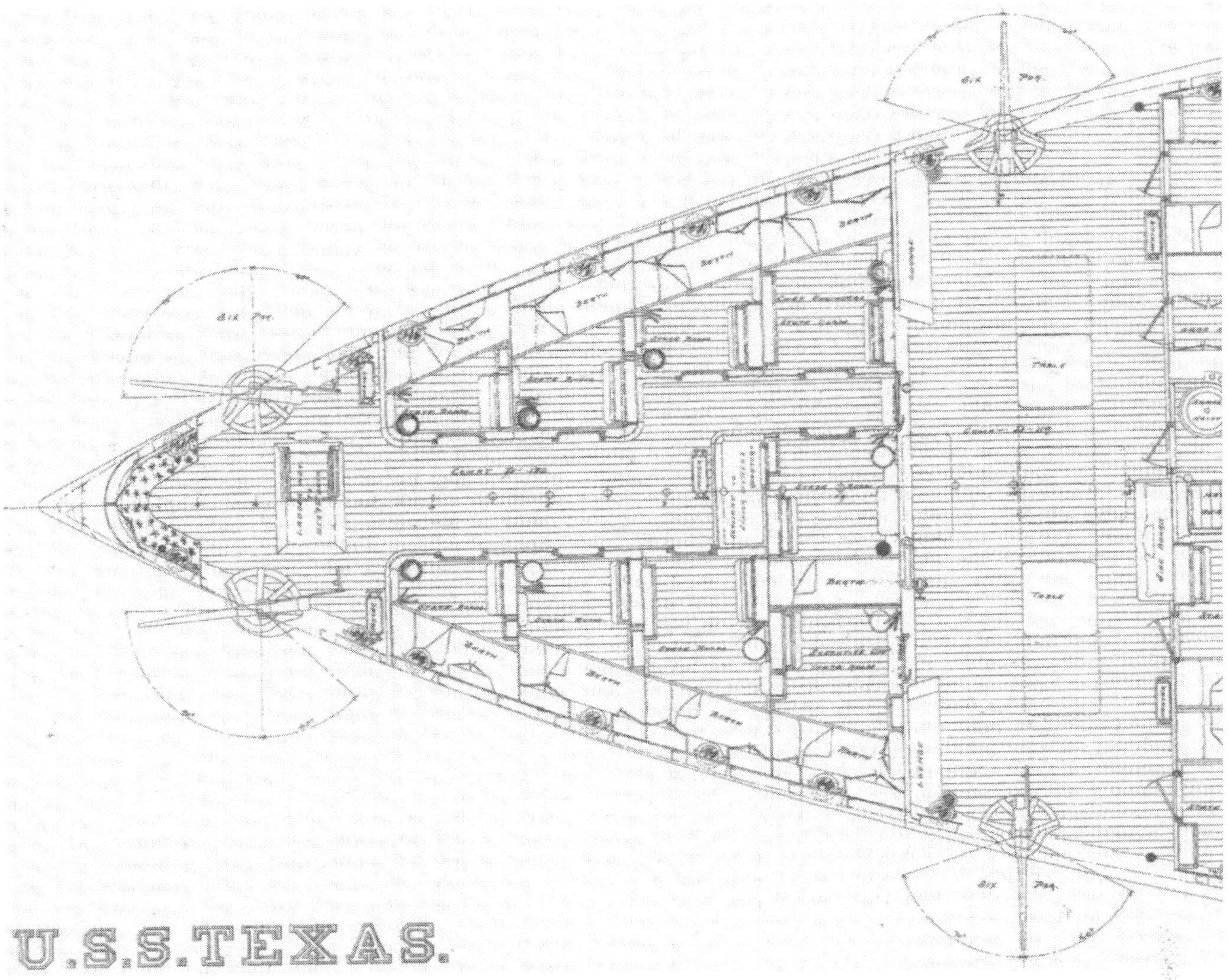

U.S.S. TEXAS.

The aft 6 pounders located in the officers quarters on the gun deck. The forward pair of guns in this battery were Hotchkiss guns, mounted in a similar manner to the amidships guns, with drop-down shutters providing protection. The aft-most pair of 6 pounders, due to the confined space they occupied and the extreme angle of the ship's hull at that point, were emplaced in sponsons projecting out of the ship's sides.

The six pounder was used almost universally by all nations, albeit with different breech mechanisms. The Spanish Navy preferred the British Nordenfelt design. The final variants of the popular naval six pounder would see service as anti-tank guns during World War II.

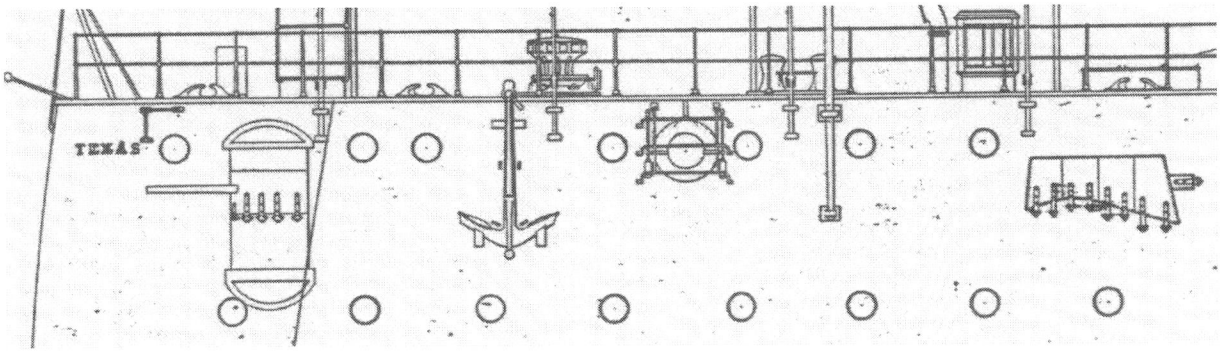

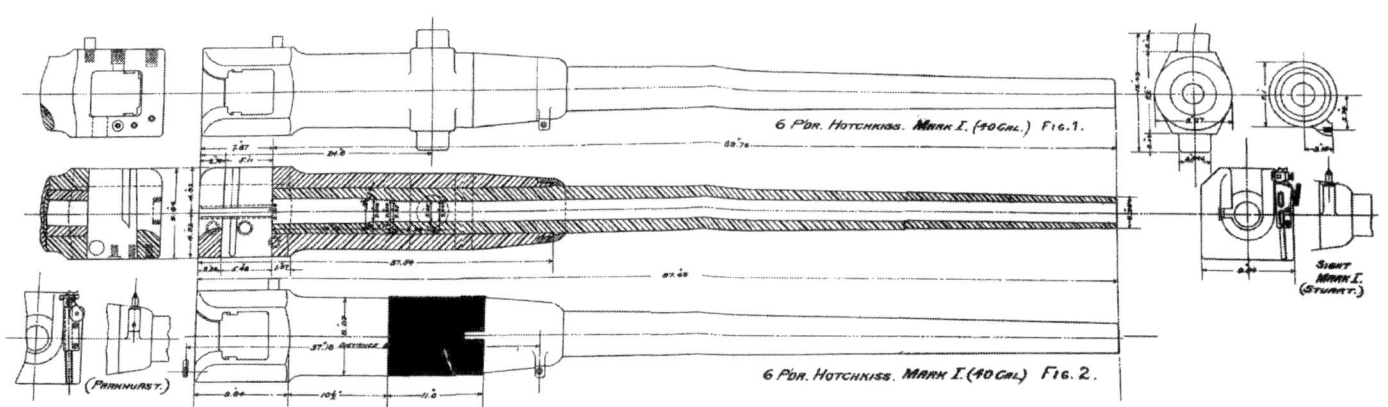

BREECH MECHANISM. Plate 6.
HOTCHKISS RAPID-FIRING GUN.

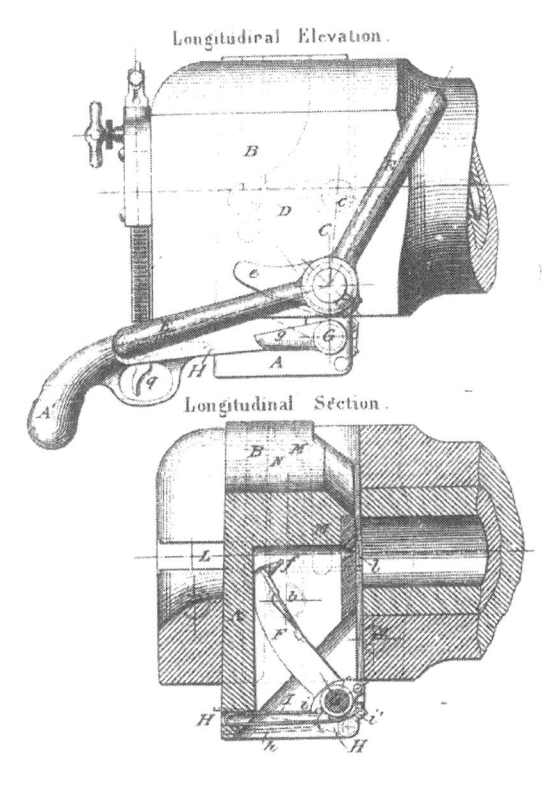

BREECH MECHANISM.
HOTCHKISS RAPID-FIRING GUN.

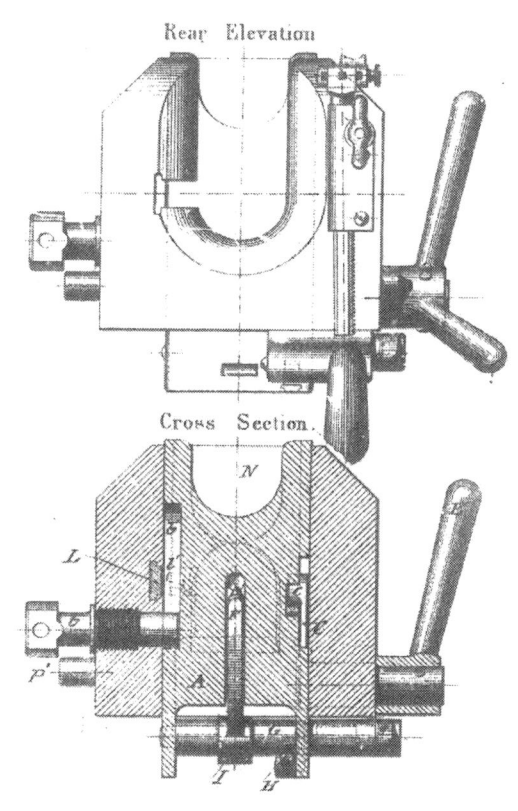

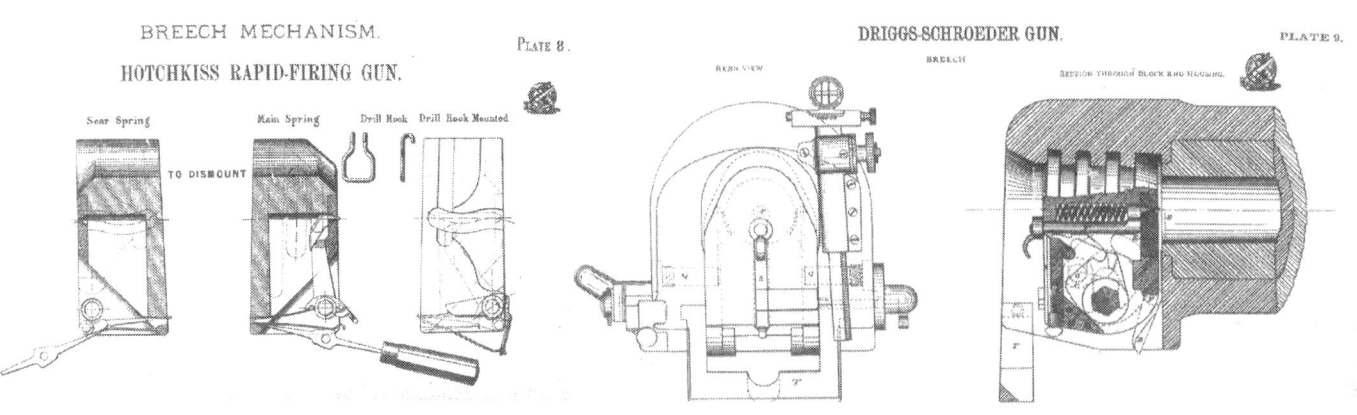

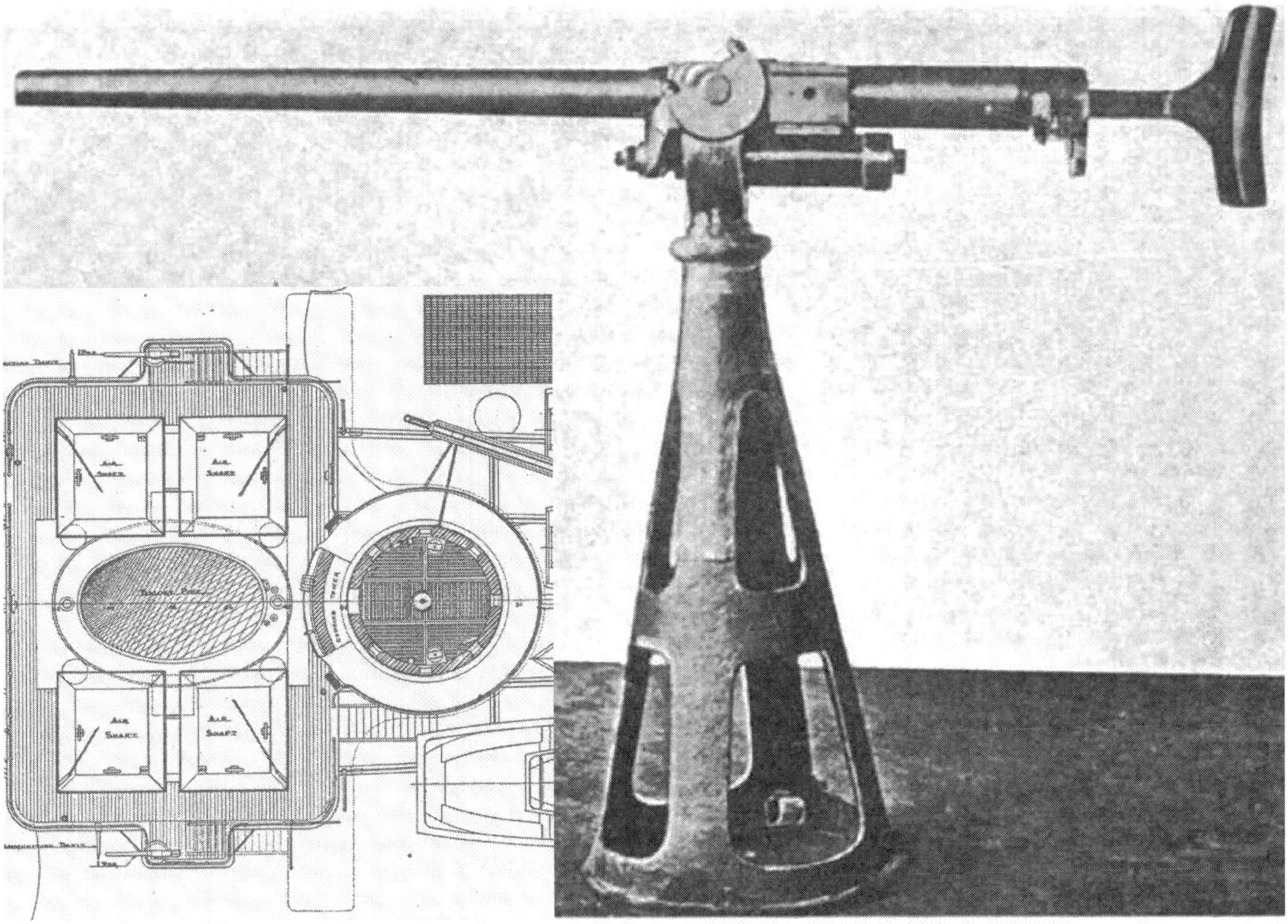

DRIGGS-SCHROEDER 1-POUNDER RAPID-FIRING GUN.

The Driggs-Schroeder 1 Pounder (Pdr) 1" 37mm rapid fire gun was for the most part, a boat gun. Six were mounted on the *Texas* but they could also be used on the ship's boats. One each were proposed to be used on the *Texas*' torpedo boats, but they had very little hitting power and a much slower rate of fire than the revolving canon of the same caliber.

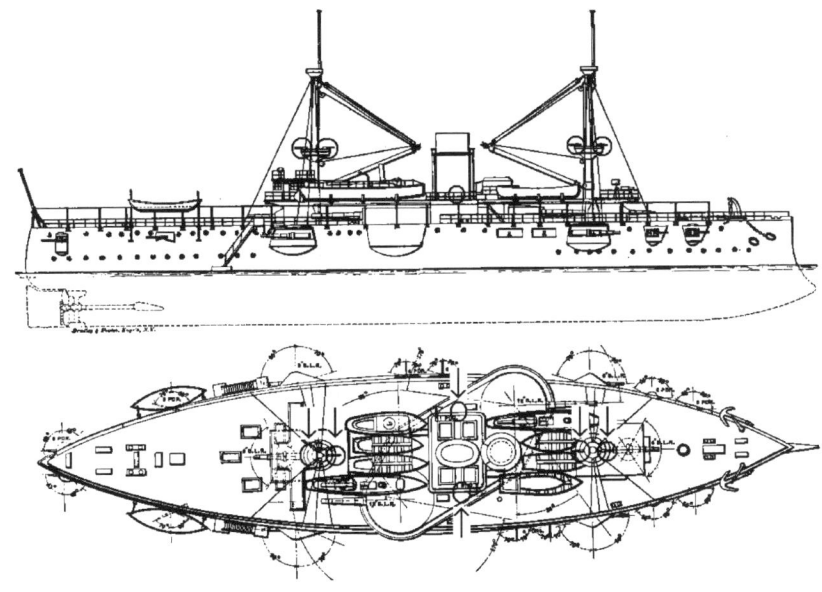

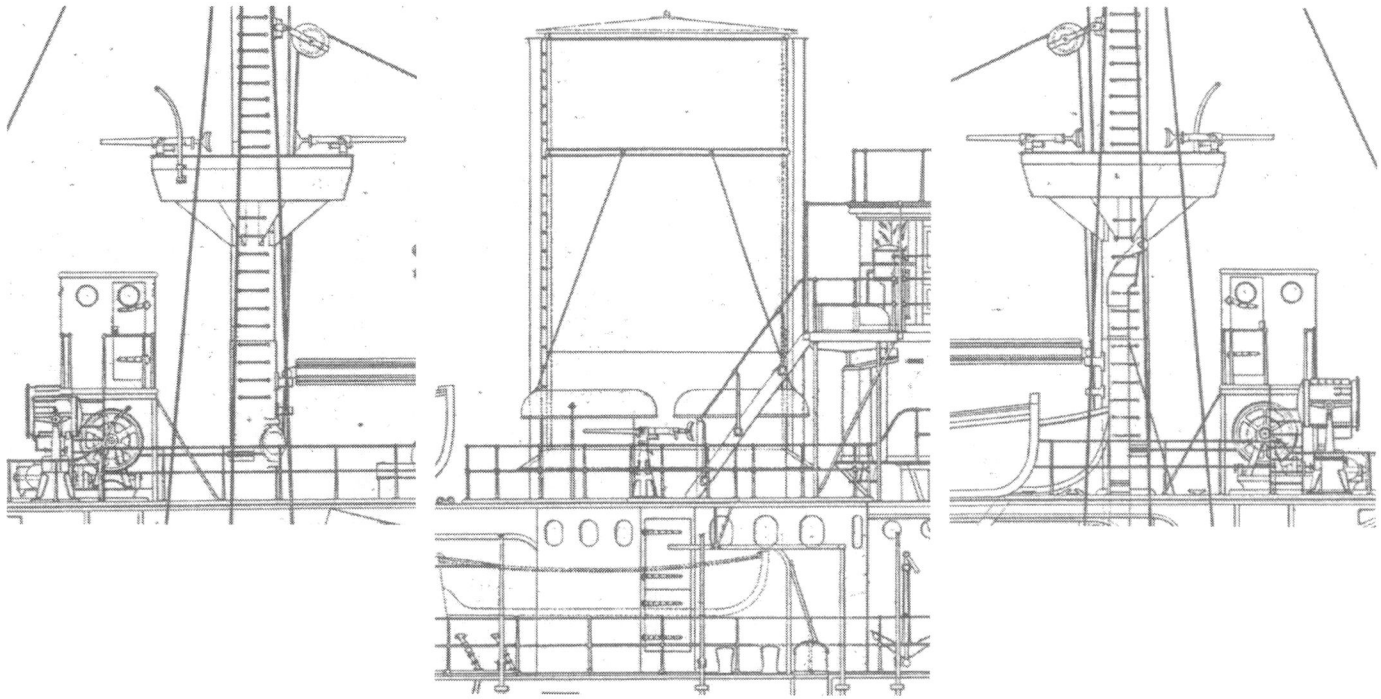

1 pounder gun positions in the aft (left) and forward (right) fighting tops as well as on the central bridge deck of the *Texas*. These rapidly worked, light-weight guns were placed in elevated positions so that they could be trained downward onto the bridge and superstructure of opposing vessels, targeting exposed navigating and command positions as well as the competing ship's gun crews.

Note in the photo below, taken at the Brooklyn Navy Yard, that the pedestal gun positions on the bridge deck adjacent to the search lights, that were normally occupied by Hotchkiss revolving cannon, have in this instance 1 pounders installed instead.

The light weight of the 1 pounders also made them usable in the fighting tops. While the *Texas* had a pair in each top, they were not the optimal weapon for this position. Machine guns would have been more effective. However, the US Navy had only just adopted the machine gun and as a result no tactics had yet been devised for their employment on ships, although some European Navies had already adopted 25MM Nordenfelt multi-barrel guns for fighting top use.

August 1898: Brooklyn, NY. Fighting top of the *Texas*. Shortly after her return from Santiago, Cuba, sailors man their combat positions for the camera.

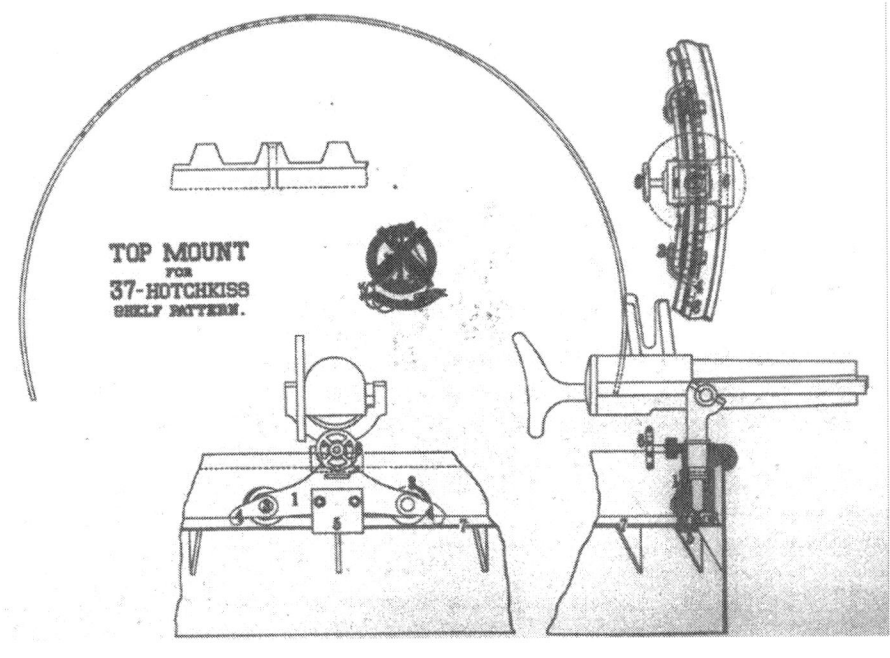

Detail of a "shelf pattern" gun mount for a ships top (in this diagram depicting the mounting of a 37mm Hotchkiss revolving cannon) similar to the mounts seen in photos of the *Texas*.

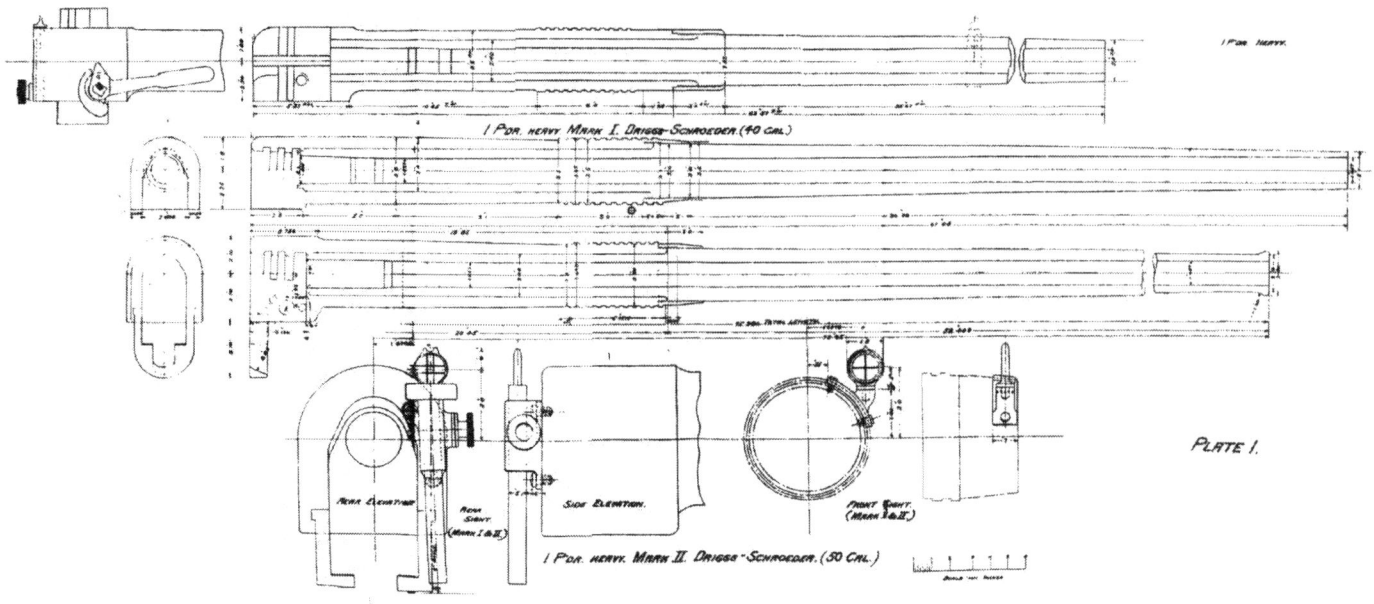

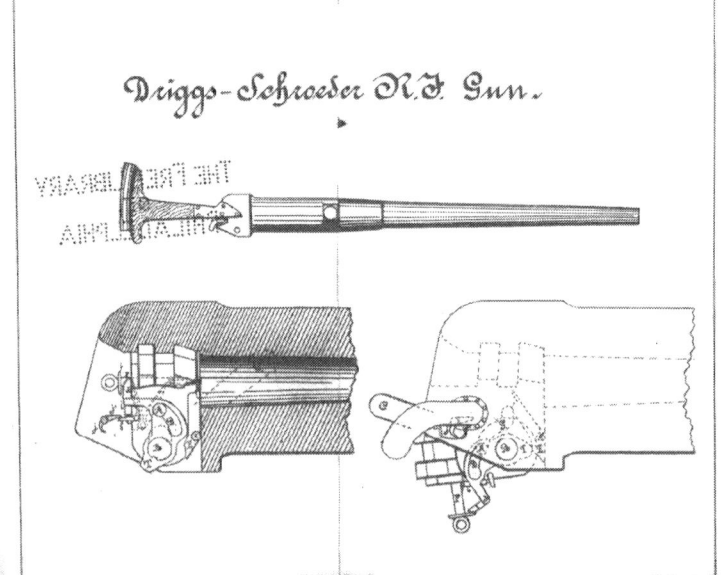

The 1 pounder Driggs-Schroeder rapid fire gun fired both armor piercing and common shells utilizing a charge of 4.9 ounces of black powder.

Sailors on the USS *Nahant* bring a 1 pounder into "action" for the cameras.

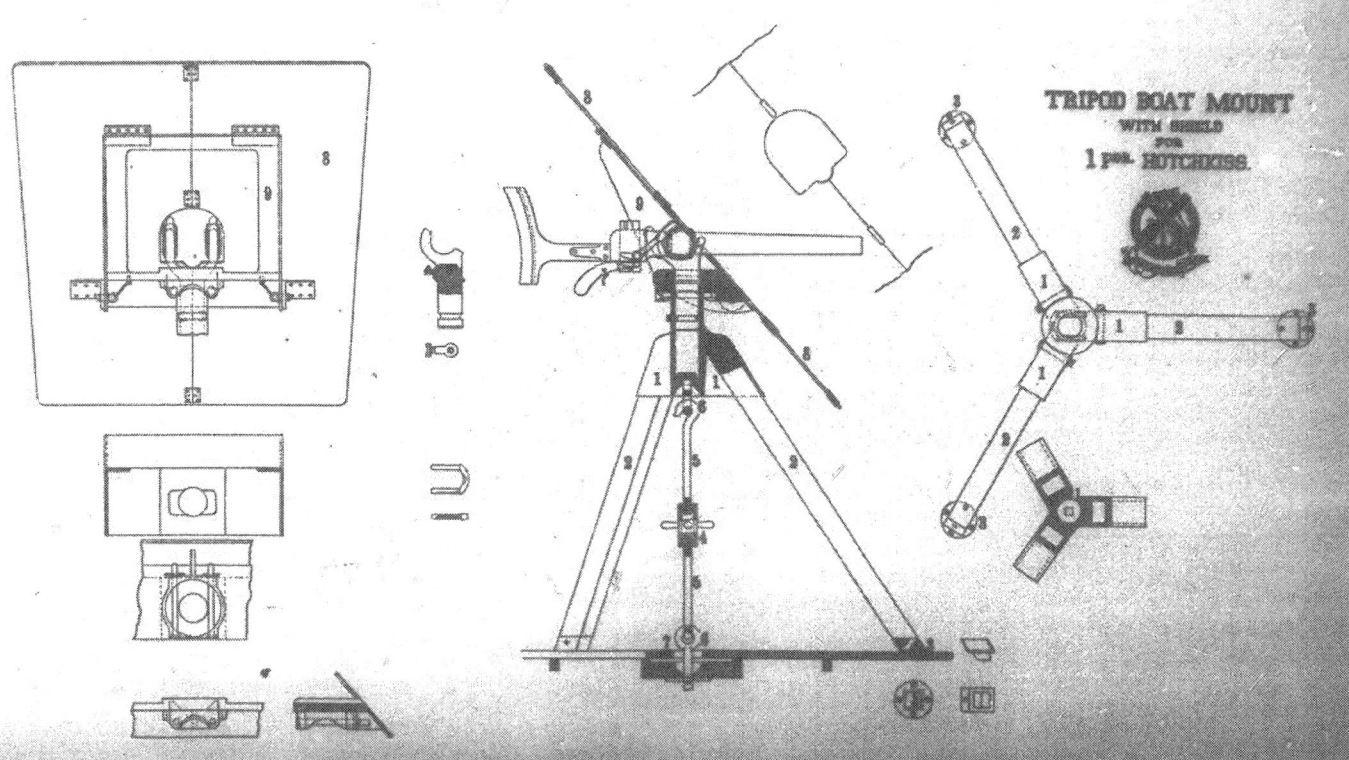

United States Navy boat and field carriages for 1 pounder guns. The size of these pieces and their shells gave them some utility as field pieces for use by the ship's Marines and shore parties. To this end the Navy developed special boat mounts and field carriages which allowed them to be carried into action ashore, outside of the area of fire support normally afforded by the ship.

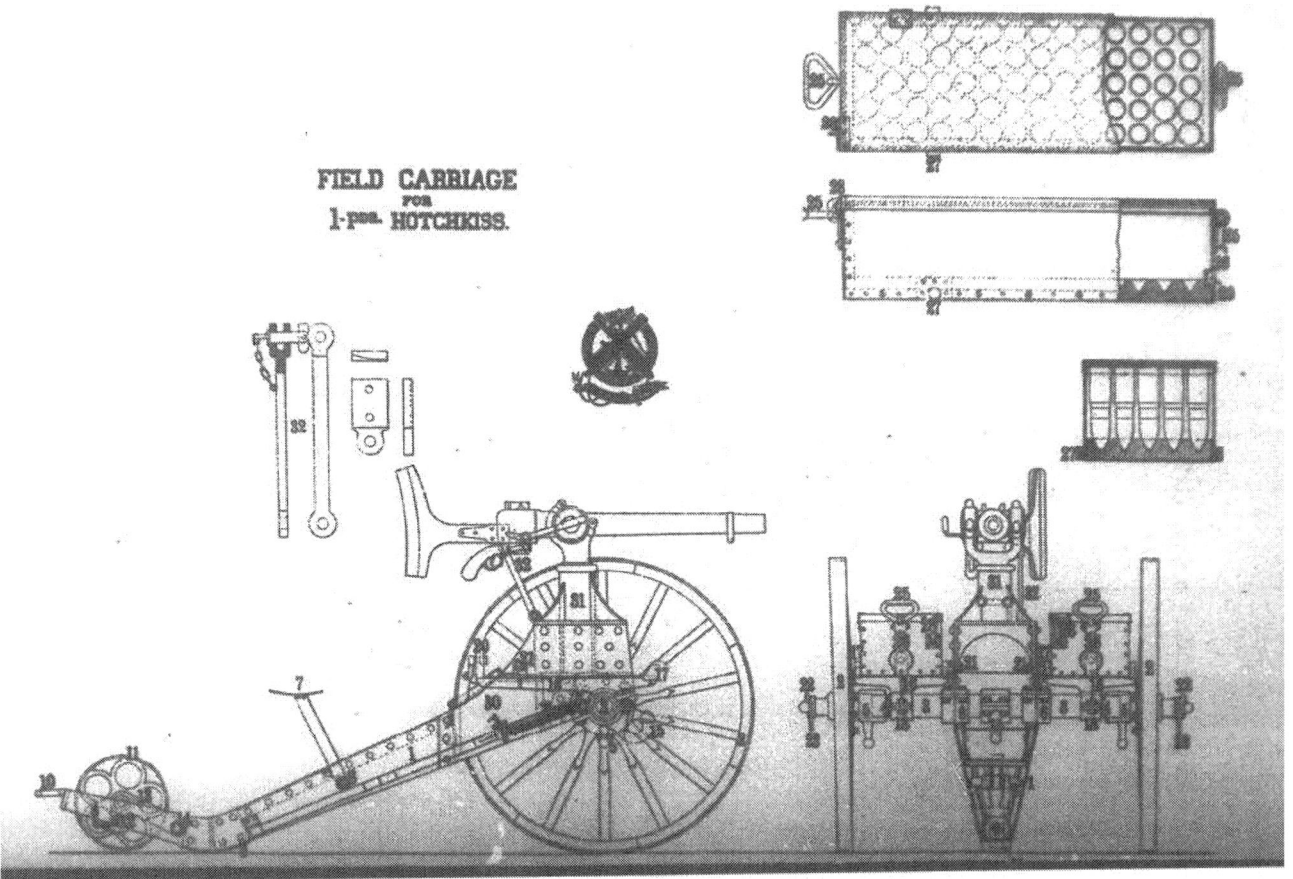

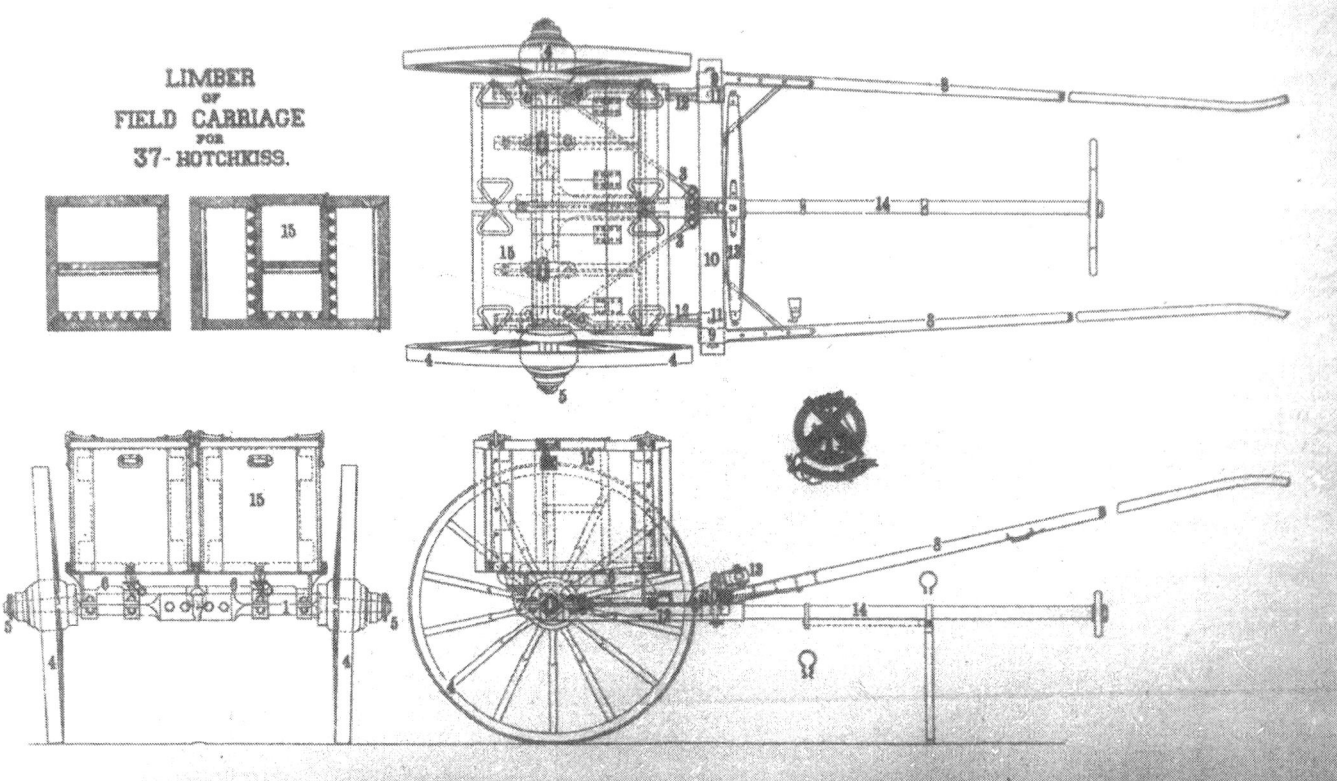

The *Texas* is known to have carried fittings for boat service for both her 1 pounder Driggs-Schroeders and her 1 pounder Hotchkiss Revolving Cannon. There is no record of the *Texas* carrying field carriages for these pieces. During the campaign in Cuba in 1898, Colt machine guns from the *Texas*, one on a lightweight field carriage the other on a field carriage, were brought into action at Guantanamo Bay by a landing party of sailors and Marines.

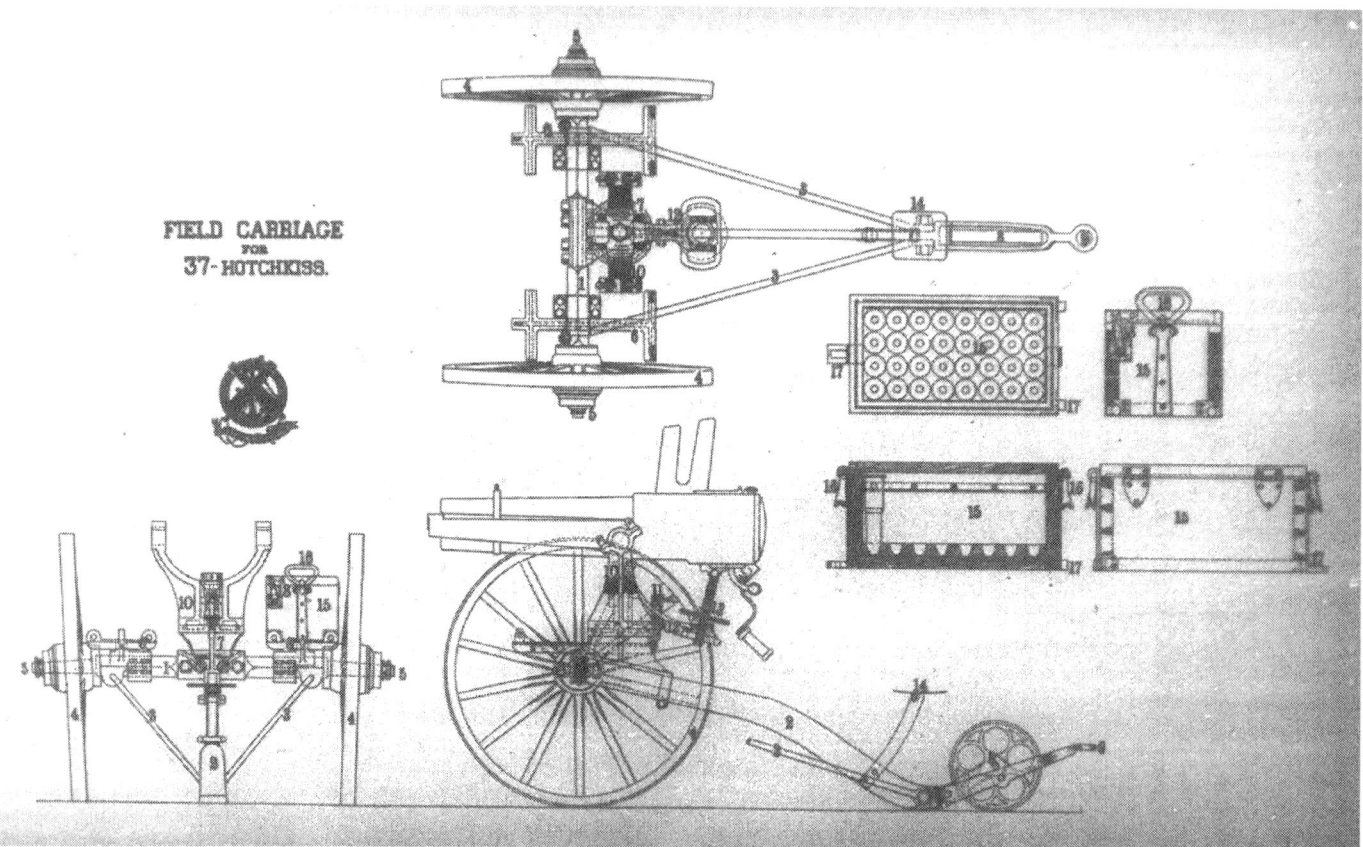

1898 ABT: Brooklyn, NY. Lt. J.G. Mark L. Bristol of the *Texas* leans against the starboard side aft 37mm Hotchkiss revolving cannon mounted to the bridge-deck.

July 3, 1898: Sailor of the *Texas* at the same gun keeping a watchful eye on the concluding moments of the naval Battle of Santiago.

William John had originally envisioned a mixture of 47MM (1.65") revolving cannon and 6 pounder rapid fire guns as the anti-torpedo armament of the *Texas*, but the 47mm gun was not favored by the US Navy. Instead, a 37mm 1 pounder revolving cannon on each quarter of the ship provided an excellent field of fire to support the 6 pounder guns firing from positions along the hull on the gun deck. These revolving guns were the last line of the *Texas'* anti-torpedo boat defensive armaments.

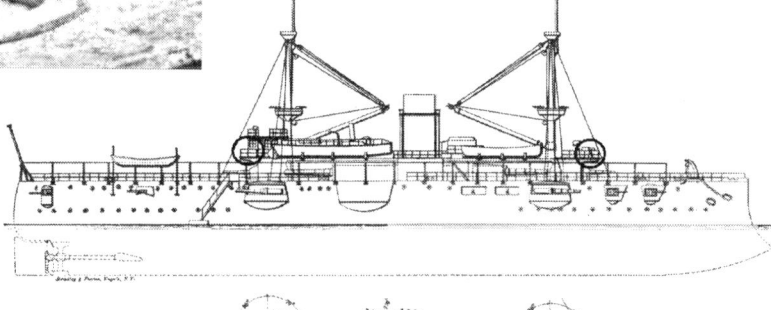

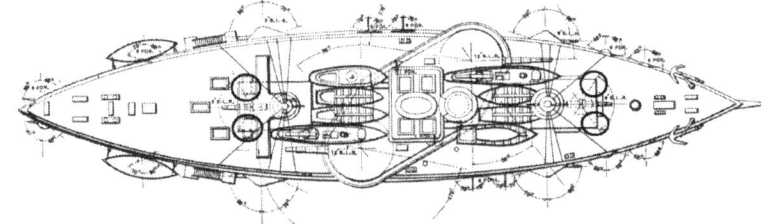

Hotchkiss guns on US Navy test range.

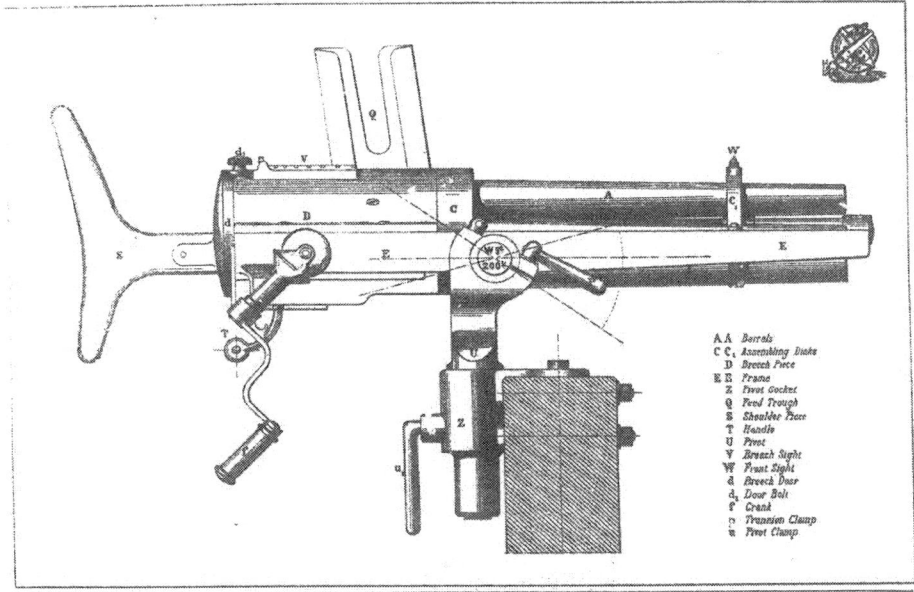

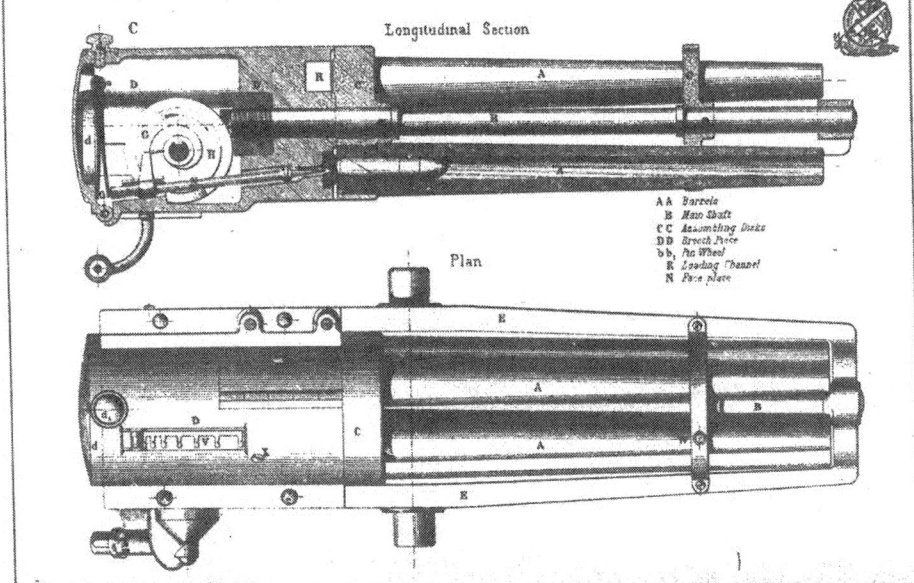

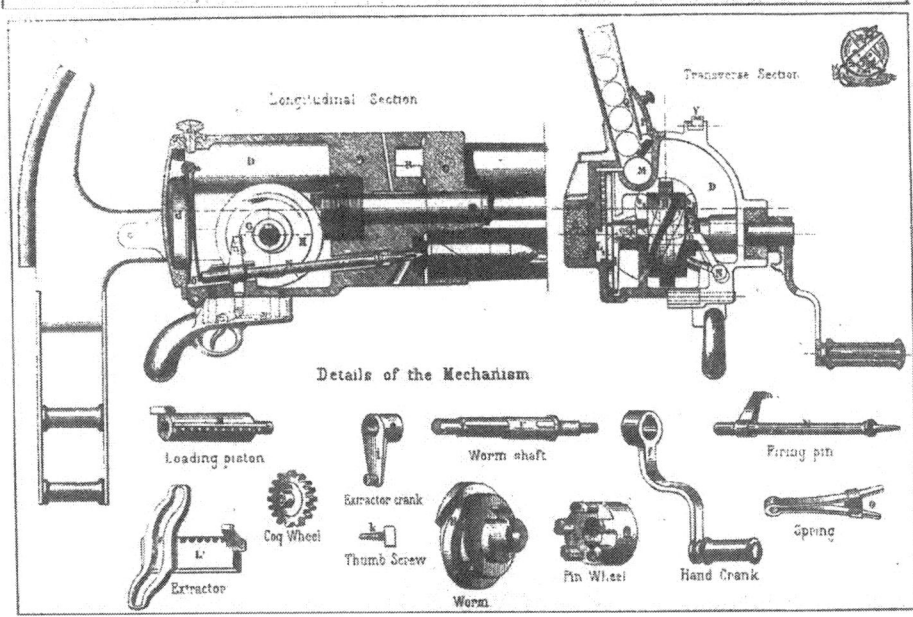

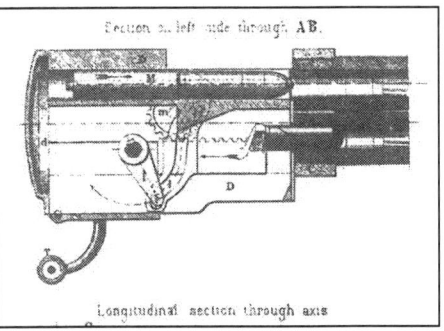

When the *Texas* was fitted out with her armaments, the 37mm 1 pounder revolving cannon was still a mainstay of warship design although its use was rapidly fading as superior machine cannons were developed. The newer guns, still firing a 37mm shell, were of considerably less weight, required less manpower, and could maintain a higher continual rate of fire.

The Hotchkiss Revolving Cannon on the *Texas* utilized cartridges containing a charge of 2.9 ounces of black powder and either an armor piercing or common shell. Hand-fed via chutes from above, the revolving cannon could put up a prodigious rate of fire, but only for a short time as they were exhausting for their crew due to the need to manually rotate the barrels while aiming simultaneously. They would see active service on the *Texas* during the war.

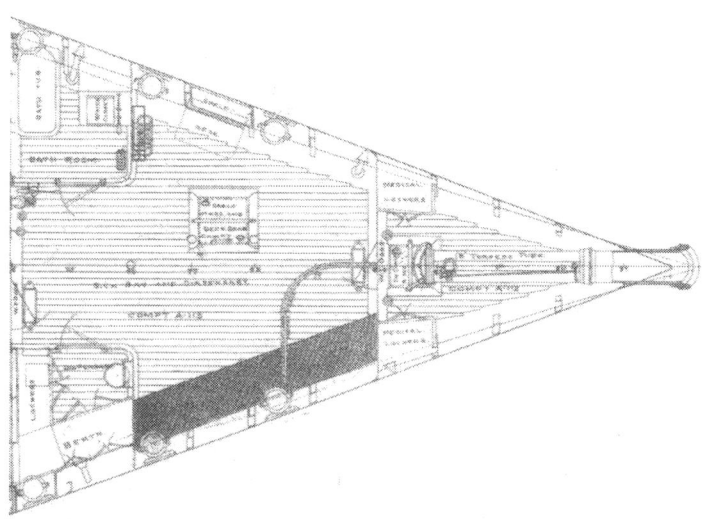

The *Texas* had four 18" Whitehead torpedo tubes; one in the bow, one in the stern, and one on each side amidships, all mounted above water line on the berth deck. The amidships tubes shared a compartment stretching across the breadth of the ship, just forward of the officers quarters. Torpedoes were moved through each of these spaces using overhead tracks and pulleys.

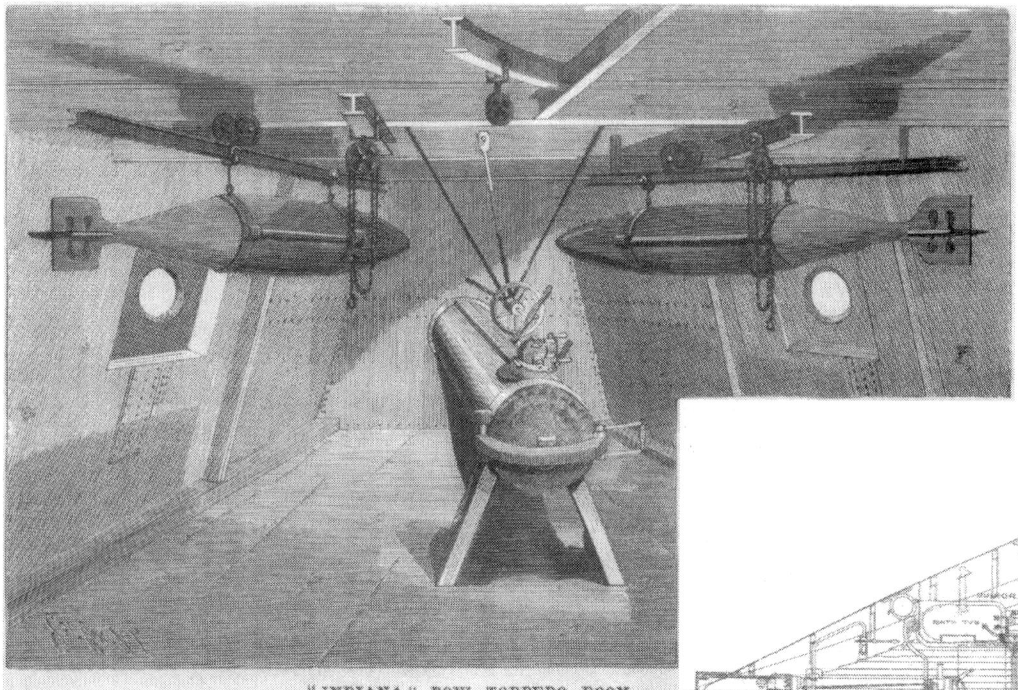

"INDIANA"—BOW TORPEDO ROOM.

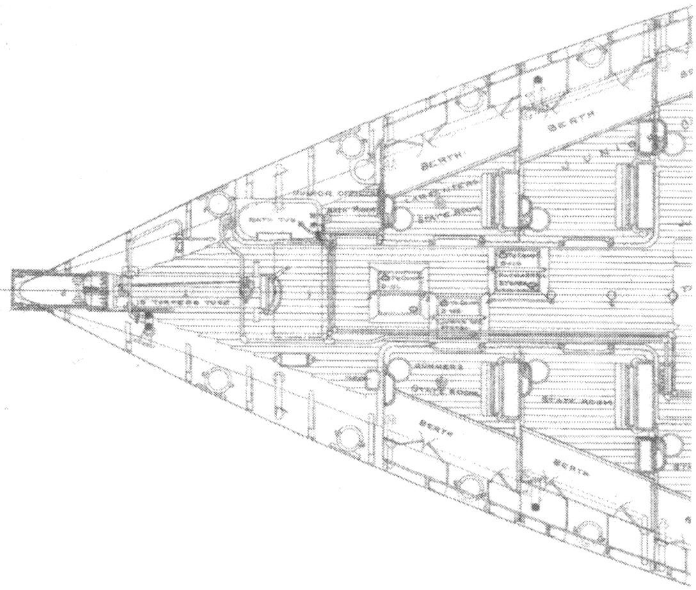

As can be seen in this view of the similar bow torpedo room on the USS *Indiana* (above), the torpedo compartments fore and aft provided little space in which to work and correspondingly limited firing angles. The aft torpedo tube was housed in a compartment usually off limits to the crew – the junior officers bath room.

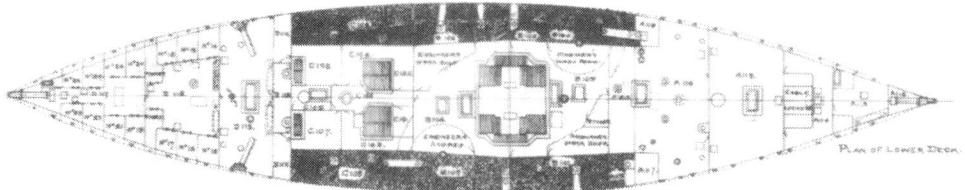

108

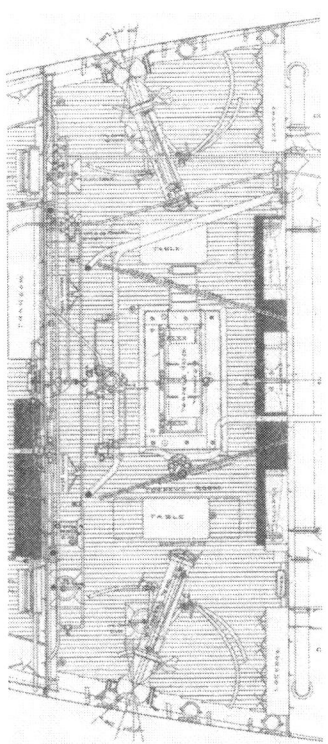

The amidships torpedo room provided much more commodious arrangements. The tubes could be pivoted along a track mounted on the deck. Extra torpedoes were stowed in lockers affixed to the forward bulkhead.

The bow and stern torpedo tubes were removed shortly before the war, but it is unclear if the side tubes were removed at the same time, the assumption is that they had not. The reason for removing the bow and stern tubes was that they were of extremely limited use due to the torpedo's short range and that they poised a potential danger to the ship as they were extremely vulnerable to shellfire. During the Battle of Santiago the Spanish cruiser *Vizcaya* had one of her bow torpedoes explode from a glancing blow of a shell near the tube, with disastrous results. The amidships torpedoes, however retained some value for delivering the coup de gras to disabled vessels.

The photo below shows the similar compartment on the contemporary USS *Maine*.

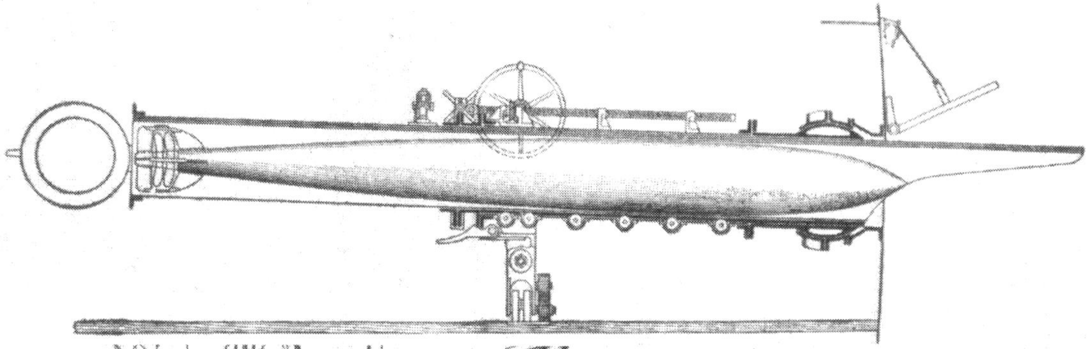

Torpedoes were aimed using simple mechanical "directors". Each torpedo was manually loaded into the breach of the torpedo tubes before being launched using compressed air, as seen in this illustration of a launching from a contemporary U.S. Navy warship.

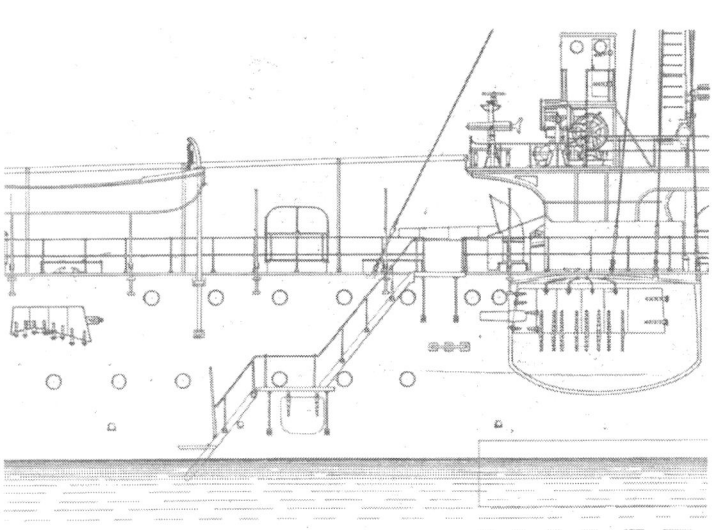

The amidships torpedo tube hatch on the *Texas* can be seen immediately below the gangway landing.

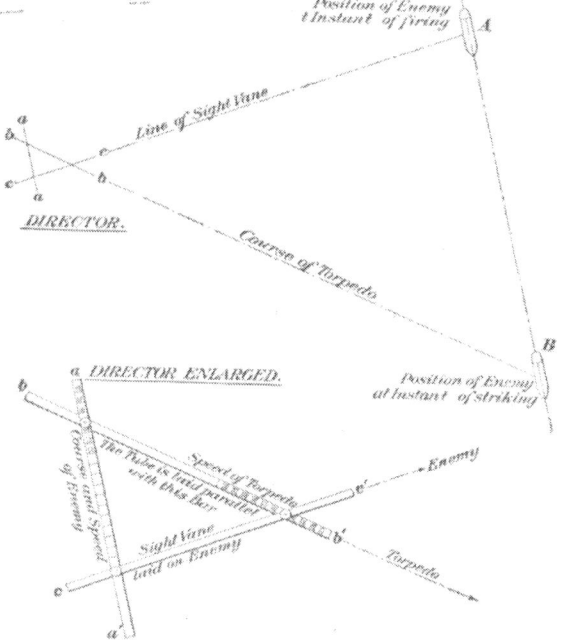

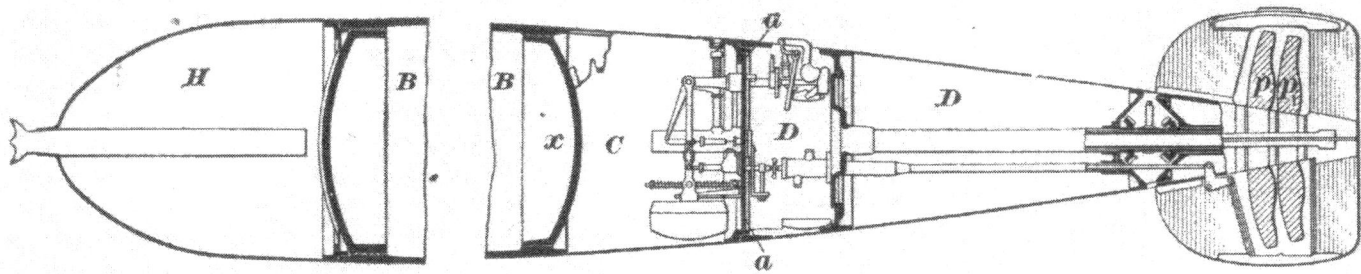

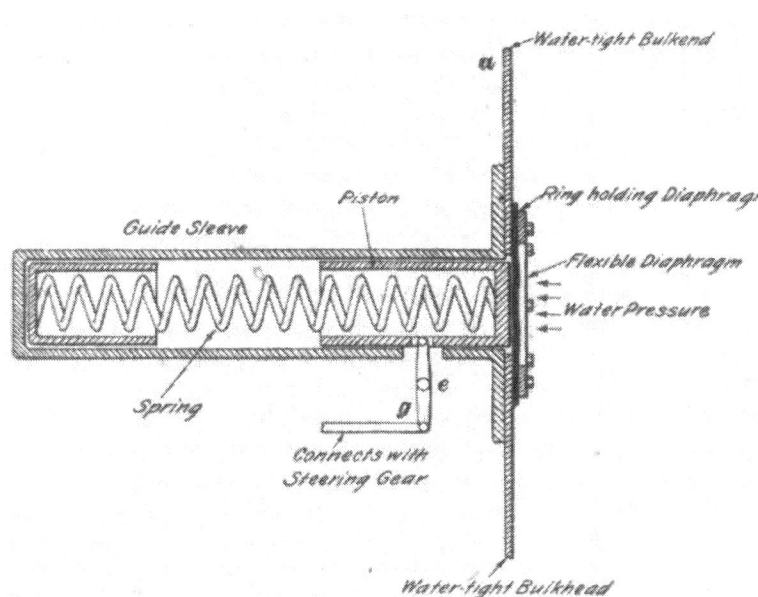

The Whitehead Automobile Torpedo was an assembly of several technologically advanced components shrouded within a streamlined housing. The torpedo was tipped with a plunger type contact fuse using fulminate of mercury to initiate the over 100 pound guncotton bursting charge of the warhead H. Aft of the warhead was the compressed air reservoir B. Once launched, the torpedo proceeded under its own power, drawing on this 2000 psi air. This reservoir or "air flask" took up almost half of the torpedo's body. Depending on the particular model, Whitehead torpedoes could carry sufficient air for a 2 mile maximum range, however practical ranges were more typically up to about 1,200 yards, over which the torpedo could maintain a speed of 35 knots. The immersion compartment C contained a hydrostatic piston depth control mechanism (left) which controlled the horizontal vanes at the tail to maintain a preset depth.

Also in the immersion compartment was the gyroscope (right). The rapidly spinning gyroscope was connected to the vertical vanes or rudder at the tail of the torpedo and controlled direction. The gyroscope could be set to a certain bearing prior to firing, allowing the torpedo to be launched at almost any angle, trusting on the gyroscope to turn the torpedo to its preset bearing upon entering the water. The aftmost compartment housed the pneumatic motor and driveshaft powering the twin, counter-rotating propellers at the tail. The propellers were shielded somewhat from potential entanglement in nets or cables by the horizontal and vertical fins. In the event that the torpedo missed its mark, it was equipped with sinking gear which would open a valve admitting water after certain number of revolutions corresponding to a specific distance was exceeded. Ships of the period, no matter how large, would usually sink after one torpedo hit as internal water tight integrity had not yet been perfected.

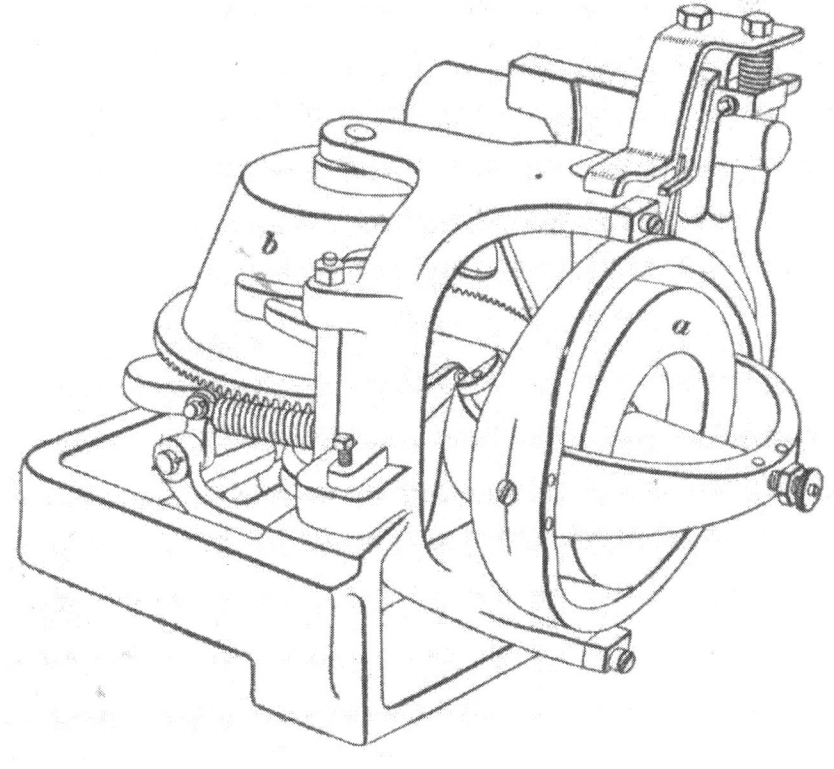

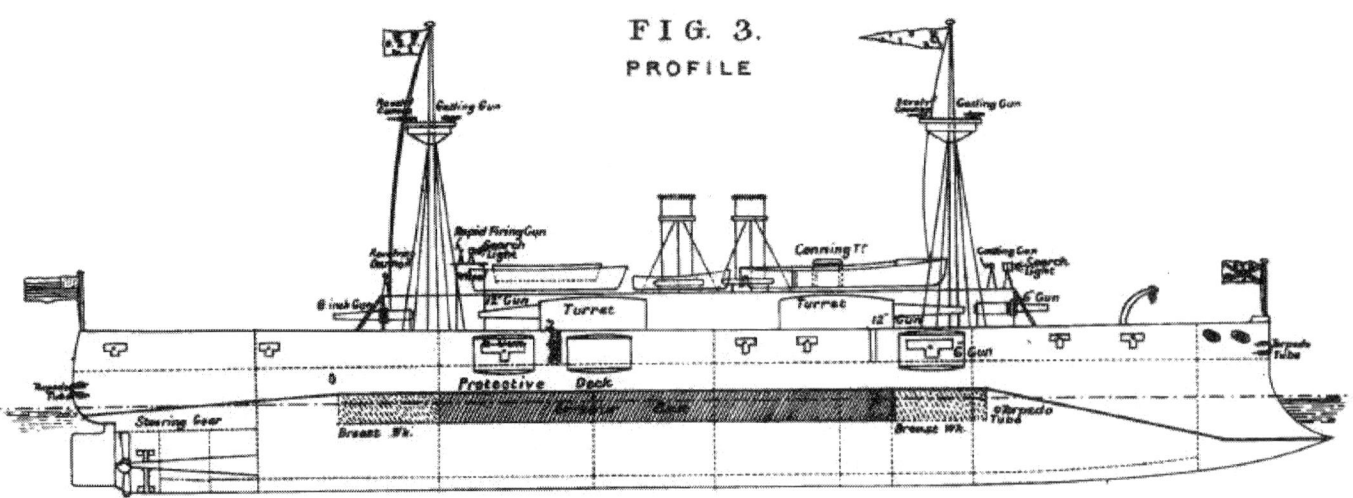

At the time of her design, prevailing opinion in naval circles held that the ram was a viable weapon, a "point" driven home visually in naval architect William John's 1888 illustration of the vessel.

The *Texas'* ram was located deep, reflecting British practice, rather than on the waterline as favored by the French. The ram was principally useful for attacking stationary or slow moving vessels. Interestingly, it was only after rams began to be deleted from warship designs that ramming tactics saw significant use. Submarines and torpedo boats were successfully rammed by larger vessels on several occasions during World War I and II.

The ram of the *Texas* was cast in steel and reinforced from below by the keel and from above by the intersection of the sloping protective deck.

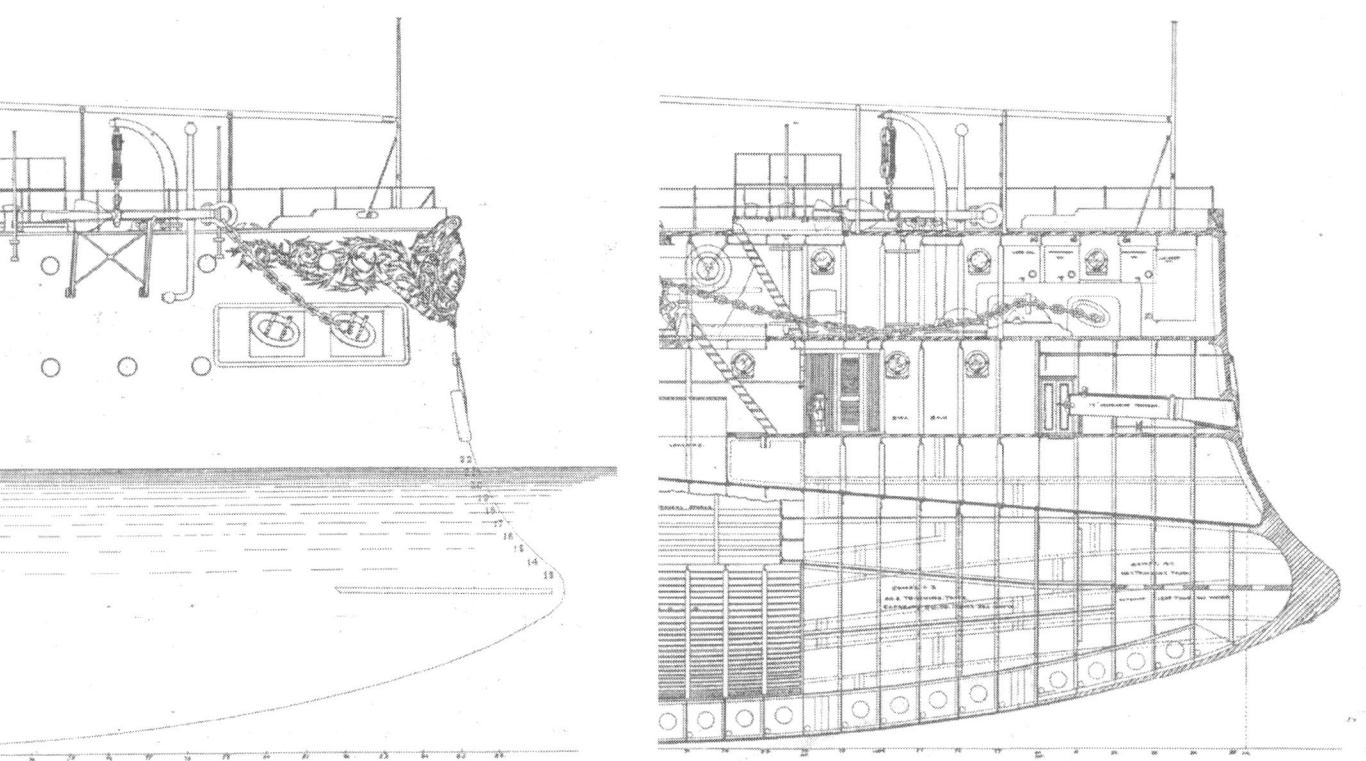

GATLING GUN, WITH CASING REMOVED.

A number of period reports indicate that the *Texas* carried a pair of .45-70 Gatling guns mounted on the bridge - but no photos or post-commissioning plans show these guns.

In April 1898, just before the *Texas* sailed, Captain Philip urgently requested and received a pair of 6mm Colt Machine Guns for the *Texas*. Whether the Gatling guns were replaced as part of this request or if they had been removed prior to it, or indeed if they had ever been installed, is an open question. The *Texas*, however, carried a large quantity of .45-70 rounds which were off-loaded in 1898 to Cuban insurgents in support of the US Marines at Guantanamo when the *Texas* was supporting the invasion. Apparently the Cubans at Guantanamo were armed with .45-70 Model 1873 Springfields as well as 6mm 1895 Lee rifles.

The images here show a typical US Navy ship mount of the period (on another vessel) and a naval field carriage. The illustration at upper right depicts the cycle of loading, cocking, firing and extraction in the Gatling gun. Since each barrel carried its own operating mechanism, their axial arrangement relative to the fixed cam path allowed the firing cycle to be performed simultaneously and sequentially as the barrels were revolved via hand crank.

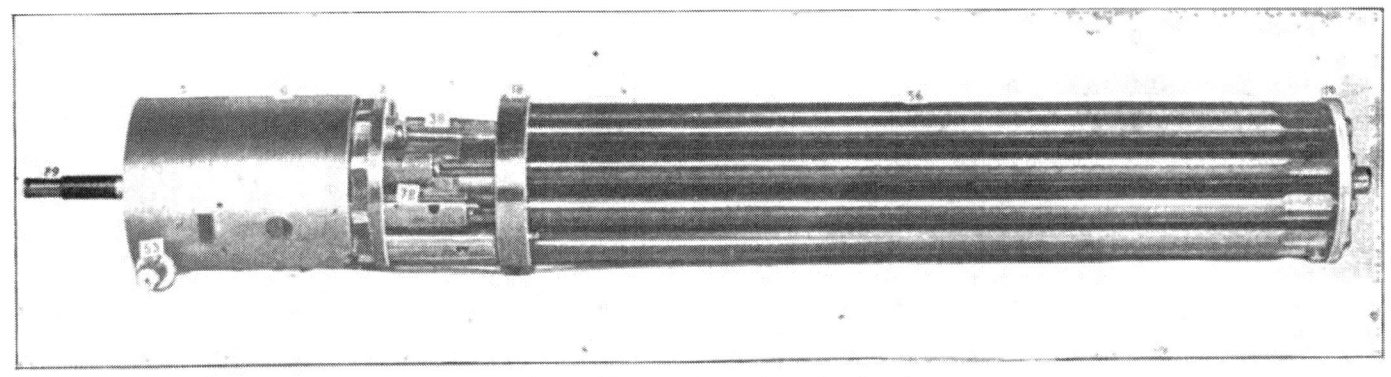

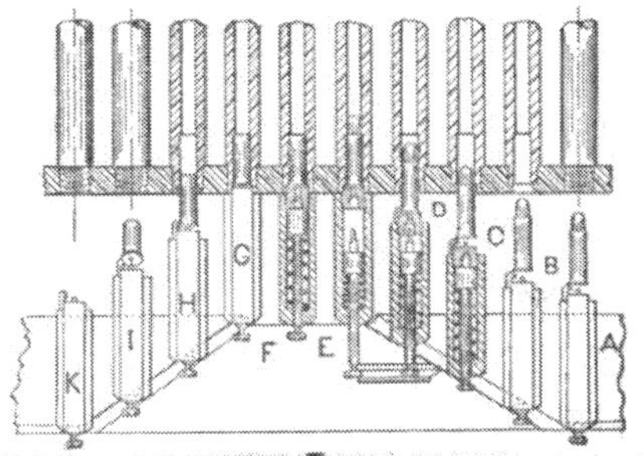

GATLING GUN, MOUNTED ON NAVY FIELD-CARRIAGE, WITH THE DIRECTING-BAR, SHOULDER-REST, CRANK, AND FEED GUIDE-WAY SHIPPED.

7 EQUIPMENT & SMALL ARMS

Lithographs of United States Navy and Marine Corps uniforms as depicted in former officer of the USS *Texas*, J.D.J. Kelly's book <u>The Navy of the United States</u> (1899).

Enlisted Men of the USS Texas (August 1895) - Authorized & On board

Rating	Auth	On
Chief Boatswain Mate	1	0
Boatswain's Mate 1st Class	3	3
Seaman Gunners	0	7
Chief Gunners Mate	1	1
Gunner's Mate 1st Class	5	1
Chief Quartermaster	1	1
Quartermaster 3rd Class	4	1
Chief Carpenters Mate	1	1
Sailmaker's Mate	0	1
Ship's cook 1st Class	2	1
Carpenters and Caulkers	2	0
Baymen	2	0
Master's At Arms	3	0
Apothecary	1	1
Ship's Yeoman	1	0
Ship's Writer		2
Painter	1	0
Bugler	1	0
Blacksmith	2	2
Plumber and Fitter	1	1
Boatswain's Mates 2nd Class	4	2
Gunner's Mate 2nd Class	5	1
Cooper-smith 3rd Class	1	0
Machinist 2nd Class	4	2
Gunner's Mate 3rd Class	4	1
Ship Wrights	2	4
Machinist Chief	4	4
Mess attendant	10	1
Cabin Steward	1	0
Cabin Cook	1	1
Ward-room Steward	1	0
Ward-room Cook	1	0
Steerage steward	1	0
Steerage Cooks	1	0
Warrant Officer's Steward	1	0
Warrant Officer's Cook	1	0
Seamen	36	56
Ordinary Seamen	26	26
Landsmen	61	68
Boys	0	0
Apprentices	30	30
Machinists 1st Class	4	1
Boiler maker	1	1
Water Tenders	3	3
Oilers	8	8
First-class Firemen	14	21
Second-class Firemen	14	14
Coal Heavers	36	36
Musician 2nd Class	0	1
	322	297

Additional For Flagship:

Master of the band	1
Chief Musician	1
First-class Musicians	6
Second-class Musicians	8
Printer	1
Steward to C in C	1
Cook to C in C	1
Coxswain to C in C	1
Seamen to C in C	6
Apprentices to C in C	6
Mess attendant	2
Yeoman	1
Marine Guard	30
	352

Seaman William E. Hinde, USS *Texas*, ca. 1897.

Annual U.S. Navy Pay Rates 1898

Rear Admirals	$6,000
Commodores	$5,000
Captains	$4,500
Commanders	$3,500
Lt. Commanders	$2,800-$3,000
Lieutenants	$2,400-$2,600
Lieutenants, j.g.	$1,800-$2,000
Ensigns	$1,200-$1,400
Naval Cadets	$950 (at sea)
Mates	$1,200
Medical Directors, Inspectors	
Pay Directors, Inspectors	
Chief Engineers (at sea)	$4,400
Fleet Surgeons,	
Fleet Paymasters,	
Fleet Engineers	$4,400
Surgeons,	
Paymasters,	
Chief Engineers	$2,800-$4,200
Naval Constructors	$3,200 - $4,200
Professors of Mathematics	
Civil Engineers	$2,400 - $3,500
Chaplains	$2,500 - $2,800
Assistant Naval Constructors	$2,000 - $2,600
Passed Assistant Surgeons	
Paymasters	$2,000-$2,200
Passed Assistant Engineers	$2,000
Assistant Surgeons,	
Paymasters	
Engineers	$1,700-$1,900
Clerks	$1,200 - $1,800
Boatswains,	
Gunners,	
Carpenters,	
Sailmakers	$1,200
Chief Machinists	$840
Chief Master-at-Arms	$780
Chief Yeoman,	
Apothecaries,	
1st Class Boilermakers	$720
1st Class Machinists	$660
Band Master	$624
Chief Boatswain's Mates,	
Chief Gunners Mates,	
Chief Gun Captains,	
Chief Carpenters Mates,	
Chief Quartermasters,	
1st Class Coppersmiths,	
1st Class Blacksmiths	$600
Plumbers and Fitters	
Stewards to Commander-in-chief	
Stewards to Commandants	$540
1st Class Boatswains Mates,	
1st Class Gunner Mates,	
1st Class Quartermasters,	
1st Class Carpenters,	
1st Class Gun Captains,	
1st Class Sailmakers' Mates,	
1st Class Yeomen	
1st Class Water Tenders,	
Masters-at-arms	
Schoolmasters,	
2nd Class Machinists	
Cooks to Commander-in-chief	
Cooks to Commandants	$480
Oilers	
Cabin Stewards	
Wardroom Stewards	$444
First Musicians	$432
2nd Class Boatswains Mates	
2nd Class Gunner Mates,	
2nd Class Quartermasters,	
2nd Class Gun Captains	
2nd Class Carpenters Mates	
2nd Class Yeomen	
1st Class Firemen	
1st Class Ships Cooks	
Printers	$420
1st Class Musicians	
Cabin Cooks	
Wardroom Cooks	$384
3rd Class Master-at-Arms	
3rd Class Gunner Mates,	
3rd Class Quartermasters,	
3rd Class Carpenters Mates	
3rd Class Yeomen	
2nd Class Musicians	
2nd Class Firemen	
2nd Class Ships Cooks	
Buglers	
Painters	
Coxswains	$360
Seamen Gunners	$312
Shipwrights	
Sailmakers	
Steerage Stewards	
3rd Class Ships Cooks	$300
Seamen	
Warrant Officers' Stewards	$288
Coal Passers	
Steerage Cooks	$264
Apprentices, 1st Class	$252
Warrant Officers' Cooks	
4th Class Ships Cooks	$240
Baymen	$216
Landsmen	
Mess Attendants	$192
Apprentices, 2nd Class	$180
Apprentices, 3rd Class	$108

The *Texas* carried a 3 Inch Mark I Rapid Fire field gun for support of her Marines and shore parties ashore. This gun used the "Fletcher breech" with integral firing lock designed by Lt. (later Admiral) Frank Friday Fletcher. A spring recoil mechanism encircled the barrel. It utilized cartridges firing 12 pound shells.

Ammunition was carried in the two large detachable boxes mounted on either side of the gun tube on the field carriage. Approximately 85 rounds per gun were provided for field use.

On June 8, 1898, during the Spanish American War, the *Texas'* 3 inch field gun along with 9 others in the blockading fleet, was offered by Admiral Sampson to General Shaftner for use with the Army ashore. While the initial offer was accepted, the number of guns was subsequently reduced and in the end none were delivered to the Army.

Marines on an unidentified vessel (above left) and midshipmen at Annapolis (below) display their 3 inch rapid fire field guns.

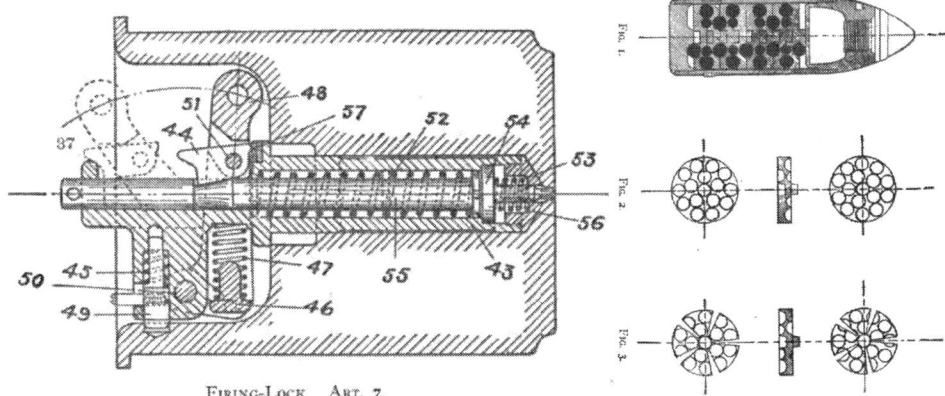

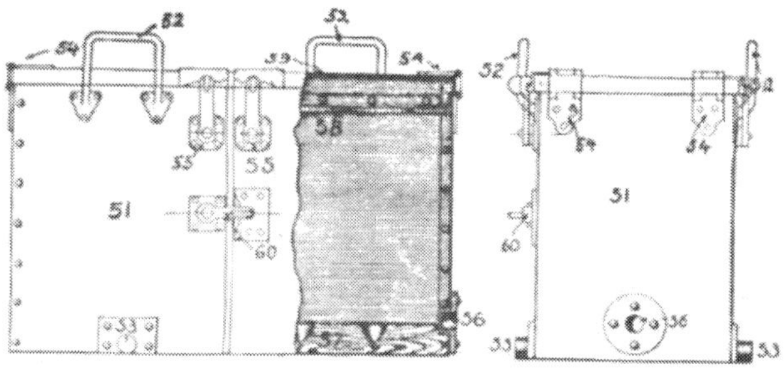

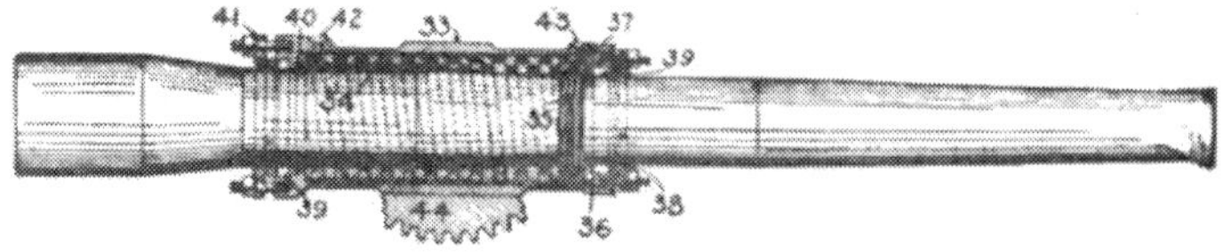

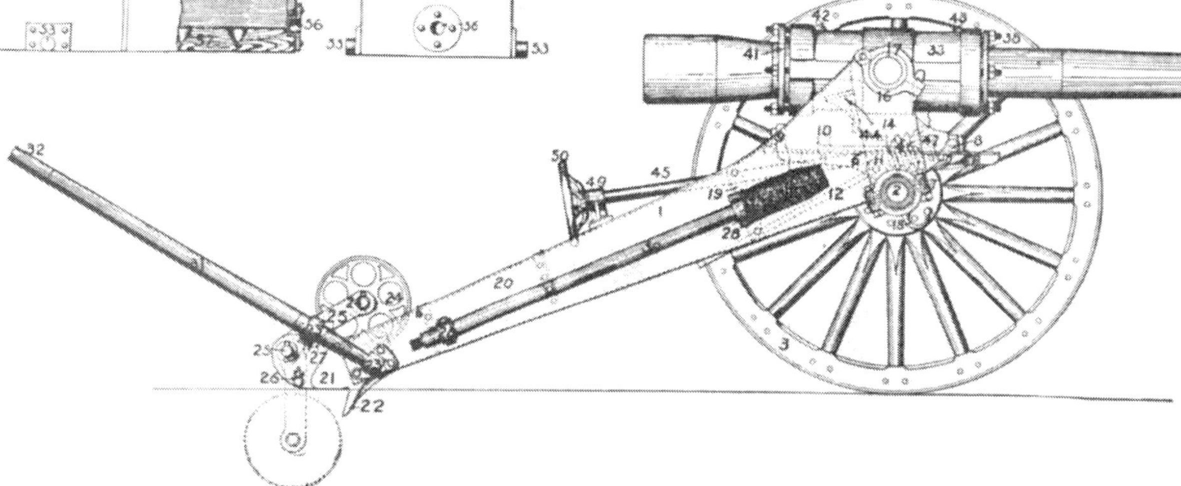

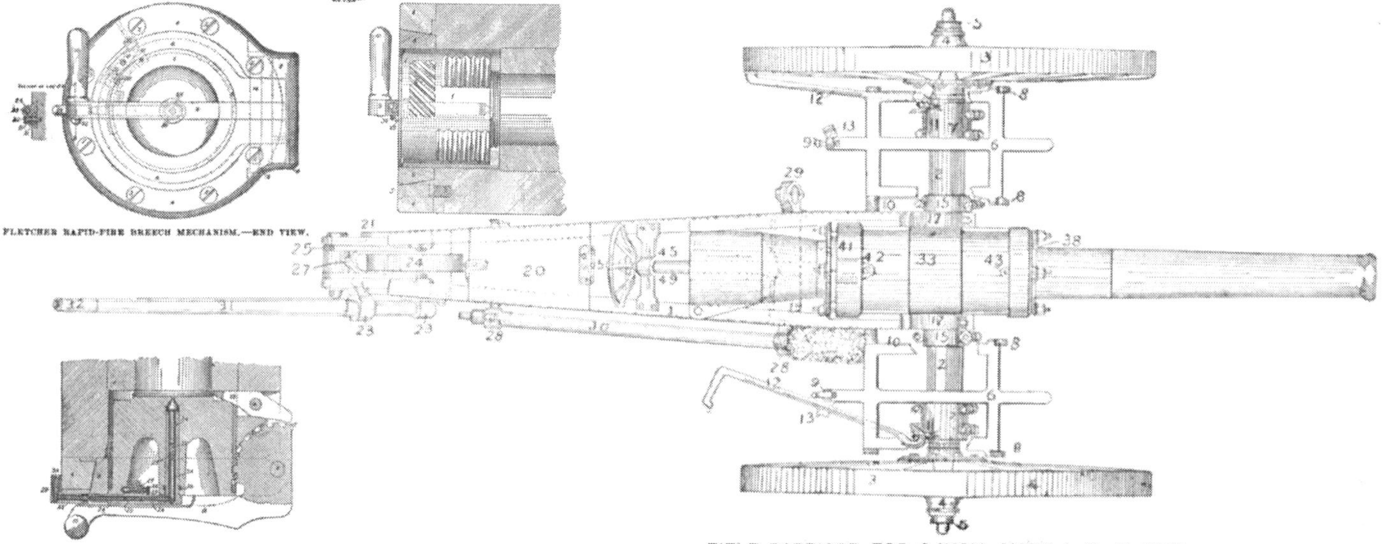

FLETCHER RAPID-FIRE BREECH MECHANISM.—END VIEW.

FIELD-CARRIAGE FOR 3-INCH, MARK I, R. F. GUN.

For service during the Spanish-American War the *Texas'* 3 inch field gun was placed on the forward bridge deck (as seen here in the photo at right) and manned by Marines.

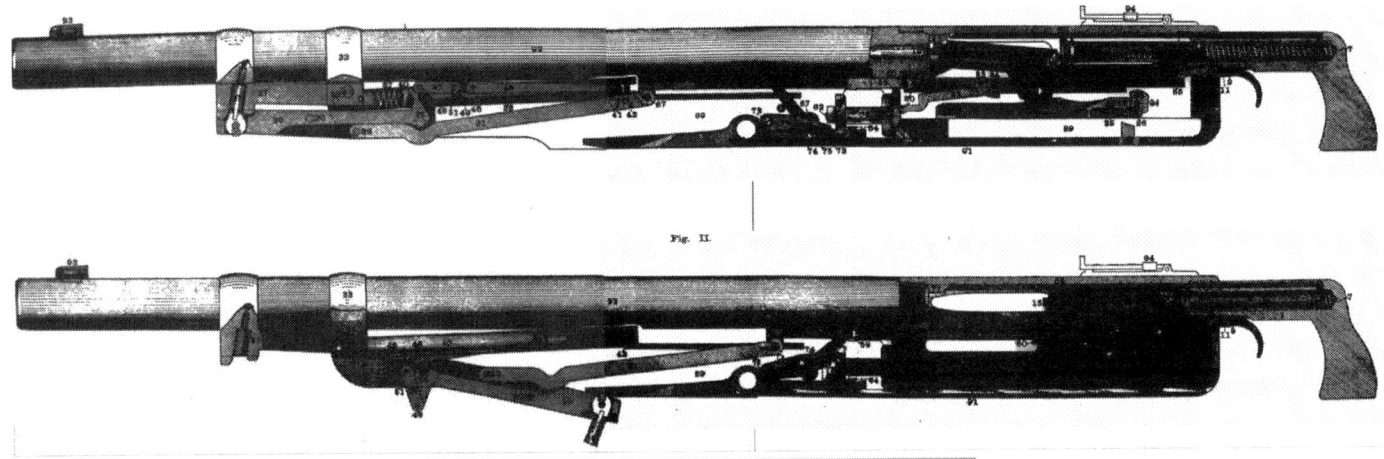

As the *Texas* was entering commission, the Navy replaced its .45-70 Gatling Guns, still a mainstay with the U.S. Army, with John Browning designed Colt 1895 "Potato Digger" machine guns. The nickname "potato digger" came from the swinging action of the exposed lever operation mechanism under the barrel, a unique characteristic of the Colt. The Colt had a theoretical rate of fire of about 400 rounds per minute but the actual rate was significantly less due to the need to keep the barrel cool and due to the limited ready ammunition available in belts. The light landing carriage, although cumbersome, carried 2,000 belted rounds in ammo boxes. Never used in large numbers as it proved a bit too light and weak for Army use, the Colt M1895 nevertheless saw useful service with the Marines and foreign powers through World War I, especially in Naval service. Chambered in the same 6mm caliber as the Lee Rifles adopted concurrently by the Navy, the Colts saw distribution in 1897-1898, just in time for war. The *Texas*, after an urgent letter from Captain Philip to the Bureau of Ordnance, received two Colt's in May 1898, just before sailing, with two light landing carriages and one tripod. The *Texas'* Colts were offloaded in Guantanamo, Cuba, doubling the number of machine guns in use by the Marines in defense of Camp McCalla. One of the *Texas'* Colts, likely on a tripod mount, also participated in the subsequent Battle of Cuzco wells.

A Colt machine gun on a naval field carriage, possibly from the *Texas*, is seen at right in a photo taken during a subsequent midshipmen's cruise.

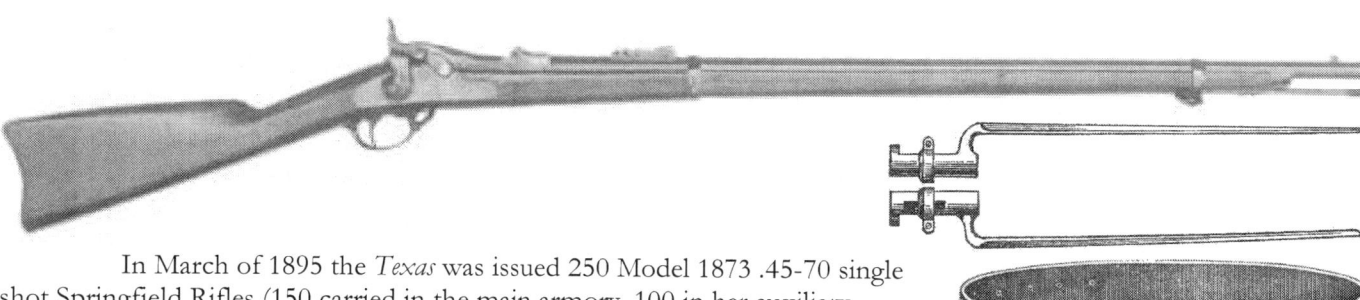

In March of 1895 the *Texas* was issued 250 Model 1873 .45-70 single shot Springfield Rifles (150 carried in the main armory, 100 in her auxiliary armory). This design was a relic by this date, the US Army having already replaced them in first-line use with Krag-Jorgensen turn-bolt action magazine rifles in 1892.

The Navy followed suit and develop its own modern rifle, the Winchester-made Lee five shot Model 1895 straight-pull bolt action rifle in 6mm caliber. The Lee rifles were adopted in May of 1895 and first issued in 1897 to naval vessels, including the *Texas,* and to shore-based Marines and were very much an unproven design at the initiation of hostilities with Spain.

The Lee Navy Rifle proved far superior to the old Springfield Model 1873 rifles still carried by many Army units in Cuba and were near equals of the 7mm Model 1893 Mausers carried by the Spanish. The Lee's failings included a problematic extractor/ejector, firing pin lock, and bolt lock actuator. The Model 1895 did not last long in government service as it did not prove to be a durable design, although it gave satisfactory service in the relatively short and sharp engagements of the Spanish American War and Boxer rebellion.

The Lee rifles issued to the *Texas* had already had their baptism by fire, so to speak, being damaged in a conflagration at the Brooklyn Navy Yard in June of 1897 which had unfortunately been extinguished with seawater. On October 18, 1897 Capt. Phillip of the *Texas* reported that all 222 of the newly issued rifles onboard had rough bores, some had charred stocks, and that their bayonets were pitted. The Bureau replied that they were not sufficiently damaged to warrant refinishing.

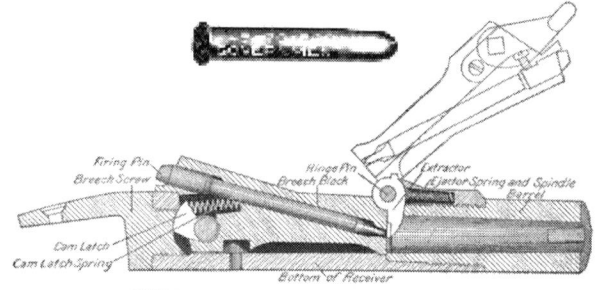

As equipped for the Spanish-American War the *Texas* carried Lee Navy Rifles but also retained her 250 Springfield 45 caliber rifles, possibly for the express purpose of handing them over to the Cuban insurgents. She also carried two .22 caliber practice rifles.

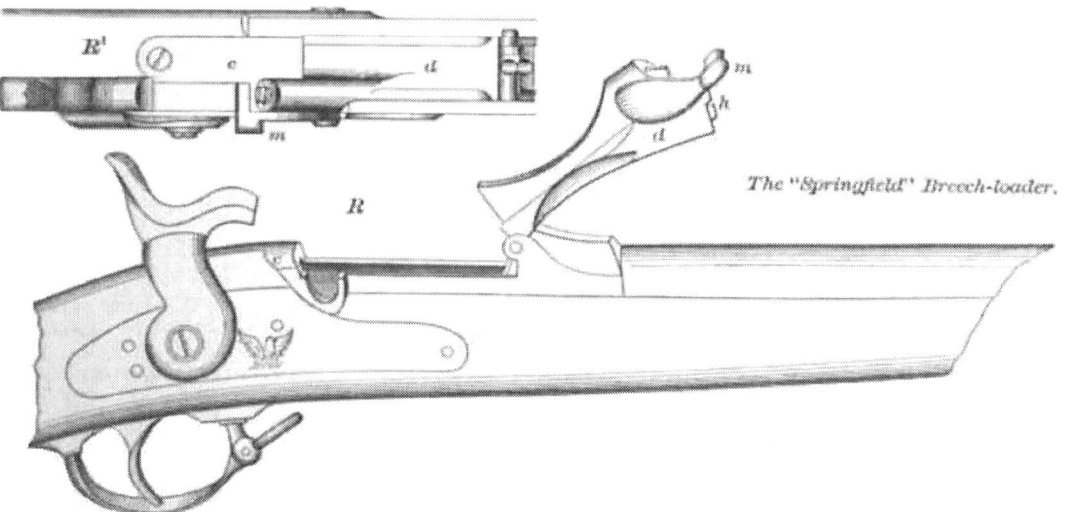

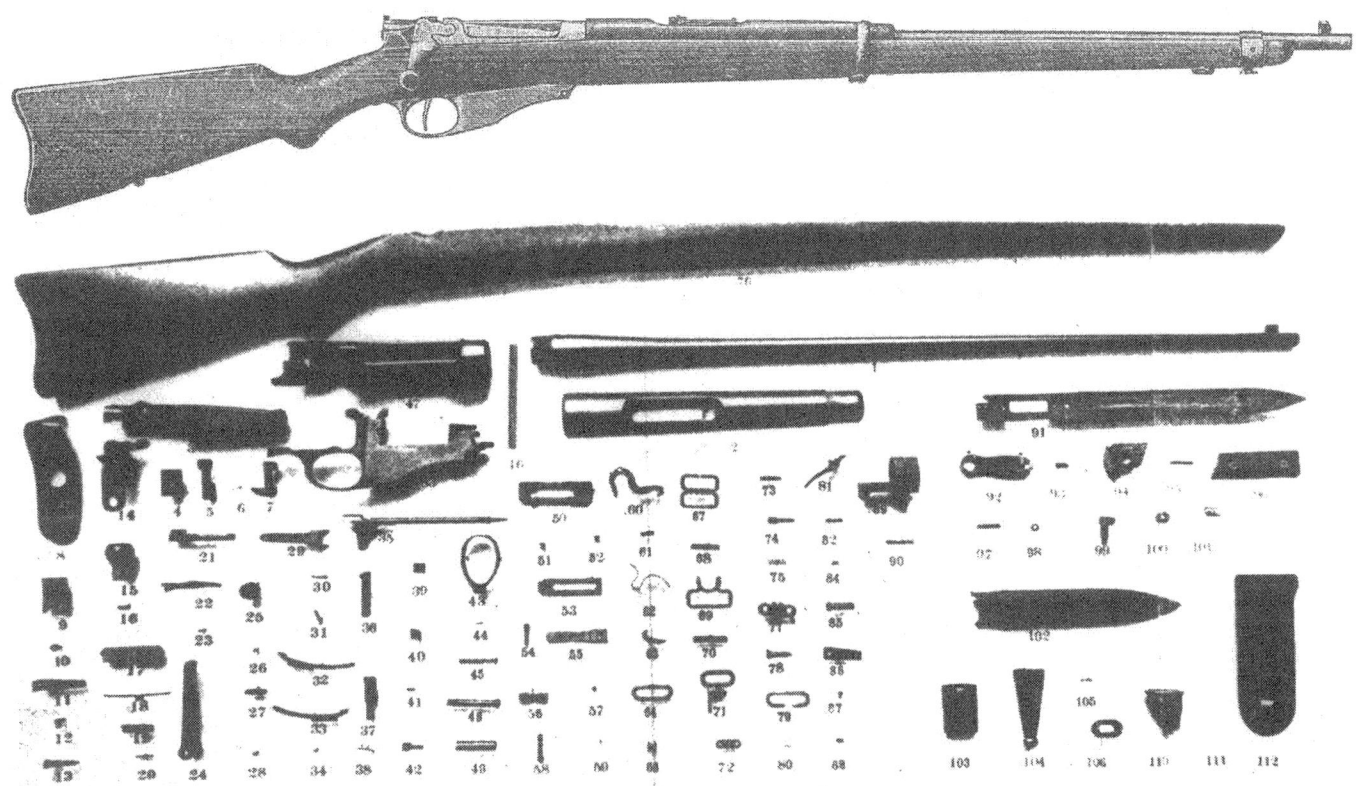

"THE NEW NAVY RIFLE

Its Efficiency as Demonstrated by the Guantanamo Fights. Camp McCalla, June 22. - The active service on the field which the marine corps has seen during the past ten days has put the new navy rifle to a test severe enough to bring out its bad and good points and to give the officers and men an opportunity to judge its effectiveness and practibility for use in the field. Its range and accuracy were long ago determined, and the only question to be decided was whether it was so constructed as to withstand the treatment it must be subjected to when handled in the field in the heat of battle. The question is yet debated. The officers say it is a good arm, and that all is required is to familiarize the men with it. The mechanics who are called upon to keep the pieces in order say that it is too complicated an arm for field use and that it cannot be satisfactory until it has been simplified. Since the marines have been here many arms have been in the hands of the gunsmiths for repairs, and their records show that the main weakness in the arm is in the ejecting mechanism and in the bolt stop.

    The bolt stop is intended to prevent the breech block from slipping from the slot in which it works. It is operated by the thumb, and when in position its head is elevated slightly above the top of the block. To release the block the stop is pushed down, and then the block may be pulled back and freed from the rifle. It has been the experience of the gunsmiths that working their way through the brush this stop is knocked down, and when the block is opened it falls out, letting the ejector fall to the ground. This has been the main complaint, and by far the greatest number of repairs have made have been in the replacing of ejectors.

    The loss of the ejectors disables the pieces. In some cases the Cubans, who have never seen the rifle before, lost the blocks entirely and then threw the arms away, disgusted with them. It was noticeable that the Cubans reported a much larger percentage of disabled pieces than the marines. This bears out the contention of the officers that the arm is all right, and that familiarity with it will lessen the number of accidents.

    The officers point out that the marines occupied and held their present position, went through three days of continual fighting, and engaged in a pitch battle, all with a rifle with which they were practically unfamiliar. They say that the battalion had had but little peace experience and no war experience with the arm and that it is admittedly in an experimental stage as yet…

…The officers are pleased with the arm. In spite of the defects in the block mechanism, they say it is more effective than any other arm that has been placed in their hands. They expect that its effectiveness will develop as the men become accustomed to it and learn to handle it properly. In the field they were frequently appealed to by the men who said their pieces were out of order. They found that many of the complaints were groundless, the men, who in the heat of action, having neglected to take the proper measures to work the arm.

    As to the effects of the bullet from the gun, it is too early to make any definite tissues of the body at long range is known. Two skulls recovered from the battlefield at Cuzco show that the wound of entry in the skull is about the size of the bullet, while the wound of exit is very much larger. In one skull the bullet entered the skull in the back of the head, below the crown, and pierced the brain, leaving the skull through the eye. The wound of exit was an inch and a half in diameter. This was due to the enormous velocity of the projectile, which caused an explosive effect. The surgeons hope for a better opportunity to observe the effects of the bullet." - New York Sun, June 1898.

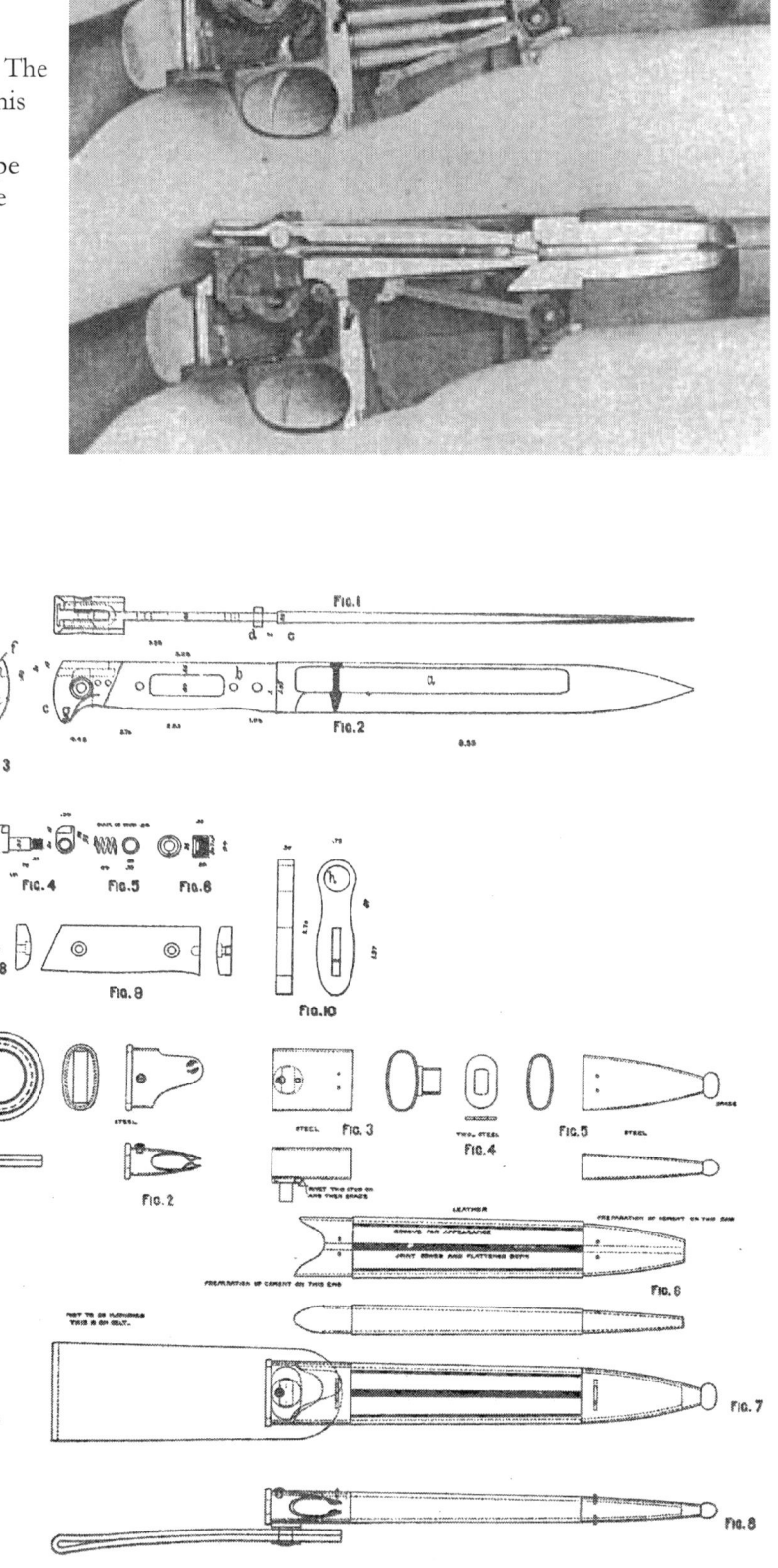

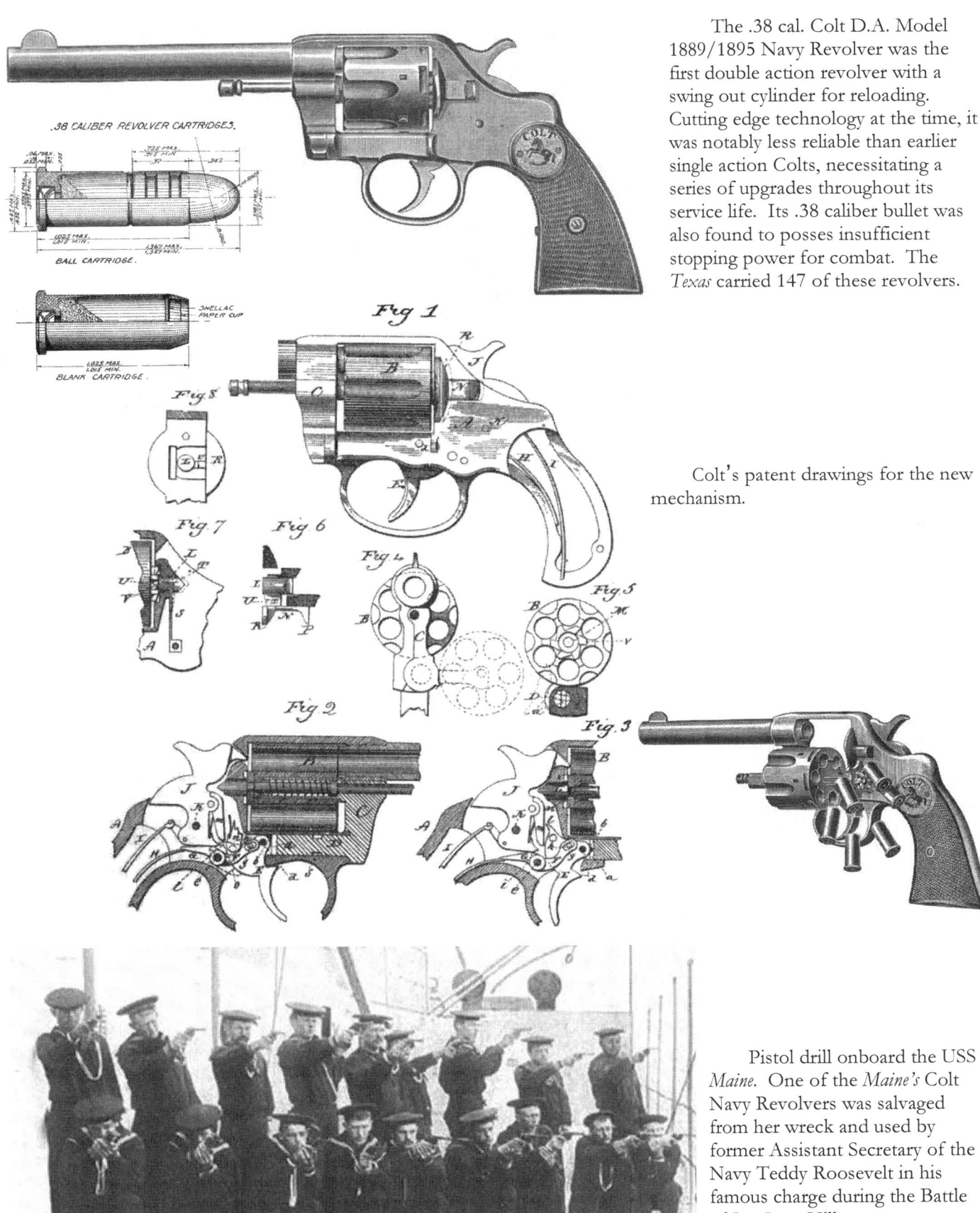

The .38 cal. Colt D.A. Model 1889/1895 Navy Revolver was the first double action revolver with a swing out cylinder for reloading. Cutting edge technology at the time, it was notably less reliable than earlier single action Colts, necessitating a series of upgrades throughout its service life. Its .38 caliber bullet was also found to posses insufficient stopping power for combat. The *Texas* carried 147 of these revolvers.

Colt's patent drawings for the new mechanism.

Pistol drill onboard the USS *Maine*. One of the *Maine's* Colt Navy Revolvers was salvaged from her wreck and used by former Assistant Secretary of the Navy Teddy Roosevelt in his famous charge during the Battle of San Juan Hill.

With the transition to steam powered steel warships and the resulting rarity of opportunity for hand to hand combat, the utility of the cutlass as a weapon of war was limited. It never the less remained standard equipment on US Navy warships for many years, primarily for its role in helping to maintain the crew's physical fitness. Regular practice was held onboard and ashore for the exercise and amusement of the junior officers and men. The *Texas* was equipped with 72 M1860 cutlasses.

The M1860 cutlass was 32 inches in length overall, with a 26 inch blade and a brass half basket hand guard. Most of these weapons were produced by the Ames Manufacturing Company during the Civil War. The last of these Civil War relics was not removed from official service until the beginning of World War II.

THE SILVER SERVICE PRESENTED TO THE TEXAS.

The citizens of the State of Texas contributed donations amounting to approximately $5,000 to commission an elaborate silver service for use on the USS *Texas*. The Whiting Manufacturing Company produced the set described in the Dallas Morning News of October 16, 1896 as including "a large punch bowl in the form of ripe cotton with heavy scrollwork and color enamel panel showing the Alamo supported by a steer and surmounted by the Texas State Seal. The reverse of the punch bowl has a steer supporting a panel (to be inscribed) and the seal of the US Navy. The bowl is supported by four dolphin heads and entwined with a pennant labeled "Be sure you are right, Then go ahead". Also included in the service are candelabra, meat and fish platters, four vegetable dishes, ice dish , "and lesser pieces" all in character with the punch bowl and inscribed with panels depicting Texas scenes such as a ranch, a stampede, Alamo Plaza, University of Texas, & etc. Each piece is inscribed "Presented to the Battleship *Texas* by the Citizens of Texas."

This service was presented to the officers of the ship at a ceremony in Galveston, Texas. It is presently on display aboard the USS *Texas* BB 35, permanently moored at the San Jacinto Battlefield in Texas.

SIX THOUSAND POUNDS U. S. NAVY BUNTING SIGNAL FLAGS used on Board Navy Battleships made of the highest grade special quality all wool bunting as per Navy Specifications. Made up into flags at the N. Y. Navy Yard by Widows of Navy Sailors. Flags furnished as part of the navigation equipment to U. S. Warships. No doubt many of these flags are historical as they were sold to us after the close of the Spanish War. Navy Regulations forbid marking on the flags of the battle engagements. Those who have witnessed a ship in port on holidays dressed with the many colored Navy signal flags, know what a beautiful sight they present. To those who wish to decorate for any celebration, these flags are more desirable than any others and will give great satisfaction. We have for over 45 years supplied flags for decorating New York City, especially since 1889 when the late Stanford White as Chairman of a Committee, gave contract for flags to a theatrical decorator. The morning before the celebration a slight rain storm destroyed all the flags which were not of fast colors and as a party said they looked like a field of carnage "DESECRATION" instead of "DECORATION." We were called upon, and furnished flags within 6 hours time, which decorated 11 blocks of Fifth Avenue, from 23rd to 34th Streets, including the President's stand at Madison Square.

Our Flags are fast colors, no amount of rain can change them. They were only sold by reason of the change in the U. S. N. Signal Code. Some of the flags are entirely new. We have packed them into bales, consisting of 10 Steamer Flags from 3 to 5 feet wide and 10 to 20 feet long, with 15 square flags from 3 to 9 feet wide and from 5 to 15 feet long. Assorted colors and patterns complete, with ropes ready for hoisting. These bales of 25 flags weigh from 35 to 75 pounds per bale according to the sizes of the different flags. OUR BARGAIN PRICE PER BALE IS 90c PER POUND.

The US Navy employed two different system of flag signals at the time of the Spanish-American war. The first was "wig-wag," a two-flag system also employed by the US Army. This system utilized a binary (dot and dash) code called Myers code, similar to civilian Morse code. In this system waving a flag to the right meant a dot, while waving a flag to the left signified a dash. This system was employed in the Navy for most daytime, short-distance, point-to-point communications as well as in cooperation with the Army. The same system could also be used at night or in the fog by substituting long or short blasts on the ship's steam whistle.

ADMIRAL DEWEY'S BATTLE FLAGS.

U. S. Signal Flags from the Olympia. These flags when turned in would under general orders have been condemned to be burned. We found this out and wrote the Honorable Secretary of the Navy, asking that they be given to us for our Museum collection. The Secretary gave us an order for them, but upon presenting the order to the storekeeper of the Boston Navy Yard we were told that we were "too fresh, the flags had not yet been surveyed and condemned." We said we would wait until they were surveyed and condemned. After waiting several months the Board of Officers reported that the flags should be sold at auction. At the auction sale, June 5, 1900, lot No. 17, we were the purchasers not only of the three sets of Signal Flags, but also a few Pennants and U. S. Flags, all from the famous ship. Had these flags been given to us gratis for our Museum we should have held them and offered none for sale, but now we feel free and will offer one set of Signals from the U. S. Flagship Olympia and the price is $800.00 for the 19 flags. The other two sets are not for sale; will be added to our Museum collection. Neither is the large blue flag with the four white stars which was on the ship as a Rear Admiral's flag. But when Commodore Dewey was made Admiral the necessary two extra stars were sewed on this flag, thus making it an Admiral's flag, and as such flown from the masthead of the Olympia at Manila and on Dewey's triumphal voyage home until he arrived at New York, when Admiral Farragut's old flag was presented to Dewey and this flag was turned in, eventually finding its way to our Museum, where it is now and is not for sale.

These flags were used on the Olympia at the Battle of Manila Bay to signal to the fleet. Commodore Dewey's orders among the many signals were, as we understand it, "Remember the Maine," "Engage the enemy," "Haul off for breakfast," "Report casualties," "Renew battle," etc., etc. Also the orders at the taking of Manila in connection with the Army. We have had these flags preserved in moth-proof preparation. It is a rare chance to obtain one set of these 19 flags for $800.00. Flags are fully authenticated.

Also from Admiral Dewey's Flagship, the Olympia, we purchased 1 British flag, 2 German flags, 2 narrow pennants. Prices upon application.

The second signaling system used by the US Navy was the flag hoist system. A number of flags of different shapes, colors, and designs were each assigned a specific meaning in a carefully guarded code book that was issued to each ship. By stringing several specific flags together a numeric code was communicated which was cross referenced to the code book to reveal the message. Often in wartime an additional cipher was added to the numeric code, making the enemy's interception and interpretation of the signal difficult.

At night pyrotechnic signals consisting of red and green flares or "stars," fired from a Very signal pistol, were substituted for the flag system.

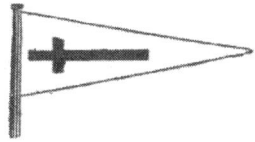

In addition to signal flags, flags denoting the rank and presence of the commanding officer on station were displayed. During battle special "battle flags" were run up the mast and when religious services were to be held a chaplain's flag was raised, inviting officers and men from neighboring vessels without a chaplain to come aboard and attend.

This was a period of transition in ship-to-ship communications. Old systems depending on hoists were being overtaken by systems made possible by the invention of the electric light, and some experimentation had begun into the possibility of shipboard wireless radio.

These illustrations from a 1898 Navy manual describe the means by which signals could be communicated under varying conditions when vessels were out of the range of the human voice. Flags could be used over short to medium ranges when there was good visibility. At longer ranges a system of cones, tops and drums could be more easily distinguished. While the ease of use and vastly superior range of radio was soon to change naval communications as well as strategy, it was with these systems that the *Texas* operated as she embarked on her career.

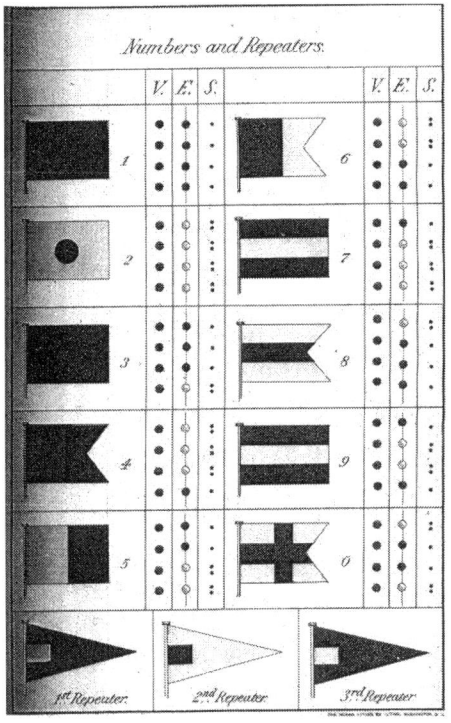
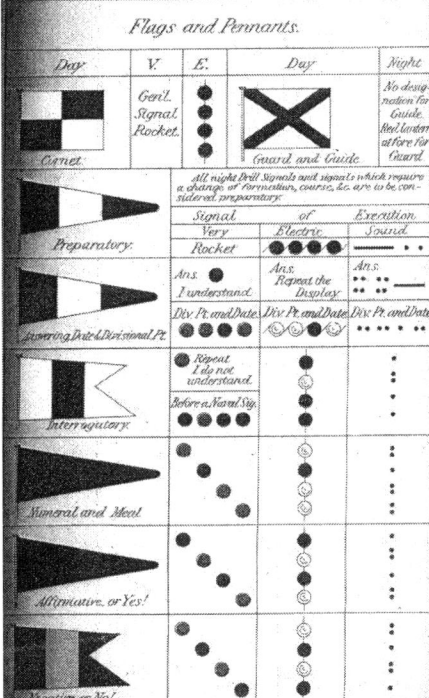
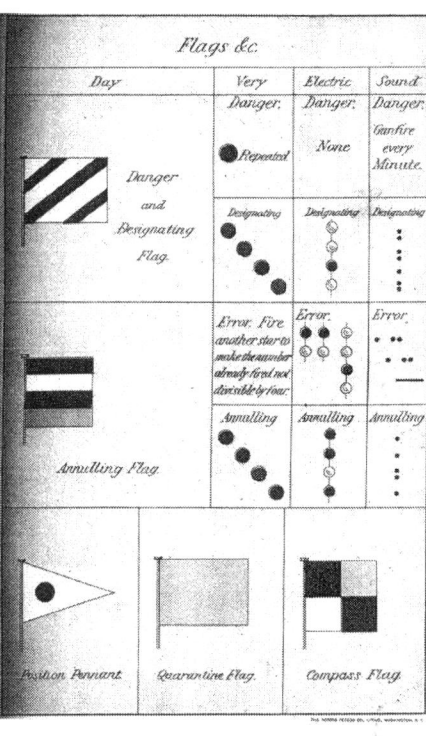
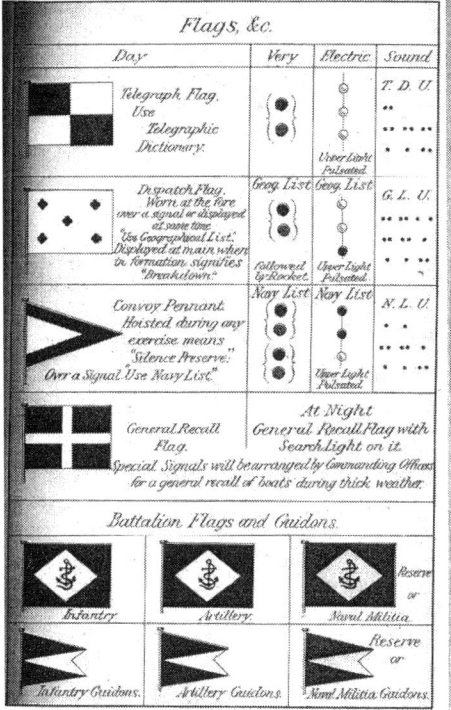
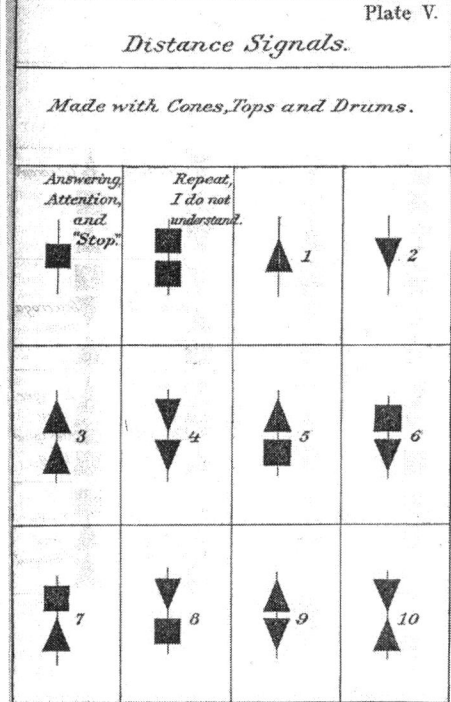
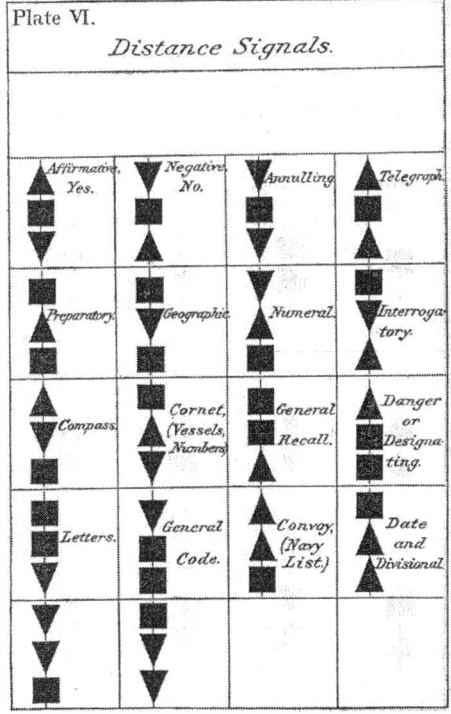

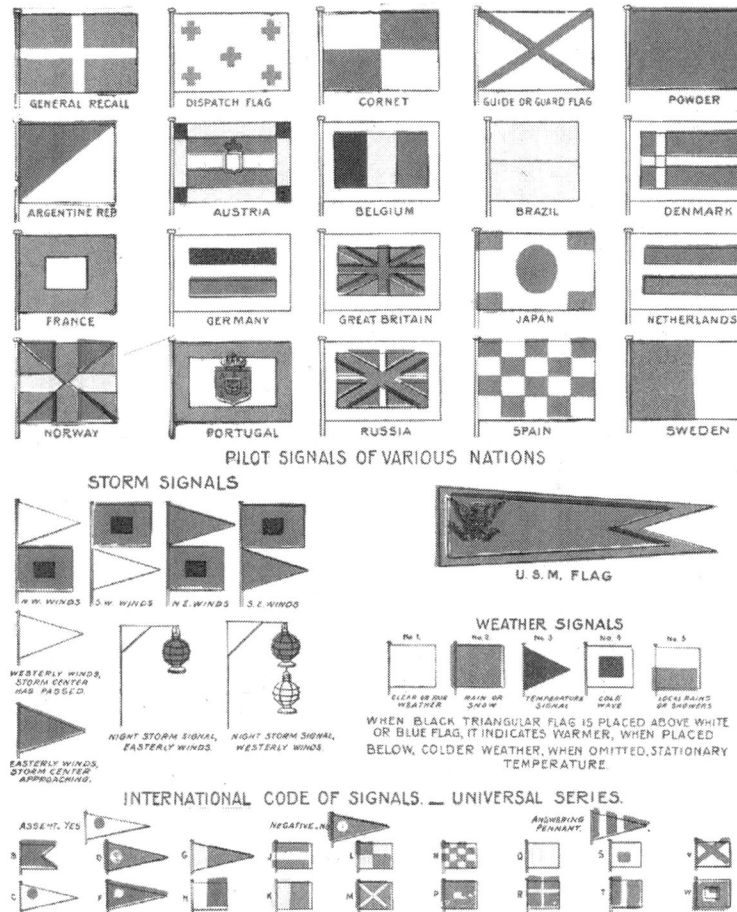

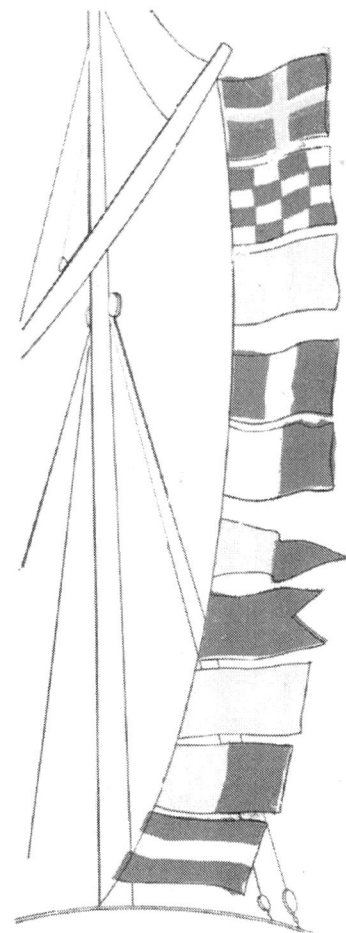

Battle Cry of Americans.

"Remember the Maine," as It is Signaled From the Flagship.

Upon the assignment of Sampson's fleet to Cuban waters it was understood that whenever the enemy came within range ten flags signifying "Remember the Maine" were to be kept floating from the signal top of the flagship until the last shot was fired.

The signal is meant to be read as easily by the Spaniards as by the Americans, for it is taken from the international code of signals, which has a place in the captain's cabin of every vessel that floats.

The flags are grouped to spell the words. The topmast flag is of red with a cross of yellow on it; the next is a blue-and-white checker-board and the third is yellow. The three make up "RNQ," meaning "remember." The next group is of two flags—the first of red, white and blue, meaning "T," and the other of red and white, floating for "H." Inasmuch as there are no vowels in the code, the "e" in "the" is omitted. The last group of flags is headed by a yellow and blue pennant, which is recognized by the tarsas "G." Its presence signifies that the following word is the name of a man-of war instead of a State. Following in order are red, yellow; yellow and blue, and blue and white flags, which spell "BQKJ," or "Maine."

Marine guard of the *Texas* aboard the USS *Maine* circa 1895, led by 2nd Lt. Wendell C. Neville.

Neville went on to become one of the most decorated Marines in history and the Commandant of the Marine Corps in 1929. These Marines signify an end of an era. The uniforms are hardly different than those worn during the Civil War and their rifles are the single shot 1873 Springfield. In the course of a few years, equipped with the bolt-action 1895 Lee Rifle and the Colt machine gun, a new "Marine" would step onto the world stage as an independent fighting force in and of itself.

8 USS TEXAS & USS MAINE: A COMPARISON

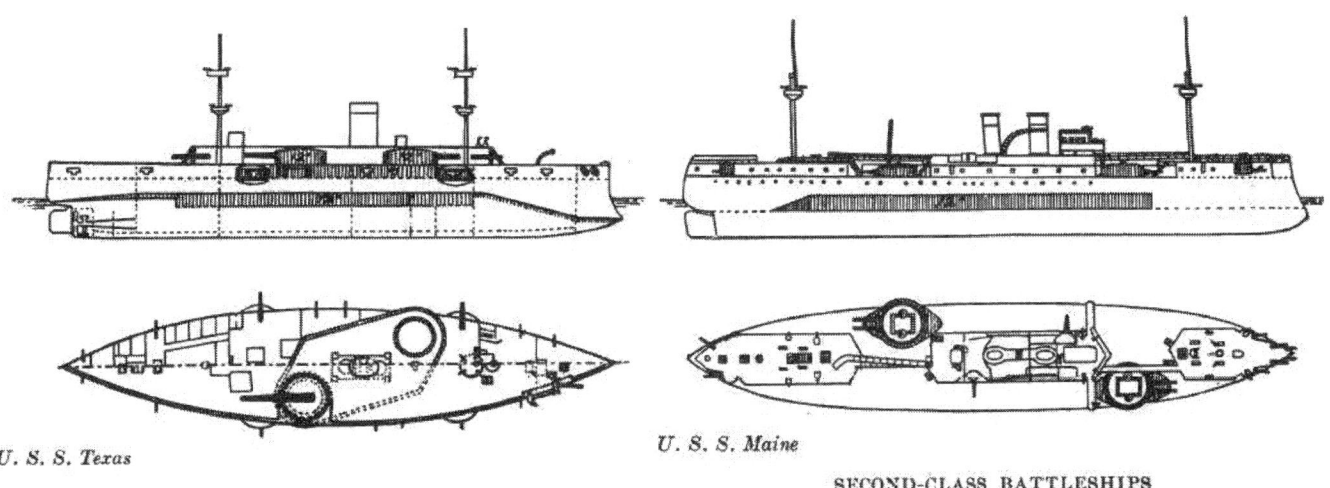

U. S. S. Texas

U. S. S. Maine

SECOND-CLASS BATTLESHIPS

The *Texas* (in the distance on the left) and the *Maine* (wreckage in the foreground) rendezvous for the final time. Havana Harbor, December 1898. In Cuba both ships found their place in history that tumultuous year.

Cross section and plan of the *Maine*. Note the torpedo boats on deck, like those of the *Texas* destined never to join the ship. Also note the yard-arms suspended by chains beneath the crow's nests on each mast. The Navy's design for the *Maine* embodied the latest thoughts in naval architecture but struggled to escape the last vestiges of sail. Note the open-topped turrets. The en echelon arrangement of the main armament was arrived at independently from that of the *Texas*. Also apparent is the transverse arrangement of the *Maine's* boilers in contrast to axial arrangement of the boilers in the *Texas*.

Cross section and plan of the *Texas* as originally designed. The overall similarities in general layout with the *Maine* are apparent, although the *Texas's* turrets were echeloned mirror image to those on the *Maine*. The *Texas'* design, like that of the *Maine*, also originally featured two stacks, but in the case of the *Texas* this was revised during construction in favor of a single, large diameter stack.

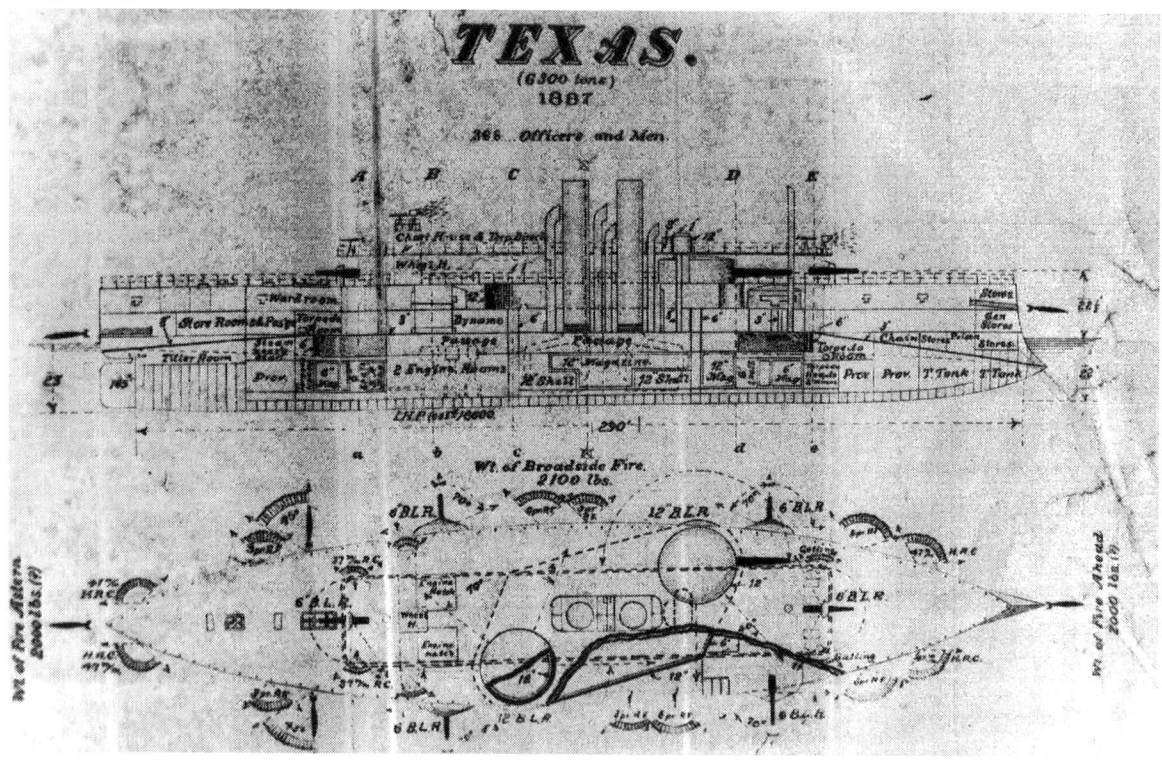

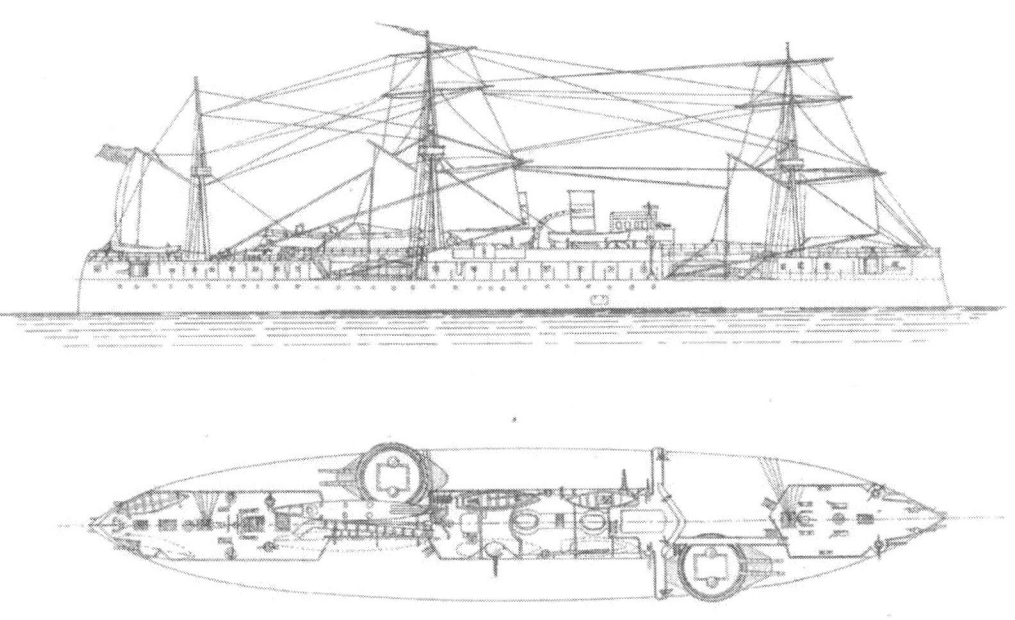

Designed as a cruiser, the *Maine* was expected to sail far from the US shores to overseas ports where the Navy had no coaling stations. To achieve this the designers envisioned the use of sails for propulsion on long voyages so that coal could be conserved for combat and maneuvering. This early illustration of the armored cruiser *Maine* shows the full sailing rig which in the end was never fitted. The *Maine* was instead reclassified a 2nd Class Battleship in which role she, like the *Texas*, was expected to operate in home waters. Note the differing stowage locations for the ship's boats when compared to the previous plan for the *Maine*. The *Maine*, like the *Texas*, had turrets in her main battery designed to fire full ahead, full astern, or to either broadside, making it difficult for her designers to find a location to safely store the ship's boats away from muzzle blast.

Diagram of the *Texas* showing the arrangement of her armor. The armored turrets sit atop an armored citadel, protecting her main guns. The ships buoyancy and vital machinery are protected by a belt of side armor and an armored deck, seen angling down to the bow and stern. The masts support fighting platforms with no provision for sailing rig. The *Texas* was designed for defending the coast of the United States from attack, not for cruising to the enemy's shores to seek combat. Subsequent US battleships favored increased size and range, capabilities which led to the forming of a true battle fleet. Reflecting their reduced role in future battle plans, the *Texas* like the *Maine* was reclassified a 2nd Class Battleship.

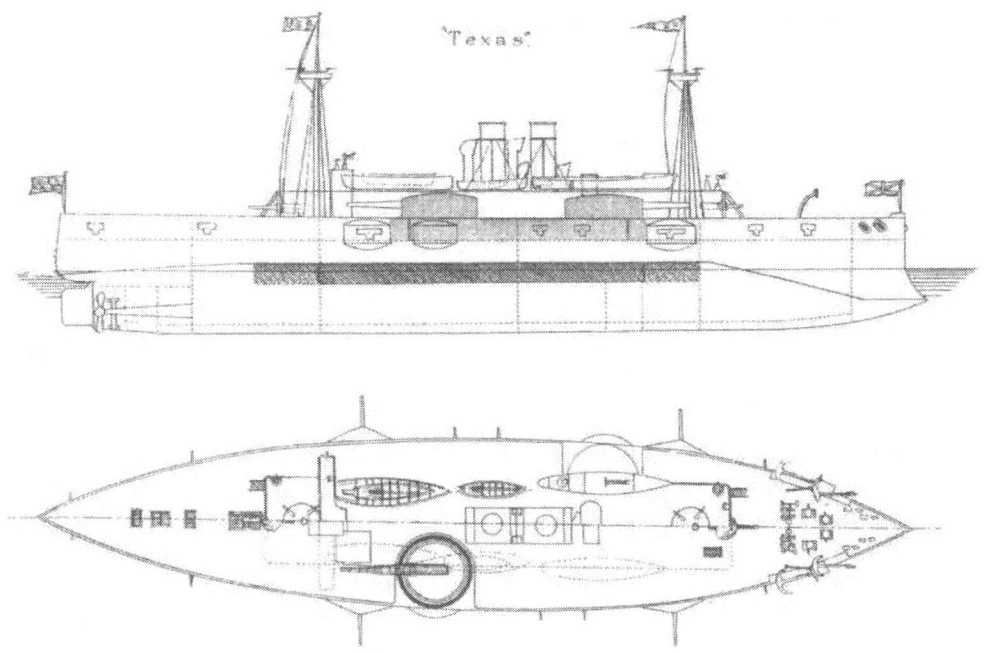

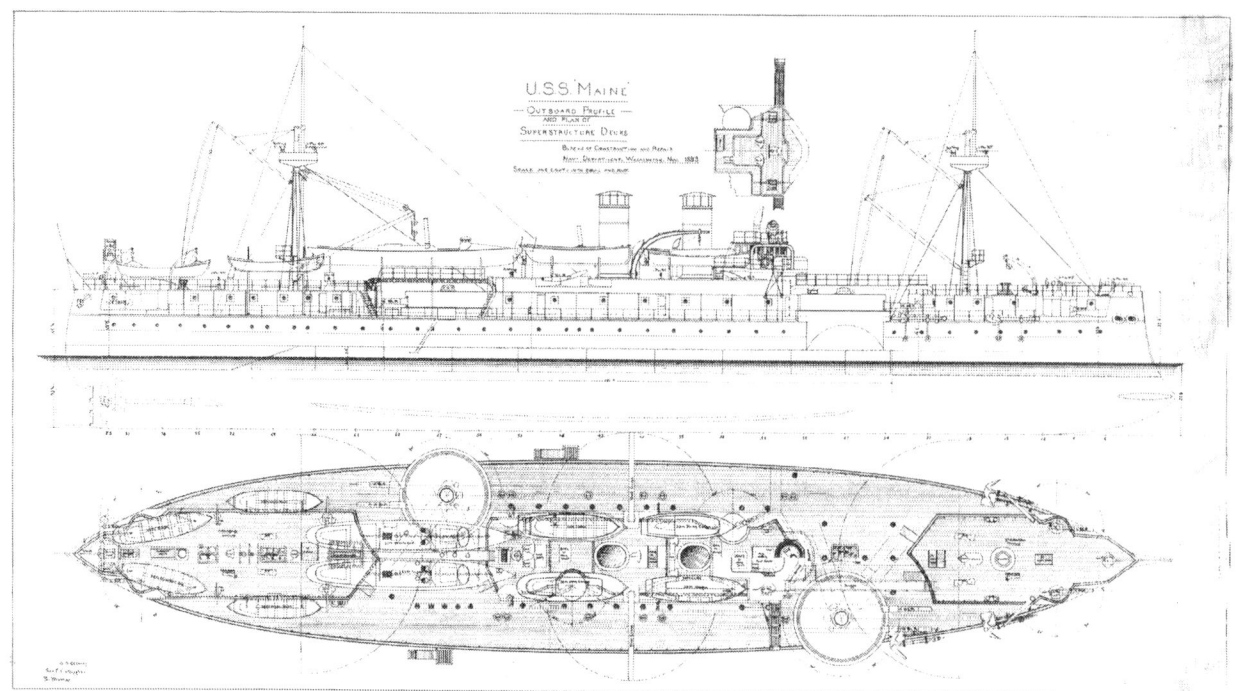

Shown here essentially in her ultimate form, the *Maine* has lost the final vestiges of a sailing rig in favor of fighting tops like those of the *Texas*. The *Texas'* design in contrast has lost its second funnel. While this reduced the number of penetrations through the armored deck, the stack's diminished slenderness may have reduced its draft somewhat, costing the *Texas* some speed. The *Maine's* gun turrets shared the gun deck, while those on the *Texas* were carried a deck higher. The turret location on the *Maine* increased the danger of an accidental discharge while the turrets were turning but lowered the *Maine's* center of gravity, increasing stability.

In practice carrying the turrets higher on the *Texas* was found to create no stability issues. Both plans still show the intended torpedo boats stowed on deck. The torpedo boats would not be deleted from the proposed equipment of these vessels until 1895.

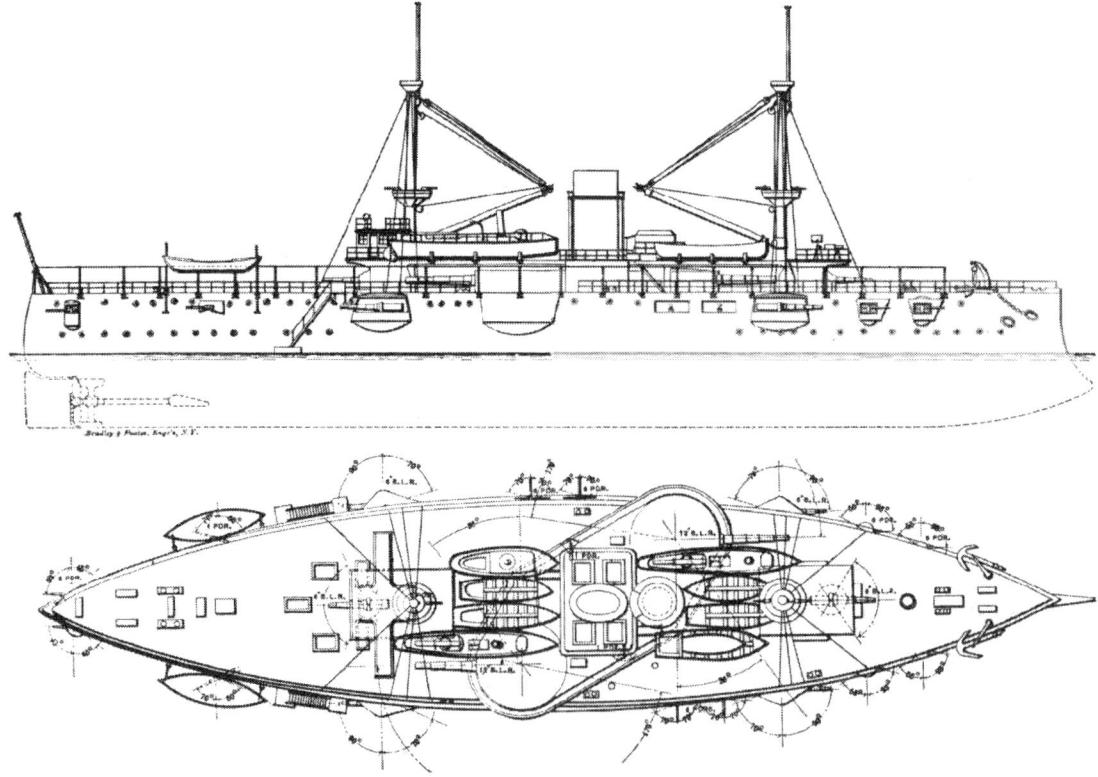

Although the USS *Texas* received her fair share of fame at Santiago, within a generation she was forgotten by the public while the USS *Maine* has gained lasting remembrance as the tragic, albeit spectacular, trigger for the Spanish American War. These two vessels were never "sisters." Their designs originated from two different specifications and from naval architects on two different sides of the Atlantic. The facts that they  were authorized simultaneously, were of approximately the same tonnage, and shared the en echelon turret arrangement were their notable points of commonality. There is no question that as a second class battleship the *Texas* was the better of the two vessels in all respects, for the *Maine* was simply not designed to be a battleship.

The *Texas* was in essence a British warship, taking advantage of a design discipline and heritage second to none. The *Maine* was a wholly American project, arising from naval architects who had never previously built heavy steel warships. While the *Texas* suffered somewhat in the translation from British to American technology, the *Maine* lacked a pedigree entirely. Had the two ships been built side-by-side, perhaps both may have benefited, but the construction of these ships was purposefully separated in an effort to spread knowledge and experience across a developing military-industrial complex. Even before their belated commissioning ceremonies in 1895 (with the *Texas* gaining the honor first), they had already served the U.S. Navy well. Newer, heavier, and much more impressive vessels followed hard on the heels of the *Maine* and *Texas*, vessels which benefited from the lessons learned during the building of these pioneering warships.

In comparing the design of these warships, it is ironic that had the *Texas* been selected for duty in Havana Harbor in 1898 instead of the *Maine*, the Spanish American War may never have begun, at least not in the dramatic fashion than it did. There is no question that either warship would have sunk had a mine indeed ripped open her hold - no pre-dreadnought in

existence was mine proof. However, if a coal fire adjacent to one of the *Maine's* six inch magazines actually initiated the explosion, the war might have been averted on the drawing boards as the *Texas'* design rendered her immune from this danger. The *Texas* did not have any of her magazines adjacent to coal bunkers, which were a well-known fire hazard in coal-fired steamships of the day.

The *Maine's* big guns, four Ten inchers which each threw a 550 lb shell, gave the her a bit more long range clout than her bigger, faster, and much more capable armored cruiser cousins, the *Brooklyn* and *New York*. She did not have the range or the hitting power of the *Texas*, however. After the turret and ammunition handling improvements were made on the *Texas* shortly before the war, the *Maine* probably would not even have had the advantage of rate of fire.

The *Maine* had more in common with her cruiser cousins that the *Texas*. She had a long, narrow cruiser hull, significantly different than the wide-beamed *Texas*, a design feature that should have made her faster. Unfortunately the *Maine* had a problem with her weight distribution that unbalanced and slowed her, a fatal defect in a cruiser. Her twin gun mounts, although also placed en echelon, were mounted awkwardly on a cut-away gun deck which made them near awash in bad weather. They were also mounted further forward and aft, away from the center of the ship and therefore more subject to greater motion in rough seas. Although both ships were considered seaworthy, the high hulled *Texas* with her gun turrets on the main deck was the drier and more stable ship.

As the *Maine* was clearly no cruiser, she was artificially re-designated a second class battleship, but in this role she did not have the measure of the *Texas*. Although there are those that would argue that the *Maine* served more in her first year than the *Texas* and only missed beating the *Texas* into commission by a hairs breadth, the fact is that she was a battleship in designation only, while the *Texas* was first and always a battleship, indeed the *Texas* was the first battleship of the "New Navy."

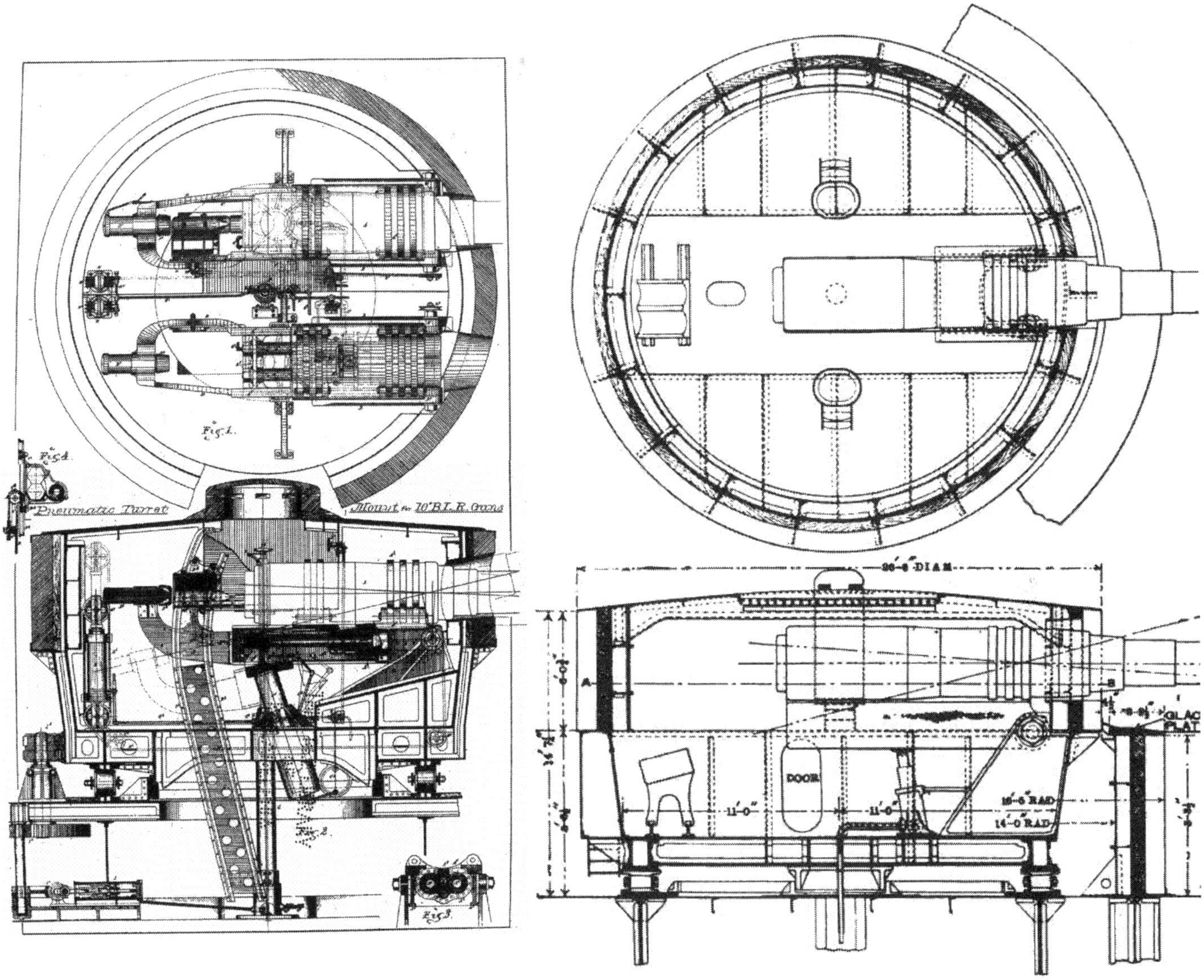

Plans and sections of the turrets on the *Maine* (above left) and the *Texas* (above right). The *Maine's* 10" gun and its mounting is shown enlarged below.

In many ways a battleship's main guns are the ultimate measure of the vessel and in the *Maine's* case these were two pairs of 10" guns mounted in armored turrets. On the *Texas* each turret held a single 12" gun. As both the *Texas* and the *Maine* were equipped with the best contemporary naval ordnance made in the United States at that time, the designs of the guns shared many similarities, as can be seen in the photos of the 10" gun above and the 12" gun below being tested at the Navy's proving range.

A triple expansion steam engine of the *Maine* (above) and of the *Texas* (below). The twin engines of the *Maine* were rated at a total of 9,000 horsepower while those of the *Texas* were rated at 8,600. In her trails the *Maine* officially achieved 9,293 HP and 17.4 knots, while the *Texas* achieved 8,900 HP and 17.82 knots during her trials. At one point in her trials, the *Texas* reportedly hit an impressive maximum speed of 18.8 knots. Unexpectedly, the Navy's new battleship was faster than its higher-powered armored cruiser cousin.

The boilers of the *Maine* (above) and those of the *Texas* (below).

The *Maine* (above) and the *Texas* (below) as each appeared in 1911. While they were not true sister ships, in the end they shared a similar fate in making the ultimate sacrifice for their country. In the process both warships contributed to the development of the United States as a naval and a world power.

9 TROUBLESOME TORPEDO BOATS

Early torpedoes began as floating water-tight casks containing gunpowder explosive. These moored torpedoes (of Civil War "damn the torpedoes" infamy) proved capable of severely damaging or destroying a warship but depended upon unreliable contact triggers or direct electrical firing by an observer on shore. Constant exposure to the elements necessitated correspondingly constant maintenance and replacement. After the Civil War more powerful guncotton-based explosives increased their potential threat but their deterrent value often outweighed their combat effectiveness except, perhaps, in confined, well-defended waters where maintenance could be conducted under the protection of shore batteries and attacking ships would be obliged to pass directly over them.

During the American Civil War the strictly defensive nature of these moored or free floating torpedoes lead both blockaded Southerners and the Northern blockaders to resort to spar torpedo-equipped boats in an effort to carry the war to the enemy. Stealth and small silhouette were the key characteristics of these boats. Propulsion was provided by manpower or steam. The Confederate "Davids" were the culmination of this type of torpedo boat.

Following the Civil War the development in Europe of the Whitehead "automobile torpedo" resulted in a self-propelled, self-guided torpedo capable of being launched at an opposing vessel from distances of up to 1000 yards and carrying a warhead of approximately 100 pounds of guncotton. Warships of all sizes up to the mighty battleships then being developed soon incorporated torpedo firing apparatus, but it was clear that the promise of the torpedo was in the capability it gave to a small, inexpensive vessel to cripple or sink even the largest warships afloat. Navies around the world, began development of a new class of high-speed, small boats to carry these torpedoes into action.

Post-Civil War torpedo boat developments in the United States were lead by the Herreshoff Manufacturing Company of Bristol, Rhode Island. Unlike many foreign navies which invested in hundreds of the new torpedo boats, the U.S. Navy's interest was focused on a limited number of largely experimental vessels, trusting no doubt that in time of war large numbers of additional boats could be quickly constructed if they proved successful.

With only limited Navy development, much of the experimentation into high-speed boats was initiated by wealthy businessmen along the north-east seaboard. William Randolf Hearst, Charles R. Flint, and other yacht club members commissioned and raced boat after boat, attempting to out-speed and out-spend one another. These competitions drove the technology, and creative minds like that of designer Charles Dell Mosher answered the call for speed on the waves.

C.D. Mosher gained public notoriety in the early 1890's for the amazingly fast boats he designed with his business partner William Gardner, including the *Still Alarm* and the *Feisen*. Mosher designed and built steam engines and boilers of previously unheard-of lightness and strength. The *Feisen* set a new world's record pace of 31.6 mph on August 25, 1893,

before being sold to the Brazilian Navy and converted into a torpedo boat. Mosher's talent for engine and boiler design was well appreciated at the time, however his innovative hull design remained something of a trade secret. Mosher had taken over a portion of a disused mill race for private hydrological research. By replacing the sides of the mill race with glass and affixing tufts of string to model boat hulls, he was able to determine which hull forms resulted in the least resistance. These studies led him to pioneer the development of hulls designed to rise up out of the water as their speed climbed, resulting in a marked reduction in drag. These were among the first hydroplaning hulls ever developed.

Mosher's boat designs culminated in 1902 with the *Arrow*, which set the world's record for a piston-engined, steam-propelled vessel at 42.9 mph, though there are unconfirmed contemporary reports claiming that speeds of up to 50 mph were obtained on occasion. This world record still stands to this day.

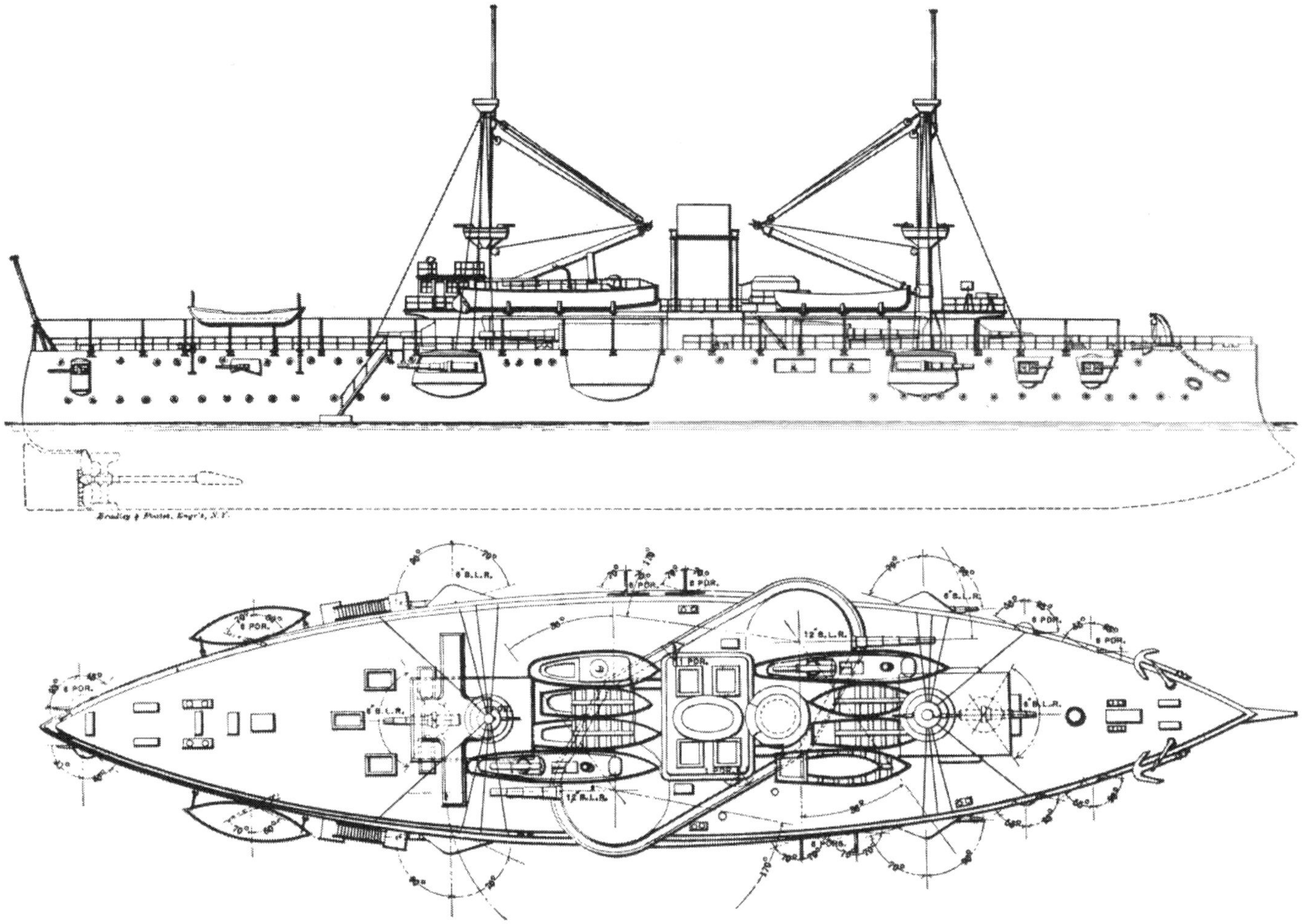

SIDE ELEVATION AND DECK-PLAN OF UNITED STATES BATTLESHIP "TEXAS."

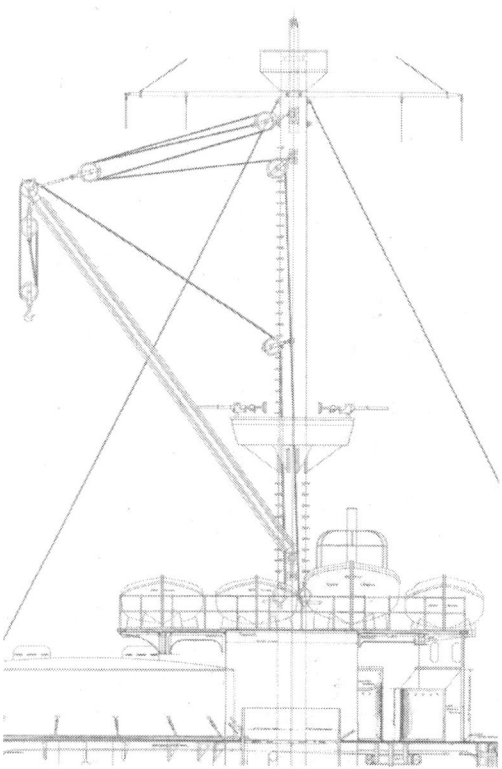

Plans for the *Texas* showing the proposed pair of 50 foot "third class" (i.e. ship transported) torpedo boats, stowed on the platform deck. It is apparent that the torpedo boats would have had to have been launched prior to action, as in their stowed position they would have been well within the muzzle blast of the big 12" guns.

The inclusion of the torpedo boats was an important design consideration in laying out the *Texas* and necessitated the installation of large mast-mounted cranes, capable of lifting the 9,900 pounds boats.

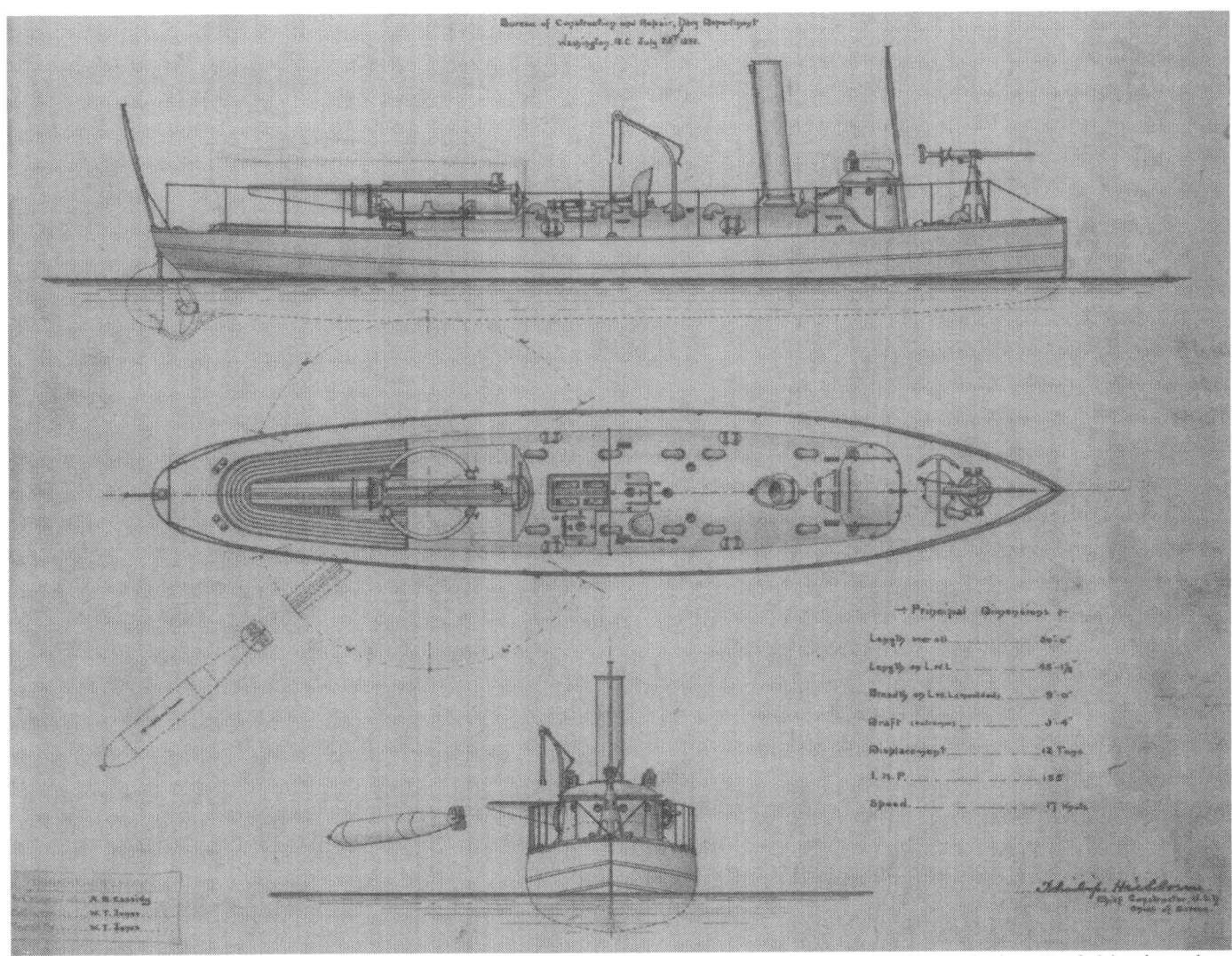

Plans of the torpedo boats for the USS *Texas*. These boats were based upon the "best designs" of this class then being built abroad, incorporating many advanced features including a flush-plated steel hull, experimental lightweight aluminum fittings, linoleum covered steel decks, forced-draft air supply to Mosher boilers (the type in use in the record holding racing yachts *Norwood*, *Nada*, and *Feisen*), pedestal mounted Whitehead torpedo tube at the stern, and a 1-pdr rapid-fire bow gun. The special lightweight, Mosher-designed quadruple-expansion engine in each boat was rated at 155 hp. The expected speed of the boats was to be in the 17 to 18 knot range. It was anticipated that they would see service as fast dispatch vessels in addition to their combat role, so they were provided with officers' bench seating aft - there being no interior accommodations other than engine room, fire room, armored conn, and the forward storage space.

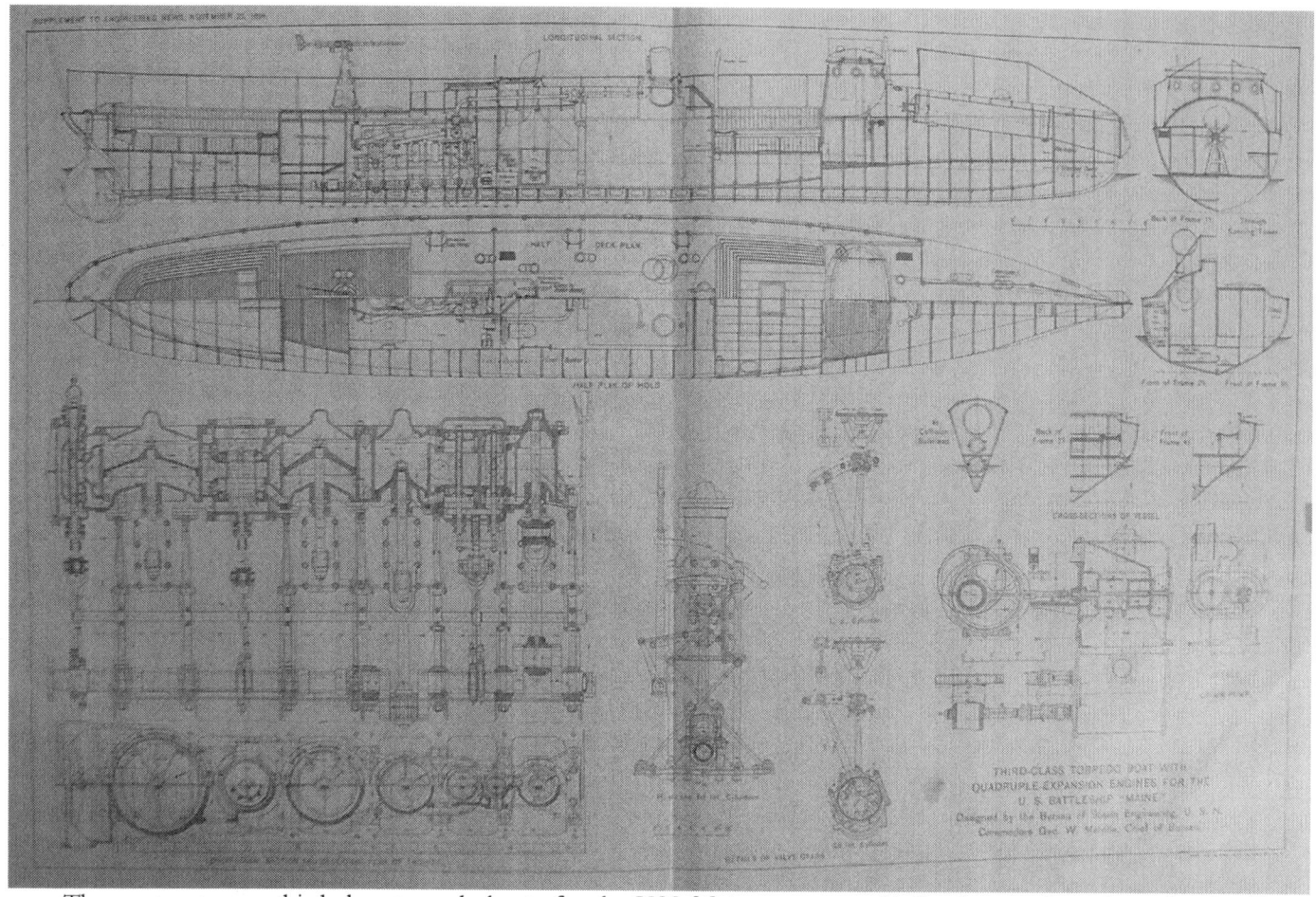

The contemporary third class torpedo boats for the USS *Maine* were over 11 feet longer than those for the *Texas*, and featured a bow mounted torpedo tube rather than a pivoting stern mount. In attempt to compensate for their larger size and still achieve comparable performance, a somewhat larger Mosher-designed boiler and engine were used on the *Maine's* boats. The boats for the *Texas* and the *Maine* were developed concurrently and shared many details of design in their fittings and machinery. Each of the torpedo boats for both warships held a crew of 5.

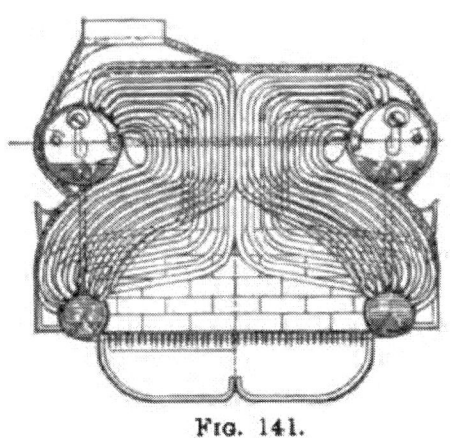 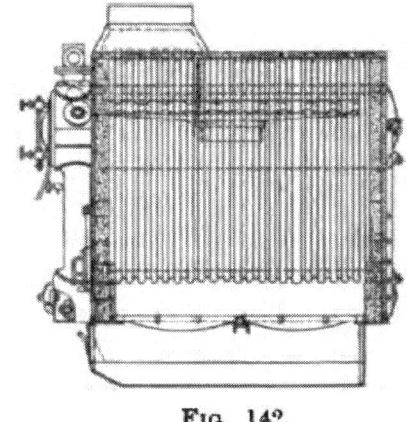 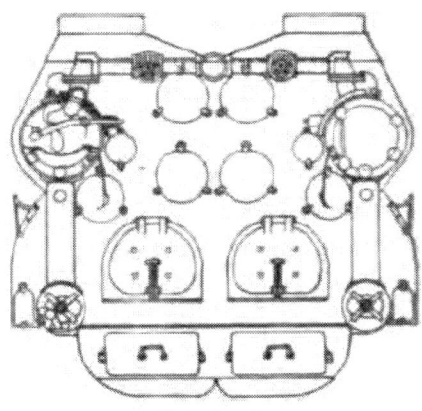

Fig. 141. **Fig. 142.** **Fig. 143.**
Mosher's Water-Tube Boiler.

Charles Dell Mosher's designs for the boilers of the torpedo boats for the *Maine*. The boilers of the *Texas'* and the *Maine's* torpedo boats differed somewhat in size and exhaust, but were otherwise essential similar. The *Maine's* torpedo boats were each fitted with two stacks, while those of the *Texas* had but a single stack.

Comparative Statistics for the Machinery of the Torpedo Boats for the USS *Texas* and the USS *Maine*:

	Texas:	*Maine*:
Engine:	Mosher Quadruple Expansion	Mosher Quadruple Expansion
	5.25", 7.35", 10" & 14" bores x 8" stroke	6", 8.87", 11.75" & 15.75" bores x 8" stroke
Horsepower:	155 hp @ 250 psi	200hp @ 250 psi
Boilers:	Mosher Water Tube	Mosher Water Tube
	375 sq. ft. heating surface	485 sq. ft. heating surface
	10.3 sq. ft. grate surface	12.6 sq. ft. grate surface
	3,500 lbs.	4,130 lbs.
Screw:	1 – 4 bladed, manganese bronze	1 – 4 bladed, manganese bronze

Unfortunately for the Navy, while they had obtained from C.D. Mosher the latest design in machinery for their new torpedo boats, they had not obtained his innovative "rising" hull design, an omission that seriously compromised the boats' performance.

Plan showing the design of the forced-draft blowers used on the torpedo boats of both the *Texas* and the *Maine*. The blower was situated on the aft bulkhead of the fire room and discharged air into the space to increase the rate of burning in the fireboxes, thereby raising boiler pressure, horsepower, and speed.

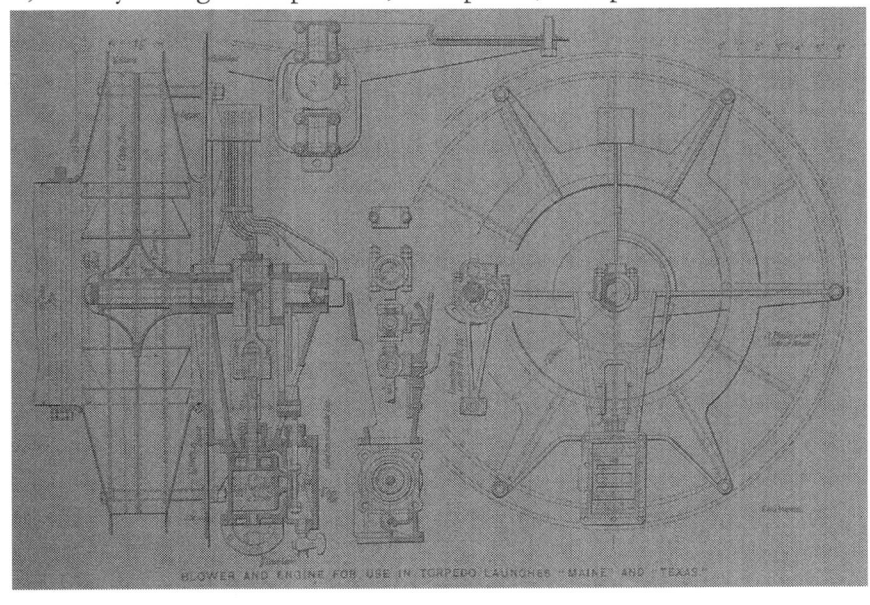

Trials of the *Texas Torpedo Boat #2*, held at the Norfolk Navy Yard in the summer of 1895, proved to be a disappointment. The boat would not exceed 11 knots, produced only about 120 horsepower, and showed excessively high propeller "slip" for the rpm. A subsequent change to a different propeller and other adjustments allowed the engine to reach its rated horsepower, but resulted in a speed increase of less than a quarter of a knot over previous tests. The Secretary of the Navy reported to Congress that "The failure of the *Texas'* third class torpedo boats to develop more than a moderate speed precludes the idea of their usefulness to that vessel in time of war. Ill adapted as they are for ships' use, it is possible that they may be made use of elsewhere for purposes of torpedo instruction."

The *Maine's* torpedo boats likewise were a failure. Neither warship received her torpedo boats.

Texas Torpedo Boat #1 was last recorded as being on display at the Cotton States Exposition in Atlanta, Georgia in 1895. *Texas Torpedo Boat #2* was towed to the Naval Academy at Annapolis for use in instruction of the midshipmen. In this photograph midshipmen at Annapolis work on a lightweight steam engine similar to that of *Texas Torpedo Boat #2*.

10 EARLY SERVICE

The USS *Texas* was placed into commission at the Norfolk Navy Yard at 1:30 PM on August 15, 1895, under the command of Captain Henry Glass, an able officer and Civil War combat veteran who had demonstrated his technical savvy and ability to bring a modern warship to its peak efficiency during his preceding service as captain of the USS *Cincinnati*.

In the tradition of naval vessels around the world the *Texas* had a figurehead. However, in keeping with the growing minimalist movement in nautical design, that of the *Texas* was an understated American eagle with shield. On each side acanthus and ribbon streamed back from the eagle and encircled a Lone Star of Texas. Also visible in this view is the hatch covering the forward torpedo tube, on the bow just above the waterline.

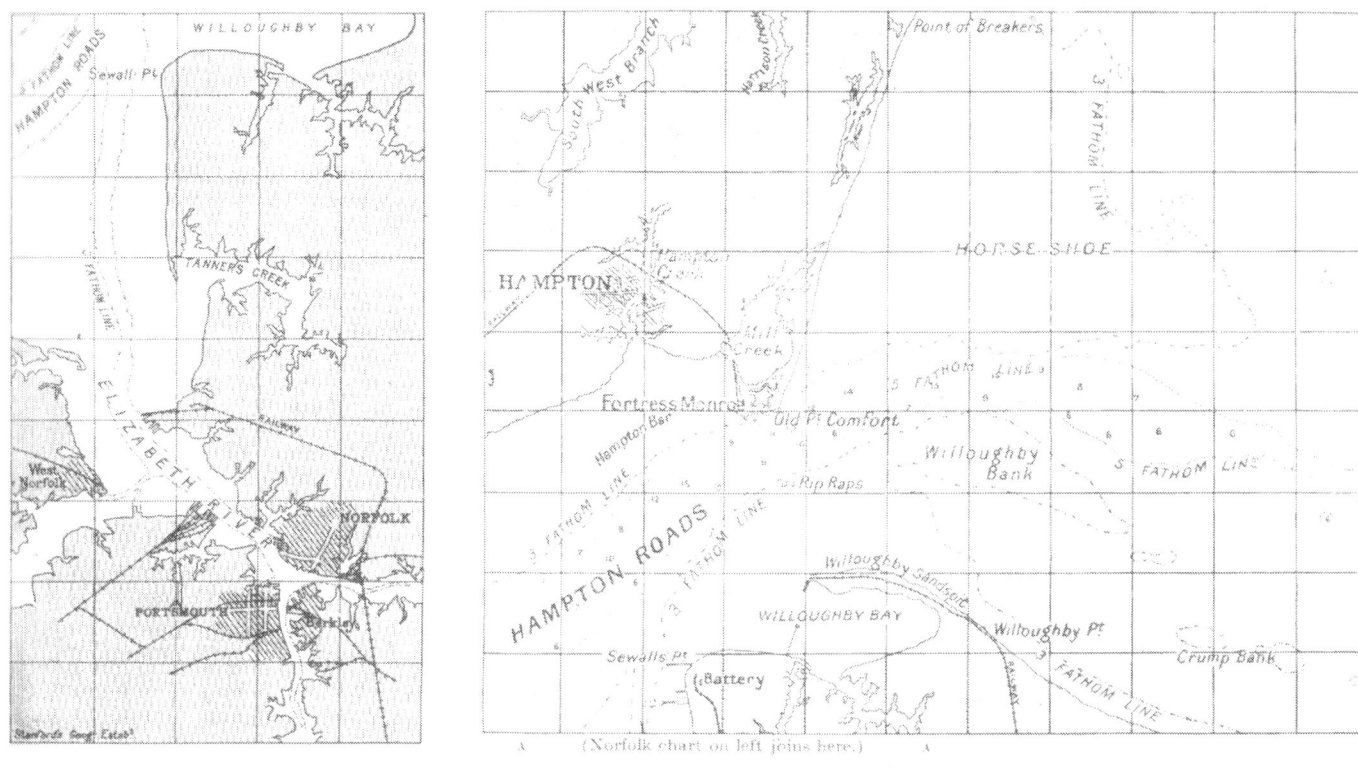

NORFOLK, VA. (HAMPTON ROADS AS ABOVE MAP.)

The *Texas'* first duty was the completion of her sea trials. These tests of the ship and her machinery were to be conducted in and around Hampton Roads, near the Norfolk Navy Yard where any repairs and adjustments too complicated to be made at sea could be readily accomplished. On September 5 at 7:45 am the *Texas* left Norfolk to commence her trials. By 8:45 am the port engine bearings were overheating, necessitating that the engine be slowed and then, 20 minutes later, stopped.

The *Texas* is visible anchored off of the Government Wharf at Fort Monroe, Old Point Comfort, Hampton Roads, Virginia circa 1895. Note the four-masted bark in the background. While the trade had begun the transition to steam, for reasons of economy a large portion of ocean going transport was still under sail in tall ships. It was not until after World War I that these ships would fade away and become a rarity.

At 9:55 am on September 5th, 1895 during the first hours of her maiden voyage, the *Texas* anchored off of Fort Monroe for an official visit.

On the night of September 5th, a party of 22 men from the Richmond Locomotive and Machine Works came aboard to participate in the trials, beginning the next day. Having built the ship's machinery, these personnel were on hand to help conduct the trials and make adjustments. These men were presumably well-motivated as exceeding the design performance specifications would result in substantial monetary reward, while failing to meet them entailed a financial penalty.

Visible in this photo on the platform deck adjacent to the masts are the fore and aft lookout compartments. These were intended to provide shelter to the lookouts, but in practice blocked the view from the bridge. These compartments were removed during the first refit in 1896. Also seen, suspended from the side of the hull in its extended position, is the portside boat boom. This pole had lines hanging from it to aid boats coming alongside. It could also be used to support a torpedo net that, deployed around the vessel, provided protection against "automobile" torpedoes.

The *Texas* off of Old Point Comfort, Hampton Roads during the 1895-6 period. In the background can be seen the first Chamberlin Hotel.

Failures of several pumps and ventilators in the mechanical spaces on the second day of the trials resulted in their early end, as well as in the heat prostration of several engineers and crew. Supply pipe sizing issues and mud in her condensers further extended the delays.

The Chamberlin Hotel, an extravagant beachside palace designed by Smithmeyer and Pelz, architects of the Library of Congress, and built in 1890 adjacent to Fort Monroe, was the backdrop for many early photos of the *Texas* and witness to her early trials. The hotel burned to the ground in 1920.

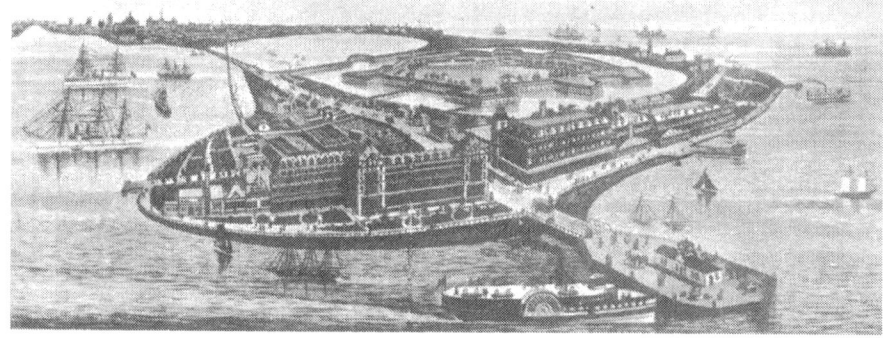

The *Texas* off of Old Point Comfort, Hampton Roads, Virginia during the 1895-6 period.

In late October 1895, the *Texas* embarked on her first voyage away from the port where she had been built, bound for Brooklyn Navy Yard, New York.

A subsequent shake-down cruise got her machinery in order, but Navy Department officials instructed that her hull be cleaned and painted prior to the speed trials. This relatively routine procedure grew in significance as it was subsequently decided to send her to the deeper dry dock in Brooklyn instead of using the one at the Norfolk Navy Yard. When the *Texas* had previously been dry docked at the Norfolk Yard, she had not been fully armed, giving her a shallower draft. Now fully loaded, there was some concern about the suitability of the Norfolk dry dock to accommodate the *Texas*.

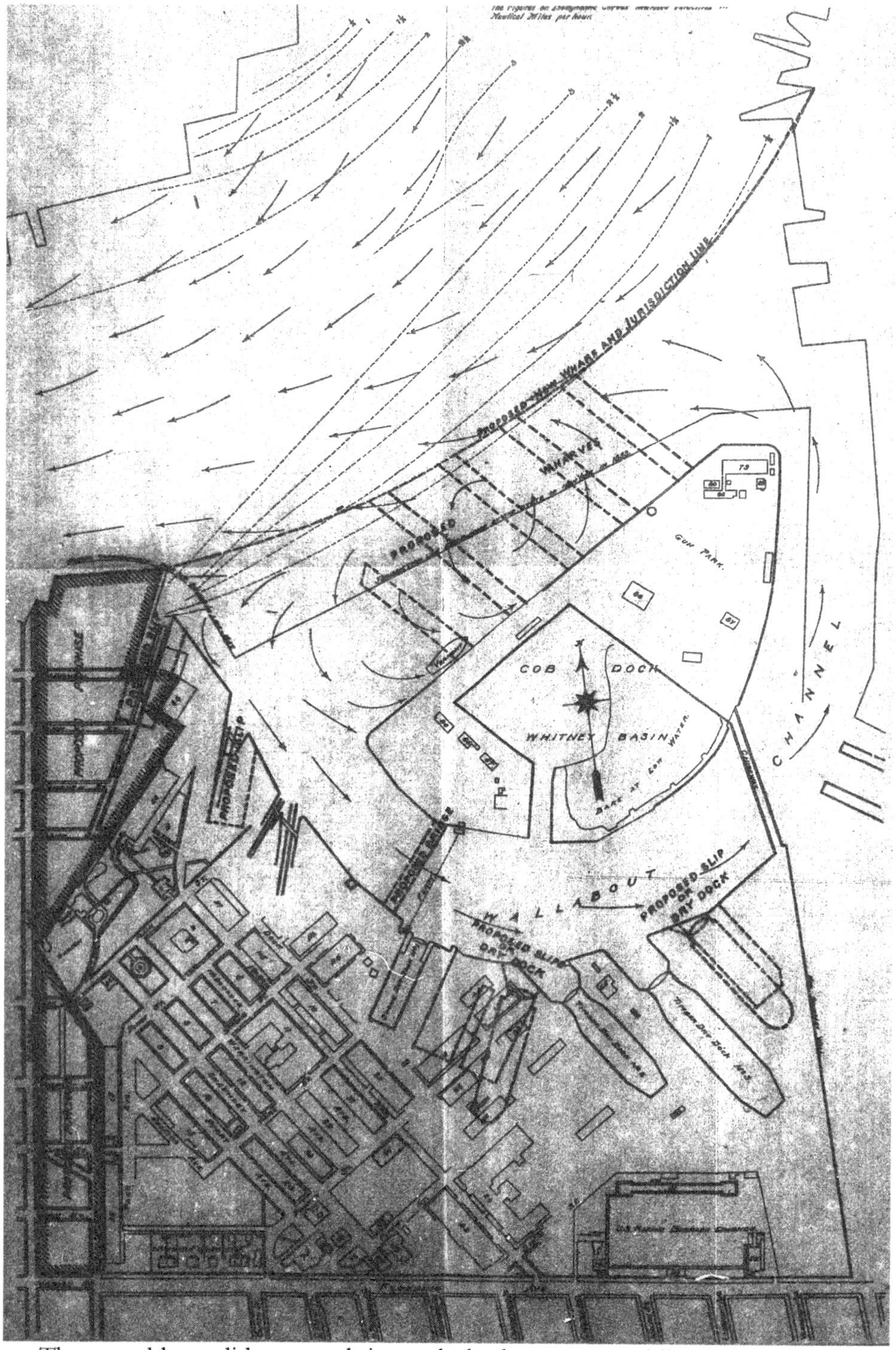

Upon arrival at the Brooklyn Navy yard, officials once again grew wary of the prospect of dry docking the *Texas*. Although the dock should have been able to handle the *Texas* under any normal tide, it was relatively narrow and steep sided. Navy officials decided that it would be prudent to await the next spring tide, to allow maximum clearance, not only for her keel but also for the *Texas'* bulging turret sponsons.

When dry docked on November 4th it was soon noted, as the water slowly drained away, that the both of ship's propellers were badly chipped, necessitating their replacement. As the water drained further it became increasingly apparent that the hull was resting heavily upon the wooden keel blocks on the floor of the dry dock. While the hull was being cleaned and painted over the following days, slight but steady settling was observed in the hull plates. On the 8th floor plates at frame 45 were found to be buckling and it was ordered that the next day water should be allowed into the dock up to the level of the propeller shafts in attempt to relieve the strain. On the 11th the water level was again raised when cracks in the cement of the bottom plating and buckling in the floor plates was found over a 144 foot length of the bottom.

These problems did not result in any leaks, but were troubling indicators of possible structural weakness. Although critics expounded on the weakness of the *Texas'* hull, Constructor Francis T. Bowles attributed the damage to improper placement of the blocks in the dry-dock.

Relatively minor hull repairs were made and the ship removed from the dry dock on November 21st, following which improvements and repairs to her machinery were also made in attempt to rectify the unacceptable conditions in the mechanical spaces noted during her initial trials.

FRANCIS T. BOWLES

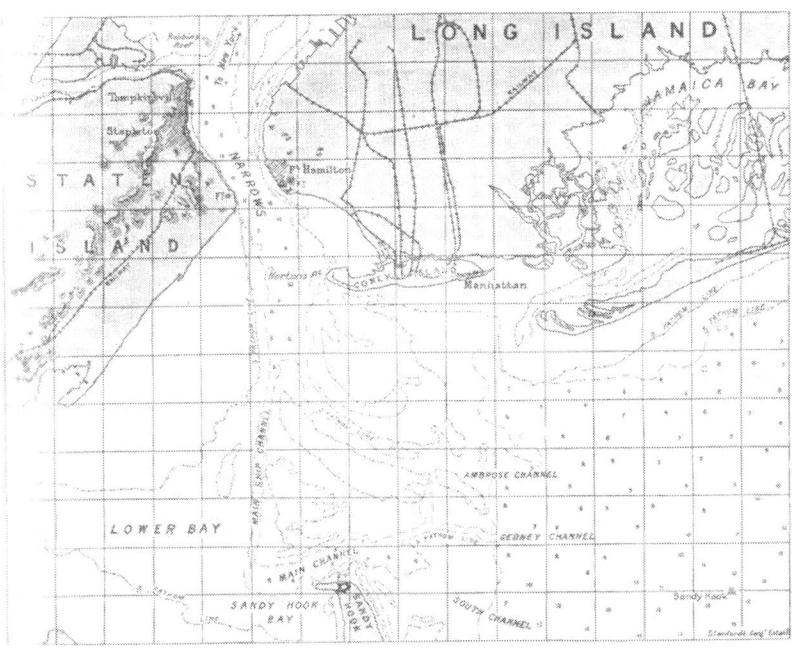

On December 5th the *Texas* left the Brooklyn Navy Yard for a preliminary test of her engines and promptly broke down off Tompkinsville, Staten Island when her steering gear failed. Repairs were quickly made but it was becoming apparent, in late December of 1895, that the *Texas* was in no condition to materially contribute in a rapidly developing potential confrontation with Venezuela that chose this moment to flare-up.

Operating off of Tompkinsville, the *Texas* once again embarked engineers from the Richmond Locomotive and Machine Works and was put through her paces. She achieved a sustained speed of 17.82 knots at 123 revolutions, exceeding her design speed of 17 knots, and reached a maximum speed of 18.8 knots. A maximum 8,900 horsepower was obtained at 126 revolutions, exceeding her design by 300 horsepower. It was found that the *Texas* was quite steady and free of excess vibration at speed. These four-hour sustained speed trials had to be cut short however at three hours and 5 minutes due to an overheating bearing in one of the circulating pumps. During this trial the engine's crank pits filled with oil and water which was thrown in showers with each revolution of the engine, making the taking of measurements in the engine room impossible.

In spite of this minor setback, Captain Glass reported the *Texas* ready to face the Board of Survey and Inspection with the coming of the new year.

The Board of Inspection, headed by Captain George Dewey, arrived on December 23rd and boarded ship at Tompkinsville to make its survey. While the ship's propulsion system appears to have met expectations, the board focused strong criticism of the hydraulic system operating the main guns and their turrets. Hydraulic leakage in the pump room was found to be so severe that the crew was unable to remain in the compartment. Turret machinery, ammunition hoists, and electrical firing appliances were also found to be wanting. The 12" gun magazines located between the boilers were found to be too hot and the hull required various bracket plates to increase its stiffness. The *Texas* departed for Norfolk, home, and an uncertain future.

Subsequently, in January of 1896, a Board of Survey was commissioned to make recommendations for remedial repairs and improvements to the *Texas*. They recommended strengthening of the hull that would add 31 tons to the displacement of the ship, including the replacement of the outer keel plate on the bottom of the hull. Not surprisingly many of their structural recommendations focused on replacing or reinforcing the first steel components that had gone into the hull, a reflection perhaps on the quality of the early steel as much as upon the design. The ship's propulsion machinery was accepted without penalty.

While these modifications were being made at the Norfolk Navy Yard, the Navy Department ordered the ship placed out of commission. Other than a skeleton crew that remained with the ship, Captain Glass, the officers, and men of the *Texas* were reassigned to other duties.

11 "OLD HOODOO" IN THE NEW NAVY

Once again with the *Texas* unfit for duty, foreign tensions raised their head, this time with Spain over Cuba. Growing animosity in American public opinion, inflamed by an active Cuban exile community and a enthusiast yellow press, fed rumors of impending conflict. In May 1896 the *New York Times* reported that US Naval vessels were under orders to keep their coal bunkers and ships' stored filled, ready for instant service, if called upon. The *Times* further noted that work on the *Texas* was soon to be completed and that she would be ready for action in June. As had happened in the past, this timetable slipped. The USS *Texas* was placed back into commission on July 20, 1896. September would find the ship still completing her stores and equipment.

USS *Texas* at the Norfolk Navy Yard, undergoing a refit to address problems in her turret operating hydraulics and in the ventilation of her magazines as well hull strengthening. Navy constructors took the opportunity to survey and correct many of the problems found during the *Texas*' brief first commission.

The 1896 refit resulted in few external changes to the appearance of the *Texas*. Most notably, the lookout platforms and their cabins, previously located adjacent to the fore and main masts, were removed.

On September 16th the *Texas* arrived off of the torpedo station at Tompkinsville, Staten Island to receive her torpedo outfit. Due to confusion in the engine room, the signal to back the port engine was missed and the ship ran hard aground on the sandy bottom. As one of the ships junior officers, future admiral Albert Gleaves, later described in his memoirs, "I recall how well I thought the captain was handling the ship in the crowded channel way. When we rounded to for our own anchorage, I could see the officers at the War College on the lawn and steps of the college watching us. All went well until we swung halfway around to floodtide. The captain and executive were on the bridge and we had a good deal of way on. All the officers were at their stations. I was on the forecastle. I heard the orders, 'Full speed astern. Let go the port anchor.' The ship continued to forge ahead and a stream of sparks poured from the hawse pipe as the anchor took the chain. By the time the whole cable was laid out the ship was aground almost in the inspector's garden." According to Gleaves, "At the moment the reverse signal was rung up, a fuse had burned out in the engine room, the lights all went out and the mechanic at the throttle got gallied and put the lever *ahead* full speed." Adding insult to injury as the ship sat helpless off of the War College, "the captain received an unofficial visit from Mr. Henry White and Mr. Bourke Cochrane in company with Lord Russell, the chief justice of England. These gentlemen remained some time on board and seemed to enjoy their stay, although the decks were covered with mud from 120 fathoms of chain cable."

The *Texas* was successfully floated off the following morning by the combined efforts of four tugboats. Censure and reprimand for several of the engineering officers was recommended by a subsequent Court of Inquiry.

The following month the *Texas* rode-out a hurricane in company with the USS *Maine* and USS *Indiana*, demonstrating noteworthy stability, a testament to designer William John's experience with the *HMS Captain* incident, many years before.

![U.S.S. Texas, an Officer's Room]

An officer's cabin aboard the *Texas*, complete with extensive woodwork, electric light fixtures, and private wash basin.

On November 9th, while undergoing repairs to an outboard delivery pipe alongside the dock at the Brooklyn Navy Yard, the *Texas* suffered yet another well-publicized indignity. A sea-cock valve failed and the compartment quickly flooded. Closing the water tight doors led to the discovery that they and the bulkheads themselves leaked, allowing sufficient flooding into 61 compartments to put out her fires in one fire room within half and hour and to bring the hull to rest on the filthy but fortuitously shallow bottom, effectively sunk.

She would spend much the remainder of the month in dry dock being "scoured" of the evidence of her emersion while yet another Court of Inquiry reviewed the incident.

Repairs were effected quickly, spurred by the ongoing tensions with Spain over Cuba. The Navy Department ordered all repairs and work on naval vessels at the Brooklyn Navy Yard to be completed before January 1897, so that the fleet could gather at Hampton Roads. In early February the fleet engaged in blockade maneuvers off of Charleston, S.C. before detaching the *Texas* to Galveston to receive her silver service.

Texas arrived in Galveston for her first visit to her namesake state on February 17, 1897, initiating a week-long series of events, presentations, celebratory dinners, and public tours.

As the anchor was let go inside the harbor, the *Texas'* stern swung to the tide and promptly grounded. Composing his report to the Secretary of the Navy that evening, Capt. Glass said to his executive officer J.D.J. Kelly, "This is the end of my career, Kelley. Read what I shall wire the secretary: 'In entering Galveston Harbor, got ashore on Pelican Spit. Am hard and fast aground. If ship does not come off in the morning with the tide, shall remove guns, stores, etc.'"

Kelley a respected writer of essays and books replied, 'If you send that dispatch, Captain, your career will be ended. Let me suggest this.' 'Have touched lightly on Pelican Spit. Will be off next high tide." The *Texas* indeed floated off and the local pilot publically apologized for the incident.

Illustration and photos of the *Texas* at Galveston, 1897.

On February 19, 1897 on the plaza of the Galveston Beach Hotel, an estimated 10,000 people witnessed the presentation of the silver service to the officers of the USS *Texas*. The Texas Legislature in Austin recessed and special trains were arranged so that officials and citizens from across the state could attend the festivities. Texas Gov. Charles Culberson delivered an address followed by presentations of the silver service, a Texas flag, portraits of Stephen F. Austin and Sam Houston, a collection of books including Texas histories and works by Texas authors, and an additional silver service composed of cracker dish, sugar bowl, and cream pitcher contributed by the San Antonio Chapter of the Daughters of the Republic of Texas.

Captain Henry Glass of the USS *Texas* opened the vessel to visitors and thoughtfully accepted the presentations stating, "She has been called an unlucky ship, a "hoodoo" but the facts of her history contradict this most decidedly. While it is true that she was injured the first time she was taken into a dry dock, has been ashore, has sunk in harbor, and had many minor accidents, it is also true that on every occasion she has risen superior to mishaps that would have ruined other ships, and that in her case have led only to improvements. - She is a very lucky ship, I think…"

Would-be tourists had to arrange their own transport to the battleship as the Captain declined to attempt to dock, reportedly due to the danger to the docks presented by the ship's overhanging turret sponsons. It was never-the-less estimated that 10,000 people from all walks of life toured the vessel while it lay at anchor at Galveston. One visitor was "none other than the macrocephalous and megalophonous favorite son of the commonwealth of Texas" former Governor James Stephen Hogg who finding the gangway barred to him during the current Governor's visit, circled the battleship, at one point bellowing "Ahoy there! Ahoy there, Mr. Commander, or whoever you are. By gatlins, just tell Capt. Glass that Mr. Hogg is here and is in a hurry to get aboard. I could have come in any one of those darned pomp parties, but I'm a plain American citizen, and I didn't want any red tape in mine. See?" - *Dallas Morning News*: November 10, 1896.

One officer of the *Texas* received a special commendation at an oyster roast held at Galveston in their honor. The leather medal was inscribed "Battleship *Texas*. Presented to Lieut. Commander J.D.J. Kelly for running the blockade and seizing and devouring in the presence of the governor and members of the legislature of Texas 1544 oysters, without firing a gun. Galveston harbor, Feb. 20, 1897."

Departing Galveston on February 24, 1898, the *Texas* steamed to her next assignment, rendezvous with the USS *Maine* for joint participation in the New Orleans Mardi Gras celebrations.

When leaving New Orleans with the *Maine* on March 11, bound for torpedo practice and Port Royal, South Carolina, the *Texas'* anchor cable parted, forcing her to leave her anchor "resting forever in the bottom of the Mississippi River at a depth of over 100 feet." Photo of USS *Texas* in 1897.

Captain Henry Glass turned over command of the *Texas* to Captain William Clinton Wise in April of 1897. Her next assignment under her new commander would be as socially arduous as her last, participation in a "water parade" at the dedication of Grant's Tomb in New York on April 27th. This naval review carried unusual significance for the *Texas'* future service a scant fifteen months hence, as she steamed in company with the visiting Spanish cruiser the *Infanta Maria Teresa* (right), past the recently-inaugurated President William McKinley, reviewing the proceedings from the deck of the USS *Dolphin*.

The string of social calls continued with attendance at the dedication of Philadelphia's Washington Monument, a bronze equestrian sculpture by Rudolf Siemering, on May 15, 1897.

This was followed by a trip to Boston, where Marines from the Texas participated in the June 1st parade celebrating the dedication of the memorial monument to the 54th Massachusetts Volunteer Infantry Regiment.

The 54th Massachusetts or "Shaw's" Regiment was one of the first official black units to serve in the U.S. Army during the Civil War. The climatic, defining engagement for the 54th Regiment was the failed attack on Battery Wagner, located on a sand bar outside of Charleston, South Carolina. Captain W. C. Wise, now commanding the *Texas* but then an ensign, had himself participated in subsequent Union attacks on Fort Wagner while aboard the USS *New Ironsides*. The story of the 54th and its commander Col. Richard Gould Shaw, was recounted in the 1989 Academy Award-winning movie "Glory" in which this notable monument, by sculptor Augustus Saint-Gaudens, was featured.

Asst. Secretary of the Navy Theodore Roosevelt then order the USS *Texas* south to exhibit her machinery at the Railroad Master Mechanics convention, held at Old Point Comfort, Hampton Roads, Virginia on June 7-15, 1897. The *Texas*, whose machinery had been built by the Richmond Locomotive and Machine Works, was presented with the Richmond loving cup at the conclusion of the event.

In July, in company with the USS *New Hampshire*, the *Texas* participated in New York Naval Militia training in Long Island Sound. Despite heavy weather Asst. Secretary of the Navy Roosevelt rowed out to observe and inspect the *Texas*. In speaking to the sailors aboard the ship, Roosevelt stated "No nation is worthy to be called a nation that is not fit to fight when fighting is needed. No nation deserves the respect of the world if it cannot, when necessary, command peace at home and regard abroad with a strong hand."

Aboard the *Texas* on August 8, 1897 Ensign Walter R. Gherardi, son of Admiral Gherardi USN, was awarded the silver Maltese cross of the International Order of King's Daughters, along with a medal, recognizing his bravery during a severe cyclonic storm that struck the Atlantic Squadron while at sea off Cape Hatteras in February of 1897 when, while serving aboard the USS *Maine* he commanded the boat sent to rescue a seaman who had gone overboard. The boat was dashed to pieces but Ensign Gherardi was credited with saving the sailor single handed. Ensign Gherardi went on to save another overboard seaman while serving on the *Texas*, receiving his first command, the armed tug USS *Sioux*, in recognition for his acts of heroism and thus becoming the youngest officer in command of a vessel in the US Navy at that time. After serving blockade duty as Captain of the *Sioux* during the Spanish-American War he was given a shore command, being placed in charge of the lighthouses on Puerto Rico, where he was again credited with personally leading lifesaving efforts, this time helping to save nearly 150 people during a hurricane in 1899. This was just the beginning of Gherardi's long and distinguished naval career in which he rose to the rank of rear-admiral.

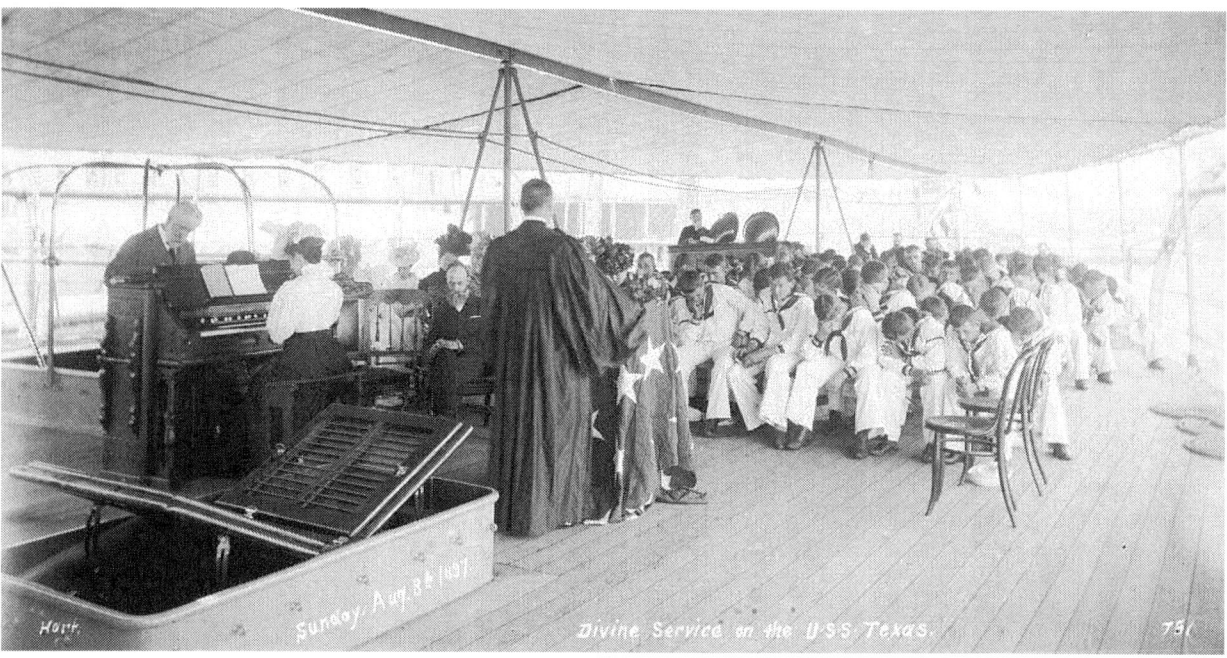

The long boom seen here extending down the centerline of the ship was for use in supporting canvas awnings that could be unfurled to roof the entire main deck forward and aft of the 6" guns, as seen in the photo taken during a worship service aboard (opposite). This awning would typically be used when at anchor to provide weather protection from rain or sun – a consideration that was particularly important to a vessel that was notoriously hot below decks in summertime. On September 30, 1897, the New York Times Reported "Twenty of the crew of the *Texas* deserted her while she was in the dry dock [at the Brooklyn Navy Yard]…They have deserted at every opportunity. The vessel is uncomfortable. The engine rooms are so situated that it is impossible to keep them cool, and the living quarters of the crew are also unnecessarily heated."

Port and starboard views of the aft main deck of the *Texas* taken in late 1897 or early 1898.

The remainder of the summer of 1897 was filled with drills and evolutions ranging from Portsmouth, New Hampshire to Hampton Roads, Virginia and the southern drill grounds. A series of visits to the Brooklyn Navy Yard and its dry docks resulted in additional modifications and repairs to the turret machinery, hull, propellers, propeller shafts, yard arms, and outboard delivery pipes. At the end of September, 1897 the ship's bow and stern torpedo tubes were removed as they had been found to be "practically useless" and "a danger to the vessel" – a lesson the Spanish would soon learn at Santiago.

The *Texas* then steamed to Boston to attend the centennial celebration of the launch of the USS *Constitution*, held on October 17th, 1897. On the 18th Captain W. C. Wise of the Texas turned over his command to Captain John W. Philip.

Capt. Phillip, also a Civil War veteran, had been assigned to the USS *Constitution* as a midshipman in early 1861, meteorically rising to the rank of Lieutenant in just over a year.

At Boston the boiler of the *Texas'* steam launch exploded while the boat was alongside the ship. The ship's surgeon, Dr. W. R. Dubose had two teeth knocked out and two other officers and several men were slightly injured.

The crew of the *Texas* at the aft 6" gun. The tubing framework over the hatch held a canvas awning and was quickly removable. Visible in both photographs is the ship's dog, a rat terrier named Daisy. Ship's dogs were common in the Navy. Daisy met her end in combat, dying on deck during the *Texas*' bombardment of Santiago.

October 1897 - Feb 1898: The officers of the *Texas* gather at the forward 6" gun. Officers present include: Captain John Woodward Philip, Lt. Commander Giles Bates Harber, Lt. Lewis Cass Heilner, Lt. Harry Phelps, Lt. Francis J. Haeseler, Lt. Harrison Augustus Bispham, Lt. j.g. Mark Lambert Bristol, Ensign William Kern Gise, Naval Cadet Alfred Warren Pressy, Naval Cadet William Herbert Reynolds, Naval Cadet Frederic Ralph Holman, Naval Cadet Robert William Henderson, Naval Cadet Morris Hamilton Brown, Naval Cadet Henry Tutweiler Wright, Naval Cadet Guy William Faller, Surgeon Clement Biddle, Asst. Surgeon Harold Hamilton Haas, Paymaster John Slaughter Carpenter, Chief Engineer Alexander Berry Bates, Passed Assistant Engineer Kenneth McAlpine, Assistant Engineer Chester Wells, Assistant Engineer Alfred Watson Hinds, Chaplain William Harry Jones, 1st Lt. of Marines Cyrus S. Radford, Boatswain John Francis Brooks, Gunner Francis Martin, Carpenter Ellis Washington Craig. Captain Philip is seated directly in front of the ship's dog, Daisy.

In January of 1898 the Atlantic Fleet, including the *Texas*, gathered at Hampton Roads in preparation for winter maneuvers.

These evolutions were to be held at the southern drill ground centering on Key West, Florida. Maneuvers this close to the coast of Cuba had been avoided since the elevation of tensions with Spain in the preceding years, but it was decided to resume use of the traditional practice zone so that U.S. ships would be in the area to protect United States interest and citizens in Cuba as well as to interdict filibuster expositions attempting to reach the island from the U.S.

The USS *Texas* was subsequently ordered to rendezvous with the USS *Maine* and USS *Indiana* at Dry Tortugas. The *Maine* was to take the ship's boys from both vessels on her cruise. Immediately after the *Maine's* arrival the thirty nine boys from the *Indiana* transferred to the *Maine* but the eighteen boys on the *Texas* were instructed to wait until the next day. That night the *Maine* was ordered to Havana, at the request of U.S. counsel-general there, General Fitzhugh Lee. The boys remained aboard the *Texas*, much to their disappointment at having missed a Caribbean cruise to exotic Cuba.

The *Texas* proceeded in company with the USS *Nashville* to Galveston, arriving on February 15, 1898.

The *Texas* in late 1897 – early 1898

The evening of February 15, 1898 the USS *Maine* exploded in the harbor at Havana, Cuba, sending 266 officers and men to their deaths. Learning of the event from reporters in Galveston the next day, Captain Philip of the *Texas* stated. "I cannot see how an explosion on board the *Maine* would be possible. Neither can I imagine the possibility that a torpedo was exploded under the *Maine*. It is unreasonable that any one would have done such a thing, and thereby incur the enmity of the whole world."

On February 23rd the *Texas* departed Galveston, bound for Florida, Hampton Roads and finally the Brooklyn Navy yard to be refit for possible combat actions.

The *Texas* docked in Brooklyn – probably February, 1898.

12 PREPARING FOR WAR: FEBURARY – APRIL 1898

The United States Navy, thanks to the fevered preparations of bellicose administrators and politicians including Assistant Secretary of the Navy Theodore Roosevelt, found itself able to get on a war footing in a comparatively short period of time. Naval thinkers had no doubt that sea power would ultimately determine the outcome of the conflict. Captain Alfred Thayer Mahon's exponents stressed the need for control of the sea through the concentration of force into powerful fleets, while local politicians from up and down the East Coast clamored in the halls of the capitol in Washington for a warship to be sent to their home waters to provide naval protection for each of their coastal towns. As US naval vessels concentrated from all points of the globe, they coalesced into powerful squadrons capable of executing the new naval strategies recently developed and espoused by Mahon.

In a contemporary illustration, a portion of the US fleet gathers off the East Coast as the world prepares to receive the results of the investigations into the loss of the *Maine* and the subsequent debates in Washington and Seville that would determine the fate of nations. Pictured above are the vessels of the "Flying Squadron" comprised of the *Texas*, *Brooklyn* (flagship), *Minneapolis*, *Columbia*, and *Massachusetts*.

THE IMPROVED TURRETS OF THE BATTLESHIP *TEXAS*.

In an article printed in *Scientific American* and the *Proceedings of the United States Naval Institute* after the war, R. W. Henderson of the USS *Texas* wrote, "the efficiency of her large guns is due chiefly to the improvements on her turrets, instigated by Lieut. F. J. Haeseler… The turrets, ammunition hoists, and rammers are all worked by hydraulic power, the engines being of the three cylinder Brotherhood type. The power is furnished by four powerful hydraulic pumps, all the machinery being inside the armored redoubt.

When the *Texas* went into commission, it was impossible to load these 12-inch guns except in two positions, pointed directly ahead or directly abeam, the rammers for these two positions being outside the turrets. When firing in intermediate positions, it was necessary to train the gun off the target to load, picking the target up again after loading. This consumed much time, the interval between two shots from the same gun being at that time about seven minutes…"

"…Lieut. Haeseler advanced the idea of carrying a light but strong telescopic rammer inside, which was to revolve with the turret, thus enabling the gun's crew to load from any position. To accomplish this it was necessary, besides securing a strong rammer that could be easily handled, to change the lead of many of the hydraulic pipes, secure a "change" or "balance pressure" valve, and to devise a means of loading inside the turret. A "balance pressure" valve that could be used as a supply, exhaust, and reversing valve was obtained by a slight modification of a "Sellers" valve, and the

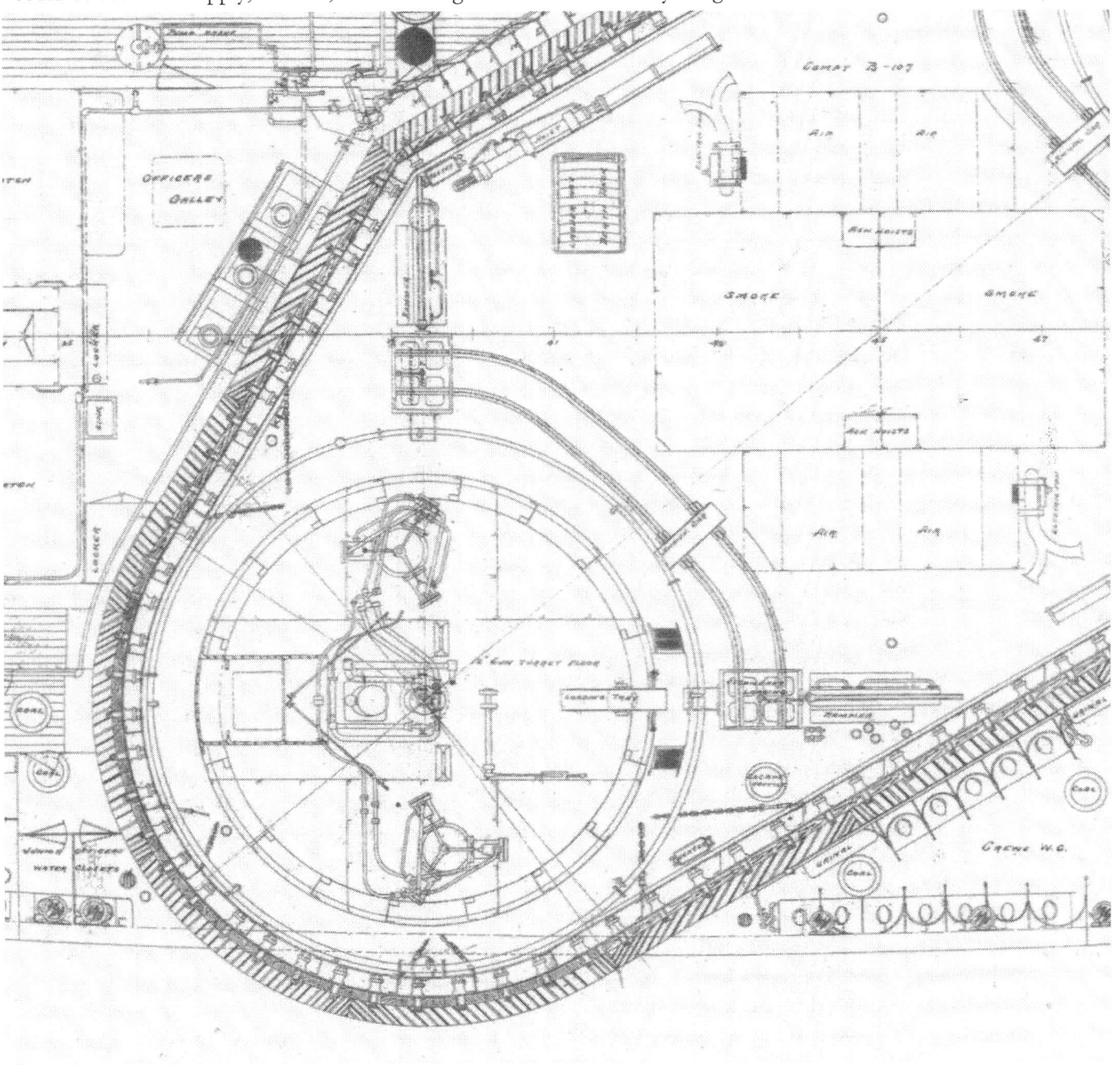

THE IMPROVED TURRETS AND THE AMMUNITION HOISTS OF THE BATTLESHIP TEXAS.—[See page 190.]

hydraulic plant was changed accordingly. Immediately behind the breech of the gun, when level, a strong but light telescopic rammer was balanced on trunnions, which permitted its being raised or lowered into working position by one man.

The next problem was to devise a means of transporting the 12-inch shell, which weighs 850 pounds, from the ammunition hoist outside the turret to the breech of gun, as formerly they were hoisted into a loading position forward of the stationary rammers. A circular track carrying a small traveling car was placed entirely around the turret inside the redoubt and a grooved table was put just inside the turret opening. When a shell was sent up from the ammunition room below, it was whipped by a chain strap and differential pulley into the traveling car, run around to the turret opening by one man, and shoved into the stationary table.

Inside the turret another ammunition lift was placed, running by hydraulic power, and fixed so that in its upper position the shell table on it was level with the bore of the gun in its loading position. One man pushes the shell into the shell table; the powder, which is in four sections, is

placed in stands beside the shell; the car is hoisted; the shell and powder are run home by the rammer, and the car lowered for another charge. A small loading platform, working on hinges and secured by a hook, was placed under the breech of the gun, to allow a man to wipe out the powder chamber after the gun has been fired…"

"The crew of the *Texas* showed their appreciation of his services by presenting Mr. Haeseler with a beautiful gold watch with the following inscription: " Presented to Lieut. F. J. Haeseler by the crew of the *Texas*, in appreciation of his services in creating the 'Old Hoodoo' into the 'New Hero.'"

While the new loading system was being devised and installed, "…an interesting experiment was tried in regard to sighting the turret guns, which would have been very useful in case of accident to the regular sights. The gun is sighted by means of telescopic sights placed in hoods on each side of the breech, the officer in charge being in this hood and sighting gun. Ordinarily, in case this hood were to be demolished by a shot, the gunners would be unable to obtain anything like an accurate aim.

Through an aperture in the turret, near the gun, a small tube was placed which was laid exactly parallel with the bore of the gun. Cross wires were fitted in the ends of this tube for sighting. Near the elevating slide, at the side of the gun, an arc was fixed firmly, graduated in yards, and a pointer attached to the slide pointed out the yards on this arc, the accuracy of the arc having been tested by the regular sights. To aim the gun by this improvised sight, the gun was trained on the target by means of the fixed tube, and the gun was elevated or lowered until the pointer on the slide showed on the arc the number of yards indicated on the range finder. The test shots with these sights gave very accurate results." "This constituted the repairs that were made on the guns in the New York Navy Yard, and after preliminary drills the *Texas* went out beyond Cape Henry, at Old Point, to test the work. The result was even more than expected. A mean between the intervals of five shots was one minute and fifty-five seconds, a vast improvement on the old record, while one interval was as low as eighty-five seconds. The *Texas* returned to Old Point ready for whatever was to come, and her record during the late trouble showed how completely she can be relied upon."

Service History of the Officers of the USS Texas Who Served Aboard During the Spanish-American War, 1898:

Captain John Woodward Philip was born on August 26, 1840 in Kinderhook, N.Y. and raised in a Dutch-speaking home. Appointed to the Naval Academy on September 20, 1856, he narrowly avoided dismissal for excessive demerits resulting from high spirited though non-malicious behavior. Graduating in 1860, he began his service on the USS *Constitution* but was soon transferred to the USS *Santee*, then promoted to acting-master of the sloop of war USS *Marion* on duty with the Gulf Blockading Squadron. Shortly thereafter he was attached to the USS *Sonoma* of the James River Fleet. On July 16, 1862 Philip was commissioned a lieutenant and from September 1862 to January 1865 was executive officer of the steam gunboat USS *Chippewa*, screw sloop USS *Pawnee*, and the monitor *Montauk*, being actively involved in operations at the siege of Charleston. On July 16, 1863, in an action in which the *Pawnee* was struck forty-six times, he was wounded, being struck by splintered wood and knocked ten feet across the deck. Philip stood up and stayed in the action, firing one of the ships nine inch guns that had become partially disabled.

In 1865 he was made executive officer on the steam frigate USS *Wachusett* and began a three years cruise in the far East. Philip was a very well-balanced officer and, although deeply religious and a non-drinker (he had sworn off liquor while at Annapolis), he got along well both professionally and socially with his fellow officers. He was noted as an excellent navigator.

In 1867, he transferred to the steam frigate USS *Hartford* on the China station, as an executive officer. He later transferred to the steam frigate USS *Richmond* in the Mediterranean where for a brief time he served as navigator, but was soon elevated to executive officer.

Because of the Civil War Philip advanced to executive officer very quickly, but unlike others he maintained the position after the war by his merit, though considered young for the post. Philip developed a considerable reputation as an effective executive officer and was generally permitted to manage the ship's routine and discipline without interference from his captains. When Philip became captain of his own vessel, he was noted for following this same style of management with his own executive officers.

Philip's first command, in 1873, was the old side-wheeler USS *Monocacy*. He was commissioned a commander in December 1874, then from 1876 through 1884 he commanded the bark-rigged armed steamer USS *Adams*, the USS *Tuscarora*, and the iron hulled USS *Ranger*.

In 1884 he married at the age of 44 and fathered two children during a period in which he was assigned as Lighthouse Inspector of the 12th District. In 1887 he was placed in command in the receiving ship USS *Independence*. Commissioned captain March 31, 1889, he was given command of the steel cruiser USS *Atlanta* in 1890, but was reassigned to be the inspector of the armored cruiser *New York* that was then building. He was subsequently placed in command of the *New York* and was her captain until August 1894 when he was made captain of the Boston Navy Yard. He held that post until his appointment as captain of the USS *Texas* on October 17, 1897. Promoted to commodore September 1898 and rear-admiral on March 3, 1899, Philip died at his home at the Brooklyn Navy Yard on June 30, 1900 and is buried at the US Naval Academy Cemetery. Two destroyers have been named in his honor.

Lt. Cmdr. Giles Bates Harber, Executive Officer - Midshipman, 24 July, 1865. Graduated June, 1869. Ensign, 12 July, 1870. Master, 12 July, 1871. Lieutenant, 19 September, 1874. Commanded the Jeannette Search Expedition to Siberia. Lieutenant Commander, 4 September, 1896. Commander, 25 September, 1899. (Recognized by the US Congress and promoted five numbers for "conspicuous conduct in battle" for his service at Santiago) Naval attaché at Paris, France and St. Petersburg, Russia. Rear Admiral, 24 July, 1909. Commander of Atlantic Fleet. Commander of Pacific Fleet. President of the Naval Examining and Retiring Boards, 1911. Retired 24 September, 1912. Died 29 December 1926. Buried Arlington National Cemetery.

Lt. Lewis Cass Heilner, Navigator - Midshipman, 25 July, 1866. Graduated 7 June, 1870. Ensign, 13 July, 1871. Master, 27 September, 1873. Lieutenant, 2 June, 1879. Lieutenant Commander, 9 December, 1898. Rear Admiral 16 November 1909. Retired 29 January, 1911. Died 25 January, 1912. Buried Arlington National Cemetery.

Lt. Harry Phelps, Magazine Commander - Cadet Midshipman, 22 September, 1876. Graduated 22 June, 1882. Ensign, Junior Grade, 3 March, 1883. Ensign, 26 June, 1884. Author of <u>Practical Marine Surveying</u> 1889. Lieutenant, Junior Grade, 19 June, 1892. Lieutenant, 10 May, 1896. Commodore 30 June, 1911. Retired 30 June, 1911. Recalled to active duty 18 April 1918. Died 23 December 1919. Buried Arlington National Cemetery.

Lt. Francis Joy Haeseler, Starboard 12" Gun Commander - Cadet Midshipman, 22 September, 1876. Graduated 22 June, 1882. Ensign, Junior Grade, 3 March, 1883. Ensign, 26 June, 1884. Instructor US Naval Academy 1885-1889, 1892. Lieutenant, Junior Grade, 9 January, 1893. Lieutenant, 11 October, 1896. Died 20 October, 1900. Held several US patents on ordnance and rotary engines. Buried Arlington National Cemetery.

Lt. j.g. Harrison Augustus Bispham, Forward 6" Gun Commander – Born 10 February 1865 Philadelphia, Pa. Cadet Engineer/Naval Cadet, 1 October, 1881-1885. Ensign, 1 July, 1887. Lieutenant, Junior Grade, 4 May, 1896. Lieutenant, 3 March, 1899. Lt. Commander, 25 October 1908. Commander, 1911. Died 24 April 1960. Buried Arlington National Cemetery.

Lt. j.g. Mark Lambert Bristol, Port 12" Gun Commander - Naval Cadet, 19 May, 1883. Ensign, 1 July, 1889. Lieutenant, Junior Grade, 14 March, 1897. Lieutenant, 3 March, 1899. 1901 to 1903 aide to the Commander-in-Chief North Atlantic Fleet. Captain USS *Oklahoma* (BB-37) during World War I for which he received the Distinguished Service Medal. US High Commissioner in Turkey 1919-27. Rear Admiral commanding Asiatic Fleet 1927. Died 13 May 1939. Buried Arlington National Cemetery. Two US Navy destroyers have been named in his honor.

No Photo Available –
Ensign William Kern Gise,. Aft 6" Gun Commander - Naval Cadet, 14 June, 1889. Ensign, 1 July, 1895. Lieutenant, Junior Grade, 3 March, 1899. Lt. Commander 8 February 1907. Died Tutulia, Samoa 5 July, 1909.

Lt. Cyrus Sugg Radford, USMC Commander Secondary Battery Above Decks – Naval Cadet, 1885-1889. 2nd Lieutenant, 1891. Co-authored Handbook of Naval Gunnery 1898. Awarded Navy Cross for service as officer-in-charge of the supply depot at Philadelphia 1917-1918. Brigadier General 1929. Quartermaster-General of the Corps 1929. Resigned 1929. Died 19 January 1951. Buried Arlington National Cemetery.

Dr. William Richards DuBose, Surgeon – Born 12 September 1854, Sparta, Georgia. University of Georgia 1871-73, transferred to University of Virginia 1874, earning M.D. in 1875. Post-graduate studies with the Medical Department of the University of the City of New York. Commissioned Assistant Surgeon in the US Navy 1875. Served aboard a number of ships as well as at the Naval Academy. Bureau of Medicine and Surgery, 1903. Commander Yokahama Naval Hospital, Japan 1907. Commander Naval Medical Center Portsmouth, Va. 1909-1911. Naval Retiring Board, 1915. Commodore, Medical Corps. Died February 1937. Buried US Naval Academy Cemetery. Father of Rear Admiral William G. DuBose.

Rev. Harry W. Jones, Chaplain – Born 1865? YMCA minister 1886. Chaplain, US Navy 1896. Ordained in the Baptist Church 9 March 1893. PhD in Divinity Wake Forrest College 1899. M.A. Bucknell University 1900. Author of A Chaplain's Experience Ashore and Afloat: The "Texas" Under Fire (1901) and various social/religious works. Ordained in the Episcopal Church 13 November 1904. Court-martialed 1907 and discharged from the Navy for passing checks on an account with insufficient funds during a controversy between Navy chaplains. Subsequently pastor of churches of various denominations in the New York area and founder of the "People's Church" on Long Island in 1911. Volunteer lecturer/chaplain with the Salvation Army in France WWI. Last known residence in Los Angles, California, 1930.

At the Brooklyn Navy Yard final preparations were made to the *Texas* prior to her sailing to join the Flying Squadron forming at Hampton Roads. The ship was painted battleship gray, much of her woodwork was removed to reduce the risk of fire, and the ship was loaded with powder and ammunition.

An hour before the *Texas'* departure from Brooklyn, a woman visiting onboard asked for the captain, saying "I would like to shake hands with the captain of the *Texas*." Capt. Philip extended his hand as the woman continued, "I was the last person to shake hands with the captain of the *Huron* before she sailed, and wish to shake hands with you before you sail." As was well known to the officers of the *Texas*, the *Huron* had been lost with all hands within hours of leaving port. - Capt. Philip's reaction is unrecorded.

On Wednesday April 13th as the Flying Squadron lay in Hampton Roads, a signal gun was fired and the ships ordered to get underway for an undisclosed destination. Officers said their last goodbyes to their weeping wives bobbing in boats in the wake of the departing warships. Instead of battle there followed several days of battery and maneuver drills before the ships returned to Hampton Roads.

THE FLYING SQUADRON PERFORMING "SHIPS LEFT"—TAKEN FROM THE QUARTER-DECK OF THE FLAGSHIP "BROOKLYN."

No gladiator ever looked more fit for a combat than the Texas as she steamed into Hampton Roads and cast anchor with the flying squadron. The Texas and the Massachusetts are designed to do the heavy fighting, and it is figured that the new flying squadron is amply sufficient to oppose the one now coming from Cadiz. The machinery of the Texas was made by the Richmond Locomotive and Machine Works and has never given the least cause for complaint.

With her destiny clearly beckoning, the "Old Hoodoo" *Texas* began to attract a measure of respect from the press. Nevertheless this Richmond newspaper still felt the need to defend the quality of her locally-made machinery.

At Hampton Roads the ships of the Flying Squadron awaited their orders from the Navy Department in Washington to sail.

The *Texas* with the Flying Squadron at Hampton Roads (below left) and as seen in the distance from the deck of the USS *Minneapolis* (below right).

The Flying Squadron under Commodore Winfield S. Schley, consisting of the armored cruiser *Brooklyn* (flagship), battleships *Texas* and *Massachusetts*, and the protected cruisers *Columbia* and *Minneapolis*, as well as several auxiliary cruisers. Initially this squadron, independent from the North Atlantic Squadron, was intended to protect the US coast against an attack by the Spanish fleet.

One of the advantages that Spain had at the beginning of the war was simply the uncertainty of her fleet's mission. Most of the Spanish cruisers, individually comparable to second class battleships like the *Texas*, had good theoretical top speed and, had they had coal and other logistical matters effectively managed, they could have conducted a *guerre de course* off the US coast, tying up the entire US fleet and preventing it from conducting effective offensive operations while threatening the safety of any troop transports the US might consider sending to Cuba. The Spanish cruisers, in many cases, could outgun anything that could catch them in the open sea and their 11" guns could wreck havoc against an unprotected harbor or troop ship.

Port side view of the *Texas* as fitted out for war.

Starboard side view of the *Texas* as fitted out for war.

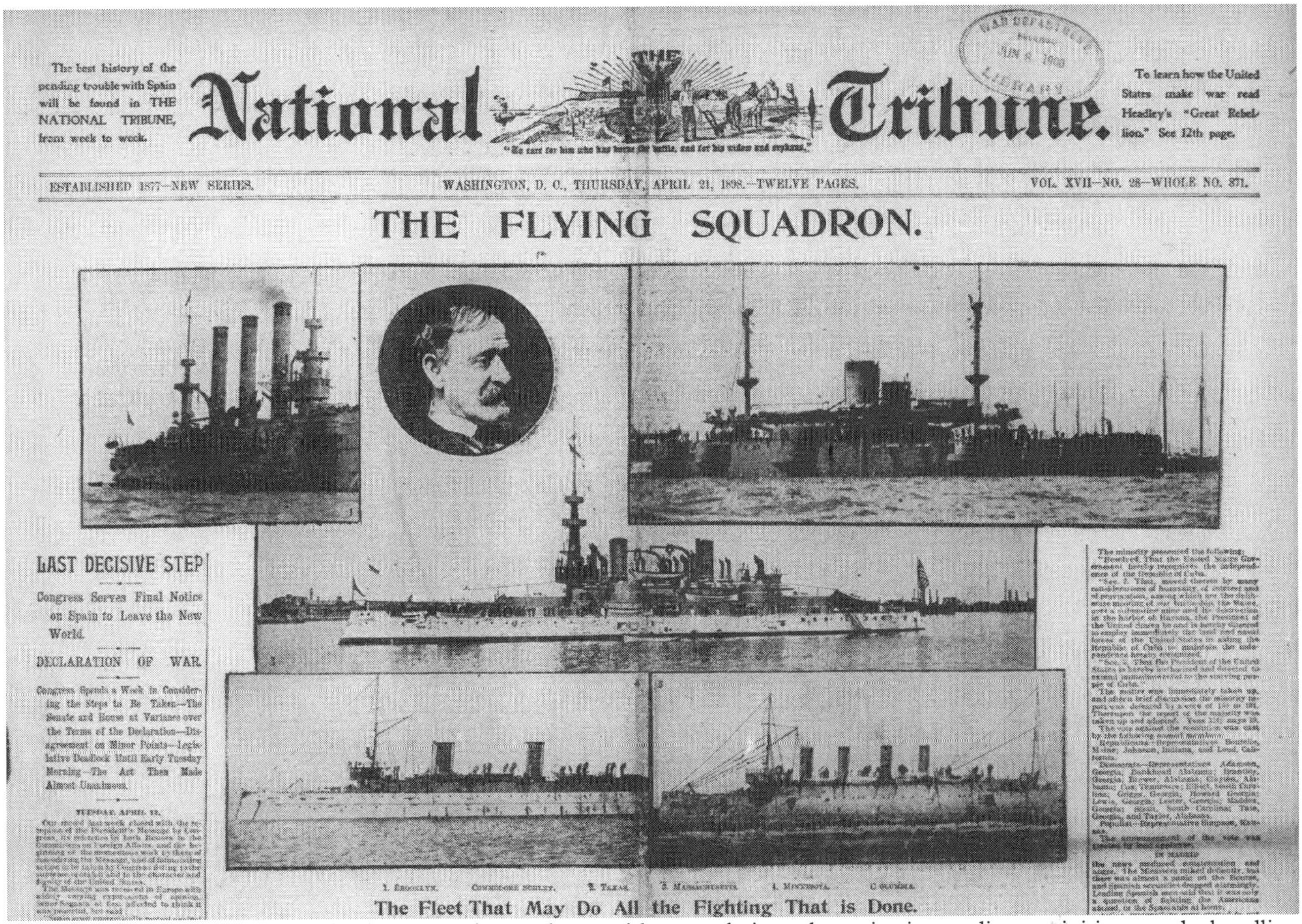

The best history of the pending trouble with Spain will be found in THE NATIONAL TRIBUNE, from week to week.

The National Tribune.

To learn how the United States make war read Headley's "Great Rebellion." See 12th page.

ESTABLISHED 1877—NEW SERIES. WASHINGTON, D. C., THURSDAY, APRIL 21, 1898.—TWELVE PAGES. VOL. XVII—NO. 28—WHOLE NO. 871.

THE FLYING SQUADRON.

1. BROOKLYN. COMMODORE SCHLEY. 2. TEXAS. 3. MASSACHUSETTS. 4. MINNEAPOLIS. 5. COLUMBIA.

The Fleet That May Do All the Fighting That is Done.

LAST DECISIVE STEP

Congress Serves Final Notice on Spain to Leave the New World.

DECLARATION OF WAR.

Congress Spends a Week in Considering the Steps to Be Taken—The Senate and House at Variance over the Terms of the Declaration—Disagreement on Minor Points—Legislative Deadlock Until Early Tuesday Morning—The Act Then Made Almost Unanimous.

TUESDAY, APRIL 12.

The minority presented the following:

The Flying Squadron's final preparations, along with speculation about its impending activities, made headline news across the nation.

The *Texas* sits at anchor behind the USS *Minneapolis*.

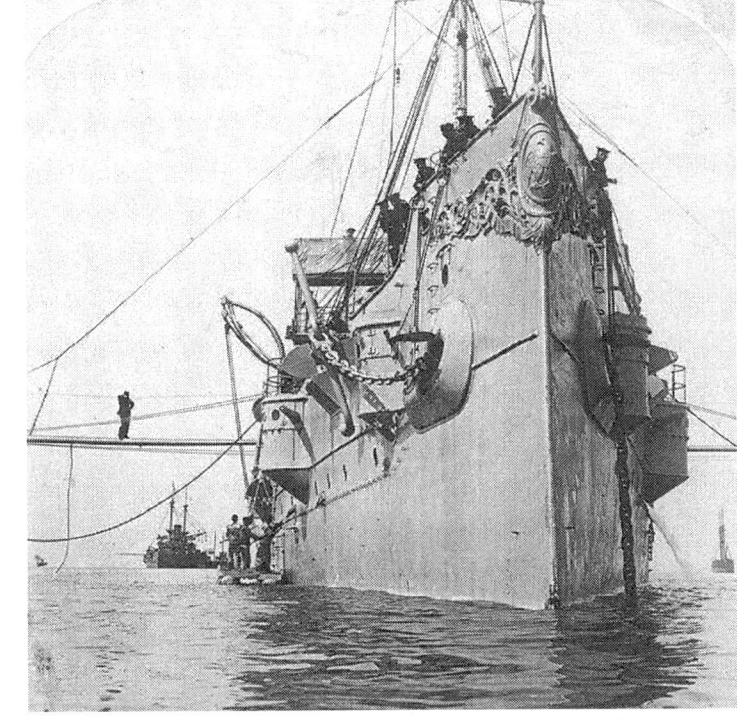

On April 24th, 1898 Spain, seeing the deteriorating diplomatic situation and facing strong internal pressures to defend Spanish honor, declared war on the United States. The U. S. responded with its own declaration of war against Spain the following day.

Hardly had the war begun when news was received of a major U.S. Navy victory against the Spanish naval forces at Manila Bay in the Philippines. Commodore Dewey, acting under orders from the Navy Department, had attacked and defeated the Spanish squadron in a one-sided victory that left him in de-facto control of the Philippine capitol. All he lacked, it appeared, were the Army forces needed to occupy the islands, a shortcoming quickly rectified as transports on the west coast of the U.S. were rapidly loaded and dispatched to his support.

On May 13th the "Flying Squadron" departed Hampton Roads for the last time, bound for Key West, Florida, a scant 90 nautical miles from the Cuban capitol Havana, the presumed destination of the Spanish fleet that had last been seen departing the Cape Verde Islands on April 30th.

Along her route to war the *Texas* exercised her guns as well as her crew. Lt. Haeseler commented, "On the way down to Key West and until we actually took the ship into battle the captain was most energetic and painstaking in carrying on drills, tending to fit us for action, and he showed his great tact and knowledge of human nature by not having useless, tiresome drills and inspections which could only kill the men's interest."

13 THE SPANISH FLEET: CUBA

SPAIN'S TORPEDO-BOAT FLOTILLA EN ROUTE FROM THE CANARIES TO PUERTO RICO.—By W. Louis Sonntag, Jr.

The *Cristobal Colon*, launched in 1896, was an Italian-built 6,800 ton armored cruiser of the Giuseppe Garibaldi class capable of 19 knots. She was fitted with a turret forward and another aft, each intended to carry a 254mm gun. As the photo of her empty turret reveals (below left) however, these were not installed prior to her deployment to Cuba, rendered her extremely vulnerable to combat with anything more powerful than a protected cruiser. She was armed with 10 x 152 mm (6 inch) guns; 6 x 120 mm guns, 10 x 57 mm guns, 10 x 37 mm guns, 2 machine guns, and 5 torpedo tubes. *Colon's* cruising range was 8,300 miles at 10 knots, using 1,000 tons of coal.

The gun deck of the *Colon* (above right). The *Colon's* 6 inch guns were made in Britain by Armstrong and fired a 105 pound shell using the new smokeless powder in a separate metallic cartridge. Modern and efficient, these guns significantly outclassed the 6 inch guns of the *Texas*.

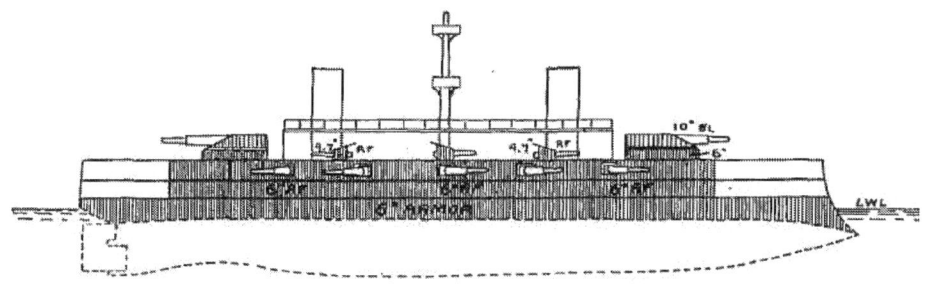

DIAGRAM OF GUNS AND ARMOR OF ARMORED CRUISER "CRISTOBAL COLON."

The Spanish had three 6,890 ton protected cruisers of the Maria Teresa Class: *Infanta Maria Teresa* (1890), *Vizcaya* (1891), and *Almirante Oquendo* (1891). Each was armed with 2 x 11" Hontoria guns in turrets fore and aft, 10 x 14cm Hontoria guns, 10 x 3pdr Hotchkiss guns, 8 x 37mm Hotchkiss guns, 6 submerged torpedo tubes, and 2 above-water tubes. Range was 9,700 nm on 1,050 tons of coal. These cruisers were built by La Sociedad Anonima de los Astilleros del Nervion, Bilbao, Spain.

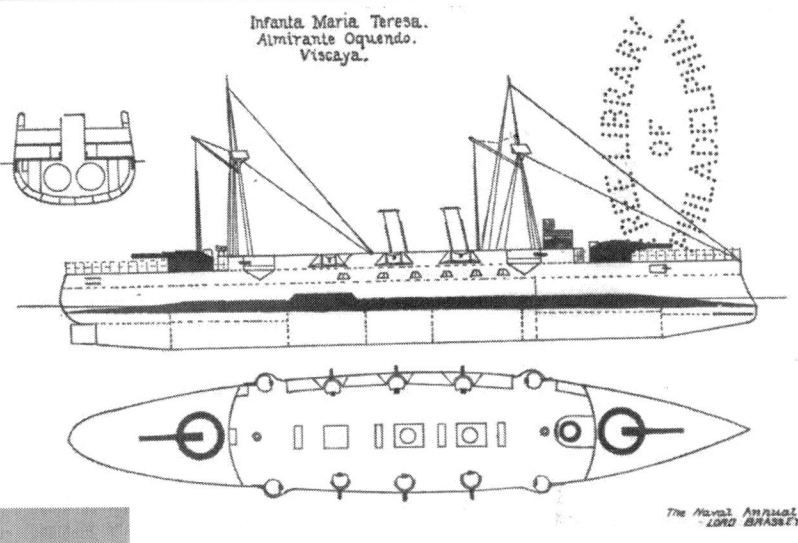

The three Spanish heavy cruisers were all theoretically capable of 20 knots. In action, however, inferior coal, and in the case of the *Vizcaya* a severely fouled bottom, lowered their speed to significantly less than that of the *Texas*.

The *Vizcaya* is seen here in New York taking on coal during her prewar visit to the United States.

The *Almirante Oquendo* seen alone prior to the war (above). The *Vizcaya* in the Canary Islands during her prewar trip to the United States and Cuba (below).

The 11" compound armor of these warships could not stop the larger shells of the American battleships at any range. However, they were imposing cruisers capable of absorbing significant damage.

Spanish sailors aboard the *Infanta Maria Teresa*. In battle, the wooden decks and upper works proved dangerously prone to fire.

The *Vizcaya* (above) during her good will call at New York in February 1898.

Upon arrival on the 18th her officers were informed of the USS *Maine* tragedy. For security reasons she was anchored off the Tompkinsville Naval Station where police boats guarded her without incident until she departed on February 25th.

Views of the *Vizcaya* (below and right).

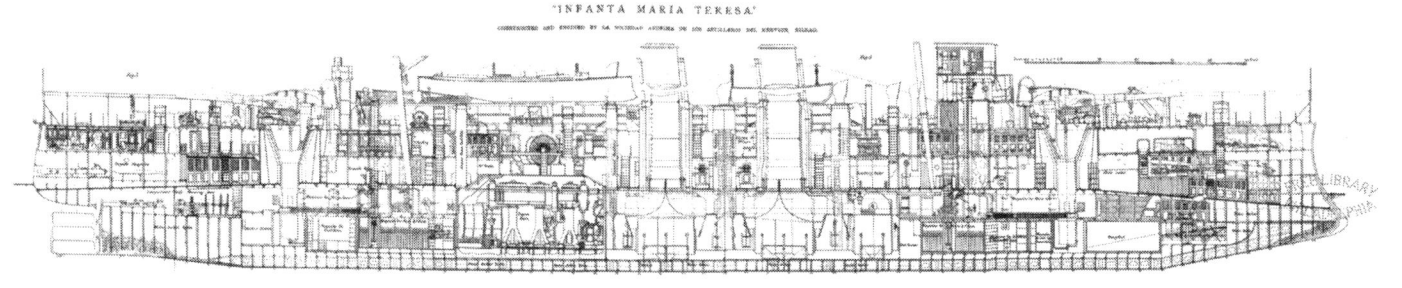

"INFANTA MARIA TERESA."
CONSTRUCTED AND ENGINED BY LA SOCIEDAD ANONIMA DE LOS ASTILLEROS DEL NERVION, BILBAO.

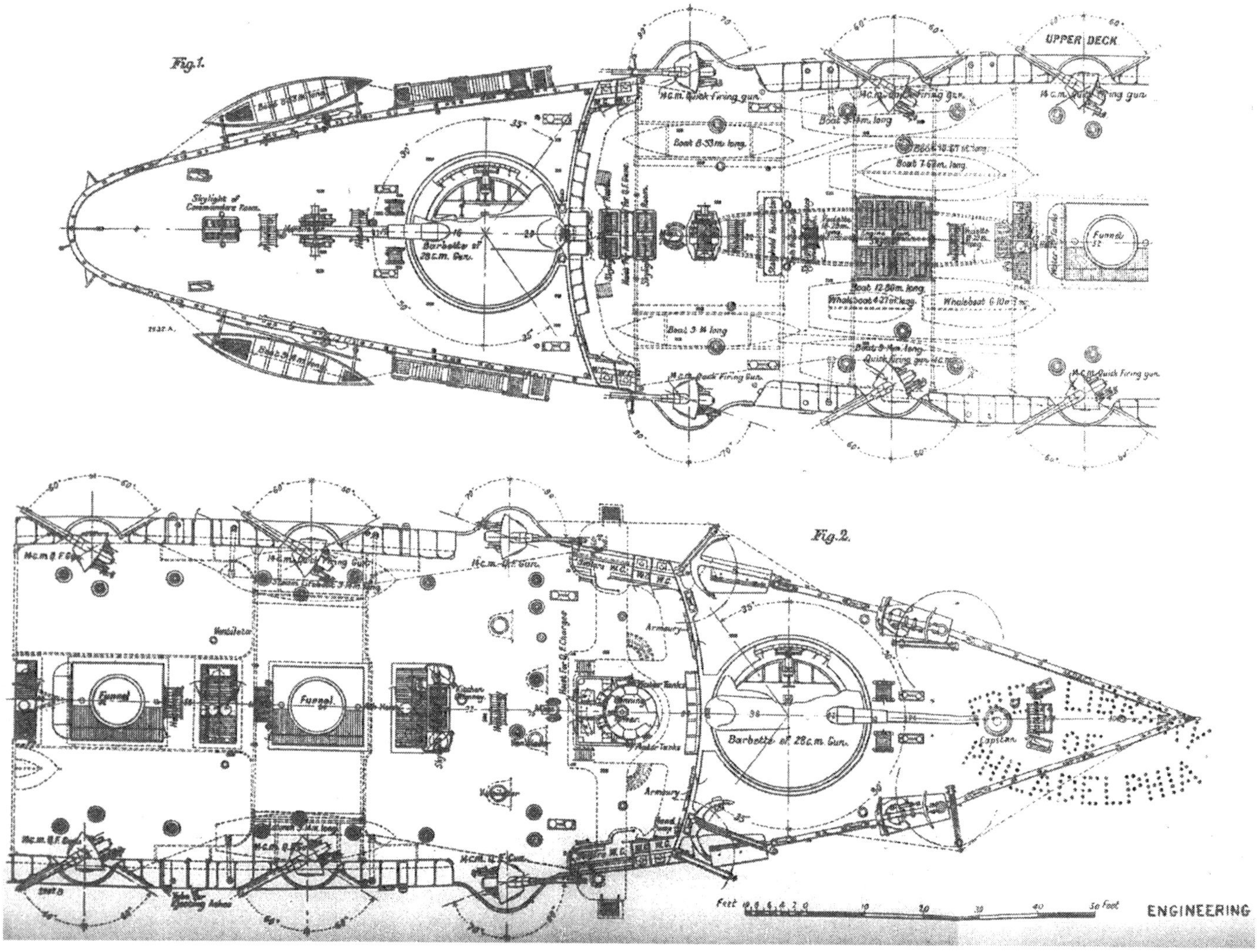

GENERAL ARRANGEMENT OF THE MACHINERY OF THE SPANISH CRUISER "INFANTA MARIA TERESA."
CONSTRUCTED BY LA SOCIEDAD ANONIMA DE LOS ASTILLEROS DEL NERVION, BILBAO.

The Maria Teresa class warships were each equipped with two triple-expansion steam engines delivering a total of 13,700 hp, driving the vessels at a top speed of 20 knots. Note that these ships were originally designed to carry 3rd class torpedo boats on their decks but, as in the case of the USS *Texas*, this was not done.

The forward 11" Hontoria gun on the *Vizcaya*. These turrets featured heavy, vertical barbette armor to resist large caliber shells with a thin, sloped top designed to protect the crew from light rapid fire guns and the elements. In practice the covers proved to be shell traps and most navies eventually discarded them. Armored turrets, although adding much weight, supplanted barbette mounts by the mid 1890's.

Gun crews at practice with their rapid-fire 14cm Hontoria guns on a Maria Teresa class cruiser. The ten 14cm 5.5" Hontoria guns per ship mounted on the *Maria Teresa*, *Oquendo*, and *Vizcaya* were these vessels' most effective weapons, with a very high theoretical rate of fire for the 78 pound shell firing from a fixed cartridge. The 14cm guns were mounted atop the main deck behind light shields which rotated with the guns. The fore and aft-most pairs of guns projected out from the sides of the hull in sponsons in order to maximize their fields of fire. Note the cartridges and shells being carried to the guns using dollies. Even at close range the shells of these guns could not penetrate battleship armor but they could cause significant damage to unprotected areas of the ship.

The planked, angled objects visible in the deck above are the bottoms of the ship's boats. Like on the USS *Texas*, the ship's boats were carried in cradles on an open-framed bridge deck located above the main deck. Note the boat's recognizable form in the shadow it casts onto the deck below.

Unfortunately, these guns had been recently converted from bag loading to cartridge loading prior to the equipping of these ships for war and all the "bugs" had not been worked out. Initial problems with bad extractors had to some extent been alleviated, but many of the metallic cartridge cases themselves proved defective, sticking in the chamber. The problem had been recognized before the advent of war, however, only 100 improved cartridge cases had been delivered to the three ships, leaving a scant 33 reliable rounds per ship. in the initial action of the Battle of Santiago these guns gave good service, but as soon as the improved ammunition gave out, which was in minutes, the Spanish gun crews immediately experienced trouble operating their weapons effectively. Many guns were silenced and the rate of fire dropped rapidly as crews struggled with defective ammunition often sticking in the breech.

Close-up photo of a Spanish 14 cm gun. Compare this photo to the detail plan on the following page and note that the gun in this instance differs somewhat from the plan in that both the elevating and traversing gear are on the left side of the mount.

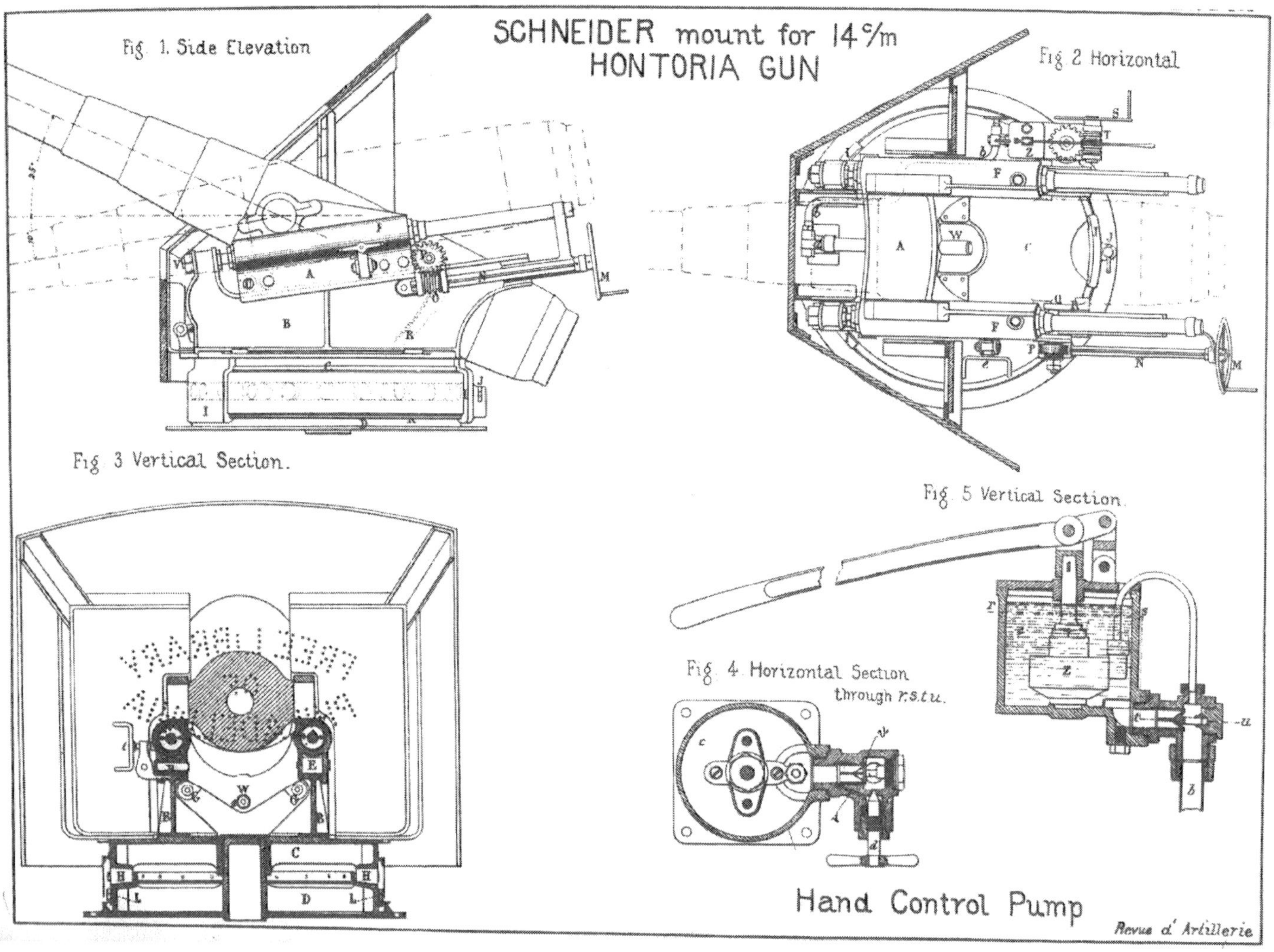

14 cm Hontoria gun as carried by the Maria Teresa class cruisers.

Shells being manufactured at the Cartegena Arsenal in Spain. Manufacturing problems with ammunition would prove disastrous in battle.

Spanish automotive torpedoes being assembled and maintained in the Cartegena Arsenal, Spain, prior to the outbreak of hostilities. Despite their great promise as giant killers, the torpedo not only failed to level the field between the fleets, it proved a vulnerable Achilles heel as it sat in its exposed launch tube.

Torpedo recovered from the wreck of the *Almirante Oquendo* after the battle. This particular torpedo subsequently found its way to the showroom of the Bannermans surplus store in New York.

Referred to in the press at the time as "torpedo boats," the *Furor*, *Pluton*, and *Terror* were in fact among the first generation of torpedo boat *destroyers*. The destroyer class of light warships was developed in Spain and England during the late 19th Century in direct response to the threat posed by small torpedo boats, the first such vessel *El Destructor* (1887) being designed by the innovative Spanish naval officer Fernando Villaamil. Light and fast but large enough to operate effectively with the fleet at sea, this new class of vessels went on to largely supplant the role of the small torpedo boat. These three Spanish destroyers were built by the Thomson yard in Clydebank, Scotland. The *Furor*, seen in the photo above, was completed on November 21, 1896. On her deck Villaamil would meet his death during the naval battle of at Santiago in 1898.

The *Pluton*, seen at right with her auxiliary sailing masts erected, was completed on November 4, 1897.

During the blockade of Santiago, *Furor* and *Pluton* were a constant source of concern to the US Fleet. One torpedo from these small vessels was quite capable of sinking a battleship of the period. Their presence forced the US Navy ships to maintain a heightened state of alert, requiring them to keep their portholes closed during the blockade, causing significant stress and heat fatigue in the blockading fleet.

The *Terror* was completed on November 20, 1896. Mechanical problems kept the *Terror* from reaching Cuba with Cervera's squadron. Detached at Martinique, she saw action on June 22, 1898 against US Navy ships blockading Puerto Rico. Damaged by the converted cruiser USS *St. Paul* to the extent that she had to be beached, repairs were completed in time for her to steam back to Spain on September 14, 1898, after the end of hostilities.

Armament of these destroyers consisted of 2 x 12 pdrs, 2 x 6 pdrs, 2 x 1 pdrs, and two torpedo tubes. Their twin engines developed 6,000 hp and drove them to 28 knots. They carried a coal capacity of 100 tons.

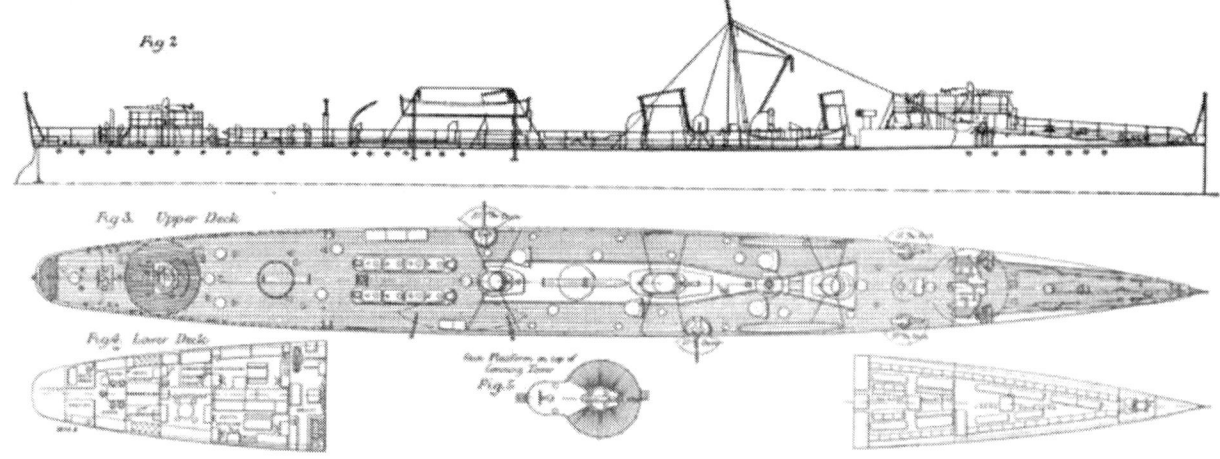

THE SPANISH TORPEDO BOAT DESTROYERS FUROR AND TERROR.

The *Reina Mercedes* was launched on September 12, 1887 at Cartagena, Spain. By the time of the Spanish-American War she had served 5 years in Cuban waters and was in desperate need of a refit, with only three of her ten boilers serviceable. She was rigged for sail as well as steam and was rated as being capable of 9 knots.

The *Reina Mercedes'* armaments consisted of six 16 cm Hontoria guns, two guns of 7-10 cm, ten rapid fire guns, and torpedoes.

The *Reina Mercedes* was not originally part of Cervera's Squadron, but she was in the harbor at Santiago when the squadron arrived. Her slow speed and the poor condition of her machinery precluded any attempt by her to leave the harbor with the more modern vessels of the squadron, however throughout the siege she supported the land batteries near the entrance of the harbor and took many hits from the US fleet as result.

During the blockade and siege of Santiago, four of her 16 cm (6.3 inch) guns were removed and emplaced in the shore defenses of Santiago. Two of her guns mounted on the Socapa battery proved to be the most effective Spanish shore guns in the campaign, hitting the *Texas* on June 6, 1898.

Reina Mercedes used her two remaining 16 cm guns and her torpedoes against the *Merrimack* during that vessels attempt to bottle up the Spanish fleet and she was heavily engaged with the *Texas* and *Massachusetts* in her own subsequent attempt to block the harbor. Raised after the war, she served the US Navy for over fifty years as a station ship at Annapolis.

The Spanish navy employed a number of gunboats along the coast of Cuba. Twenty-five of these gunboats were built in 1895 by Thompson & Co. in Clydebank, Scotland for the Spanish government in response to escalating tensions between the US and Spain over the revolution underway in Cuba. The primary use of these small vessels was to interdict gun runners operating between Florida, or US-flagged civilian vessels, and the Cuban revolutionaries. They also contributed gunfire support for Spanish actions ashore.

The *Alvarado* (above left), based at Santiago, and the *Sandoval* (center left), based at Guantanamo Bay, were 108 ton steel hulled sisters. The 137 horsepower engines propelled these craft to over 12 knots. Each gunboat carried one 57mm Nordenfelt cannon and one 37mm Maxim. Both vessels took part in the mining of the channels at their respective bases. *Alvarado* saw action against a cable cutting attempt by the USS *Wompatuck* on the night of May 16, 1898 and participated in patrols at the mouth of Santiago Bay during the blockade. She also removed six Spanish mines the night before Cevera's attempted escape from the harbor. *Sandoval* also saw action against a cable cutting incursions first by the USS *Wompatuck* and USS *St. Louis* and later by the same vessels acting with the USS *Marblehead*, after which the *Sandoval* retired to the upper reaches of Guantanamo Bay. Both vessels were captured prior to the cessation of hostilities and commissioned into the US Navy.

The *Diego Velazquez* (below left) was a 200 ton steel hulled vessel of 228 horsepower with a 12.5 knot maximum speed. She carried two 57mm Nordenfelt cannon and two 37mm Maxim guns. *Velazquez* operated from Cienfuegos, Cuba and saw action during the war against the USS *Yankee*. The *Velazquez* attempted to return to Spain after the conflict but ended up in Martinique where she was sold to Venezuela.

Cevera's squadron at the Cape Verde Islands during the period of March 14th – April 30th, 1898. By Mahon's doctrines, while it remained at the Cape Verde Islands, this squadron served as a "fleet in being", tying the hands of the stronger US fleet by its mere existence and its theoretical ability to appear at any point from Puerto Rico to Cuba - or even off the East Coast of the United States.

Despite Admiral Cevera's strong personal misgivings about the wisdom of seeking a direct confrontation with the US Navy, acting on orders from the Spanish civilian government, Cevera's squadron left the Cape Verde Islands on April 30th. True to Mahon's theories, until the Spanish squadron's destination could be determined, the US was unable to embark troops for its planned invasion of Cuba and was forced by domestic political pressure to keep its "Flying Squadron", including the USS *Texas*, in home waters.

The torpedo boat destroyer *Terror* or *Furor* at the Cape Verde Islands.

Colon (left) and *Vizcaya* (right) at St. Vincent in the Cape Verde Islands, March-April 1898.

Vizcaya and *Maria Teresa* in Santiago Bay, Cuba 1898.

Reserve / Camara's Squadron: A Threat in Being 1898

Andes   Proserpina   Osado   Pelayo, flagship
THE SPANISH RESERVE SQUADRON, UNDER COMMAND OF ADMIRAL CÁMARA, ON ITS WAY TO PORT SAID.—Drawn by L. A. Shafer

The remaining modern ships of the Spanish Fleet, her reserve, were lead by the battleships *Pelayo* and *Carlos V* under Rear Admiral Manuel de la Camara. This fleet was initially held ready to defend the coast of Spain from depredations of US warships and to threaten US shipping in the Atlantic. As a fleet in being, it remained a threat to US Navy plans.

The Battle of Manila Bay on May 1, 1898 changed the Spanish plans, however. In that battle, the American Asiatic squadron under Admiral Dewey, made up of light cruisers and spearheaded by the protected cruiser *Olympia*, overwhelmed the outdated and weak cruisers and gunboats of the Spanish Philippines fleet. Once the news of the outcome of the Battle of Manila Bay was received, the Spanish determined that an attempt should be made to retrieve the situation in the Philippines by sending Camera's reserve fleet through the Suez Canal to confront the American cruisers.

"Patria."   "Rapido."   "Alfonso XIII."   "Emperador Carlos V."   "Giralda."   "Pelayo."   "Proserpina."   "Osado."
ADMIRAL CAMARA'S SHIPS ON THE WAY TO MANILA

The *Pelayo* was the only battleship in the Spanish navy. Built and launched by Forges et Chanters, at La Seyne, France on February 5, 1887, her design, even more so than that of the USS *Texas*, was considered outdated, being a combination broadside and turret ship and being rigged for sails as well as steam. She was propelled to a maximum speed of 16 knots by a pair of engines developing 9,600 hp.

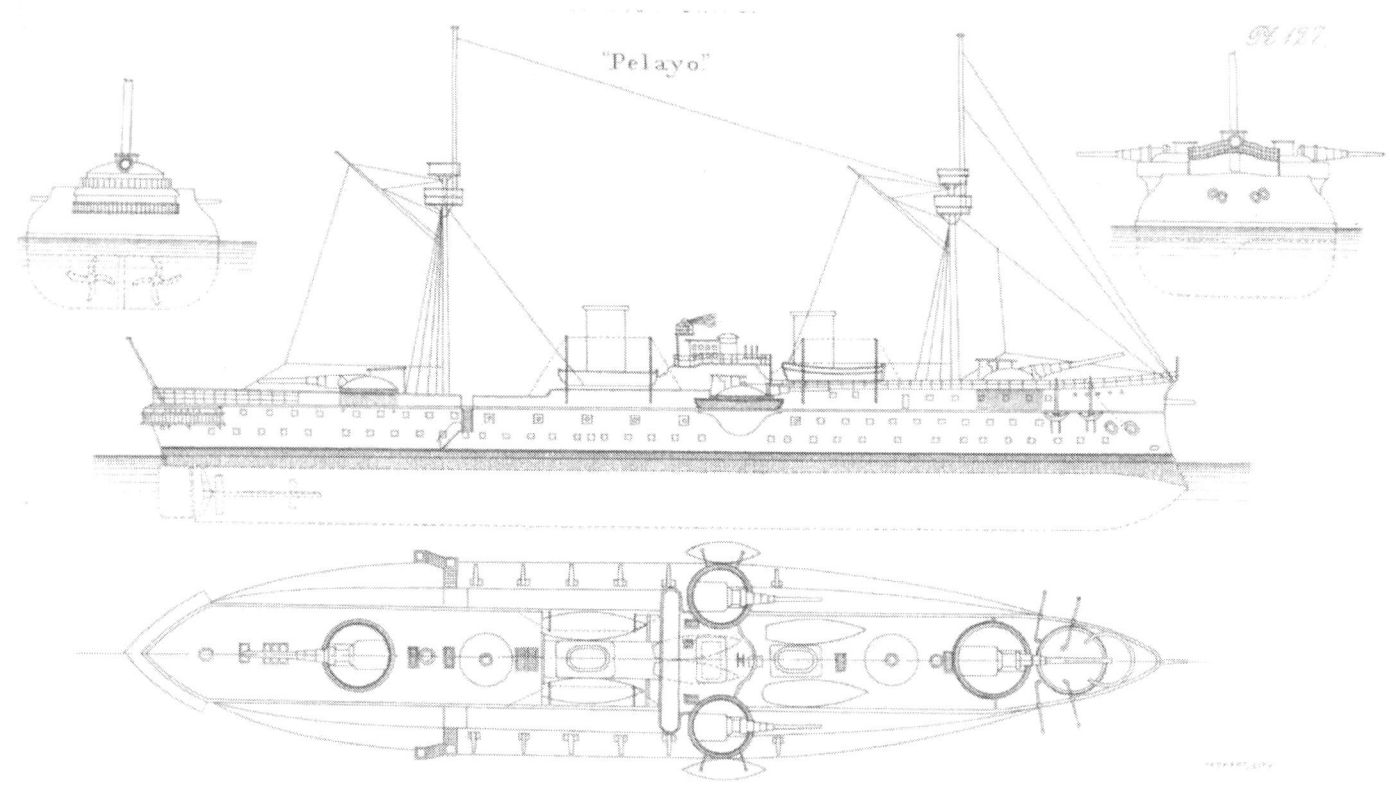

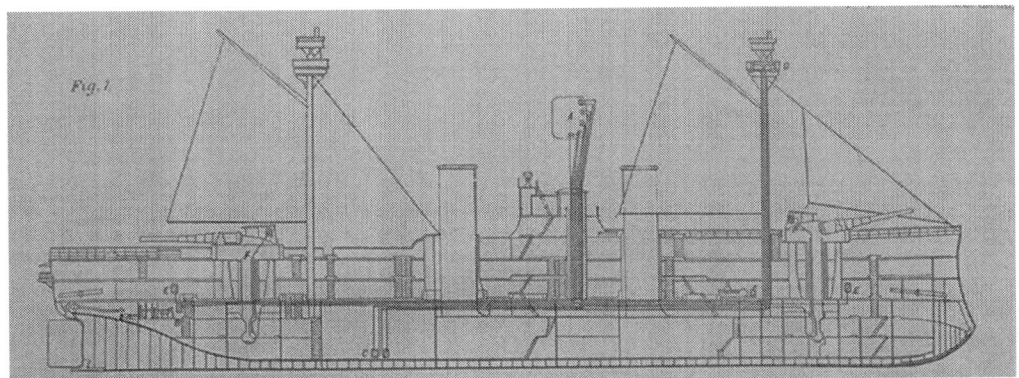

The 9,745 ton *Pelayo* was under refit at La Seyne, France when the war broke out, requiring that the work be rushed to completion. As result, she was launched without her new secondary armament of nine 5.5 inch guns, her original secondary armament having been removed. *Pelayo* had 11" belt armor, 12" barbette armor, and a 2.75" armored deck. In addition *Pelayo* had received 3" of new Harveyized armor for her midships battery during her reconstruction.

HONTORIA CHASE GUN OF "PELAYO."—6.29 INCHES CALIBER.

As equipped during the Spanish-American War, the *Pelayo* had 2 x 12 ½" guns in turrets fore and aft, 2 x 11" guns in turrets on each side amidships, 1 x 16 cm Hontoria gun, 12 x 12 cm guns (some sources state 9 x 14 cm guns), 5 x 6 pdrs, machine guns, and seven torpedo tubes. The *Pelayo* carried 800 tons of coal and had a range of 3000nm at 10 knots.

The *Emperador Carlos V* was constructed in Cadiz, Spain and completed in June of 1898. Classified by the Spanish as a 1st class battleship, she was actually an armored cruiser. The *Carlos V* was the largest warship built in Spain until that time, but many of her major components were produced at shipyards and armories across Europe, a fact that delayed her completion.

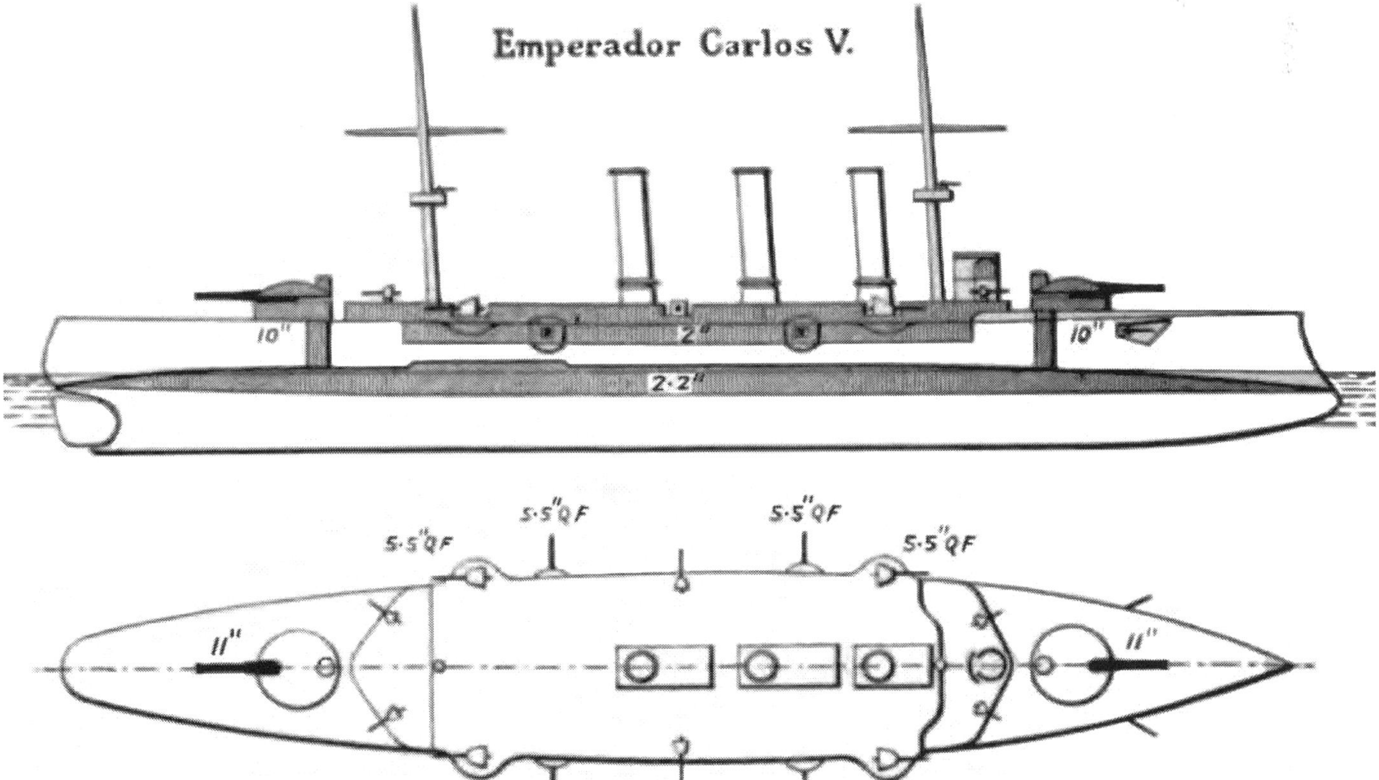

Not fully operational at the outbreak of hostilities with the United States, the *Carlos V* was never-the-less attached to Camara's Squadron. Armaments included 2 x 28 cm guns in turrets fore and aft, 8 x 14 cm guns, 4 x 10 cm guns, 2 x 70 mm guns, 2 x 55 mm guns, and 6 torpedo tubes. The Carlos V had only a thin 2" belt armor, 9" armored barbettes, and 6" deck armor, but had much greater coal capacity than other Spanish capital ships.

The large auxiliary cruisers *Patriota* (former Hamburg-Amerika Line Normannia, left) and *Rapido* (former Hamburg-Amerika Line Columbia, below) were passenger liners purchased by the Spanish government and converted into commerce raiders. While potentially useful in that role or as fast transports, they would be of little use in a naval battle.

These ships were photographed in Port Said, Egypt in 1898.

The modern 400-ton torpedo boat destroyers *Audaz* (left) and *Proserpina* (below), both built in Scotland and completed in 1897, as seen in Port Said, Egypt in 1898.

The remaining vessels making up Camara's Squadron were "auxiliary cruiser" transports. They included the *Buenos Aires* (1887, left), the *Colon* (1885-85, below), the *Covadonga* (1883-85, below left), and the *Isla de Panay* (1882, bottom) seen here at Port Said, Egypt in 1898.

Significantly delayed by neutrality laws enforced by Egypt and the well considered purchase by American agents of existing coal stockpiles along the projected route of the Spanish fleet, the warships moved slowly, taking a week to transit the Suez Canal, from June 26 to July 2 before news of the decisive naval Battle of Santiago was received. On July 7th the fleet was hastily recalled to defend the coast of Spain. US Navy actions had virtually eliminated the Spanish naval presence in the Philippines and Caribbean which had existed for over three hundred years.

Photos of the *Carlos V* (left) and the *Pelayo* (below) at Port Said, Egypt in 1898.

14 SEEK THE ENEMY: MAY-JUNE, 1898

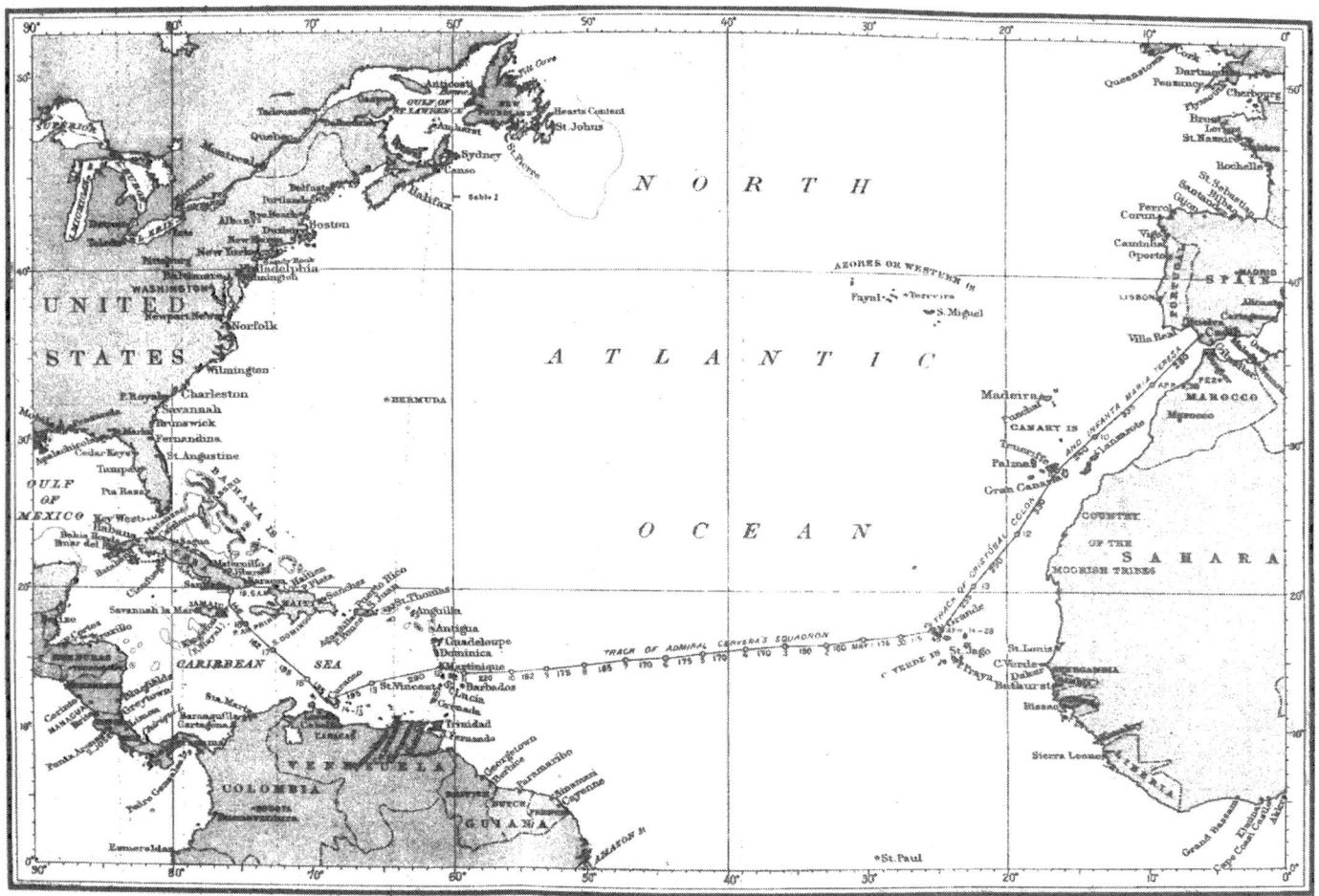

On April 14th, the main elements Admiral Cevera's fleet organized at the Cape Verde Islands, the *Cristobal Colon* and *Maria Teresa* having come southwestward from Cadiz, Spain and the *Vizcaya* and *Oquendo* all the way from Puerto Rico. (*Vizcaya* having just returned from her unfortunately timed "good will" call to New York.) Immediately, logistic problems developed for the Spanish with once-abundant coal now suddenly hard to find. On August 29th, the fleet sailed for the West Indies, heading first to Martinique where the fleet's destroyers scouted for coal and news of American naval movements. It was at Martinique in the second week of May that the Spanish fleet learned of the disastrous results of the May 1st battle of Manila Bay. The torpedo boat destroyer *Terror*, suffering problems with her machinery, was detached to Puerto Rico for repairs. The remaining ships of the fleet touched at Curacao on May 14-15, then cruised directly northwest between Haiti and Jamaica to arrive in Santiago, Cuba on May 19.

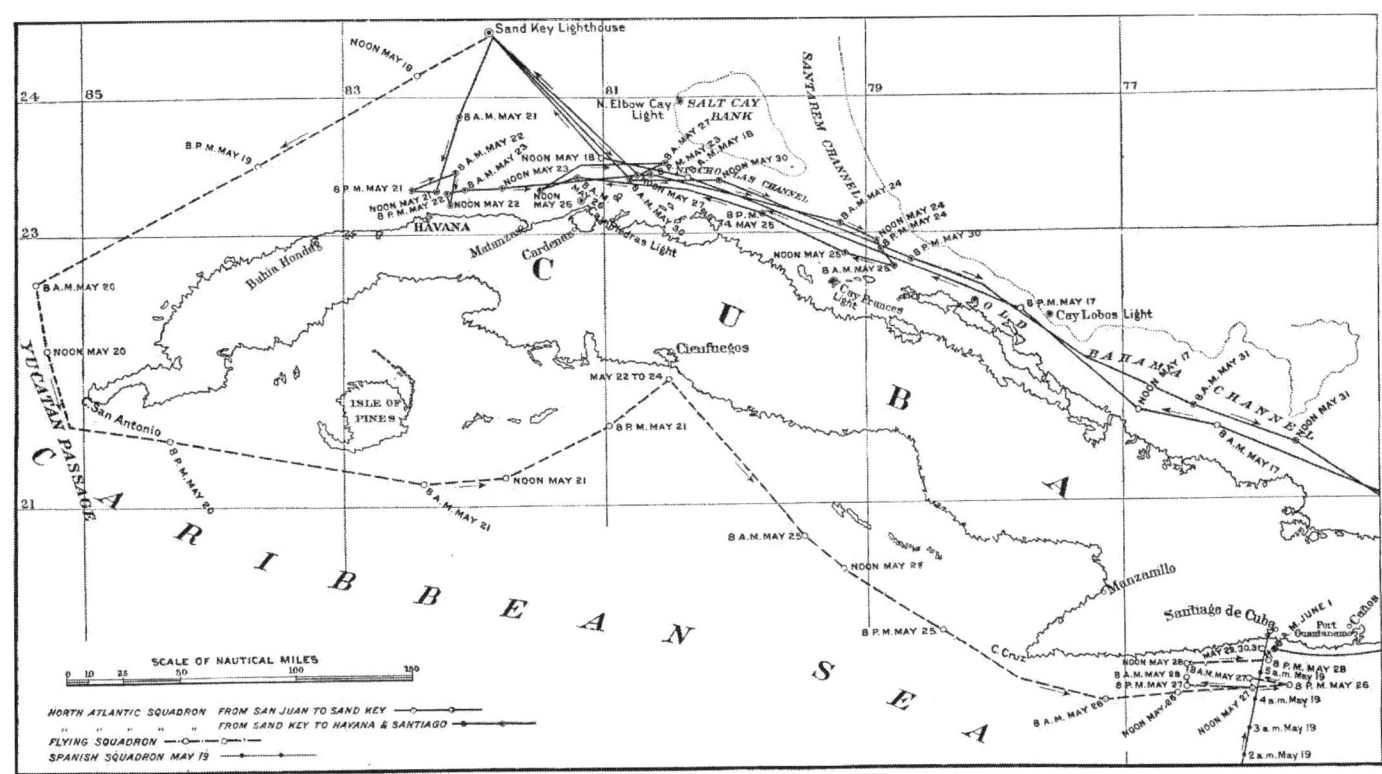

American intelligence reported that Cervera had left the Cape Verde Islands, destination unknown, forcing the Flying Squadron to remain in its central, defensive position at Hampton Roads. After Cervera appeared near Martinique, rather than off the US coast, the Flying Squadron left Hampton Roads for Key West on May 13, to better position itself to interdict the Spanish fleet. When Cervera reached Curacao, his presence was quickly reported. It was erroneously believed that he was making a run to Cienfuegos to escort a convoy of cargo ships (which it turned out did not exist). The Flying Squadron, under Commodore Schley, left Key West on May 19 with orders to blockade Cienfuegos, by which time Cervera's fleet had already slipped into Santiago de Cuba undetected. Telegram intercepts from Cuba quickly leaked that the Spanish fleet had arrived at Santiago, but this intelligence was discounted as the auxiliary cruiser *St. Louis* had just left Santiago a short time before Cervera arrived and reported no sign of the fleet.

On departing Key West for Cuba, the *Texas* and the *Iowa* promptly hit a reef off the Dry Tortugas, in a location marked on their charts as being forty-eight feet deep, both vessels listing noticeably as they passed over it and continued on their way. Capt. Phillip of the *Texas* signaled Capt. Higginson of the Massachusetts "*Texas* luck - struck bottom in eight fathoms." Months later when the *Texas* was dry docked it was found that the hull had received a dent 8 feet long and 6 inches deep.

On May 20 the Navy Department reconsidered and instructed Admiral Sampson to pass information to Schley regarding the likelihood of Cervera being at Santiago. Sampson, unaware of the Navy's reliable source, ordered Schley to continue to Cienfuegos. Schley had received his own intelligence on May 19th that Cervera was at Santiago, but reports the next day stated Cervera had departed.

DRAWN BY HOWARD F. SPRAGUE FROM A PHOTOGRAPH FOUND IN SANTIAGO BY T. R. DAWLEY.

THE SPANISH FLEET IN SANTIAGO HARBOR.

THE CASTLE AT CIENFUEGOS

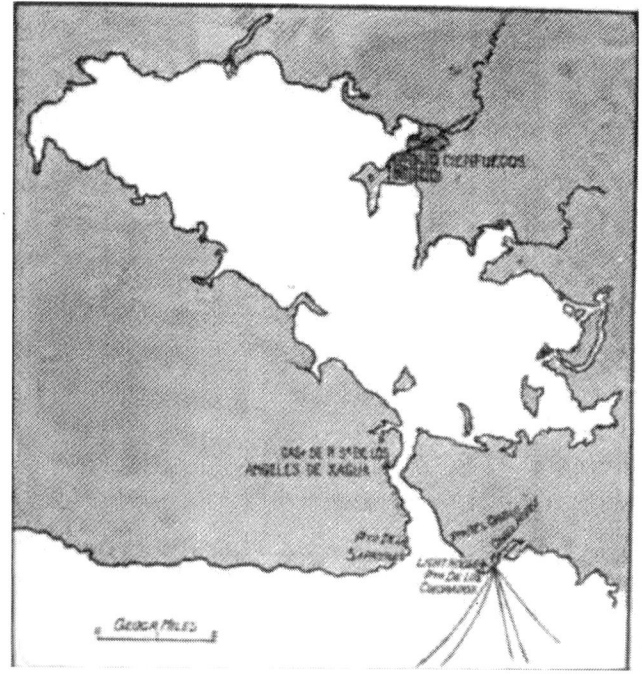

On the night of May 21st, Schley arrived off Cienfuegos. The harbor at Cienfuegos, like that at Santiago, was protected by a Morro Castle and shore batteries as well as high headlands, effectively blocking observation of its interior from hostile warships at sea. Schley could confirm neither the presence nor the absence of the missing Spanish warships.

SANTIAGO, FROM THE HARBOR

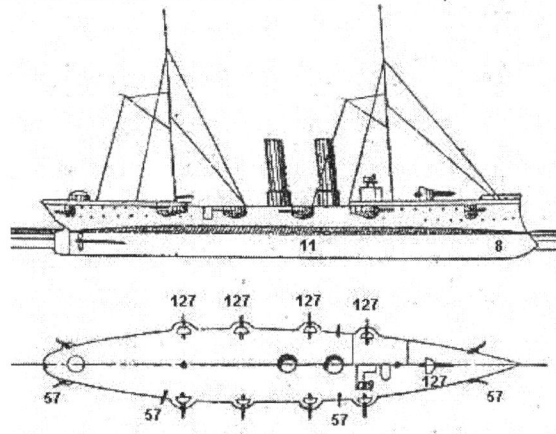

On the same day that Commodore Schley reached Cienfuegos, the Navy Department confirmed that Cervera's squadron was at Santiago through intelligence sources in Cuba. Schley received this information from Admiral Sampson on May 22nd, but considered it to be old news, believing that Cervera had subsequently gone on to Cienfuegos. As Sampson did not specifically order Commodore Schley to go to Santiago, the flying squadron remained at Cienfuegos.

On May 24, Commander McCalla of the cruiser *Marblehead*, acting on his own initiative, responded to light signals ashore and contacted Cuban insurgents at Ceinfuegos, learning that the Spanish fleet was indeed at Santiago. Commodore Schley was still unconvinced but on May 25 ordered the Flying Squadron to proceed to Santiago at a very reduced speed.

The photo below shows the *Marblehead* during her subsequent activities off Guantanamo.

On May 26, just under the horizon from Santiago, Schley stopped his squadron to await new intelligence from the cruisers operating in the area. Captain Sigsbee, formerly captain of the *Maine* but now commanding the auxiliary cruiser *St. Paul*, seen above in wartime photographs, off the mouth of Santiago Bay reported that the Spanish fleet was not there. He had not seen any sign of the Spanish fleet in the area for a week and failed to realize that the they had slipped in before his arrival on scene. The report received from Captain Sigsbee reinforced Commodore Schley's own doubts. Commodore Schley immediately turned his squadron back for Cienfuegos.

About four hours later, however, Commodore Schley reconsidered and the squadron stopped while he vacillated. Sixteen hours later, on May 27, Commodore Schley surprisingly ordered the Flying Squadron to return to Key West for coal, even though some of his ships had already used the halt to begin coaling at sea. – This decision was all the more confusing as all of the American vessels still carried aboard enough coal to stand blockade for at least ten days while leaving an ample reserve to steam to a sheltered bay in a neutral port closer to the action for coaling from the colliers in the squadron.

Commodore Schley's communication of his intention to return to Key West was received by his superiors in the Navy Department and in the War Office at the White House with trepidation, incomprehension, and dismay.

The response within the squadron anticipated and echoed these feelings. Using his megaphone, Capt. Evans aboard the *Iowa* (left) hailed Capt. Philip on the *Texas* (below) asking "Say, Jack, what the devil does it mean?" "Beats me," responded Capt. Philip, "What do you think, Bob?" "Damned if I know anything," returned Capt. Evans, "except that I am the most disgusted man afloat." Just an hour and a half later however, Commodore Schley again turned back for Santiago. What prompted him to go back is unknown, but his indecision was apparent to the officers and men throughout the squadron.

On the evening of May 27, the Flying Squadron finally appeared off Santiago harbor. The following morning, the *Cristobal Colon* was seen anchored in a defensive position near the top end of the harbor entrance, while the other Spanish ships remained hidden from view. Cervera was cornered, although the strength of the Flying Squadron was not yet sufficient to ensure that the Spanish could not fight their way out. Cervera had missed his opportunity to escape unmolested during the US Navy's initial period of vacillation and poor communications and did not immediately choose to force the issue. With the Spanish squadron pinpointed, if not effectively blockaded, the Atlantic Fleet could now sortie and the Army's invasion force could be safely embarked for Cuba.

At the time Schley's difficulties were appreciated as being part of the "fog of war", especially considering his ultimately successful "trapping" of Cervera. However, Schley's hesitant performance during the hunt, taken into consideration with a later command decision during the campaign, would cause him significant postwar grief and great controversy within the Navy and in the court of public opinion.

Ironically, the arrival of the Spanish fleet at Santiago shifted the target of the US invasion from the well-defended and largely pro-Spanish capitol at Havana to the isolated city of Santiago, deep within a territory controlled by Cuban revolutionaries. As result, destruction of the Spanish Fleet and hence Spain's ability to project its power overseas, rather than the capture of the colonial capitol, Havana, became the strategic goal defining success or failure in the US prosecution of the war.

Coaling ship was very labor intensive. Bags of filthy coal were brought up to the *Texas*' deck, while the side of the ship was covered in protective canvas, and dumped by hand through the open scuttles leading to the coal bunkers below. This was difficult in a protected harbor but much more challenging in any kind of sea. The need to secure a nearby coaling station in sheltered waters in order to effectively maintain the squadron on blockade was a priority.

The large vertical pipe visible behind the 12" gun sponson is the ash chute, used to dump overboard the coal ash produced by the boilers, bucket by a bucket, funneling the ash as close as possible to the sea so as to keep it from dirtying the ship's sides.

The *Texas'* overhanging sponsons made coaling difficult at sea, however her oversize booms, initially designed to lift heavy torpedo boats, allowed provisioning vessels to stand off a bit.

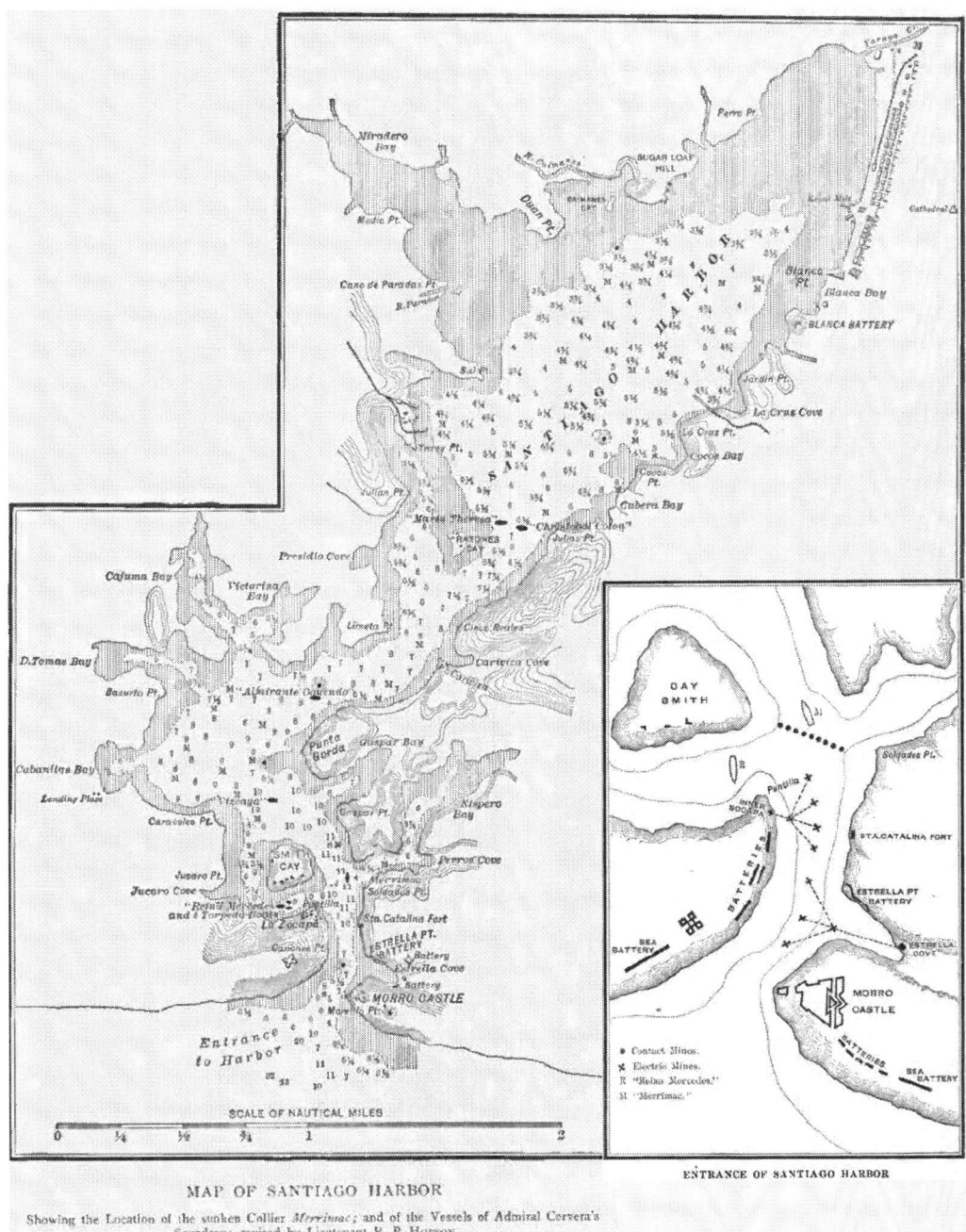

MAP OF SANTIAGO HARBOR
Showing the Location of the sunken Collier *Merrimac*; and of the Vessels of Admiral Cervera's Squadron; revised by Lieutenant R. P. Hobson.

ENTRANCE OF SANTIAGO HARBOR

While the Navy could attempt to maintain its blockade of Cervera's warships, it could not reasonably be expected to run the gantlet of the harbor's forts and minefields to engage the Spanish ships in the bay. It was therefore decided that an invasion force be sent to Santiago to threaten the port from the landward side and force the Spanish ships to either attempt to run the blockade or eventually surrender in the besieged port.

Because his government had not equipped his squadron with any colliers or supply vessels, Admiral Cervera had been given little choice but to tie down US forces by taking a defensive position, rather than a potentially more effective offensive tactic of raiding the US coast. As a defensive position Santiago harbor was ideal as it possessed rugged terrain and Army forces large enough to deter all but a major invasion. In addition the large harbor with its narrow entrance and screening headlands allowed him to safely disperse his ships out of sight of the US fleet, safe it appeared, from bombardment.

The guns of the land defenses were not strong, but supplemented by the guns and automobile torpedoes of the old cruiser *Reina Mercedes* that already sheltered there, they had just enough bite to deter any but the most aggressive of attacking warships. Coupled with the fixed torpedo (mine) defenses, and with the memory of the USS *Maine's* demise - presumed at that time to have been destroyed by a mine - fresh in the minds of the US commanders, the defenses suggested caution on the part of the US fleet. Now added to the harbor's existing defenses were the massed main guns of the Spanish fleet totaling 6-11", 5-6", and 15-5.5" guns as well as smaller guns and torpedoes from the cruisers and the two destroyers. A US Navy attempt to penetrate the harbor's mouth would at best present 2-13", 2-12" or 4-8" forward firing guns presented one at a time by each successive American warship as they steamed slowly up the narrow, mined channel and into a close-range onslaught.

While the Spanish Fleet's position was virtually impregnable from naval attack, the reverse was not true. Unless the US Navy maintained a very large fleet to blockade it, there was a chance that some or all of the Spanish cruisers could escape in appropriate conditions. They were, in theory, faster than any of the major US warships except for the *Brooklyn* and *New York*, and as a group effectively outgunned these two ships. The US Navy was forced to invest virtually all it's major naval assets in the blockade of Santiago, a force at least three times that Cervera possessed.

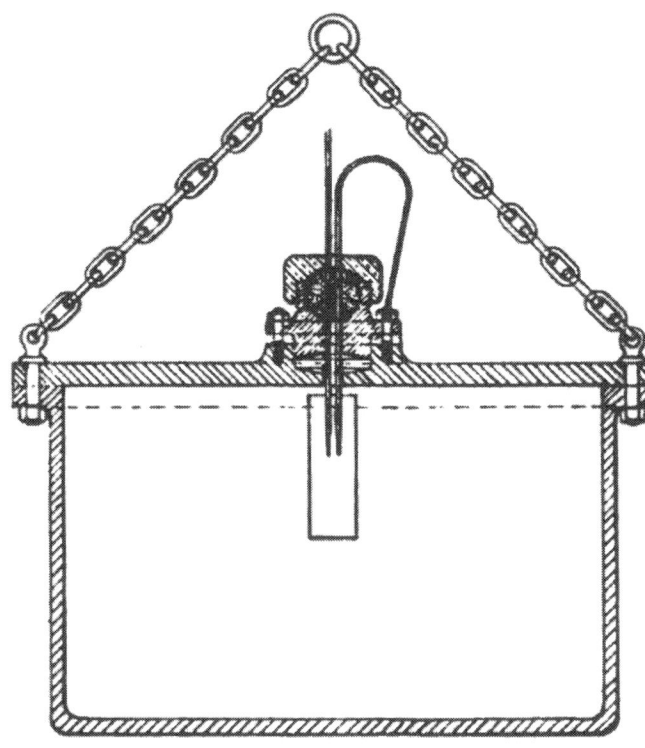

Observation Mine.

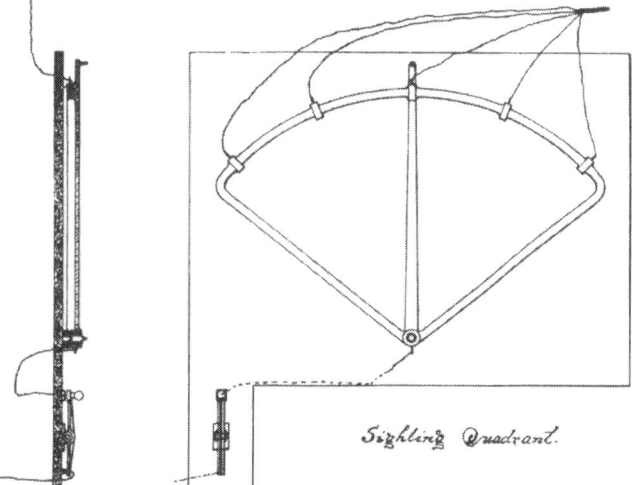

Sighting Quadrant.

The mines employed by the Spanish forces in Cuba were of two types, Bustamente contact mines and Latimer-Clark observation mines. As their names imply, contact mines were triggered when their "horns" or "plungers" were directly impacted by a vessel's hull, while observation mines were discharged via electrical signal from a shore based control station monitoring the minefield.

At Santiago Bay, the Spanish mines were deployed in three fields. In the channel between Morro Castle and the Lower Socapa Battery, which was as narrow as 125 yards, was a mine field consisting of observation mines operated from a control station sheltered deep in Estrella Cove.

A second field of observation mines was deployed just up the channel from the first, between the Lower Socapa Battery and the Battery on Estrella Point. This minefield was operated from a control station located on Socapa Point. These electrically operated mines were planted on the bottom in water ranging from 7 to 11 fathoms.

The Latimer-Clark observation mine was made of a cast iron cylindrical pot approximately ¾" thick capped with a cast iron cover, filled with explosive, and sealed with a rubber gasket. A chain was fitted to the top of the mine to allow it to be placed and removed. Each mine contained a massive 226 kilo charge of guncotton, necessary due to the fact that the mine would likely not be ideally located relative to the enemy vessel being targeted. Fusing was an electrically initiated fulminate of mercury detonator. The control stations were small camouflaged wooden huts with slits in their walls enabling their occupants to view the breadth of the minefield they controlled. The firing of the mines was accomplished through the use of a quadrant sighting bar hooked via electrical connections to each mine in the channel. When activated by connecting the circuit to the firing battery, simply pivoting the sighting bar to visually align with the enemy vessel steaming up the channel and then pressing the firing key would detonate the appropriate mine beneath the ship.

This type of minefield could be cleared by severing the connection to its control station. Although this might be possible using well directed gunfire aimed at the station, assuming its location was known, the only way to be certain that the connection was permanently broken would be to capture the station or the control cables themselves.

New mines at the Cartegena Arsenal in Spain, prior to the war.

The third minefield in Santiago Bay consisted of 9 un-controlled Bustamente contact mines anchored to float at a depth of approximately 11 feet beneath the surface of the water. As contact mines required periodic cleaning and maintenance of their trigger mechanism and would have to be removed and reinstalled installed via small boats to allow the Spanish warships to sortie, their sheltered location up the channel allowed this delicate work to occur under cover from the observation and gunfire from the blockading fleet.

The Bustamente contact mine consisted of a conical buoy 32" in diameter at the top and 12 ½" at the bottom, 36" high. A centrally mounted internal cylinder 11" in diameter housed 45 kilos of wet guncotton, a priming charge of dry guncotton, and the fusing mechanism consisting of a glass tube filled with sulphuric acid in a bed of potash, sugar, and possibly mercury fulminate (no mercury fulminate was positively identified after the war in undetonated captured mines however). At the base of each mine was an iron plate to which was attached a reel that held about 120 feet of wire rope used to anchor the mine. The floating depth of the mine was adjustable via cable attached to a pawl on the reel.

This type of minefield was theoretically removable by an attacking force via small boats trawling for each mine's anchor cables using chains; clearly an unworkable option at Santiago given the inevitable defensive fire from shore batteries and warships within the harbor.

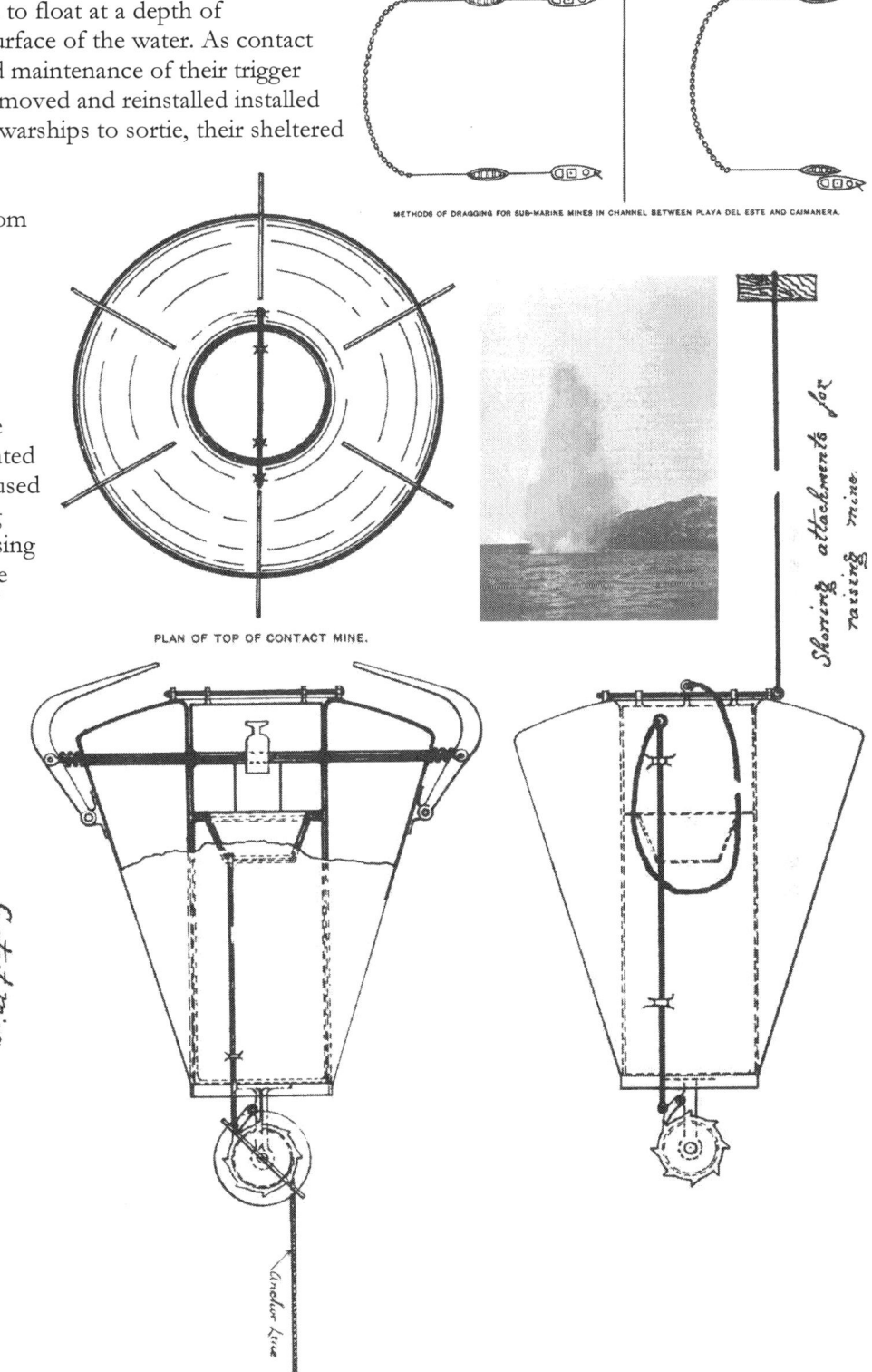

In addition to the three minefields, Spanish defenders deployed a log boom secured by 5" steel hawsers across the secondary channel that separated Cay Smith from Socapa Point. Behind this boom sheltered the Reina Mercedes, moored with her broadside facing the main channel.

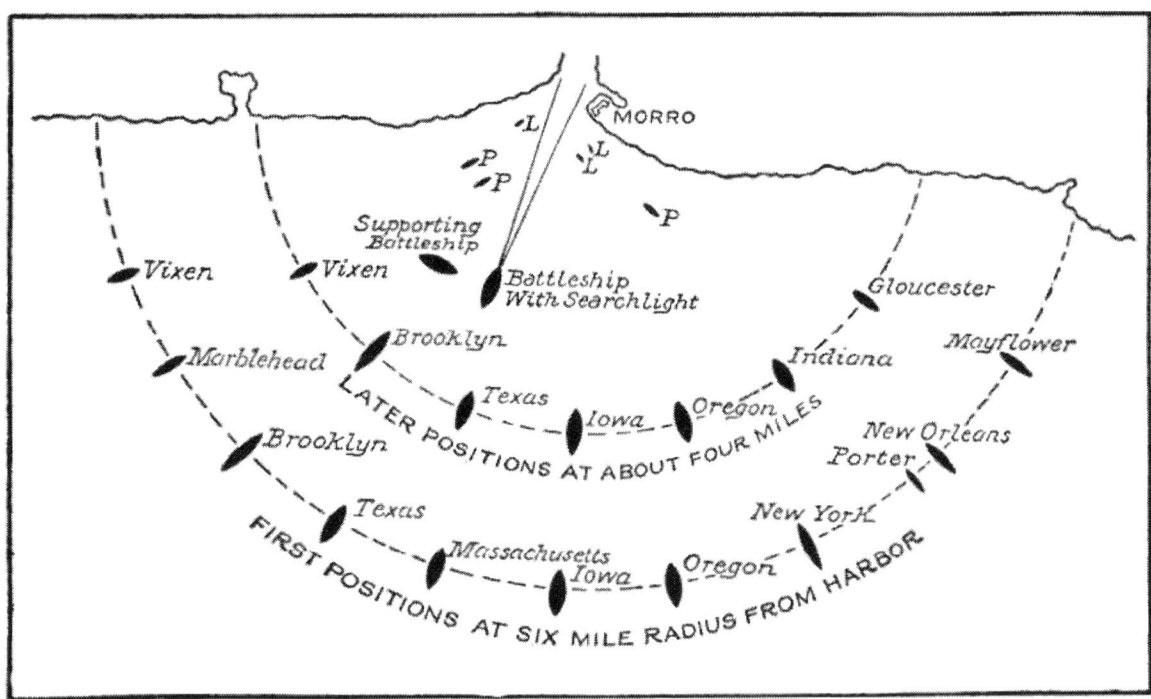

DIAGRAM ILLUSTRATING THE BLOCKADE OF SANTIAGO BY ADMIRAL SAMPSON'S FLEET.

P, P, P, Customary picket-stations of two or three of the smaller craft at night; L, L, L, Launches engaged in close picket-duty at night. The "later positions" also represent the relative positions of the six ships encountered by Admiral Cervera, July 3, 1898. The two dotted lines represent the earlier and later day positions. At night the line was accustomed to move in about a mile closer.

Sampson in his flag ship, the *New York* devised a simple semi-circular plan for blockading Santiago Harbor. In the event of a Spanish sortie the fleet was to move quickly to smother the lead vessels with heavy gunfire The *Texas* and *Brooklyn*, two of his fastest ships, were stationed to the west so that they could run down any Spanish cruisers that survived the gauntlet and attempted to escape in that direction. The slower battleships were stationed south and east, the direction the Spanish squadron would take should they attempt to attack the Army transports off Daiquiri. The battleships, including the *Texas*, rotated inshore duties at night playing searchlights up the mouth of the harbor in order to detect as early as possible any nocturnal sortie by the Spanish, the torpedo boats being considered a constant threat to the fleet. At any given time, several blockading ships would not be in position, either on detached duty or coaling. Coal consumption was high during the blockade of Santiago due to the need to keep boilers fired up for emergencies. In harbor during peacetime, the *Texas* power needs could be maintained by one boiler but at Santiago she normally maintained all four boilers burning. After the capture of Guantanamo Bay, ships would shuttle there a few at a time to take on coal, keeping their bunkers as full as possible.

In addition to the guns of Cevera's Squadron, the US Navy had to deal with several fortifications guarding the mouth of Santiago harbor. Supplementing these shore batteries was the Spanish cruiser *Reina Mercedes*. Her machinery in no condition to operate with Cervera's Squadron, she lent her guns and crew to the defense of the harbor. A number of her guns were removed during the campaign and emplaced ashore, the first such naval battery becoming active on May 18th and the last on June 17th. The *Mercedes* retained a portion of her battery aboard along with her torpedoes and was capable of slow movement. - As the relative ineffectiveness of the Spanish shore based artillery became apparent over time, Sampson moved his ships closer in.

The plan did not anticipate the US fleet becoming entangled on converging courses upon a Spanish attempt to break out. Although Schley was criticized for some of his tactics during the eventual battle, it was Sampson's plan that created the scenario with which Schley and his captains had to work.

Reina Mercedes (moored in the channel):
Two 16 CM Hontoria guns (mounted in the forward positions)
Four 57MM guns
Nordenfelt Machine guns
Whitehead torpedoes

Morro Castle and the sea batteries on Marvilla Point as seen from the south or ocean side. The point of land to the west, opposite the Morro, is Canones Point, home to the Upper and Lower Socapa Batteries. The already restricted view into Santiago Harbor between these features is completely blocked by Gaspar Point and Gorda Point, over ½ mile further up the bay.

Morro Castle and Sea Batteries seen from the west. The lighter feature crossing diagonally down from left to right is the road cut providing access to the Morro Sea Battery.

Morro Castle and road cut to the Sea Batteries as viewed from the Estrella Battery, located inside Santiago Bay. The open sea is visible at right beyond Marvilla Point.

Morro Battery:
Five 16 cm guns (muzzle loading)
Two 21 cm guns (muzzle loading)

Interior of Morro Castle showing typical construction dating back to the Eighteenth Century.

View of Morro Castle taken from the Sea Battery. Note the rings inset into the platform floor upon which guns on pivoting mounts traversed. Also note the semi-ruinous state of the fortifications.

Much of the castle's artillery was of similar vintage, as can be seen in the photo below, taken on the roof of the tower. The photos on this page were taken after the battle.

Located just to the east of the Morro Castle was this lighthouse, a prominent feature visible from the sea. Adjacent to the lighthouse was a signal mast erected by the Spanish to allow the latest positions of the American warships to be relayed to the City of Santiago and the ships of Admiral Cervera's squadron. Note the damage caused by shells fired by U.S. warships on June 6th.

Estrella Battery:
Two 21CM howitzers (muzzle loading)
Two 8 cm Plasencia Guns (breech loading)
Two short 12 cm rifled bronze guns (muzzle loading)

Inside the eastern side of the mouth of the bay was Estrella Point, seen in the distance on the left in the photo above. Morro Castle is seen on the right, separated from Estrella Point by Estrella cove.

Estrella Point was topped by Fort Santa Catalina, while the sea approaches were guarded by the Estrella Battery (left), located just below the fort along a road descending to the outer minefield control station in the upper reaches of Estrella Cove.

From its protected location up Estrella Cove, Spanish forces at the outer minefield control station could electrically fire mines located in the channel between the cove and Canones Point to the west.

"OLD HOODOO": THE BATTLESHIP TEXAS

(clockwise from above) 1. The old Sea Battery on Socapa Point, opposite Morro Castle. 2. Hut from which the inner minefield, located in the channel between Socapa Point and Fort Santa Catalina, could be activated. 3. Examining recovered Spanish mines after the capitulation. 4. Recovered Spanish Bustamente mines and electrical cable spools at Socapa Point.

221

Guns and earthworks of the Upper Socapa Battery. The two relatively modern Hontoria 6.3 inch guns in this position had been removed from the unserviceable Spanish cruiser, the *Reina Mercedes*. This position provided a commanding view of the channel entrance just to the east, as well as the blockading U.S. fleet to the south. It was one of the guns of this battery that would find the *Texas* on June 22. Although repeatedly shelled, it was found that earthen fortifications were much more rapidly repaired than the older masonry structures. These photos taken after the capitulation show the battery remained in good condition.

Not all of the guns in the Upper Socapa Battery were modern, as these muzzle-loading examples attest. The pieces with banded barrels seen above date from the mid-Nineteenth Century. Their pivoting carriage may identify them as having originated in the Morro Sea Battery or at the old Socapa Sea Battery. The guns seen in the photo at left are "modernized" examples of even earlier vintage. Unable to penetrate contemporary armor they could still inconvenience a warship's unarmored upper works or destroy lighter vessels that approached within their limited range. They also served by their presence in the batteries as a useful distraction to would-be blockaders who, not knowing their limitations, were forced to divide their efforts, shelling modern gun and museum piece alike.

Additional views of the Upper Socapa Battery showing muzzle-loading guns on pivoting carriages.

Modern guns like the Hotchkiss revolving cannon found on most of the blockading U.S. warships were capable of prodigious rates of fire. Without cover, Spanish gun crews attempting to work their slow and archaic muzzle loaders would have easily been driven from their guns.

In some locations earth-filled wooden barrels were used to form breastworks for the protection of the gun crews from smaller caliber counter-battery fire. Although earthen fortifications could be rapidly rebuilt after each bombardment, a direct hit to a gun or its carriage could knock it out of action for good. Unserviceable guns were none-the-less returned to their position in the battery to serve as "Quaker guns", dummy positions intended to draw fire away from the remaining serviceable guns and conceal the reduction in the battery's strength.

Upper Socapa Battery:
Three 21 cm howitzers (muzzle loading)
Later two 16 cm Hontoria breech loading guns added (from *Reina Mercedes*)

View from Smith Cay to the south-east towards the harbor entrance and the sea. Fortifications on each point (from left to right) include the Fort Santa Catalina/Estrella Battery, Morro Castle, and – hidden beyond the brush on right – the Lower Socapa Battery. The inner minefield lay in the channel between Fort Santa Catalina and the Lower Socapa Battery.

Lower Socapa Battery:
Two 57 mm Nordenfelt Guns (some sources state one, from *Reina Mercedes*) Four 37 MM Hotchkiss Revolving Cannon (from *Reina Mercedes*) One 25MM Nordenfelt Machine gun (belonging to the mine unit)

Guns in the Lower Socapa Battery. This position was located somewhat further up the bay than the Upper Socapa Battery and commanded the channel at its narrowest point. Reflecting the shorter ranges involved, smaller caliber, rapid firing guns taken from the Reina Mercedes were placed here. Shown in the photo below are two 57mm rapid fire Nordenfelt guns on naval mounts. A Nordenfelt four-barrel gun on a field carriage is flanked by a pair of 47mm Hotchkiss revolving cannon. These guns, crewed by sailors of the Reina Mercedes, saw action versus the USS *Merrimac* on June 2nd.

Earthworks again provided cover, though in this case some measure of concealment was also available. - Unlike at the Upper Socapa Battery, surrounding vegetation was not removed from this position. Whether this represented a deliberate attempt at camouflage or merely reflected the short time taken to prepare this position is not clear, but since this battery was in the line of sight of blockading vessels outside of the bay, the cover no doubt aided the Spanish defenders.

The blockhouse atop Canones Point, above the Socapa Batteries. From this position the Spanish could monitor the first mile of the channel entering Santiago Bay as well as provide protection from attack on the landward side of the Socapa Batteries. The disposition of the blockading American warships was communicated from this location, as well as from the Morro Castle on the opposite headland, back to Spanish Army headquarters in Santiago and to the Spanish fleet sheltering in the harbor.

The Spanish defenders of Santiago employed signal flags and the heliograph for communications. The heliograph was a signal light that flashed a message encoded in dots and dashes that could, under favorable conditions, be read up to 125 miles away. Unlike the signal lamps employed on naval vessels, the heliograph used sunlight focused and reflected on mirrors to produce a bright beam of light. At night the heliograph could be operated using moonlight or an artificial light source. US Army Signal Corps soldiers pose during the Spanish-American War with their American-issue Heliograph equipment.

Spanish forces in Santiago were also in communication with Madrid, Spain via telegraph through Havana. Despite the best efforts of the US Navy, some undersea telegraph cables linking Cuba to the rest of the world remained uncut throughout the war. This situation actually worked in favor of US forces though as the telegraph system in Cuba employed a number of foreign nationals and Cubans who were only too happy to pass the content of official Spanish communications to the Americans and insurgents.

View from the top of Canones Point, near the blockhouse, looking back up the bay to the north. The island in the foreground is Smith Cay where a small mortar battery (left) was located. To the right is Gaspar Point and beyond that, in the center, is Gorda Point, site of the Punta Gorda Battery. The water just visible between the hills of Point Gorda is the Harbor of Santiago, itself guarded by several more small batteries located on points of land and yet another battery on Raton Cay.

The position atop a hill at the end of Gorda Point commanded a sharp turn in the channel leading into Santiago Harbor. Virtually the entire sweep of the channel and bay was visible, from the Morro Castle to the south all of the way through approximately 230 degrees to the city of Santiago to the north-east.

Like at the Socapa Batteries, two 6.3 inch Hontoria guns had been taken from the *Reina Mercedes* and placed in earthworks in this position. The guns on field carriages were breech-loading army pieces of somewhat smaller caliber. This type of heavy field carriage remained in common usage in most armies through WWI.

This battery saw action against the *Merrimac* during her attempt to block the channel on June 2nd. The *Merrimac* came to a halt and sank directly before the guns of this position.

Punta Gorda Battery:
Two 15 CM Mata Howitzers (breech loading)
Two 9 CM breech loading Krupp Guns
Later two 16 cm Hontoria breech loading guns added

LED BY THE SEARCH-LIGHT OF THE "TEXAS"—TWO SPANISH TORPEDO-BOAT DESTROYERS, WHICH CREPT FROM UNDER THE SHELTER OF MORRO CASTLE, AT SANTIAGO, AT MIDNIGHT, TO ATTACK COMMODORE SCHLEY'S FLEET, WERE PROMPTLY CAUGHT IN THE ACT AND COMPELLED TO RETIRE.

One lurking threat to large warships in the pre-radar era was the fear of torpedo boats operating at night. While torpedo technology had not yet been perfected, especially in terms of range, an automobile torpedo in 1898 delivered at about 500 yards had a good chance of hitting and sinking even the largest battleship. The giant-slaying threat of the torpedo was the reason for the prodigious amount of light, rapid fire armament on warships, up through and including the 6 pounder/57mm guns. While virtually all warships of the period were capable of destroying a torpedo boat before it entered torpedo range, darkness was a time of high potential danger. Warships were equipped with powerful searchlights for night action, but even these could not cover all the angles. The possibility of a night time excursion of the Spanish destroyers *Furor* and *Pluton* was the primary reason for stationing two ships with searchlights in close blockade, to carefully watch far up Santiago bay.

Despite precautions like these, night actions, with all the smoke and glare, could quickly turn into a chaotic affair. It is possible, especially in the light of the chaos of the daytime action of the battle of Santiago, that, had the Spanish attempted a night attack on the US fleet, the torpedoes carried by both the Spanish destroyers and the cruisers might have caused significant loss and embarrassment to the US Navy. As the *Texas* had demonstrated in the Brooklyn Navy Yard not long before, the internal water-tight integrity of US warships had not yet been truly achieved.

During the blockade, the crews of US ships were significantly inconvenienced by the practice of keeping portholes closed in the war zone. This was a precaution against torpedo damage as an open porthole would let a huge amount of water into a damaged, listing ship. (During WWI a British hospital ship, the converted liner *Britannic* sister to the *Titanic*, took a single torpedo or mine and sunk in only fifteen minutes, largely as result of having open portholes.) The summer heat was a great burden on US personnel. The poorly-ventilated warships sitting stationary on blockade duty had very little effective air flow. Interior temperatures aboard ship were measured at over 110 degrees.

This period illustration dramatizes an incident on the night of June 3rd when a torpedo armed Spanish destroyer approached the blockading fleet under the cover of darkness, but was compelled to withdraw when spotted.

In Washington, American strategy had been focused upon landing the larger part of the Army on Cuba's northern shore and then capturing Havana via siege. It was deemed unwise however to place the bulk of the Army aboard transports as long as Cevera's squadron posed a threat of breaking out and intercepting them. Some means was needed to neutralize this potential threat. If the Spanish would not come out to fight a decisive battle and the US Fleet could not attempt to force the defended harbor mouth, the Spanish warships remained an effective "fleet in being." The Navy Department sought cooperation from the Army to land troops near Santiago and take the defenses that blocked the Navy from entering the harbor.

On blockade off Santiago, Admiral Sampson conceived of the idea of turning Santiago's chief asset, its easily defended land-locked anchorage, to American advantage in a way that would avoid the necessity of an Army landing on the southern coast. The collier *Merrimac* had been the bane of the squadron, being slow and suffering repeated mechanical breakdowns. Admiral Sampson ordered the ship to be stripped of all useful armaments and equipment and then run under the guns of the Spanish defenders and intentionally sunk in the narrowest part of the channel at the entrance to Santiago Bay, effectively neutralizing the threat posed by the Spanish squadron trapped within.

For this job he selected naval constructor Richard Hobson to prepare the ship with scuttling charges and anchors, and with a small volunteer crew steam the vessel into position and sink her. A call for volunteers from the fleet went out. Aboard the *Texas* every man responded, leaving the captain to choose a large Irishman named P. J. O'Boyle, who was in charge of the *Texas'* generator, to be the ship's representative in this risky endeavor.

The *Merrimac* (above) on April 23, 1898. The *Texas* alongside the *Merrimac* (right) as preparations are underway.

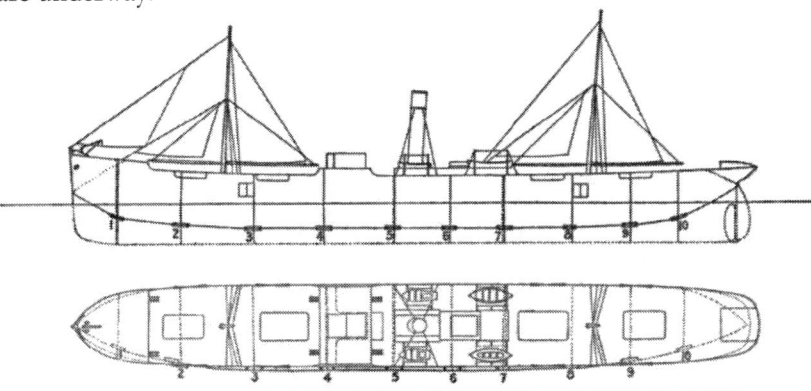

PLAN AND ELEVATION OF THE "MERRIMAC," SHOWING ARRANGEMENT OF THE TORPEDOES, ON THE PORT SIDE.
Before entering the channel Nos. 7, 9, and 10 were reported useless. The ones actually exploded were Nos. 1 and 5. The batteries of the others were shattered by the Spanish fire.

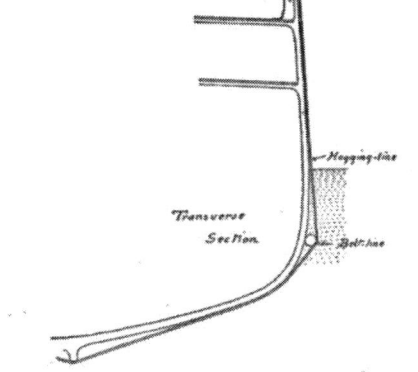

TRANSVERSE SECTION OF THE "MERRIMAC," SHOWING POSITION OF THE BELT-LINE HOLDING THE TORPEDOES AND OF THE HOGGING-LINE.

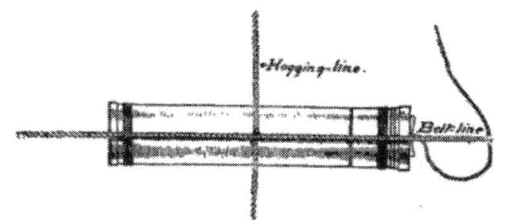

DIAGRAM SHOWING THE ATTACHMENT OF THE TORPEDOES TO THE BELT-LINE AND THE HOGGING-LINE.

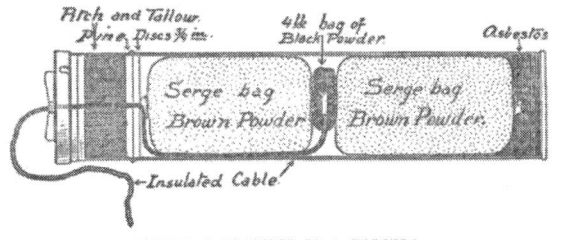

SECTIONAL DRAWING OF A TORPEDO.

"These men helped to prepare the Merrimac."

Preparations took longer than anticipated due to repeated mechanical breakdowns in the *Merrimac's* machinery. The volunteers and the work parties from the fleet performed Herculean tasks but finished just as the sun rose on the morning of June 2nd, too late to proceed. Due to the original volunteer's fatigue, a new set were selected and the *Texas'* representative returned to his ship, exhausted and depressed that he could not participate in the attack.

As the *Merrimac* moved up the channel early the morning of June 3rd, intense gunfire erupted from the Spanish defenses. Five observation mines in the outer minefield were triggered by the control station in Estrella Cove, of which only two discharged. At the middle minefield another mine was triggered from the Socapa control station. Two torpedoes fired by the *Reina Mercedes* may have struck the *Merrimac* as well. Hobson stated that the ship was lifted out of the water and almost rent asunder by the explosions.

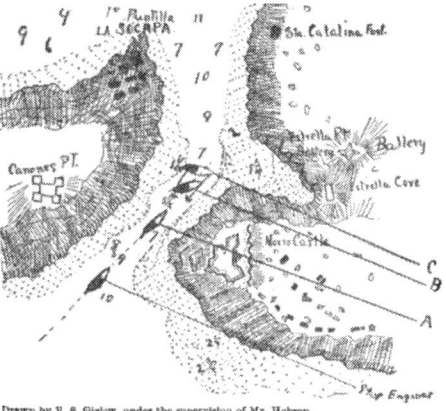
PLAN OF THE MANŒUVER AS PROJECTED.
A, Position for putting helm aport and dropping bow-anchor; B, Position for dropping stern-anchor; C, Position athwart, riding to span.

THE "MERRIMAC" AGROUND AND UNDER FIRE OFF ESTRELLA POINT.

The *Merrimac* sank just inside the inner minefield, in the channel but not fully blocking it.

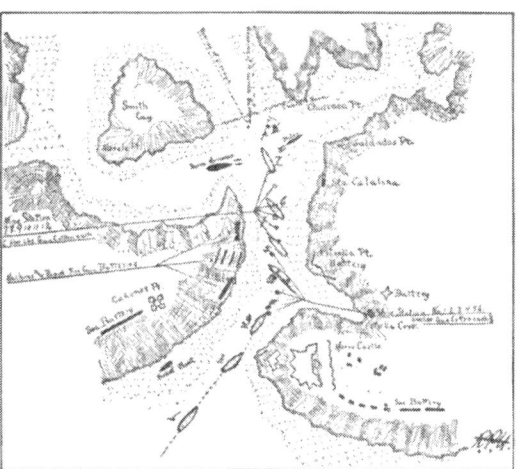
PLAN OF THE MANŒUVER AS EXECUTED JUNE 3, 1898.
EXPLANATIONS.
1, Position when engine was stopped.
2, Position when helm was last in operation.
3, Position when bow-anchor was let go and torpedoes were fired.
4, Position when struck by mine explosion, just before starboard quarter grounded on Estrella Point.
5-7, Positions as the tide wrenched vessel off Estrella Point, and set her down channel — vessel gradually straightening out.
8, Position when sunk.
□, Submarine mines unexploded, mines Nos. 9, 10, 11, 12.
■, Submarine mines fired at vessel, Nos. 1, 2, 3, 4, 6, 6, 7, 8.
※, Submarine mine that struck vessel, No. 5.
→, Automatic torpedoes fired by *Reina Mercedes* and *Pluton*.
NOTE.— The exact location of mines is not known. It would be perhaps fairly accurate to subdivide the distance between the extreme positions into eight equal parts, following the middle of the channel.

Spanish defenders quickly incorporated the obstacle into their defenses, stretching two additional steel hawser log booms from the wreck to shore in order to narrow the main channel at the mouth of Nispero Bay. The wreck and the new booms neatly closed what had been a gap in the eastern end of the inner minefield.

REAR-ADMIRAL WILLIAM T. SAMPSON.
PHOTOGRAPH BY HOLLINGER & CO.

Admiral Sampson called the captains to a conference to discuss the initiation of offensive action in support of the blockade of Santiago Harbor. This action would consist of a bombardment of the Spanish fortifications guarding the mouth of the harbor, the bombardment to begin on Sunday, June 5th.

Captain Philip, a staunchly religious man, was aghast and objected strongly to the idea of commencing battle on the Sabbath, stating his conviction that any force initiating action on a Sunday was condemned to defeat. His fellow captains took Capt. Philip's objections lightly and with some humor, but Admiral Sampson deferred to Capt. Philip's judgment and postponed the initiation of the bombardment until Monday, June 6th.

Commodore Schley, USS *Brooklyn*

(from left to right) Captain Higginson USS *Massachusetts*, Captain Clark USS *Oregon*, Captain Philip USS *Texas*, Captain Chadwick USS *New York*, Captain Evans USS *Iowa*

The US squadron opened fire at 7:41 am. "It could always be told when a shot struck, as a great cloud of dirt, smoke, and debris would rise in the air as a shot exploded. Several times, most notably during the engagement of the *Texas* and La Socopa battery, the guns of the Spaniards were completely buried by the earth thrown up by these shells, but the Spanish soldiers had discreetly retired to a pit on the opposite side of the hill, smoking in calm safety, to return, when the ships had retired, with mules and workmen, hauling out and remounting their guns." -R.W. Henderson aboard the USS *Texas*, for *Scientific American*

In addition to hitting the fortifications on shore, the US fleet also shelled the Spanish naval vessels sheltering in the harbor. Admiral Cervera reported that the *Reina Mercedes* (below left) was hit thirty-five times and her commander, Capt. Emilio Acosta y Eyermann mortally wounded. The *Vizcaya* (below right) took two hits. The *Furor* (bottom) also took a shot in her coal bunker which apparently failed to explode. The Spanish vessels hit are shown here in prewar photographs.

Casualties aboard the US vessels in this action were limited to two pets. Aboard the *Iowa*, Captain Evans' Scottish terrier, startled by the gunfire, ran the length of the ship and over the side, drowning. Aboard the *Texas* the ship's much-loved mascot, Daisy, was knocked into convulsions by the concussion of the guns and died, being committed to the deep in traditional Navy fashion.

In this action, the *Texas* expended 21 12-inch common shells, 59 6-inch common shells, 4 shrapnel 6-inch shells, 122 6-pdr common shells, and 3 armor piercing 6-pdr shells.

15 INVASION: GUANTANAMO, DAIQURI & SIBONEY – JUNE 1898

One of the two Colt Machine Guns loaned to the Marines at Camp McCalla by the USS *Texas* seen on June 12th, 1898, shortly after its arrival. Cuban insurgents with a mixture of US Navy, US Marines, and local peasant clothing and equipment sit resting, holding their recently acquired rifles in anticipation of renewed Spanish sniper fire. (Getty Images photo)

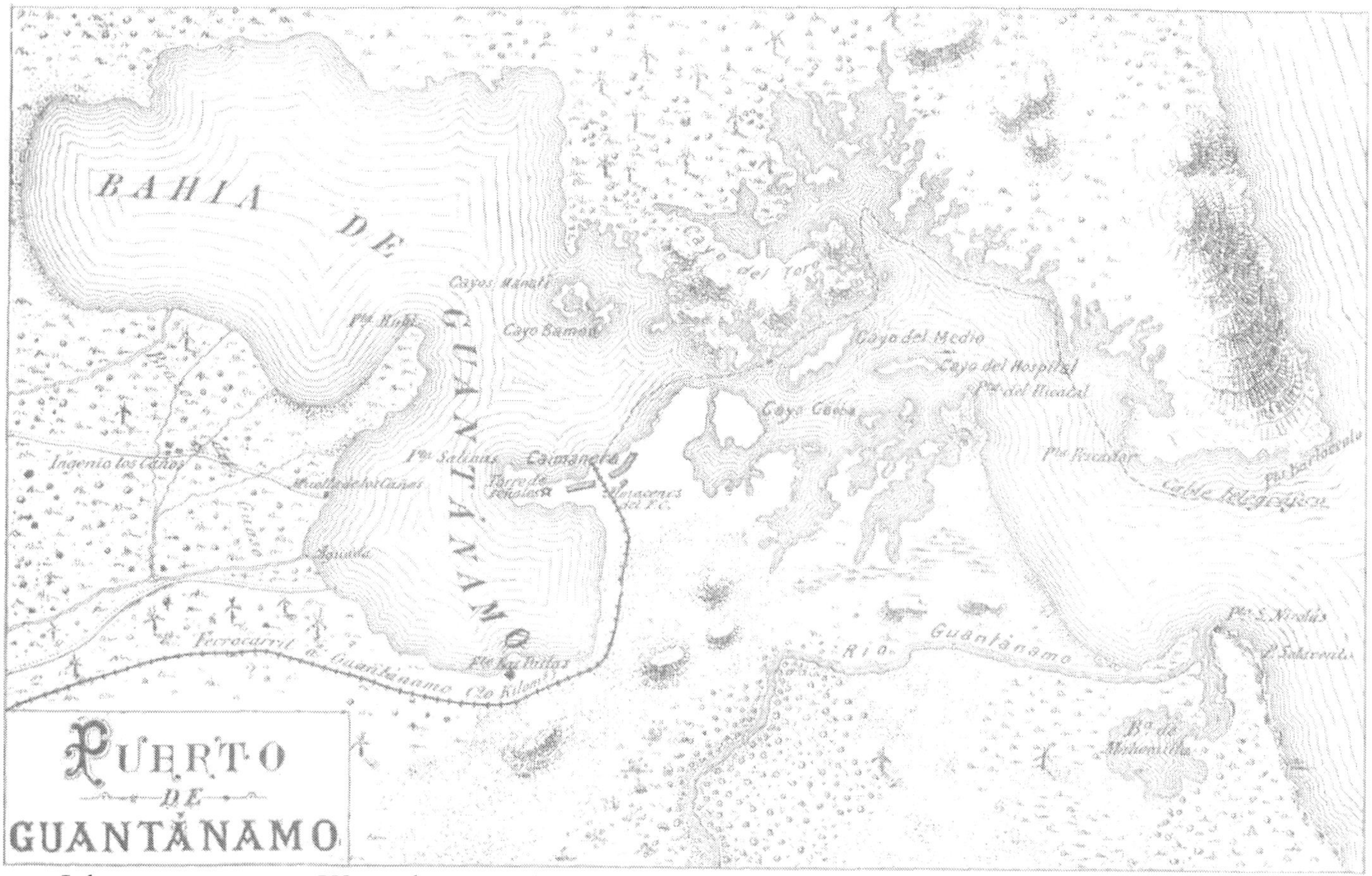

It became apparent to US naval commanders that in order to maintain an effective blockade, they would need protected waters in which to transfer coal from their colliers to the warships. Significant Spanish forces controlled the harbors at Santiago and Cienfuegos. Guantanamo Bay to the east of Santiago offered a large protected anchorage that was relatively lightly held by a single small gunboat and scattered land forces. The Spanish fort at Caimanera in Guantanamo Bay was a strongpoint protecting the narrows outside of the inner Bay of Joa, but the peninsula at the mouth of the outer bay was out of effective range of its guns. Any attempt by Spanish soldiers from the fort to move on to the peninsula would be made difficult by the activities of Cuban insurgents in the surrounding countryside, the lack of sources of fresh water, and their exposure to naval gunfire. It was here, therefore, that the Navy decided to claim its protected anchorage in Cuba.

On June 10th, the 1st Battalion of US Marine Corps disembarked from the transport *Panther* and, supported by the light cruiser *Marblehead* and the auxiliary cruiser *Yosemite*, landed at the eastern point guarding the entrance to Guantanamo Bay. Raising the United States flag for the first time on Cuban soil atop a rise immediately behind Playa del Este, they established Camp McCalla, named in honor of the *Marblehead's* Captain, Bowman Henry McCalla.

Faced with increasing Spanish resistance in the form of snipers, the Marines, with the assistance of Cuban rebels, consolidated their position at Camp McCalla, protected under the guns of the *Marblehead* and, on the 12th, the *Texas*, which had arrived on scene to provide additional support. A perimeter had by that time been established and trenches dug for cover.

Playa del Este, Guantanamo Bay. (below).

The *Texas* and *Marblehead*, along with several smaller support vessels, provided direct-fire support to the Marines dug in atop the hill at Camp McCalla at Guantanamo. The Marines' tents are visible lining the ridge in the photograph above, taken from the mouth of the bay.

The photo below was taken from further up the bay. The Marines' position is to the right, behind the smoke.

The *Texas* also shelled Spanish forces on the western shore opposite the landing area occupied by the Marines and close observation was made along both shorelines for signs of Spanish activity. Spanish soldiers made good use of natural cover though and maintained harassing fire on the Marines position at Camp McCalla day and night.

Chaplain Harry Jones of the *Texas* volunteered to assist the Marines at Camp McCalla. On June 12th he went ashore with Marines from the *Texas* in support of the Marine Corps' 1st Battalion and in this capacity conducted a funeral under Spanish sniper fire.

The *Texas* also sent ashore two Colt machine guns as well as 10,000 rounds of 6mm and 45 caliber ammunition (6mm for the Marines and 45 caliber for the 45 caliber Springfield rifles supplied to the Cuban insurgents). Although there were no casualties among the *Texas'* officers and Marines during their activities ashore, they were under frequent harassing fire.

The boats from the *Texas* carrying ashore the ship's Marines as well as Chaplain Jones.

In an article published by the *New York Sun* on June 13, 1898, the following incident was recorded: "...Between 1 and 1:30 o'clock [A.M.] the general fire was hottest. Every fresh shot or volley from the bush was followed by the rattling clatter of the Colt [machine] gun, which made the rapid discharge of the rifles seem slow shooting. Private Frick, one of the marines from the *Texas*, under Lt. Radford, was on the hill. He challenged a man he saw moving near a clump of bushes, between him and the new camp quarters, For reply the sight was shot off his gun before he could fire..."

The field carriage-mounted Colt machine gun from the *Texas* was positioned in the trenches atop the hill at Camp McCalla, Guantanamo Bay, Cuba. The other Colt machine gun loaned by the *Texas* to the Marines, as well as the two additional Colts already in use there, are believed to have been tripod-mounted. These guns were used by the Marines of the 1st Battalion in decisive and dramatic fashion in the subsequent Battle of Cuzco Wells.

The Marines manning the trenches at Camp McCalla also had the use of a naval 3 pounder field gun, seen emplaced in the image below.

The 3 pounder field gun of the *Texas* was not off loaded during the war. It remained aboard the battleship, positioned on the forward boat deck, manned and operated under fire by the ship's Marine contingent.

The Marines served under great hardship at Guantanamo. Spanish sniping was virtually continuous, the heat was oppressive, and water was in short supply. This last factor might have been a blessing in disguise however, as the Marines used fresh water provided by the distillation plants on the Navy's ships and therefore did not suffer from the illnesses which would contribute to the US Army's heavy casualties in the Santiago campaign.

The primary naval/marine rifle was the 6mm Lee straight pull bolt action rifle The Marine shore parties were supported by 6mm Colt Machine Guns and light field pieces. Although the Lee rifle proved short-lived in US government service, it served the Marines well-enough in the short Cuban campaign.

To guarantee the security of their position and eliminate the sniper threat, the Marines of the 1st Battalion carried the war to the enemy, moving eastward up the peninsula and meeting the advancing Spanish troops at Cuzco Wells. Company "C", armed with three of the four Colt machine guns available to the forces at Camp McCalla (including one from the *Texas*), out-gunned the Spanish and through this action ended any significant opposition to the Marine position at Guantanamo Bay.

Marines entered combat in Cuba wearing their traditional kepis, but soon replaced these with broad brimmed hats more suitable to action ashore under an oppressive tropical sun, as seen in these images.

On June 15th the *Texas* returned to Guantanamo Bay where she and *Marblehead*, accompanied by the *Suwannee*, aggressively steamed 2.5 miles up the bay to engage the Spanish guns of the fort at Caimanera. The fort at Caimanera overlooked a relatively narrow neck of water and protected the entrance to the Bay of Joa and Upper Guantanamo bay.

Navigation under fire in these restrictive waters was difficult, made more so by the likelihood of a Spanish mine field in the waters adjacent to the fort. Captain McCalla of the *Marblehead* provided a local pilot to help guide the *Texas*. The insurgent pilot informed Captain Philip of the *Texas* that there were no mines and that there was plenty of depth to the water in the bay near the fort. Apparently unimpressed with the pilot's reliability, Captain Philip informed him, "You run me aground, and I will swing you on the yard arm." Moments later the *Marblehead* signalled "There is something afoul with my propeller." She had encountered the first of many Spanish mines to be seen that day.

In the words of Chaplain Jones, the "poor insurgent…was frightened almost to death."

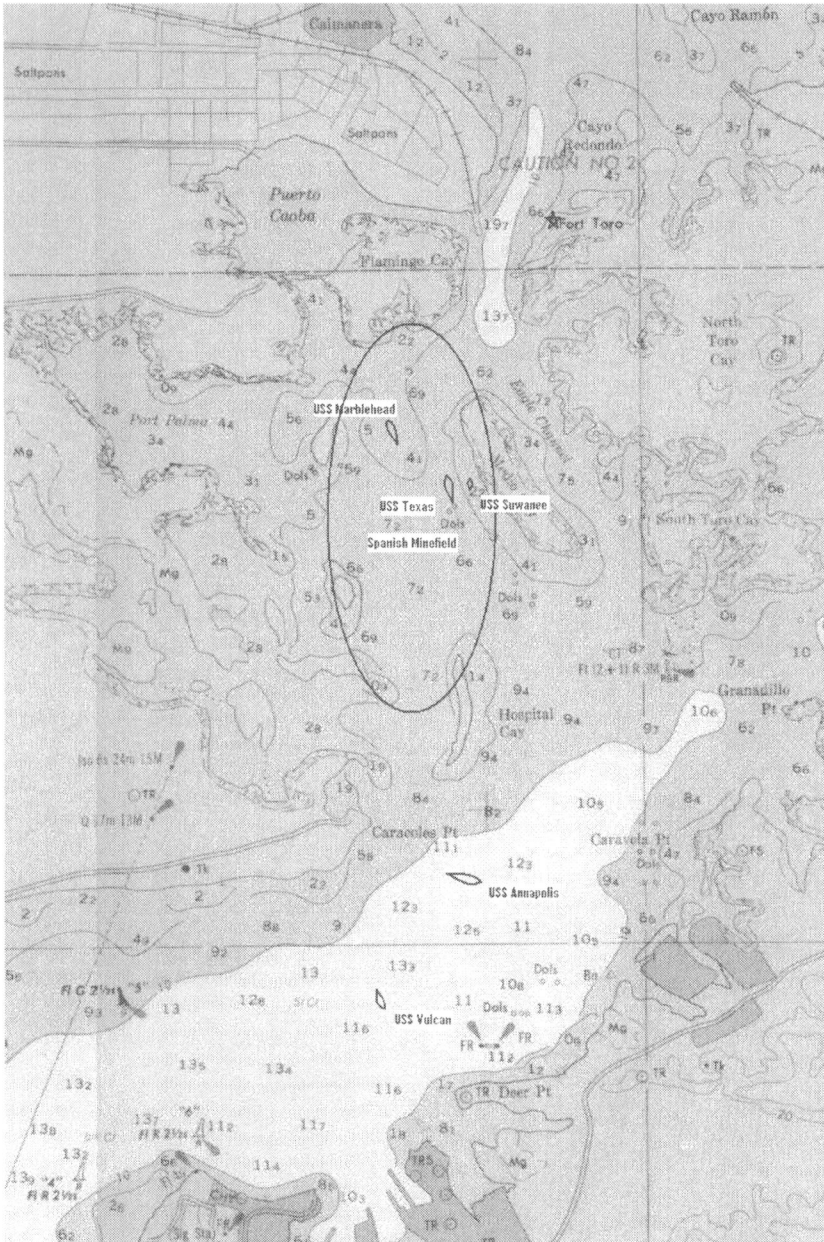

Detail of modern map of the middle Guantanamo Bay, annotated with ship positions as per an 1898 hand drawn map in a private collection.

The Chaplain, going below found the ship's barber standing in the passageway. The barber said "Well Chaplain, if the Dagoes shoot across our decks today, they won't hit me; I have been sent down here to stand by to assist when the magazines are opened" to which the Chaplain somewhat insensitively replied "No…the Spaniards won't hit you down here; but if we should happen to strike a mine, you will not be around to tell the story of how it happened."

Returning topside the Chaplin found to his horror that while he had been conversing flippantly with the barber near the magazines below, the Texas had in fact struck two mines and fouled another on its propeller – none of which exploded.

The twelve inch guns of the *Texas* dominated the action and the guns of the fort were silenced.

In this action the *Texas* narrowly escaped destruction by Spanish mines, actually fouling one in her propellers, as seen in the illustration at left from a contemporary newspaper. Fortunately the Spanish mines were poorly maintained and did not explode.

By securing Guantanamo Bay, the *Texas* and *Marblehead* ensured that a safe and calm harbor was available for the coaling of warships, greatly increasing the efficiency and therefore the security of the fleet. Capt. Philip submitted his report:

"U. S. S. '*Texas*,' off Santiago, June 16, 1898. Sir: I respectfully submit the following statement: Yesterday at 8:45 A. M. the flag-ship signaled the '*Texas*:' 'Proceed without delay, Guantanamo; destroy fort; resume blockade station this evening.' At 8:50 went ahead at full speed, steam, under three boilers only. At 1:07 beat to general quarters for action, and stood up through the narrow channel, followed by the '*Marblehead*,' to the westward of Cayo del Hospital in order to get within effective range of the fort on Cayo del Toro. Went ahead until in 25 feet water, dropped anchor under foot, and at 2:06 P. M. opened fire on the fort at 2,300 yards, the fort having opened fire on us as we passed the Hospital Cove. About 2:45 the fort ceased firing, and at 3:20 we ceased to fire, having destroyed in obedience to orders, though in all probability the enemy will remount guns, again in three or four days. Being ordered to resume station on blockade the same evening, we got under way about 3:30, stood out the channel and down the harbor and returned to this place, reporting to the commander-in-chief in person about 8:45 P. M. I would state that in going through the narrow channel to the westward of Cayo del Hospital the '*Texas*' broke adrift a contact submarine mine, and the '*Marblehead*' picked up one on her starboard propeller, each containing about 106 pounds of gun cotton, but owing to Divine care neither of them exploded.

There was no casualty nor injury of any kind, but I trust the action of the '*Texas*' will meet with your approbation. Very Respectfully, J. W. PHILLIP, Captain U. S. N., Commanding.
(to) The Commander-in-Chief, North Atlantic Squadron."

The Spanish Bustamente mine that might have sunk the *Texas*, seen onboard the ship next to the aft six inch deck gun. On raising the fouled mine to the deck it was observed that the mine had a visible dent in it where the spinning blade of the *Texas'* propeller had struck it directly between two of the contact triggers. Seeing the dent, Captain Philip remarked, "Cracky, but that was a close call."

The mine is resting upside down with the charge at the top having been removed. The horns, which if contacted would have set off the charge, are seen ringing the top of the inverted mine.

Mines were widely considered to be the greatest threat to a warship trying to force her way into a defended harbor. The *Texas* was extremely lucky, but fortune sometimes does favor the bold, and Captain Philip of the *Texas* and Captain McCalla of the *Marblehead* were bold indeed to steam into the unfamiliar, restricted, and mined waters to engage the guns of a fort. Captain Philip's aggressiveness, in consideration with his well known religious zeal, does not appear to have been fostered by any lust for glory, but rather stemmed from a determination to see the job done.

A contemporary illustration of a Bustamente mine with the complete outfit necessary for its emplacement and use is shown below.

The horns of the mine contained glass ampoules, which if broken by contact would create a chemical mix that would excite an electric charge to detonate the mines. Despite the lack of success by Spanish mines during the war, similar devices would wreck havoc in future conflicts.

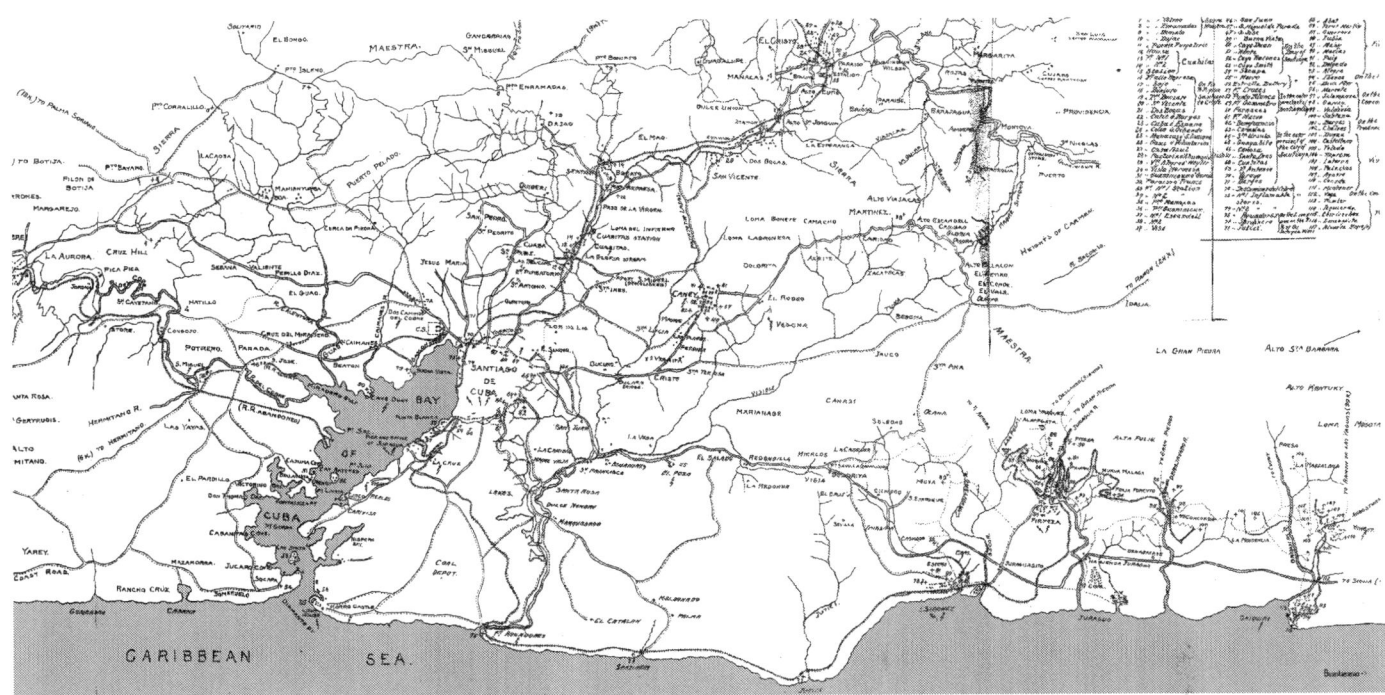

In the Santiago region, like most of Cuba, Spanish forces were concentrated around population centers, forts, and guard houses. Communications with neighboring forces was moderately good but receiving actual support from other regions was difficult due to the activities of Cuban insurgents in the countryside. Supplies, particularly food and coal, were severely limited and of low quality.

The US plan of action was for the Navy to guard the mouth of the harbor against any attempt by the Spanish warships to leave while the Army would land an invasion force at Daiquiri to the east of Santiago, well away from the Spaniards' concentrated defences. As the Army advanced to the west, a subsequent landing could then be made at Siboney to secure the Army's left flank and shorten its supply lines to the sea. Cuban revolutionary forces would be tasked with preventing the Spanish forces from receiving re-supply from the north or west and with keeping steady pressure on the Spanish to compel them to spread their forces completely around the perimeter of the city. This plan of action was essentially similar to that of the English, who were defeated in their attempt to take Santiago from the Spanish in the Eighteenth Century. The English effort had succumbed to tropical disease that arose annually in the late summer. It was the goal of the US Army to complete their campaign before a similar fate befell it.

While the Spanish forces were compelled to form a complete perimeter around the city, they concentrated their strength in trenches and fortified guardhouses along the ridges which ran perpendicular to the US Army's path of approach. Their ground forces were reinforced by sailors and guns from the naval vessels in the harbor and a relief column from Havana was expected. Their goal was to hold out until the disease season descended upon and defeated the Americans, as it had the English over a century before.

US Navy Order of Battle for the Landing at Daiquiri

NORTH ATLANTIC STATION

U.S. FLAGSHIP NEW YORK (1st Rate)

Off Santiago de Cuba, Cuba,

June 21, 1898.

ORDER OF BATTLE.

1.--The Army Corps will land tomorrow morning, the entire force landing at Daiquiri. The landing will begin at daylight, or as soon thereafter as practicable. General Castillo with a thousand men coming from the Eastward of Daiquiri will assist in clearing the way for an unopposed landing, by flanking out the Spanish forces at that point.

2.--Simultaneously with the shelling of the beach and blockhouses at Daiquiri, the Ensenada de los Altares, and Aguadores, both to the Eastward of Santiago, and the small bay of Cabanas about two and one-half miles to the Westward of Santiago will be shelled by the ships stationed there for that purpose.

3.--A feint in force of landing at Cabanas will be made, about ten of the transports, the last to disembark their forces at Daiquiri remaining during the day or greater part of the day, about two miles to the Southward of Cabanas, lowering boats, and making apparent preparations for disembarking a large body of troops; at the same time General Rabi with 500 Cuban troops will make a demonstration on the West side of Cabanas.

4.--The following vessels are assigned to bombard the four points mentioned above:

At Cabanas, the SCORPION, VIXEN and TEXAS.
At Aguadores, the EAGLE and GLOUCESTER.
At Ensenada de los Altares, the HORNET, HELENA and BANCROFT.
At Daiquiri, the DETROIT, CASTINE, WASP and NEW ORLEANS, the DETROIT and CASTINE on the Western flank, the WASP and NEW ORLEANS on the Eastern flank. All the vessels named will be in their position by daylight.

5.--Great care will be taken to avoid the wasteful expenditure of ammunition. The firing at Daiquiri will begin on signal from the NEW ORLEANS.
At Cabanas it is probable that, after a few minutes, unless the firing is returned, occasional dropping shots from the smaller vessels will be sufficient, but the semblance of covering a landing should be maintained, the ships keeping close in.
At Aguadores and Ensenada de los Altares the same rule should prevail. At Daiquiri, the point of actual landing, vessels will of course use their artillery until they have reason to believe that the landing is clear. They will take care to make the firing deliberate and effective. As General Castillo's column, approaching from the Eastward, is likely to come within range of the guns, sharp-eyed quartermasters with good glasses will be stationed to look out for the Cuban flag, and care will be taken not to direct the fire towards any point where that flag is shown.

6.--The TEXAS and BROOKLYN will exchange blockading stations, the TEXAS going inside to be near Cabanas. The BROOKLYN, MASSACHUSETTS, IOWA and OREGON will retain their blockading positions, and will keep a vigilant watch on the harbor mouth. The INDIANA will take the NEW ORLEANS' position in the blockading line West of Santiago, and between the flagship NEW YORK and the shore. This is only a temporary assignment for the INDIANA, to strengthen the blockading line during the landing, and avoid any possibility of the enemy's breaking through should he attempt to get out of the Port.

7.--The SUWANEE, OSCEOLA and SAUPATUCK will be prepared to tow boats. Each will be provided with two five or six-inch lines, one on each quarter; each long enough to take in tow a dozen or more boats.

8.--These vessels will report at the NEW YORK at 3.00 a.m. on June 22nd, prepared to take in tow the ships' boats which are to assist in the landing of troops and convey them to Daiquiri.

9.--The TEXAS, BROOKLYN, MASSACHUSETTS, IOWA, OREGON, NEW YORK and INDIANA will send all their steam cutters and all their pulling boats with the exception of one retained on board each ship, to assist in the landing. These boats will report at the NEW YORK at 3.00 a.m.

10.--Each boat, whaleboat and cutter will have three men; each launch five men, and each steam cutter its full crew and an officer for their own management. In addition to these men, each boat will carry five men, including one capable of acting as coxswain to manage and direct the transports' boats. Each steam launch will be in charge of an officer, who will report to Captain Goodrich. Care will be taken in the selection of boat-keepers and coxswains, to take no men who are gun-pointers, or who occupy positions of special importance at the battery.

11.--Unnecessary oars and impedimenta should be removed from the pulling boats, for the greater convenience of the transportation of troops; but each boat should retain its anchor and chain.

12.--Captain Goodrich, commanding the ST. LOUIS, will have, on the part of the Navy, general charge of the landing.

13.--The NEW ORLEANS will send her boats to report to Captain Goodrich upon her arrival at Daiquiri.

14.--The attention of Commanding officers of all vessels engaged in blockading Santiago de Cuba is earnestly called to the necessity of the utmost vigilance from this time forward--both as to maintaining stations and readiness for action, and as to keeping a close watch upon the harbor mouth. If the Spanish Admiral ever intends to attempt to escape that attempt will be made soon.

WILLIAM T. SAMPSON,
REAR ADMIRAL,
COMMANDER-IN-CHIEF U.S. NAVAL FORCE,
NORTH ATLANTIC STATION.

The US invasion fleet gathers off of Daiquiri.

The *Texas*, like the other Navy vessels, supported the Army's landing by loaning boats and boat crews. Her second steam launch along with both the first and second cutter, under the command of Naval Cadet Reynolds carried Army personnel from the transport ships to the shore.

The Daiquiri landing on June 22nd, compared to the smooth efficiency of the Marine landing at Guantanamo, was accomplished with great difficulty. Fortunately there was no resistance from the Spanish forces who retired to prepared positions surrounding the city of Santiago.

The lack of a dock that could be approached by ocean-going ships necessitated that all of the soldiers and equipment had to be brought ashore in boats. Horses were made to swim from the transports to the beach. According to reports, when panicked Army horses became disoriented and began swimming out to sea, a quick thinking bugler sounded "Recall" and the well-drilled horses turned back to land.

During this chaotic processes, one of Colonel Roosevelt's horses was drowned. His second horse, named "Little Texas", made it to the beach and went on to fame carrying Roosevelt in his charge up Kettle Hill during the "Battle of San Juan Hill".

METHOD OF LANDING HORSES FROM TRANSPORTS

LANDING AT THE PIER, DAIQUIRI.—Photograph by James Burton

The *Texas'* steam launch returned to the ship off Santiago on June 24th, while the cutters remained at Daiquiri with the Army transports.

"We watched the Texas silence the battery"

While the Army landed at Daiquiri, the *Texas*, along with the *Brooklyn* and two transport vessels engaged the Socapa batteries west of the mouth of Santiago Bay from 5:45 pm until 7 pm, in a diversionary attack intended to divide Spanish attention between their eastern and western approaches.

Sailors aboard the *Brooklyn* (left) watch the *Texas*' gunners in action in what was described by a witness as a "spectacular" show of marksmanship as "she dropped shell after shell right on the ridge of the hill where the enemy's guns lay."

In this engagement the *Texas* incurred its most serious loss of the war. The last 6.3 inch Spanish shell fired from the Socapa battery hit her port gun deck forward of the armored redoubt, passed between two engaged gun crews, cut through a four-inch stanchion and exploded killing seaman F.J. Blakely and wounding G. F. Mullen, R. Russel, R. Errgel, H.E. Lee, J. F. Lively, J. Nelson, J.J. Simonsea, and A. Sivgrist, who were standing by their guns on the disengaged starboard side. Seaman Blakely was buried at sea that afternoon. Blakely, whose enlistment expired earlier, had volunteered to stay aboard for the war cruise, in the hope of seeing action. Though one gun at the Socapa battery had been buried beneath the dirt kicked up by the 12-inch shells of the *Texas*, it was back in action within hours.

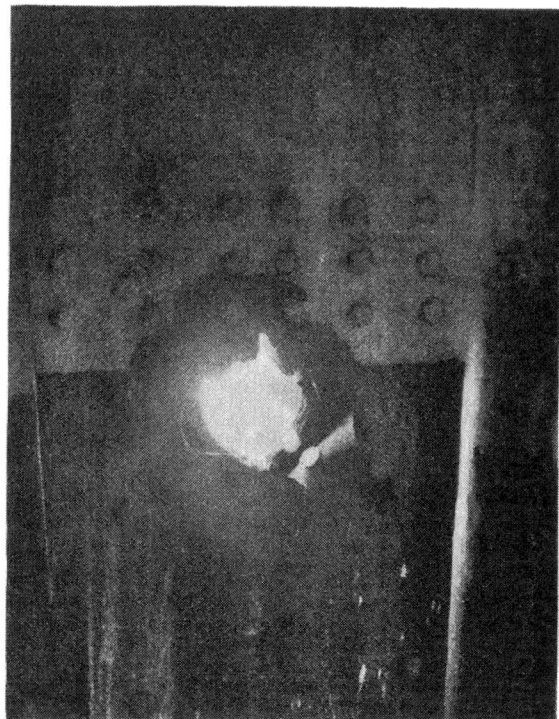

3.—Hole Made by 6-inch Shell in Port Bow on Gun Deck.

1.—Starboard Ship's Frame on Gun Deck Cut in Two Places by Fragments of 6-inch Shell.

"OLD HOODOO": THE BATTLESHIP TEXAS

ENGAGEMENT OFF SANTIAGO, JUNE 22, 1898.
U. S. S. TEXAS.

Case No. 1.—Lacerated wounds from explosion of a 6-inch shell. The body was mangled and partly dismembered. Death was instantaneous.

Case No. 2.—Lacerated wound in front of right ear from fragment of shell. Wound dressed and patient discharged to duty same day. Number of days on sick list, one.

Case No. 3.—Lacerated wound of left forearm and contusion of left popliteal space from fragments of shell. The wound of forearm involved only soft parts. Upon exploration no fragments of shell could be found. Discharged to duty July 3. Number of days on sick list, nine.

Case No. 4.—Lacerated wound of right great toe. Fragment of shell removed from wound and aseptic dressing applied. Discharged to duty June 22, 1898. Number of days on sick list, one.

Case No. 5.—Contused wound behind right ear from fragment of shell. Not serious. Discharged to duty June 22. Number of days on sick list, one.

Case No. 6.—Lacerated wounds of right thigh and left leg from fragments of shell. Careful exploration failed to reveal any of the fragments in the wounds. Gauze drainage was employed and aseptic dressings applied. Patient was transferred to *Solace*, thence to naval hospital, Norfolk, where he was admitted July 16, and discharged to duty July 23. Number of days on sick list, thirty-one.

Case No. 7.—Flesh wound about 2½ inches in length, extending down to great trochanter of left femur. Patient transferred to *Solace*, thence to naval hospital, Norfolk, where he was admitted July 16. The wound healed perfectly, and he was discharged to duty August 29 in excellent condition. Number of days on sick list, sixty-eight.

Case No. 8.—Burns of forehead, eyelids, right ear, nose, lips, left hand, and right wrist from powder flash of bursting shell. Injuries superficial and shock very slight. Patient transferred to *Solace*, thence to naval hospital, Norfolk, where he was admitted July 16 and discharged to duty July 22. This man was assigned to duty on the U. S. S. *Cæsar*, where he was surveyed July 31 for persistent headache resulting from the concussion of the exploding shell on June 22. A second survey was held September 1, and in accordance therewith he was invalided from the service by reason of chronic inflammation of right ear and persistent headache. Number of days on sick list for burns, thirty.

Case No. 9.—Seventeen lacerated wounds from shell fragments; principal injuries located as follows: One of right thigh, 3½ inches in length, below groin, extending deeply into outer muscles; one near insertion of patellar ligament, lacerating and bruising soft tissues to outer side of left tibia; one 3½ inches above left ankle down to the tendons; one of left eyelid, the iris being torn and hæmorrhage into ocular humours caused, although no external wound of eyeball produced; several trivial wounds of wrists and feet. Patient was transferred to *Solace*, thence to naval hospital, Norfolk, and later on to naval hospital, Philadelphia, where he was admitted on August 3. On admission the wounds below left knee and outer side of thigh were found unhealed and the outer quadrant of left iris detached. On September 1 wounds were recorded as healed. September 17 the detached portion of iris fixed by adhesions and the lens becoming cloudy. The cloudiness of the lens has progressed and vision has steadily failed. Patient surveyed October 10, and recommended to be invalided from the service. Number of days on sick list, one hundred and ten.

Photo of the *Texas* taken after her return from Cuban waters showing what appears to be the patched entry hole left by the 6.3-inch shell that killed Seaman Blakely, seen directly below the cross arm of the stowed anchor. The section inset shows the location of the hit.

It appears that the hole was plugged using a Colmes Stopper, a piece of damage control equipment carried by Navy vessels during the war, as seen in a contemporary issue of Scientific American.

One dead and eight wounded crewmen made the "butcher's bill" from the *Texas'* surgeon.

Shortly after the funeral of Seaman Blakely, while the blockading squadron lay off Santiago, one of the guns of the USS *Massachusetts* suddenly and unintentionally discharged, its shell passing harmlessly over the *Texas*. Capt. Philip displaying his characteristic wit, wryly signaled his close friend Capt. Higginson of the *Massachusetts*, "Good line shot, but a little high."

The USS *Massachusetts* as she appeared in 1898.

As the campaign proceeded, the Army and Navy strategies diverged. The Navy considered the Army's principal goal to be the silencing of the forts at the mouth of the bay so that the Navy could disable the Spanish minefields and then sail in and attack the Spanish ships. The army instead focused on the capture of the city of Santiago, hoping in this way to secure the surrender of the Spanish warships to the Army. Inter-service rivalry would play a role in the campaign, as well as in joint operations for many years to come.

16 BATTLE OF SANTIAGO: JULY 3, 1898

"Crewmen of my Squadron! The solemn moment of fighting has come. The sacred name of Spain and the glorious honor of her flag so demands. I want you to assist me in this rendezvous with the enemy dressed in our full-dress uniforms. I know my order has surprised you because of its inadequacy but it is the uniform which Spanish sailors dress in the great solemnities and I do not believe that there is a more solemn time than that when a soldier is going to die for his fatherland. The enemy covets our old and glorious hulls. They have sent the whole power of their young navy against us so as to achieve this goal, but they will be only able to take the splinters of our ships, and they will only be able to take our sabers from us when, as corpses, we remain floating in this waters which belonged and belongs to Spain. My sons, the enemy is superior to us in strength but they are not in courage. Hoist the flag and surrender no ship. Crewmen of my squadron, up with Spain!" – Admiral Cervera

Some fight, eh Jack? – Admiral Schley

COMBINED SEA AND LAND ATTACK AT AGUADORES, JULY 1. — Drawn by Carlton T. Chapman

DESTRUCTION OF THE FORT AT AGUADORES, JULY 1. — Drawn by Carlton T. Chapman
The *Suwanee's* three splendid shots: the first tilted the flag-staff; the second tore the flag in two; the third carried it away

US Army forces safely ashore at Daiquiri and advancing inland from the beachhead, American naval attention once again focused on the harbor fortifications that stood between themselves and the Spanish fleet.

At 10 am on the morning of July 1st, as US Army forces advanced from the east along the railroad line from Daiquiri in the direction of the mouth of Santiago Bay, US warships including the *New York* and several smaller vessels closed on the fort at Aguadores to provide fire support, shelling the fort to destruction over the course of the next five hours. The *Texas* simultaneously closed on the Upper Socapa Battery west of Santiago in a feint before retiring to a position off of the mouth of the harbor to watch for any potential response from the Spanish fleet.

NAVAL BOMBARDMENT OF SANTIAGO'S HARBOR DEFENCES, JULY 2.—Drawn by Carlton T. Chapman

At 5:30 am on July 2nd warships including the *Texas*, *New York*, *Newark*, *Brooklyn*, *Oregon*, *Indiana*, *Iowa*, *Massachusetts*, and *Vixen* once again closed on the Spanish fortifications, this time shelling Morro Castle and the Battery on Punta Gordo until 7:30 am. In this action the *Texas* expended 6 common and 2 armor piercing 12-inch shells, 104 common and 1 shrapnel 6-inch shells, and 55 common 6-pdr shells.

The Navy viewed these actions as a prelude to a combined Army-Navy attack on the Morro Castle guarding the entrance to the harbor. If the Castle could be taken by US troops, the Navy could then neutralize the minefields and attempt to force the mouth of the harbor and engage the Spanish fleet within and force the city's surrender. The Army, on the other hand saw these actions as little more than a feint, or at best an extension of its lines to the coast to complete its encirclement of the city of Santiago in preparation for laying siege to the city. The Army intended to capture the city, simultaneously capturing the Spanish warships sheltering in the harbor as a one of the terms of the city's surrender. The fundamental difference in strategy had come to a head, necessitating a coordination meeting between the Army and Navy commanders. This meeting was scheduled to take place at Daiquiri the next day.

To Cevera and the Spanish naval forces, these attacks underscored the futility in remaining in the false security of Santiago Bay and telegrams from Madrid ordered him to sortie. The only honorable course would be to make a breakout, or die in the attempt.

Vessels involved in the Naval Battle of Santiago

Scale illustrations from Brasseys Naval Annual, the leading contemporary naval digest. Modern rendered illustrations of the *Vixen*, *Gloucester*, and *Reina Mercedes* provided courtesy of Jullio Pillet. No scale views of the Spanish gunboat *Alvarado*, which was present in Santiago Bay but did not directly participate in the sortie, are available.

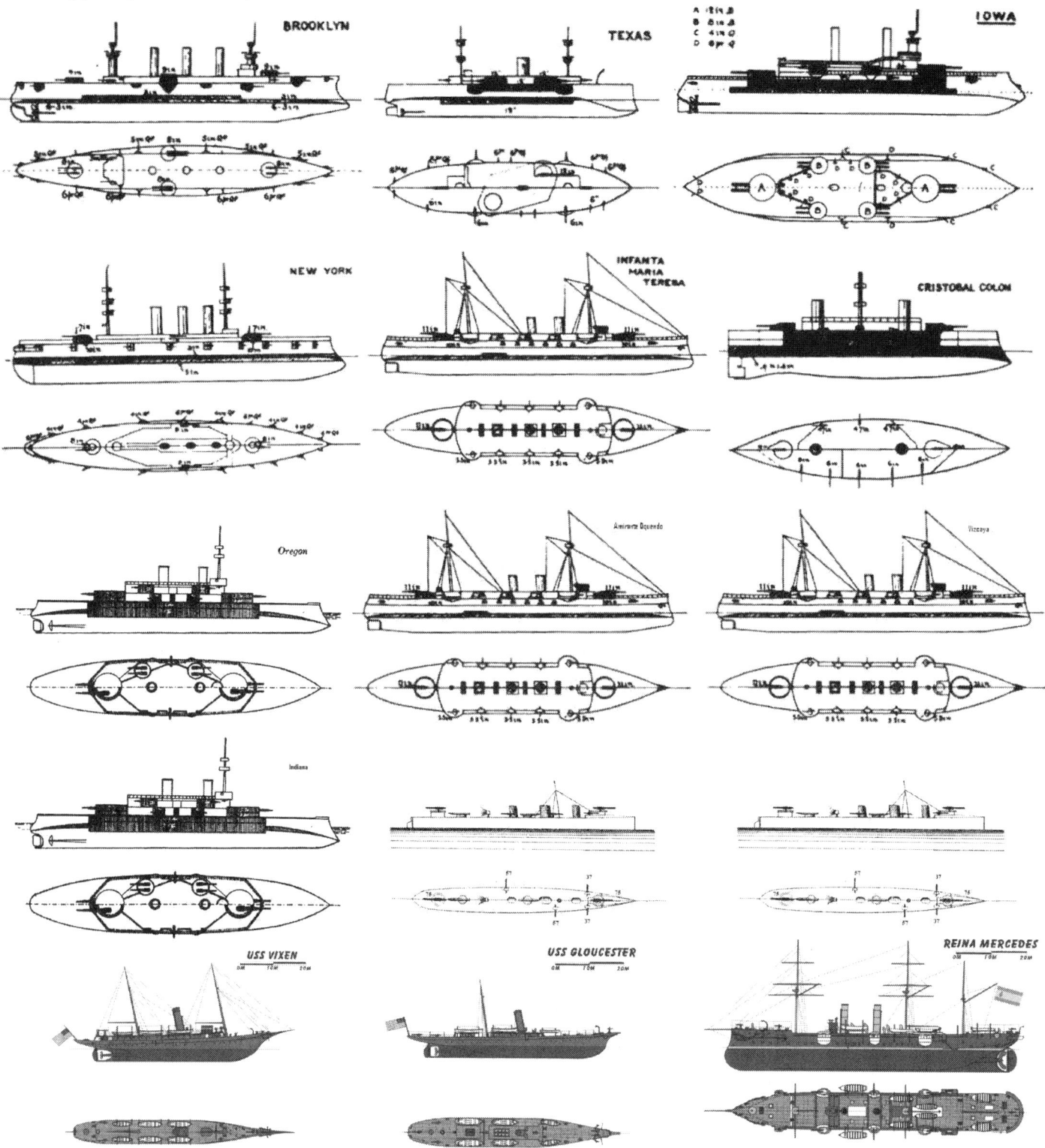

With the investment of Santiago from the east by the US Army and from the west by Cuban irregulars, it was apparent that, should the Spanish Fleet remain in Santiago Harbor, it would suffer the same fate as the besieged city. Admiral Cervera called a council of his captains and resolved that a daylight sortie would give most of the Spanish ships a chance to escape capture. As the heavy American battleships stood to the east protecting the American beachhead, Cervera, in the *Maria Teresa*, would lead a breakout to the west (view to the west along the Cuban coast shown above). His intent was to sacrifice his flagship by directly attacking and torpedoing or ramming the *Brooklyn*, well known to be the fastest American ship engaged. The remainder of the Spanish fleet would then outrun the slow US battleships and out-fight the cruisers. With good luck the remaining Spanish vessels would not be subject to the big guns for long.

The choice of July 3 turned out to be opportune for the Spanish, as the cruiser *New York* with Admiral Sampson aboard, hoisted the signal "Disregard movements of Commander-in-Chief" and left her position in the blockade to deliver Admiral Sampson to a meeting with the Army commander ashore, and the *Massachusetts* was away coaling at Guantanamo Bay.

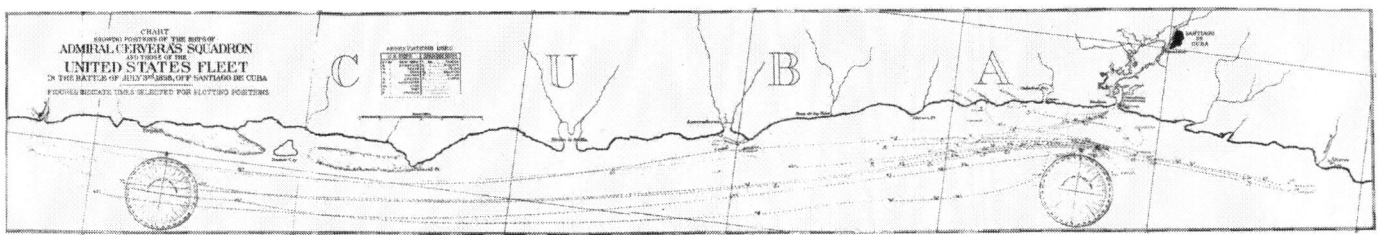

*The precise movements of the US vessels during the initial stage of the action, as depicted in this official chart, came under intense criticism several years later during the Sampson-Schley Hearings and is still a matter of some debate.

At 9:35 am on Sunday, July 3rd, as the *Texas* lay facing east 5,000 yards off the harbor mouth, Lt. Bristol on the bridge of the *Texas* saw smoke above Socapa Point and then the bow of a Spanish warship emerging around the bend in the channel.

Signal 2.5.0. "The enemy is trying to escape," was hoisted on the American ships as the Spanish fleet came out in single file. Lt. Bristol sounded the general alarm and called the engine room via the speaking tube saying, "hustle as the enemy is coming out." Capt. Philip was on the bridge within moments of the alarm. Aboard the *Texas* the men sprang into action. Ammunition hoists and magazines were opened, the ammunition handlers sliding down the hoist cables to their stations in their anxiety to get into the fight. The first 12" shell was brought up for Lt. Haeseler's starboard turret, on its side was written in chalk the rhyme, "In God we trust, This shell will bust, And blow the Dagoes into dust."

As Admiral Cevera had planned, the *Maria Teresa* aggressively charged the *Brooklyn*, which lay about 7,000 yards from shore, immediately to the west of the *Texas*. Within three minutes of the sounding of her general alarm the *Texas* was making maximum revolutions with guns firing and all posts manned. As the *Texas'* port batteries opened fire on the lead Spanish cruiser at a range of 4,200 yards the American ships accelerated in attempt to close in on the harbor

mouth in a pre-planned effort to block the Spanish warships before they could all emerge. Admiral Sampson's written instructions had been, "If the enemy tries to escape, the ships must close and engage as soon as possible, and endeavor to sink his vessels or force them to run ashore in the channel." The accelerating *Texas* turned to port to close on the harbor mouth and then, as the direction of the attempted Spanish escape became clear, continued her turn to port to cut off or parallel the Spanish course to the west.

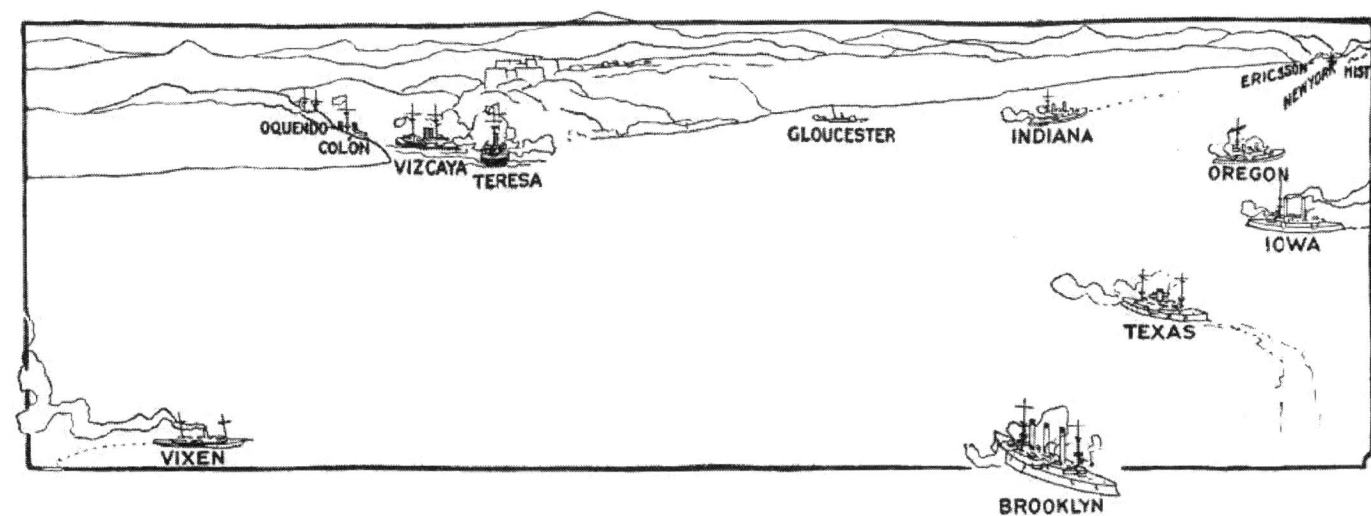

POSITION NO. 1. THE SPANISH SHIPS COMING OUT.

As the gunfire increased, the wind, blowing from behind the Spanish vessels and towards the American ships, caused the smoke from the Spanish guns to act as a smokescreen, partially masking the ships, obscuring the fall of individual shots, and making correction of aim for the American gunners difficult. Compounding this problem, the smoke from the American's own guns blew back over the US ships limiting even their ability to see one another. Spanish shots were for the most part passing high, the Spanish also being prevented from taking accurate aim due to the smoke enveloping the American ships.

While the *Maria Teresa* charged on an intercept course with the *Brooklyn*, her guns blazing, the *Vizcaya*, *Oquendo*, and *Colon* steamed out of the harbor and turned to the west accelerating and opening fire "with mechanical rapidity" on the encircling American warships.

Following the cruisers were the torpedo boat destroyers *Furor* and *Pluton* which, as purveyors of the much feared automobile torpedo, received special attention from the American gunners undue their diminutive size and limited firepower. Capt. Philip ordered all of the *Texas*' smaller guns to be turned upon them.

Onboard the flagship *Brooklyn* the onrushing Spanish warships prompted a quick conference between Commodore Schley, Captain Cook, and Lt. Hodgson, the *Brooklyn's* navigator, regarding how best to proceed. Schley first advocated a turn to port but then quickly assented to Cook's and Hodgson's suggested turn to the starboard.

Turning to port to block the escape of the Spanish cruisers would have placed the *Brooklyn* directly into a close range fight where Spanish torpedo or ramming attacks were a real possibility. The *Brooklyn's* turn to starboard took her away from the Spanish and directly into the path of the onrushing US warships which were picking up speed as they converged towards an increasingly congested bit of water.

Hodgson pointed out the danger the turn to starboard posed to the onrushing *Texas*, to which Schley snapped, "Damn the *Texas*! I can't help that. She must look out for herself."

The *Texas* and, immediately to the east of her the *Iowa*, were turning to port and increasing speed. The *Texas*, having initiated her turn from a more easterly bearing than the *Iowa*, was also moving faster than the *Iowa* and thus swinging through a wider-radius. Admiral Schley's words were being echoed on the bridge of the *Iowa* as her navigator alerted Capt. Evans that if they did not take care in their turn to the west they would "be into the *Texas*." Capt. Evans responded, "Let Philip look out for the *Texas*." Notwithstanding his comment, the *Iowa* eased her helm to swing wide and avoid turning into the *Texas*.

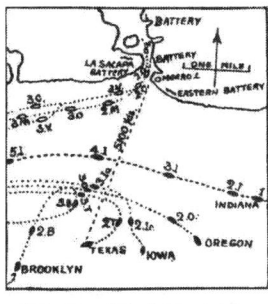

First phase of the Battle according to the New York *Sun*.

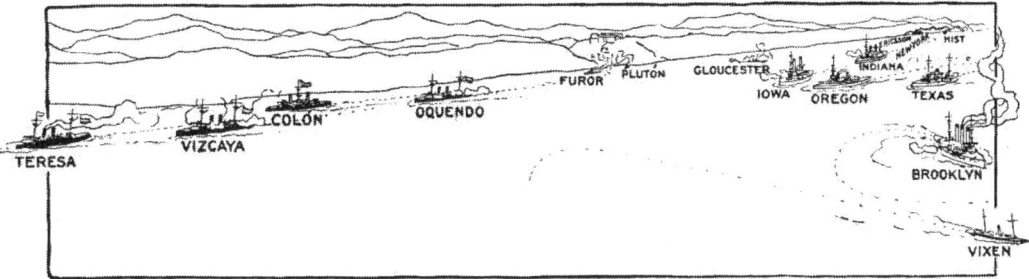

POSITION NO. 2. THE AMERICAN FLEET CLOSING IN.

In this opening phase of the battle, the *Texas* was rapidly coming up to speed while simultaneously engaging several Spanish ships at around 2000 yards range. Turning to port as did the *Iowa* and the *Oregon* on it's right, the *Texas* was ideally placed to engage the *Vizcaya*, but was suddenly forced to back engines full for three minutes as the *Brooklyn* appeared out of the smoke in the middle of her unexpected turn to starboard, the course of her bow sweeping across the onrushing *Texas*. The *Brooklyn*, making full speed, crossed the *Texas*' bow barely 150 yards ahead. The *Texas*, coming to a complete stop, caused the trailing *Oregon*, now at nearly 16 knots, to run up on the *Texas* and mask the fire of the *Texas*' gunners as she passed close by to starboard.

After the war Capt. Philip wrote: "The smoke from our guns began to hang so heavily and densely over the ship that for a few minutes we could see nothing...Suddenly a whiff of breeze and a lull in the firing lifted the pall, and there, bearing towards us and across our bows, turning on her port helm, with big waves curling over her bows and great clouds of smoke pouring from her funnels, was the *Brooklyn*. She looked as big as half a dozen *Great Easterns*, and seemed so near as to take our breath away. 'Back both engines hard!' went down the tube to the astonished engineers, and in a twinkling the old ship was racing against herself. The collision which seemed imminent, even if it was not, was averted, and as the big cruiser glided past, all of us on the bridge gave a sigh of relief".

These words and the accompanying dramatic illustration below appeared in *The Century Magazine* and fueled post-war criticism of Schley's performance.

Texas nearly colliding with Brooklyn, by F. Cresson Schell

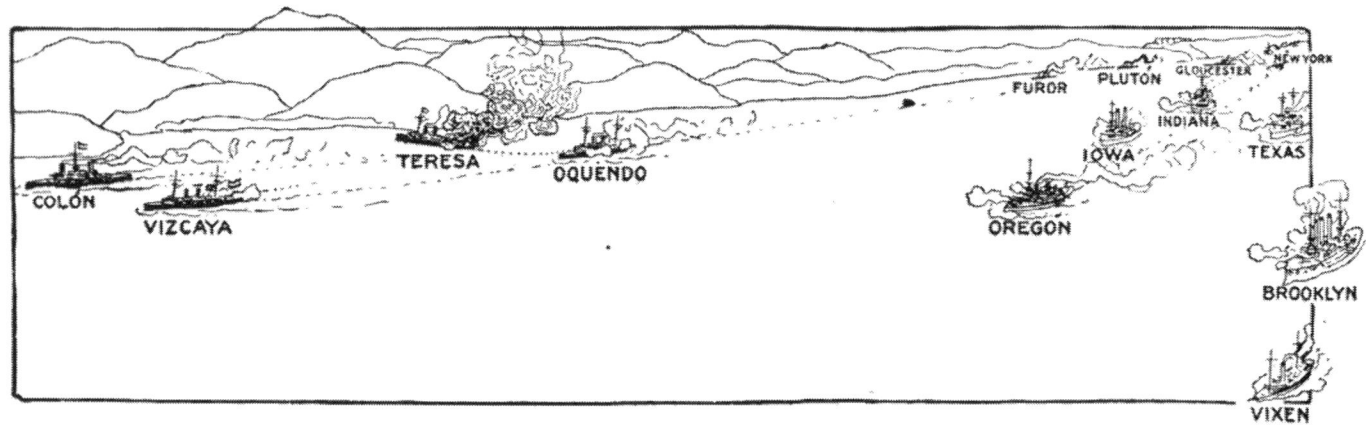

POSITION NO. 3. THE BATTLE AT ITS HEIGHT.

The *Maria Teresa*, as the lead ship out of the harbor and the initial target of every gun in the American fleet, was soon overcome by the deluge of shells and turned away to beach herself, a disabled and burning pyre. At this time the action was compressed as the *Vizcaya*, *Colon*, and the trailing *Oquendo* with the two destroyers, *Pluton* and *Furor*, were aligned parallel and somewhat ahead of the pursuing American warships. At about 9:50, with Spanish shells tearing the air above the flying bridge, Capt. Philip ordered the officers and men present to move to the lower bridge at the conning tower. As they descended the ladder a Spanish shell struck the jamb of the starboard door of the pilot house spraying the interior with splinters and fragments and carrying away the aft bulkhead. Philip's timely order to descend to the lower bridge had saved the lives of those who had occupied this space only moments before. Soon Spanish fire slackened as a defect in the 5.5" ammunition asserted itself.

The *Brooklyn*, having completed it's turn out to sea, now bore back into the battle and engaged the *Vizcaya* which was also engaged with the *Oregon*. The *Colon*, the newest and fastest of the Spanish ships had slipped past the *Vizcaya* and quickly separated herself from action.

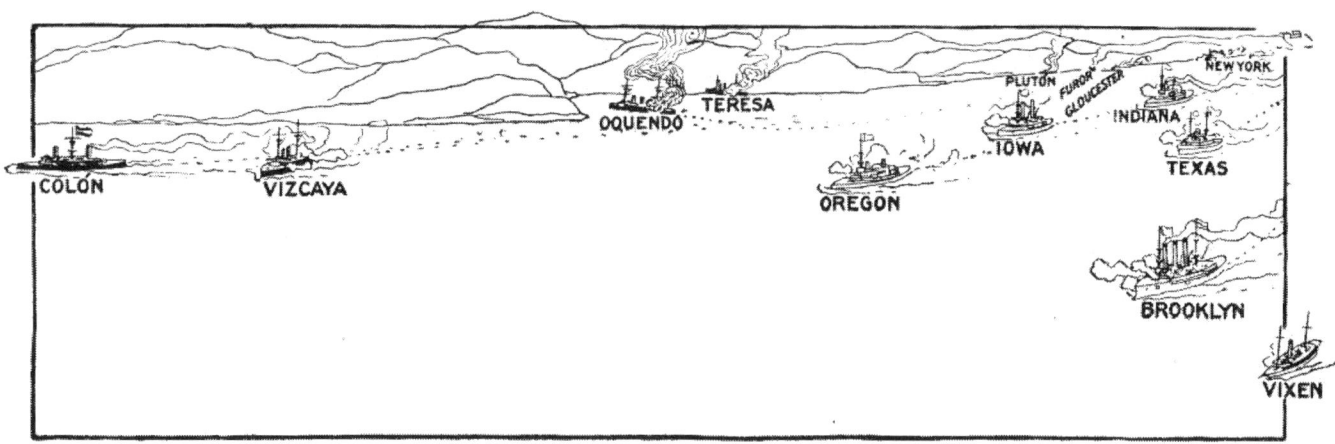

POSITION NO. 4. FOUR SPANISH VESSELS DISABLED.

The Spanish gun batteries ashore were not idle during the sortie, springing into action as the battle commenced and peppering the waters around the American ships with shrapnel for as long as they were within range.

The Spanish destroyers, trailing the Spanish squadron, now bore the brunt of the American secondary battery fire. As the *Texas* pulled away Ensign Gise and his gunners at the *Texas'* aft 6" gun claimed the hit that sank the *Furor*, several other ships also claiming the decisive strike.

THE "GLOUCESTER" AND THE SPANISH TORPEDO-BOATS.
The *Furor* is in a sinking condition, and the *Plutón* is heading for shore.

THE SINKING OF THE "FUROR."
The boats to the right going to the wreck of the *Plutón* are those under command of Assistant Engineer A. M. Procter (nearest the wreck) and of Lieutenant Thomas C. Wood. The smoke above the point of land is from the wrecks of the *Teresa* and the *Oquendo*. The other vessels of the fleets are shown in the distance.

THE SINKING OF THE DESTROYER "FUROR," AS SEEN FROM THE "GLOUCESTER." FROM A PHOTOGRAPH

The destroyer *Pluton* faired little better, harassed not only the secondary batteries of the large warships but also the smaller American vessels in the action. While the *Furor* sank in dramatic fashion in deep water, the burning *Pluton* ran up a white flag and turned for shore.

For a moment it appeared that Cervera's strategy might bear some fruit as both the *Vizcaya* and *Colon* broke out ahead of the American squadron. The trailing *Almirante Oquendo* and the destroyers were catching the attention of the *Texas*, now accelerating again. The ponderous *Iowa* and the *Indiana*, though on the eastern edge of the engagement, also answered.

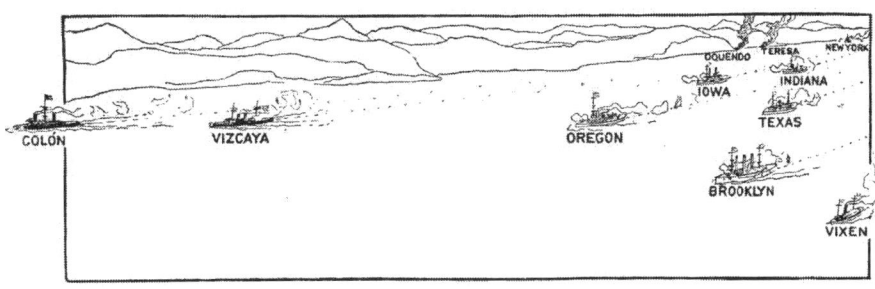

POSITION NO. 5. THE BEGINNING OF THE CHASE.

261

The *Oquendo* put up a spirited fight with her short supply of good ammunition. Shots from her initial 5.5 inch salvoes hit the *Texas* at least twice, one round entering her superstructure below the conning tower and exploding in her funnel, another striking the curved armored barbette sponson below the starboard turret, both rounds causing only superficial damage. A shot of unknown caliber also destroyed the starboard side aft searchlight.

Shortly before 11am the *Texas* began to disengage from the flaming *Oquendo*, which was joining the *Maria Teresa* in making a final turn to beach.

THE "GLOUCESTER'S" BOAT UNDER LIEUTENANT WOOD RESCUING THE CREW OF THE "OQUENDO."

By this time the *Brooklyn* was engaged in close action with a slower but pugnacious *Vizcaya*, which maneuvered to get within torpedo range. The *Brooklyn*, firing rapidly and effectively with her 8" and 5" guns, managed a hit on one of the *Vizcaya's* armed bow tube torpedoes, causing a spectacular explosion and forcing the *Vizcaya* to turn to the beach. Supporting the *Brooklyn*, the *Oregon* fired it's bow guns and at least one 13.5 inch shell was observed to rake the length of the *Vizcaya's* superstructure.

The *Vizcaya* had put up a spectacular fight against great odds, made worse by her fouled hull and short supply of good ammunition for her 5.5 inch guns. Within minutes of beaching, as her crew took to the boats, her burning hull was again racked by a massive explosion.

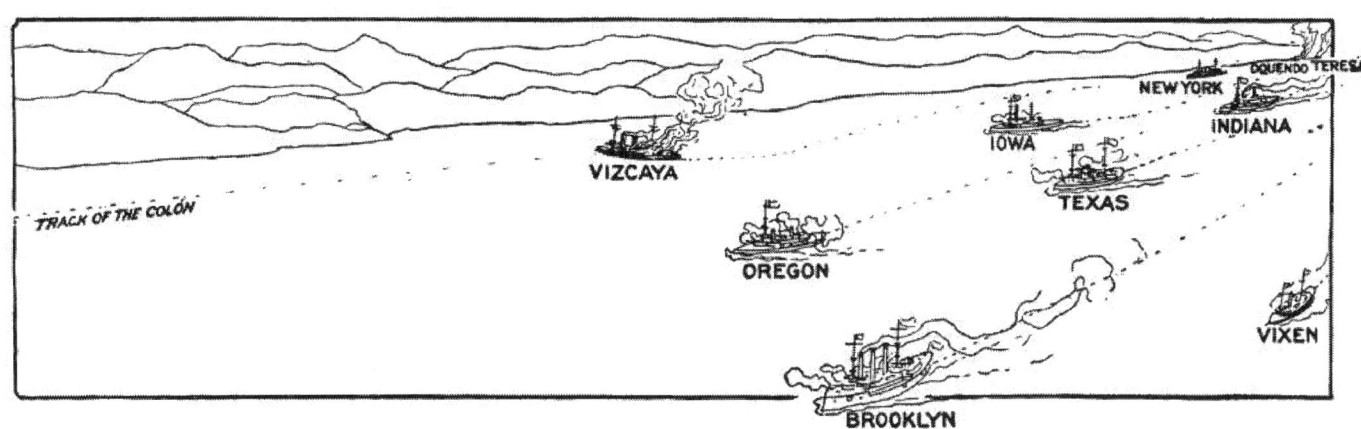

POSITION NO. 6. THE END OF THE "VIZCAYA."

The *Oregon* and *Brooklyn* had pounded the *Vizcaya* into submission but the fight was not over. The *Brooklyn*, the surprisingly fast *Oregon*, and the *Texas*, now again up to speed but a bit behind, continued the chase of the *Cristobal Colon*.

As the *Texas* passed the burning *Vizcaya*, her men lifted up a cheer of victory only to be remonstrated by Capt. Philip, "Don't cheer men, those devils are dying."

Pushing a foaming white "bone in her teeth" at her bow and with smoke belching from her stacks the *Colon* makes a dash. Pre-war photograph of the *Cristobal Colon* appearing much as she did during battle. The original publisher of the image apparently touched it up to accent the ship's 152 mm (6 inch) Armstrong guns along her sides. Note the lack of the main guns in the turrets.

With the *Vizcaya* out of the fight, the only remaining target was the *Cristobal Colon*, which had she escaped, would have caused significant embarrassment to the US Navy.

The *Brooklyn*, followed by the *Oregon* and the *Texas*, all of which were able to keep pace with the *Colon* once she ran out of her British coal, kept up the chase for about 75 miles with the *Brooklyn* in the lead out to seaward and the *Oregon* ahead of the *Texas*. By now the *Iowa*, knowing it could not keep up had turned back to the burning and beached Spanish ships to lend rescue assistance. Among the many survivors rescued was Admiral Cervera (opposite).

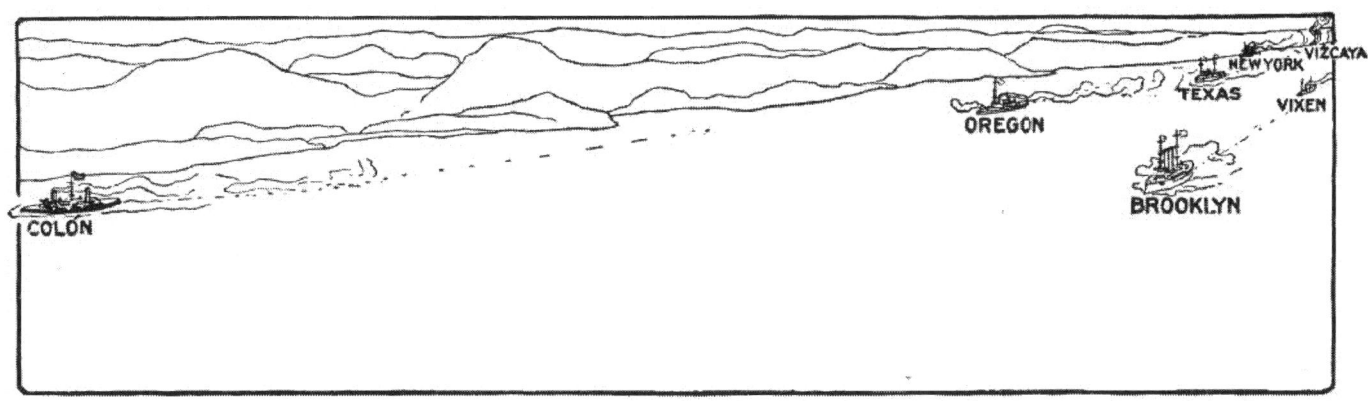

POSITION NO. 7. OVERHAULING THE "COLÓN"

As the battle transformed into a pursuit, the order went out aboard the *Texas*, "All hands aft!" The engines of the *Texas* raced at 114 revolutions.

Captain Philip watching the chase of the *Colon* from the battle scarred bridge of the *Texas* (right) while one of the *Texas'* 37MM Hotchkiss gunners stands ready (below right).

ADMIRAL CERVERA'S RECEPTION ON BOARD THE "IOWA."
The officer on the left is Captain Evans, the one on the right is Lieutenant-Commander Wainwright. The admiral's son, Lieutenant Angel Cervera, is just back of him.

Cristobal Colon   *Oregon*   *Brooklyn*

Had the *Colon* possessed a larger store of British coal, she might have out-run the American ships. Unfortunately for her, she used up her limited supply of Cardiff coal very quickly. The leading American warship, the *Brooklyn*, pursued a course straight for a distant headland, knowing that the *Colon* would eventually have to alter course and turn out to sea and into her guns. The *Oregon* and the *Texas* held a more direct course for the Spanish vessel. Behind the *Texas* now appeared the *New York* with Admiral Sampson in command, coming up fast and desperate to get a shot in the battle. Once the *Colon's* good coal was gone, all four pursing American vessels were gaining on her.

The chase was ended by the *Colon* being forced seaward by the prominent headland and, due to the turn, coming into range of the *Oregon's* 13.5 inch guns. It quickly became apparent to the captain of the *Colon* that further flight or resistance was futile, especially as the *Colon* did not have it's main battery 10" guns fitted. At 1:15 pm he beached the *Colon*, opening the cruiser's sea cocks in a final act of defiance. The Naval Battle of Santiago was over.

THE SURRENDER OF THE "COLÓN."

The Spanish vessel is shown on the point of turning for the beach and pulling down the flag. The American vessels from right to left are the *Brooklyn*, *Texas*, *Oregon*, and in the distance the *New York*. In the foreground is shown the column of water raised by the *Oregon's* last shot.

FROM A PHOTOGRAPH TAKEN AT 11:45 BY T. M. DIEUAIDE.
GROUP OF SAILORS ON THE PORT TURRET OF THE "TEXAS" WATCHING THE "COLÓN," AT WHICH THE "OREGON" HAS JUST FIRED.

CAPTAIN PHILIP GIVING THANKS ON THE DECK OF THE TEXAS.—Drawn by T. de Thulstrup.

Aboard the *Texas* Captain Philip gathered his crew on the quarter deck, removed his hat and offered thanks to God for the American victory saying, "I wish to make public acknowledgement that I believe in God the Father Almighty. I ask that all you officers and men lift your hats and from your hearts offer silent thanks to the Almighty." Every man removed his hat and bowed his head in a moment of silence then, unable to contain themselves they lifted three cheers for the captain.

DRAWN BY GEORGE VARIAN, FROM A PHOTOGRAPH TAKEN DURING THE ENGAGEMENT BY S. G. MAGILL.
THE CREW OF THE "OREGON" RETURNING CHEERS FROM THE "TEXAS" AFTER THE "COLÓN'S" SURRENDER.
The *New York* is shown in the distance, the *Colón* farther to the left.

DRAWN BY H. REUTERDAHL, FROM A PHOTOGRAPH TAKEN ON THE "NEW YORK," BY G. W. STROLLUM, AT 2 P.M., JULY 3.
THE "COLÓN" AFTER THE SURRENDER, SHOWING THE WATER POURING OUT OF HER TORPEDO-TUBE

American efforts immediately after the battle focused on rescuing Spanish naval personnel from the burning, explosion-racked vessels and the equally dangerous Cuban insurgents ashore. In stark contrast to the chaotic scenes played out on the burning decks of the other Spanish warships, the *Colon's* officers had their baggage brought up while aboard the *Oregon* the ship's band provided musical accompaniment to the surrender of the virtually intact *Colon*.

The Naval Battle of Santiago was a glorious US naval victory, although hardly an unexpected one. The US Navy had only one fatality, on the *Brooklyn*, although all the warships engaged had sustained some damage.

Damage to the *Texas* and casualties aboard were relatively minor and largely self-inflicted. The USS *Texas* and her crew had acquitted themselves well, although at least one officer aboard was unhappy that the *Brooklyn's* turn early in the battle had hampered the *Texas'* progress and had stolen some of her glory.

Men aboard the *Texas* watch the surrender of the Spanish cruiser *Colon*. On deck are charred hammocks that had lined the ship's railings, stained with the smoke of battle.

After the Battle, Admiral Schley, in a small boat, looked up to Captain Philip on the bridge of the *Texas* and shouted "Some fight, eh, Jack?" The heady atmosphere would gradually fade as the action was further evaluated over the ensuing years and a controversy grew over the near collision between the *Texas* and the *Brooklyn* due to what became known as the "Schley Turn." This controversy arose not due to any difficulties between Schley and Philip, who understood the uncertainty of battle and did not intend any rebuff, but in a dispute that came to a head years later between then-Admirals Sampson and Schley.

Aboard the *Oregon*, powder-stained gunners emerge from their turret to see the outcome of their handiwork while in the distance the silhouette of the *Texas* appears amid the smoke of the burning Spanish ships that line the Cuban shore.

The exhaustion and post-battle fatigue of the *Texas'* crew is obvious in these photos taken shortly after the *Colon's* surrender. Detritus of battle was strewn across the decks of the *Texas*. Witnesses aboard the *Texas* reported that the powder residue and ash accumulated on the decks during the battle gave the vessel the appearance of having weathered a snow storm. The officers and sailors were exhausted and formalities were for a time forgotten. The *Texas*, however, was shortly flying the fresh flag of the World's newest naval power.

In the opening phase of the battle the *Texas'* navigator, Lt. Heilner, had remarked to the captain on the large battle flags displayed by the Spanish warships and, noting that the *Texas* flew only her national flag at her stern, asked "Where are our battle flags?" Captain Philip, observing the fall of a 6" shell from the *Texas* raising a spray of water across the decks of the *Maria Teresa*, quipped, "I guess they won't have any misconceptions about our being in battle" to which Lt. Heilner replied "What's a battle without battle flags?" and ordered the signal-quartermaster's locker smashed open and the battle flags raised.

The battle was summed up by Ensign Joseph Pulver of the *New York*, "What a day's work! ... What a Sunday this has been. Sunday fights always go our way, and this one beats the record."

As the US warships provided rescue assistance to the officers and men of the wrecked and burning Spanish vessels, a renewed wave of excitement swept the squadron. At 7pm the *Vixen* returned to the scene of the *Colon's* beaching to report the appearance of an unknown warship off of the entrance to Santiago Bay. The US flagship *New York* hoisted the signal "Prepare to chase", but this newcomer turned out to be an Austrio-Hungarian warship, coincidentally also named the *Maria Theresa* (above).

Hardly had the smoke of the battle cleared from the waters off Santiago, before the location became a popular destination for warships from the principle naval powers in Europe. The British Navy's cruiser *HMS Indefatigable* (below) arrived off Santiago the day after the naval battle, the Imperial German Navy's cruiser *SMS Geier* (right) arrived two days later, and the French *Amiral Rigault de Genouilly* arrived by the 16th (below right).

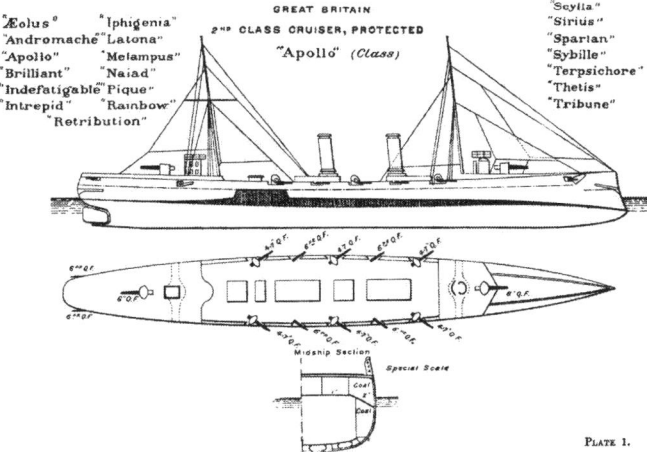

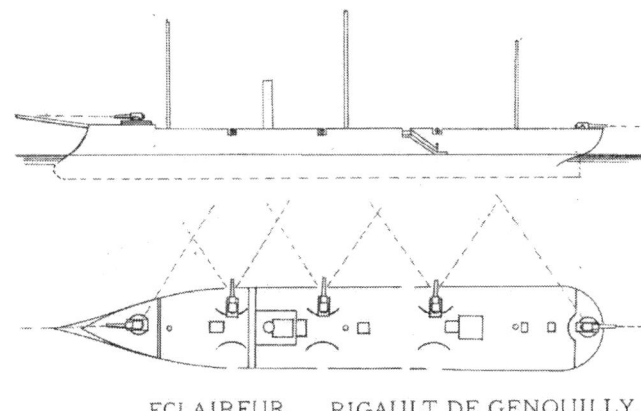

Vessels that had been sent to test the US blockade and observe the American fleet's effectiveness in bottling up the Spanish squadron witnessed instead the demise of the Spanish Navy and with it Spain's power to assert itself in the Western Hemisphere. Europe took note of the new American naval power.

17 AFTER THE BATTLE

Captain Philip confided to Rev. H.W. Jones, the *Texas'* chaplain, that he knew that the battle was theirs from the onset saying, "I was sure of it when I went to the bridge, for surely God has been with us, and it has been all on account

of prayer." As Chaplain Jones recalled in an article that appeared in the New York Herald, "Captain Philip always spoke about the late war [the American Civil War], and reminded us that the side that opened fire first on the Sabbath would lose every time; so I was very glad last Sabbath when I saw the *Maria Teresa* fire the first shot."

USS *Texas* off Cuba shortly after the naval battle of July 3rd. Note the powder stained sides of the ship's hull and the ghost of the high bow wave it reveals: evidence of her part in the running battle. This photo also reveals the stub of her starboard side searchlight which had been shot off. Also just discernable is a bright spot surrounded by a star-shaped scar on the face of the starboard 12" turret sponson, marking the impact point of a 5.5-inch Spanish shell which failed to penetrate the Texas' armor.

"NORTH ATLANTIC FLEET, SFCOND SQUADRON
U. S. FLAGSHIP *BROOKLYN*
Guantanamo Bay, Cuba, July 6, 1898

SIR: I have the honor to make the following report of that part of the squadron under your command which came under my observation during the engagement with the Spanish fleet on July 3, 1898.

At 9.35 a. m. Admiral Cervera, with the *Infanta Maria Teresa*, *Viscaya*, *Oquendo*, *Cristobal Colon*, and two torpedo boat destroyers, came out of the harbor of Santiago de Cuba in column at distance and attempted to escape to the westward. Signal was made from the *Iowa* that the enemy was coming out, but his movement had been discovered from this ship at the same moment. This vessel was the farthest west, except the *Vixen*, in the blockading line. Signal was made to the western division, as prescribed in your general orders, and there was immediate and rapid movement inward by your squadron and a general engagement at 1,100 yards and varying to 3,000 [yards] until the *Vizcaya* was destroyed, about 10.50,a.m. The concentration of the fire upon the ships coming out was most furious and terrific, and great damage was done them.

About twenty or twenty-five minutes after the engagement began two vessels, thought to be the *Teresa* and *Oquendo*, and since verified as such, took fire from the effective shell fire of the squadron and were forced to run on the beach some 6 or 7 miles west of the harbor entrance, where they burned and blew up later. The torpedo boat destroyers were destroyed early in the action, but the smoke was so dense in the direction that I can not say to which vessel or vessels the credit belongs. This, doubtless, was better seen from your flagship.

The *Vizcaya* and *Colon*, perceiving the disaster to their consorts, continued at full speed to the westward to escape and were followed and engaged in a running fight with the *Brooklyn*, *Texas*, *Iowa*, and *Oregon* until 10.50, when the *Vizcaya* took fire from our shells. She

COMMODORE SCHLEY IN HIS CABIN.

put her helm to port and, with a heavy list to port, stood in shore and ran aground at Asseraderos, about 21 miles west of Santiago, on fire fore and aft, and where she blew up during the night. Observing that she had struck her colors, and that several vessels were nearing her to capture and save her crew, signal was made to cease firing, The *Oregon* having proved vastly faster than the other battleships, she and the *Brooklyn*, together with the *Texas* and another vessel which proved to be your flagship, continued westward in pursuit of the *Colon*, which had run close in shore, evidently seeking some good spot to beach if she should fail to elude her pursuers.

This pursuit continued with increasing speed in the *Brooklyn*, *Oregon*, and other ships, and soon the *Brooklyn* and *Oregon* were within long range of the *Colon*, when the *Oregon* opened fire with her 13-inch guns, landing a shell close to the *Colon*. A moment afterwards the *Brooklyn* opened fire with her 8-inch guns, landing a shell just ahead of her. Several other shells were fired at the *Colon*, now in range of the *Brooklyn's* and *Oregon's* guns. Her commander, seeing all chances of escape cut off, and destruction awaiting his ship, fired a lee gun and struck her flag at 1.15 p. m., and ran ashore at a point some 50 miles west of Santiago Harbor. Your flagship was coming up rapidly at the time, as was also the *Texas* and *Vixen*. A little later, after your arrival, the *Cristobal Colon*, which had struck to the *Brooklyn* and the *Oregon*, was turned over to you as one of the trophies of this great victory of the squadron under your command.

During my official visit, a little later, Commander Eaton, of the *Resolute*, appeared and reported to you the presence of a Spanish battle ship near Altares. Your orders to me were to take the *Oregon* and go eastward to meet her, and this was done by the Brooklyn, with the result that the vessel reported as an enemy was discovered to be the Austrian cruiser *Infanta Maria Teresa*, seeking the commander in chief.

I would mention, for your consideration, that the *Brooklyn* occupied the most westward blockading position, with the *Vixen*, and, being more directly in the route taken b the Spanish squadron, was exposed for some minutes, possible ten to the gun fire of three of the Spanish ships and the west battery, as a range of 1,500 yards from the ships an about

3,000 yards from the batteries, but the vessels of the entire squadron, closing in rapidly, soon diverted this fire and did magnificent work at close range. I have never before witnessed such deadly and fatally accurate shooting as was done by the ships of your command as they closed in on the Spanish squadron, and I deem it a high privilege to commend to you, for, such action as you may deem proper, the gallantry and dashing courage, the prompt decision and the skillful handling of their respective vessels of Captain Philip, Captain Evans, Captain Clark, and especially of my chief of staff, Captain Cook, who was directly under my personal observation and whose coolness, promptness, and courage were of the highest order. The dense smoke of the combat shut out from my view the Indiana and the *Gloucester*, but, as these vessels were closer to your flagship, no doubt their part in the conflict was under your immediate observation.

Lieutenant Sharp, commanding the *Vixen*, acted with conspicuous courage; although unable to engage the heavier ships of the enemy with his light guns, nevertheless was close in to the battle line under heavy fire, and many of the enemy's shot passed beyond his vessel.

I beg to invite special attention to the conduct of my flag lieutenant James H. Sears, and Ensign Edward McCauley, jr., aid, who were constantly at my side during the engagement and who exposed themselves fearlessly in discharging their duties; and also to the splendid of my secretary, Lieut. B. W. Wells, Jr., who commanded and directed the fighting of the fourth division with splendid effect.

I would commend the highly meritorious conduct and courage in the engagement of Lieut. Commander N. E. Mason, the executive officer whose presence everywhere over the ship during its continuance did much to secure the good result of this ship's part in the victory.

The navigator, Lieut. A. C. Hodgson, and the division officers, Lieut. T. D. Griffin, Lieut. W. R. Rush, Lieut. Edward Simpson, Lieut. J. G. Doyle, Ensign Charles Webster, and. the junior divisional officers were most steady and conspicuous in every detail of duty contributing to the accurate firing of this ship in her part of the great victory of your forces.

The officers of the Medical, Pay, Engineer, and Marine Corps responded to every demand of the occasion, and were fearless in exposing themselves. The warrant officers, Boatswain William L. Hill, Carpenter G. H. Warford, and Gunner F. T. Applegate, were everywhere exposed, in watching for damage, reports of which were promptly conveyed to me.

I have never in my life served with a braver, better, or worthier crew than that of the *Brooklyn*. During the combat, lasting from 9.35 until 1.15 p. m., much of the time under fire, they never flagged for a moment, and were apparently undisturbed by the storm of projectiles passing ahead, astern, and over the ship.

The result of the engagement was the destruction of the Spanish squadron and the capture of the admiral and some thirteen to fifteen hundred prisoners, with the loss of several hundred killed, estimated by Admiral Cervera at 600 men.

The casualties on board. this ship were: G. H. Ellis, chief yeoman, killed; J. Burns, fireman, first class, severely wounded. The marks and scars show that the ship was struck about twenty-five times, and she bears in all forty-one scars as the result of her participation in the great victory of your force on July 3, 1898. The speed-cone halyards were shot away, and nearly all the signal halyards. The ensign at the main was so shattered that in hauling it down at the close of the action it fell in pieces.

I congratulate you most sincerely upon this great victory to the squadron under your command, and I am glad that I had an opportunity to contribute in the least to a victory that seems big enough for all of us.

I have the honor to transmit herewith the report of the commanding officer, and a drawing, in profile, of the ship, showing the location of hits and scars, also a memorandum of the ammunition expended and the amount to fill her allowance.

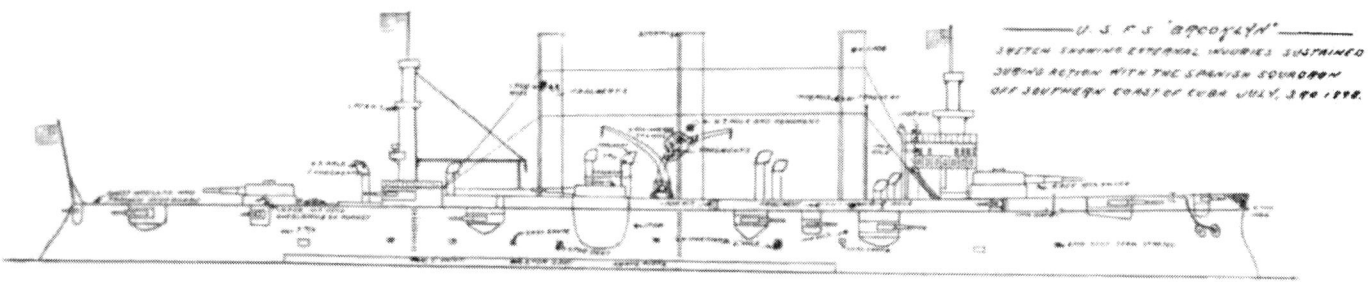

Since reaching this place and holding conversation with several of the captains, viz, Captain Eulate, of the *Vizcaya*, and the second in command of the *Colon*, Commander Contreras, I have learned that the Spanish admirals scheme was to concentrate all fire for awhile on the *Brooklyn* and the *Vizcaya* to ram her, in hopes that if they could destroy her the chance of escape would be increased, as it was supposed she was the swiftest ship of your squadron. This explains the heavy fire mentioned and the *Vizcaya's* action in the earlier moments of the engagement. The execution of this purpose was promptly defeated, by the fact that all the ships of the squadron advanced into close range and opened an irresistibly furious and terrific fire upon the enemy's squadron as it was coming out of the harbor.

I am glad to say that the injury supposed to be below the waterline was due to a water valve being opened from some unknown cause and flooding the compartment. The injury to the belt is found to be only slight and the leak small.

I beg to enclose a list of the officers and crew who participated in the combat of July 3, 1898.

I cannot close this report without mentioning in high terms of praise the splendid conduct and support of Capt. C. E. Clark, of the *Oregon*. Her speed was wonderful and her accurate fire splendidly destructive.

Very respectfully,
W. S. SCHLEY,
Commodore, United States Navy,
Commanding Second Squadron, North Atlantic Fleet.

THE COMMANDER IN CHIEF U.S. NAVAL FORCE
North Atlantic Station."

THE SPANISH OFFICERS.
1. Fernando Villaamil. 2. John Antonio Eulate. 3. Don Pedro Vazquez. 4. Don Emilio Diaz Moreu. 5. Pasquale Cervera. 6. Don Diego Carlier. 7. Don Victor Concas. 8. Don Juan Bautista Lazaga.

Captain Philip (seated at left) and Commodore Schley (seated at right) in conference with Captain Cook of the *Brooklyn* (standing at left) aboard the *Brooklyn* off Santiago, 1898.

CAPTAIN JOHN W. PHILIP, U.S.N.,
2d Class Battle-Ship "Texas."

"*U. S. S. "TEXAS,"*
off Santiago, July 4, 1898.

SIR: In accordance with the requirements of Article 437, Navy Regulations, I respectfully submit the following statement in regard to the part the "*Texas*" took in the engagement with the enemy yesterday. At daylight on the morning of the 3rd, the "*Texas*" stood out from entrance, to harbor, taking day blockading position, about three miles from the Morro (the Morro bearing north-northeast).

At 9:30 the Morro bearing N. by E. 1/2 E., distant 5,100 yards, the enemy's ships were sighted standing out of the harbor. Immediately general signal 250 was made; this signal was followed by the "*Iowa's*" almost at the same time. The ship as per order was heading in toward the entrance; went ahead full speed, putting helm, hard astarboard, and ordering forced draft on all boilers, the officer of the deck, Lieut. M. L. Bristol, having given the general alarm and beat to quarters for action at the same time. As the leader, bearing the Admiral's flag, appeared in the entrance she opened fire, which was, at 9:40, returned by the "*Texas*" at range of 4,200 yards while closing in. The ship leading was of the "*Vizcaya*" class and the flagship.

Four ships came out, evidently the "*Vizcaya*," the "*Oquendo*," "*Maria Teresa*" and "*Colon*," followed by two torpedo-boat destroyers. Upon seeing these two, we immediately opened fire upon them with our secondary battery, the main battery at the time being engaged with the second and third ships in line. Owing to our secondary battery, together with the "*Iowa*" and "*Gloucester*," these two destroyers were forced to beach and sink.

Whilst warmly engaged with the third in line, which was abreast and engaging the "*Texas*," our fire was blanketed for a short time by the "*Oregon*" forging ahead and engaging the second ships. This third ship, after a spirited fire, sheered inshore, and at 10:35 ran up a white flag. We then ceased fire on the third and opened fire with our forward guns at long range (6,600 yards) on the second ship (which was then engaged with the "*Oregon*") until 11:05, when she (enemy's second ship) sheered into the beach, on fire. At 11:10 she struck her colors. We ceased fire and gave chase, with "*Brooklyn*" and "*Oregon*," for the leading ship until 1:20, when the "*Colon*" sheered in to the beach and hauled down her colors, leaving them on deck at foot of her flag-staff. We shut off forced draft and proceeded at moderate speed to close up.

I would state that during this chase the "*Texas*" was holding her own with the "*Colon*," she leading about four miles at the start.

The reports of the executive officer and the surgeon are transmitted. I have the pleasure of stating that the entire battery of the "*Texas*" is in a most excellent condition and ready for any service required by the commander-in-chief, especially calling attention to the efficiency of the two turret-guns, due to the alterations recently made by Lieut. F. J. Haeseler, of this ship. The bearing and performance of duty of all officers met with my entire approval.

Very respectfully submitted,
J. W. PHILIP,
Captain U. S. N., Commanding.
(to) The Commander-in-Chief, North Atlantic Squadron."

"U. S. S. "TEXAS," 1st Rate,
off Santiago, de Cuba, July 4, 1898.

SIR: I beg leave to make the following report on the injuries received by this vessel during the engagement with the Spanish fleet near Santiago de Cuba, July 3, 1898. A shell about six inches in diameter entered the starboard side above the main-deck near top of hammock berthing, immediately forward of ash-hoist, angle of entrance being about 20 degrees forward of the beam; shell apparently exploded immediately after passing through the outer plating of hammock berthing, passing into the forward air-shaft to forced-draft blower, destroying doors of both air-shafts and the adjacent bulkheads. Several pieces passed through the doorway of after shaft and penetrated the after bulkhead of the shaft. The mass of shell pieces passed on through bulkhead and casing of starboard smoke-box, producing an aperture therein irregular in form, measuring about three feet vertically, two feet fore and aft. The ash-hoist machinery was badly damaged.

A piece of shell struck forward jamb of starboard door of pilot house, smashing it and carrying away considerable of paneling and framing, and passed out through after bulkhead.

The bulkhead forming the after part of forward gun-house is bulged forward about six inches. This bulge extends over the entire starboard side of bulkhead. A large number of rivets passing through the stiffening bars and frames are shorn off or broken. At the base of the gun-house the margin pieces of main-deck have been lifted up and separated from the steel-deck. A galley ventilator, which passed through berthing abaft the above-mentioned bulkhead, was destroyed.

A number of hammocks and bedding stowed in the berthing, of which above-mentioned bulkhead formed the forward plating, were badly burned. The deck planking and frames of the after part of the bridge deck over a surface about six by 12 feet have been torn up and destroyed. The starboard forward part of the third cutter was blown away, keel broken, planking and framing of the port side badly damaged, leaving it unfit for repairs. One ladder leading to bridge deck forward was badly damaged. One main-hatch ladder leading to gun-deck was destroyed. The boat covers and awning-curtains used as splinter protection over the forward boats were blown away, burned and destroyed. The hammocks, cloths, and battens securing same to bulkheads, were carried away from six compartments of hammock berthing.

The electric wire battens and fittings were carried away in a great many places on main and gun-decks forward. The starboard side of the main-deck between frames 53 and 56 shows marked depressions, beams and stanchions being bent and buckled, the crown of some of the beams no longer existing. The steel-deck has in several places become separated from the beam's through the stretching or breaking of rivets, and there are now leaks in several places.

The rivets securing the head of midship stanchions to the web of beams of frames 55 and 56 have been sheared off. The condition of starboard side of the main-deck is attributed partly to the firing of the 12-inch turret-guns over the deck during the engagement, as mentioned in my report of June 6, but mainly by similar causes during the battle of yesterday.

The marked increase in the injuries to the deck may be attributed not only to the repetition of great strains over a surface whose support was already weakened, but to an increase in the charge of powder, i. e., reduced charge previously used to full charge used during this battle. I am of the opinion that the framing of the deck in this ship is too light to permit the further firing of the 12-inch guns over the decks without serious injury.

GILES B. HARBER, Lieut. Com. U. S. N., Executive Officer.
(to) The Commanding Officer."

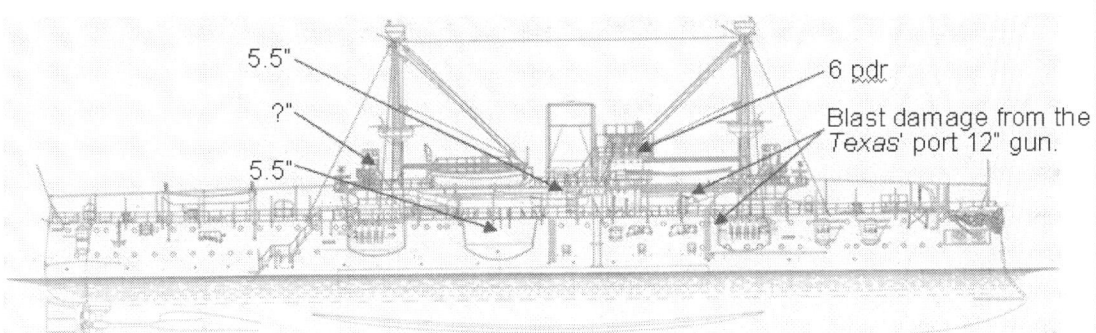

Blast damage from the *Texas'* port 12" gun.

ENGAGEMENT OFF SANTIAGO, JULY 3, 1898.

U. S. S. TEXAS.

Case No. 1.—Fracture of right fibula, as result of blast of great gun throwing him from gun deck to handling room through ammunition hoist. Patient transferred to naval hospital, New York, August 6, and discharged to duty September 7. Number of days on sick list, sixty-five.

Case No. 2.—Rupture of left tympanic membrane from blast of great gun. Discharged to duty same day. Number of days on sick list, one.

Case No. 3.—Rupture of left tympanic membrane and contusion of left great toe. Not admitted to sick list.

Case No. 4.—Conjunctivitis, resulting from powder burn during engagement. Discharged to duty July 5. Number of days on sick list, two.

BURYING THE SPANISH DEAD.

U. S. S. TEXAS (first rate).
Navy-Yard, New York, August 11, 1898.

SIR: I have the honor to submit the following report of the stations and services of the marine guard of this vessel on July 3, and other engagements participated in by the *Texas*:

Stations.—In the fore-top, 6 men, two 1-pounders; on forward superstructure, 6 men at two Hotchkiss revolving cannon; on forward superstructure, 5 men at 3-millimeter rapid-firing gun; in port and starboard waists, 6 men at two 1-pounders; on after superstructure, 6 men at two Hotchkiss revolving cannon; on after superstructure, 6 men at two Colt automatic guns; in maintop, 6 men at two 1-pounders; 1 man at central station; 2 orderlies for commanding officer; 2 sentries in engine room.

In all the bombardments the men went to and remained at their stations. The *Texas* was in the bombardments of Santiago of June 6, 16, and July 2. On June 15 forced the mined entrance to Guantanamo (14–100 pound gun-cotton mine afterwards recovered) and reduced the fortifications. Without assistance silenced the Socapa battery on June 22, which had successfully withstood the combined fire of the western squadron on the 6th and 16th. Played a conspicuous part in the destruction of the Spanish fleet on July 3, engaging the *Infanta Maria Teresa*, the first to leave the harbor, and was present at the successive surrender of the remaining vessels, including the *Cristobal Colon*, 50 miles to the westward of Santiago. Total secondary battery fire, 730 shots, the marines firing 330.

As all secondary battery guns were manned every night with two men of each crew, one man of each gun always on lookout, the service was hard but cheerfully performed. The regular post duty was in no way neglected. The guard of this vessel, by direction of Capt. J. W. Philip, U. S. N., was landed at Guantanamo on June 12 (taking ashore two Colt automatic guns), and assisted in the defense of Camp McCalla on June 12 and 13, the men behaving well under fire. The funeral escort, for the burial of Dr. Gibbs and two privates, remained at parade rest and perfectly cool under the stray firing of the Spanish sharpshooters.

The guard has done all that was required, and in a cheerful and satisfactory manner.

Very respectfully, CYRUS S. RADFORD,
First Lieutenant, United States Marine Corps.

COLONEL COMMANDANT UNITED STATES MARINE CORPS,
Headquarters, Washington, D. C.

[First indorsement.]

U. S. S. TEXAS,
Navy-Yard, New York, August 12, 1898.

Forwarded approved.

The performance of all duty of the marine guard under command of Lieutenant Radford met with my approval and commendation.

Besides their work at the secondary battery in all engagements, I desire to call attention to special instances:

During the chase on July 3 it was reported to me that the firemen and coal heavers were giving out, and the engineers desired more men from the deck. The main battery having been already drawn upon for this extra work, I directed Lieutenant Radford to detail 15 or 20 men to go in the fire room to shovel coal. Immediately, and with a rush to be first, all the marines started for the fire room to aid the *Texas* to maintain her speed in the chase.

On arrival in Guantanamo Bay, June 12, Colonel Huntington asked that the guard of the *Texas* be sent ashore to reinforce and assist his command. It was landed at once, and on arrival on the hill I noticed it was stationed on picket duty immediately and under fire at once.

The valuable service rendered by Lieutenant Radford on the 12th and 13th was later especially commended to me by both Commander McCalla and Colonel Huntington; and in this connection I desire to call attention of the colonel commandant not only to the gallant conduct of Lieutenant Radford, but to the fact that he has the distinction of being the only officer in the Marine Corps who has done service both ashore and afloat during this war, a fact that should be brought to the attention of the Navy Department for its consideration.

J. W. PHILIP,
Captain, United States Navy, Commanding.

[Second indorsement.]

NAVY-YARD, NEW YORK, *August 12, 1898.*

Forwarded.

F. M. BUNCE,
Rear-Admiral, U. S. N., Commandant, Navy-Yard and Station.

[Third indorsement.]

HEADQUARTERS UNITED STATES MARINE CORPS,
Washington, D. C., August 22, 1898.

Respectfully referred to the Secretary of the Navy, inviting attention to the attached report and indorsement, and requesting the return of the papers to this office.

CHARLES HEYWOOD,
Colonel, Commandant.

 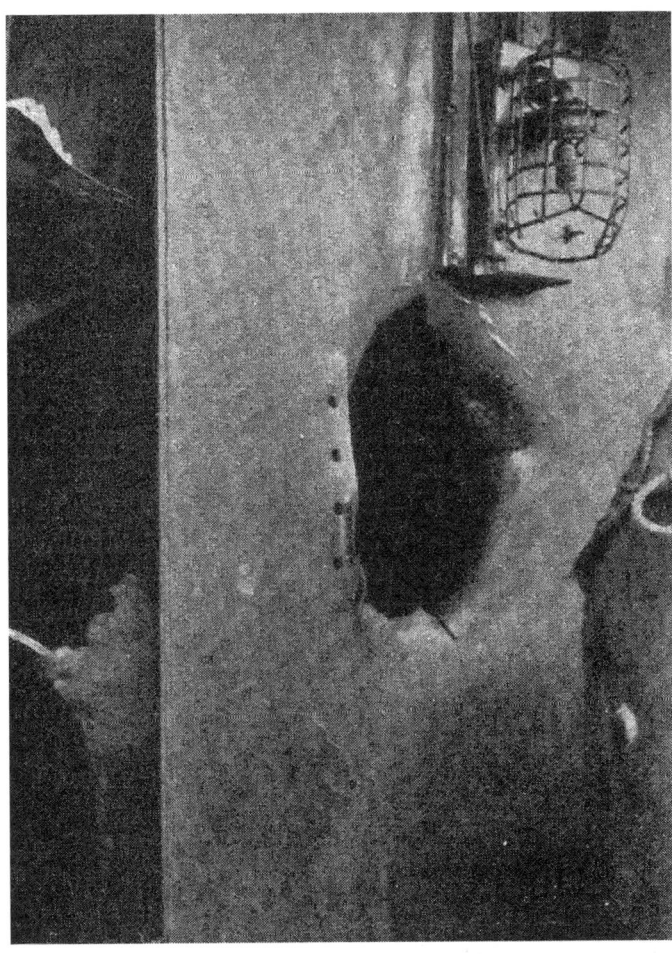

Holes marking the course of a single Spanish 5.5-inch shell that penetrated the steel bulkhead plating on the starboard superstructure amidships then tumbled through the hammock netting on the main deck. The shell then struck a heavy steel hatch, tearing off its upper half before bursting in the ash hoist, destroying the hoist engine and sending fragments through another steel bulkhead and the stack. The shock from the explosion of this shell and the large fragments that fell down the stack onto the uptake blew a large cloud of smoke and ashes from the ship, causing witnesses to fear that she had been critically damaged.

Another hit, registered by a Spanish 6 pounder gun, struck the pilot house, passing through the recently vacated space with a shower of wooden splinters, but without exploding, as recorded in this period newspaper illustration.

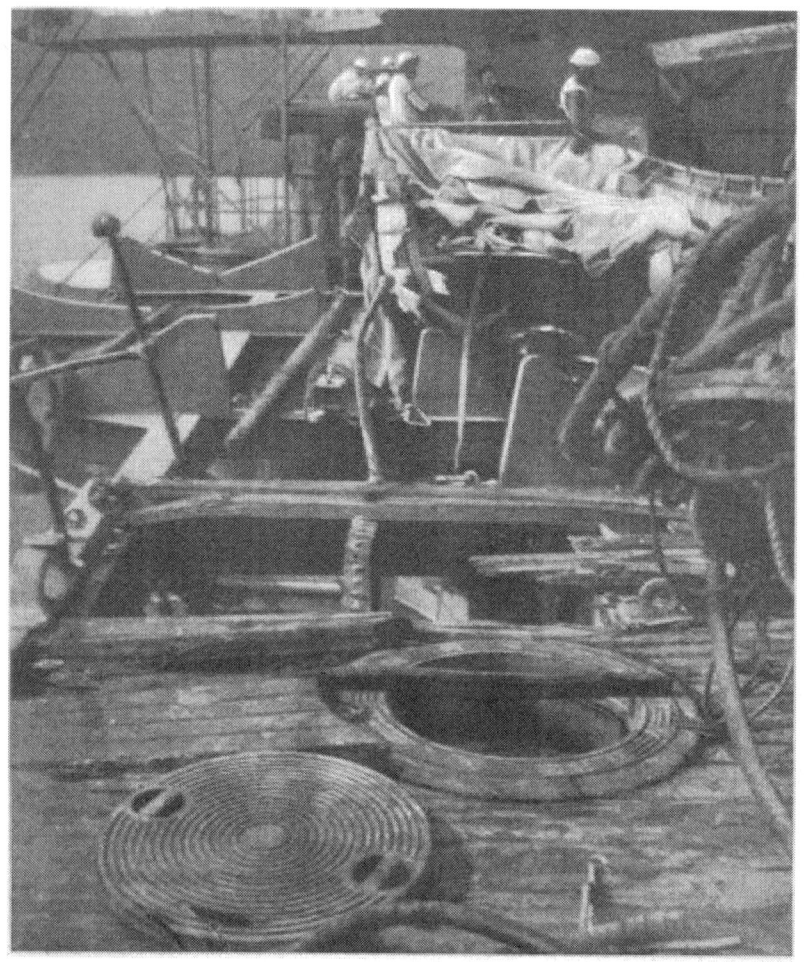

Battle damage was not limited to the effects of Spanish gunfire. The *Texas'* own guns affected the ship to an even greater degree. As pre-war testing had indicated, the decision to fire the 12-inch guns across the deck was not to be taken lightly. The above photographs, facing aft from the front of the *Texas's* forward boat deck, reveal the destruction wrought due to the blast of her port 12-inch gun firing across the main deck below.

According to a report in *Scientific American*, "During the action the port gun was swung over and fired at the Spanish fleet. The terrific blast of the gases forced down the main deck, twisting the deck beams, and forcing the heavy stanchions out of line." This type of damage was in fact typical of what occurred on ships with the en echelon gun arrangement when cross deck firing was attempted. The photo at left, taken on the gun deck shows the results of the cross deck gunfire. One can imagine the effect of this massive blast on crewmen manning their guns in this space.

The ship's only casualties during the July 3rd battle were due to the shock of the ship's own 12-inch guns. Seaman D.S. Schwarm, was thrown through an ammunition hoist from the gun deck to the handling room and received a broken leg and a concussion while others, including the ship's chaplain, suffered burst eardrums or blurred vision.

5.—Stanchions Bent by Blast of 12-inch Gun on Deck Above.

The much-photographed searchlight captured from the *Vizcaya* which replaced the starboard side, aft unit shot off the boat deck of the *Texas* during the battle of June 3rd.

The advertisement below is from an 1897 Spanish-language naval review journal and shows a virtually identical searchlight, manufactured by Maison Breguet of Paris, France.)

VAIN ATTEMPT OF THE SPANISH TO BLOCK SANTIAGO HARBOR AFTER THE BATTLE, BY RUNNING THE CRUISER "REINA MERCEDES" ASHORE IN THE NARROW CHANNEL.

With the demise of Cervera's squadron, the tables had been turned in the seaborne defense of Santiago. The Bustamonte mines had been removed from the channel in preparation for Cevera's sortie. Rather than attempt to refit and reinstall the mines, Spanish fears that the US Navy would immediately force the entrance to the harbor and attack the city from the bay resulted in another bold nocturnal attempt to block the channel, this time by the Spanish. On the night of July 5th the *Reina Mercedes* and her resourceful crew put out into the channel with the intent to block it at its mouth by scuttling the ship, also thereby preventing her capture in the event of the surrender of the city.

The USS *Texas* and *Massachusetts* were in night station close to the entrance playing their powerful searchlights up the channel when, at 11:15 pm, the Spanish cruiser was spotted heading out.

The *Texas* fired two red star signal rockets and went to general quarters. As the *Texas* and *Massachusetts* opened fire they were answered by the Spanish battery on Socapa to the west of the harbor's mouth.

Action was initiated with the *Texas*' port side 12-inch gun engaged, switching to her starboard 12-inch at 12:05 am. The Socapa battery ceased fire at 12:20 am and at 12:45 am it was noted in the log of the *Texas* that the Spanish vessel was sunk on the eastern side of the channel. While accuracy once again was an issue for the American ships, in this action at 3,500 yards range, it was sufficient to prevent the *Reina Mercedes* from achieving her goal.

The *Reina Mercedes* had been struck by large caliber rounds five times, including at least two 12-inch shells from the *Texas* (out of eight 12-inch shells fired). Three 13-inch shells from the Massachusetts also struck home. Given her unprotected sides, it is likely that these heavy shells passed right through the *Reina Mercedes*. A shell of unknown caliber and origin parted her spring cable causing her to drift out of position in the main channel. She ended up aground with her decks awash, but in a location that failed to block the channel.

After initial negotiations for Santiago's surrender reached an impasse, on July 10th and again on the 11th, guns of the US fleet joined the guns of the Army encircling Santiago in bombarding the city. Commencing at 4:45 pm the *Texas*, along with the *Brooklyn* and *Indiana*, opened fire on the city of Santiago at a range of 10,000 yards. The city was out of sight of the navy's gunners due to the intervening hills so a telephone system was installed  connecting General Shafter's headquarters to the captured railway bridge at Aguadores. From there wig-wag signals were transmitted to the *Brooklyn*, flagship of the squadron. Two minutes interval was allowed between each shot to allow its fall to be communicated back to the squadron. Throughout the latter part of the bombardment the thunder of the guns and the explosion of the shells was joined by that of a violent thunderstorm that swept across the area. At 6:05 firing ceased after General Shafter reported that the shells were falling too close to American lines.

This action was the first shelling of a city by naval vessels since the British bombardment of Alexandria, Egypt in 1884.

On July 11th the *Brooklyn* and *New York* closed in further and from a range of 8,500 yards reopened the barrage of the city at 6am. In an attempt to improve the accuracy of the naval gunfire, the Navy's wig-wag signalmen were repositioned atop the ridge over which the shots were being fired, from whence they could directly observe the fall of the shots from that angle. A slow series of shots were fired and the locations where hey had fallen were reported back for correction. Within three shots the shells were falling within the city and the general bombardment picked up to a steady pace. The *Indiana* joined the attack which continued until almost 1pm when a flag of truce was sent out by the Spanish forces in Santiago to General Shafter. 106 shells had been fired by the American warships, all but 5 landing within the city.

Photos taken during and after the bombardment of Santiago. Guns of the Navy and Army joined together to force the capitulation of the Spanish garrison. Even the novel pneumatic dynamite field gun brought along by Army volunteers joined in the fight.

SANTIAGO—WHERE AN AMERICAN SHELL STRUCK

The Spanish forces in Santiago capitulated on July 17, bringing the siege to an end and freeing the American fleet from blockade duties at that port - but the war was not yet over. On the same day that Santiago surrendered, Admiral Camara's reserve squadron was recalled to Spain from the Red Sea, where it had been slowly making its way to the relief of the Philippines. Substantial Spanish ground forces remained in Cuba and on Puerto Rico. The fleets remained on a war footing and American focus turned to Spain's other remaining toehold in the Western Hemisphere, Puerto Rico, which was invaded by U.S. forces on July 25th.

HOISTING THE AMERICAN FLAG OVER THE MUNICIPAL BUILDING AT SANTIAGO.

In the days following the battle the beached Spanish warships were inspected by numerous officers and men of the Navy and then on July 10 by an American Board of Survey to asses the their condition for possible salvage and to determine the effectiveness of American gunnery. The *Cristobal Colon* and the *Infanta Maria Teresa* were initially identified as worthy of salvage.

Wreck of the *Pluton* ashore outside of the mouth of Santiago Bay. The ship's safe and other easily movable objects were salvaged by the US Navy. The second Spanish destroyer, the *Furor*, sank in deep water and was not salvaged.

It was quickly determined both from inspecting the wrecks and discussions with captured Spanish officers that the cruisers of the *Infanta Maria Teresa* class suffered from critical design flaws. Their decks were wood, rather than wood over steel as was the design practice followed in the American vessels. Without the steel, the wooden decks quickly burned once ignited, driving the crews from their guns and rapidly spreading the flames. This problem was compounded by the vulnerability of the fire fighting pumps which were found in most cases to have been rendered inoperable by battle damage.

The US Navy had anticipated the danger of fire and ordered all unnecessary flammable materials removed from its ships during the buildup to war. Hand-carved woodwork and fine furniture had been left behind. In the case of the *Texas*, much of what little furniture remained, including even the ship's refrigerator, had been mercilessly jettisoned on May 20th en route to Cuba by an overly enthusiastic crew when the ship was stripped for action after "strange vessels on the horizon" had been sighted. The "strange" ships were the *Cincinnati* and *Vesuvius*.

The outdated compound armor of the Spanish vessels, similar to that initially specified for the *Texas*, was also found to be inferior, as Capt. Evans quipped, "The sides of the cruisers were just thick enough to explode our common shells with the most disastrous effect to the gun's crews of the Spanish ships."

The *Texas* (at left) lies next to the *Hist*, just off shore from the beached *Infanta Maria Teresa* (above). The *Maria Teresa* was found to have suffered 33 confirmed hits above the beached vessel's waterline.

"While armor-piercing shells are meant to be used against protected vessels, the "semi" shells, carrying an explosive charge, were used principally during the battle, July 3. Of these shots there is a record of but two, both of which struck the *Infanta Maria Teresa* on the port quarter, entering just under the berth deck. A remarkable feature was that the holes made by these two shells were so close together that they lapped each other, giving a convincing proof that "lightning" does strike twice in the same place. These shots entered and exploded in the after torpedo handling room, and the effect, as seen by the writer, was

something awful. Stanchions were cut to ribbons, frames wrenched from the side plating, and the deck beams were severely twisted. Everything in this part of the ship was wrecked, and a large jagged hole, about 4 feet square, was made in the starboard side." - R.W. Henderson of the USS *Texas* for *Scientific American*.

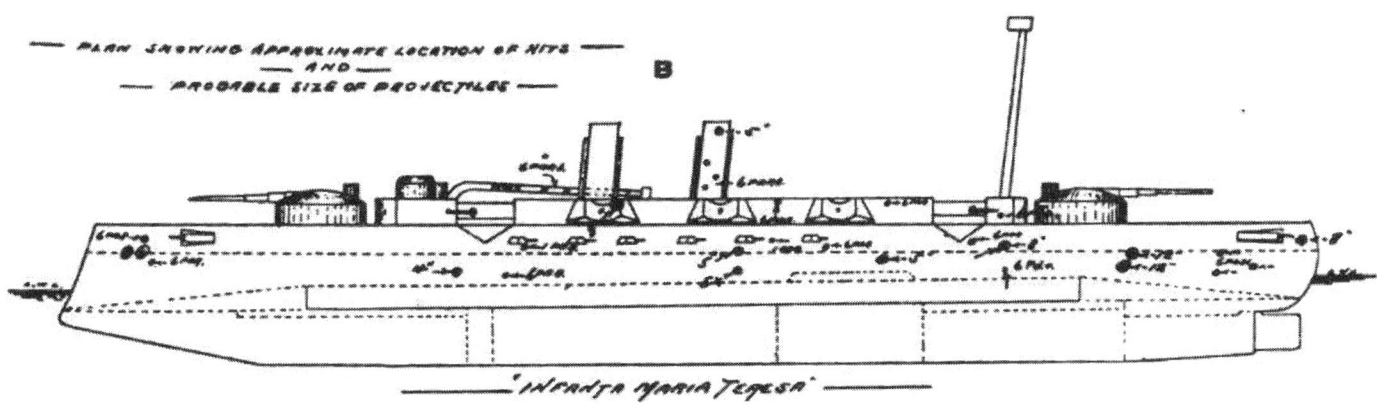

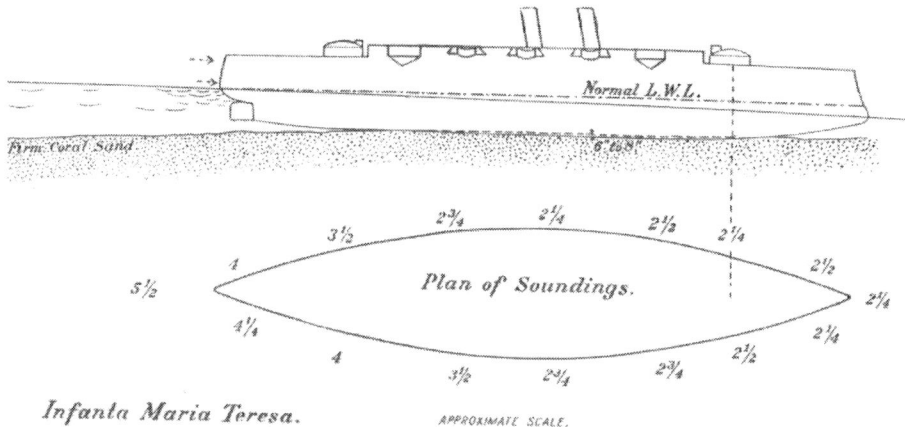

Infanta Maria Teresa.

The *Infanta Maria Teresa* was re-floated after the end of hostilities by a US Navy salvage team under the command of war-hero Lieut. R.P. Hobson. While in tow back to the United States, the captured warship was lost in a squall off of Cat Island in the West Indies. She was subsequently found aground with her back broken and declared unworthy of any additional attempt at salvage.

The *Almirante Oquendo* was found to have suffered the most hits of the vessels surveyed, with 66 hits noted in the portion of the hull that remained above water. The only recorded hit from a large caliber gun that was found was that of a 12" shell from the *Texas* which created a large hole in the hull.

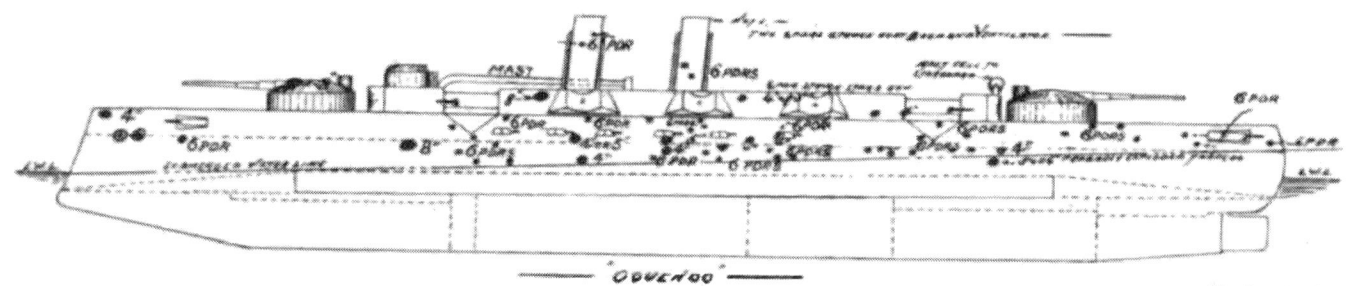

"The effect of some of the 8-inch shots was nearly as great. The one exploding in the forward turret of the *Oquendo* alone wiped out the entire gun's crew, and put the gun out of commission." - R.W. Henderson of the USS *Texas* for *Scientific American*

Vizcaya had been raked from end to end by an 8" shell from the *Brooklyn* and had suffered a massive explosion in her bow torpedo room resulting from another hit by the *Brooklyn* on one of her torpedoes. This damage and the resulting fire and explosions made her, in the opinion of one of the observers, "the worst wreck of all."

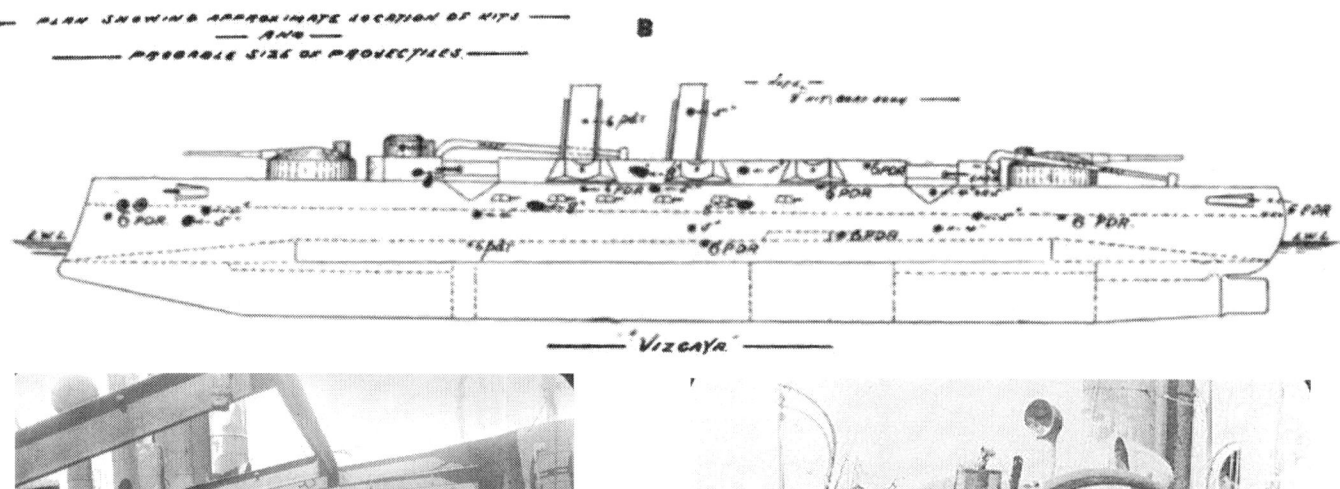

The *Critobal Colon* had struck her colors and beached herself having suffered relatively little battle damage. Rather than see his ship taken into the US Navy after its surrender, the captain of the *Colon*, in apparent violation of international convention, ordered the breech mechanisms of all of her guns thrown overboard and the sea valves broken before the Americans could come aboard and take control of the vessel. The *Colon* gradually settled onto the bottom.

As the ship slowly filled with water, she slid off the rocks on which she sat and momentarily refloated though still taking on water. The *New York* nudged up to the *Colon* and pushed the Spanish vessel back ashore but the Spanish warship subsequently capsized, a total loss.

"That the large guns of the *Texas* did most efficient work is shown by the attitude of the Spanish officers, who not only feared the marksmanship of the *Texas*, but were surprised to hear that she was not one of our best and most formidable ships." -R.W. Henderson of the USS *Texas* for *Scientific American*.

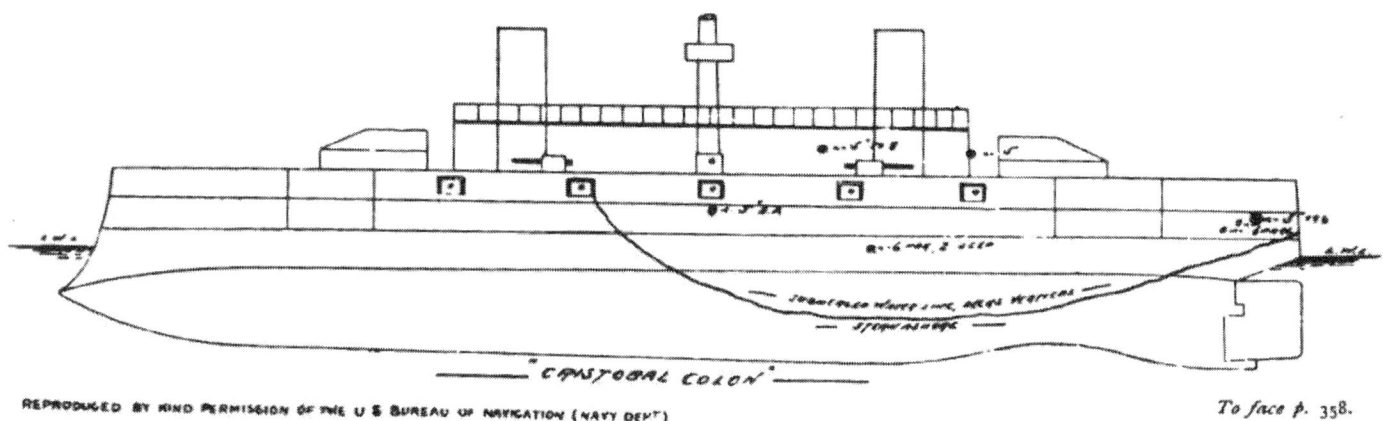

Post-war US Navy analysis of the observable hits on the Spanish ships revealed a somewhat different story about US Navy marksmanship. This survey identified 2 12" or 13" hits (2% hit ratio), 10 8" hits (5%), 17 5" or 6" hits (3.25%), 13 4" hits (5%), 76 6 pdr hits (1.5%), and 2 1 pdr hits (0%). It should be noted however that this survey recorded only the hits that remained above the waterline on the partly submerged wrecks. Hits that were below the waterline, that were obscured by other damage (such as secondary explosions and fire), and those on the sunken torpedo boat *Furor* were not included and thus reduced the hit percentage.

The low hit percentage registered by the smaller guns probably reflects the relative difficulty in identifying these hits among the wreckage and the fact that the smaller guns had targeted the torpedo boat destroyers during the early stages of the battle. With the *Furor* sunk beyond observation to the survey party and the *Pluton* heavily damaged, few of the hits on these vessels could be confirmed and recorded. It was also noted that much of the battle had occurred at ranges of 3,000 to 6,000 yards while prewar American training had focused on 1,400 to 1,800 battle ranges.

Lt. Bristol observed after the battle to a reporter from the Sun that "useful as the range finders are at long distances, they seem to have been forgotten entirely in the hurried work at Santiago, the guns being sighted in the 'old style'". Spanish officers noted that American gunfire had first fallen short then steadily climbed over the course of the battle.

As in the case of the *Infanta Maria Teresa*, the *Reina Mercedes* was refloated by the US Navy. She was successfully towed back to the United States and refitted as a station ship for the Naval Academy at Annapolis.

The "USS *Reina Mercedes*" served the Navy well at Annapolis before being sent to the scrap yard in 1957. Over those years many a naval midshipman served time aboard the *Mercedes* for infractions of discipline.

ADMIRAL CERVERA AND HIS PRINCIPAL OFFICERS—SURVIVORS OF THE SPANISH FLEET.

SPANISH PRISONERS FROM ADMIRAL CERVERA'S FLEET AT SEAVEY'S ISLAND, PORTSMOUTH, NEW HAMPSHIRE

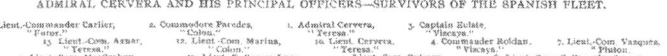

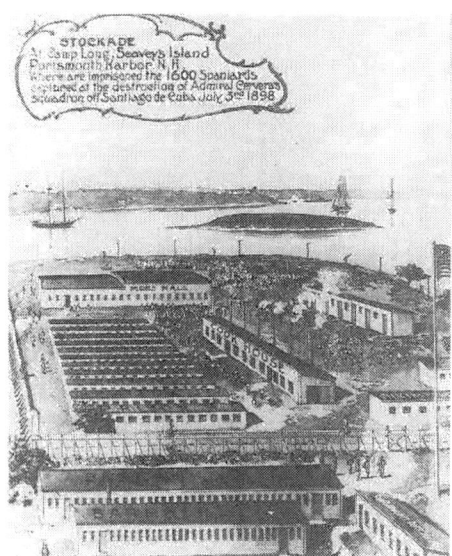
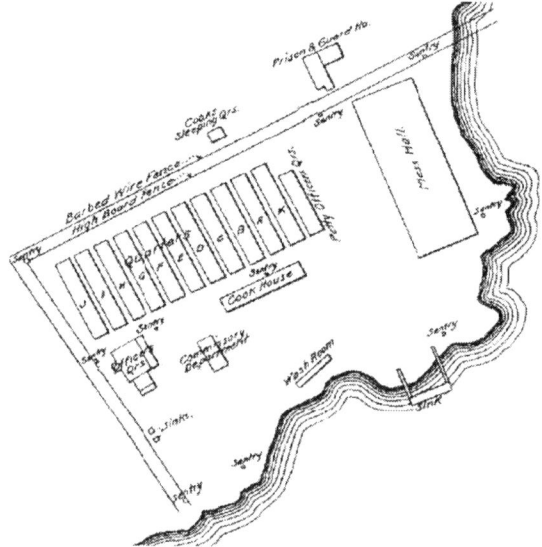

While captured officers were wined and dined through the victorious fleet, in Washington D.C., and at Annapolis; rank and file naval prisoners were transported aboard the USS *Saint Louis* and USS *Harvard* to Camp Long, located on Seavey's Island, in Portsmouth Harbor, New Hampshire for weeks of internment.

In September 1898 the Spanish officers rejoined their crew at Camp Long to make final arrangements for their repatriation to Spain. Ironically, Spanish sailors who had been captured thanks in part to the USS *Texas*, which had been designed by naval architect William John, were transported back to Spain aboard another vessel of his design, the leased steamship *City of Rome*, seen here in Kittery, Maine.

18 VICTORIOUS RETURN

The USS *Texas* steams beneath the Brooklyn Bridge with an escort of harbor tugs, en route to the Brooklyn Navy Yard for repairs following the naval Battle of Santiago. The *Texas* was the first major warship to return to a mainland port in the US following the defeat of the Spanish squadron at Cuba and therefore the focus of a wildly enthusiastic public greeting.

The *Texas* enters the dry-dock at the Brooklyn Navy Yard on August 3, 1898. As the first vessel to return to the mainland United States following the victory at Santiago, the press converged to provide detailed coverage of the ship, its officers and men, and the damage she had received in battle. Evidence of her recent service can be seen in her weathered grey paint and fouled hull. Also visible are replaced wooden panels in the pilot house where it was struck by a Spanish 6 pdr shot.

Note that the ship's boats have been removed from the bridge deck. Their extensive use in tropical waters and the damages they suffered during battle had left them in a sorry state.

Sailors standing atop floating platforms in the dry dock at the Brooklyn Navy yard begin cleaning the port bow of the *Texas*. Note the dark circle just aft of and partly obscured by the ball tipped stock of the anchor. This appears to be the hole left by the Spanish 6.3-inch shell that struck the *Texas* during her duel with the Socapa Battery during the blockade of Santiago, temporarily plugged with a "Colmes Stopper". This shot killed one seaman aboard the *Texas* and wounded eight others.

Captain Philip poses on the bridge deck next to the searchlight "captured" from the Spanish at the Battle of Santiago (left). The *Texas'* own searchlight (right) had been damaged during the battle, but her continuing blockade duties required its immediate replacement. A suitable searchlight unit was located and recovered from the *Vizcaya* and adapted to fit the *Texas*. The *Texas'* searchlights had played an important role in her subsequent action against the *Riena Mercedes*.

While at Brooklyn, the hull of the *Texas* was cleaned and painted. Here repairs are under way in the dry dock even as a ship's boilers remains lit, as revealed by the smoke rising from her stack. Spanish Admiral Camera's Squadron was still a threat to US interests. Conversely, a strong US naval squadron active in the Atlantic presented a credible "fleet in being" risk to the Spanish mainland. Repairs were conducted rapidly to help keep the pressure on the Spanish to finalize an agreement ending the war.

Captain Philip examines the hull of the *Texas* as repairs are underway. One wonders if he would have performed this duty in his "dress whites" had the press not been present.

Photos taken at the Brooklyn Navy Yard, August 1898 (clockwise from right): 1. Manning the guns of the foremast top for the cameras. 2. Sailors peer through the hole in the midships hammock berthing, left by a Spanish shell. 3. Captain Philip's son climbs the foremast to the bell with Mr. Riley, the ship's mascot. Mr. Riley had been born aboard and served through the combat actions off Cuba.

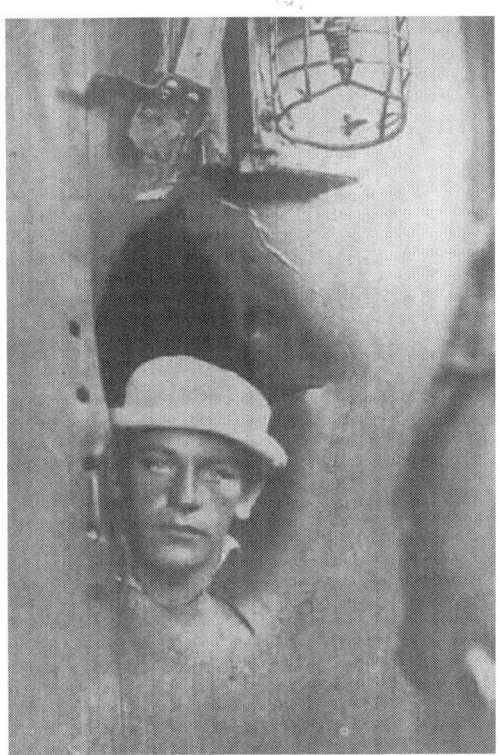

Following the destruction of both its Pacific and West Indies squadrons, as well as the successful U.S. Army landings on Cuba and Puerto Rico, Spain sought an exit from the costly conflict, signing an armistice treaty with the United States on August 12th.

On August 20, 1898 the remainder of the US fleet arrived at New York to an even more thunderous reception concluding with a naval parade past Grant's Tomb. The repaired *Texas* participated in these events which were witnessed by hundreds of thousands of spectators ashore and a veritable fleet of civilian vessels filling the harbor.

THE "TEXAS," COMMODORE PHILIP'S REFORMED HOODOO.

Looking noticeably darker in her fresh paint than the weathered vessels returning from Cuba, the *Texas* approaches the reviewing area during the naval parade at Grant's Tomb on August 20, 1898. The *Texas* would remain in the New York vicinity, near the refitting US fleet, until late October.

While anchoring off of Grants Tomb on September 9th, Thomas Edison's camera team captured movie footage of the *Texas*. Written records indicate that this was only one of a number of times the *Texas* was appeared in early motion pictures.

The USS *Texas* flies her flags during post-war celebrations, late 1898.

The *Texas* attended the Philadelphia Peace Jubilee, October 25-28, 1898. Sailors from the *Texas* marched in the parade through a specially-designed neo-classical "court of honor". The *Texas* herself was extensively lighted in a dazzling display of electric lights. The *Texas*, back in her peacetime colors, fires a salute, while a stern view taken in 1899 shows a ship's boat tied to a boom.

On January 22, 1899 Captain Philip turned over command of the *Texas* to Captain Charles D. Sigsbee. Captain Sigsbee was a Civil War veteran whose career was punctuated by his command of the USS *Maine* at the time of her explosion in Havana. During the subsequent conflict, he had successfully commanded the converted cruiser USS *St Paul* in action off of Puerto Rico and Cuba.

The ship's petty officers gather on the main deck in the shelter of the bridge deck amidships, near the engine room hatches. Note the open deck structure supporting the ship's boats. The forward/port turret can be seen in the distance at left while the aft/starboard turret is in silhouette in the shadows of the bridge deck at right.

The crew of the *Texas* at the forward 6" gun.

In 1899 US warships paid calls to ports across the Caribbean, visibly expanding the US sphere of influence across the region. In addition to stops at Cuba and Puerto Rico, the *Texas* visited Jamaica, Trinidad, Barbados, St. Lucia, Martinique, and, as seen above in April 1899, La Guaira, Venezuela. The two-stacked warships at left are the USS *Raleigh* and the USS *Cincinnati*, while the two-stacked ship in the far distance is the USS *Newark*. The three-stacked warship at center is the USS *New York* while the USS *Brooklyn* is at right. Between the *New York* and the *Newark* is the USS *Texas*.

September 1899, the *Texas* returns to Grant's Tomb.

New York celebrates yet again on September 9, 1899 - this time marking the return of Admiral Dewey from his extended service in the Philippines. Once more sailors from the USS *Texas* march through a triumphal neo-classical "court of honor."

The *Texas*, in her fresh peace-time color scheme of white hull and buff superstructure, fires salutes to the returning hero.

By late 1899 the last of the victory celebrations were over, but the *Texas* had one final war-related duty to perform – the re-interment of the victims of the USS *Maine* disaster. The *Texas* sailed for Havana, Cuba, arriving on December 17, 1899.

Immediately following the disaster, the *Maine* dead had been buried as a group in a cemetery at Havana, Cuba. It was decided to remove the remains for re-burial to a more honorific setting at the Arlington National Cemetery. For this sober task the *Texas*, under the command of Captain Sigsbee, the former captain of the *Maine*, was selected.

Wreckage of the *Maine* with the *Texas* in the distance.

As the caskets were transported by boat to the *Texas*, local residents covered them with flowers. A casket holding the remains of a sailor from the USS *Maine* is carefully carried aboard the USS *Texas* and past her starboard 12" gun.

Once back in the United States, the remains were transported through Washington D.C. to Arlington in flag-draped caskets, escorted by sailors from the *Texas*.

On a cold winter's day at the Arlington National Cemetery services were read over the caskets and the sailors finally laid to rest. Later a memorial fashioned from artifacts salvaged from the *Maine* would be erected on the site.

19 LATER CAREER: 1901-1911

Starboard 12" gun tampion on the *Texas* inscribed with her engagements and the names of enemy vessels she had faced in action radiating from a Texas lone star. "Santiago de Cuba," "Guantanamo," "Cabanas," "*Maria Teresa*," "*Vizcaya*," "*Oquendo*," "*Cristobal Colon*," "*Pluton & Furor*," "*Reina Mercedes*," "La Socopa." This tampion was made of metal recovered from the Spanish cruiser *Vizcaya*. Though considered out-of-date even before the Spanish-American War, the *Texas*' performance during the conflict had earned the former "Hoodoo" the respect of the public and naval officers alike.

Captain Sigsbee turned over command of the *Texas* to Captain W. C. Gibson on January 22, 1900. Captain Gibson directed a cruise through the Caribbean before turning over the ship to Captain M.R.S. MacKenzie that summer. On November 3, 1900 the *Texas* was decommissioned for a major overhaul at the Norfolk Navy Yard.

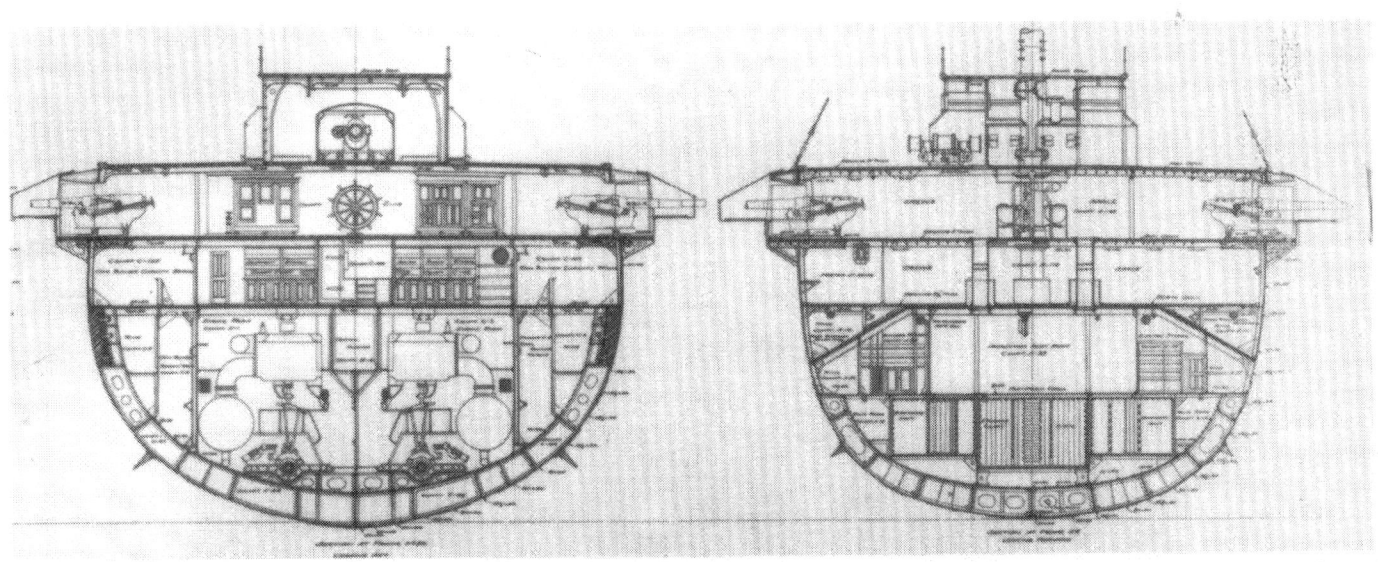

This was a thorough top-to-bottom refit, the most obvious external alterations being the raising of the stack and taller masts. These plans depict the ship upon completion of the 1901-02 refit.

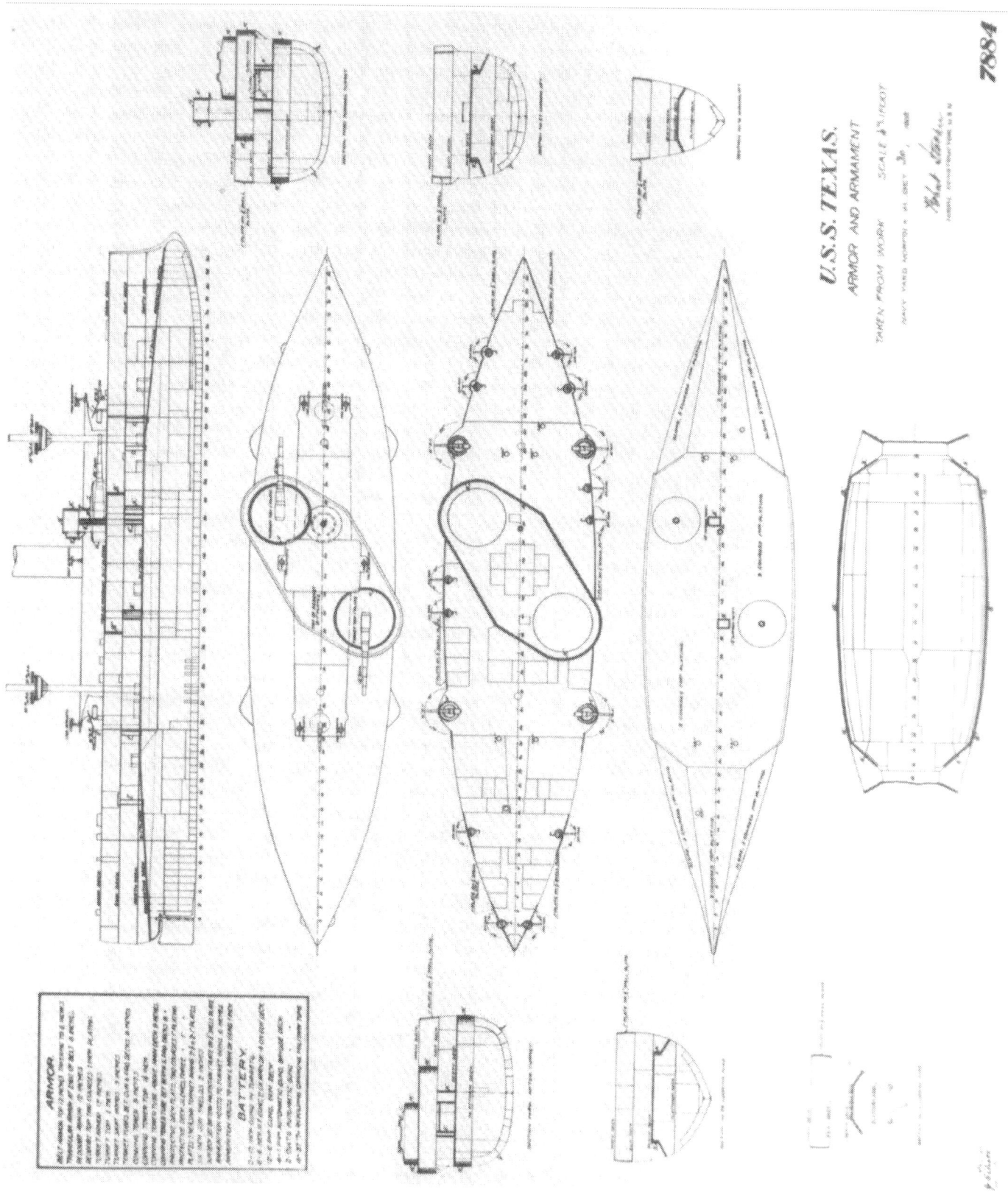

The refurbished USS *Texas* was re-commissioned at the Norfolk Navy Yard on November 3, 1902, under the command of Captain William T. Swinburne. On May 1, 1903 the *Texas* became the flagship of the Coast Squadron, North Atlantic Fleet, a distinction she maintained until 1905.

The need to raise the height of the funnel may have had its roots in the decision made during construction to change from the twin, slender funnels called for in the initial design to the single, fat funnel eventually built. Slender stacks naturally draw hot exhaust gases upwards more efficiently than fat ones. By retroactively increasing the height of the single stack, its proportions were changed making it slender and more efficient.

Port side view of the USS *Texas* after the 1901-02 refit. Less visible alterations had been carried out including the removal of her broadside torpedo battery. Raising the funnel and masts visually emphasized the short length of the ship. New post-Dreadnaught battleships grew to dwarf the *Texas*, once the largest warship ever launched in the US.

Naval design had progressed far beyond the technology embodied in the *Texas*, but she continued to serve the Navy as a valuable training tool while new, more powerful warships were under construction. The *Texas* spent much of her post-war career taking part in training exercises along the East Coast of the United States, from Maine to Texas. More exotic destinations included visits to Jamaica (Mar. 26-31, 1899), Venezuela (Apr. 4-7, 1899), Trinidad (Apr. 9-12, 1899), Barbados (Apr 13-16, 1899), St. Lucia (Apr 17-21, 1899), Martinique (Apr. 21-24, 1899), Bermuda (Apr. 1-2, 1900), Santo Domingo (Apr. 25-26, 1900), and St. Kitts (Feb. 2-5, 1903), as well as multiple trips to Puerto Rico (1898, 1900, 1902, 1903) and Cuba (1898, 1899, 1900, 1904, 1906).

In 1902 a crisis once again arose in Venezuela. Venezuela had descended into civil war from 1898 to 1900 and, during that conflict, many British, German and Italian foreign nationals had sustained large financial damages. Diplomatic efforts having failed, on December 10, 1902 Germany, Britain and Italy proceeded to establish a naval blockade of Venezuela's coast. Venezuela responded by requesting United States arbitration.

President Roosevelt accepted that Venezuela must pay her debts, but seeing the deteriorating diplomatic situation and concerned about potential imperialistic actions in the Caribbean by an increasingly belligerent Germany, Roosevelt ordered the concentration of US naval forces at Culebra Island of Puerto Rico, under the guise of conducting annual fleet maneuvers, to establish a fleet-in-being within striking range of the blockading warships off of the Venezuelan coast. This fleet was to be the "big stick" of America's defense of the little-tested Monroe Doctrine. Arrayed against the Venezuelan coast, and potentially against the US fleet, was a fleet of German and British warships.

Following her extensive 1901-02 refit at the Norfolk Navy Yard, the *Texas* had only been recommissioned on November 3rd and had only days to complete testing before rushing to join the fleet off Culebra Island, where she arrived on December 16th. The "maneuvers" conducted included the first coordinated amphibious landing and ground maneuver exercises conducted by the United States Navy and Marine Corps.

On January 17th, 1903 the *SMS Panther* destroyed the Venezuelan Fort San Carlos at Maraciabo, after that fort had fired on the gunboat. This bellicose action injured Germany's position in both the United States and Britain, driving a philosophic wedge between the German and English ships making up the blockading squadron. In secret diplomatic conversations with the German ambassador Roosevelt expressed to Kaiser Wilhelm I that it was unacceptable to the United States for a European power to threaten the territory of a nation in the Americas and that on this issue the United States was prepared to go to war. Roosevelt's threat was serious, for it was clear that neither Britain nor Italy was prepared to enter into a conflict with the United States and Germany by herself was incapable of imperialistic actions in the Western Hemisphere, against the wishes of the United States. Germany backed down and Roosevelt arbitrated a settlement of the debt issue.

Panther. Vineta. H. M. S. Ariadne. H. M. S. Indefatigable.
H. M. S. Quail. H. M. S. Charybdis.

THE ANGLO-GERMAN FLEET IN VENEZUELAN WATERS.

Of the British and German warships in Venezuelan waters the British are the more powerful, though there is only one vessel which is in the front rank. The British ships are:—*Ariadne*, 1st-class cruiser, 11,000 tons; *Charybdis*, 2nd-class cruiser, 4,360 tons; *Retribution*, 2nd-class cruiser, 3,600 tons; *Tribune*, 2nd-class cruiser, 3,400 tons; *Indefatigable*, 2nd-class cruiser, 3,600 tons; *Pallas*, 3rd-class cruiser, 2,575 tons; *Alert*, sloop, 960 tons; *Quail*, torpedo-boat destroyer, 360 tons. The German ships are as follows:— *Vineta*, 2nd class cruiser, 5,885 tons; *Amazon*, 3rd-class cruiser, 2,660 tons; *Ariadne*, 3rd-class cruiser, 2,660 tons; *Niobe*, 3rd-class cruiser, 2,645 tons; *Gazelle*, 3rd-class cruiser, 2,645 tons; *Falke*, 3rd-class cruiser, 1,574 tons; *Panther*, gunboat, 899 tons.

This gunboat diplomacy led to the "Roosevelt Corollary" to the Monroe Doctrine, as he declared in his 1904 message to Congress: "Chronic wrongdoing, or an impotence which results in a general loosening of the ties of civilized society, may in America, as elsewhere, ultimately require intervention by some civilized nation, and in the Western Hemisphere the adherence of the United States to the Monroe Doctrine may force the United States, however reluctantly, in flagrant cases of such wrongdoing or impotence, to the exercise of an international police power."

President Teddy Roosevelt doffs his hat, returning a salute from the USS *Texas* during the August 17, 1903 naval review near his home "Sagamore Hill" at Oyster Bay, New York. Visible in the ship's rigging are Ardois and Telephotos signal lights as well as newly installed Slaby-Arco wireless aerials

Voyages to the West Indies could sometimes take on the character of a "Caribbean Cruise" showing that sea duty was not always unending work, vicious storms, and thunderous battles. The photos above were taken aboard the *Texas* while in Havana, Cuba. The empty cradles indicate that the ship's boats are deployed. The barrel and sighting hoods of the 12" gun are wrapped in tarps.

The *Texas* at San Juan Puerto Rico, enjoying the fruits of her labors.

Football team of the USS *Texas*, circa 1904.

B Bâtir des phrases sur les modèles suivants :

1. Whose car is this ? Is it yours ? — No, it's John's. — 2. He is an old friend of ours. — 3. Ours is a very small flat (= Our flat is very small). — 4. They all had their hats on their heads. — 5. The blue car is John's and the black one is mine.

C Traduire :

1. Les filles de Mr Jenkins. — 2. Le prix de ce livre. — 3. Une perruque de juge anglais. — 4. Des chapeaux de Galloises. — 5. Le concert de ce soir. — 6. Les coutumes curieuses des Irlandais. — 7. L'ami de tout le monde. — 8. Les cousins hollandais de mon beau-père. — 9. Les poèmes de Wordsworth et ceux de Coleridge. — 10. Le piano des Macpherson; le piano de Mrs Macpherson.

D Traduire :

1. Charles Lamb et sa sœur; le portrait d'Emily Brontë par son frère; la lampe et son abat-jour; la chatte et ses petits. — 2. Ils avançaient lentement, tête baissée, un lourd sac tyrolien sur le dos. — 3. La seule chose à faire était de prendre ses jambes à son cou. — 4. On est encore jeune jusqu'à quarante ans. — 5. On doit aimer et aider ses semblables. — 6. A qui sont les jouets qui traînent sur le tapis ? — 7. Avec les enfants de qui jouais-tu ? — 8. Pourquoi te sers-tu de mon stylo et non du tien ? — 9. Ils cultivent leurs légumes eux-mêmes. — 10. Un camarade de classe de Dick a téléphoné pour demander s'il voulait jouer au tennis avec lui.

Leçon 39. — *Démonstratifs, relatifs et interrogatifs*

A Compléter avec le pronom relatif qui convient. Le mettre entre parenthèses s'il peut être omis.

1. The film ... we saw last night was very good. — 2. That film, ... I had seen before, is about a man ... is hunted by the police in Belfast. — 3. This is the worst winter ... we have had for ten years. — 4. Mr Thomson, with ... I play bridge on Saturdays, is the man ... I introduced to you at the party. — 5. Bob, ... plays the oboe in our orchestra, knows Benjamin Britten. — 6. The noise ... we had to put up with got on our nerves. — 7. Their front-garden, ... is very small, is full of flowers. — 8. The man in ... car I came is a town-councillor. — 9. The only advice ... I can give you is to give up the attempt. — 10. Will the person ... car is parked in front of our garage be so kind as to move it ?

B Rejeter la préposition (et omettre le pronom relatif quand c'est possible).

1. The record to which we were listening was given us by Tim. — 2. John's wife, with whom we had tea, is a very good pianist. — 3. The lady with whom we had tea is a very good pianist. — 4. The friends for whom we are waiting are always late. — 5. Their house, in which ten people could live comfortably, stands at the top of the cliff. — 6. The chair in which you are sitting is two hundred years old. — 7. The people to whom this house belongs live in Glasgow. — 8. Brian, with whom I never agree, is very narrow-minded. — 9. The film about which I told you is on at the Odeon this week. — 10. He is a friend on whom you can always rely.

C Traduire :

1. La maladie de foie dont il souffre est incurable. — 2. John Morgan, dont je suis le cousin germain, doit venir la semaine prochaine. — 3. Les femmes dont le mari était prisonnier en Allemagne se faisaient beaucoup de mauvais sang. —

4. L'église dont vous apercevez le clocher a été bâtie au 12e siècle. — 5. Le dictionnaire dont j'ai besoin coûte très cher. — 6. Sa femme, dont vous vous souvenez certainement, a passé son enfance en Afrique du Sud. — 7. Il m'a prêté plusieurs livres, dont aucun ne m'a plu. — 8. Ils emportèrent de nombreux bijoux, dont la plupart valaient plusieurs centaines de livres. — 9. J'y fis la connaissance de plusieurs Anglais, dont trois sont devenus mes amis. — 10. Notre voisin est un homme très instruit, dont deux des fils sont professeurs de mathématiques.

D   Traduire :

1. Ce qui me tracasse, c'est que je ne retrouve pas mon passeport. — 2. Tout ce que nous mangions provenait de boîtes de conserves. — 3. Son voisin joue du violon, ce qui l'agace terriblement. — 4. J'ai oublié ce dont vous m'avez parlé. — 5. Ce que vous allez apprendre vous étonnera. — 6. L'assassin était le fils du pasteur, ce qui nous a tous beaucoup surpris. — 7. Nous avons ri, ce qui l'a rendu furieux. — 8. Ce qui l'a vexé, c'est que nous avons ri. — 9. Ils nous ont permis de visiter leur jardin, ce dont nous les avons remerciés. — 10. Il fait tout ce qui lui plaît et ne se soucie pas de ce qu'en pensent ses parents.

E   Traduire :

1. Lequel d'entre vous a cassé ce carreau ? — 2. A qui voulez-vous parler ? — 3. Pourquoi Fred ne nous a-t-il pas écrit pendant les vacances ? — 4. Qui attendez-vous ? — 5. Devinez qui a gagné la course. — 6. Qui est venu pendant que j'étais sorti ? — 7. Avec quoi allons-nous ouvrir ces boîtes de conserves ? — 8. Quel a été à votre avis le plus grand roi de France ? — 9. Mais pour qui donc se prend-il ? (Commencer la phrase par : Who :). — 10. Pourquoi diable criez-vous si fort ?

Leçon 40. — *Les indéfinis. Notion de quantité*

A   Traduire :

1. J'ai beaucoup de travail à faire et trop peu de temps pour le faire. — 2. Combien d'essence consomme votre voiture ? — 3. Combien de bagages emportez-vous ? — Je n'emporte presque pas de bagages. — 4. Nous voyons très peu de touristes dans notre ville. Nous ne voyons presque pas de touristes dans notre ville. — 5. Arrêtons-nous quelques minutes et mangeons un peu de chocolat. — 6. Il nous reste peu d'argent. — 7. Nous aurons moins de cerises que l'an dernier. — 8. Nous avons trop peu de clients et trop d'impôts à payer. — 9. Je n'ai pas autant de disques que lui mais j'en ai quand même un bon nombre. — 10. Il nous a dit tant de mensonges que personne ne veut plus le croire.

B   Traduire :

1. La plupart des maisons anglaises ont un jardin. — 2. La plupart des gens du village ont la télévision. — 3. J'ai lu tous ces livres; tous m'ont plu. — 4. Certains disent que j'ai raison, d'autres que j'ai tort. — 5. Toute la ville voulait voir la reine. — 6. Il lit tous les livres, quels qu'ils soient, qui lui tombent sous la main. — 7. Il ne dit jamais rien à personne. — 8. Vous ne trouverez pas de climat plus sain ailleurs. — 9. Ils sont fous tous les deux. Ils ne se conduisent raisonnablement ni l'un ni l'autre. — 10. Si tu n'as rien d'autre à faire, tu pourrais tondre la pelouse.

Leçon 41. — *Les adjectifs numéraux*

A Lire (et écrire en lettres) :
1. 35 — 14 — 43 — 54 — 15 — 92 — 13 — 74 — 60 — 18.
2. 475 — 690 — 102 — 653 — 934 — 8,367 — 4,813 — 15,145 — 72,893 — 81,050.
The 11.53 train; the 9.34 train.

B Lire les dates :
1. 1215 — 1534 — 1649 — 1746 — 1832.
2. 1066 — 1453 — 1603 — 1666 — 1805.
3. 1170 — 1485 — 1611 — 1688 — 1815.
4. 1356 — 1558 — 1763 — 1901 — 1936.
5. 1415 — 1588 — 1783 — 1904 — 1911.

C Lire (et écrire en les faisant suivre de **th, st, nd** ou **rd**) les nombres ordinaux correspondant à :
13 — 27 — 40 — 53 — 74 — 11 — 81 — 14 — 62 — 12 — 20 — 500.

D Lire :
1. James I — George III — Edward VIII — Henry V — Richard II; — William IV — Elizabeth I — Richard III — Charles II — John XXIII.
2. 2/3 — 3/4 — 4/5 — 7/8 — 50 % — 75 % — 1·732 — 1·414.
3. Les sommes : £6.90 — £199.50 — £2,500 — £6'19'11 — 7'9 — $23.75 — $3,000,000.
4. Les numéros de téléphone : 999 (police station) — Whitehall 1212 (Scotland Yard).

E Traduire :
1. Plusieurs centaines de pages. — 2. Plus de cinquante personnes. — 3. Il y a deux mois et demi. — 4. Au moins cent livres sterling. — 5. Près d'un demi-million d'habitants. — 6. Moins de 30 miles à l'heure. — 7. Il a une vingtaine d'années. — 8. Des centaines de moutons. — 9. Il y a à peine dix minutes. — 10. Il y a environ une demi-heure.

F Traduire :
1. La guerre a éclaté le 1ᵉʳ septembre 1939; elle s'est terminée en Europe le 8 mai 1945 et en Extrême-Orient le 15 août 1945. — 2. Ces livres sont intéressants tous les deux. Les voulez-vous tous les deux ? — 3. Ils jouent du piano l'un et l'autre. — 4. Ils ont deux fils, qui sont ingénieurs l'un et l'autre. — 5. Deux hommes sur trois ne mangent pas assez. — 6. La terre est environ cinquante fois plus grosse que la lune. — 7. L'Empire State Building a 102 étages; Il a 1 250 pieds de haut. — 8. Les Alliés débarquèrent en Normandie le 6 juin 1944. — 9. Les trois dernières années du règne de Victoria furent attristées par la guerre du Transvaal. — 10. Ils se mirent à table à 8 heures 10, et dès la demie ils étaient déjà en train de faire la vaisselle.

Leçon 42. — *Phrases exclamatives*

A Transformer les phrases suivantes suivant le modèle :
She is very nice (a) **She is so nice** (avec *so* ou *such*);
(b) **How nice she is !** (avec *how* ou *what*);
(c) **You can't imagine how nice she is** (avec une exclamative indirecte (Structure 7).
1. They have a very nice house. — 2. He worked very hard. — 3. He is indeed a hypocrite. — 4. He looked very tired. — 5. They are very selfish.

B Traduire :

1. Quel petit gourmand ! Comme tu vas être malade demain ! — 2. Nous avons eu une de ces tempêtes ! — 3. Quel esprit logique a ce garçon ! — 4. Comme il nous a menti ! Quelle crapule ! — 5. Quelle fatuité ! Comme il méprise ses semblables ! — 6. Comme nous l'avons trouvé aigri et déprimé ! — 7. Ils ont tous bien ri quand je leur ai raconté à quel point il s'était rendu ridicule. — 8. Nous n'avons même pas pensé à les inviter, tellement nous étions surpris de les voir. — 9. Quelle gaffe épouvantable ! Comme tout le monde se sentait gêné ! — 10. Quelle nostalgie il éprouvait en entendant ces chansons !

Leçons 43, 44 et 45. — *Adverbes, prépositions et conjonctions*

A Traduire *(que)* :

1. Nous n'avons que dix minutes pour nous rendre à la gare. — 2. Il n'est pas aussi studieux que sa sœur, mais il est plus intelligent qu'elle. — 3. Qu'il repose en paix ! — 4. Qu'ils disent ce qu'ils veulent ! — 5. Qu'ils viennent ou non, cela m'est indifférent. — 6. Un jour qu'il se sentait fatigué, nous lui avons proposé de faire venir le docteur. — 7. Que de gens dans la rue ! Que de bruit ! — 8. C'est la meilleure pièce que vous puissiez voir à Londres en ce moment. — 9. Que cet homme est rusé ! — 10. Puisque les garages sont très chers et qu'il est impossible de stationner le long des trottoirs, tu ferais mieux de vendre ta voiture.

B Traduire *(aussi, comme)* :

1. Il aime les mathématiques et aussi les langues. — 2. Il aime les mathématiques ; moi aussi. — 3. Le malade dort, aussi vais-je vous demander de marcher sur la pointe des pieds. — 4. Ils jouent au cricket et aussi au rugby. — 5. A l'âge de six ans il nageait comme un poisson. — 6. Pourquoi n'êtes-vous pas venus hier, comme je vous l'ai demandé. — 7. Il a passé trois ans en Angleterre comme précepteur. — 8. Comme il était en colère ! Il hurlait comme un fou. — 9. Comme il était fort en colère, j'ai préféré ne pas discuter. — 10 Les boissons alcoolisées, comme la bière et le cidre, ne sont pas vendues aux jeunes de moins de dix-huit ans.

C Traduire *(chez, jusqu'à, pour)* :

1. Je dois rentrer chez moi pour finir mon travail, je passerai chez vous vers six heures. — 2. Le correspondant anglais de mon fils est chez nous en ce moment. — 3. Il y a de moins en moins d'alcoolisme chez les jeunes. — 4. Vous ne pouvez aller en voiture que jusqu'au vieux moulin. — 5. Il y avait jusqu'à cinq cents personnes qui venaient l'écouter prêcher. — 6. Les cabarets ne sont ouverts que jusqu'à 22 heures 30. — 7. Il nous a menti pour ne pas être puni. — 8. Nous l'avons puni pour nous avoir menti. — 9. Il a menti pour que son père ne le punisse pas. — 10. Pour qui est ce disque ? — Il est pour vous.

D Traduire *(encore, même, si)* :

1. A une heure du matin il n'était pas encore couché, il travaillait encore — 2. Encore dix miles et nous serons arrivés. — 3. La réunion a duré encore plus longtemps que je ne m'y attendais. — 4. Il sortit sans même dire au revoir. — 5. C'est ici même, dans cette pièce, que le traité fut signé. — 6. Nous sommes nés dans le même village. — 7. Il n'est pas si riche qu'on le dit. — Oh, mais si. — 8. Demandez-lui si cela le dérangerait que je vienne. — 9. C'est un film si bon que je l'ai vu trois fois. — 10. Ne marchez pas si vite. Ne soyez pas si pressé.

VERBES IRRÉGULIERS

LISTE 1

(80 verbes très employés)

to be	I was [wɔz] / we were [wə:]	been	être
to have	I had	had	avoir
to beat [i:]	I beat [i:]	beaten	battre
to begin	I began [æ]	begun [ʌ]	commencer
to bend	I bent	bent	courber, se pencher
to blow [ou]	I blew [blu:]	blown	souffler
to break [ei]	I broke [ou]	broken	briser
to bring	I brought [ɔ:t]	brought	apporter
to build [bild]	I built	built	bâtir
to burn	I burnt	burnt	brûler
to burst	I burst	burst	éclater
10 to buy [ai]	I bought [ɔ:t]	bought	acheter
to catch	I caught [ɔ:t]	caught	attraper
to choose [u:]	I chose [ou]	chosen [ou]	choisir
to come [ʌ]	I came [ei]	come [ʌ]	venir (1)
to cut	I cut	cut	couper
to do	I did	done [ʌ]	faire
to draw [ɔ:]	I drew [dru:]	drawn	tirer, dessiner
to drink	I drank [æ]	drunk [ʌ]	boire
to drive [ai]	I drove [ou]	driven [i]	conduire, aller en voiture
to eat	I ate [et]	eaten	manger
20 to fall [ɔ:]	I fell	fallen	tomber
to feel	I felt	felt	(se) sentir, éprouver
to fight	I fought [ɔ:t]	fought	combattre
to find [ai]	I found [au]	found	trouver
to fly	I flew [flu:]	flown [ou]	voler, aller en avion
to forget	I forgot	forgotten	oublier
to get	I got	got (Amer, gotten)	obtenir, devenir
to give	I gave	given	donner (2)
to go [ou]	I went	gone [ɔ]	aller
to grow [ou]	I grew [gru:]	grown	grandir, (faire) pousser
30 to hang [æ]	I hung [ʌ]	hung	pendre, accrocher (3)
to hear [iə]	I heard [ə:]	heard	entendre
to hide [ai]	I hid [i]	hidden [i]	(se) cacher
to hold [ou]	I held	held	tenir
to keep	I kept	kept	garder
to know [nou]	I knew [nju:]	known [noun]	savoir, connaître

(1) de même : **to become**, devenir.
(2) de même : **to forgive**, pardonner.
(3) Régulier dans le sens de « exécuter (un condamné) par pendaison ».

	to lead [i:]	I led	led	mener
	to learn [ə:]	I learnt (ou rég.)	learnt (ou rég.)	apprendre
	to leave	I left	left	laisser, quitter, partir
	to let	I let	let	laisser, permettre
40	to lie [ai]	I lay [ei]	lain [ei]	être étendu (ou couché)
	to light	I lit (ou rég.)	lit (ou rég.)	allumer, éclairer
	to lose [u:z]	I lost [ɔ]	lost	perdre
	to make	I made	made	faire, fabriquer
	to meet	I met	met	(se) rencontrer
	to pay [ei]	I paid [ei]	paid	payer
	to put	I put	put	mettre
	to read [i:]	I read [e]	read [e]	lire
	to ride [ai]	I rode [ou]	ridden [i]	aller à cheval (ou à bicyclette)
	to ring	I rang [æ]	rung [ʌ]	sonner
50	to run [ʌ]	I ran [æ]	run [ʌ]	courir
	to say [ei]	I said [e] (1)	said [e]	dire, réciter
	to see	I saw [ɔ:]	seen	voir
	to sell	I sold [ou]	sold	vendre
	to send	I sent	sent	envoyer
	to shake	I shook	shaken	secouer
	to shine [ai]	I shone [ɔ]	shone [ɔ]	briller
	to shoot	I shot	shot	tirer (arme à feu), fusiller
	to show [ou]	I showed	shown [ou] (2)	montrer
	to shut	I shut	shut	fermer
60	to sing	I sang [æ]	sung [ʌ]	chanter
	to sit	I sat	sat	être assis
	to sleep	I slept	slept	dormir
	to speak	I spoke	spoken	parler
	to spend	I spent	spent	dépenser, passer (temps)
	to spread [e]	I spread [e]	spread [e]	étendre, répandre
	to stand	I stood	stood	être debout (3)
	to steal	I stole [ou]	stolen	voler, dérober
	to stick	I stuck [ʌ]	stuck	coller
	to strike [ai]	I struck [ʌ]	struck	frapper
70	to swim	I swam [æ]	swum [ʌ]	nager
	to take	I took	taken	prendre
	to teach	I taught [ɔ:t]	taught	enseigner
	to tear [ɛə]	I tore [ɔ:]	torn	déchirer
	to tell	I told [ou]	told	dire, raconter
	to think	I thought [ɔ:t]	thought	penser
	to throw [ou]	I threw [u:]	thrown	jeter, lancer
	to wake (up)	I woke (up)	woken (up) (ou rég.)	(se) réveiller
	to wear [ɛə]	I wore [ɔ:]	worn	porter (vêtements)

(1) La 3ᵉ personne du singulier du présent (says) se prononce également avec une voyelle courte [sez]. Comparer said [e] avec laid [ei] et paid [ei], qui sont réguliers pour l'oreille.

(2) Ne pas confondre les prononciations de shone [ɔ] et de shown [ou].

(3) De même : to **understand**, comprendre.

	to win	I won [ʌ]	won [ʌ]	gagner
80	to write [ai]	I wrote [ou]	written [i]	écrire

LISTE 2 (60 verbes d'emploi assez courant)

	to awake	I awoke	awoke (ou rég.)	(se) réveiller (1)
	to bear [ɛə]	I bore [ɔ:]	borne (2)	supporter
	to bet	I bet	bet	parier
	to bind [ai]	I bound [au]	bound	lier, relier
	to bite [ai]	I bit [i]	bitten [i]	mordre
	to bleed	I bled	bled	saigner
	to breed	I bred	bred	élever (enfants, bétail) (3)
	to cast	I cast	cast	jeter (surtout sens fig.)
	to cling	I clung [ʌ]	clung	s'accrocher
10	to cost	I cost	cost	coûter
	to creep	I crept	crept	ramper
	to deal [i:]	I dealt [e]	dealt [e]	distribuer
	to dig	I dug	dug	creuser
	to dream [i:]	I dreamt [e] (ou rég.)	dreamt [e] (ou rég.)	rêver
	to feed	I fed	fed	nourrir
	to flee	I fled	fled	s'enfuir
	to fling	I flung [ʌ]	flung	jeter (violemment)
	to forbid	I forbade [ei] ou [æ]	forbidden	interdire
	to freeze	I froze	frozen	geler
20	to grind [ai]	I ground	ground	moudre
	to hit	I hit	hit	frapper, atteindre
	to hurt	I hurt	hurt	blesser, faire mal
	to kneel	I knelt	knelt	s'agenouiller
	to knit	I knit (ou rég.)	knit (ou rég.)	tricoter
	to lay	I laid [ei]	laid	poser à plat
	to lean [i:]	I leant [e] (ou rég.)	leant [e] (ou rég.)	s'appuyer
	to leap [i:]	I leapt [e]	leapt [e]	sauter (4)
	to lend	I lent	lent	prêter
	to mean [i:]	I meant [e]	meant [e]	signifier, vouloir dire
30	to mow	I mowed	mown (ou rég.)	faucher
	to rise [ai]	I rose [ou]	risen [i]	s'élever, se lever (5)
	to saw [ɔ:]	I sawed	sawn	scier
	to seek	I sought [ɔ:t]	sought	chercher (sens abstraits) (6)
	to set	I set	set	fixer
	to sew [ou]	I sewed	sewn	coudre

(1) Dans la langue courante on se sert surtout du verbe **to wake up** (liste 1).
(2) **To be born** (sans e) : *naître* (verbe passif).
(3) Plus couramment **to bring up** quand il s'agit d'enfants.
(4) Moins courant que **to jump** au sens propre.
(5) Se lever du lit : **to get up**. Se lever de sa chaise : **to stand up**.
(6) Chercher ce qu'on a égaré : **to look for**

to shed	I shed	shed	verser (larmes, sang)
to shrink	I shrank [æ]	shrunk [ʌ]	rétrécir
to sink	I sank [æ]	sunk [ʌ]	sombrer, couler
to slide [ai]	I slid [i]	slid	glisser
40 to smell	I smelt	smelt	sentir (odorat)
to sow [ou]	I sowed	sown (ou rég.)	semer
to spell	I spelt (ou rég.)	spelt (ou rég.)	épeler
to spill	I spilt (ou rég.)	spilt (ou rég.)	renverser (un liquide)
to spin	I spun [ʌ] (ou span)	spun	filer
to spit	I spat	spat	cracher
to split	I split	split	fendre
to spoil	I spoilt (ou rég.)	spoilt (ou rég.)	gâter, gâcher
to spring	I sprang [æ]	sprung [ʌ]	bondir, jaillir
to sting	I stung [ʌ]	stung	piquer (insectes)
50 to stink	I stank [æ] (ou stunk)	stunk [ʌ]	puer
to strive [ai]	I strove [ou]	striven [i]	s'efforcer
to swear [ɛə]	I swore [ɔ:]	sworn	jurer
to sweep	I swept	swept	balayer
to swell	I swelled	swollen [ou]	enfler
to swing	I swung [ʌ]	swung	(se) balancer
to thrust	I thrust	thrust	fourrer, enfoncer
to tread [e]	I trod	trodden	fouler aux pieds
to weave	I wove	woven	tisser
to weep	I wept	wept	pleurer
60 to wring	I wrung [ʌ]	wrung	tordre

Verbes à ne pas confondre :
a — **to lie** (être étendu) et **to lay** (poser à plat);
b — **to feel** (ressentir), **to fall** (tomber) et **to fell** (rég. : **to fell a tree**, abattre un arbre);
c — **to fly** (voler), **to flee** (fuir, qui se dit aussi : **to fly away**) et **to flow** (rég. couler, s'écouler);
d — **to find** (trouver) et **to found** (rég., fonder);
e — **to forget** (oublier), **to forgive** (pardonner) et **to forbid** (interdire, qui se dit aussi : **to prohibit**, rég.);
f — **to sew** (coudre), **to sow** (semer) et **to saw** (scier), qui se conjuguent de même; les deux premiers se prononcent de même.

LISTE 3

30 verbes plus rares (La plupart sont archaïques ou ont des synonymes plus courants dans la langue parlée. Ne les employer qu'avec précautions)

to abide [ai] (by)	I abode	abode	rester fidèle (à)
to beget	I begot (Bibl. : begat)	begotten	engendrer
to beseech	I besought [ɔ:t]	besought	supplier
to bid	I bade [æ] ou [ei]	bidden (ou : bid)	ordonner
to bid	I bid	bid	offrir (prix, enchère)
to blend	I blent (ou rég.)	blent (ou rég.)	mélanger
to chide [ai]	I chid	chidden (ou : chid)	réprimander

213

to cleave	I cleft (ou : clove)	cleft (ou : cloven)	fendre
to crow	I crew (ou rég.)	crowed	chanter (coq)
to dare	I durst (ou rég.)	dared	oser (voir § 69)
to dwell	I dwelt	dwelt	habiter
to forsake	I forsook	forsaken	abandonner
to gild [g]	I gilded	gilt (ou rég.)	dorer
to gird [g]	I girt (ou rég.)	girt (ou rég.)	ceindre
to hew	I hewed	hewn (ou rég.)	tailler à coups de hache
to quit [kwit] (1)	I quit (ou rég.)	quit (ou rég.)	cesser (de...)
to rend	I rent	rent	déchirer
to rid	I rid (ou rég.)	rid	débarrasser (2)
to shear [iə]	I sheared	shorn (ou rég.)	tondre (les moutons)
to shoe	I shod [ɔ]	shod	ferrer, chausser
to slay	I slew [slu:]	slain	massacrer
to sling	I slung [ʌ]	slung	lancer avec une fronde
to slink	I slunk [ʌ]	slunk	aller furtivement
to slit	I slit	slit	fendre, déchirer
to smite [ai]	I smote [ou]	smitten [i]	frapper
to speed	I sped	sped	se hâter
to strew [stru:]	I strewed	strewn	joncher
to stride [ai]	I strode [ou]	stridden [i]	marcher à grandes enjambées.
to string	I strung [ʌ]	strung	enfiler
to thrive [ai]	I throve [ou]	thriven [i]	prospérer
to wind [ai]	I wound [au]	wound [au]	enrouler, remonter (horloge)

(1) Rare en Angleterre, courant en Amérique.

(2) S'emploie surtout au participe passé, dans les expressions : **to be rid of** (être débarrassé de) et : **to get rid of** (se débarrasser de).

Remarques. (1) Les verbes à préfixe se conjuguent comme les verbes qui leur servent de radical (ex. : to become, to forgive, to understand; voir liste I).

De même: **to arise** (s'élever, survenir); **to befall** (survenir); **to behold** (contempler); **to foresee** (prévoir); **to foretell** (prédire); **to overcome** (surmonter, vaincre); **to overtake** (rattraper, doubler); **to withdraw** (retirer, se retirer).

Exceptions (formes différentes au participe passé) : to get, to forget (liste 1) et to beget (liste 3); to bid (liste 3) et to forbid (liste 2).

To broadcast (radiodiffuser) est régulier au preterite. Le participe passé est **broadcast** ou **broadcasted**.

To behave (se comporter) et **to welcome** (accueillir) sont réguliers. (Dans « **to be welcome** », être le bienvenu, **welcome** est un adjectif).

(2) Participes passés irréguliers à valeur d'adjectifs :

Wrought iron (de : to work), *le fer forgé*.
A clean-**shaven** face (de : to shave), *un visage rasé de frais*.
Poorly **clad** (de : to clothe = to dress), *pauvrement vêtu*.
Laden with (de : to lade, synonyme rare de **to load**), *chargé de, accablé de*.
Molten lead (de : to melt), *du plomb fondu*.

Mais les participes passés à valeur verbale sont réguliers **(You haven't shaved. The gun was not loaded. The snow has melted away).**

(3) Quelques verbes dont les temps irréguliers se terminent par un *t* (**to burn, to smell...**) sont réguliers en Amérique (**burned, smelled**). Ces formes s'emploient aussi en Angleterre.

INDEX

such et so, 398.
suffixes, 637 à 642.
suggest (to -), 183, 335.
sujet, sa place, 87 à 93.
   gérondif ou infinitif sujet, 220 et 232.
suit (to -), 286.
superlatifs, leçon 35.
supply (to -), 295.
suppose (to -), 263, 279, 281, 299.
supposition avec if, 176, 188.
— avec if + should, 181.
— avec inversion, 91.
sure, sure to, 351, 453.
surprise, 59, 60, 184, 449.

tags, leçon 5.
tant de, 555.
tant que, 612.
tantôt... tantôt..., 614 (now).
teach (to -), 208, 259, 260, 283, 291, 478.
-teen, -ty, 568.
tell (to -), 208, 258, 260, 291, 307 à 309.
than, RF 20; 446, 447.
thank (to -), 344.
that, conjonction, 618, 279, 459, 460.
— pronom relatif, 527-530.
— démonstratif, 520 à 524.
the, article défini, leçon 32.
— adverbe, devant un comparatif, 444, 445.
there is, 23, 24.
there is no + gérondif, 225.
these, 520 à 523.
think (to -), 111, 254, 263, 279, 281, 288, 458, 461.
this, 520 à 523.
those, 520 à 524.
thou, thee, thy, thine, 2.
thousand, 569, 570.
threaten (to -), 243, 305.
through, 85, 619.
throw (to -), 593 (§ 4).
times, 152.
to, 620.
— exprimant le but, 228.
— suivi d'un gérondif, 224.
— anaphorique, 233.
too, 398, 599.
too many, too much, 100, 556.
toujours, 598 (always et still), 606 (ever).
tout, tous, 560 à 565.
très, 433.
trop, 100, 599 (§ 3).
trop de, 556.
trust (to -), 262, 295.
tutoiement, 2.
twice, 152, 437.
understand (to -), 111, 279.

up, 86, 621.
use (to -), 286, 534, 649.
use (it's no -), 225, 649.
used to, 162, 163, 168.

venir de, 142, 146.
verbes auxiliaires, leçon 3.
— défectifs, leçon 4.
— composés, leçon 6.
vers, 591 (about), 621 (towards), 622 (-wards).
very, 433, 621.
— avec un superlatif, 438.
(very) much, 101, 433.
voici, voilà, 25, 90.
volonté, 118, 119 (will), 243, 261 (to want).
volonté d'agir, 243.

wait (to -), 262, 287, 315.
want (to -), 111, 243, 252, 261.
warn (to -), 258.
-wards, 622.
watch (to -), 593 (§ 3).
well et good, 648.
   place de (very) well, 94, 101.
were, 17, 175 à 178.
what, 397, 536, 541 à 544, 588.
whatever, 180.
when, 131, 132, 622.
whether, 623, 282, 283.
which et that, 527 à 529.
which et what (= ce que), 536 à 539.
which et what (= quel), 543.
who et whom, interrogatifs, 542.
who et whom, relatifs, RF 26; 526.
whoever, who ever, 545, 567.
whose, 514 à 516, 532, 533.
why, 345, 462, 623.
will, leçons 9 et 5; 165, 351.
wish (to -), 177, 243, 261, 333, 336, 341.
woman, 381.
wonder (to -), 282.
worry, 284, 476 (§ 2).
worth, 225, 464.
would, leçons 9 et 5; 176, 177, 351.
would rather, 55, 340.
wrong (to be -), 22.

-y (suffixe ajouté à), RF 1.
y (traduction de), 477.
il y a, 23 à 26, 156 à 160.
yes, 57, 58.
yet, 600.
you + impératif, 199.
yours (sincerely), 513.

zéro, 574.

---

able to, 49.
about, 75, 591.
about to, 124.
abstraits (noms), 367, 375, 383, 421.
account for, 287.
accusation, 296.
adjectif démonstratif, 520.
— indéfini, leçon 40.
— interrogatif, 541, 543.
— numéral, leçon 41.
— possessif, 505 à 512.
— qualificatif, leçon 34.
   — composé, 411 à 416.
   — substantivé, 417 à 422.
   — place, 408 à 410.
   — construction, leçon 36.
— relatif, 544.
— verbal, 214.
admit (to -), 250, 279.
adverbe, leçon 43 à 45.
— en -ly, 624.
— place, 96 à 102.
— comparatif et superlatif, 430, 435.
advice, 367, 649.
advise (to-), 258, 335, 649.
afford (to -), 245.
afin de, afin que, 345, 346.
afraid, 449, 460.
âge, 21.
ago, 157.
agree (to -), 111, 243.
ainsi, 597 (§ 5), 620.
alive et living, 636.
all, 560, 562, 564.
allow (to-), 246, 259, 49.
alone et lonely, 636.
and entre adjectif, 407.
— après hundred, 569.
— après come, go, try, 314, 315.
animaux, 355.
another, 154, 557.
answer (to -), 286.
any, 403 à 406, 551, 558, 562, 603.
— (composés de), 565.
apparence (verbe + as if), 326, 327.
around, voir round, 616.
article défini, leçon 32.
— indéfini, 391 à 401.
— partitif, 402 à 406.
as, 592.
— avec article indéfini, 398.
as et than, 446, 447; RF 21.
as..., as, 439; RF 21.
as if, as though, 176.
look (sound) as if, 326.
as et like, 592 (§ 4).
ask (to -), 243, 258, 260, 282, 287, 295.
asleep et sleeping, 409, 636.
aspect, 104.

assez, 100, 605.
assez de, 556.
at, 593.
at all, 593 (§ 5).
attempt (to -), 243.
attend (to -), 262.
attribut, 297, 299.
   adjectif attribut, 409.
   nom attribut, 395.
aucun, 562, 563.
aussi, 626.
   moi aussi, 61.
autant de, 552.
autre, 557, 558, 566.
auxiliaires, leçons 2, 3 et 5.
— be ou have, 19.
avoid (to -), 248.

baby, 355.
be (to -), leçons 3 et 5.
   to be to, 125, 126.
bear (I can't -), 255.
beaucoup de, 546.
beg (to -), 258.
begin (to -), 251.
behave (to -), 481.
believe (to -), 111, 263, 279, 281, 288.
belong (to -), 111, 491.
besoin de (avoir -), 54.
better, best, 440.
better (I had -), 55.
born (to be -), 204.
borrow (to -), 294.
both, 563, 564, 572, 604.
bound to, 352.
brothers et brethren, 359.
burst out (to -), 251.
business, 357.
busy, 214.
but, 594, 236.
but d'une action, 345, 346.
buy (to -), 292.
by, 595.

can, leçons 4 et 5; 179.
car, 342.
cas possessif, 492 à 503.
case (in -), 182.
cat, 355.
catch (to -), 270.
cattle, 365.
causatifs (verbes -), 267, 272.
cause, 342 à 344.
ce, 520 à 522.
— traduit par the, 379.
c'est... que (ou qui), 189, 467.
ce qui, ce que, 536 à 538.
celui de, 501, 523.
celui qui, 523.
chacun, chaque, 560.
challenge (to -), 258.
chance (to -), 353.
change (to -), 366.

charge (to -), 296.
chez, 627.
child, 355; RF 12.
choix (what et which), 543.
choose (to -), 243.
clothes, cloths, 369, 372.
collectifs (noms -), 368 à 370.
combien de, 548.
come (to -), 312, 314, 298.
comme, 628.
comparatifs, leçon 35.
compel (to -), 328.
compléments du nom, leçon 36.
— de l'adjectif, leçon 36.
— directs et indirects, 286 à 288.
— d'objet et d'attribution (291 à 293).
— du comparatif et du superlatif, RF. 20 et 21; 434.
— place, 94, 95.
concordance des temps, leçon 15.
condition (avec if), 188.
conditionnel, 128 à 130.
— passé, 188.
— des défectifs, 37.
— français traduit par un preterite, 131.
confiance, 262.
congratulate (to -), 296.
conjonctions de temps, 131.
conseils, 334, 335.
consentement (will), 118.
conséquence, 347, 348.
consider (to -), 263, 299, 458.
contemplate (to -), 243.
continuation, 251.
contractions avec not, 13.
— des auxiliaires ('s, 'd), 18, 28, 29, 116.
conversion, 643 à 649.
could, leçons 4 et 5; 177, 179.
craft, 360.
croire, 263, 279, 281.
crowd, 370.

'd, 29.
dare (to -), 52, 53, 258.
daresay (I -), 350.
dates, 504, 580.
date d'une action, 149 à 151.
dead et died, 159.
deal of (a great -), 546.
decide (to -), 243.
décimales, 573.
déclaration, 263, 279, 299.
défectifs (verbes -), leçons 4 et 5.
demandes, 330 à 333.
démonstratifs, 520 à 525.
depend (to -), 262, 288.
déplacements, 300.
depuis, 155, 157.
depuis que, 159 (§ 4).
dérivation, 634 à 642.
dès, 151.

215

dès que (as soon as), 131, 618.
describe (to -), 294.
deserve (to -), 245.
destination d'un objet, 229.
devoir, leçon 27; 351.
dimension, 21.
dire, 307 à 309.
discuss (to -), 282.
dislike (to -), 255.
distance, 26, 504.
distributif (sens -) de a(n), 399.
do (to -), leçons 2, 5 et 13; 172.
dog, 355.
dont, 534, 535, 539.
dozen, 570.
dress (to -), 285, 481.
durée, 154 à 160, 504.

each, 560.
each other, 484 à 486.
échec, 244.
-ed, prononciation RF 8; 5.
either, 563, 605.
elder, eldest, 431, 441.
elliptiques (phrases -), 66, 196, 198, 233, 281.
emphatique (forme -), leçon 13.
— du futur, 118 à 122.
— de l'impératif, 199 à 201.
en (traduction de -), 476.
en + participe présent, 215.
enable (to -), 246.
encore, 629.
English, 423, 428.
enjoy (to -), 249, 286, 481.
enough, 100, 230, 556, 605.
enter (to -), 286.
épithète, sa place, 407, 408.
équivalents des défectifs, 49.
étonnement, 60, 194.
even, 102, 606.
éventualité, 43, 349.
ever, 545, 567, 606.
every, 560.
— avec idée de fréquence, 153.
— composés de every, 565.
except, 236.
exclamatives (phrases -), leçon 42.
excuses, 250, 296.
expect (to -), 243, 262, 279, 281, 286, 350.
explain (to -), 280, 294.

-f, -fe → -ves RF 12; 359.
fail (to -), 244.
faillir, 353.
faire + infinitif, 275 à 278.
falloir, 328, 329.
far, 431, 606.
fear (to -), 255.
fed up with, 449.
feel (to -), 266, 269, 319 à 327.
féminin, 354 à 357.
few, 547.
  a few, 549.
fewer et less, 554.
fight (to -), 285.
find (to -), 270, 458, 461.
finish (to -), 251.
first, 582, 607.
fish, 369.
fois (nombre de -), 152.
folk, 365.
for, 596, 154, 157, 160, 223.
for et to, 344, 345.
for fear, 182.
forbid (to -), 261, 330.
forget (to -), 253.
forgive (to -), 223, 250, 296.
former (the -), 441.
fractions, 583.
French, 423, 428.
fréquence, 152, 153.
fruit, 369.

furniture, 368.
futur, leçon 9.
— proche, 123, 124.
— antérieur, 147.
— emphatique, 118 à 122.
— ou présent ? 131, 132.

génitif, 492, 504.
genre des noms, 354 à 357.
géographiques (noms -), 385.
gérondif, leçon 18 (216 à 225).
— après for, 223.
— après to, 224.
— après un verbe, leçon 20.
— après un cas possessif, 218.
get (to -), 70, 211, 272, 276, 277, 298, 443.
give (to -), 291, 293, 208.
give up (to -), 248.
given to, 224.
go (to -), 298, 312 à 314, 596 (§ 1).
go on (to -), 251.
going to, 123.
good, 648, RF 20.
  a good + nombre, 571.
goods, 369, 372.
got (I've got, I've got to), 32, 33.
grown-up(s), 373.

h muette, 374, 391.
hair, 369.
half, 102, 398, 583.
habitude, leçon 12; 168.
happen (to -), 245, 353.
hard et hardly, 608, 648.
hardly + ever, any, etc., 12, 608.
hasard, 353.
hate (to -), 255, 261, 484.
have (to -), leçons 3 et 5; 272, 276, 277, 643.
had better, had sooner, 55.
had rather, 55, 178, 340.
hear (to -), 265, 266, 269, 319 à 323.
help (can't -), 248, 352.
hesitate (to -), 244.
heures, 579.
hope (to -), 243, 281.
hope (nom), 448.
house(s), 359.
how interrogatif, 541.
— exclamatif, 584, 587.
how long (durée), 154.
how much, how many, 548.
how often, 152, 153.
however, 180, 567, 609.
hundred, 569, 570.

if, 176, 188.
ill et sick, 409.
imparfait (trad. de l'), 169.
impératif, leçon 16.
impersonnels (verbes -), 475.
impression (verbes d'-), 324 à 327.
in, 79, 609.
— après le superlatif, RF 20.
incertitude, 349.
inchoatifs (verbes -), 298.
indéfini (article), 391 à 401.
indéfinis (pronoms et adjectifs), leçon 40.
indénombrables (noms), 367, 368.
indirect (style -), 190 à 193.
inévitable (action -), 352.
infinitif, leçon 19.
— dans une interrogative indirecte, 283.
— ou gérondif ? leçon 20.
infinitive (proposition -), leçon 21; 231, 456.
information, 367.

-ing (formes verbales en -), leçon 18.
insist (to -), 331, 183, 279.
insistance (voir : emphatique).
intend (to -), 243, 261.
intention, 118, 123.
interdiction, 41, 46, 122, 330, 332.
interrogatifs (termes), 540 à 545.
interrogative (forme), leçon 2.
interrogative indirecte, 87, 282 à 284.
interro-négative (forme -), leçon 2.
inversion, 87 à 93.
invraisemblance, 181, 184.
irréel, 175 à 178.
irréguliers (verbes), liste page 210.
irréguliers (pluriels), RF 12; 359.
it, 470 à 475.

jamais (never et ever), 606, 613, 12.
jusqu'à, 630.
just, 610, 142, 146.
justement, cf. just, 610.

keep (to -), 270, 297.
keep on (to -), 251.
kill (to -), 478, 484.
know (to -), 111, 263, 279, 283.
knowledge, 367.

laisser, 316 à 318.
langues (noms de -), 428.
last, 386, 582, 611.
late et lately, 611, 648.
latter (the -), 441.
lead (to -), 258.
learn (to -), 245, 283.
least (the -), 432.
leave (to -), 316, 317.
left (to be -), 204.
lend (to -), 291.
lequel (choix), 543.
less et fewer, 554.
less, RF 21.
less (the -), 444, 445.
less and less, 443.
lest, 182.
let (to -), leçon 16; 265, 268, 318.
liable to, 449.
like (to), 111, 255, 261, 286, 338, 341.
like et as, 611, 592 (§ 4).
likely to, 350.
listen (to -), 287, 285.
little, 92, 547, 611.
  a little, 549.
long (adverbe), 430, 648.
  how long, 154, 158, 160.
  no longer, 613.
look (to -), 287, 285, 324 à 326, 596 (§ 2).
look forward to (to -), 224.
lot of (a-), 546.
love (to -), 255, 261.
luggage, 368.
-ly (adverbes en -), 624.

make (to -), 265, 267, 273, 276, 292.
make up one's mind (to -), 490.
maladies (noms de -), 387.
malgré, 604 (despite), 609 (-in spite of).
man, 379, 381.
manage (to -), 243.
manière (adverbes de -), 99, 624.
many, 546.
masculin, 354 à 357.
may, leçons 4 et 5; 179, 180, 349, 353.
maybe, 88, 612.
me et I, 434.

means, 363.
même, 102, 631.
might, voir may.
mind (nom), 383, 490.
mind (to -), 111, 249, 286.
mine, 507.
miss (to -), 286.
mode, 104.
moi, je..., RF 10.
moi aussi, moi non plus, 61.
moi si, moi non, 62.
moins, RF 21.
moins de, 554.
moins... moins..., 444.
  de moins en moins, 443.
  d'autant moins, 445.
more, RF 20; 429, 553.
  more and more, 443.
  the more, 444, 445.
  no more, 613.
mort, 159 (§ 5).
most (the -), RF 20; 429.
most (of), 561.
most (= very), 433.
mouvements, 300.
much, 433, 546.
must, leçons 4 et 5; 328, 351.

narration, 114, 134.
nationalités (noms et adjectifs de -), 423 à 428.
ne... plus (no more et no longer), 613.
nécessité, 46, 54, 120, 126, 328, 329.
need (nom), 448, 456.
need (to -), 52, 54, 252, 286, 328, 534.
négative (forme -), leçon 2.
— de l'impératif, 197, 198.
négation en tête de phrase, 92.
neither, 61, 563, 613.
n'est-ce pas ? 64, 65.
neutre, 354, 355.
never, 92, 613.
news, 363, 372.
next, 386, 582, 613.
ni moi non plus, 61.
ni l'un ni l'autre, 563.
ni ... ni ... (neither ... nor ...), 613.
no, 57, 392, 405, 436, 562.
  composés de no, 565.
nom, 31.
  noms abstraits, 367, 369.
  noms collectifs, 368 à 370.
  noms composés, 371 à 373.
non, 57, 58.
  moi non, 62.
  moi non plus, 61.
none, 562.
nor, 61, 93, 613.
not, leçon 2; 281.
not any, 404, 405.
numéraux (adjectifs -), leçon 41.

-o → -os, -oes, RF 12; 359.
obey (to -), 286.
object (to -), 224, 249.
obligation, 328, 329.
of, 519, 396, 457.
off, 82, 614.
offer, 243, 291, 208.
older et elder, 431.
on (traduction de -), 212.
on, 81, 614.
once, 615.
one (numéral), 394, 569.
— (pronom personnel), 487 à 490.
— (pronom indéfini), 557.
— remplaçant un nom, 422, 501.
  the one, 524.
one another, 484 à 486.
one's oneself, 488 à 490.
only, 102, 615.

onomatopées, 644.
opinion (verbes d'), 263,
order (to -), 261, 330, 33
  in order to, in order
  346.
ordinaires (verbes -), 1.
ordinaux (nombres), 575
ordres, 183, 261, 330 à
orthographe des termin
  bales, RF 1, 7 et 8; 6
other, RF 6; 557, 558, 5
  every other, 153.
où traduit par when, 62
ought to, 48, 51, 334, 3
oui, 57, 58.
out, 80.
out of, 615, 302, 305.
over, 83, 615.
owing to, 343.
own, 517, 518.
own (to -), 491.

pair of, 364.
Parliament, 382.
participe passé, leçon
  272 à 274, 413.
participe présent, le
  269 à 271, 412.
passé récent, 142.
passer-by, 373.
passif, leçon 17.
— progressif, 210.
— avec l'auxiliaire
pay (to -), 287.
pays (noms de -), 38
pendant, pendant q
  605; while, 62
  612.
penny, pennies, pen
people, 365.
perhaps, 88.
perception (verbes
  323.
permission, 41, 46
permit (to -), 246,
person, 354.
personne du singul
personnifications, 3
persuade (to -), 2
peu de, 547.
  un peu de, 549
peuples (noms de
piece of, 367, 36
plan (to -), 243.
play (to -), 389.
pleased with, ple
plenty of, 546.
plupart (la -), 56
pluriel et singul
pluriel des noms
pluriels irréguliè
plus (de), 553.
plus... plus..., 44
  de plus en pl
  d'autant plus
plus-que-parfai
— modal, 175
politics, 362.
possessifs, 505
possessif (cas -
possession, leç
possibilité, 38,
postpone (to -
postpositions,
potentiel, 176
pour, 632.
pouvoir, 38 à
prefer (to -),
préférence, 3
préfixes, 634
prepare (to -
prépositions,
— avec ver
— avec arti

request (to -), 2
require (to -), 2
resent (to -), 24
resist (to -), 286
reste (il -), 204.
rich, riches, 417
right (to be -),
rob (to -), 295.
round, 84, 616.

-s, -es, RF 1
's (génitif), RF
  504; (pluriel)
  (= is ou has),
same, 447, 559.
sans, sans que, 2
savings, 369, 372
savoir + verbe 3
say (to -), 307
  597 (§ 6).
Scotch, Scots, Sco
see (to -), 266, 26
seem (to -), 244, 26
send (to -), 208, 2
set (to -), 270.
semi-défectif, 52 à
seulement, 102.
shall, 115 à 122;
should, 48, 51, 28
  186, 334, 350,
show (to -), 208, 29
si, 633.
since, 617.
so, 597.
so much, so many,
soit... soit... (either
soit que (whether),
some, 402 à 406, 5
  composés de som
souhaits, 44, 177, 3
sound, 297, 3
souvenir, 253.
souvenir (se -), 310,
spend (to -), 214.
stand (to -), 214.
start (to -), 251, 270
still, 598.
stop (to -), 251.
strike (to -), 536.
structures (définition
— du verbe, leçons
— du nom et de l'
  36.
styles direct et in
subjonctif, leçon 14.
  traduction du sub
  çais, 187.
succeed in (to -), 222
such, 397, 525, 589.

TABLE DES MATIÈRES

PREFACE	3
INTRODUCTION : REVISION DES REGLES FONDAMENTALES	5
Corrigés des exercices des leçons de révision	23
Première liste d'adverbes, prépositions et conjonctions	26

PREMIERE PARTIE : LE VERBE ET LES STRUCTURES VERBALES.

A. LE VERBE. GENERALITES

1. Conjugaison d'un verbe ordinaire	31
2. Formes interrogative, négative, interro-négative	33
3. Les auxiliaires *to be* et *to have*	35
4. Les auxiliaires de modalité (verbes défectifs)	38
5. Emplois idiomatiques des auxiliaires	42
6. Les postpositions	45
7. Place des mots accompagnant le verbe	50

B. TEMPS, MODES ET ASPECTS

8. Forme progressive. Présent progressif et présent simple	53
9. Futur et conditionnel	56
10. Temps du passé	60
11. Comment situer une action dans le temps : date, fréquence, durée	64
12. Forme fréquentative	68
13. Forme emphatique	71
14. Le subjonctif	72
15. Concordance des temps et style indirect	76
16. L'impératif	78
17. La voix passive	79
18. Les formes verbales en *-ing*	82
19. L'infinitif	85

C. STRUCTURES VERBALES

Les structures du verbe, leur classification	87
20. Les structures 1a et 3	89
21. La structure 1b	92
22. Les structures 2a, 2b, 4b et 5b	94
23. Les structures 6 et 7	97
24. Les structures O, A, B, C, D	98
25. Les structures E et F	100
26. Constructions spéciales à certains verbes	102

D. EXPRESSION DE CERTAINES NOTIONS

27. Nécessité, ordres, conseils 105
28. Souhaits, préférences, regrets 107
29. Cause, but, conséquence 109
30. Incertitude, probabilité, hasard 111

DEUXIEME PARTIE : LES AUTRES ELEMENTS DE LA PHRASE

A. LE NOM, L'ARTICLE ET L'ADJECTIF QUALIFICATIF

31. Le nom 114
32. L'article défini 119
33. L'article indéfini et l'article partitif 124
34. L'adjectif qualificatif 127
35. Comparatifs et superlatifs 131
36. Structures du nom et de l'adjectif 134

B. PRONOMS ET ADJECTIFS

37. Les pronoms personnels, réfléchis et réciproques 137
38. Notion de possession 141
39. Démonstratifs, relatifs et interrogatifs 146
40. Les indéfinis. Notion de quantité 151
41. Les adjectifs numéraux 155
42. Phrases exclamatives 158

C. ADVERBES, PREPOSITIONS ET CONJONCTIONS

43. Dix mots-charnières à sens multiples : *about, as, at, but, by, for, so, still, too, yet* 160
44. Adverbes, prépositions et conjonctions. Liste alphabétique 166
45. Traduction de quelques mots invariables français 174

ADDENDUM : Dérivation et conversion 177

EXERCICES 180

VERBES IRREGULIERS 210

INDEX 215

Tableau : STRUCTURES DU VERBE (sur marque-pages inséré dans l'ouvrage)

Photocomposition et impression
IMPRIMERIE LOUIS-JEAN
BP 87 — 05003 GAP Cedex
Tél. : 92.51.35.23
Dépôt légal : 125 — Février 1990
Imprimé en France

Dépôt initial : 1967

With the successful conclusion of the Spanish-American War, US interests had expanded globally. European powers had finally departed, or had been expelled, from the Western Hemisphere but ever-improving warship technology meant that vessels based in once far-away Europe could still potentially harass the eastern seaboard. In the Pacific the United States had gained possessions that were uncomfortably close to the borders of the aggressively expanding Japanese Empire.

A two-ocean Navy linked by a Central American canal was required, and Roosevelt set out with his naval "big stick" to achieve it. The first decade of the 20th Century was a period of exponential growth for the US Navy, a fact reflected in these scenes of the USS *Texas* in the busy Brooklyn Navy Yard.

The USS *Texas* in the Brooklyn Navy Yard, 1904. Note the gun turrets on the wharf awaiting installation in a more modern warship. Officers and crew of the USS *Texas* gather for a group photo and for worship service, circa 1904.

The *Texas* rides out rough seas.

At the same time that warships grew larger, the world grew smaller for ship's captains. Wireless sets made their appearance on US Navy warships in this period. The USS *Texas* received a set in 1903, as evidenced by the appearance of aerial antenna cables on her masts. Note also that on her starboard aft bridge deck the *Texas* appears to retain the non-standard searchlight, captured from the *Vizcaya* in 1898, even after her refit. (?)

International relations, once largely at the discretion of captains when operating at foreign ports, could now be directed in-detail by politicians and senior Navy staff in Washington D.C. and relayed to ships around the globe. As one officer was heard to grumble, "Now we have become mere messenger boys at the end of the cable." Strategic and tactical ship-to-shore and ship-to-ship communications expanded beyond direct line of sight, allowing for coordinated actions on a scale previously only imagined.

The German made Slaby-Arco wireless system as installed on the *Texas* and other vessels in 1903 for evaluation during the summer maneuvers that year.

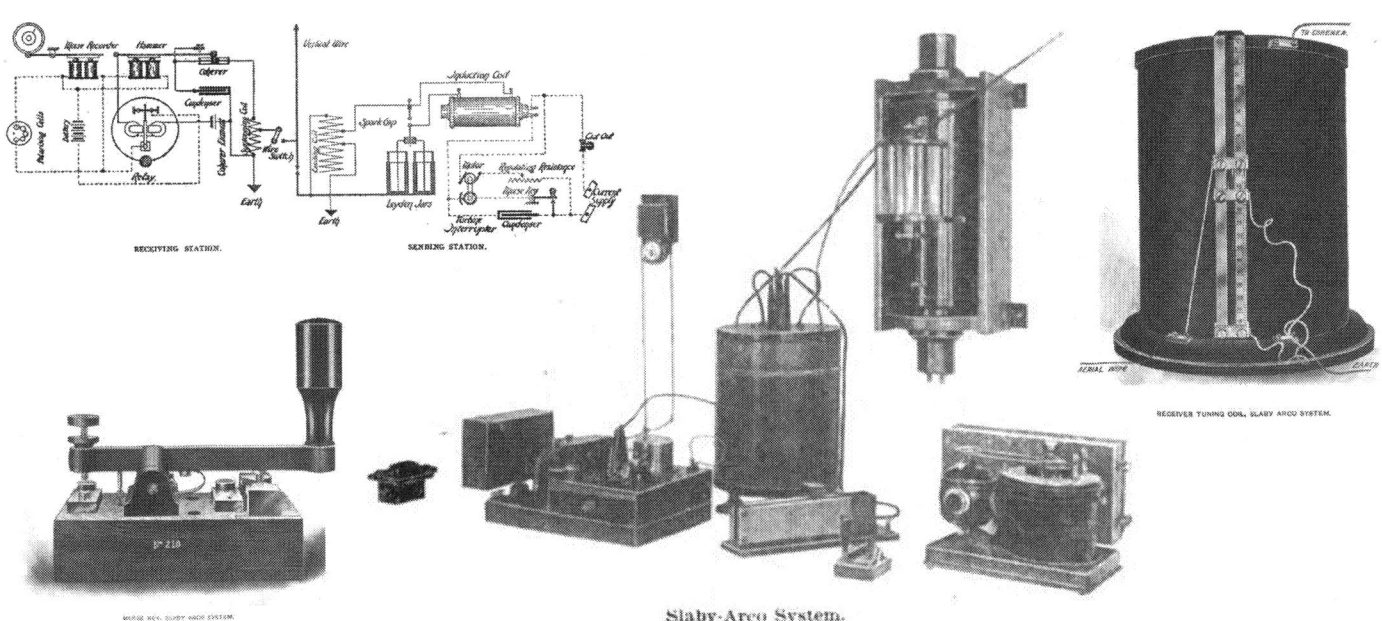

The Navy purchased 20 Slaby-Arco wireless sets in 1903 and installed them on a number of vessels of the North Atlantic Fleet to evaluate their impact and utility in fleet actions. During the summer maneuvers, the fleet was divided into two squadrons the defending Blue Squadron had several radio equipped vessels while only the *Texas* in the attacking White Squadron had a radio. Blue Squadron was required to preface its messages with specific "metal" code words, while White used "flower" code words to begin their messages. As the Blue Squadron attempted to locate and intercept the White Squadron, the operator on the *Texas* was ordered by exercise officials to attempt to jamb Blue Squadron's metal-prefaced communications. Eight days into the exercise a message prefaced with "gold", revealing that a Blue squadron vessel had located the attacking White Squadron, came through clearly and without jamming by the *Texas*. Within hours the defending Blue Squadron had rendezvoused and captured the attacking White Squadron. Exercise officials went onboard the *Texas* as soon as she returned to determine why she had not attempted to jam the critical transmission, only to discover that the radio operator was in the brig. The incarcerated sailor reported the following: "I was on watch and everything was working fine. I heard a message begin, and the first three letters were G, O, and L, so I knew it was going to be "gold" and that it was from the other side. I reached for the key, but the Flag Lieutenant, who was with me said 'No don't do that I want to get the entire message.' When the message was ended, the Lieutenant said 'Make interference,' and I said 'Sir, it's no use now. The message has gone out with a speed of 186,000 miles a second and we can't catch up with it.' So here I am on bread and water." The lieutenant in question was Lt. (later rear admiral) T.P. Magruder.

The fleet then departed for a presidential review at Oyster Bay, New York. The Navy's radio technician, who was embarked on board the *Texas* to help check and adjust her radio, discovered that Lt. Magruder had taken exception to the unsymmetrical appearance of the ship's newly installed antenna and had ordered it rerouted so close to the ship's stack that corona discharges were noted when it transmitted. The Navy's technician related that Lt. Magruder had communicated that "he didn't give a damn about wireless…but he did give a damn for the appearance of the ship." The Navy Department won in the end and the antenna was relocated away from the stack and rigging.

Wireless towers located outside of Washington D.C. in Arlington, Virginia (above).

Texas displays her "wireless" aerials off New London, CN.

Visits were made from New England to the Gulf coast on several occasions. In this view the *Texas*, passed by an earlier form of steamship, the paddle-wheel riverboat, rests in the Mississippi at New Orleans, decked out with flags in celebration of Mardi Gras.

In the photo below numerous vessels utilizing an even older form of propulsion share company with the *Texas*.)

Midshipmen from the Naval Academy at Annapolis were shipped aboard the *Texas* on occasion, including an extended cruise in the summer of 1903.

The photos on the following page are from the Naval Academy's yearbook <u>The Lucky Bag</u> and show the USS *Texas* during a midshipmen cruise. The photos at left and right show future admirals on their midshipmen cruises during the period. Through cruises such as these midshipmen with names like Nimitz, Stewart, and Ingersoll were introduced to a life at sea.

On February 13, 1906 the *Texas* sank the derelict schooner *Sakata*, a floating wreck deemed a hazard to navigation, while steaming from Charleston, SC to Key West, FL. In June of that year she visited Rockland Harbor, Maine. Note the wash hanging out to dry, up-wind of the thick coal smoke rising from the ship's funnel.

In the spring of 1906, as the *Texas* was being prepared to be placed in reserve at Norfolk, a succession of commanding officers came and went. Captain George A. Bicknell was replaced on June 26, 1906 by Captain Charles Plunkett, who was subsequently replaced by Commander George R. Clark on August 25th.

Routines quickly changed in September though, as threatening hostilities in Cuba caused the Navy to place the *Texas* back into commission and dispatch her to Havana, carrying Marines. By late October the threat had dissipated. The *Texas* brought the Marines back to the United States and, on November 9, 1906 she was placed in reserve at the Norfolk Navy Yard.

The *Texas* surrounded by new torpedo boats operating from Norfolk Navy Yard.

The Texas peeks from behind the torpedo boats stationed at the Norfolk Navy Yard?

The *Texas* briefly came back into commission on August 17, 1907 to participate in the Jamestown Exposition. Under the command of Lt. Cmdr. Edward T. Witherspoon, the *Texas* engaged in Exposition activities while the more modern vessels of the US Navy gathered around her and prepared for the celebrated around-the-world cruise of the Great White Fleet.

The Great White Fleet consisted of 16 battleships and numerous other vessels which circumnavigated the globe in a demonstration of US naval prowess. Setting sail from Hampton Roads on December 16, 1907, soon after the close of the Jamestown Exposition, the Great White Fleet stopped at major ports on six continents including Trinidad, British West Indies, Rio de Janeiro, Brazil; Punta Arenas, Chile; Callao, Peru; Magdalena Bay, Mexico, Monterey, Ca.; San Francisco, Ca.; Puget Sound; Honolulu; Auckland, New Zealand; Sydney, Albany, and Melbourne, Australia; Manila, Philippines; Yokohama, Japan; Amoy, China; Colombo, Ceylon; Suez, Egypt; Messina, Sicily; Naples, Italia; and Gibraltar, returning to Hampton Roads, Va. on February 22, 1909.

While the Great White Fleet steamed to exotic ports, the *Texas* and her crew completed their duties at the Exposition and prepared the ship once more to go into reserve. The *Texas* was taken out of commission again on January 11, 1908.

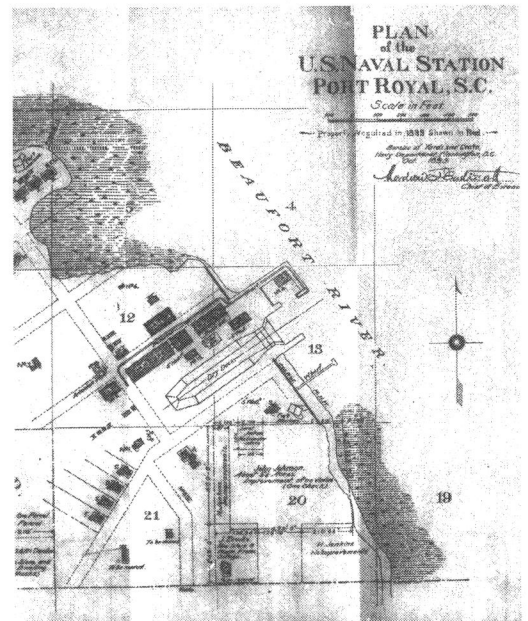

At Norfolk, the *Texas* was fitted out as a station ship and then dispatched to Charleston, SC under the command of Cmdr. William A. Gill, arriving there on September 26, 1908. The *Texas* served as a station ship in Charleston until 1910, then returned to the Norfolk Navy Yard for her final decommissioning.

19 A FITTING END: 1911-

The USS *San Marcos*, formerly the USS *Texas* (left) makes the cover of Scientific American for the final time in a feature story describing the test of modern gunnery versus an armored warship.

Although there had been talk of presenting the aged battleship to a state Naval Militia for use as a training ship, the vessel's antiquated design and equally out-of-date equipment was judged a poor instrument by which to train new sailors in 20th century seamanship. It was instead decided that the warship would be expended in a manner consistent with her fighting spirit as well as her status as the prototype for the battleship fleet. She would serve as a target, testing the probability of sub-surface hits by naval guns, the transmission of shock through a vessel, the comparative damage to inflammatory materials, the orientation of shells upon hitting at long range, and the effects of high-explosive and other shells upon the armor, ship's structure, and unarmored spaces and fittings.

Decommissioned on February 11, 1911, the USS *Texas* was renamed the USS *San Marcos*, freeing up her original name for the new "Super-Dreadnaught" USS *Texas* BB-35, then under construction at the Newport News Shipbuilding Company (seen below on October 23, 1913 undergoing trials).

Final preparations for the tests were made at the Norfolk Navy Yard, where the *Texas* had been completed less than twenty years previously. Modifications included the removal of all articles that would normally have been landed prior to expected action. It was originally recommended that the 12" guns be removed and placed in reserve, but in the event these were left in place, along with the 6" guns, of which the Navy appears to have had a surplus already in reserve. All other armaments were removed, but beyond this the only other fittings removed were those related to her previous duty as a station ship at Charleston.

Prior to the test large canvas sheets were suspended from the masts and stack.

On March 21, 1911 the USS *New Hampshire* opens fire, initiating a series of firings using both 12" and 8" guns that would extend over the course of two days.

In the photo below tall geysers of water can be seen, raised by 12" shells striking the sea. Smaller splashes are from 8" shells. The USS *New Hampshire* was firing from off camera, to the right.

A hit is registered midships on the *San Marcos/Texas*. It is noteworthy that these tests were conducted at a range of approximately six miles, far beyond the battle ranges envisioned by the *Texas's* original designer back in 1889.

More shells strike the USS *San Marcos/Texas* as the ship begins to list. Clearly, a below-waterline penetration has been achieved and the vessel is taking on water.

Shells strike home again, this time producing a spray of fragments extending well beyond the ship. Targeting on the *New Hampshire* was performed using range-finding instruments and corrected via spotters noting the fall of shells from the *New Hampshire's* tall cage masts.

After each firing session, inspection parties headed to the *San Marcos/Texas* to survey the effects and make minor repairs to help maximize the benefits of subsequent tests.

These photos, taken after the first firing sequence, reveal that the *San Marcos/Texas* is already holed to the extent that her bow is resting on the shallow bottom of Chesapeake Bay. Numbers were noted on these photos by the Navy to identify individual hits.

Of interest was the fact that almost all of the hits recorded were from 12" shells. Only one hit in the first series was confirmed as being from an 8" shell. The big guns were establishing their preeminence at long range.

By the second inspection period, the decks of the warship were becoming a jumble of damaged equipment, railings and bulkheads, as the USS *New Hampshire's* guns systematically disassembled the *San Marcos/Texas*.

In the background can be seen the tug USS *Mohawk* which ferried observers to and from the ship during the tests. The *Mohawk* served the Navy from 1898 until 1948.

The *San Marcos/Texas* lists to port and down by the bow. Note the glancing hit to the funnel seen in this photo taken from the tug USS *Mohawk*.

The scarred aft deck of the *San Marcos/Texas*.

Inspection parties made their way below decks as well, where they recorded hits and the resulting effects on the ship, its equipment and crew. – In this test crewmen were represented by dummies suspended at action stations around the 6" guns in port-side compartment A-123 on the gun deck. Damage in this space was caused by a 12" shell ricocheting off the water short of the ship, passing into this compartment and fragmenting on impact with the redoubt. Fragments swept the area "wounding" the test dummies. Damage to the 6" gun in compartment C-110 on the gun deck was even more severe.

Sunlight streams in through the missing plating and the dummy is, itself, largely missing below the knees. It was estimated that, had they been in place, the gun sights would have been destroyed by this hit as well.

Photo taken in compartment C-110 demonstrating the destruction wrought by the fragmentation of a 12" shell on impact with the ship's redoubt armor. The shell hit in the space above and blew downwards destroying wooden lockers and leaving the deck knee-deep in places with splinters and fragments of equipment.

Compartment C-110, facing port showing the damage associated with the passage of two shells through this space. Note the base of the main mast with a rack for rifles. The shiny object to the left of the mast was the auxiliary steering position.

Shell hole in the berth deck, space A-16. Note the extensive wood splinters created when the 12" shell from the *New Hampshire* struck the protective deck below and fragmented. While a portion of the shell penetrated the protective deck, another fragment ricocheted up through the berth deck. This occurrence illustrates the danger of wooden decks on a warship. "Battleship" linoleum on a metal deck would have been far less dangerous to crewmen unfortunate enough to have been in this space.

Photos of the riddled port side taken on the second day of the test. Note in the photo at right that shot E-38 penetrated the turret redoubt while the adjacent shot F-63 did not.

The port side of the *San Marcos/Texas*, showing the vessel resting on the bottom of Chesapeake Bay as waves wash in and out of shell holes along the waterline.

Starboard side view identifying the numerous hits and gaping holes caused by the repeated bombardments.

Destruction of the pilot house resulting from the detonation of an 8" shell atop the armored conning tower below. Note the ship's wheel as well as the navigation and control equipment visible inside the pilot house and on its roof. A subsequent strike by a 12" shell later finished the job (middle right).

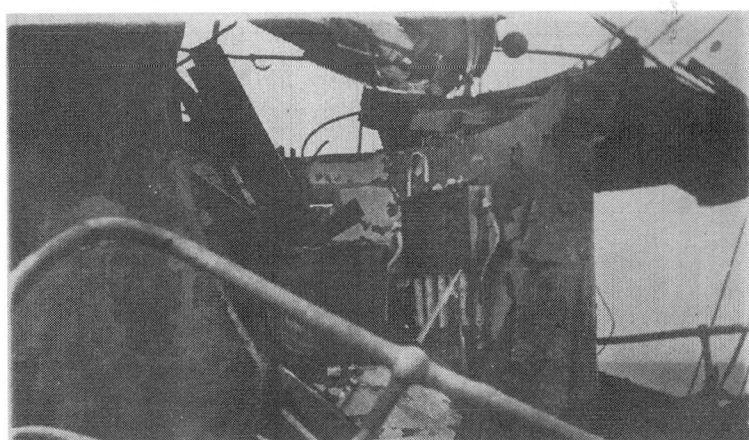

An inspection crew clambers aboard the *San Marcos/Texas* from an attending vessel (above left) and examines the area beneath the aft bridge deck (above right).

View looking aft on the main deck (below left) showing a 20 ton fragment of the armored conning tower laying where it was blown by a hit from a 12" shell. Hole in hull near the water line caused by 12" shell (below right).

Nose of a shell resting on the handrail of a 12" gun turret (below right), later revealed to have been jokingly balanced there by a mischievous sailor in an attempt to confound the gunnery experts. Note the direct hit below the rail, effectively stopped by the ship's armor.

Deck winch of the *Texas* sitting next to a 12" turret (below left). This winch was blown to this location from the opposite side of the ship.

"The experimental firings at the *Katahdin* and *San Marcos* have been very instructive in the matter of armor and have furnished information of value in connection with the design of later vessels. Two of the most important facts that have been clearly demonstrated are that a projectile while in flight is at all times tangent to the trajectory, and that penetrative effects of projectiles at battle ranges on modern armor are in accordance with previously calculated data. These two points have been consistently disputed by some inventors of high explosives, their claim being that the axis of a projectile in flight was parallel to it's position at the time of leaving the gun and that therefore at high angles of fall it would be impossible to penetrate armor. These claims have been completely discredited by the firing at the *Katahdin*. The firings at the *San Marcos* have been less instructive, since the quality of her armor was not high enough to give a severe test to the projectiles with which it was attacked. The efficiency of the projectiles against her armor, however, have been demonstrated." – Excerpt from: *Report of the Secretary of the Bureau of Ordnance to the Secretary of the Navy, October 1, 1911.*

Furrow carved by a shell along the deck of the *San Marcos* /*Texas*.

6" gun compartment, immediately below the "furrow" seen at left.

The ship that had taken so long to build had been effectively neutralized in two days. To the end, though, she continued to push the frontiers of American naval science and helped to educate two generations of naval officers.

On April 6, 1911 the *San Marcos/ Texas* was used as a target once again, this time for torpedoes fired by the USS *Flusser*. In late 1911 a proposal was made to use the sunken warship for aerial bombing tests, but it is unknown if these were carried out. On October 10, 1911, the vessel was struck from Navy lists.

Mast That Is Target for Big Guns

In the summer of 1912 further gunnery tests were conducted on the *San Marcos/Texas*. The new battleships being built for the Navy required tall masts from which to spot the fall of shots and debates were ongoing in naval circles as to whether a rigid, heavy tripod mast (like that on the precedent-setting *HMS Dreadnaught*) or a light, flexible cage mast would prove superior. For these tests a standard 90 foot cage mast was erected on the *San Marcos/Texas*, of the same type as that used in the latest US battleships the *Florida*, *Utah*, *Arkansas*, *Wyoming*, *New York*, and the new USS *Texas*.

Fired at from 1,000 yards by the 12" guns of the monitor USS *Tallahassee*, the mast succumbed after an estimated 12 direct hits. Three additional shells fired at the mast either missed or passed through the mesh of the mast without damage. The mast collapsed to port during the test but was judged to have shown remarkable resilience to 12" gunfire directly targeting it. The wreckage also proved easy to clear, being removed by a repair party from the USS *Idaho* in only twenty minutes. Cage masts would be used by the US Navy until after WWI.

These images show the remains of the cage mast on the battered hulk of the *San Marcos/Texas* after the trials. The stubs of the tubes that comprised the body of the cage mast can be seen in the lower right foreground in the above image. The base to which the cage mast was affixed is visible on the main deck in the image below.

The *Texas* proved as stubborn to destroy as she had been to build. Repeated use as a target rendered her profile unrecognizable, but the battered hull (seen mast-less at left) witnessed Army Air Corps General Billy Mitchell's famous experiments in the aerial bombardment of warships in 1921. The *Texas* remained a target ship for years, finally being blown to fragments not by gunfire or bombs but by a Navy demolitions team in order to clear the hazard to navigation. Fishermen and divers willing to brave cold murky currents and unexploded ordinance still occasionally visit her Chesapeake Bay grave located at 37 degrees 43' 10" N, 76 degrees 05' 00" W.

APPENDIX I: 1895 USS TEXAS PLANS

The following are U.S. Navy plans depicting the ship as originally completed and placed into commission in 1895.

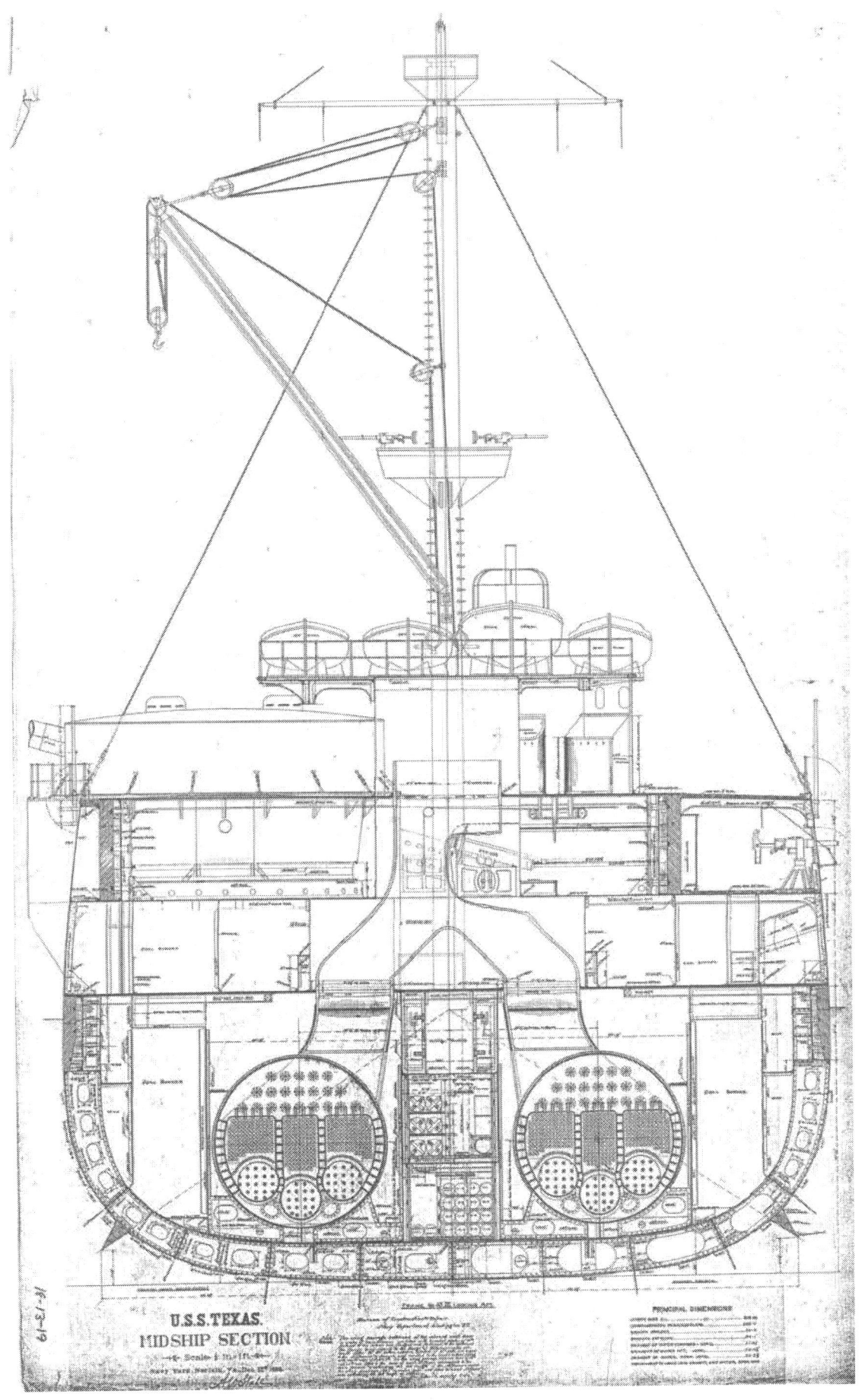

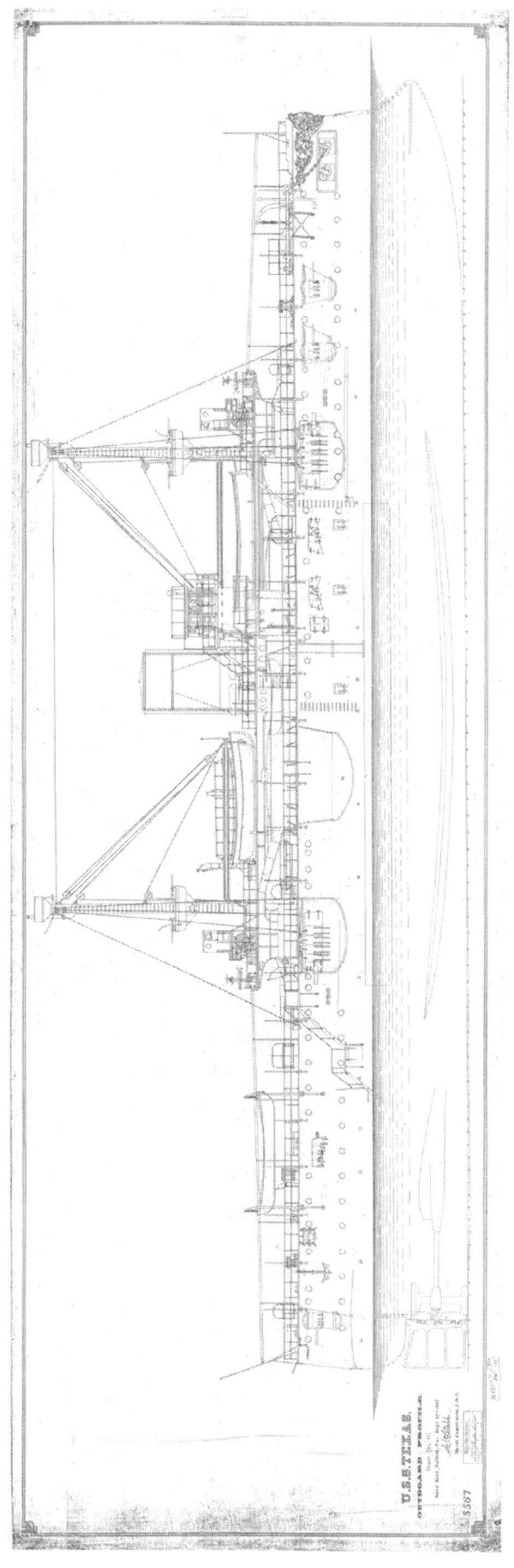
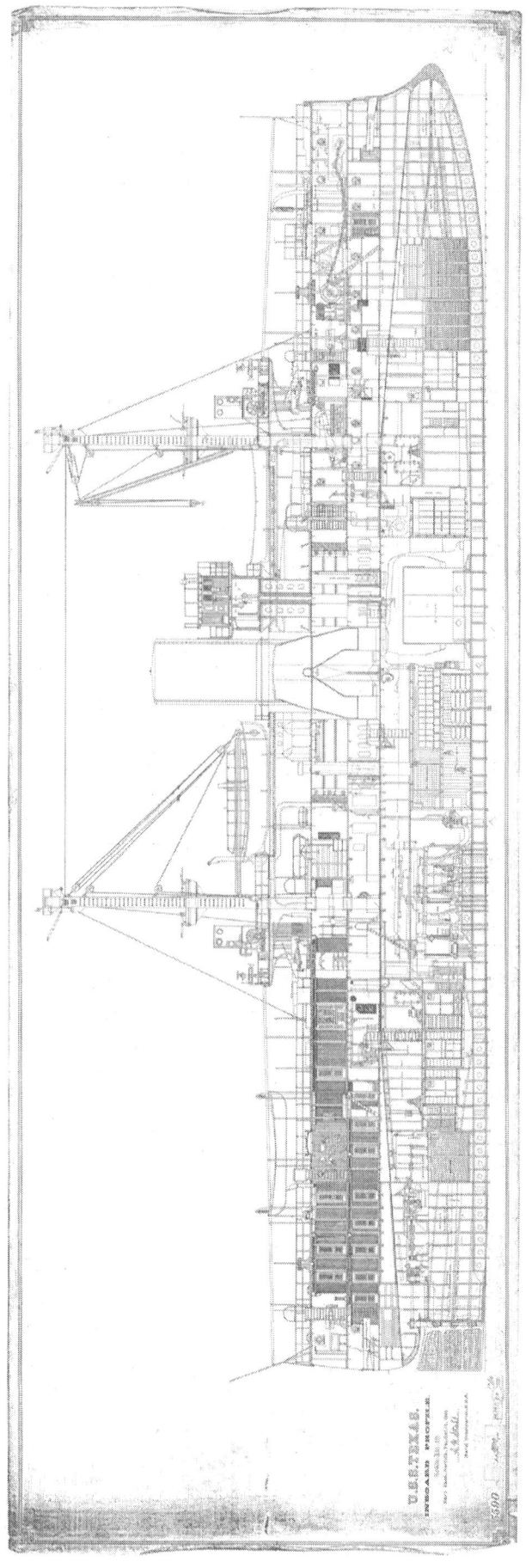

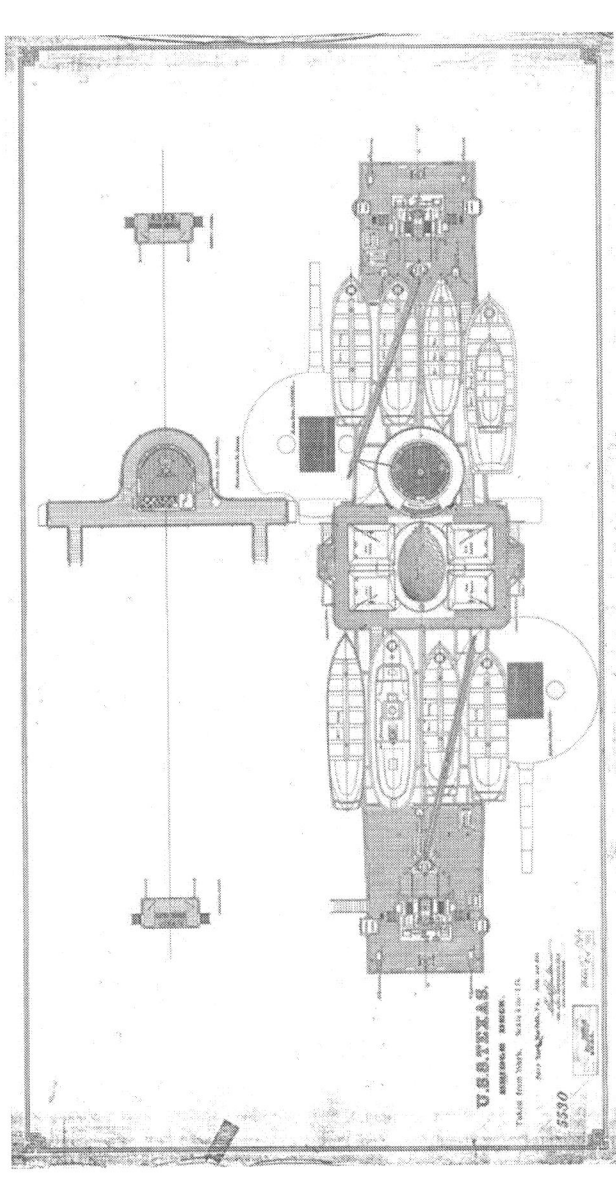
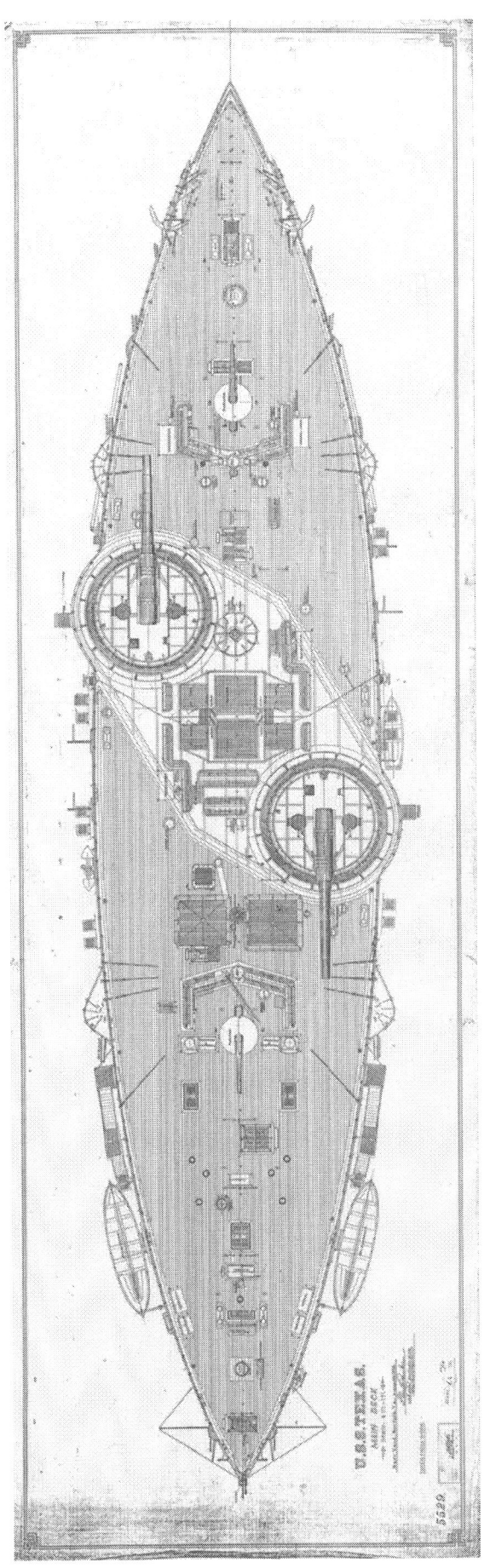

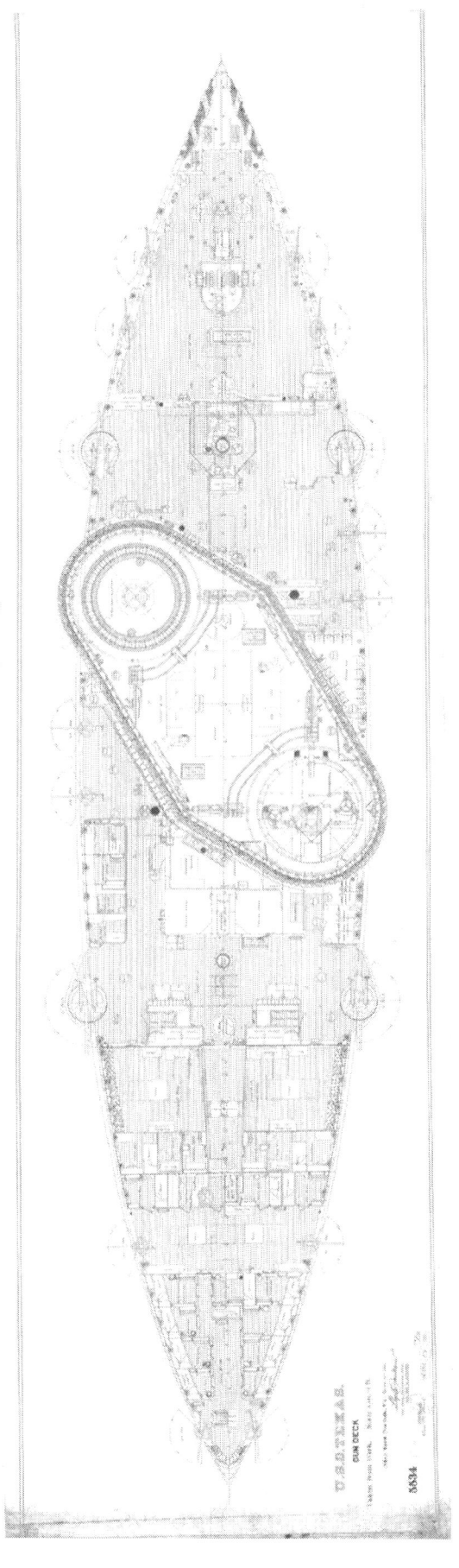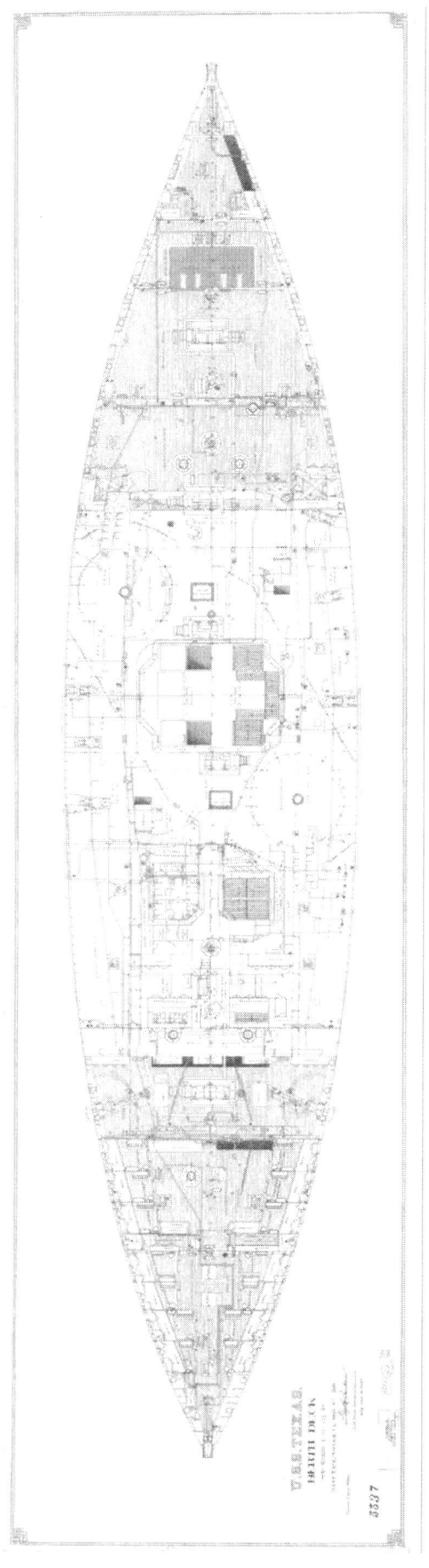

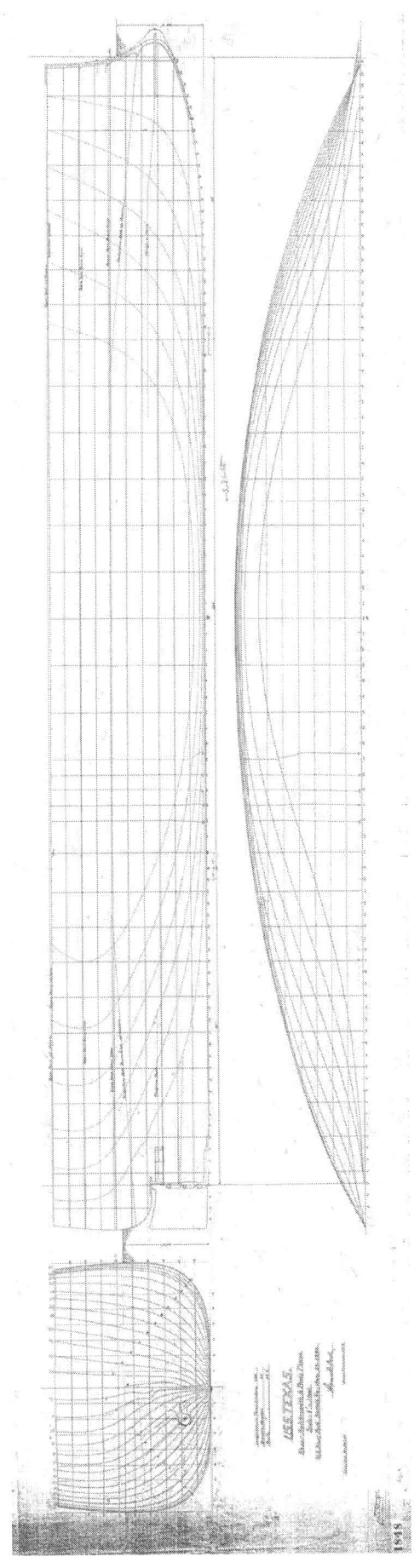

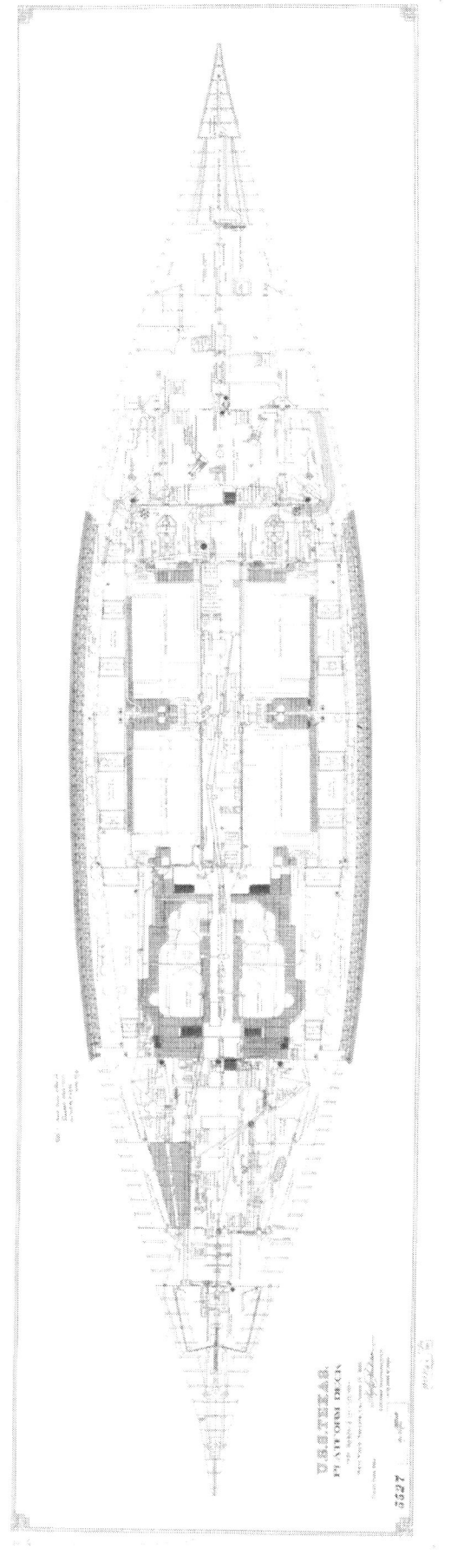
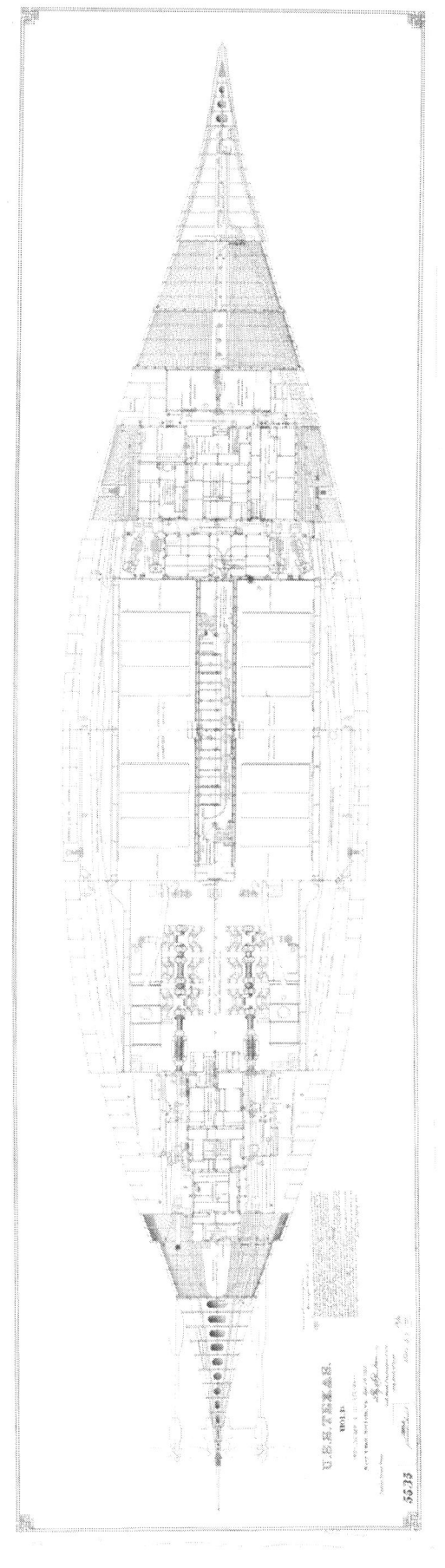

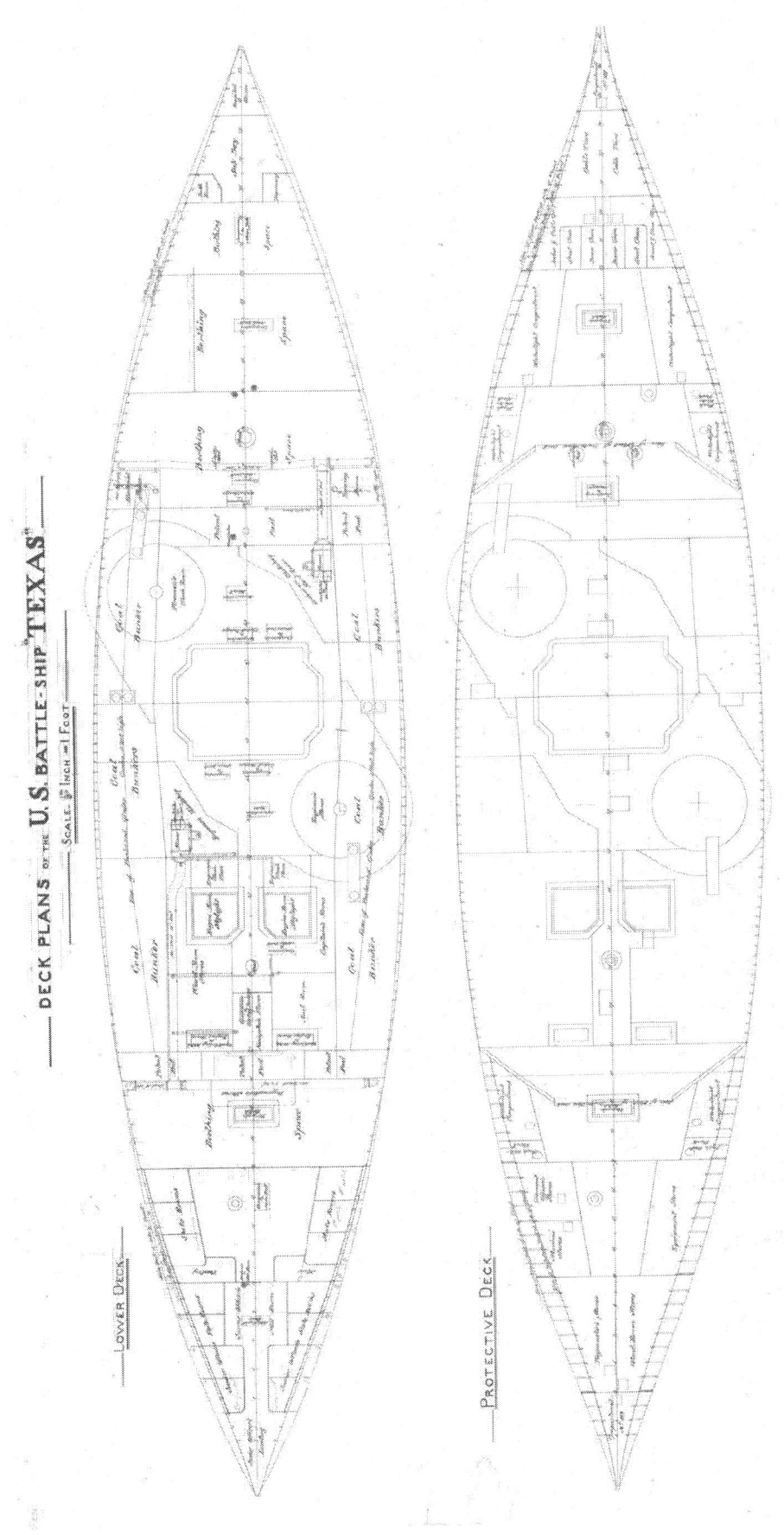

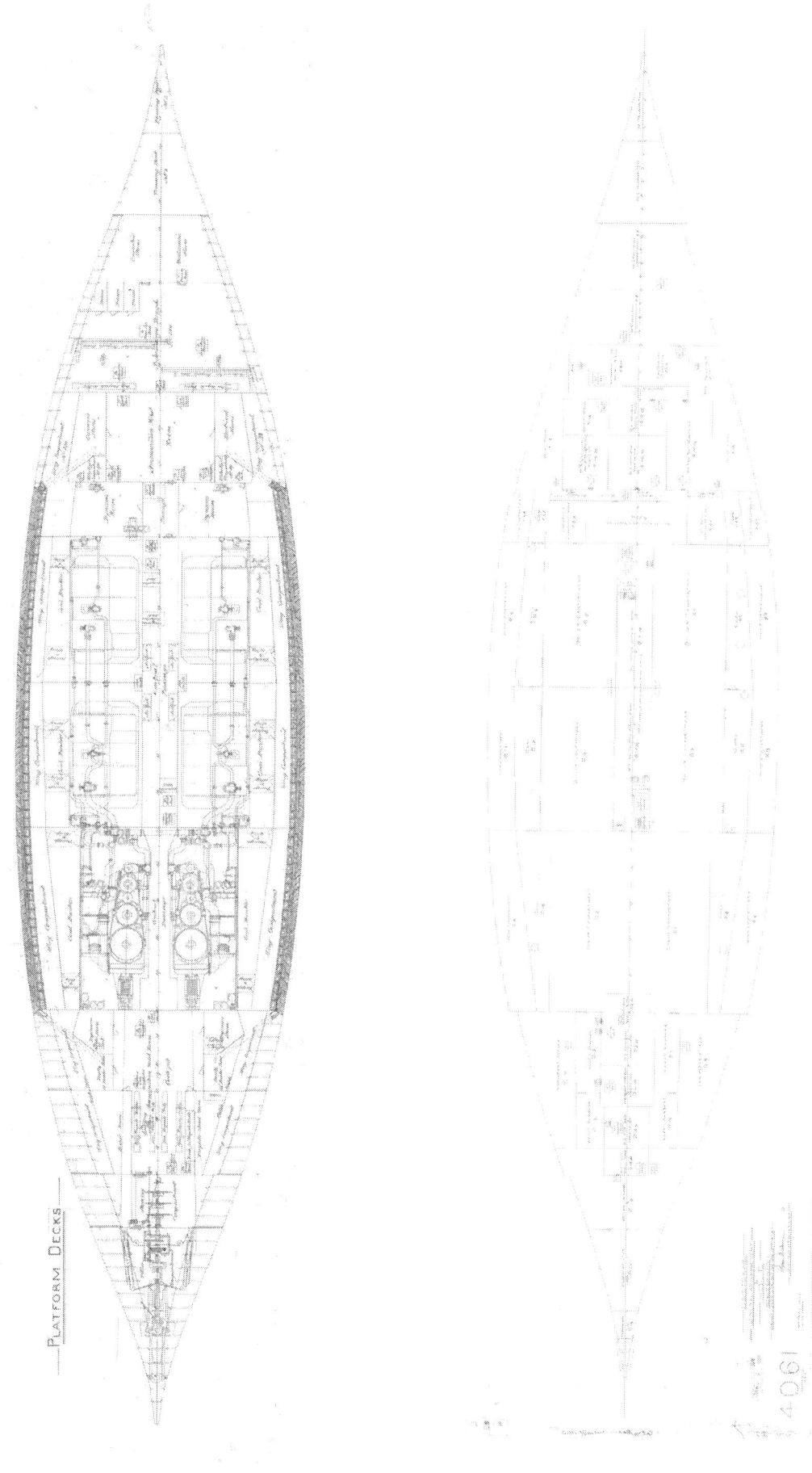

Platform Decks

APPENDIX II: OFFICIAL DESCRIPTION & FACTS

The following detailed description of the battleship *Texas*, furnished by the US Navy's Chief Constructor Phillip Hichborn, was printed in newspapers across the country in December of 1897:

"This twin screw vessel, built at Norfolk, on the design of the Barrow shipbuilding company, is of the belted type, that is, with a belt of armor amidships to protect the vitals of the ship and under water decks from the ends of the armor to the extremities of the vessel.

Length between perpendiculars 290 feet, breadth extreme 61 feet 1 inch, depth molded to upper deck 39 feet 8 inches, draught of water forward 22 feet, draught of water aft 23 feet, mean 22 feet 6 inches, displacement to above draught, 6300 tons, transverse metacenter above center of gravity 3 feet 1 ½ inches, longitudinal metacenter above center of gravity 237 feet, tons per inch at load line 30, moment to change the trim one inch in foot tons 432, indicated horsepower 8600, maximum speed 17 knots, complement of officers and men 300.

<u>Scantling and general construction:</u>
The vertical keel is 20 pounds per square foot, reduced to 11 ½ pounds at ends, 39 inches amidships, with double angles at top 3 ½ by 3 inches of 8 pounds per foot, and at the bottom 4 ½ by 3 ½ inches of 12 pounds per foot.

The outer flat keel plate is 25 pounds per square foot, the inner 17 ½ pounds per square foot.

The transverse framing in wake of and below the armor belt has an outer angle of 4 by 3 ½ inches of 8 ½ pounds per foot, and an inner angle of 4 by 3 inches of 8 pounds pre foot, extending from the vertical keel to the fourth longitudinal, with bracket plates of 10 pounds per foot, secured to the longitudinal by clips of 3 by 3 inches, of 7 pounds per foot.

From the fourth longitudinal to the armor shelf the outer and inner angles are 3 ½ by 3 inches of 8 pounds per foot, with a 10 pound plate between, lightened with holes.

The framing above and before and abaft the armor belt consists of two bars of 6 by 3 ½ by 3 inches, of 15 pounds per foot, with lower ends, where landing on the armor deck, secured by a 15 pound plate, and where coming down to the keel, split and a 10-pound floor plate riveted in.

There are four longitudinals on each side in wake of the double bottom, the inner two of 12 ½ pound plating, the outer two of 15 pound plating, with 3 ½ by 3 inches of 8 pounds per foot angles on the outer edges, and 3 by 3 inches of 7 pounds per foot angles on the inner edges. At the extremities there are three longitudinals, the first and second from the keel being 12-pound plates extending above the floors, with double angles 4 by 3 inches of 10 pounds on the upper edges.

The outer longitudinal is a Z bar 10 by 3 ½ by 3 inches of 20 pounds per foot, scoring over the frames, with a reverse angle on the back 3 ½ by 3 inches of 7 pounds per foot.

The bottom plating is 17 ½ pounds per square foot up to the armor belt and protective deck, above then 15 pounds increased to 60 pounds in wake of machine guns. The inner bottom is 10 pounds per square foot.

The bridge deck beams are angle bulbs, 5 by 3 inches of 9 pounds per foot, the upper deck beams 9 by 5 ½ inches of 30 pounds per foot, reduced to 8 by 5 ¼ inches of 22 pounds per foot at the ends of the main deck beams 9 by 5 ½ inches of 30 pounds per foot , reduced to 8 by 5 ¼ inches of 22 pounds per foot at the ends, the berth deck beams in the wake of the armor belt 9 by 2 ¼ [this number difficult to read in the original] inches of 24 ½ pounds, reduced to 6 by 5 inches of 16 pounds before and abaft the armor belt. The protective deck beams before and abaft the belt are 9 by 3 ½ inches of 24 ½-pound angles.

The bulkheads are 10 to 15 pounds, well stiffened by Z bars and angles. There are two masts with military tops.

Armored protection:
The vital parts of the vessel are protected by a steel armor belt 12 inches thick, 2 feet above and 4 ½ feet below the water. This embraces the engines, boilers and magazines, and is terminated at each end by a steel breastwork 6 inches thick, extending diagonally across the vessel. The backing is of wood, 6 inches thick, behind which are two thicknesses of 25-pound plating.

The shelf plate is 25 pounds, and back of the plating behind the backing are worked two horizontal girders formed of 15-pound plating, secured to the plating behind the backing by 3 ½ x 3 inches of 8-pound angles, and to 15-pound plate at their inner edges by similar angles.

An armored protective deck is worked over the armor belt, sloping down from the ends of the belt to the bow and stern. This deck is throughout 3 inches in thickness.

The lower parts of the turrets and the machinery for working the guns are enclosed in armored redoubts 12 inches thick, backed by 6 inches of wood. The turrets are plated with 12-inch armor.

There is an armored conning tower 12 inches thick placed forward on a level with the bridge with an armored tube leading from it 3 inches thick. The ammunition hoists are 6 inches thick.

Armament:
The main battery consists of two 12-inch guns in turrets and 6 6-inch guns protected by shields. The 12 inch guns are mounted in turrets placed en echelon to give each a fore and aft fire: each has a complete broadside fire on one side and has a train on the opposite side of 40 degrees for the forward gun and 70 degrees for the after gun.

A 6-inch gun is placed forward and on aft on the same level as the 12 inch guns, having each a train of 120 degrees. The remaining four 6-inch guns are mounted in sponsons of the main deck, two having a train from directly forward to 25 degrees abaft the beam, and two from directly aft to 25 degrees forward of the beam.

On the main deck the secondary battery consists of four 6-pounders, four 3-pounders, and four 47mm revolving cannon, protected by 1 ½ inch steel plating. Two Gatlings and two 37mm revolving cannon are placed on the bridge deck and two 1-pounders are placed on the flying bridge. Two 37mm rapid-firing guns are fitted in the steam cutters.

The magazines for the main battery are placed in the center of the vessel below the protective deck. The ammunition for the secondary battery is stowed in magazines placed forward and aft, the ammunition being passed up to the main deck through an armored tube 3 inches thick. Torpedoes can be projected through six tubes, one through the bow, one through the stern, two through the side aft above the water and two through the side forward below the water.

Machinery:
The motive power is furnished by two triple-expansion engines, placed in separate water-tight compartments. The cylinders are 36, 51, and 78 inches in diameter, with a stroke of 39 inches. There are four double-ended boilers 14 feet in diameter by 17 feet long. The steam pressure id 150 pounds; grate surface, 504 square feet; indicated horsepower, with an air pressure of two inches of water, 8600.

At the normal draft of 22 feet 6 inches, the coal supply is 500 tons. With this supply the endurance for a speed of 17 knots, 1110 knots; 15 knots, 2050 knots; 12 knots 3179 knots. With a coal supply of 850 tons the endurance is for a speed of 16.5 knots, 2180 knots; 14.75 knots, 3900 knots; 11.8 knots, 6000 knots.

Quarters for officers and crew:
This vessel is fitted as a flagship. Directly aft on the gun deck is the admiral's private cabin; forward of this his dining saloon and sleeping cabin; next the admiral's bath and water closet and pantry. Forward of these are similar accommodations for the captain. Forward of this is an open space extending across the vessel, with two passages leading forward from it. The passages enclose the wardroom, and the staterooms open into them from the outer sides. There are nine staterooms opening into these passages. Beyond the wardroom bulkhead is a large open space, which can be used by the steerage officers. The crew are berthed forward on the gun and berth decks. The seaman's heads are on the berth deck."   (DMN 2/17/1897)

USS Texas - "Hoodoo" and Mishaps

January 14, 1891: Major fire at the Richmond Locomotive and Machine Works where the engines and machinery for the *Texas* are under construction.

June 1891: Strike at the Richmond Locomotive and Machine Works.

Date Unknown: 2 workmen killed when lightning strikes the *Texas* while she is still on the ways at Norfolk Navy Yard.

Date Unknown: Ship "nearly capsizes" during installation of turrets.

November 1893: Boiler supports fail while boilers are being filled with water at Norfolk. Boilers "almost" drop through the bottom, causing the ship to list.

May 1894: During dockside engine trials at Norfolk a passing schooner, ironically named the "Henry W. Slicer", is drawn into the spinning propellers of the *Texas* and destroyed.

August 15, 1895: On her first night in commission, fire breaks out in her steam launch due to "live ashes being left in boat when fires were hauled." Damage to the boat was minor.

September 5, 1895: First sea trials canceled due to mud ingestion and numerous mechanical deficiencies.

November 7, 1895: In her first dry-docking since commissioning, it is discovered that both of the *Texas'* propellers are chipped. The propellers are replaced by the contractor who had originally cast them.

November 7-11, 1895: While in dry dock in the Brooklyn Navy Yard, the hull begins to "settle" resulting in dents, buckling, and cracking of cement along her hull seams. A Navy board of inspection, headed by Captain George Dewey, is subsequently named to investigate the serviceability of the *Texas*.

December 5, 1895: Having left the Brooklyn Navy Yard to resume sea trials, the steering gear is crippled during full-power trials. Tests halted at Tompkinsville, Staten Island. Repairs are made and tests begin again.

December 11, 1895: US Representative Fisher of New York (where the Maine had been built) offers a resolution in the House of Representatives calling for an investigation into the condition and construction of the *Texas*.

December 31, 1895: On recommendation of Dewey's board of inspection, numerous alterations to the *Texas* are ordered. Principal items to be reworked include the hydraulics operating the 12" turrets and the reinforcing of the keel and floor plates. These portions of the hull had been among the first pieces of steel assembled between 1889-1890. The *Texas* is placed out of commission while modifications are made.

September 16, 1896: On reporting to Newport to receive her torpedo outfit, a miscommunication occurs between the bridge and the engine room resulting in the *Texas* running hard aground. She is pulled free by four tugs on the following morning. The ship's engineer is officially censured and the assistant engineer and chief machinist are officially reprimanded for failure to observe and respond to engine signals from the bridge.

November 9, 1896: *Texas* sinks at the dock in the Brooklyn Navy Yard when an outboard delivery pipe being serviced breaks, rapidly flooding the compartment. It is then discovered that the compartment is not in fact water tight, leading to flooding in the adjacent fire room and the ship's settling onto the (fortunately) shallow bottom. An officer's subsequent report finds the damage was not extensive, leading Secretary of the Navy Herbert to publicly remark that he was "glad to find one man pleased with the *Texas*." A "bacteriologist of the naval surgeon's corps", however, publicly expresses his concern to the New York Times that the crevasses of the ship may never be cleaned of the accumulated sewage taken aboard by the sinking. He recommends restricting the Texas service to northern waters for a year.

February 17, 1897: On her first visit to the state of Texas, the USS *Texas* runs aground in Bolivar Roads, Galveston Bay. The local pilot assumes full responsibility. The *Texas* floats off of the bar at the next high tide, without damage.

October 21, 1897: While present in Boston harbor for celebrations relating to the 100th anniversary of the launching of the USS *Constitution*, the boiler of the *Texas'* steam launch explodes while alongside the *Texas* with 35 men on board, injuring two officers and several sailors.

February 16, 1898: The USS *Maine*, seen by many as a near-sister ship to the *Texas*, explodes at Havana, Cuba beginning a chain of events leading to the Spanish-American War.

May 19, 1898: As she leaves the naval anchorage at Dry Tortuga to begin her first cruise into combat, the *Texas* strikes an uncharted reef. - But then the USS *Texas'* fortunes begin to take a dramatic turn...

"The Texas was the first battleship built in this country and it cannot be denied that some mistakes were made in her construction from want of experience, but these mistakes have now been entirely corrected and she is today, thanks to the confidence felt by Secretary [of the Navy] Herbert in her final success and in his determination to leave nothing undone to bring about that result, one of the soundest, most seaworthy, and efficient vessels of war under our flag or any other in the world. She has been called an unlucky ship, a "hoodoo" but the facts of her history contradict this most decidedly. While it is true that she was injured the first time she was taken into a dry dock, has been ashore, has sunk in harbor, and had many minor accidents, it is also true that on every occasion she has risen superior to mishaps that would have ruined other ships, and that in her case have led only to improvements.

She is a very lucky ship, I think..." - Capt. Henry Glass (DMN 2/20/1897)

Ship's Routine as Recorded by the New York Times, November 3, 1895

"…the steel-clad battleship *Texas*, the first of her class ever to float the flag of the United States. Right hansom she is to look at, but there is no mistaking her for anything but what she is, Man-of-war is written in every uncompromising line. The cavernous muzzles of two twelve-inch rifles glower ahead and astern, and where her citadel rises amidships, the Gatling, the dainty Hotchkiss, and the glint of her long-barreled six-inch rifles can be seen. Where the prow dips into the water the outward curve of the steel spur underneath has a sinister suggestiveness.

The *Texas* is the first of her type to have been commissioned, and a description of the vessel and the every-day life on board the mobile fortress may be of interest. A reporter for the New-York Times visited the ship and found as much to marvel at as to admire.

To Capt. Henry Glass, who, as Commander of the cruiser *Cincinnati*, brought that vessel to the highest state of perfection that could be reached, was accorded the honor of commanding the first battleship of the new navy. The high state of efficiency and discipline in which the *Cincinnati* was kept won from a somewhat exacting Admiral unqualified praise. Therefore, the action of the Navy Department, in detaching him from the command of that vessel before his "cruise" had been half finished, and ordering him to the more important one of the *Texas*, was not so surprising as the innovation would have been. A marked tribute to the ability of Lieut. Commander J. D. J. Kelly, the former executive officer of the *Cincinnati*, was also paid by the department, when that efficient officer was directed to accompany Capt. Glass to his new command."

"In the little time that the *Texas* has been in commission, she has been brought to the standard that the Cincinnati was when the commander of the North Atlantic station described the vessel as the crack cruiser of the fleet. In external appearance, she looks as though she had just come out of some titanic bandbox. Her milk white sides show never a blemish, and a myriad of suns dance in the polished brass-work of her fittings. Internally, there is a place for everything, and everything is in its place.

Onboard, life runs in ordered grooves; interdependence absolute; Mr. Kipling probably would have described it. Reveille is sounded at daybreak, and the men who have not been on watch during the night turn out of their hammocks, lash and stow their bedding, and get "early coffee" and biscuit. Then clothes are scrubbed, decks washed down and dried; side-cleaners wash off the white paintwork of the side, boat-keepers run wet swabs over the white planking of their individual charges to remove any coal dust that may have settled there, and when the breakfast call is sounded at 7:30, most of the ship's morning toilet has been made. Breakfast over, the men light their pipes and lull at ease until the uniform of the day is announced. When in the company of a flagship this is made known by signal.

The men array themselves in the uniform prescribed – there are several worn by the wearers of the navy blue – and when the "turn to" call has been sounded, proceed to their various tasks. Arms and accoutrements have to be cleaned daily, the big guns kept free from rust and stain, and the brasswork kept polished. While this is going on the bugle sounds another note. It is recognized as the "sick call," and all who feel the need of the Surgeon's care repair to the sick bay, where their wants are attended to. A list of those judged to be incapacitated is furnished the officer of the deck, so that their duties can be attended to by their "opposite number." Every man on the ship has a number, and certain duties attaching thereto. For instance, if No. 21 is sick or absent, No. 22 takes his place, and so on.

About an hour is given for cleaning up the guns, oiling the mechanism of the big pieces, and putting the finishing touches to the brasswork of the ship, and then comes the order to "clear up the decks of the ship for inspection." Cleaning rags are put away, hands washed, an extra hitch given to the trousers, - for in the navy sailors do hitch their trousers – and then the call to quarters is sounded.

The men go to their stations at the various guns, their officers appear, a swift inspection of their appearance is made, and then the several divisional officers report to the executive officer. He is armed with a list of the men who are legitimately absent, of those who are sick or excused by the Surgeon, and checks off the absentees reported by the division officers. When all reports are in, the executive reports to the Captain, who is standing near. The latter then makes a tour of the ship, and inspects battery and crew. When the inspection is finished, the men are drilled for an hour – one division at great guns, another with revolvers, some with signals, some with small arms, and so on, the drills rotating with divisions.

Then comes dinner at noon, an hour for its discussion and smoking, and more drills during the afternoon. Just before supper is the setting-up drill. After that the men are at liberty to do very much as they please, unless there is a searchlight or night-signal drill scheduled for that special evening. With 9 P.M. comes taps, and the cry of the master at arms, "Turn in your hammocks and keep silence!" The order about keeping silence is mandatory, for, on a man-of-war, the sleep of the crew when the hour comes is a sacred thing and must not be disturbed. But there are a number of shaded lights about the birth deck, and such of the men as are studiously inclined may sit near them after taps and finish the book they are reading or the letter they are writing, with none to say them nay. Such is the routine in port. Shore leave, of course, is interpolated in it, all who live up to the regulations going onshore whenever their presence is not necessary. At sea the routine is considerably varied, as watches have to be stood.

Battleships are built, commissioned, and maintained for the purpose of action with an enemy whenever such contest may be necessary. That being the chief purpose in life, it is natural that the drill of "clearing ship for action" is one to which particular attention is given. Following it always is a mimic encounter with an imaginary foe. Not the slightest detail in preparation is ever neglected, and nothing but blood and shrieks and wounds is lacking to make the imaginary battle that follows as realistic as any actual one would be.

The only thing old about the work of preparing a modern battleship for action is the way in which the order is communicated to the crew. In the old days the call of the boatswain's mate summoned the crew to quarters, and in the new ships of the American Navy the men are trained to respond to the same call. As soon as the cry echoes from the main deck the bugle sounds the "assembly" on the gun and birth decks. Officers and men at once hurry to their allotted stations. Quiet is insisted upon, and in a well-disciplined ship but little noise is heard.

If the order to clear ship for action is given at night, as it frequently is for drill purposes, hammocks are stowed in the nettings, unnecessary lighting circuits are shut off, lamps, globes, and shades liable to destruction by gun shock are removed, and the battle circuit is connected. Such of the crew as are in confinement are released and made "prisoners at large."

As fast as the various divisions are made ready the officer in charge reports to the executive officer. When all divisional officers have reported ready, the executive reports to the commanding officer that the ship is ready for action. There is an enormous amount of work to be done before a battleship can be got in readiness. On one recent occasion the Admiral of a French fleet made signal to clear ship for action, commanding officers to report when ready. Some of the vessels, it is related, did not report for three days after.

But on the *Texas* the work is more expeditious, and it is made so from the fact that the duties are nicely and evenly distributed. The swirling human tide which is set in motion by the boatswain's call has no conflicting currents. Men rushing in one direction are not met by others struggling to go the opposite way. So far as possible the separate divisions are birthed and messed in their own part of the ships, and their duties lie in that special section.

For instance, the marine guard, which on the *Texas* is included in the first division, improvise, as soon as the call is sounded, a breastwork for sharpshooters, using hammocks and awnings. Meanwhile others of the same division rig collision mats, unship railing around the forecastle, lower anchor davits in cradles, and carry below and secure levers and tackles. There are a score of other duties to be performed by the men of this division, all looking to the expeditious and unencumbered slaughtering of a foe.

Other divisions lower and unship awning stanchions and railing in wake of the guns, close water-tight compartments, rig in and secure danger booms, unship ladders, and supply buckets of fresh water for drinking purposes. Magazines are opened and lanterns trimmed, battle bucklers are fitted to air ports, and those who are detailed to attend the speaking tubes in the wake of the torpedo tubes go to their stations. An officer goes to the central station, calls up and gets a clear response by voice and signal from each branch station.

The Surgeon's division converts the wardroom into a temporary operating room, removes rugs and curtains, and sees that all adjoining staterooms are made ready for the reception of wounded.

There are other duties to be preformed – too many to enumerate here - before the Captain hears from his executive officer the report, "Ship is ready for action, Sir." When that report is made the call to general quarters is sounded, the battery is cast loose, the pieces are trained upon an imaginary foe – then exercise with torpedoes, collision drill, and many others of different sort follow. For instance, the executive officer will suddenly shout, "No. 3 at No. 6 gun is wounded!" The officer commanding that gun division says sharply, "No. 3, you are wounded." No. 3 promptly sinks to the deck, his opposite number steps into the vacated place, the "aids to wounded" hurry the man below after the prescribed manner.

Besides the exercise of "clearing ship for action," there are many others to be gone through with at stated intervals. These are "fire quarters," and its logical follower, "abandon ship"; boat drills of many kinds, under sail and under oars; battalion drill, when the ship's company is formed as infantry; drill with single-sticks, and open "aiming drill," with small arms. All in all, the life of the modern man-of-war's man is a rather busy one."

APPENDIX III: SHIP'S BOATS

Author's Note: The USS *Texas* was fitted out over an extended period, a number of years before the Navy standardized its ship's boats. She went in and out of commission on several occasions, during which times boats would likely have been modified or replaced, and it is known that she lost several of her boats during operations in Cuba. These factors make it difficult to document the exact plans of her boats at any given time. The boats depicted in this appendix are of the types and approximate sizes called out for the *Texas*. These plans reproduced here are from Chief Constructor Phillip Hichborn's book Standard Designs for Boats of the United States Navy, published in 1900.

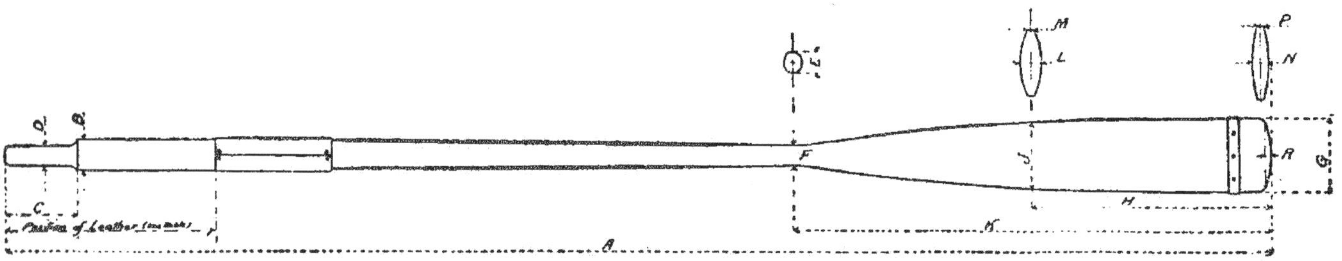

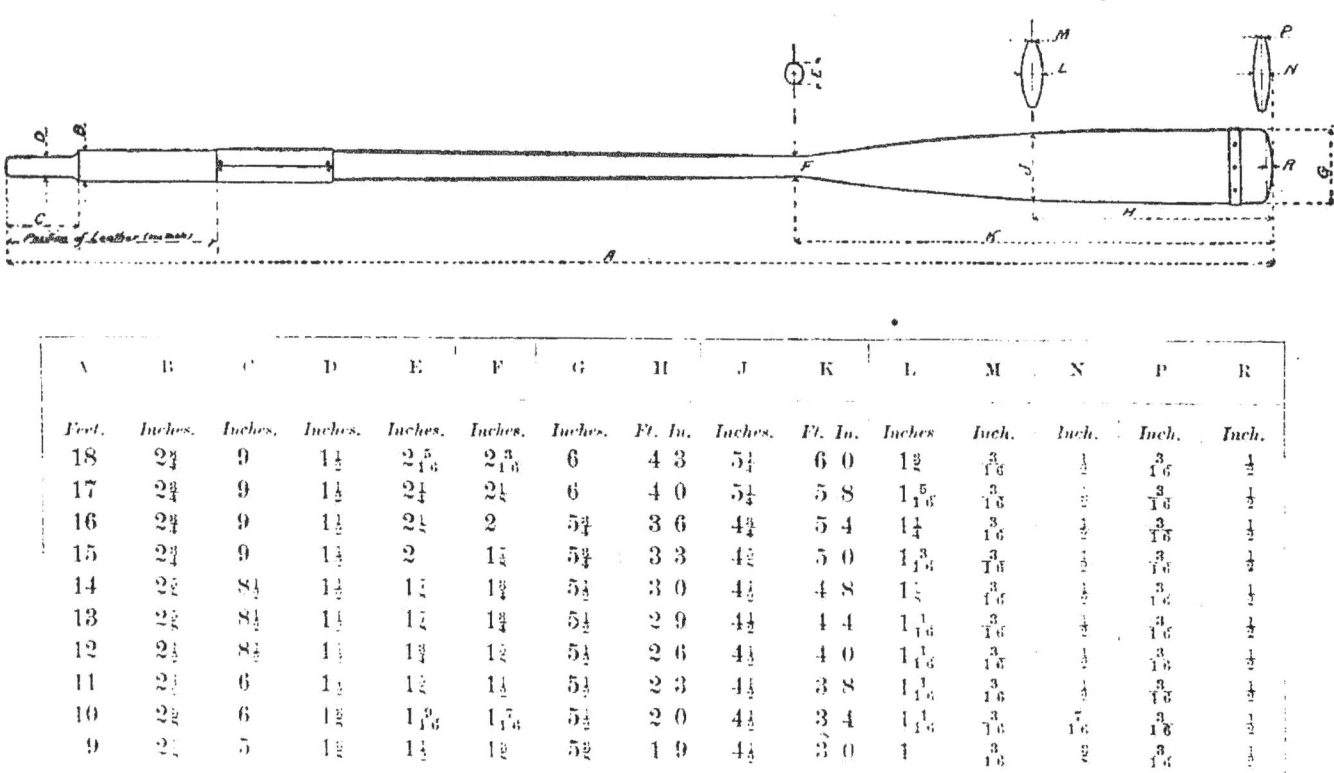

A	B	C	D	E	F	G	H	J	K	L	M	N	P	R
Feet.	*Inches.*	*Inches.*	*Inches.*	*Inches.*	*Inches.*	*Inches.*	*Ft. In.*	*Inches.*	*Ft. In.*	*Inches*	*Inch.*	*Inch.*	*Inch.*	*Inch.*
18	2 3/4	9	1 1/2	2 5/16	2 3/16	6	4 3	5 1/4	6 0	1 3/8	3/16	1/2	3/16	1/2
17	2 3/4	9	1 1/2	2 1/4	2 1/8	6	4 0	5 1/4	5 8	1 5/16	3/16	1/2	3/16	1/2
16	2 3/4	9	1 1/2	2 1/8	2	5 3/4	3 6	4 3/4	5 4	1 1/4	3/16	1/2	3/16	1/2
15	2 3/4	9	1 1/2	2	1 7/8	5 3/4	3 3	4 5/8	5 0	1 3/16	3/16	1/2	3/16	1/2
14	2 5/8	8 1/2	1 1/2	1 7/8	1 3/4	5 1/2	3 0	4 1/2	4 8	1 1/8	3/16	1/2	3/16	1/2
13	2 5/8	8 1/2	1 1/2	1 7/8	1 3/4	5 1/2	2 9	4 1/2	4 4	1 1/16	3/16	1/2	3/16	1/2
12	2 1/2	8 1/2	1 1/2	1 3/4	1 5/8	5 1/2	2 6	4 1/2	4 0	1 1/16	3/16	1/2	3/16	1/2
11	2 1/2	6	1 1/2	1 5/8	1 1/2	5 1/2	2 3	4 1/2	3 8	1 1/16	3/16	1/2	3/16	1/2
10	2 3/8	6	1 3/8	1 9/16	1 7/16	5 1/2	2 0	4 1/2	3 4	1 1/16	3/16	7/16	3/16	1/2
9	2 1/4	5	1 3/8	1 1/2	1 3/8	5 3/8	1 9	4 1/2	3 0	1	3/16	3/8	3/16	1/2

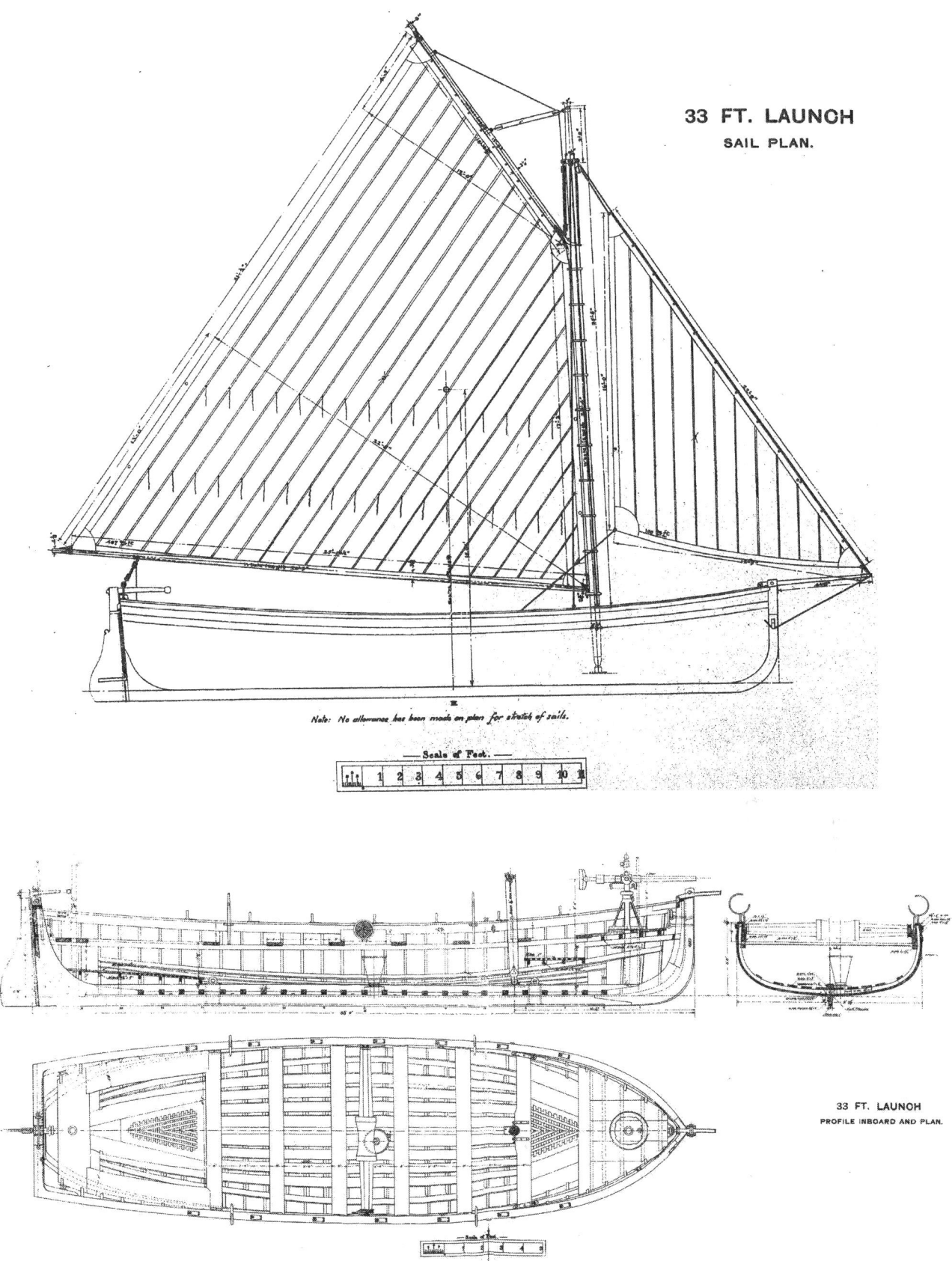

33 FT. LAUNCH
SAIL PLAN.

33 FT. LAUNCH
PROFILE INBOARD AND PLAN.

33 FT. STEAM CUTTER
SAIL PLAN.

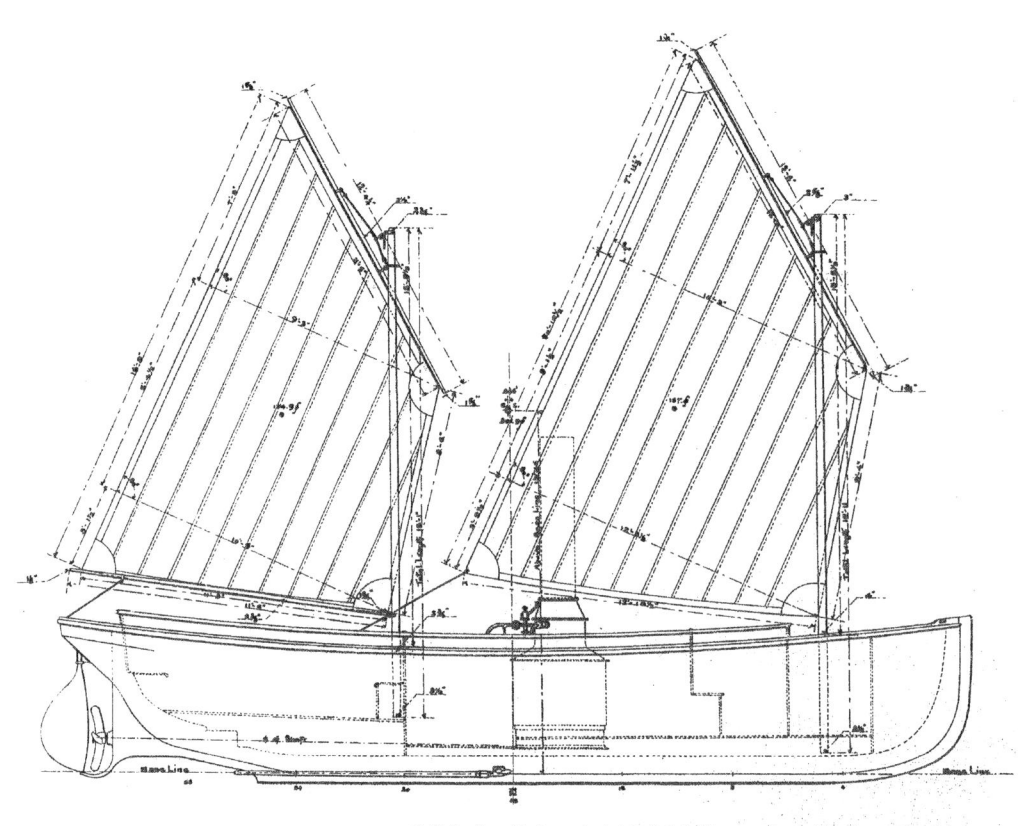

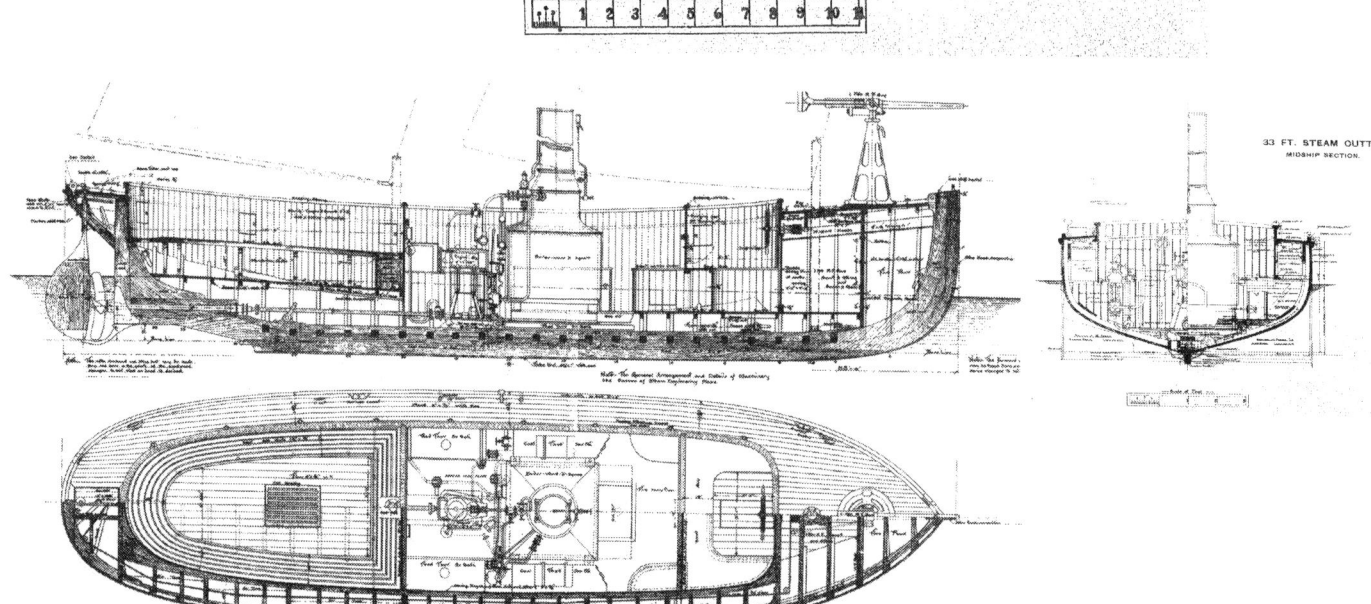

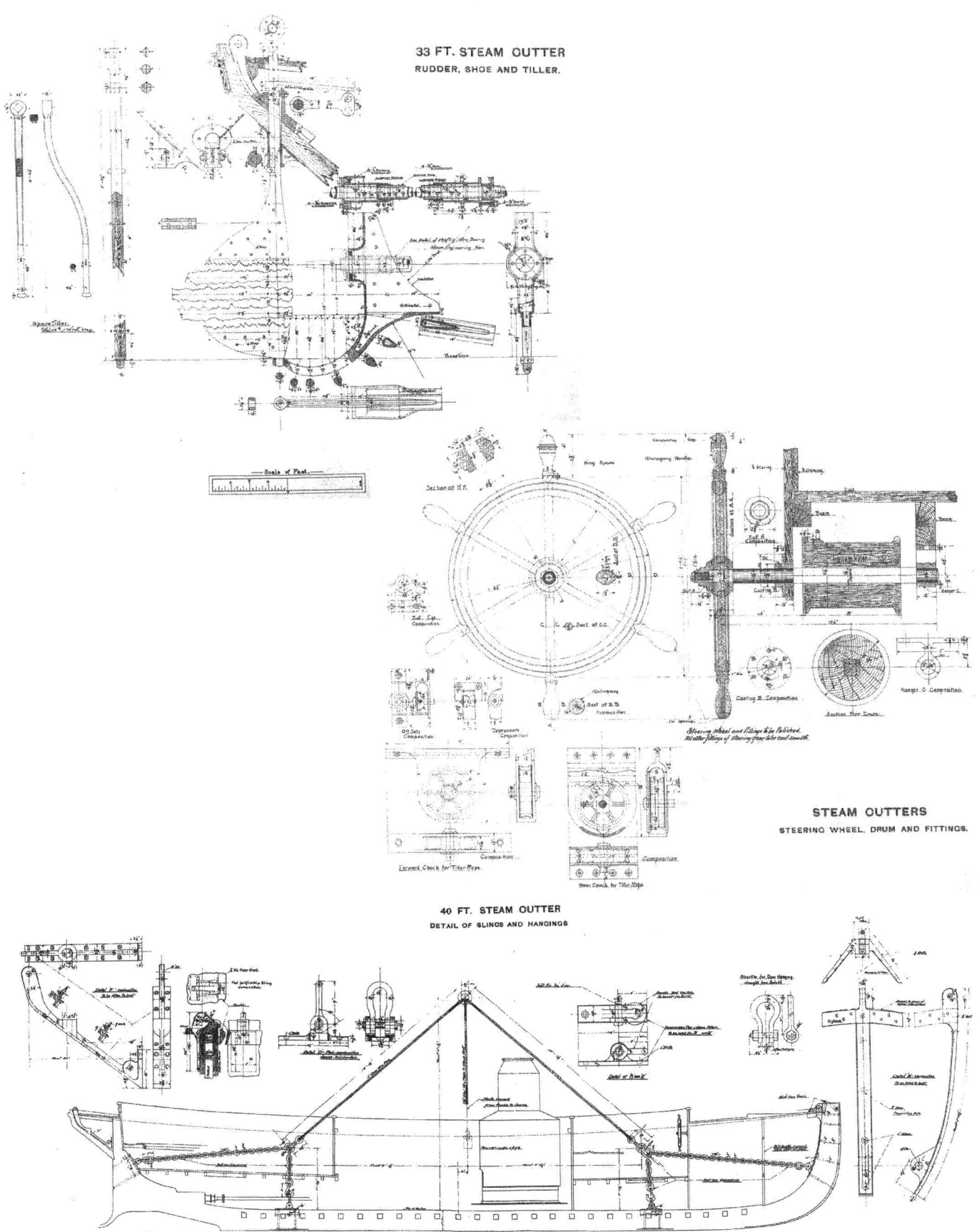

The above "40 Ft. Steam Cutter" drawing above is included as it shows typical details of boat lifting apparatus.

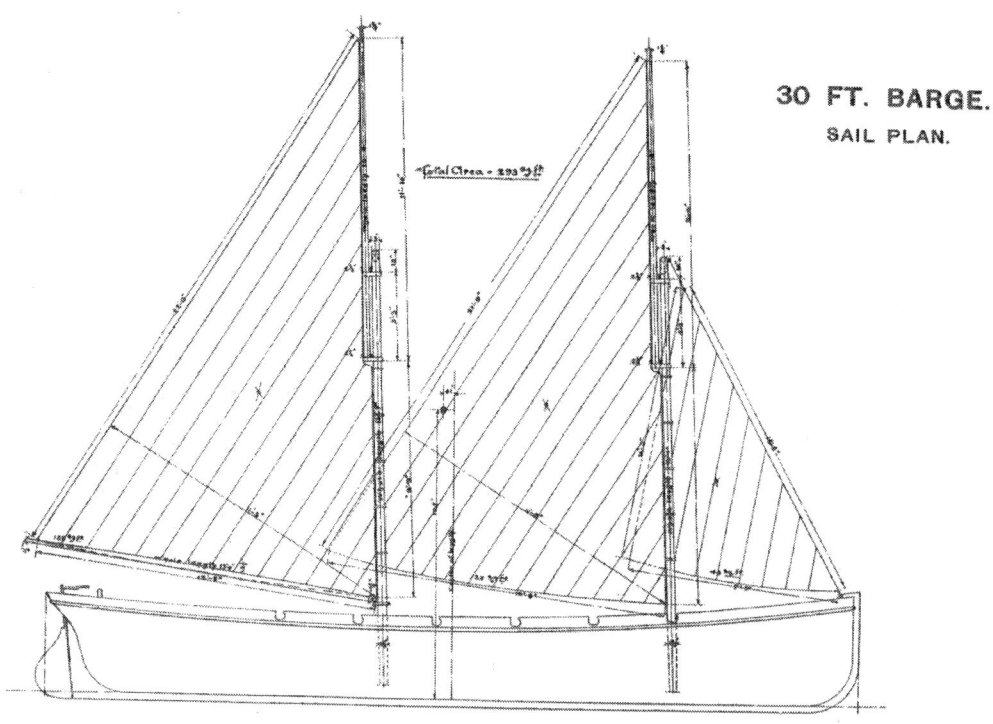

30 FT. BARGE.
SAIL PLAN.

Note: No allowance has been made on plan for stretch of sails.

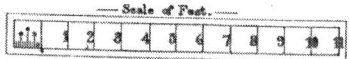

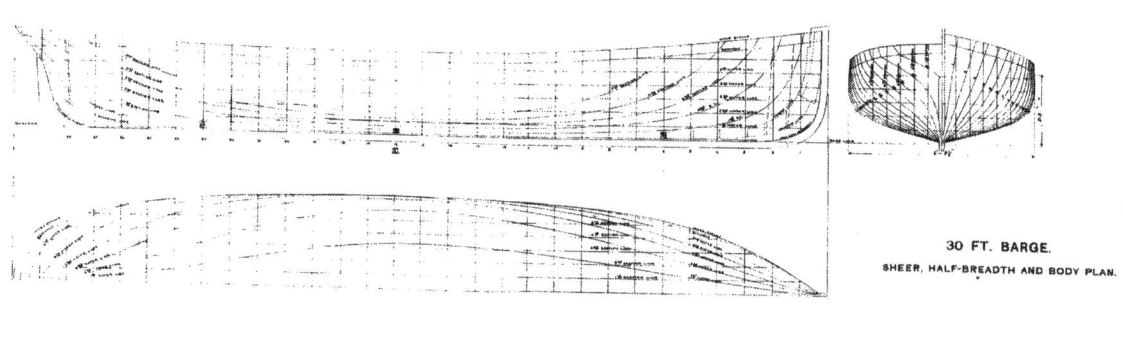

30 FT. BARGE.
SHEER, HALF-BREADTH AND BODY PLAN.

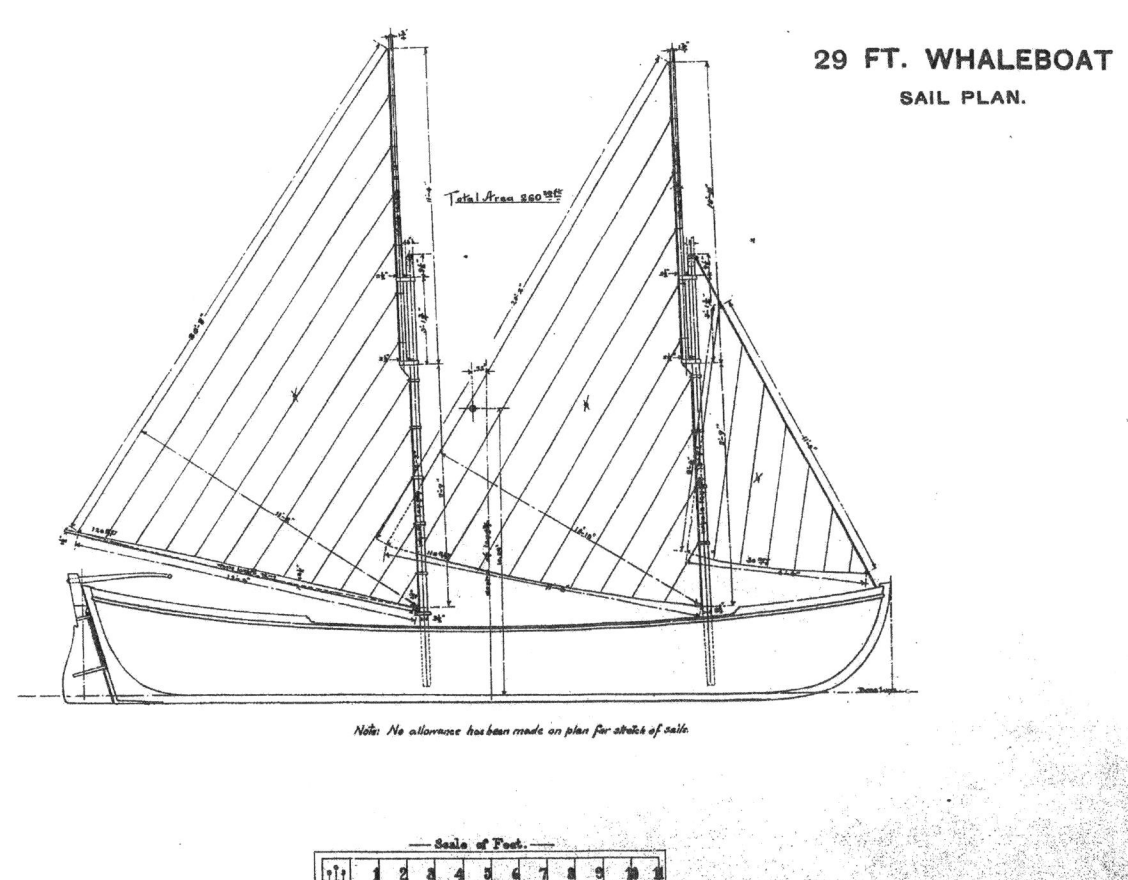

29 FT. WHALEBOAT
SAIL PLAN.

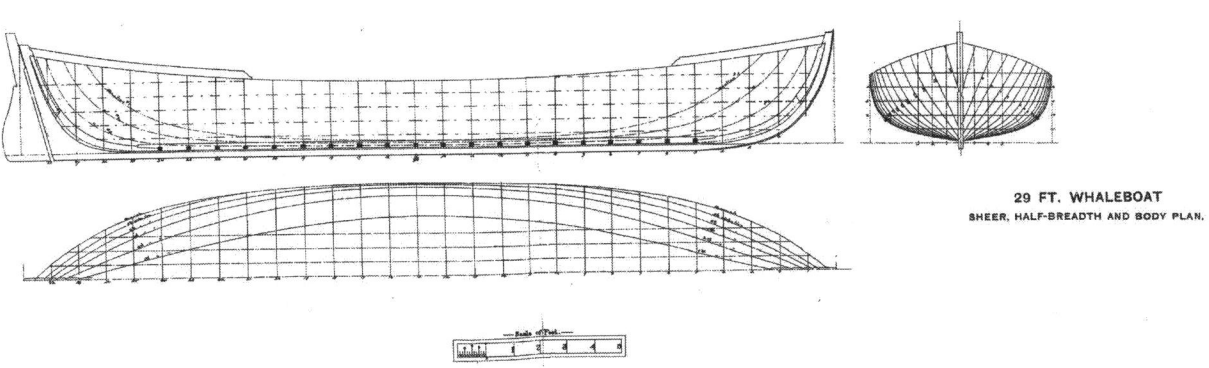

29 FT. WHALEBOAT
SHEER, HALF-BREADTH AND BODY PLAN.

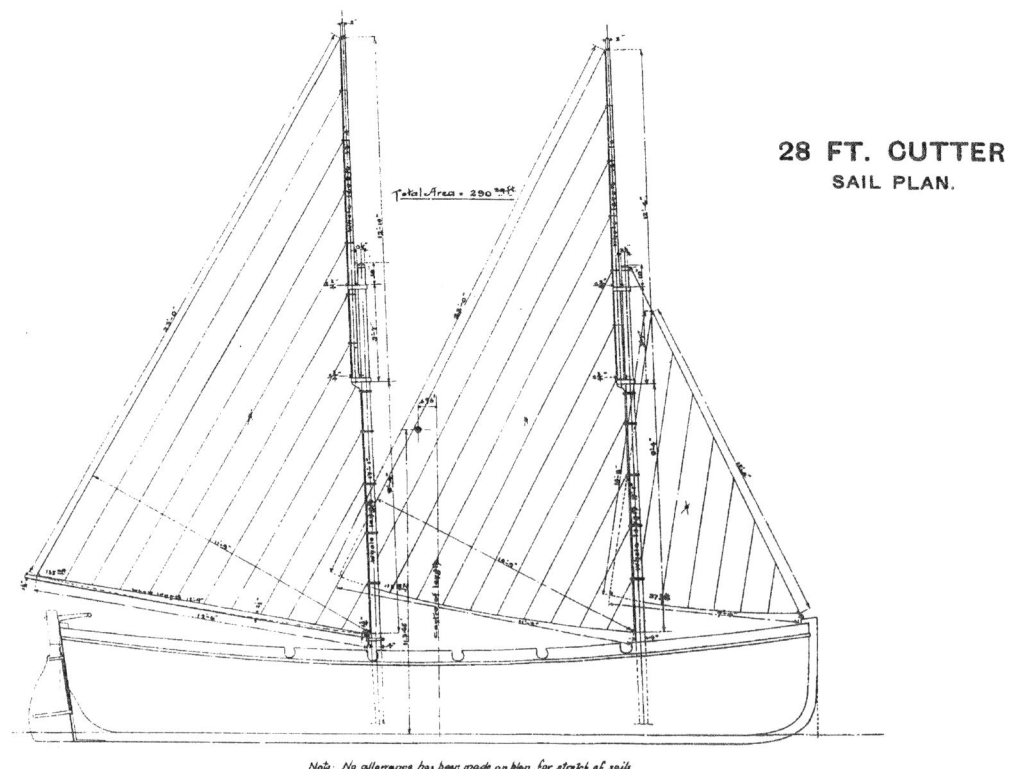

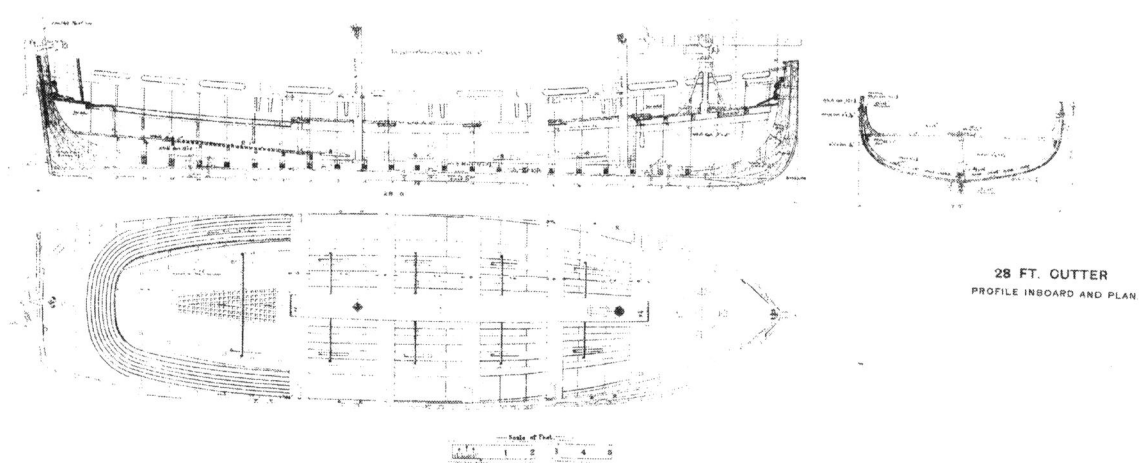

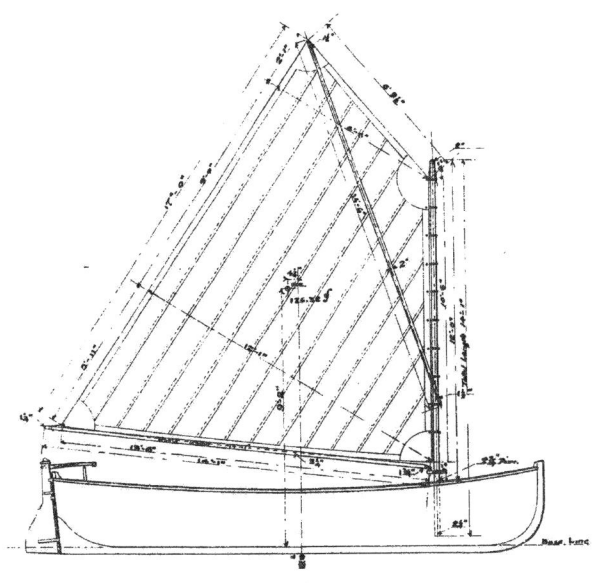

18 FT. DINGHY.

SAIL PLAN.

Note: No allowance has been made on plan for stretch of sails.
Keel for 18 ft. Special Dinghy to be 1¾" below Garboard.

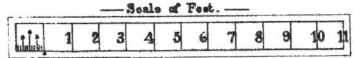

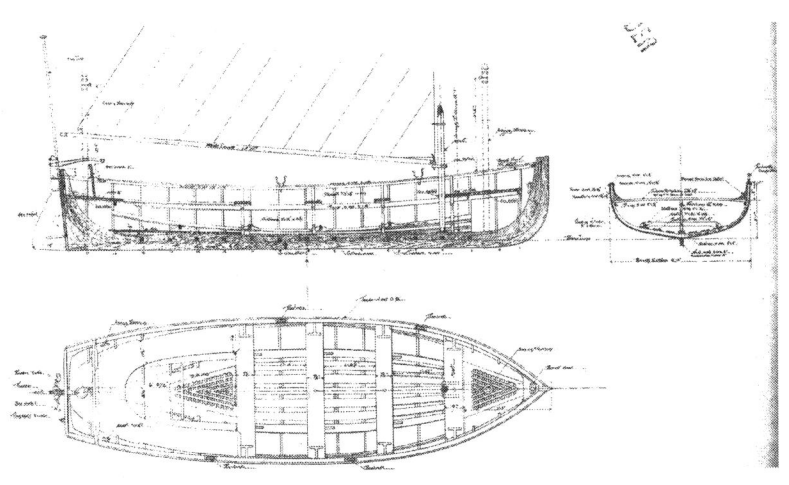

AWNING STANCHIONS AND FLAG STAFF TRUCKS.

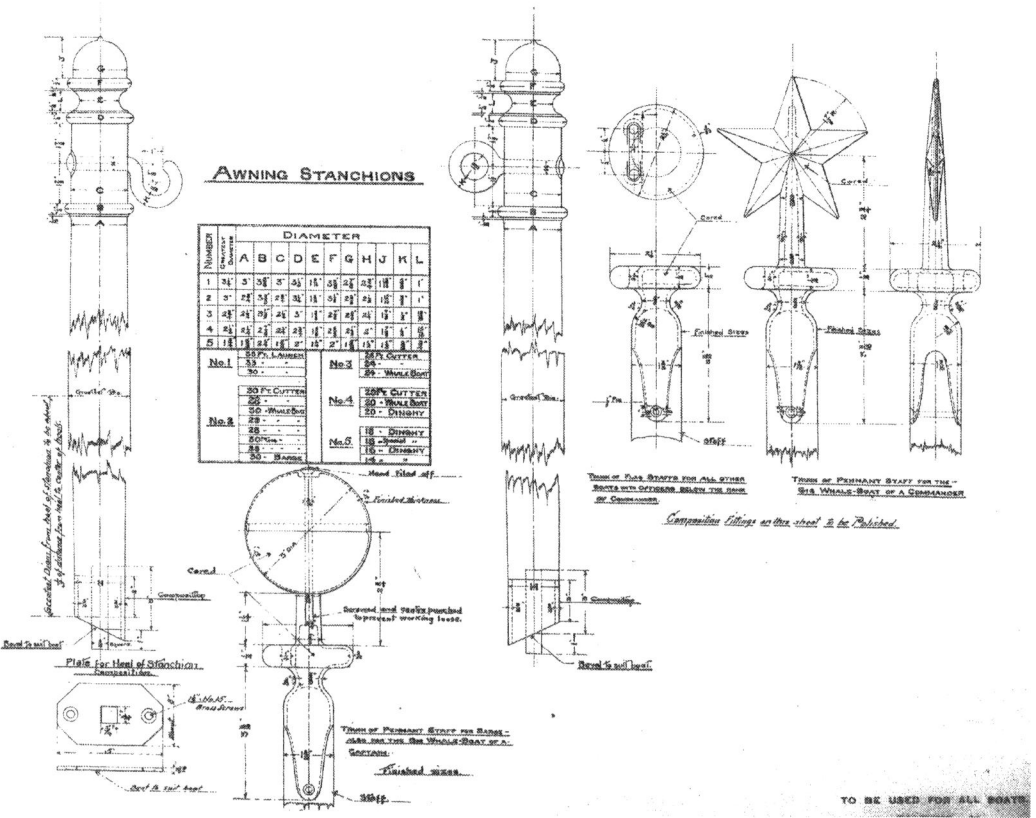

TILLERS, YOKES, BACKBOARDS AND STOPS

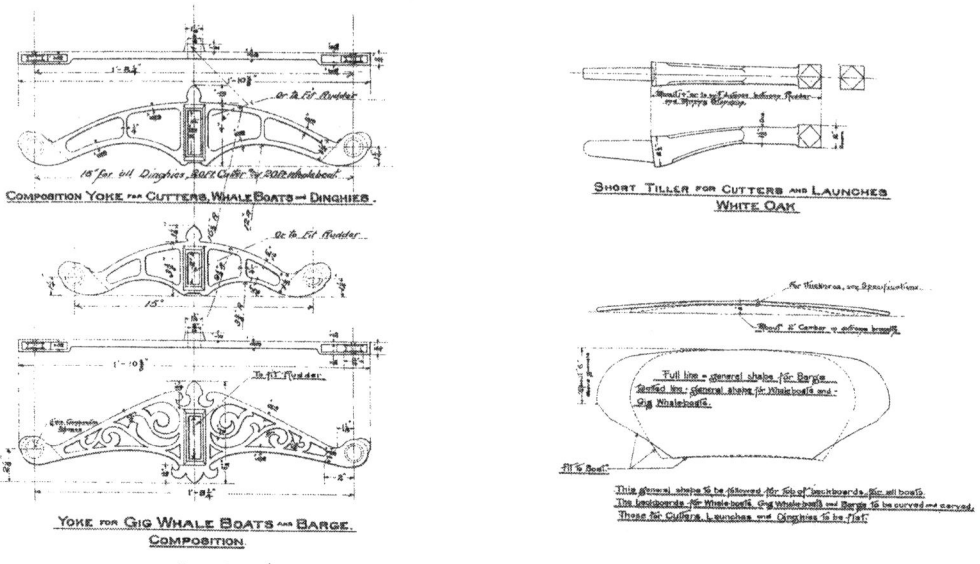

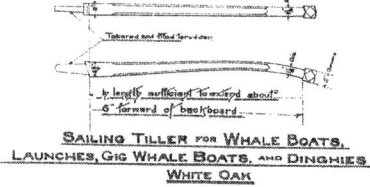

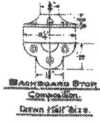

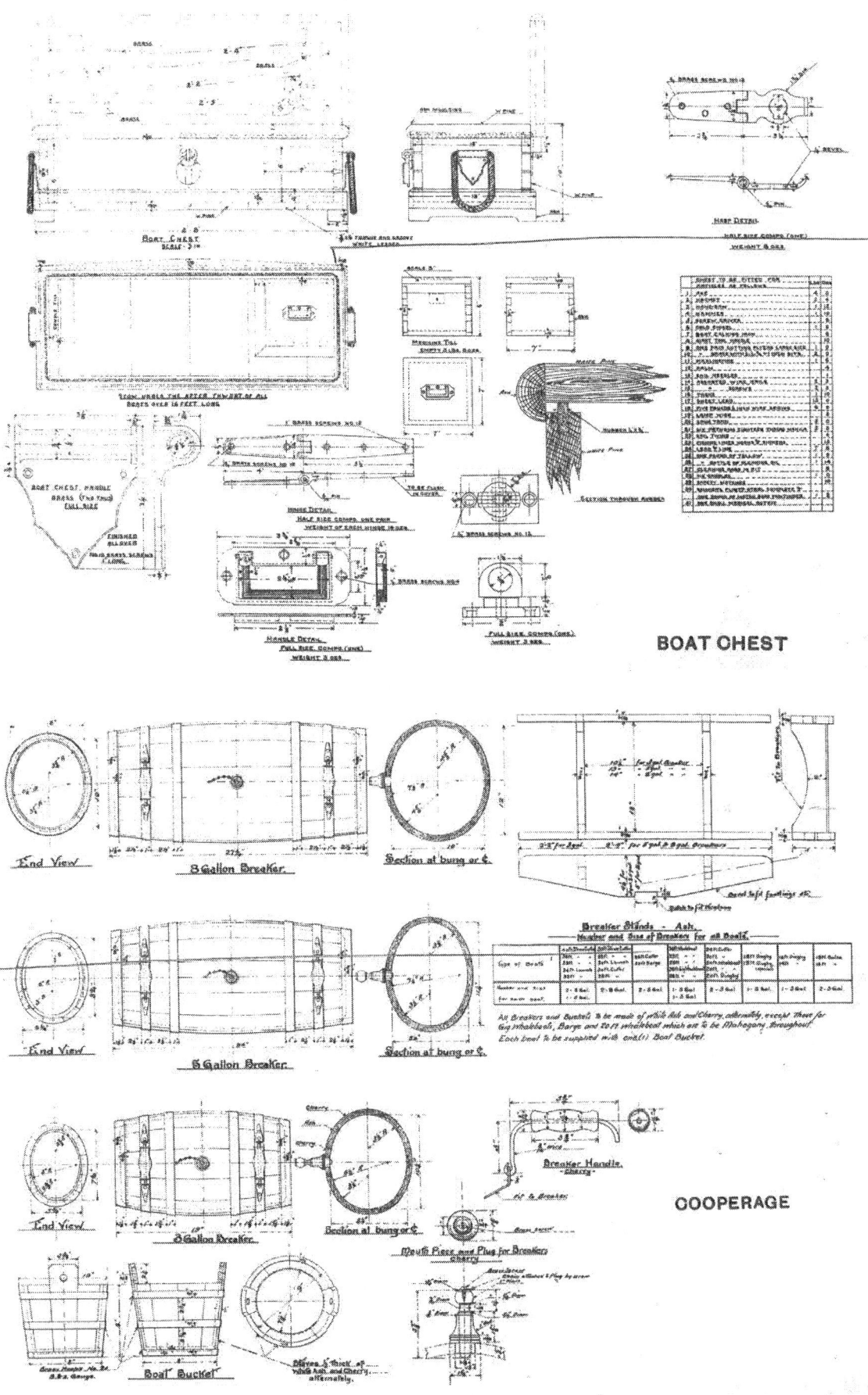

APPENDIX IV: COMPARISON OF THE USS SAN MARCOS (1895 USS TEXAS) AND THE NEW (1912) USS TEXAS, BB35

Excerpt from "Armor and Ships: A Brief Resume of Twenty Years Progress and Its Effect on Coast Defense" by Captain John W. Gulick, Coast Defense Artillery Corps, *Journal of the United States Artillery* Vol. 38 No. 3 November-December, 1912.

JOURNAL
OF THE
UNITED STATES ARTILLERY

"La guerre est un métier pour les ignorans et une Science pour les habiles gens."

Vol. 38 No. 3   NOVEMBER—DECEMBER, 1912   Whole No. 117

ARMOR AND SHIPS

A BRIEF RÉSUMÉ OF TWENTY YEARS PROGRESS AND ITS EFFECT ON COAST DEFENSE

By Captain JOHN W. GULICK, Coast Artillery Corps

In examining the files of the JOURNAL U. S. ARTILLERY, 1892-1911, one is impressed with the great mass of current information which has been placed before the readers of the JOURNAL on the general subject of Armor and Ships. In fact, no event in the progress of naval affairs has been overlooked, and with the limited space allotted this paper nothing more than a brief résumé of progress during the past twenty years is considered practicable or desirable. In the JOURNAL, No. 2, Vol. I, and No. 4, Vol. II, may be found two notable articles on armor, armor attack, and armored ships*. In these articles the contest between guns and armor and the characteristics of the principal fighting ships of the world are ably reviewed from 1854 to 1893. These articles possess more than ordinary interest for the coast artilleryman, in that the importance of the subject is fully recognized and the conclusions of the writer are substantiated by a thorough discussion.

---
* "Seacoast Guns and Steel Armor" and "Notes on Armor" by E. M. Weaver, 1st Lieut. and R. Q. M., 2d U. S. Artillery, now Brigadier General and Chief of Coast Artillery, U. S. A.

ARMOR

At the time the articles above referred to were written, the Annapolis and Ochta trials of 1890 had established the superiority of the homogeneous nickel-steel plate over the compound plate with hard-steel face and wrought-iron back, when attacked by chilled cast-iron projectiles, that armor being superior to such projectiles.

About the same time, however, Holtzer in France and Hadfield in England successfully produced forged, chrome-steel, armor-piercing projectiles, which marked the downfall of the steel and compound plates and restored the attack to the same relative position it had held ten years before. Figures 1 and 2 show typical plates of about this period.

The next important advance in armor was the introduction of Harvey Cemented Armor, in which the compound armor principle was perfected in a homogeneous plate. This was accomplished by the application of the well known principle of cementation, or face hardening, to steel or nickel-steel plates, and was the invention of an American, Mr. H. A. Harvey of the Harvey Steel Company of Newark, N. J. Harvey Nickel-Steel Cemented Armor easily established its superiority over any armor previously tested. The first ships to which it was applied were the U. S. S. *Oregon* and *Brooklyn*.

In 1895, when there were not more than half a dozen ships in the world which had benefited by the Harvey process, Krupp came forward with a method of cementation which for many years stood unrivaled and has only recently been equaled by other processes, which are probably similar in principle. The superiority of Krupp armor was not due essentially to its chemical composition, although chrome and nickel predominated, but to its "*treatment*," or manner of heating and cooling, the differential heat treatment being a feature of the Krupp process.

Figure 3, shows the high development of a typical Krupp Cemented plate produced by the Bethlehem Steel Company and used for acceptance test of projectiles. This plate is a standard Krupp plate of recent manufacture and is 14.0 feet, by 7 feet 6 inches, by 6 inches. It has been attacked 31 times and perforated 29 times. The impacts all show the characteristic Krupp appearance; and in some cases, notably at the two holes to the right and below the wooden brace, though the wall was not more than one-half caliber thick, it was not cracked.

The relative resistance of the different classes of armor (1892-1900), when attacked by uncapped projectiles, is shown by Figure 4, the standard of comparison, being the usual homogeneous wrought-iron plate with the caliber of the projectile just equaling the thickness of the plate.

Fig. 1.
Ballistic test of compound armor plate

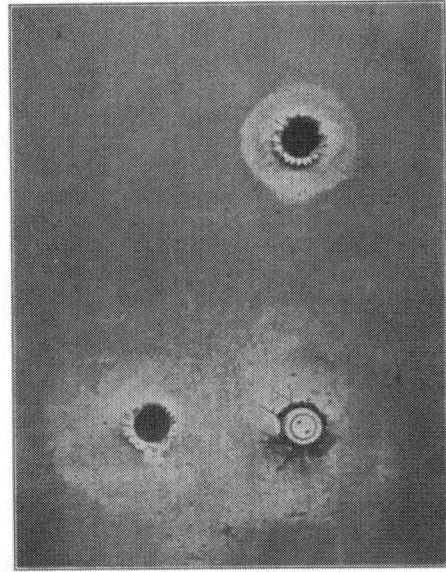

Fig. 2.
Creusot steel plate

CAPPED PROJECTILES

In 1877 it was found that a chilled shot which was defeated by a compound plate would perforate, when an additional 2.5 inches of iron was placed in front of the plate. In 1894 ad-

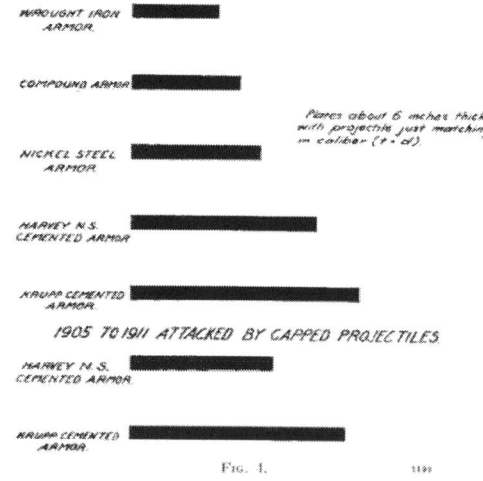

FIG. 3.
Typical Krupp plate

vantage was taken of this knowledge to cover the point of the projectile with a cap of mild steel, which materially reduced the resisting power of hard-faced armor. But, although experiments were undertaken at once by all naval powers, it was not until about 1901 that the utility of the cap was fully recognized.

RELATIVE RESISTANCE OF ARMOR IN TERMS OF WROUGHT IRON. 1892 TO 1903 ATTACKED BY UNCAPPED PROJECTILES.

WROUGHT IRON ARMOR.

COMPOUND ARMOR.

NICKEL STEEL ARMOR.

Plates about 6 inches thick with projectile just matching in caliber (t = d).

HARVEY N.S. CEMENTED ARMOR.

KRUPP CEMENTED ARMOR.

1905 TO 1911 ATTACKED BY CAPPED PROJECTILES

HARVEY N.S. CEMENTED ARMOR.

KRUPP CEMENTED ARMOR.

FIG. 4.

In October and December of that year an important trial which illustrated the efficiency of the cap was held at Messrs. Vickers' range at Eskmeals, when a 6-inch hard-faced plate was attacked by 6-inch uncapped projectiles, weight 100 lbs., with the following results:

In four shots fired in October with striking velocities varying from 1996 to 2177 f.s., the projectile was wrecked on the face of the plate. In the fifth shot, also fired in October, with a striking velocity of 2261 f.s., the projectile just perforated the plate. The plate was of excellent quality as shown by the fifth shot, which fixed its F.M.* at 2.77. A sixth shot was fired in December, 1901, using a projectile fitted with a Johnson cap, weight 105 lbs. This shot was fired with a striking velocity of 1945 f.s., and the projectile completely perforated the plate and was found unbroken and in excellent condition. The F.M. of the plate was thus reduced by the action of the cap to less than 2.3, and the perforating power of the projectile was increased more than 20 per cent.

In May, 1902, a trial at the same range attracted considerable attention. In this trial 6-inch uncapped and capped projectiles were fired against an 11.8-inch Krupp Cemented plate. Uncapped projectiles fired with striking velocities as high as 2827 f.s. broke up on the face of the plate without perforating, while capped projectiles with striking velocities as low as 2799 f.s. completely perforated the plate without breaking up.

During the early experiments it was assumed that the cap was efficient only when the angle of impact was normal, or nearly so, and that at angles of incidence exceeding 30 degrees the cap was of no assistance. But from a series of shots fired at Redington, Pa., the proving ground of the Bethlehem Steel Company, in April, 1904, and at Sandy Hook in 1905, it appeared that the cap was efficient at all angles, and that the tendency of capped projectiles to "bite" at angles of incidence exceeding 45 degrees was marked, it being noted that all capped projectiles perforating the plate at such angles turned in toward the normal to an angle of about two-thirds the angle of incidence before perforating.

Most authorities now agree that the use of a cap against soft homogeneous plates will add nothing to the penetrative power of the projectile, and that there is a velocity below which the cap is useless, or nearly so. This velocity appears to be about 1800 f.s.

Since the introduction of the capped, forged, chrome-steel projectile, improvements in armor-piercing projectiles have been in the direction of material and methods rather than in design. Progress along these lines has enabled the forged steel projectile to hold its position with the best armor plate, the efficiency of modern, armor-piercing projectiles being now fully recognized as due as much to the excellent material employed,

* Ratio of thickness of plate to thickness of wrought-iron the projectile would have just perforated.

and the methods of manufacture, as to the efficiency of the cap. The above statement may be appreciated when more recent designs of armor-piercing projectiles are considered. The latest design, both in this country and abroad appears to be in the direction of a projectile body with an ogival head of from 2½ to 3 calibers radius, with a blunt point and provided with a thin cap or envelope, covering a large portion of the

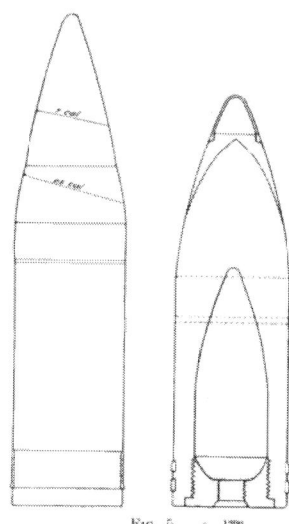

FIG. 5.
Modern A. P. projectiles.—
American and British types

head, with a radius of about 7 calibers. The ballistic efficiency of the projectile is thus increased by reducing the co-efficient of form, c, about 50 per cent; and the blunt point, assisted more or less by the envelope, or cap, is depended upon for perforating hard-faced plates. In Figure 5 are shown two types of such projectiles, each designed to perforate a thickness of hard-faced armor equal to the caliber of the projectile. Such projectiles, as manufactured abroad, carry a bursting charge equal to 3 to 4½ per cent of the projectile weight.

Armor Attack

The problem of armor attack has always been one of great complexity and is impossible of strict analytical investigation. When we consider the complicated and difficult treatment of large armor plates, and the secrecy preserved with regard to the processes and composition of materials, etc., it is evident that considerable diversity is to be expected in the results published from time to time. If in nothing else, this diversity would be clearly shown in the great number and variety of empirical formulas proposed for the perforation of armor. It is doubtful if it is possible to express the law of resistance of any armor plate and the power of any projectile to overcome that resistance by an exact formula, on account of the many conditions that escape calculation. Since the publication of Lieut. Weaver's articles, previously referred to, two important formulas have been brought forward. The first was proposed by Captain Tressider in the "Naval Annual" for 1905 and published in the JOURNAL, No. 1, Vol. XXVI.

The second formula was proposed by Major Alston Hamilton, U. S. Coast Artillery Corps, and published in the JOURNAL, No. 2, Vol. XXVII.

The practical coast artilleryman is chiefly concerned with the behavior of modern armor plates when attacked by service projectiles, under battle or service conditions; and, unfortunately, there is but a limited amount of data concerning tests of armor and projectiles under such conditions. Governments conducting tests of this nature very properly regard information obtained as confidential, and the publication of results is repressed or discouraged. Proving ground experiments were formerly made public; but recently, details of such experiments are generally withheld, and such data now available for publication is derived from results of acceptance tests of armor and projectiles. But, as is well known, conditions for acceptance tests are far from simulating battle or service conditions. The projectile arrives at the plate usually horizontal and with normal impact, while under battle conditions we should not expect more favorable angles than 35 degrees, measured from the normal. If, however, we accept the striking velocities allowed for acceptance tests of armor-piercing projectiles as the minimum velocities which will insure perforation by projectiles supplied under present specifications, we may determine the striking velocities the same projectiles will require under battle conditions and the corresponding ranges. This has been worked out in the following table, using Hamilton's method for oblique impact and the present test velocities as the basis. The corresponding ranges are correct only for the short nose projectiles. No range tables have been issued for the long nose projectile, therefore the corresponding ranges should be increased for such projectiles about 65 per cent.

Limiting Ranges for Perforation of K. C. Armor, 1 Cal. Thick.

Caliber in inches.	Weight in pounds.	Thickness in inches.	Striking velocity, normal impact, ft. per sec.	Range, normal impact, yards.	Striking velocity, battle conditions, ft. per sec.	Range, battle conditions, yards.
6 (2600)	106	6	2040	1357	2346	598
8 (2200)	316	8	1800	3096	2070	884
10 (2250)	604	10	1790	4210	2058	1700
12 (2250)	1046	12	1760	5389	2024	2433
14 (2150)	1660	14	1745	4550	2007	1400

ARMORED SHIPS

The evolution of the armored ship during the past twenty years may be brought out by a brief description of two battleships, the U. S. S. San Marcos (formerly *Texas*), launched in 1892, and the U. S. S. *Texas*, launched in 1912.

The *San Marcos* (old *Texas*) has recently been used as a target for experimental purposes, details of which appeared in the JOURNAL for July-August, 1911. The ship was stricken from the navy list on October 11, 1911.

The *San Marcos* (old *Texas*) was laid down at Norfolk, June, 1889, and was launched June 28, 1892. The design was purchased by the Navy Department from the Barrow Ship Building Company of England. The final trials of the ship were completed in December, 1895.

The *San Marcos* (old *Texas*) was 301 feet in length, 64 feet beam, 22 feet 6 inches draft, with a displacement of 6327 tons. The I. H. P. developed on trial was 8422, which compared favorably with the designed I. H. P. The designed speed was 17.8 knots; but this speed was never attained, and three years later, at Santiago, 13 knots was the best that could be attained.

The armor protection was essentially as follows: A waterline belt of the early Harvey type, 12 inches thick at the top

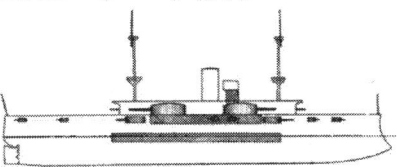

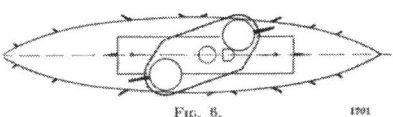

Fig. 8.
U. S. S. San Marcos (old Texas), 1892

and tapering to 7 inches at the bottom, extending 4 feet below and 3 feet above the waterline, protected the engine and boiler spaces for a length of 118 feet. This side armor was extended inboard diagonally at the ends to protect against a raking fire, the diagonal armor being 8 inches thick and 17 feet long. The protective deck, steel, 2 inches thick, rested on the armor belt and was 3 inches thick on the slopes at the bow and stern. On the lower deck above the protective deck, was an armored redoubt extending diagonally across the ship, the turrets being mounted at the ends, the port turret forward. The redoubt armor was 12 inches thick and of nickel-steel. The turrets were of 12-inch Harvey steel and the ammunition hoists to the turrets were protected by 6 inches of steel. The conning tower, located just forward of the smokepipe was of steel, 9 inches thick.

The general arrangement of the armament is shown in Figure 6, and consisted of:

Two 12-inch, 35-caliber guns, M.V. 2100 f.s.; one mounted in each turret.

Six 6-inch, 35-caliber guns, M.V. 2300 f.s.; distributed as shown, and unprotected by heavy armor.

Twelve 6-pounder guns.

Ten 1-pounder guns.

Two Gatling guns.

Two torpedo tubes, both above water.

The *Texas* was laid down at Newport News in 1911 and has been launched in 1912.

The *Texas* is 565 feet in length, 95 feet beam, about 24 feet draft, with a displacement of 27,000 tons. The designed speed is 21 knots. The *Texas* will carry the following armament:

Ten 14-inch, 45-caliber guns, M. V. 2600 f.s.

Twenty-one 5-inch, 50-caliber guns, M. V. 3000 f.s.

The 14-inch guns will be mounted in five elliptical turrets, located on the center line, two forward of the smokepipe and three abaft. One after and one forward turret will be elevated to allow four 14-inch guns to be trained dead ahead or dead astern. All of the ten 14-inch guns will be available for either broadside. The 5-inch guns for protection against torpedo attack will be distributed as shown in the plan.

The armor protection is essentially as follows, all of K. C. armor:

A main waterline belt 8 feet wide protects the engine and boiler spaces, extending for about 478 feet amidships. This belt is 12 inches thick at the top and 10 inches thick at the bottom, uniformly tapered for 418 feet, and 6 inches thick for about 60 feet.

An armored bulkhead, 10 to 11 inches thick, extends entirely across the ship at the forward end of the main belt, and a triangular bulkhead, 9 to 11 inches thick, extends entirely across the ship at the after end of the main belt.

The lower casemate armor, resting on the main belt, extends the limits of the magazine spaces. This armor is about 7 feet wide and is 9 inches thick at the top and 11 inches thick at the bottom, and is provided with transverse bulkheads, 10 inches thick, extending entirely across the ship.

The upper casemate armor, resting on the lower casemate armor, extends about 129 feet. This armor is about 4 feet wide, and is 6½ inches thick throughout. Diagonal bulkheads, 6½ to 9 inches in thickness, extend across the ship to Nos. 2 and 5 barbettes, thus clearing the ends.

The 14-inch barbettes are from 4 to 14 inches thick. The 14-inch turrets have front plates 14 inches thick, sides and rears 8 inches thick, and tops 4 inches thick.

The central station is surrounded on three sides with armor 6 inches thick. The conning tower is 12 inches thick with a top 5 inches thick. The conning tower tube is 36 inches in inside diameter and is 11 inches thick.

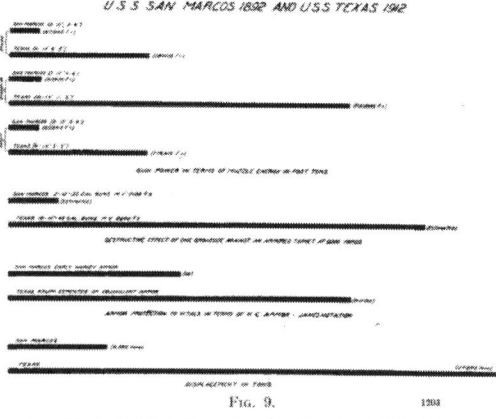

FIG. 9.
Comparison of U. S. S. San Marcos (old Texas) and U. S. S. Texas

A comparison of gun power, protection, etc., of the *San Marcos* (old *Texas*) and *Texas* is shown by the graphic chart, Figure 9.

EFFECT OF RECENT NAVAL DEVELOPMENT ON COAST DEFENSE

In theory, fleets never attack coast fortifications; in practice they have almost invariably done so when the naval situation has admitted of it. Therefore, it is well to consider the

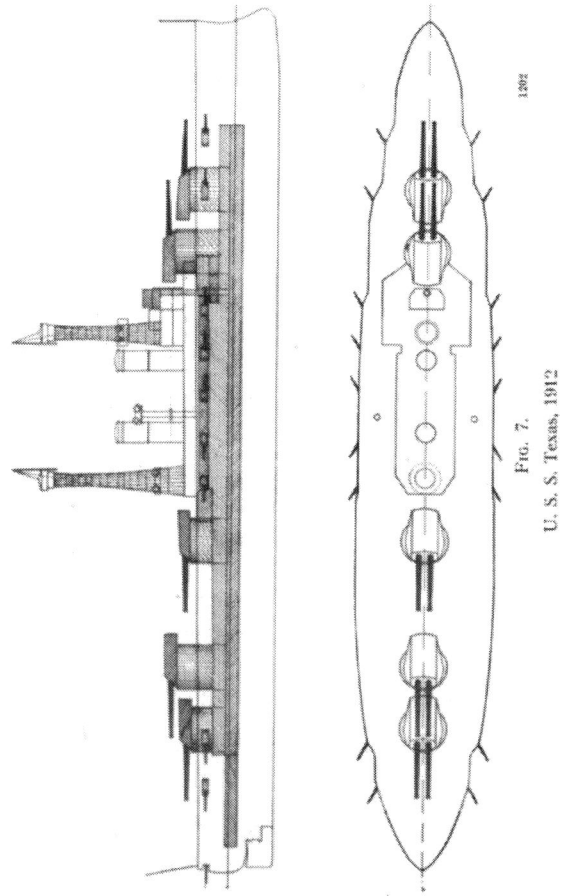

FIG. 7. U. S. S. Texas, 1912

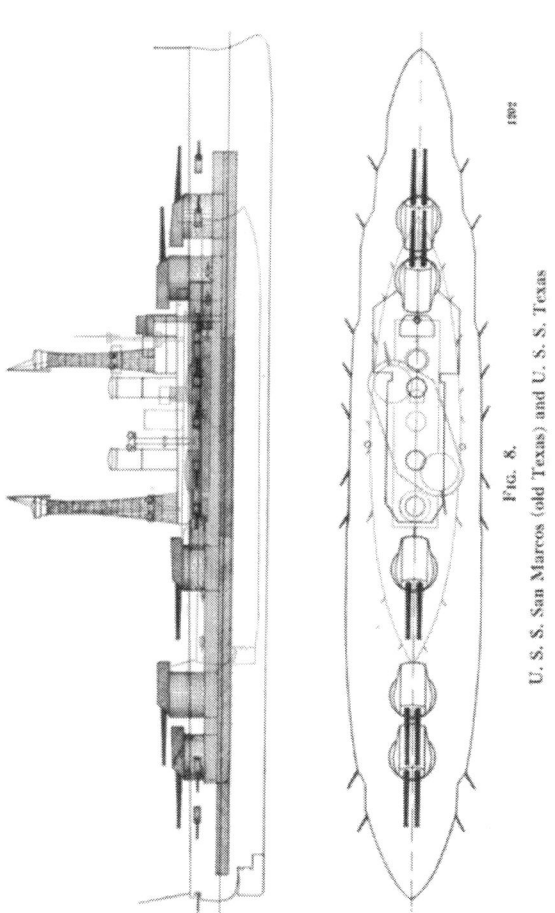

FIG. 8. U. S. S. San Marcos (old Texas) and U. S. S. Texas

effects of the present development of the big-gun-big-ship on defense. These may be briefly summed up as follows:

1. *Armament.*—The policy of most navies at the present time is to include in the assigned weight of battery the largest guns that can be readily handled, or to mount on all armored ships nothing but heavy guns (12 to 14 inches in caliber) in turrets, and an adequate secondary battery, 3 to 6 inches in caliber, for torpedo defense. This policy is necessary on account of the great thickness and extent of armor carried by modern armored ships, and because a gun below 12 inches in caliber will not do effective work against such armor at battle ranges. From a naval point of view this policy has the following distinct advantages:

 a. Better protection for guns and personnel.
 b. Fewer expert gun pointers required.
 c. Better communications and easier fire control.
 d. Simplified ammunition supply.
 e. Increased accuracy of fire due to flatter trajectories.

The destructive effect of the old, 35-caliber, 12-inch guns of the *San Marcos* (old *Texas*) has been compared with that of the new, 45-caliber, 14-inch guns of the *Texas*. As this destructive effect is computed for an armored target, it is well to consider the effect of the 45-caliber, 14-inch gun, firing a 1400 lb. projectile against sand and concrete targets. Using the U. S. Engineer formula, we find that, at 9000 yards, 63 feet of sand or 21 feet of concrete will not stop the projectile. Therefore, if our coast guns are to be adequately protected, the parapets of batteries must be increased in thickness. In addition to the increased destructive effect of the heavy guns now being mounted on modern battleships, the adoption of improved mountings for such guns which admit of fire being carried on at ranges up to 18,000 yards, and improvements in naval gunnery which will make the fire of attacking ships effective at such ranges, are matters of great importance to the coast artillery. The accuracy of such guns is indicated by recent firings with the type 14-inch gun of the U. S. Navy.

For 15 rounds fired after 11 rounds had been previously fired, the following results were obtained:

Elevation, 8 degrees.
Angle of fall, 10 degrees.
Mean range, about 14,000 yards.
Average variation in range from mean range, 53 yards.
Average variation in velocity from mean velocity, 3 f.s.

It used to be held that guns on high sites were better protected than guns on low sites. This was mainly based on the proposition that mountings of guns on board ship would not permit of sufficient elevation at the then considered fighting ranges. But that this is a fallacy now, will be evident when we consider modern fighting ranges, the slight increase in elevation required to reach a site 1000 feet high, and modern methods of fire control by which a group of calibrated guns may be "spotted" up the face of a high site to the crest, where the batteries are usually located.

The increased range of guns now being mounted on modern battleships, give a fleet much more latitude as to positions from which a fortified place may be bombarded. In order to cope with guns of the attacking fleet under such conditions, the guns of coast forts must be of such a nature and so sited as to be able to fire on any position open to the fleet. With the limited range permitted by existing mounts, it is necessary that guns ashore be pushed well to the front. When however, as is often the case, this cannot be done, they should be supplanted by guns of greater power, or 12-inch mortars ranging up to 17,000 yards should be installed to cover the position.

The great displacement of modern battleships also means a corresponding increase in the number of rounds of ammunition carried by each ship. Thus, in the case of the *San Marcos* (old *Texas*), or taking one of the later ships of that period as an example, a fleet of 6 ships carried 24 heavy guns or 4 heavy guns each, with 60 rounds of ammunition per gun, or 1440 rounds for the fleet. A fleet of 6 ships of the *Texas* type carry 60 heavy guns, or 10 guns each, with 100 rounds of ammunition per gun, or 6000 rounds for the fleet. If we assume that in attacking a particular target it will require an expenditure of 1000 rounds, it is evident that upon the conclusion of the action, the fleet of 4-gun ships will have fired more than 40 rounds per gun and will have only 440 rounds on hand, while the fleet of 10-gun ships will have fired less than 17 rounds per gun and will have 5000 rounds on hand.

Assuming that the rates of fire are the same, without taking into account superior speed, it is evident also that the fleet of 10-gun ships will be under fire from the coast batteries about one-third the time of the fleet of 4-gun ships.

In addition to all of the above, the fleet of 10-gun ships will be at no disadvantage as regards the accuracy life of its guns, due to the limited number of rounds fired; so the probability of attack from such fleets is greater than it was from the old fleets of 4-gun ships, when the firing of a large number of rounds would impair the accuracy life of the guns and render the fleet incapable of resisting a hostile fleet on equal terms.

In actions between forts and ships, there has always been a disparity of armament. If the calibers and ballistics of the guns have been equal, superiority of numbers has usually been with the fleet. Therefore, if the use of coast guns in action is anticipated, it is important that the number of guns mounted ashore should not be too small in comparison with those that an enemy can bring to bear; and, if they are limited in number, as is usually the case, they should be of such power and so mounted as to make up in caliber and ballistics, the disparity in numbers.

Equality in striking velocity is not necessary, but equality or superiority in range is necessary.

2. *Armor Protection.*—The great displacement of modern battleships also means increased protection to the guns, the personnel, and the vitals of the ship. The modern battleship of the big-gun type is so well protected, not only by armor but by watertight subdivision, that it is doubtful if a single impact on the waterline would seriously affect the trim of the ship. Taking the *Texas* as an example, we find that of the total displacement, nearly 7000 tons is devoted to armor. Of this, one-third may be assumed to be devoted to the protection of the guns and the personnel, and two-thirds to the hull for the preservation of buoyancy and stability and for the protection of the vitals of the ship. All heavy guns are mounted in turrets and protected by 14 inches of armor on the exposed sides. This protection is superior to any hitherto given to guns; and when we consider the thickness of waterline armor, with internal bulkhead construction, it may be frankly stated that the sinking of such a ship by long range fire of coast guns is entirely out of the question.

Actions between forts and ships will not be so decisive as actions between ships, as far as destruction of material is concerned; for, taking into account the peculiar functions of shore defenses, all that can be expected is so to cripple the attacking ships as to cause them to draw off, thus preventing them from accomplishing their object.

It should be remembered that an accurate and rapid fire has never failed to cripple vessels, however heavily armored, through damage to upper works, funnels, smoke-pipes, masts, and top-hamper.

The experiences of Tsushima show that perforation of belt and turret armor is not essential, and that frequent hitting by H. E. shell may be decisive. In the case of the *Texas*, the exposed area that is protected by armor 9 inches thick, or armor superior at battle ranges to any coast gun now mounted, is about 50 per cent of the total exposed area, which includes masts, funnels, etc.

The increased size of the target is an important advantage for the shore guns, the larger target increasing the chances of hitting. As a result of development, of naval actions of the Russo-Japanese war, and of recent tests conducted in this country and abroad, the old question of shell fire vs. armor perforation is still under discussion. It is probable that, as far as this country is concerned, the policy will be, as heretofore, to supply two types of armor-piercing projectiles: one designed to carry its bursting charge behind the heaviest armor before bursting, to be used at those ranges at which perforation may be expected; the other to carry a large bursting charge and designed to perforate armor about one-half caliber thick, to be used against personnel and matériel at those ranges at which perforation of the heaviest armor may not be expected. It is evident, referring to the table given on page 268 that projectiles of the first type should be supplied only to the most powerful guns; *i.e.*, 10, 12, and 14-inch; and that for such guns the proportion of the two types of projectiles should be not more than one of the first type to four of the other type.

APPENDIX V: SUMMARY OF SERVICE & STATISTICS

1886
3 Aug: Authorized by Congress.

1887
19 Dec: Contract for plans signed with Barrow Shipbuilding.
June: Steel Contract Let.

1888
10 Mar: US government issues $15,000 check to Barrow Shipbuilding for plans.

1889
1 June: Keel laid at Norfolk Navy Yard, Norfolk, VA.
7 Oct: Stem casting arrives at Norfolk Navy Yard, VA.

1890
1 July: Constructor reports 25% of total work completed.

1891
1 Aug: Constructor reports 47% of total work completed.
1 Sep: Constructor reports 49% of total work completed.
1 Oct: Constructor reports 50% of total work completed.
1 Dec: Constructor reports 54% of total work completed.

1892
1 Jan: Constructor reports 56% of total work completed.
1 Mar: Constructor reports 60% of total work completed.
1 May: Constructor reports 64% of total work completed.
11:10 am 28 June: Launched.
1 July: Constructor reports 68% of total work completed.
16 July: Constructor reports 69% of total work completed.
Aug: Installation of main engines begins.
1 Sep: Constructor reports 72% of total work completed.
1 Nov: Constructor reports 76% of total work completed.
Dec: Installation of boilers begins.

1893
1 Jan: Constructor reports 79% of total work completed.
1 Feb: Constructor reports 80% of total work completed.
1 Apr: Constructor reports 81% of total work completed.
4 Nov: Boiler supports fail as boilers are filled causing ship to list alongside dock. Accident attributed to insufficient strength of plates below boilers.

1894
1 Apr: Constructor reports 91% of total work completed.
12 May: Starboard engine trial at Norfolk Navy Yard, VA.
15 May: Port engine trial at Norfolk Navy Yard, VA.
1 July: Constructor reports 93% of total work completed.
1 Dec: Constructor reports 95% of total work completed.
1894: Re-designated second-class battleship.

1895
1 Apr: Constructor reports 96% of total work completed.
1:30 pm 15 Aug: Commissioned.

4 May: Machinery trials board appointed.
8 May: Dock trials of machinery, Norfolk, VA.
16 June: In dry dock, Norfolk Navy Yard, VA.
BEF 30 July: Capt. Henry Glass appointed to command the USS Texas. Lt. Cmdr. J.D.J. Kelly appointed as executive officer.
8 Aug: Draft of 260 bluejackets leave the USS Vermont for the receiving ship Franklin at the Norfolk Navy Yard, VA. They are intended for the battleship USS Texas.
31 July: Bids for stores opened.
1:30 pm, 15 Aug: Placed in commission at Norfolk Navy Yard, VA. Capt. Henry Glass assumed command.
6-7 Sept: Preliminary engine trials begin off Hampton Roads, Va. Condensers fill with mud.
11 Sept: Chief Engineer A. Kirby relieved on medical grounds, replaced by Chief Engineer J. A. B. Smith.
13 Sept: Preliminary engine trials resume off Hampton Roads, VA.
3 Oct: 'Shake down' prior to the official trial off Hampton Roads, VA.
5 Oct: Ordered to Norfolk Navy Yard, VA for replacement of eccentric strap.
9 Oct: Off Hampton Roads, VA.
21 Oct: Orders revised prior to entering Norfolk dry dock.
22 Oct: Ordered to Brooklyn Navy Yard, NY.
10:00, 23 Oct: Departs Fort Monroe, VA for Tompkinsville, NY.
23 Oct: Arrives Tompkinsville, NY.
28 Oct: Enters Brooklyn Navy Yard, NY for inspection, repairs, and minor modifications.
4 Nov: Enters dry dock at the Brooklyn Navy Yard, NY.
5 Nov: Dent observed in hull as result of dry docking at the Brooklyn Navy Yard, NY.
5-7 Nov: Ship painted in dry dock at the Brooklyn Navy Yard, NY.
7 Nov: Buckling observed in bottom plate in dry dock at the Brooklyn Navy Yard, NY.
8 Nov: Buckling of floor plate of frame 45 and signs of straining observed at the Brooklyn Navy Yard, NY.
9 Nov: Dock partly refilled to ease strain at the Brooklyn Navy Yard, NY.
10 Nov: Dock refilled further to ease strain.
11 Nov: Buckling and cracks observed for 144 feet amidships.
15 Nov: Repairs of cracks and installation of stiffening brackets ordered. Investigation of docking incident by the inspection board ordered.
17 Nov: Still in dry dock for installation of new propellers at Brooklyn Navy Yard, NY.
AFT 17 Nov: Capt. George Dewey heads board of inspection to investigate hull
20 Nov: Work on lower hull continues. Additional water let into dry dock at Brooklyn Navy Yard, NY.
10:00 am, 20 Nov: Removed from dry dock and warped alongside the big crane wharf at Brooklyn Navy Yard, NY.
ABT 23 Nov: Dock trials of engines.
3 Dec: Departs Brooklyn for preliminary test of engines. Arrives at Tompkinsville, NY with broken steering gear.
7 Dec: Went outside Sandy Hook, NY and returned in preparations for sea trial
12 Dec: Departs Tompkinsville, NY for preliminary sea trials. Returns after nightfall.
14 Dec: Capt. Glass reports that the ship is ready for official trials at Tompkinsville, NY pending the overhaul of the journals.
18 Dec: Four hours horsepower trial postponed due to fog off Tompkinsville, NY.
19 Dec: Steam trials begun.
20 Dec: Four hours horsepower trial off Tompkinsville, NY called off after three hours due to insufficient drainage in engine room.
23 Dec: Departs Tompkinsville, NY for a short sea run beyond Sandy Hook, NY. Board of Inspection and Survey, Capt. George Dewey, President onboard. Returns after nightfall. Members of the board sent to shore then conducts searchlight tests.
31 Dec: Board of Inspection's report released. Ship ordered to navy yard for modifications.

1896
1:20 pm, 3 Jan: Passed out at Sandy Hook, NY bound for Norfolk Navy Yard, VA.
10 Jan: At Norfolk Navy Yard, VA.
12 Jan: SecNav recommends officers and men be detached to other duties.
27 Jan: Norfolk Navy Yard, VA. Decommissioned.
8 Feb: 165 former USS Texas sailors and several officers transferred by train from Norfolk, VA to Mare Island Navy Yard, CA.
14 Feb: Dry docked at Norfolk Navy Yard, VA for formal survey and modifications to main gun turret hydraulic systems and magazine ventilation.
21 Mar: Norfolk Navy Yard, VA undergoing modifications.
8 May-9 May: Dry docked at Norfolk Navy Yard, VA having hull strengthened.
22 June: Repairs completed at Norfolk Navy Yard, VA.
20 July: Recommissioned with her former officers. Assigned to North Atlantic Squadron.
25 Aug: Departs Norfolk Navy Yard, VA for Tompkinsville, NY.
26 Aug: Arrives Tompkinsville, NY.
1 Sep: Departs Tompkinsville for Fisher's Island, NY.
7 Sep: Arrives Fisher's Island, NY.
16 Sep: With North Atlantic Squadron at Gardiner's Bay. Departs for Newport, RI.
5:50, 16 Sept: Arrives Newport to receive torpedo outfit. Grounds off westerly shore of torpedo station.
2:30 am, 17 Sept: Pulled off ground at high tide by 4 tugs from Providence, RI.
25 Sep: Departs Newport for Tompkinsville, NY.
26 Sep: Arrives Tompkinsville, NY.
1 Oct: Depart Tompkinsville for Fort Monroe, VA.
5 Oct: Arrives Fort Monroe, VA.
12 Oct: Departs Fort Monroe for Tompkinsville. Rides out hurricane with USS Maine and USS Indiana (North Atlantic Squadron?)
14 Oct: Arrives Tompkinsville, NY.
23 Oct: Departs Tompkinsville, NY, arrives at the Brooklyn Navy Yard, NY.
9 Nov: Sinks at dock at Brooklyn Navy Yard, NY while undergoing repairs to the outboard delivery pipe.
15 Nov: In dry dock for cleaning and repairs related to sinking and changes to the turning gear of the turrets.
BEF 26 Nov: Court of inquiry called to fix the responsibility for sinking.
3 Dec: Leaves dry dock.
20 Dec: Due to "international complications" ordered to complete repairs prior to Jan 1, 1897 and proceed to Hampton Roads, VA to join the fleet.

1897

10 Jan: Ordered to proceed to Galveston to receive silver service on Feb. 16 following fleet blockading maneuvers off Charleston in the first week of February.
8:00 am, 9 Feb: Departs New York for Galveston, TX.
4 pm, 16 Feb: Arrives at Galveston, TX. Grounds on mud bank on south side of Bolivar Roads. Comes off at next tide. Pilot assumes responsibility.
17 Feb: Gov. Culberson of Texas visits the USS Texas at Galveston.
19 Feb: Presentation of silver service from State of Texas on the plaza of the Beach Hotel at Galveston, TX.
21 Feb: Relocates three miles outside the Bolivar Roads jetties at Galveston, TX.
10:00, 24 Feb: Departs Galveston, TX for New Orleans, LA.
26 Feb: Arrives in New Orleans, LA for Mardi Gras celebration.
11 Mar: Departs New Orleans, LA with USS Maine for Port Royal, SC. Loses anchor in Mississippi River.
16 Mar: Arrives at Port Royal, SC with Maine.
3 Apr: Departs Port Royal, SC with the Maine to join Adm. Bunce's squadron at Hampton Roads, VA.
5 Apr: Arrives at Newport News, VA.
9 Apr: Departs Newport News, VA, arrives Fort Monroe, VA.
19 Apr: Departs Fort Monroe, VA.
20 Apr: Arrives Tompkinsville, NY.
25 Apr: Departs Tompkinsville, NY for Grant's Tomb, NY.
27 Apr: Participates with fleet in Grant Day naval parade celebrations at the dedication of Grant's Tomb, NY.
28 Apr: Departs Grant's Tomb for Tompkinsville, NY.
10 May: Departs Tompkinsville, NY for Philadelphia, PA.
13 May: Arrives Philadelphia, PA.
15 May: Takes part in celebration for dedication of Washington Monument.
18 May: Departs Philadelphia, PA for Boston, MA.
23 May: Arrives Boston, MA
1 June: Marines from USS Texas participate in Memorial Day / Shaw 54th Mass Memorial Dedication in Boston, MA.
2 June: Ordered by Asst. SecNav Roosevelt to Old Point Comfort, Hampton Roads, VA to exhibit machinery to the Railroad Master Mechanics annual convention on June 7-15th.
4 June: Departs Boston, MA for Newport News, VA.
7 June: Arrives Newport News, VA.
9 June: Removal of the bow and stern torpedo tubes ordered.
10 June: Departs Newport News, VA, arrives Fort Monroe, Va.
15 June: Richmond loving cup presented to the USS Texas. Ordered to Norfolk Navy Yard, VA.
15-17 June: Bow and stern torpedo tubes dismounted and delivered ashore. Bow tube port covered, stern tube port hatch fixed closed.
30 June: Departs Hampton Roads, VA for Tompkinsville, NY.
4 July: Arrives Tompkinsville, NY.
13 July: Departs Tompkinsville, NY, arrives Brooklyn Navy Yard, NY.
14 July (and intermittingly through 12 Aug): Brooklyn Navy Yard, NY. Right aiming hood of aft turret and left hood of forward turret altered to equip them with telescopic sights similar to existing sights in primary hoods.
23 July: Departs Brooklyn Navy Yard, NY, arrives Tompkinsville, NY.
24 July: Departs Tompkinsville, NY for Fisher's Island, NY.
25 July: Arrives Fisher's Island, Long Island Sound, NY for fleet maneuvers with the USS New Hampshire of the Naval Militia of New York (25-30 July).
28 July: Departs Fisher's Island, NY for Gravesend Bay, NY.
29 July: Arrives Gravesend Bay, NY.
30 July: Off New York. Conducts searchlight exercises with fleet.
31 July: Departs Gravesend Bay, NY. Arrives with fleet at Fort Hamilton, NY(?). Inspected by Asst. SecNav Roosevelt. Arrives Tompkinsville, NY. Departs Tompkinsville, NY, arrives Brooklyn Navy Yard, NY.
2 Aug: At Brooklyn Navy Yard, NY for repairs to main gun system.
12 Aug: Departs Brooklyn Navy Yard, NY for Provincetown, MA.
14 Aug: Arrives Provincetown, MA, departs for Portsmouth, NH to participate in fleet drills and evolutions.
16 Aug: Arrives Portsmouth, NH, departs for Portland, ME participating in fleet drills and evolutions.
23 Aug: Departs Portland, ME for Bar Harbor, ME participating in fleet drills and evolutions.
24 Aug: Arrives Bar Harbor, ME participating in fleet drills and evolutions.
31 Aug: Departs Bar Harbor, ME for Hampton Roads, VA.
3 Sept: Arrives Hampton Roads, VA, departs for Newport News, VA.
4 Sept: Arrives Newport News, VA.
6 Sept: Departs Newport News, VA, arrives Southern Drill Grounds.
12 Sept: Departs Southern Drill Grounds, arrives Hampton Roads, VA.
15 Sept: Departs Hampton Roads, VA for Tompkinsville, NY.
16 Sept: Arrives Tompkinsville, NY. Departs Tompkinsville, NY, arrives Brooklyn Navy Yard, NY.
25 Sept: Enters timber dry dock at Brooklyn Navy Yard, NY to clean and paint hull, work on main gun machinery, repair propellers and shafts, and outboard delivery pipes. Battle hatches near main guns probably installed at this time.
29 Sept: Moved from dry dock to Cobb Dock at Brooklyn Navy Yard, NY to have bow and stern torpedo outfits removed.
4 Oct: Ordered to join squadron and to participate in centenary celebration at Boston, MA of the launching of the USS Constitution.
9 Oct: Departs Brooklyn Navy Yard, NY for Provincetown, MA to await North Atlantic Squadron.
10 Oct: Arrives Provincetown, MA.
14 Oct: Departs Provincetown, MA, arrives Boston, MA.
17 Oct: Takes part in centenary celebration at Boston, MA of the launching of the USS Constitution with North Atlantic Squadron.
18 Oct: Boston Harbor, MA. Capt. W. C. Wise relieved by Capt. John W. Philip.
22 Oct: Boiler of USS Texas' steam launch explodes alongside ship in Boston Harbor, MA. Departs Boston, MA for Tompkinsville, NY.
24 Oct: Arrives with White Squadron at Tompkinsville, NY.
12 Nov: Departs Tompkinsville, NY, arrives Northern Drill Grounds.
16 Nov: Departs Northern Drill Grounds, arrives Tompkinsville, NY.
18 Nov: Target practice off Tompkinsville, NY. Salutes Commodore Dewey on the USS Iowa.
20 Nov: Departs Tompkinsville, NY, arrives Brooklyn Navy Yard, NY.
26 Nov: Takes part in Thanksgiving celebration at Brooklyn Navy Yard, NY.

"OLD HOODOO": THE BATTLESHIP TEXAS

19 Dec: Undergoing repairs at Brooklyn Navy Yard, NY. Articles of War read.

1898
15 Jan: Work completed at Brooklyn Navy Yard, NY. Departs New York at 2 pm for the Chesapeake Capes to join North Atlantic Squadron bound for the southern training area.
16 Jan: Passed out Sandy Hook with USS Massachusetts to join fleet assembling at Hampton Roads, VA. Fleet is to proceed to Southern Drill Grounds off Key West, FL. Fleet ordered to apprehend filibusters off coast of Florida and be available should a "situation" arise.
18 Jan: Arrives Cape Fear, NC.
20 Jan: Departs Cape Fear, NC for Key West, FL.
23 Jan: Arrives Key West, FL.
24 Jan: Departs Key West, FL, off Jacksonville, FL.
25 Jan: Arrives with fleet for maneuvers off Dry Tortugas, FL.
27 Jan: Off Dry Tortugas, FL.
29 Jan: Ordered to proceed to New Orleans, LA after repairs to meet the USS Maine (currently at Havana, Cuba).
29 Jan: Arrives off Key West, FL.
9 Feb: Maneuvers at Dry Tortugas, FL.
12 Feb: Departs Dry Tortugas, FL for Galveston, TX.
15 Feb: Arrives with Cruiser USS Nashville at Galveston, TX from the Dry Tortugas, FL.
17 Feb: While at Galveston, TX receives word of the destruction of the USS Maine.
23 Feb: Departs Galveston, TX for Dry Tortugas, FL.
26 Feb: Arrives Dry Tortugas, FL.
21 Mar: Departs Dry Tortugas, FL for Hampton Roads, VA.
24 Mar: Arrives in Hampton Roads, VA from Dry Tortugas, FL.
25 Mar: Departs Hampton Roads, VA, arrives Newport News, VA. Departs Newport News for Tompkinsville, NY.
26 Mar: Arrives Tompkinsville, NY.
27 Mar: Departs Tompkinsville, NY, arrives Brooklyn Navy Yard, NY.
6 Apr: Departs Brooklyn Navy Yard, NY for Hampton Roads, VA.
7 Apr: Arrives Hampton Roads, VA.
24 Apr: Spanish-American War begins.
13 May: Departs Hampton Roads, VA for Key West, FL.
18 May: Arrives Key West, FL.
19 May: Departs Key West, FL for Cienfuegos, Cuba. Strikes uncharted reef. USS Iowa also strikes same reef.
21 May: Arrives off Cienfuegos, Cuba.
24 May: Departs Cienfuegos, Cuba for Santiago, Cuba.
27 May: Arrives off Santiago, Cuba to begin blockade duty.
4 June: Accidental discharge of starboard 12" gun.
6 June: Bombards forts at mouth of Santiago Bay.
11 June: Departs Santiago, Cuba, arrives Guantanamo Bay, Cuba for reconnaissance. Engaged Spanish troops ashore, in support of Marine landing. Departs Guantanamo, Cuba and returns to Santiago, Cuba.
12 June: Departs Santiago, Cuba, arrives Guantanamo Bay, Cuba. Departs Guantanamo Bay, Cuba, arrives Santiago, Cuba.
13 June: Departs Santiago, Cuba, arrives Guantanamo Bay, Cuba. Departs Guantanamo Bay, Cuba, arrives Santiago, Cuba.
15 June: Departs Santiago, Cuba, arrives Guantanamo Bay, Cuba.
1400-1516 hrs, 15 June: Shore bombardment of the fort on Cayo del Tore with USS Marblehead in support of Marine shore operations at Caimanera, Guantanamo Bay, Cuba.
15 June: Departs Guantanamo Bay, Cuba, arrives Santiago, Cuba.
16 June: Bombards Socapa Battery at Santiago, Cuba.
17 June: Bombards Somervelos Battery at Santiago, Cuba.
22 June: Bombards Socapa Battery at Santiago, Cuba. Struck by Spanish 6.3" shell, killing seaman F.J. Blakley.
23 June: Departs Santiago, Cuba, arrives Guantanamo Bay, Cuba. Departs Guantanamo Bay, Cuba, arrives Santiago, Cuba.
29 June: Departs Santiago, Cuba, arrives Guantanamo Bay, Cuba. Departs Guantanamo Bay, Cuba, arrives Santiago, Cuba.
30 June: Departs Santiago, Cuba, arrives Guantanamo Bay, Cuba. Departs Guantanamo Bay, Cuba, arrives Santiago, Cuba.
2 July: Bombards Socapa Battery at Santiago, Cuba.
3 July: Participates in naval Battle of Santiago with Flying Squadron. Spanish cruisers Cristobal Colon, Infanta Maria Teresa, Almirante Oquendo, and Viscaya as well as Furor and Pluton destroyed.
4-5 July: Engages Spanish cruiser Reina Mercedes during her nocturnal attempt to block mouth of Santiago harbor. Reina Mercedes runs aground out of position and surrenders to USS Massachusetts and USS Texas.
10 July: Bombards city of Santiago, Cuba.
12 July: Departs Santiago, Cuba, arrives Rio Tarquina, Cuba.
13 July: Departs Rio Tarquina, Cuba, arrives Santiago, Cuba. Departs Santiago, Cuba, arrives Guantanamo, Cuba.
25 July: Departs Guantanamo, Cuba for Brooklyn Navy Yard, NY.
31 July: Arrives Brooklyn Navy Yard, NY.
19 Aug: Departs Brooklyn Navy Yard, NY, arrives Tompkinsville, NY.
4 Sept: Tompkinsville, NY. Capt. John W. Philip relieved by Capt. Charles D. Sigsbee.
8 Sept: Departs Tompkinsville, NY, arrives Brooklyn Navy Yard, NY.
10 Oct: Departs Brooklyn Navy Yard, NY, arrives Tompkinsville, NY.
20 Oct: Departs Tompkinsville, NY for Philadelphia, PA.
22 Oct: Arrives Philadelphia, PA to participate in the Peace Jubilee.
1 Nov: Departs Philadelphia, PA for Tompkinsville, NY.
3 Nov: Arrives Tompkinsville, NY.
11 Nov: Departs Tompkinsville, NY, arrives Brooklyn Navy Yard, NY.
24 Nov: Departs Brooklyn Navy Yard, NY, arrives Tompkinsville, NY.
1 Dec: Departs Tompkinsville, NY for Hampton Roads, VA.
2 Dec: Arrives Hampton Roads, VA.
14 Dec: Departs Hampton Roads, VA for Havana, Cuba.
17 Dec: Arrives Havana, Cuba.

1899

9 Feb: Departs Havana, Cuba for Galveston, TX.
13 Feb: Arrives Galveston, TX.
17 Feb: Departs Galveston, TX for Havana, Cuba.
20 Feb: Arrives Havana, Cuba.
10 Mar: Departs Havana, Cuba for Cienfuegos, Cuba.
13 Mar: Arrives Cienfuegos, Cuba.
16 Mar: Departs Cienfuegos, Cuba for Guantanamo Bay, Cuba.
18 Mar: Arrives Guantanamo Bay, Cuba.
25 Mar: Departs Guantanamo Bay, Cuba for Kingston, Jamaica, cruising with the Atlantic Fleet.
26 Mar: Arrives Kingston, Jamaica.
31 Mar: Departs Kingston, Jamaica for La Guaira, Venezuela.
4 Apr: Arrives La Guaira, Venezuela.
7 Apr: Departs La Guaira, Venezuela for Trinidad, British West Indies.
9 Apr: Arrives Trinidad, British West Indies.
12 Apr: Departs Trinidad, British West Indies for Bridgetown, Barbados.
13 Apr: Arrives Bridgetown, Barbados.
16 Apr: Departs Bridgetown, Barbados for Port Castries, St. Lucia.
17 Apr: Arrives Port Castries, St. Lucia.
21 Apr: Departs Port Castries, St. Lucia, arrives St. Pierre, Martinique.
24 Apr: Departs St. Pierre, Martinique for San Juan, Puerto Rico.
25 Apr: Arrives San Juan, Puerto Rico.
26 Apr: Departs Puerto Rico for Tompkinsville, NY.
2 May: Arrives Tompkinsville, NY.
9 May: Departs Tompkinsville, NY, arrives Brooklyn Navy Yard, NY.
28 May: Departs Brooklyn Navy Yard, NY for Newport, RI.
29 May: Arrives Newport, RI.
15 June: Departs Newport, RI for Boston, MA.
16 June: Arrives Boston, MA.
22 June: Departs Boston, MA for Newport, RI.
23 June: Arrives Newport, RI.
7 July: Departs Newport, RI for Rockport, MA with North Atlantic Squadron.
8 July: Arrives Rockport, MA with North Atlantic Squadron.
9 July: Departs Rockport, MA, arrives Portsmouth, NH with North Atlantic Squadron.
12 July: Departs Portsmouth, NH, arrives Portland, ME with North Atlantic Squadron.
16 July: Departs Portland, ME, arrives Boothbay, ME with North Atlantic Squadron.
17 July: Departs Boothbay, ME for Newport, RI for squadron evolutions.
20 July: Arrives Newport, RI.
4 Aug: Departs Newport, RI for Rockland, ME.
6 Aug: Arrives Rockland, ME.
7 Aug: Departs Rockland, ME for Bar Harbor, ME.
8 Aug: Arrives Bar Harbor, ME.
13 Aug: Departs Bar Harbor, ME for Belfast, ME.
14 Aug: Arrives Belfast, ME.
17 Aug: Departs Belfast, ME, arrives Northport, ME.
18 Aug: Departs Northport, ME, arrives Castine, ME.
19 Aug: Departs Castine, ME, arrives Rockland, ME.
20 Aug: Departs Rockland, ME for Newport, RI.
21 Aug: Arrives Newport, RI.
25 Aug: Record target practice off Newport, RI.
27 Aug: Arrives Newport, RI.
1 Sept: Departs Newport, RI for Philadelphia, PA
3 Sept: Arrives Philadelphia, PA.
15 Sept: Departs Philadelphia, PA for Tompkinsville, NY.
16 Sept: Arrives Tompkinsville, NY.
29 Sept: Departs Tompkinsville, NY, arrives North River, NY.
3 Oct: Departs North River, NY for Hampton Roads, VA.
5 Oct: Arrives Hampton Roads, VA.
13 Oct: Departs Hampton Roads, VA for Norfolk Navy Yard. Destroys wreck off Cape Hatteras.
16 Oct: Arrives Norfolk Navy Yard.
13 Nov: Departs Norfolk Navy Yard, arrives Hampton Roads, VA.
14 Nov: Departs Hampton Roads, VA for Boston, MA.
16 Nov: Arrives Boston, MA.
22 Nov: Departs Boston, MA for Gloucester, MA. Duty in connection with trial of USS Kentucky.
23 Nov: Arrives Gloucester, MA.
24 Nov: Departs Gloucester, MA for Newport, RI. Stakeboat for USS Kentucky.
25 Nov: Arrives Newport, RI. Departs Newport, RI for Hampton Roads, VA.
27 Nov: Arrives Hampton Roads, VA.
28 Nov: Departs Hampton Roads, VA for Brunswick, GA.
30 Nov: Arrives Brunswick, GA.
5 Dec: Departs Brunswick, GA for Hampton Roads, VA.
7 Dec: Arrives Hampton Roads, VA. Target practice.
13 Dec: Departs Hampton Roads, VA for Havana, Cuba.
17 Dec: Arrives Havana, Cuba to take on board remains of USS Maine dead.
21 Dec: Departs Havana, Cuba for Newport News, VA.
23 Dec: Arrives Newport News, VA to disembark remains of USS Maine dead.

27 Dec: Departs Newport News, VA, arrives Hampton Roads, VA.
30 Dec: Departs Hampton Roads, VA for Brooklyn Navy Yard, NY.

1900
2 Jan: Arrives Brooklyn Navy Yard, NY.
22 Jan: Brooklyn Navy Yard, NY. Capt. Charles D. Sigsbee relieved by Capt. W. C. Gibson.
26 Jan: Departs Brooklyn Navy Yard, NY, arrives Tompkinsville, NY.
27 Jan: Departs Tompkinsville, NY, arrives Norton's Point, NY.
28 Jan: Departs Norton's Point, NY for San Juan, Puerto Rico.
3 Feb: Arrives San Juan, Puerto Rico.
12 Feb: Departs San Juan, Puerto Rico, arrives Culebra Island, Puerto Rico.
15 Feb: Departs Culebra Island, Puerto Rico.
19 Feb: Arrives Key West, FL.
20 Feb: Departs Key West, FL for New Orleans, LA.
24 Feb: Arrives New Orleans, LA.
4 Mar: Departs New Orleans, LA for Key West, FL.
7 Mar: Arrives Key West, FL.
11 Mar: Departs Key West, FL for Havana, Cuba.
12 Mar: Arrives Havana, Cuba.
15 Mar: Departs Havana, Cuba for Galveston, TX.
18 Mar: Arrives Galveston, TX.
27 Mar: Departs Galveston, TX for Pensacola, FL.
30 Mar: Arrives Pensacola, FL.
4 Apr: Departs Pensacola, FL.
6 Apr: Arrives Key West, FL. Departs for Bermuda.
12 Apr: Arrives Bermuda.
21 Apr: Departs Bermuda for Samana Bay, Santo Domingo.
25 Apr: Arrives Samana Bay, Santo Domingo.
26 Apr: Departs Samana Bay, Santo Domingo for San Juan, Puerto Rico.
27 Apr: Arrives San Juan, Puerto Rico.
1 May: Departs San Juan, Puerto Rico for Hampton Roads, VA.
6 May: Arrives Hampton Roads, VA.
17 May: Departs Hampton Roads, VA for Tompkinsville, NY.
18 May: Arrives Tompkinsville, NY.
19 May: Departs Tompkinsville, NY, arrives Brooklyn Navy Yard, NY.
30 May: Departs Brooklyn Navy Yard, NY, arrives North River, NY, departs for Newport, RI.
31 May: Arrives Newport, RI.
13 June: Departs Newport, RI for Boston, MA.
14 June: Arrives Boston, MA.
25 June: Departs Boston, MA for Newport, RI.
26 June: Arrives Newport, RI.
NOTE: Gap in record of movements. Also note that Capt. M.R.S. Mackenzie is listed as commanding w/o record date of change of command.
10 July: Arrives Jamestown, VA.
23 July: Departs Jamestown, VA for New London, CT.
24 July: Arrives New London, CT.
29 July: Departs New London, CT, arrives Gardiners Bay.
1 Aug: Departs Gardiners Bay for Portland, ME.
2 Aug: Arrives Portland, ME.
8 Aug: Departs Portland, ME, arrives Belfast, ME.
11 Aug: Departs Belfast, ME, arrives Bath, ME.
15 Aug: Departs Bath, ME for Gloucester, MA.
18 Aug: Arrives Gloucester, MA.
19 Aug: Departs Gloucester, MA, arrives Boston, MA.
27 Aug: Departs Boston, MA to act as stakeboat for USS Alabama's trials.
29 Aug: Arrives Boston, MA.
2 Sept: Departs Boston, MA for Bar Harbor, ME.
3 Sept: Arrives Bar Harbor, ME.
13 Sept: Departs Bar Harbor, ME for Portsmouth, NH.
14 Sept: Arrives Portsmouth, NH.
20 Sept: Departs Portsmouth, NH for Newport, RI.
21 Sept: Arrives Newport, RI.
24 Sept: Departs for maneuvers with North Atlantic Squadron then returns to Newport, RI.
25 Sept: Departs for maneuvers with North Atlantic Squadron off Newport, RI.
26 Sept: Arrives Newport, RI. Departs for Norfolk, VA.
28 Sept: Arrives Norfolk Navy Yard, VA for major overhaul.
3 Nov: Decommissioned for repairs at Norfolk. (This work probably included the removal of the broadside torpedo tubes as well as the extension and alterations to the masts, and the extension of the funnel.)

1901
Norfolk Navy Yard. Out of commission.

1902
3 Nov: Re-commissioned, Capt. William T. Swinburne, commanding.
28 Nov: Departs Norfolk Navy Yard for trial speed run and test of battery following major refit.
1 Dec: Arrives Norfolk Navy Yard.
11 Dec: Departs Norfolk Navy Yard for Culebra Island, Puerto Rico to join fleet.

16 Dec: Arrives off Culebra Island, Puerto Rico.
17 Dec: Participates in fleet maneuvers off Culebra Island, Puerto Rico.
20 Dec: Enters Great Harbor, Culebra Island, Puerto Rico.
21 Dec: Departs Great Harbor, Culebra Island, Puerto Rico for Pointe a Pitre, Guadeloupe.
22 Dec: Arrives Pointe a Pitre, Guadeloupe.
27 Dec: Departs Pointe a Pitre, Guadeloupe for Culebra Island, Puerto Rico.
29 Dec: Arrives Culebra Island, Puerto Rico to rejoin fleet then proceeds to Great Harbor, Culebra Island, Puerto Rico for coal.
30 Dec: Departs Great Harbor, Culebra Island, Puerto Rico and rejoins fleet off Culebra Island, Puerto Rico.
31 Dec: Participates in fleet maneuvers off Culebra Island, Puerto Rico.

1903

1 Jan: Participates in fleet maneuvers off Culebra Island, Puerto Rico.
2 Jan: Participates in fleet duties off Culebra Island, Puerto Rico.
27 Jan: Departs Culebra Island, Puerto Rico, arrives San Juan, Puerto Rico.
30 Jan: Departs San Juan, Puerto Rico, arrives Culebra Island, Puerto Rico.
1 Feb: Departs Culebra Island, Puerto Rico for Basseterre, St. Kitts.
2 Feb: Arrives Basseterre, St. Kitts.
5 Feb: Departs Basseterre, St. Kitts for Ponce, Puerto Rico.
6 Feb: Arrives Ponce, Puerto Rico.
11 Feb: Departs Ponce, Puerto Rico for New Orleans, LA.
19 Feb: Arrives New Orleans, LA.
27 Feb: Departs New Orleans, LA for Pensacola, FL.
28 Feb: Arrives Pensacola, FL.
23 Mar: Departs Pensacola, FL for target practice.
28 Mar: Returns to Pensacola, FL.
15 Apr: Departs Pensacola, FL for Hampton Roads, VA.
20 Apr: Arrives Hampton Roads, VA.
22 Apr: Departs Hampton Roads, VA, arrives Lambert's Point, VA.
27 Apr: Departs Lambert's Point, VA, arrives Hampton Roads, VA.
28 Apr: Departs Hampton Roads, VA, arrives Southern Drill Grounds, VA.
30 Apr: Departs Southern Drill Grounds, VA, arrives Hampton Roads, VA.
1 May: Departs Hampton Roads, VA, arrives Norfolk Navy Yard, VA. Flagship of Coast Squadron, North Atlantic Fleet (through 1905).
19 May: Departs Norfolk Navy Yard, VA, arrives Newport News, Va.
24 May: Departs Newport News, VA, arrives Annapolis, MD.
8 June: Departs Annapolis, MD, arrives Solomon's Island, Patuxent River, MD.
12 June: Departs Solomon's Island, Patuxent River, MD, arrives Newport News, VA.
18 June: Departs Newport News, VA for Boston, MA.
21 June: Arrives Boston, MA.
26 June: Departs Boston, MA for Orient Point, NY.
27 June: Arrives Orient Point, NY.
29 June: Departs Hampton Roads, VA for New London, CN.
1 July: Arrives New London, CN.
19 July: Departs New London, CN, arrives Horton's Point, NY. Departs Horton's Point, NY, arrives Falkner Island, NY(?).
20 July: Departs Falkner Island, NY(?), arrives Horton's Point, NY. Departs Horton's Point, NY, arrives Falkner Island, NY(?).
21 July: Departs Falkner Island, NY(?), arrives New London, CN.
22 July: Departs New London, CN, arrives New London, CN.
26 July: Departs New London, CN, arrives off Fisher's Island, CN(?). Departs Fisher's Island, CN(?), arrives New London, CN.
27 July: Departs New London, CN, arrives New London, CN.
28 July: Departs New London, CN, arrives New London, CN.
3 Aug: Departs New London, CN, arrives Fort Pond Bay, CN.
5 Aug: Departs Fort Pond Bay, CN, arrives New London, CN.
8 Aug: Departs New London, CN, arrives Fort Pond Bay, CN.
10 Aug: Departs Fort Pond Bay, CN, arrives New London, CN.
15 Aug: Departs New London, CN, arrives Bradford, RI.
16 Aug: Departs Bradford, RI for St. Mary, MD.
20 Aug: Arrives St. Mary, MD.
24 Aug: Departs St. Mary, MD, arrives Solomon's Island, MD(?).
30 Aug: Departs Solomon's Island, MD(?) for Annapolis, MD. Midshipmen returned to the Naval Academy.
1 Sept: Departs Annapolis, MD, arrives Old Point Comfort, VA.
3 Sept: Departs Old Point Comfort, VA for Bradford, RI.
5 Sept: Arrives Bradford, RI.
7 Sept: Departs Bradford, RI, arrives Woods Hole, MA.
11 Sept: Departs Woods Hole, MA, arrives at target range No. 1, south of Martha's Vineyard.
23 Sept: Departs target range No. 1 for Tompkinsville, NY.
24 Sept: Arrives Tompkinsville, NY. Arrives Brooklyn Navy Yard, NY for repairs.

1904

7 Jan: Departs Brooklyn Navy Yard, NY for Hampton Roads, VA.
8 Jan: Arrives Hampton Roads, VA.
9 Jan: Departs Hampton Roads, VA for Key West, FL.
13 Jan: Arrives Key West, FL.
25 Jan: Departs Key West, FL for Guantanamo Bay, Cuba.
28 Jan: Arrives Guantanamo Bay, Cuba.
22 Mar: Departs Guantanamo Bay, Cuba for Key West, FL.
25 Mar: Arrives Key West, FL.
29 Mar: Departs Key West, FL for Pensacola, FL.

31 Mar: Arrives Pensacola, FL.
1 Apr-7 Apr: Conducts target practice at target range off Pensacola, FL.
10 Apr: Departs Pensacola, FL for Key West, FL.
12 Apr: Arrives Key West, FL.
14 Apr: Departs Key West, FL for Norfolk, VA.
18 Apr: Arrives Norfolk, VA.
22 Apr: Departs Norfolk, VA, arrives Newport New, VA.
24 Apr: Departs Newport News, VA, arrives Hampton Roads, VA.
9 May: Departs Hampton Roads, VA, arrives Annapolis, MD.
11 May: Departs Annapolis, MD for tactical data trial at Tangier Island trial course.
12 May: Arrives Annapolis, MD.
5 June: Departs Annapolis, MD for Solomons, MD.
7 June: Arrives Solomons, MD.
11 June: Departs Solomons, MD for joint exercises.
17 June-24 June: Off Baltimore, MD; Hampton Roads, VA; the mouth of the Potomac, VA; and Newport News, VA.
29 June: Arrives Rockland, ME.
31 June: Departs Rockland, ME for East Lamoine, ME.
1 Aug: Arrives Lamoine, ME.
2 Aug: Departs Lamoine, ME, arrives Rockland, ME.
14 Aug: Departs Rockland, ME for New London, CN.
16 Aug: Arrives New London, CN.
24 Aug: Departs New London, CN for Solomons, MD.
26 Aug: Arrives Solomons, MD.
30 Aug: Departs Solomons, MD, arrives Annapolis, MD.
31 Aug: Departs Annapolis, MD for Newport News, VA.
1 Sept: Arrives Newport News, VA for Perry Day Celebration.
2 Sept: Departs Newport News, VA, arrives Lynnhaven, VA.
3 Sept: Departs Lynnhaven, VA for Provincetown, MA.
5 Sept: Arrives Provincetown, MA.
9 Sept: Departs Provincetown, MA for Newport, RI.
10 Sept: Arrives Newport, RI.
11 Sept: Departs Newport, RI, arrives Bradford, RI.
12 Sept: Departs Bradford, RI, arrives at target grounds in Cape Cod Bay, MA.
23 Sept: Departs Cape Cod Bay, MA for Norfolk, VA.
25 Sept: Arrives Norfolk, VA for repairs.
2 Nov: Departs Norfolk, VA for Tompkinsville, NY.
3 Nov: Arrives Tompkinsville, NY.
4 Nov: Departs Tompkinsville, NY, arrives Brooklyn Navy Yard, NY for docking.
14 Nov: Departs Brooklyn Navy Yard, NY for Newport News, VA.
15 Nov: Arrives Newport News, VA to assemble Coast Squadron.
26 Nov: Departs Newport News, VA for Hatteras Cove, NC.
27 Nov: Arrives Hatteras Cove, NC, departs and arrives Lookout Bight, NC.
28 Nov: Departs Lookout Bight, NC for Charleston, SC.
29 Nov: Arrives Charleston, SC.
18 Dec-19 Dec: Cruising off Charleston, SC.

1905*
24 June: Departs Newport News, VA for Rockland, [ME?] to conduct summer cruise for midshipmen from US Naval Academy.
29-30 June: Arrives Rockland, [ME?]
5 Jul: Cruise in vicinity of Rockland, [ME?]
15-18 through 24 Aug: Arrives New London, CT and conducts cruises in vicinity.
24-25 Aug: Departs New London, CT for Solomons, MD.
30 Aug: Departs Solomons, MD for Annapolis, MD.
31 Aug: Arrives Annapolis, MD. Midshipmen disembarked.

*Author's Note: This is a partial record covering the period June 24, 1905 – August 31, 1905 based on excerpts found in the Annual Register of the US Naval Academy, 1904-1905. The complete "Summary of Service" record for the year 1905 has not been found.

1906
2 Jan-4 Jan: Cruising off Charleston, SC.
15 Jan-16 Jan: Cruising off Charleston, SC.
13 Feb: Departs Charleston, SC for Key West, FL. Destroys derelict schooner Sakata en route.
17 Feb: Arrives Key West, FL.
19 Feb: Departs Key West, FL for Pensacola, FL.
21 Feb: Arrives Pensacola, FL, departs for New Orleans, LA.
22 Feb: Arrives New Orleans, LA to participate in Mardi Gras celebrations.
1 Mar: Departs New Orleans, LA for Pensacola, FL.
3 Mar: Arrives Pensacola, FL.
22 Mar-24 Mar: Conducts target practice off Pensacola, FL.
2 Apr: Departs Pensacola, FL for target practice off Santa Rosa Island, FL.
3 Apr: Departs Santa Rosa Island, FL, returns to Pensacola, FL.
4 Apr: Departs Pensacola, FL for Key West, FL.
6 Apr: Arrives Key West, FL.
8 Apr: Departs Key West, FL for Charleston, SC.
10 Apr: Arrives Charleston, SC.
21 Apr: Departs Charleston, SC for Boston Navy Yard, MA. Searches for reported derelict vessel en route.

26 Apr: Arrives Boston Navy Yard, MA for repairs in preparation for being placed in reserve.
10 May: Departs Boston Navy Yard, MA for Norfolk Navy Yard, VA.
12 May: Arrives Norfolk Navy Yard, VA to be placed in reserve.
24 May: Norfolk Navy Yard. Placed in reserve.
26 Jun: Norfolk Navy Yard, VA. Capt. George A. Bicknell relieved of command by Capt. Charles P. Plunkett.
25 Aug: Norfolk Navy Yard, VA. Capt. Charles P. Plunkett relieved of command by Cmdr. George R. Clark.
29 Sept: Norfolk Navy Yard, VA. Placed in full commission for mission to deliver Marines to Cuba.
30 Sept: Departs Norfolk Navy Yard, VA, arrives Cape Henry, VA.
2 Oct: Departs Cape Henry, VA for Charleston, SC.
5 Oct: Arrives Charleston, SC.
6 Oct: Departs Charleston, SC for Havana, Cuba.
9 Oct: Arrives Havana, Cuba.
30 Oct: Departs Havana, Cuba with Marines. Bound for Hampton Roads, VA.
3 Nov: Arrives Hampton Roads, VA.
4 Nov: Departs Hampton Roads, VA, arrives Norfolk Navy Yard, VA to be placed in reserve.
9 Nov: Norfolk Navy Yard, VA. Placed in reserve.

1907
17 Aug: Norfolk Navy Yard, VA. Cmdr. George R. Clark relieved of command by Lt. Cmdr. Edward T. Witherspoon.
? Nov-? Dec: Hampton Roads, VA. Duty in connection with Jamestown Exposition.
2 Dec: Departs Hampton Roads, VA, arrives Norfolk Navy Yard to be placed out of commission.

1908
11 Jan: Norfolk Navy Yard, VA. Decommissioned.
1 Sep: Norfolk Navy Yard, VA. Placed in commission.
1- 26 Sept: Norfolk Navy Yard, VA. Fitting out as station ship.
26 Sept: Departs Norfolk Navy Yard, VA for Charleston, SC. Cmdr. William A Gill commanding.
29 Sept: Arrives Charleston, SC. Assigned to station ship duty at Charleston Navy Yard, SC.

1909
Charleston Navy Yard station ship.

1910
Jan-?: Charleston Navy Yard station ship.
?: Returned to Norfolk Navy Yard.

1911
11 Feb: Decommissioned at Norfolk Navy Yard.
15 Feb: Name changed to San Marcos.
Feb-Mar: Ship "cleared for action" in preparation for tests as gunnery target.
22 Mar: Sunk as target ship at lat. 37 43 10N, long. 76 05 00W off Tangier Island in Chesapeake Bay by 12" gunfire from the USS New Hampshire.
6 Apr: Used as target for torpedo tests by USS Flusser.
Late 1911: Proposed as target for aerial bombing tests.
10 Oct: Struck from Navy list.

1912
1912: "Standard" fully equipped battleship 90' cage mast erected on deck for gunnery damage trials.
21 Aug: Cage mast trials. 12" guns at 1000 yards fired from USS Tallahassee. Cage mast destroyed and removed.

1913
AFT 15 March: Proposed for use for erection of canvas target screens.

1917
Aug: Recognized as a "Hazard to Navigation."

1924
24 Sep: Placed on sale list.

1940
Freighter Lexington hits wreckage and sinks.

1944
Last portions of wreckage fully above water shot away during naval gunnery practice.

1949
Oyster boat T.H. Anderson hits wreckage and sinks.

1955
No portion of wreckage visible above water, even at low tide.

1959
Final attempt at demolition by U.S. Navy

Timeline Overview:

8 Aug 1886: Authorized.

1 June 1889: Keel laid.

28 June 1892: Launched.

15 Aug 1895: Commissioned.

1895-Feb 1897: Atlantic coast cruising.

Feb-May 1898: War preparations.

21 May-Aug 1898: US Flying Squadron off Cuba.

2 Dec 1898: Atlantic Fleet based at Hampton Roads. (Cruises to Cuba in 1898 and 1899.)

1901: Decommissioned for repairs at Norfolk.

3 Nov 1902: Re-commissioned.

1902-1905: Flagship of Atlantic Coast Squadron of Atlantic Fleet.

1905-1908: Atlantic Fleet.

1908-1910: Station ship at Charleston, SC.

11 Feb 1911: Decommissioned at Norfolk Navy Yard.

15 Feb 1911: Name changed to San Marcos.

10 Oct 1911: Decommissioned and struck from Navy list.

Mar 1911: Sunk as target ship off Tangier Island in Chesapeake Bay.

USS Texas Spanish-American War Ammunition Expenditures off Cuba:

Date:	12"	6"	6 pdr.	1 pdr.	37mm	Action:
June 4	1*					
June 6	21	63	125			Engaged forts at Morro Castle, Santiago Bay
June 12	0	1	10			Engaged troops at mouth of Guantanamo Bay
June 15	12	52	0			Engaged Caimanera fort, Guantanamo Bay
June 16	13	33	0			Engaged Socapa batteries, near Santiago Bay
June 17	0	17	24			Engaged Somervelos Battery near Santiago Bay
June 22	19	83	50	20		Engaged Socapa batteries near Santiago Bay
July 2	14	105	55			Engaged Socapa batteries near Santiago Bay
July 3	8	97	400	150	180	Naval Battle of Santiago
July 4-5	8	18	0			Engaged Reina Mercedes at Santiago Bay
July 10	6	3	0			Shelled city of Santiago
	101**	472	794	170	180	TOTAL FOR CUBAN CAMPAIGN

Main Battery (heavy and medium):	573**
Secondary battery:	794
Light guns:	350
Total rounds expended from ships cannons:	1717**
Number of engagements:	10

*Accidental Discharge due to short circuit in the electrical firing attachment. This occurred in the forward/port turret. - The danger of an accidental discharge was one of the arguments made 8 years earlier against the Texas's en echelon turret design. It was argued that an accidental discharge could occur when the gun was pointed at the superstructure with disastrous results. Fortunately, in this instance the gun was not pointed at the superstructure when it went off.

**Does not include the June 4 accidental discharge.

"OLD HOODOO": THE BATTLESHIP TEXAS

Date	Boilers	Water Expended last 24 hours	Distilled "	Remaining Noon	Coal Used Ton/lbs last 24 hours	Coal Remaining Ton/lbs Noon
June 1-2	4	2125	2800	4375	23t 2210lbs	614t 2230lbs
2-3	"	2525	2000	5050	24 740	590 1490
3-4		2125	1400	4525	22 1130	567 360
4-5		1825	2300	3800	23 180	544 180
5-6		2623	2000	4275	23 1980	520 440
6-7		1711	2800	3636	21 760	498 920
7-8		1913	2000	4725	20 1800	477 1360
8-9		1912	2000	4812	20 2100	456 1500
9-10		1600	1600	4900	21 1000	435 500
10-11		2271	2000	4900	29 1730	405 1010
11-12		1999	1200	4639	29 1000	506 10
12-13		1364	2000	3840	37 1620	638 630
13-14		2021	1400	4476	26 90	708 1240
14-15		2325	800	3855	22 1900	685 1580
15-16		1560	2000	2330	29 1290	656 1980
16-17		1745	2000	2770	20 990	635 1540
17-18		1700	570	3025	19 1800	615 1980
18-19		1700	2210	1995	22 1200	593 780
19-20		2090	2348	3702	22 1040	570 1980
20-21		1562	1140	3960	21 560	549 1420
21-22		1700	3310	3538	28 600	521 820
22-23		1800	2017	5148	31 1440	489 1620
23-24		1600	939	4396	31 2160	457 2000
24-25		1600	1965	5100	22 980	435 720
25-26		1800	2200	5500	25 1720	409 1240
26-27		2400	1700	4800	27 1680	381 1800
27-28		N/A	N/A	N/A	26 370	355 1430
28-29		1800	1605	4800	33 1640	321 2030
29-30		1800	2128	5160	41 880	532 2050
30- 01	4	2000	1800	4900	29 60	724 1870
Jul 01-02	4	1700	1200	4600	30 1440	693 1670
02-03		1900	1200	3613	31 2060	661 1850
03-04		1500	2267	4380	35 1840	621 0
04-05		2000	2145	4525	23 460	602 1790
05-06		2200	1830	4156	23 1660	579 130
06-07		1656	700	3200	24 200	554 2170
07-08	4	1800	600	2000	20 1420	534 1750
08-09	3	1200	2100	2900	18 680	516 1070
09-10		1600	1600	3000	18 1640	497 1690
10-11		1200	1600	3400	20 1000	477 670
11-12		N/A	N/A	N./A	35? 1160	449 750
12-13		1400	1100	3300	35 510	414 1240
13-14		1400	1600	3500	26 2100	387 1380
14-15	3	1500	1500	3900	28 610	359 770
15-16	1	1700	1700	3900	10 760	349 10
16-17		1500	1500	3900	10 1760	857 1610
17-18		1700	1600	3800	10 400	847 210
18-19		2300	2300	3800	10 1850	836 1600
19-20		1500	1600	3900	10 260	826 1340
20-21		2100	2300	4100	10 130	816 210
21-22		2600	2000	3500	10 810	806 400
22-23		1600	1600	3500	10 1560	795 1080
23-24		1500	1700	3700	11 440	784 640
24-25	1	1500	2000	4200	12 1560	771 1320
25-26	4	1800	2600	4800	63 1780	707 1280
26-27		1900	1400	4300	91 520	616 1260
27-28		2100	1800	4000	90 330	526 930
28-29		2200	2600	4400	100 1640	425 1530
29-30		2200	2300	4500	102 2200	322 1570

Example of Combat Patrol Expenditure of Coal per Mile:

27th	236 miles	91 tons	.6 current
28th	235.3 miles	100 tons	.4 current
29th	271 miles	102	.7 current

Example of Combat Patrol Expenditure of Coal per Time:

4.17 tons / hour = 33 pounds / minute

APPENDIX VI: USS TEXAS AT SANTIAGO DECK LOGS
JUNE 1, 1898 – JULY 16, 1898

Wednesday June 1, 1898
Commences and to 4 A.M. Clear and pleasant. Light airs to light breezes from north. In column natural order, standing back and forth in front of entrance to harbor, following movements of flagship. Temperature of coal bunkers normal. At steam pressure 140 lbs, revs stbd 21.9, port 21.1. - H.A. Bispham, Lieutenant, U.S.N.

4 to 8 A.M. Clear and warm. Rain squalls around the horizon. Light airs from N.E. to north. At 4.30 sighted three steamers at S'd and E'd and reported them to flagship. At 6.00, the New York, flying Admiral Sampson's flag, the Oregon, and the Mayflower came in. There was heavy gun firing on shore. Steam four boilers. Lying off Santiago using engines occasionally. Inspected coal bunkers. Signals per record. - Mark L. Bristol, Lieutenant, U.S.N.

8 A.M. to Mer. Partly cloudy and warm. Calm to light variable breezes. Steaming across the harbor and back to rest of watch. The Brooklyn signaled "An attempt will be made to sink the Merrimac in entrance to-night. Five volunteers enlisted men, one from each ship requested" Peter O'Boyle selected. By order of the Commanding Officer released H. Hansen (A Sea) adn M.J. Mulrey (A 2 Cl) and confined for two days in solitary confinement on bread and water Wm.Trapp ((Lds) and A Friesch (Prvb). Commanding Officer inflicted the following punishments P.J. Kenny (A2C) disrespect to an officer, and slow in obeying orders, 2 days solitary confinement on bread and water. By order of the Commanding Officer the acting appointment of J.S. Simmons (leox) was revoked, for inefficiency. Received in dept of S and A from U.S.S. Harvard, 311 1/4 lbs fresh meat. The Mayflower sent cutter ashore to entrance of harbor. The New York and Marblehead covered Vixen while last communicated with shore to westward of harbor. New York's steam launch dragging for cable to westward of entrance. Made continue reports at 12.00. Other signals as per record book. The torpedo boat Porter came in from E'd. Steam in four boilers. Avg pressure 139 lbs. Coal bunkers reported normal. Magazine temperatures as per list. - W.K. Gise, Ensign, U.S.N

Mer. to 4 P.M. Clear and warm weather. Heavy rain squalls on western horizon at intervals. Light breeze from South. Smooth sea. Ship stopped using engines at intervals to maintain position. Signals, at 12.35 from flag. "What is the name of the volunteer" Answered "Philip O'Boyle (SM2Cl) and there are many others on the Texas ready". At 12.45 to flag "Can Texas steam up to Merrimac and take those guns now" Flag answered "not yet". At 2.15 from "Send one division and 20 men to Merrimac, right away to trim coal" At 2.45 from flag, "Tel 8185-8105-9 22 At 2.30 " permission to move up to near X to land working party" Answered "granted". At 3.10 "I will have Merrimac's guns temporarily" At three 3.15 to flag. "Vessel to E'd". At 3.30 from flag, "Send mail from Harvard by 8.00 A.M. tomorrow." Sighted two steamers to E'd, appearing to be U.S.N. vessels. - Harry Phelps, Lieutenant, U.S.N.

4 to 6 P.M. Cloudy but pleasant. Gentle breeze from S.W. At 4.15 flagship made signal to form column. Vixen came within hail of this ship and transferred to her "Philip O'Boyle (GM2Cl) volunteer on service to sink Merrimac to-night. Squadron formed column heading to westward, slow speed, flagship leading. At end of watch standing to westward, slow speed, about 4 miles off entrance to Santiago Harbor. - F.J. Haeseler, Lieutenant U.S.N.

6 to 8 P.M. Cloudy, pleasant weather. Gentle breeze from N.E. shifting to S.W. in fresh squall last hour, accompanied by heavy rain and lightning. Lying off the entrance, Brooklyn leading column westwards opening to double distance. Temperature of coal bunkers normal. - H.A. Bispham, Lieutenant, U.S.N.

8 P.M. to Mid. Cloudy. Light breezes from North. Steaming slowly back and forth before entrance to Santiago in column double distance. Steam four boilers. Inspected coal bunkers and magazines. Mark Bristol, Lieutenant, U.S.N.

Thursday June 2, 1898
Commences and 4 A.M. Generally cloudy. Light airs from North. Steaming in column off Santiago. Four boilers. On pressure 137 lbs. Bunkers reported in normal condition. - W.K. Gise, Ensign U.S.N.

4 to 8 A.M. Fair and warm. Light breeze from various directions. Smooth sea. Steaming in column at steerage way under four boilers to and fro before entrance to port. At daylight sighted a steamer to W'd, and another E.by S. which came in and proved to be the cable steamer "Adria", no colors. The New York steamed off to W'd, apparently in chase of the steamer sighted to W'd. At 5.20 the fort to the E'd of Morro Castle fired four shots, which struck several miles inshore of squadron. At 7.30 sighted a steamer E.S.E. Signals as follows, At 6.00 from flags "Send mail to Harvard". At 5.00 to flag, "3720-40C" at 7.45 "3720-052". Coal bunkers reported in normal condition. Life buoys reported in good order. - Harry Phelps, Lieutenant U.S.N.

8 A.M. to Mer. Fair and warm. Light breeze from E.S.E. at 9.20 an English Tug flying Associated Press Flag came in from S.E. At 11.00 a torpedo boat came in from S.W. Steaming in column natural order, back and forth in front of Santiago Harbor, about 3 ½ miles distant At 11.00 the Harvard left the squadron, bound to the Eastward. Routine signals at 10.00 and noon. Signals as per record book. Our steam pressure 136 lbs, Revs stbd 28.5, port 37.8.- F.J. Haeseler, Lieutenant U.S.N.

Mer. to 4 P.M. Fair to cloudy. Light breeze from south and S.W. Lying to off harbor entrance. Signals as per signal record. Following "Massachusetts" in obedience to signal, the flagship having hauled ou t of position. At end of watch standing to the E'd. The "Oregon" and "Marblehead" stood to the E'd and S'd out of sight. Temperature of coal bunkers normal. Av. steam pressure 137 lbs, Av. no. of revs 22.2 stbd port 30.9. - H.A. Bispham, Lieutenant U.S.N.

4 to 6 P.M. Generally cloudy. Light breeze from S.W. Mustered at quarters at 5.00. Sent boat to flagship for P. O'Boyle (GM2cl). Steam from boilers. At end of watch taking position in blockade off Santiago. Signals as per record book. - Mark L. Bristol, Lieutenant U.S.N.

6 to 8 P.M. Partly cloudy and warm. Bright moonlight. Calms and westerly airs. Taking position in new blockade formation. Highest bunker temperature 110 degrees. Highest magazine temperature 108 degrees. (see list). Steam on four boilers av pres. - W.K. Gise, Ensign U.S.N.
8 P.M. to Mid Fair and pleasant weather. Bright moonlight. Light airs from N.E'd. Ship stopped, lying on blockade formation. Coal bunkers reported in normal condition.- Harry Phelps, Lieutenant U.S.N.

Friday, June 3, 1898
Commences and to 4 A.M. Fair and pleasant. Bright moonlight. Vessels of fleet lying in semi-circle, battle formation, blockading Santiago. At 2.45 the New York's steam launch came alongside, with Asst. Engr. R. K. Crank U.S.N. and 8 men of the Merrimac. At 3.00 the Merrimac started in for Santiago, as was fired on in the entrance at 3.15, and firing continued until 3.30 from the shore batteries at end of watch, lying with engines stopped about three miles off Santiago. - F.J. Haeseler, Lieutenant U.S.N.
4 to 8 A.M. Fair to cloudy, and warm. Light airs adn breeze from North first half . Stiff squall accompanied by heavy rain, wind, lightning and thunder come up from S.W., wind shifting to S.S.W. during third hour. Raining at end of watch. Moon set at 4.05. At daylight sighted the New York's steam launch standing to the E'd. Later launch put about, standing to the W'd. When off the entrance guns on W'n battery and along shore opened fire upon her. Launch continued to W'd uninjured, adn later stood off shore. Edged inshore a little adn launch came alongside. "New York" stood to W'd and picked up the launch. The St. Louis came in at 7.00 avg steam pressure Lbs av. revs Stbd Port. - H.A. Bispham, Lieutenant U.S.N.
8 A.M. to Mer. Clear and hot. Light breezes from East. Lying off and on the blockade station. The small boats of the enemy were seen moving around at the entrance to the harbor. The "Yankee" joined the fleet. Signals as per record. Steam from boilers. Inspected coal bunkers and magazines. The following by order of Commanding Officer, J. Simonson (Cox) disrated by Seaman., J.J. Bechtle rather to Coxswain, Wm Roff, (Sea) confined, 3 days solitary confinement on bread and water for disobedience of orders, adn insolence to P.O.: P. J. Kerrey (A 1 Cl) two days on bread and water for disrespect to an officer and slow in obeying orders. P.J. Kerry (A 1 cl) and F.J. Glazer, reported the expiration of their enlistments. - Mark L. Bristol, Lieutenant U.S.N.
Mer. to 4 P.M. Clear and warm. Light breeze from East. In obedience to orders of Commander in Chief, kept inside cable steamer "Adria" At 2.50 Spanish flag of truce boat "Ceolon", was met by U.S.S. Vixen, under flag of truce, and accompanied by U.S.S. New York. Signals as per record. Under steam four boilers, air pressure   lbs. Bunkers reported normal. Sighted masts asn smokestacks of sunken collier Merrimac. The U.S.S. Justin came in. Asst. Engr. R.K. Crank U.S.N. reported on board for duty. - W.K. Gise, Ensign U.S.N.
4 to 6P.M. Cloudy weather. Light breeze from East. Smooth sea. Lying by Cable steamer "Adria". Moving engines to keep position. At 5.00 mustered at quarters. At 6.00 started ahead full speed to resume blockading station. Signals at 5.30 from flag: "Coal vessels crew prisoners of war, two slightly wounded. All well." At 5.40 "Take blockading station." Repeated all signals. At 5.50 form flag: "Take blockading station opposite "Oregon". At 4.40 boat with flag of truce went back to port. - Harry Phelps, Lieutenant U.S.N.
6 to 8 P.M. Fair and pleasant. Calms, and light airs from N.N.E. Stood down to Westward, at at end of watch in position, blockade formation. Signals as per record book. - T.J. Haeseler, Lieutenant U.S.N.
8 P.M to Mid. Generally fair. Light airs and breezes from N.W. and N.N.W except first hour, where a heavy rain squall passes, accompanied by moderate breeze from N.N.E. veering suddenly to W.S.W. Breeze came out N. W. after squall. Moonlight at intervals. At 10.40 a vessel to the E'd signaled the approach of a torpedo boat and firing was commenced by the eastern end of the line. Went to general quarters and 11.20 secured. Lying to in assigned position. - H.A. Bispham, Lieutenant U.S.N.

Saturday June 4, 1898
Commences and to 4 A.M. Clear. Light breezes from N.N.W. Lying to on station on blockade off Santiago. Inspected coal reserves. - Mark L. Bristol, Lieutenant U.S.N.
4 to 8 A.M. Partly cloudy. Light breeze from N.E. to E.N.E. Steam four boilers. Ship lying in blockading position of Santiago. Coal bunkers in normal condition. - W.K. Gise, Ensign U.S.N.
8 A.M. to Mer. Fair and pleasant weather. Light to gentle breeze from East. Lying to on blockading station. Aired bedding. Magazine temperatures taken as per list. Life buoys reported in good order. Coal bunkers in normal condition. Signals as follows at 8.40 to flag, "Can I disable starboard engine for two hours." answered, " If you can take care of yourself on one engine." "all right." At 8.50fomr Flag "Keep fast engines." then "Is English steamer all right." answer "Steamer is chartered by N.Y. Sun." from Flag, " Shove Sun boat from out of lines." At 9.55 from Flag, "Was cable cut yesterday." answered: "When ordered to resume station last night, "Adria" had hold of cable and expected to cut it." At 10.00 and meridian, continue signals. - Harry Phelps, Lieutenant U.S.N.
Mer. to 4 P.M. Cloudy but pleasant. Light breeze form East. At 2.00 in obedience to signal from flagship resumed position on station and commenced clearing ship for action. At 3.45 flagship made signal to prepare to stand in towards entrance to harbor. At end of watch ship cleared for action and headed in towards the entrance. Signals as per record book. Bunkers reported as being normal. - F.J. Haeseler, Lieutenant U.S.N.
4 to 6 P.M. Fair and warm. Light Easterly breeze. At 4.05 went to general quarters and stood in for position for battle off harbor entrance. Expended on 12" common shell and one reduced charge, the forward turret gun having been fired by accident, owing to short circuit in electric firing attachment. Signals as per record. At end of watch off entrance to harbor. - H.A. Bispham, Lieutenant U.S.N.
6 to 8 P.M. Cloudy. Moon rose at 7.00 Light airs from East. Coal bunkers inspected. Lying to on blockade line off Santiago. - Mark L. Bristol, Lieutenant U.S.N.
8 P.M. to Mid Partly cloudy and fine. Very bright moonlight. Light Easterly breezes. In position on blockade line, of Santiago entrance. Steam from boilers. Coal bunkers reported normal. - W.K. Gise, Ensign U.S.N.

Sunday June 5, 1898
Commences and to 4 A.M. Clear and pleasant weather. Bright moonlight. Light to gentle breeze from North to N.N.E. Smooth sea. Lying with engines stopped in blockading station, moving engines as intervals to maintain position. Coal bunkers reported in normal condition. - Harry Phelps, Lieutenant U.S.N.
4 to 8 A.M. Fair and warm. Light breeze from N.N.E. At 6.30 U.S.S. Resolute came in. Signals as per record. Coal bunkers reported as normal. Working engines as necessary to preserve position on blockading line. - F.J. Haeseler, Lieutenant U.S.N.
8 A.M. to Mer. Fair and warm. Light airs from S.E. and South. At 10.30 small launch came out flying flag of truce and was spoken by the Iowa. Launch returned and Iowa left her station to communicate with flagship. Made routine signals at 10.00 and noon. Chaplain H.W. Jones held Divine Service. Magazine temperature as per list of. Coal bunkers normal. Vy order of Commanding officer released P.J. Kenny (A 1 Cl) his term of confinement having expired. - H.A. Bispham, Lieutenant U.S.N.
Mer. to 4 P.M. Cloudy and hot. Light airs from S.S.W. and S.W. Coal bunkers inspected. At 2.15 sighted enemy's large torpedo boat inside the entrance to the harbor; went ahead and went inside the the cable steamer to protect her.   Received from U.S.S. Resolve, 20 Appentices 2nd Class as follows, J.E. Spofford, A. Schmidt, H.G.Phelps, H.G. Luerke, C.H. Foster, R.A. Reck, A. Johnson, A.W. Greene, J.G. M. Johnson, G.F. Mullin, C Drubel, H.P. McColgan, J.R. Flynn, R.G. Horgan, J.G. Melmat, T. Curty, F. Hovell, H. Jones, P. May adn C.J. Trappe with bags, hammocks and necessary transfer papers. Steam from boilers. - Mark L. Bristol, Lieutenant U.S.N.
4 to 6 P.M. Cloudy and warm. Light southerly breezes. Standing by cable steamer which grappled cable at 5.45 when sent dinghy's crew to assist. Signals as per record book. Steam from boilers. Coal bunkers reported normal. - W. K. Gise, Ensign U.S.N.
6 to 8 P.M. Cloudy weather. Light breeze from E.N.E. Smooth sea. Lying to on blockading station with engines stopped. Signals as per record. Coal bunkers in normal condition. Magazine temperatures as per list. - Harry Phelps, Lieutenant U.S.N.
8 P.M. to Mid. Cloudy and warm. Calm and light breezes form North and N.E. At 8.50 the cable steamer at the cable. During at end at end of watch ship in positions in blockade formation, working engines as necessary. Coal bunkers reported in normal condition. - T.J. Haeseler, Lieutenant U.S.N.

Monday, June 6, 1898

Commences and to 4 A.M. Fair to cloudy. Light breeze from north and N.N.E. until last half hour, when breeze came out from S.E. accompanied by rain squall. Moonlight at intervals. Ship in position, lying to off entrance to harbor. Temperatures of bunkers normal.- H.A. Bispham, Lieutenant U.S.N.

4 to 8 A.M. Cloudy. Gentle breeze from East. At 6.05 the flagship made signal to form column of squadrons. At 7.15 went ahead and took position to S'd and W'd of Morro Castle. At 7.41 the two squadrons opened fire on the forts, with starboard batteries. The breech block of the starboard turret jammed for 15 minutes., then worked perfectly for remainder of action. Swung port battery to forts and engaged. The forts returned fire. Steam four boilers. - Mark L. Bristol, Lieutenant U.S.N.

8 A.M. to Mer. Cloudy and rainy first part. Warm. Calms and light variable airs. Shelling batteries at entrance until 10.21 when hauled off and resumed position on blockade line. Steam from four boilers using forced draft at times. Coal bunkers reported in normal condition. Signals as per record book. Expended 21 Common shell and 16 full charges powder for 12" guns, 59 common shell, 6" 4 shrapnel 6" 22 full charges powder 6", 41 reduced charges powder 6", 122 six pounder common shell, 3 six pounder A.P. shell, 75 electric primers, 75 percussion primers, 5 six pounder ammunition boxes. - .K. Gise, Ensign U.S.N.

Mer. to 4 P.M. Cloudy to fair weather, drizzling rain first part. Light to gentle breeze from E.S.E. to South. Lying with engines stopped on blockading station. Coal bunkers reported in normal condition. Signals as follows; At 1.00 from flagship "2nd Squadron, Well done." At 1.08 from flagship "k-108" at 1.40 "Are you sure the cable that was cut last night is not the same one the St. Louis cut before?" answered, "Do not know, shall I go to Adria and ask?" Flagship answered "Do not go." At 1.45 "Texas needs 300 tons coal tomorrow." - Harry Phelps, Lieutenant U.S.N.

4 to 6 P.M. Cloudy and pleasant. Light breeze from South. Marblehead to westward and Dolphin to eastward firing at something on shore. Moving engines to keep in position on blockading line. Signals as per record book. Coal bunkers reported as normal. - F.J. Haeseler, Lieutenant U.S.N.

6 to 8 P.M. Cloudy but pleasant. Light breezes from South. Communicated with "Porter" receiving mail from flagship. Lying to off entrance. Temperatures of coal bunkers normal and of magazines as per list. (highest 113 degrees) - H.A. Bispham, Lieutenant U.S.N.

8 P.M to Mid. Cloudy. Light airs from South and North. Lying to on blockade station. Steam four boilers. Moon rose at 9:00. Inspected coal bunkers. - Mark L. Bristol, Lieutenant U.S.N.

Tuesday June 7, 1898

Commences to 4 A.M. Cloudy and warm. Moonlight. Light northerly airs. Holding position on blockade. One of the Mosquitoes fired a red star about 12.50. Steam four boilers. Coal bunkers normal. - W.K. Gise, Ensign, U.S.N.

4 A.M to 8 A.M. Cloudy weather. Rain squall approaching last hour., breaking at end of watch. Light airs from north shifting to East at end of watch. Lying to until 7.00 when went near cable steamer "Adria" for her protection. She left to communicate with "New York" at 7.50. Resumed blockading station. Life buoys inspected and reported in good order. Coal bunkers in normal condition. Prepared to coal ship. Signals . At 5.50 from Sterling, "Orders to coal you. Will you come alongside." Answered "When and where from orders to coal. My last order not to coal." Answered "From F last evening." At 7.00 to flagship, "Orders conflicting, shall I coal or protect Adria." Flagship answered, "Protect Adria." - Harry Phelps, Lieutenant U.S.N.

8 A.M. to Mer. Overcast and cloudy. Heavy rain squall during first hour of watch. Gentle breeze fro East. Signals as per record book. Working engines as necessary to keep position on blockading line. Coal bunkers reported as normal. - F.J. Haeseler, Lieutenant U.S.N.

Mer. to 4 P.M. Cloudy and warm. Gentle to light breeze from East. Strong set to W'd and at 3.00 headed East, following flagship an d resumed station off entrance. Signals as per signal record. Realized $2.81 from Lucky Bag sale. Temperatures of coal bunkers normal. J. Delalude (G.M. 1 Cl) and J. Conley (W.I.) reported their term of enlistment having expired. - H.A. Phelps, Lieutenant U.S.N.

4 to 6 P.M. Overcast and cloudy. Light breezes from S.E. Lying to on blockade station. Inspected coal bunkers. - Mark L. Bristol, Lieutenant U.S.N.

6 to 8 P.M. Generally cloudy. Light breeze from E.N.E. In position on blockade station. Bunkers in normal conditionl. Magazine temperatures as per list. - W.K. Gise, Ensign U.S.N.

8 P.M to Mid. Fair and pleasant weather. Moonlight after 9.50. Light breeze from N.E. Smooth sea. Lying with engines stopped on blockading station. New York, Oregon, and Iowa used searchlights from 8.00 to 9.30. - Harry Phelps, Lieutenant U.S.N.

Wednesday, June 8 1898

Commences and to 4 A.M. Cloudy but pleasant. Light airs and breezes from N.N.W. and E.N.E. Fleet in night blockade formation. Working engines as necessary to preserve position. - F.J. Haeseler, Lieutenant U.S.N.

4 to 8 A.M. Fair, warm weather. Calm first hour. Light breeze to light airs from S.S.E. adn South remainder of watch. By direction of Lieut. Com'd'r Harber, Almer Armsted (Lds) and J.A. Green (C.P.) were placed under sentries charge to await investigation for fighting. Bunker temperatures oral. In position off entrance to harbor. - H.A. Bispham, Lieutenant U.S.N.

8 A.M. to Mer. Cloudy. Light breezes from E.N.E. Lying to on blockade station. Port engine disabled for an hour. A flag of truce came out of the Harbor, was met by the Massachusetts and returned. A small gunboat and a collier found the fleet. The Sterling and Marblehead left, standing to the E'd. By order of the commanding officer, G. Palmquist, ( ) was confined for 2 days on bread and water from leaving station at gun and sleeping on deck. A. Schaefer (A 1 Cl) 3 days extra duty for willfully failing to man boat. Wm Brunt (A 2 Cl) rated to A 1 Cl, to date from April 1, 1898. J.O. McCormick (A 3 Cl) rated to apprentice 2 Cl to date from April 2, 1898. Inspected coal bunkers and magazines. - Mark L. Bristol, Lieutenant U.S.N.

Mer. to 4 P.M. Cloudy and warm. Light breezes from E.N.E. and East. Holding position in blockade line, off entrance. Discovered enemy erecting a new battery to westward of entrance; which signaled to "Brooklyn". Steam on all boilers. Coal bunkers reported normal. The U.S.S. Gloucester brought mail and dispatches. The Suwanee returned from Westward. - W.K. Gise, Lieutenant U.S.N.

4 to 6 P.M. Fair and pleasant weather. Light airs from N.E. Lying to on blockading station. Coal bunkers reported in normal condition. - Harry Phelps, Lieutenant U.S.N.

6 to 8 P.M. Cloudy but pleasant. Light airs and breezes from East at 7.00 took position: night blockade formation. Vessels of squadrons using search lights on entrance to harbor. Coal bunkers normal. Temperatures of magazines as per list. - F.J. Haeseler, Lieutenant U.S.N.

8 P.M. to Mid. Cloudy and pleasant. Light breeze from East. On station off harbor. Using search lights from 10.00 to 10.50. Moon rose at 10.30. Bunker temperatures normal. - H.A. Bispham, Lieutenant U.S.N.

Friday, June 10, 1898

Commences and to 4 A.M. Fair and pleasant weather. Light airs from North. Long swell from S.E. Lying with engines stopped on blockading station. At 12.30 as vessel to the S.E. made ships number "478". Coal bunkers in normal condition. - H.A. Phelps, Lieutenant U.S.N.

4 to 8 A.M. Fair and warm. Light breeze from North. Bunkers reported as normal. Several vessels came in from the E'd. Made two of them out to be Panther and Yosemite. On blockade station. - F.J. Haeseler, Lieutenant U.S.N.

8 A.M. to Mer. Fair and warm. Light breeze from East. At 9.15 stood to W'd to communicate with flagship. Commanding Officer going on board. Sent boat to Steamer "Supply" for fresh provisions. At end of watch lying to near flagship. J.Harris (F 1 Cl) reported his term of enlistment as having expired. By order of the Commanding Officer released G. Palmquist (S) from confinement, his term of punishment having expired. Signals as per signal record. Routine signals at 10.00 and noon. Temperature in coal bunkers 115 degrees. - H.A. Bispham, Lieutenant U.S.N.

Mer. to 4 P.M. Cloudy and hot. Light airs from E.S.E. Receiving stores from the Supply. Inspected coal bunkers. Steam four boilers.- Mark L. Bristol, Lieutenant U.S.N.

4 to 6 P.M. Cloudy and warm. Light westerly airs. Received in Dept of S&A 700 lbs fresh beef, 2200 lbs fresh vegetables, 2096 pounds biscuit, 3145 lbs sugar, 3600 lbs salt pork, 1400 lbs Salt beef, 1316 lbs beans, 192 lbs tinned milk, 696 lbs tinned roast beef. Steam four boilers. Bunkers normal. - W.K. Gise, Ensign U.S.N.

6 to 8 P.M. Fair and pleasant weather. Light breeze from North. Smooth sea. Resumed blockading station at 7.00 and stopped engines lying to remainder of watch. Coal bunkers in normal condition. Temperature of magazines taken as per list. - Harry Phelps, Lieutenant U.S.N.

8 P.M. to Mid. Fair and pleasant. Gentle breeze from N.N.E. In blockading station, using search lights. Bunkers reported as normal. - F.J. Haeseler, Lieutenant U.S.N.

Sunday, June 12, 1898

Commences and to 4 A.M. Cloudy and pleasant. Light N.E. airs and breezes. At 3.30 left blockade line and stood on course E. by S. (fe) Steam on all boilers. Coal bunkers normal. - W.K. Gise, Ensign U.S.N.

4 to 8 A.M. Cloudy weather. Gentle breeze from E to E.N.E. Smooth seas. Steaming under four boilers along south coast of Cuba making various courses. At end of watch just entering Guantanamo Bay. At 7.30 exchanged numbers with U.S.S. Marblehead. Coal bunkers in normal condition. Sighted steamer "Adria" entering Bay ahead of us. Steam 165 lbs Revs. stbd 69.9 , port 69.9. - Harry Phelps, Lieutenant U.S.N.

8 A.M. to Meridian Generally cloudy. Gentle breeze from E.N.E. to calm. Arrived at Guantanamo Bay and went alongside collier "Abarenda". Took on 100 tons during watch. Sent Marine Guard ashore with arms and field pieces, also 10,000 rounds of ammunition. Fired 10-6 pdr. shots in reply to shots fired from Western shore. Colliers "Abarenda" and "Sterling" also shelled western side of entrance. Intermittent fire along eastern side. At end of watch alongside collier "Abarenda". - F.J. Haeseler, Lieutenant U.S.N.

Mer. to 4 P.M. Generally cloudy and warm. Calm first half, light airs and light breezes from S.S.E. and E.by N., remainder of watch. Coaling ship until 2.40 taking in 170 tons in all. Marine Guard returned at 2.30. Hoist out steam launch and made preparations for sending it out as a picket boat. Tried a common shell with a full charge from after main-deck B.L.R. in the direction of railway station where troops were seen disembarking. Heavy musketry firing ashore during last half of watch. - H.A. Bispham, Lieutenant U.S.N.

4 to 6 P.M. Cloudy. Gentle breezes from East. At 4.30 sent the Marine Guard in charge of Lt. C.S. Radford , U.S.M.C. were landed at Camp McCalla. The steam launch with Naval Cadet T.R. Holman U.S.N. in charge was left at Guantanamo Bay for picket duty. Got under way from collier at 5.00 and put over pilot at 5.14. Standing to Westward for Santiago. Steam four boilers. Coal bunkers inspected. - Mark L. Bristol, Lieutenant U.S.N.

6 to 8 P.M. Cloudy. Gentle easterly breezes. Standing along Cuban coast for Santiago. Met and spoke with U.S.S. Dolphin. Steam on four boilers. Av. pressure 138 lbs Revs. stbd 69.4 port 69.4. - W.K. Gise, Ensign U.S.N.

8 P.M to Mid Clear and pleasant weather. Light breeze from various directions. Smooth sea. Steaming under four boilers making various courses . At 8.30 sighted squadron off Santiago. At 9.30 passed close to and communicated with flagship New York. Later resumed blockading station and remained stopped after 10.00. Coal bunkers in normal condition.- Harry Phelps, Lieutenant U.S.N.

Tuesday, June 14

Commences and to 4 A.M. Clear. Gentle breezes from N.E. On blockade station, using search lights from 2.00 to 4.00. Moon rose at 1.45. - Mark L. Bristol, Lieutenant U.S.N.

4 to 8 A.M. Clear and fine. Gentle breezes from N.W. to North. On blockade line. Steam from all boilers. At 5.00 the New Orleans exchanged a few shots with shore batteries. Inspected life buoys. Coal bunkers normal. - W.K. Gise, Ensign U.S.N.

8 A.M. to Mer. Clear and pleasant weather. Gentle breeze from North. Smooth sea. Steam in four boilers. Lying on blockading station, moving engines at times to keep position. Magazine temperatures taken as per list. The Captain assigned the following punishments, J.G. McNamara (A 2 Cl) asleep on watch, 5 days bread and water. F.A. Bolle (A 2 Cl) Stowing himself away and not informing man he relieved 2 days bread and water. Wm. DeForest (A 3 Cl) shirking, 5 days bread and water. W. J. Glase (A 2 cl) clothes in lucky bag, 1 day extra duty. M.J. Mabry (A 2 Cl) Shirking 2 days extra duty. Confined J.G. McNamara (A 2 Cl) and Wm. DeForest (A 2 Cl) in accordance with punishment. Signals at 10.00 and meridian. Sick and coal report. Coal bunkers reported in normal condition. - Harry Phelps, Lieutenant U.S.N.

Mer. to 4 P.M. Clear and warm. Light breeze from S.E. At 1.30 the U.S.S. Solace came in from Eastward. Signals as per record book. Coal bunkers in normal condition. On blockade station as in previous watch. - F.J. Haeseler, Lieutenant U.S.N.

4 to 6 P.M. Fair and warm. Light to gentle breeze fro S.E. Mustered at quarters at 5.00. Transferred to "Solace" with necessary papers and effect T. Brott (Lds) for medical treatment. Off entrance, on blockade station. Strong set to W'd. - H.A. Bispham, Lieutenant U.S.N.

6 to 8 P.M. Fair. Gentle to light breezes from S.E. On blockade station using search light after dark. Coal bunkers inspected. Steam three boilers. - Mark L. Bristol, Lieutenant U.S.N.

8 P.M. to Mid Clear and fine. Bright starlight. Light N.N.W. breezes. On blockade line, playing search light on beach from 8 to 10. Steam on four boilers. Coal bunkers normal. - W.K. Gise, Ensign U.S.N.

Wednesday June 15, 1898

Commences and to 4 A.M. Clear and pleasant weather. Light breeze from North. Smooth Sea. Ship on blockading station. Steam in three boilers. Running engines at times to keep position. About 2.45 moon rose. Coal bunkers reported in normal condition. - Harry Phelps, Lieutenant, U.S.N.

4 to 8 A.M. Clear and pleasant. Light to gentle breeze from North. Ship on blockading station, steam in three boilers. Signals as per record book. Coal bunkers reported normal. - F.J. Haeseler, Lieutenant, U.S.N.

8 A.M. to Mer. Clear and warm. Light to gentle breeze from N.E. shifting to E.S.E. at 8.45 flagship made telegraphic signal for this vessel to proceed to Guantanamo and destroy forts, and resume blockading station this evening. Other signals as per record. At 8.50 steamed slowly toward flagship, and at 8.50 went ahead full speed for Guantanamo. Passed "Suwanee" standing to E'd . Steam in three boilers, using forced draft. At steam pressure 127 lbs, av. revs. stbd 108.2 port 70.07. Put over patent log at 9.30 reading 0.0 and at noon it read 23.8. Coal bunkers reported normal. - H.A. Bispham, Lieutenant, U.S.N.

Mer to 4 P.M. Cloudy. Light breezes from N.E. Standing in to Guantanamo Bay. At 1.07 beat to general quarters. Stood up to engage the forts in company with the "Suwanee" and Marblehead. At 2.06 opened fire at 3000 yards, with main battery. At 3.20 ceased firing: the fort was silenced. Stood out of harbor and secured, standing for Santiago. Steam in three boilers. - Mark L. Bristol, Lieutenant U.S.N.

4 to 6 P.M Partly cloudy and warm. Light N.E. breezes. Standing out of Guantanamo Bay, and for Santiago de Cuba. Put over patent log at 4.20 reading 0.0. Steam on three boilers. Lieut. H. Phelps U.S.N. inspected magazines and shell room and other compartments in his charge and tested flood cocks. Inspected coal bunkers. Expended in Ordnance Dept.

12-12" and 49-6" Common Shell, 3-6" Shrapnel, 47 full 6" charges, 4 reduced 6" charges, 9 3/4 full 12" charges, 40 electric and 40 percussion primers. - W. K. Gise, Ensign, U.S.N.

6 to 8 P.M. Clear and pleasant. Light breeze from N.E. Smooth sea. Steaming along south coast of Cuba, under three boilers, steering various courses. At 7.40 sighted squadron off Santiago. Magazine temperatures taken as per list. Bunkers reported in normal condition. - Harry Phelps, Lieutenant, U.S.N.

8 P.M. to Mid Clear and pleasant. Light breeze from N.E. and North. At 8:35 stopped and communicated with flagship. At 10.00
took position on blockade line. At 11.30 the Vesuvius fired three shots from her pneumatic guns, one of which exploded behind the hill on western side of entrance to harbor. Bunkers in normal condition. - F.J. Haeseler, Lieutenant, U.S.N.

Thursday June 16, 1898

Commences and to 4 A.M. Clear and fine. Gentle breeze form North. Ship on blockading station, steam three boilers. About 3.15 moon rose. Using search light form two until four. Bunkers in normal condition. - H.A. Bispham, Lieutenant, U.S.N.

4 to 8 A.M. Fair to clear. Light breezes from North. At 4.55 to general quarters, and stood in to engage the batteries of Santiago. At 5.23 fleet opened fire and this ship at 5.25. Firing from this ship at the western battery, using only the main battery. The fort was silenced and 6.20 ceased firing and hauled off and secured. Steam three boilers. Expended 9- 12" common and 4- 12" A.P. shells, 9 3/4- 12" full charges, 33- 6" Common Shell. 29 6" full charges, 4-6" reduced charges, 30 electric and 40 percussion primers. Coal bunkers in normal condition. - Mark L. Bristol, Lieutenant, U.S.N.

8 A.M. to Mer. Partly cloudy and fine. Light easterly airs to gentle breezes. Holding position on blockade line. Steam in three boilers. Made routine reports at 10:00 and 12:00. Other signals as per record book. Coal bunkers normal. Spanish Colors over Morro Castle half masted from 9.00 to 10.00. - W.K. Gise, Ensign, U.S.N.

Mer. to 4 P.M. Fair and pleasant weather. Moderate breeze from East. Smooth sea. Lying with engines stopped. On blockading station. Running engines at times to keep position. Issued clothing and small stores. At 3.20 U.S.S. Yankee joined squadron. Coal bunkers in normal condition. - Harry Phelps, Lieutenant, U.S.N.

4 to 6 P.M. Partly cloudy. Gentle breeze from E.N.E. Steam three boilers. Lying on blockade station off Santiago. Bunkers in normal condition. - F.J. Haeseler, Lieutenant, U.S.N.

6 to 8 P.M. Fair and warm. Gentle to light breeze from E.N.E. shifting to E'd and S'd last half hour. Tested and worked search lights after dark. On blockade station. Coal bunker temperatures normal and magazine temperature as per list, highest 107 degrees. - H.A. Bispham, Lieutenant, U.S.N.

8 P.M. to Mid Clear, Light breezes from E.N.E. On blockade station. Steam three boilers. Bunkers inspected. - Mark L. Bristol, Lieutenant, U.S.N.

<u>Friday, June 17, 2002</u>
Commences and to 4 A.M. Clear. Bright Starlight. Light westerly breezes. St. Louis dragging cable in shore of line. - W.K. Gise, Ensign, U.S.A.

4 to 8 A.M. Clear and pleasant weather. Light breeze from E.N.E. and North. Smooth sea. Lying stopped on blockading stations. At 5.00 the "Vixen" was seen to be firing at a small fort on the beach. Ran in towards her. Went to general quarters at at 2500 years range opened fire on the Somervelos Battery. Expended 17-6" Common Shell and 17-6" full charges. 24-6 pdr Common Shell and 17 electric and 8 percussion primers. At 5.45 ceased firing and resumed station. No casualties on this ship nor on "Vixen" which reported having been fired upon from the fort. Coal bunkers in normal condition. Life buoys inspected and found in good order. - Harry Phelps, Lieutenant, U.S.N.

8 A.M. to Mer. Clear and warm. Calms and light breezes from S.E. at 9.40 mustered crew at quarters. No absentees. After which exercised at divisional exercises. Routine signals as per record book. On blockade station. By directions of the Commanding officer the following punishments were inflicted; W. Byrnes (A 2 d) A Cairne (Lds), G. Walsh (Sea) Washing clothes on Spar Deck out of blouse and without permission. 1 day extra duty each. E. Sloan (W Att.) Deliberate disobedience of orders when ship was in action, 2 days bread and water. W.M Heiss (Lds) Oilskins in lucky bag, 1 day extra duty. W. H. Gordon (l.p.) Shirking. Disrated to Landsman. - F.J. Haeseler, Lieutenant U.S.N.

Mer. to 4 P.M. Clear and warm. Light breeze from S.E. On blockade station steam under three boilers. Signals per record book. Coal bunkers reported normal. - H.A. Bispham, Lieutenant U.S.N.

4 to 6 P.M. Fair and warm. Light airs from S.E. Signals as per record. Coal bunkers inspected. Quarters at 5.00. On blockade station. - Mark L. Bristol, Lieutenant, U.S.N.

6 to 8 P.M. Cloudy and warm. Light S.E. airs. On blockade line. Steam on three boilers. "Massachusetts" using search lights on entrance. - W.K. Gise, Ensign, U.S.N.

8 P.M. to Mid. Clear and pleasant weather. Starlight. Light breeze from North. Smooth sea. Lying with engines stopped on blockading station. Coal bunkers reported in normal conditions. - Harry Phelps, Lieutenant, US.N.

<u>Saturday, June 18, 1898</u>
Commences and to 4 A.M. Clear and pleasant. Light breeze from North. At 3:00 headed in for Morro Light and at 3:20 when about 1 ½ miles turned search light on entrance, and kept the entrance lit up until the end of watch. Bunkers at normal temperatures. - F.J. Haeseler, Lieutenant U.S.N.

4 to 8 A.M. Generally clear, pleasant weather. Light breezes from North. At 4.45 turned off search lights and stood out from position off entrance, and resumed blockade station. Strong sea to westward. Signals as per record. Bunker temperatures normal. - H.A. Bispham, Lieutenant, U.S.N.

8 A.M. to Mid. Generally clear and pleasant. Light and gentle breeze from S.E. On blockade station of Santiago. Signals at 10:00 " num ? ". At noon "num 20" "num 616" Coal bunkers in normal condition. Flagship New York left for Guantanamo at 9.00. Signals as per record book. - Mark L. Bristol, Lieutenant, U.S.N.

Mid to 4 P.M. Partly cloudy and warm. Light breezes to airs from S.E. Holding position on blockade. The Scorpion came in from Eastward. Steam in 3 boilers. Realized $0.95 from lucky bag effects. Coal bunkers normal. - W.K. Gise, Ensign, U.S.N.

4 to 6 P.M. Fair and warm. Light airs from S.E. Smooth sea. Lying on blockading station with engines stopped. Running engines at times to maintain position. Sighted Flagship New York, about 5.50 coming from Eastward. Coal bunkers in normal condition. - Harry Phelps, Lieutenant, U.S.N.

6 to 8 P.M. Fair and pleasant. Light airs from S.E. at 7:00 headed in for Morro Castle and at 7:15. When about 1 ½ miles from Morro headed to Eastward and turned search light on entrance, and kept it there until end of watch. At 7.30 the U.S.S. New York came in from Guantanamo and resumed station on blockade. Bunkers reported as in normal condition. Temperatures of magazines as per appended list. - F.J. Haeseler, Lieutenant U.S.N.

8 P.M. to Mid. Clear and Pleasant. Light airs to light breezes from N.N.W. Bright starlight. Discontinued using search light in entrance at 9.22., the Oregon relieving this ship in obedience to signal from Flagship. Temperature of coal bunker normal. - H.A. Bispham, Lieutenant, U.S.N.

<u>Sunday June 19, 1898</u>
Commences and to 4 A.M. Clear. Light airs from north. Blockade duty. Steam on three boilers. Coal bunkers inspected and reported at normal temperature. - Mark L. Bristol, Lieutenant, U.S.N.

4 to 8 A.M. Clear and warm. Light N.W. airs. On blockade line. Steam on three boilers. The Dixie came in from the westward, convoying the "Celtic", exchanging salutes with "New York". Coal bunkers normal. - W.K. Gise, Ensign U.S.N.

8 A.M. to noon Clear and warm. Light airs from N.W.'d. Smooth sea. Lying on blockading station, engines stopped. At 9.00 the captain inspected crew at quarters. At 9.30 the "Yosemite" joined the fleet and at 10:15 the Dixie left, steaming to westward. Life buoys reported in good order. Temperature of magazines as per list. Coal bunkers reported in normal condition. By order of Captain released W. H. Forest (A 3 d) and G. J. McNamara (A 2 d) their terms of punishment being expired, and confined F. A. Bolle (A 1 d) and E. Sloan ( ) for 2 days, in accordance with the punishment previously assigned. Signals to Flag at 8.50, "Thank you for assistance in lighting entrance last night. Texas was only 2000 yards out at the time. Your light is splendid." At 9:00 "Permission requested to repair hydraulic pumps, will disable turrets for four hours. Absolutely necessary." Answered "granted". At 10.00 and meridian, routine signals. - Harry Phelps, Lieutenant, U.S.N.

Mer. To 4 P.M. Clear first part, cloudy during latter part of watch. Light breeze from S.E. to N.W. Steam in three boilers. Lying on blockade station at Santiago. U.S.S. Yosemite left fleet at 1:00 and stood to Eastward. Coal bunkers in normal condition. - F.J. Haeseler, Lieutenant, U.S.N.

4 to 6 P.M. Fair to cloudy and pleasant. Light airs from N.W. on blockade station. Temperature of coal bunker normal. - H.A. Bispham, Lieutenant, U.S.N.

6 to 8 P.M. Clear. Light airs to light breeze from N.W. to North. Steam three boilers. Blockade duty. - Mark L. Bristol, Lieutenant, U.S.N.

8 P.M to Mid. Partly cloudy and bright starlight. Light northerly airs and breezes. Playing search lights on shore line to westward of entrance from 10:00 to 12:00. Steam in 3 boilers. Coal Bunkers normal. - W.K. Gise, Ensign, U.S.N.

<u>Monday June 20, 1898</u>
Commences and to 4 A.M. Clear and pleasant weather. Bright starlight. Light breeze from North. Smooth sea. Lying on blockade station, engines stopped. Coal bunkers in normal condition. - Harry Phelps, Lieutenant, U.S.N.

4 to 8 A.M. Clear and pleasant. Light breezes from N and N.W. The U.S.S. Resolute and U.S.S. Wompatuck came in. Naval cadet F. Morrison reported on board for duty on this ship. Lying on station in blockade, working engines occasionally. Coal bunkers reported normal. Signals as per record book. - F.J. Haeseler, Lieutenant, U.S.N.

8 to Mer. Fair and warm. Light breeze from E.S.E. Mustered and inspected at quarters. Exercised crew at divisional drills. Temperatures of coal bunkers normal and magazines as per list. Sighted fleet of transports at 10.00 the Indiana convoying same. Hoisted out steam launch, fourth cutter and whaleboat and sent them to supply steamers for provisions. Signals as per record book. - H.A. Bispham, Lieutenant, U.S.N.

Mer. to 4 P.M. Fair and cloudy. Light breezes from E.S.E. on blockade station. Coal bunkers inspected. The Dupont and Rogers joined the fleet on blockade. The "Army" transports and convoying fleet in the offing. - Mark L. Bristol, Lieutenant, U.S.N.

4 to 6 P.M. Cloudy. Light breezes from E.S.E. Holding position on blockade line. Steam on 3 boilers. The Baucroft came in from transport fleet saluting the Rear Admirals flag, which "New York" returned with 7 guns. Coal bunkers normal. - W. K. Gise, Ensign, U.S.N.

6 to 8 P.M. Clear and pleasant weather. Light airs from East. Smooth sea. Lying on blockading station, working engines when necessary. Coal bunkers normal. Harry Phelps, Lieutenant, U.S.N.

8 P.M. to Mid Clear and pleasant. Light airs from N.E. and North. In position on blockading stations, working engines when necessary. Coal bunkers normal. - F.J. Haeseler, Lieutenant, U.S.N.

<u>Monday June 21, 1898</u>
Commences to 4 A.M. Clear and pleasant. Light breeze from North. Bright starlight. Set to westward. On station off blockade. Temperature of coal bunkers normal. - H.A. Bispham, Lieutenant, U.S.N.

4 to 8 A.M. Clear and fine. Light breeze from North. Lying on blockade station, turning engines occasionally to keep position. Coal bunkers normal. Signals as per record book. - Mark L. Bristol, Lieutenant, U.S.N.

8 A.M. to Mer. Clear and warm. Light breezes from East to E.S.E. Mustered at quarters at 8.15. Exercised 2nd and 3rd divisions rifles, 1st and 4th at Battery, 5th at stations, and 7th at infantry. Made continue routine reports at 10.00 and 12.00. Coal bunkers normal. Magazine temperatures as per list. The Army transports headed by "Indiana" stood in from Westward. Bv order of Commanding Officer released F.A. Bolle (A 1 ld) and E. Sloan (m a u) and confined J.G.M. Johnson (a 2 ld) and S Edwards (F 1 lel). The following punishments were inflicted: J.G.M. Johnson, (A 2 cl) lying, 2 days bread and water, J.D. Collins ( ) dumping slops in wash house and beastly dirty, 1 day extra duty, W.S. Reapass (Lds) taking food off J.G. table and eating it in J.G. pantry, 1 day extra duty. W H Hatchett (f 1 cl) washing clothes out of hours, 2 days extra duty. S Edwards (F 1 cl) Fresh water in possession without authority, 2 days bread and water, J. Mooney (F 1cl) 2 days bread and water, Joshua Pathry (Sea) Shoes on engine room hatch, 1 day extra duty, C Hutol (F 2 cl), using bucket that did not belong to him, 1 day extra duty. - W.K. Gise, Ensign, U.S.N.

Mer. to 4 P.M. Clear and warm. Light breeze from E.S.E. Smooth sea. Lying on blockading station, engines stopped. Moving at times to keep position. Broke out fore hold. Shipped forward boat boom. Coal bunkers in normal condition. - Harry Phelps, Lieutenant U.S.N.

4 to 6 P.M. Clear and warm. Light breeze from E.S.E. lying on blockading station, working engines when necessary to keep position. Mustered at quarters at 5.00. Coal bunkers normal. - F.J. Haeseler, Lieutenant U.S.N.

6 to 8 P.M. Generally cloudy. Light breeze from E.N.E. Lightning to S'd. In blockade station of Santiago. Coal bunkers in normal condition. Signals as per record book. Temperatures of magazines as per list. Highest 110 degrees. - H.A. Bispham, Lieutenant U.S.N.

8 P.M. to Mid Cloudy. Moon set at 9.20. Light breeze from East and North. On blockade station. Steam four boilers, connecting C boiler at 8.20. Inspected magazine and coal bunkers. - Mark L. Bristol, Lieutenant, U.S.N.

<u>Wednesday June 22, 1898</u>
Commences to 4 A.M. Cloudy and warm. Sent 2nd Steam Launch 1st and 2nd cutters under charge of Naval Cadet Reynolds to Daiquiri to assist in landing army. Steam on four boilers. Coal bunkers normal. Exchanged places on blockade line with Brooklyn. - W.K. Gise, Ensign, U.S.N.

4 A.M. to 8 A.M. Fair and pleasant weather. Light breeze from N.N.E. Smooth sea. Lying on blockading station untl 7.00 when moved in to within 1500 yards of entrance to Cabanas Bay. Steam on four boilers. AT 4.30 cleared ship for action. At 6.50 exchanged numbers with U.S.S. Manning convoying two transports. At 7.20 went to general quarters. Prepared to shell beach at Cabanas but saw none of the enemy at that point. - Harry Phelps, Lieutenant, U.S.N.

8 A.M. to Mer. Clear and warm. Light breeze from S.E. at 8.03, fort on weather side of entrance to harbor opened fire, which the "Texas" immediately returned. At 8.45 as 6" shell entered port bow, this being the last shot fired by the fort, killing F. J. Blakely (A 1 cl) seriously wounding Geo. F Mullen (A 2 Cl) and R. Russel (A 2 cl) and wounding R. Errgel (Sea) H.E. Lee (A 2 cl) J.F. Lively (Lds) John Nelson (A 2 cl), J.J. Simonsea (Sea) and A. Sivgrist ( ), carried away one stanchion, two frames and two hawser reels, and bulged out plates in two places on starboard bow. At 9.32 "Brooklyn" signaled Neg 1 at 9.40 the "Brooklyn" signaled "well done". At 9.50 ceased firing and commenced again at 10.10. Ceased firing and hauled off firing line at 10.23. Expended the following ammunition, 14 ½ full 12" charges, 2-6" full charges, 103 6" reduced charges l, 19-12" A.P. shells, 22-6" A.P. shells, 66-6" common shells, 17-6" shrapnel, 50-6 pdr common shells, 20 1pdr common shells, 10 6/mm balls in clips, 90 electric and 50 percussion primers, Lieutenant H. Phelps inspected magazines and shell rooms, and other compartments in his charge at noon. Made routine signals. Coal bunkers normal. Resumed position in blockading line. - F.J. Haeseler, Lieutenant, U.S.N.

Mer to 4 P.M. Clear and warm. Light breeze from South. On station on blockade. Requested permission of Brooklyn to run out a couple of miles for burial service. Permission being granted the ships was headed out at 2.00 o'clock, and ran out about three miles. Called all hands and Chaplain H.W. Jones, U.S.N. read burial service, and committed the body of F.J. Blakely (A 1 cl) to the deep. Returned to station on blockade. Signals as per record book. Bunkers inspected. - Mark L. Bristol, Lieutenant, U.S.N.

4 to 6 P.M. Fair and warm. Light airs from South. Lying to on blockade. Quarters at 5.00 Steam four boilers. "New York" and "New Orleans" returned to blockade at 4.30. Signals as per record book. Bunkers inspected. - Mark L. Bristol, Lieutenant, U.S.N.

6 to 8 P.M. Partly cloudy and warm. Light variable airs. Steam four boilers. Coal bunkers normal. Magazine temperatures as per list. - W.K. Gise, Ensign, U.S.N.

8 P.M. to Mid Clear and pleasant weather. Light breeze from N.N.E. Lying on blockading station. Engines stopped. At 11.00 the "Vesuvius" fired three shells into the Eastern battery. Coal bunkers in the normal positions. - Harry Phelps, Lieutenant, U.S.N.

<u>**RECORD OF THE MISCELLANEOUS EVENTS OF THE DAY**</u>
<u>**WEDNESDAY, June 23 1898**</u>
Commences to 4 A.M. Clear and warm. Light breeze from North. On blockade station until 3.00 A.M. , when put ship on course E.S.E. and went ahead full speed, bound for Guantanamo. At end of watch on course E.S.E. about 5 miles off coast of Cuba. Coal bunkers in normal condition. - F.J. Haeseler, Lieutenant U.S.N.

4 to 8 A.M. Clear and pleasant. Gentle breeze from N.E. and North. Standing along coast bound for Guantanamo Bay. At end of watch, standing to go alongside U.S.S. Resolute. Temperature of magazines as per list. Coal bunkers normal. Under steam four boilers. Av. pressure 132 lbs. Av. revs stbd 60.1 port 62.6. - H.A. Bispham, Lieutenant U.S.N.

8 A.M. to Mer. Clear and hot. Gentle Breezes from N.E. to East. At 9:00 made fast alongside of the Resolute, and for remainder of watch taking on ammunition. The Vesuvius, Rogers, and Dupont came in. The Marblehead shifted berth. Coal bunkers inspected. Transferred to U.S.S. "Solace" four wounded men, names as follows: J.J. Simmons (Sea) Geo. F. Mullins (A 2 Cl) R. Russel (A 2 Cl.) H.E. Lee (A 2 Cl). - Mark L. Bristol, Lieutenant, U.S.N.

Mer. to 4 P.M. Clear and fine. Gentle breezes from East and N.E. Lying alongside the U.S.S. Resolute taking on ammunition until 3.30 when cast off and stood out of harbor. Received on board in Dept of Ordnance 16 12" Common L.F shell, 25 A.P. 12" l.f. Shell, 12-12" A.P. Shell, 200-6" common shell, 268-6" A.P. l.f. Shells, 29-6" Shrapnel l.f. 46-12" Full charges, 400 6" full charges, 22-6 pdr Cartridges Steel Shell. Received from Collier Sterling, 60 frn. 4" Manila Rope. Put on

Resolute for U.S.S. Marblehead one 800 pound steam anchor. The "Yosemite" left the harbor. The Dupont came in and anchored. Steam on four boilers. Coal bunkers normal. Received 12 bent wood chains from U.S.S. Panther. - W.K. Gise, Ensign, U.S.N.

4 to 6 P.M. Clear and pleasant weather. Gentle breeze from E.S.E. Smooth sea. Standing along South coast of Cuba under steam four boilers. At 4.20 exchanged numbers with U.S.S. Wasp, flying dispatch flag. She signaled "Wish to communicate." Stopped and received on board Naval Cadet R.S. Pope who reported for duty. At 5.30 exchanged numbers with U.S.S. Eagle heading to E'd. At 5.45 exchanged numbers with U.S.S. Castine heading to E'd. The Ericsson and Porter passed heading to W'd. Sight several sail off Daiquiri Bay. transports and gunboats. - Harry Phelps, Lieutenant, U.S.N.

6 to 8 P.M. Cloudy and warm. Light breeze from E.S.E. At 6.05 exchanged numbers with "Annapolis" and "Bancroft". Stopped and received on board for duty on this ship, Naval cadets F.H. Howe and W.E. Wood. At end of watch standing towards Santiago de Cuba, about 3 miles from land. Under steam four boilers. Av. pressure 128 lbs Av. revs stbd 70.1 port 69. Coal bunkers normal. Temperature of magazines per list. - F.J. Haeseler, Lieutenant, U.S.N.

8 P.M to Mid. Cloudy with lightning to W'd. Rain squall latter part. Light breeze to light airs from E.S.E. to N.W. Took station on blockade at 8.30. Temperature of coal bunkers normal. - H.A. Bispham [signature of Mark L. Bristol removed], Lieutenant, U.S.N.

Friday, June 24, 1898

Commences and to 4 A.M. Fair to clear. Gentle breeze from North to N.N.E. On blockade. Coal bunkers inspected. - Mark L. Bristol, Lieutenant, U.S.N.

4 to 8 A.M. Clear and warm. Gentle northerly breezes. Holding position on blockade. Steam on four boilers. Coal bunkers normal. - W.K. Gise, Ensign, U.S.N.

8 A.M. to Mer. Fair and pleasant. Light to gentle breezes from N.N.E. to E.S.E. Smooth sea. Lying on blockade station with engines stopped. At 8.15 mustered at quarters. By order of Captain, J. Mooney (F. 2 Cl) was placed in solitary confinement for two days in accordance with punishment previously assigned. At 9.00 the steam cutter returned to the ship. Naval Cadet Reynolds in charge, the other boats being with the transports. About 11.00, the Detroit, Scorpion, St. Louis and some others opened fire on the beach, hillside, etc. about three miles east of Morro Castle, and kept up an intermittent fire to end of watch. Temperatures of magazines taken as per list. Tested flood cocks. Coal bunkers in normal condition. Routine signals at 10.00 and meridian. - Harry Phelps, Lieutenant, U.S.N.

Mer. to 4 P.M. Cloudy pleasant weather. Gentle breeze to light airs from E.S.E. Lying on blockade station. Coal bunkers normal. - F.J. Haeseler, Lieutenant U.S.N.

4 to 6 P.M. Fair to cloudy, pleasant weather. Light westerly airs. On blockade station. Flagship returned from E'd. at 5.45. Mustered at quarters at 5.00. At end of watch Morro Castle bore N.N.E.1/4E. per standard compass, and distant 5300 yards, per sextant angle. Temperature of bunkers normal. - H.A. Bispham, Lieutenant, U.S.N.

6 to 8 P.M. Cloudy. Light airs from W.N.W. to North. On blockade station. Coal bunkers and magazines inspected. Morro Castle bore N & E ½ E distance 2 ½ miles. - Mark Bristol, Lieutenant, U.S.N.

8 P.M. to Mid. Clear. Bright starlight. Light northerly airs and breezes. Holding positions on blockade. Steam on all boilers. Coal bunkers normal. At of watch Morro Castle bore N by E ½ E. distance 5500 yards. - W.K. Gise, Ensign, U.S.N.

Examined and found to be correct. L. C. Strelner, Lieutenant, U.S.N., Navigator

Saturday, June 25, 1898

Commences and to 4 A.M. Clear and pleasant weather. Gentle breeze from North. Smooth sea. Ship on blockading station, engines stopped, moving at times to keep position. Coal bunkers in normal condition. At of watch Morro Castle bore N.N.E. (mag), distance about 2 3/4 miles. - Harry Phelps, Lieutenant, U.S.N.

4 to 8 A.M. Clear and fine. Gentle breeze from North. Ship on blockading position. Hospital ship "State of Texas" and USS Yankton joined fleet. At 4/10 heavy explosions were heard ashore and signals were read from some vessel to flagship, "Enemy have blown up railroad bridge in bay." At end of watch Morro bore N.N.E (mag) distance 2 ½ miles. - F.J. Haeseler, Lieutenant, U.S.N.

8 A.M. to Mer. Fair, warm weather. Calm first hour, light airs to light breeze from S.E. to S.S.E. remainder of watch. Temperature of magazines as per list (Highest 110 degrees) and of coal bunkers, normal. On blockade station. At end of watch Morro bore N.N. E. ½ E. per compass. Ships head S.W. ½ W. and distance 4500 yards, per sextant angle. The surgeon of the ship made the required weekly sanitary inspection. Naval Cadet L.S. Shapley U.S.N. reported for duty. - H.A. Bispham, Lieutenant, U.S.N.

Mer. to 4 P.M. Clear to fair. Light breeze to light airs from S.S.E. to S.E. on blockade station. Coal bunkers inspected. Morro bore N.N.E. distant 2 ½ miles at 4.00. Acting appointments were issued by Commanding Officer as per list appended. - Mark L. Bristol, Lieutenant, U.S.N.

4 to 6 P.M. Cloudy but fine. Calm and light S.S.W. airs. Holding position on blockade station. Steam on four boilers. The Quarterly Board of Survey of which Lieut. L.C. Heilner U.S.N. was senior member, condemned 150 lbs potatoes. Naval Cadet W. K. Reynolds inspected compartments of third division. The "Helena" came in from Eastward. Dense smoke from Daiquiri. The Gloucester shelling beach occasionally. At end of watch Morro Castle bore N.N.E. 4500 yards distant. Coal bunkers normal. - W.K. Gise, Ensign, U.S.N.

6 to 8 P.M. Clear and pleasant. Calm-Smooth sea. Lying on blockading station engines stopped. Signals as per record book. Temperatures of magazines taken as per list. Coal bunkers in normal condition. At 8.00 El Morro bore (N.N.E) mag. distant 2 ½ miles. - Harry Phelps, Lieutenant, U.S.N.

8 P.M. to Mid. Clear and pleasant. Light breeze from North. On blockade station. At end of watch Morro bore about N.N.E. distant 2 ½ miles. Coal bunkers in normal condition. - F.J. Haeseler, Lieutenant, U.S.N.

Saturday June 26, 1898

Commences and to 4 A.M. Clear and pleasant. Gentle breeze from North to East. On blockade station. Temperatures from bunkers normal. Bearing of Morro at end of watch N. N. E. 1/4 E. ( ) Ships head W.S.W., distant 2 ½ miles. - H.A. Bispham, Lieutenant, U.S.N.

4 to 8 A.M. Clear. Gentle breeze from N.N.E. to North. Lying to on blockade station. Steam four boilers. Inspected coal bunkers. At 8.00 Morro Castle bore N.N.E. distant 3 miles. - Mark L. Bristol, Lieutenant, U.S.N.

8 A.M. to Mer. Clear and pleasant. Gentle breeze and light airs from North to N.N.E. Ship on blockade station. Temperature of bunkers normal. Magazine temperatures as per list. J. Mooney was released from confinement by order of commanding officer. Had quarters for inspection at 9.00. at end of watch Morro Castle bore N & E 3/4 E 5300 yards. - W.K. Gise, Ensign, U.S.N.

Mer. to 4 P.M. Clear and pleasant weather. Gentle to moderate breeze from E.S.E. to S.E. Smooth sea. Lying on blockade station, engines stopped. Moving at times to keep position. Coal bunkers in normal condition. Signals to Brooklyn at 12.15 "We are now using coal from upper bunkers. Lower bunkers are empty. Upper bunkers are main protection to steam pipes." Brooklyn answered, "I will have you sent to Guantanamo as soon as I can." At end of watch El Morro bore N.N.E. distant 2 ½ miles. - Harry Phelps, Lieutenant, U.S.N.

4 to 6 P.M. Clear and pleasant. Moderate to gentle breeze from E.S.E. On blockade station, with Morro Castle bearing N.N.E. distant 2 3/4 miles at end of watch. Coal bunkers normal. - F.J. Haeseler, Lieutenant, U.S.N.

6 to 8 P.M. Fair and warm. Gentle to light breeze from E.S.E. On station on blockade. The cutters used to land army returned at seven and were hoisted in. Temperature of magazines as per list (highest 110 degrees) and of coal bunkers normal. At end of watch Morro bore N.N.E. distant about 2 ½ miles. - H.A. Bispham, Lieutenant, U.S.N.

8 P.M to Mid. Generally cloudy. Rain squalls. Light to gentle breeze from E.S.E. to N.E. On blockade station. At end of watch Morro Castle bore N.N.E. 3/4E. Distant about 2 ½ miles. Temperature of coal bunkers normal. - Mark L. Bristol, Lieutenant, U.S.N.

Monday, June 27, 1898

Commences to 4 A.M. Cloudy and warm. Light and gentle northerly breezes. Holding position on blockade. Steam four boilers. The Vesuvius fired three shots, one of which exploded. The New Orleans fired two 6" shots. At end of watch Morro bore N by E 3/4 E. 5500 yards distant. Coal bunkers normal. - W.K. Gise, Ensign, U.S.N.

4 to 8 A.M. Fair and pleasant weather. Light breeze from North. Smooth sea. Lying on blockading position, engines moving occasionally to maintain position. U.S.S. Yale joined the fleet from Eastward. Life buoys inspected and found in order. Coal bunkers reported in normal condition. At end of watch El Morro bore N.N.E., distant 3 miles. - Harry Phelps, Lieutenant, U.S.N.

8 A.M to Mer. Cloudy but pleasant. Light airs and breeze from E.N.E. At 8.15 mustered crew at quarters after which exercised at divisional drills. At 10.40, when Morro Castle bore N.N.E. distant 2 ½ miles, was directed by Brooklyn to go further out. By direction of Commanding Officer placed A. Schaefer, (A 1 Cl) in solitary confinement on bread and water for two days for sleeping on watch. Signals as per record book. Temperature of magazines as per list. Bunkers normal. At end of watch Morro Castle bore N.N.E. distant 2 3/4 miles. - F.J. Haeseler, Lieutenant, U.S.N.

Mer to 4 P.M. Fair, pleasant weather. Light breeze from E.S.E. and S.E. On blockade station, working engines frequently to keep position. Strong set to E'd and inshore. Signals as per signal record book. Held sale of the effects of the late F. J. Blakely (A 1 Cl) and realized $37.00 from same. Temperature of bunkers normal. At end of watch Morro bore N.N.E. ( ) ships head N.E. and distant 5200 yards. - H.A. Bispham, Lieutenant, U.S.N.

4 to 6 P.M. Cloudy with squalls over the land. Light breeze to light airs from S.E. Had quarters at 5.00. On blockade station. Morro Castle bore N.N.E., distant 2 ½ miles at end of watch. - Mark L. Bristol, Lieutenant, U.S.N.

6 to 8 P.M. Cloudy and warm. Calm and light airs from S.E. Holding position on blockade. Steam in four boilers. Coal bunkers normal. At end of watch Morro bore N. by E. ½ E. distant 4200 yards. - W.K. Gise, Ensign, U.S.N.

8 P.M to Mid. Cloudy weather. Gentle breeze from North. Obscured moonlight. Smooth sea. Lying on blockading station, engines moving occasionally to maintain position. Coal bunkers in normal condition. At end of watch El Morro bore N.N.E. distant about 4200 yards. - Harry Phelps, Lieutenant, U.S.N.

Tuesday, June 28, 1898

Commences to 4 A.M. Clear and pleasant. Gentle breeze from North. Bright moonlight until 12.30 when moon set. On blockade station at end of watch. Morro Castle for N.N.E. distant 4100 yards. - F.J. Haeseler, Lieutenant, U.S.N.

4 to 8 A.M. Clear and pleasant. Gentle to moderate breeze from N.N.E. At daylight stood off shore and took station three miles from entrance. At end of watch Morro bore N by E 5/8 E distant 5200 yards. Signals as per signal record. Bunker temperature normal. - H.A. Bispham, Lieutenant, U.S.N.

8 A.M. to Mer. Clear and warm. Light breezes from N.N.E. and S.S.W. Getting provisions on board from "Celtic". Wm. Sireeban reported the expiration of his term of enlistment. Lieut. H. Phelps inspected magazines, shell rooms and compartments under his charge, and tested flood cocks. Inspected coal bunkers. Morro Castle bore N by E. distant 3 ½ miles. - Mark L. Bristol, Lieutenant, U.S.N.

Mer. to 4 P.M. Cloudy. Passing showers. Light to stiff variable breezes. Provisioning from supply ship "Celtic". Received on board in Dept. of S. and A. $2000.00 and 565 lbs of fresh Beef, 284 lbs Fresh vegetables and 540 lbs fresh mutton, also 400 lbs apples, 500 gals beans, 3000 lbs Tinned Lean Beef, 1488 lbs Roast Beef, 5000 lbs biscuit, 504 lbs butter, 3000 pds coffee, 5500 lbs Wheat Flour, 1440 lbs Tinned Ham, 768 lbs Tinned Mutton, 1000 lbs Salt Pork, 220 lbs Raisins, 600 lbs Rice, 1488 lbs sausage, 152 ½ Galls. syrup, 6108 lbs sugar, 583 lbs tea, 2470 lbs Tomatoes, 2496 lbs vegetables, 32 gals. vinegar. D.F. Kronadrer (Chf.yeo) returned from the "Celtic", with his left forearm broken, caused by hatch giving way beneath him. At end of watch Morro bore N ½ E. 2 ½ miles distant. Steam four boilers. Coal bunkers normal. - W.K. Gise, Ensign, U.S.N.

4 to 6 P.M. Fair and pleasant weather. Light breeze from N.N.E. Smooth sea. Lying on blockading station, engines stopped. At 5.15 U.S.S. Waupatuck came alongside with the Flag Lieutenant of Squadron. Coal bunkers in normal condition. At end of watch El Morro bore N.N.E. distant 2 3/4 miles. - Harry Phelps, Lieutenant, U.S.N.

6 to 8 P.M. Fair and pleasant. Light breeze from N.N.E. At 7.00 went to quarters, and loaded the guns, and kept the crew at quarters. At the same time the ship moored in closer to Morro Castle, prepared to open fire if necessary. At end of watch Morro Castle bore N. by E. distant about 2 miles. Temperatures of magazines as per list. Coal bunkers normal. - F.J. Haeseler, Lieutenant, U.S.N.

8 P.M to Mid. Clear and pleasant. Bright moonlight. Light to gentle breeze from N.N.E. first hour, shifting to N.N.W. On station off entrance, distant about 3000 yards from Morro. At end of watch heading out to resume regular station. Temperature of bunkers normal. Signals as per signal record. - H.A. Bispham, Lieutenant, U.S.N.

Wednesday, June 29, 1898

Commences and to 4 A.M. Clear. Light breezes from E.N.E. to N.E. At 12.30 went ahead and headed for Guantanamo. Put over the patent log reading 0.0. Steam four boilers. Coal bunkers inspected. Moon set at 12.45. At end of watch about three miles west of Guantanamo. - Mark L. Bristol, Lieutenant, U.S.N.

4 to 8 A.M. Clear and warm. Light northerly breezes. Stood into Guantanamo Harbor and made fast to collier Rington. Commenced coaling at 6.45. Steam on four boilers. Coal bunkers normal. Received 45 tons coal. - W.K. Gise, Ensign, U.S.N.

8 A.M. to Mer. Clear and pleasant weather. Gentle breeze from East. Coaling ship, taking during watch 143 tons. The "Porter" came in. The "Manning" and "State of Texas" left the harbor. By order of the Captain, released A. Schaefer (A 1 Cl) from confinement, his term of punishment having expired. Temperature of magazines taken per list. Coal bunkers normal condition. - Harry Phelps, Lieutenant, U.S.N.

Mer. to 4 P.M. Fair and pleasant. Gentle breeze from East. At 2.10 finished coaling ship, having received 252 tons 900 lbs of coal in all. Cast off from the Rington and stood out of harbor, bound for blockade of Santiago de Cuba. At end of watch standing along the southern coast of Cuba about 1 ½ miles from shore. Signals as per record book. - F.J. Haeseler, Lieutenant, U.S.N.

4 to 6 P.M. Cloudy and pleasant. Light breeze from East to S.S.E. Standing to westward to resume station on blockade at end of watch slowed down to signal to flagship. Av. steam pressure 131 lbs Av revs stbd 61.1 port 62.8. - H.A. Bispham, Lieutenant, U.S.N.

6 to 8 P.M. Cloudy to squally. Passing thunder and squalls of rain. Light to moderate breezes from North to E.S.E. at 7.00 loaded the guns and went to quarters, and stood in to guard entrance. Steam four boilers. Bearing and distance of Morro at 8.00 was N.N.E. and 1 mile. - Mark L. Bristol, Lieutenant, U.S.N.

8 P.M. to Mid. Cloudy and rainy, to clear and moonlight. Light northerly breezes. On station off entrance to harbor. Steam on four boilers at 9.00 Morro bore N. by E. 1700 yards, and N.E. by N. 2400 yards by end of watch. Coal bunkers normal. - W.K. Gise, Ensign, U.S.N.

Thursday, June 30, 1898

Commences and to 4 A.M. Clear and pleasant weather. Light breeze from East. Smooth sea. At 12.15 stood out at slow speed from entrance to Santiago. At 12.30 went ahead full speed under four boilers, on course E.S.E. 3/4 E. and put over log reading 0. Passed several transports off Daiquiri. At 1.45 moon set. Stood along south coast of Cuba on various courses. Coal bunkers in normal condition. At end of watch approaching entrance to Guantanamo Bay at half speed. - Harry Phelps, Lieutenant, U.S.N.

4 to 8 A.M. Cloudy, with passing showers during first two hours of watch. At 5.30 entered harbor of Guantanamo, and by 6/15 made fast to U.S. collier Rington. At 7.00 commenced coaling ship. Bunker temperatures normal. Signals as per record. - F.J. Haeseler, Lieutenant, U.S.N.

8 A.M. to Mer. Fair to clear. Warm weather. Light airs from N.N.E and East. Engaged in coaling ship. Received up to noon. 176 tons. Bunker temperature normal. D. L. Lynch (0 Sea) reported his term of enlistment as having expired. Sent to "Marblehead" 7240 round cal. .45 ammunition. Lost overboard through carelessness of B.W. Kemp (App.) one box containing 1000 rounds cal. .45 Rec'd in Equip Dept 1 Hawser 8", 427 lbs Manila 3 ½", 286 lbs 2 3/4", 62 lbs 15 td, 90 lbs Hemp, 21 td and 78 lbs 9 td, 95 yards Flex Canvas Tarpaulin, 2 lbs Beeswax, 50 boxes Brushes and Handles, 48 ----r Brooms, 6 Padlocks, 6 Hasps and Hinges, 2 lengths Hose. - H.A. Bispham, Lieutenant, U.S.N.

Mer. to 4 P.M. Cloudy. Light breezes from S.E. and N.W. Coaling ship at Guantanamo until 2.15. Cast off from collier at 2.25 and stood out, the Indiana in. At 2.55 clear of the harbor and standing to the W'd. Coal bunkers inspected. Received on board 220 1000/2240 tons in all. - Mark L. Bristol, Lieutenant, U.S.N.

4 to 6 P.M. Partly cloudy and fine. Light variable breezes. Standing on various courses for blockade station. Steam in four boilers. Coal bunkers normal. - W.K. Gise, Ensign, U.S.N.

6 to 8 P.M. Fair and Pleasant weather. Light breeze from North. Smooth sea. Steaming to blockading station, reaching it 6.45 when stopped and remained so. Temperatures of magazine taken as per list. Coal bunkers in normal condition. At end of watch El Morro bore N.N.E. distant 4000 yards. - Harry Phelps, Lieutenant, U.S.N.

8 P.M. to Mid. Fair and pleasant. Light breeze from N.N.E. At 9.20 flagship signaled, "Prepare to bombard batteries from same position as sixteenth at 6.00 A.M. Army will begin general attack about same time." and at 10.00 to this ship "Take position near search light ship for the night." Sent crew to quarters, loaded all guns, spread fires, and stood in close to search light ship. At end of watch Morro Castle bore N. by E. And distant 2800 yards. - F.J. Haeseler, Lieutenant, U.S.N.

Friday, June 30, 1898

Commences and to 4 am: Fair and pleasant. Bright moonlight. Vessels of the fleet lying in semi-circle, battle formation, blockading Santiago. At 2:05 the New York's steam launch came alongside with assistant Ensign _____ U.S.N. and 8 men of the Merrimac. At 3:00 clock this morning started in for Santiago, and were fired on in the entrance at 3:15, and firing continued until 3:30 from the shore batteries. At the end of watch, lying with engines stopped, about three miles off Santiago. - F.J. Haeseler, Lieutenant, U.S.N.

4 am to 8 am: Fair to cloudy and warm. Light airs and breeze from north first half. Stiff squall accompanied by heavy rain, wind, lightning, and thunder came from S.W., wind shifting to SSW during third hour. Raining at end of watch. Moon set at 4:06. At daylight sighted sighted the New York's steam launch standing to the S'd. Later launch _____ about, standing to the w'd. When off the entrance, guns on the w's battery and along the shore, opened fire upon her. Launch continued to w'd, uninjured, and later stood offshore. Edged inshore a little, and launch came alongside. "New York" stood to W'd and picked up launch. The St. Louis came in at 7:00 _____ steam pressure _____ the _____ _____ _____ _____. - H.A. Bispham, Lieutenant, U.S.N.

8 am to noon: Clear and warm. Light breeze from east. Lying off and on in blockade station. The small boats of the enemy were seen _____ around at the entrance to the harbor. The "Yankee" joined the fleet. Signals _____ record. Steam from boilers. Inspected coal bunkers and magazines. The following by order of Commanding Officer: J S _____, (Cox) disrated to seaman, J.J. B _____ rated to
Coxswain, Wm _____ (Sea) confined _____ days solitary confinement on bread and water for disobedience of orders and insolence to P.O.; P.O. K _____, two days bread and water from disrespect to an officer and slow in obeying orders; _____ K _____ (_____) and Gl _____, reported the expiration for their enlistments. - Mark L. Bristol, Lieutenant U.S.N.

Friday, June 30, 1898

Noon to 4 AM Clear and warm. Light breeze from East. In obedience to orders of Commander in Chief, kept inside cable steamer "Ad____" at 2:50 Spanish flag of truce boat "C____", was met by USS Vixen under flag of truce, and accompanied to USS New York. ____ _____ under steam from boilers ____ pressure _____ _____. Bunkers reported normal. Sighted masts and smokestacks of sunken collier Merrimac. The USS _____ came in. Asst. Engr. A.K. C_____ reported ____ _____ _____. - W.K. Gise, Ensign U.S.N.

4 to 6 PM _____ _____. Light breeze from East. Smooth sea. Lying by the cable steamer "A____" working engine to keep position. At 5:09 mustered at quarters. At 6:00 started ahead full speed to _____ blockading squadron. Signals at 5:20 from flag _____ _____ prisoners of war two_____ _____ _____. At 5:40 "Take blockading station". Repeated all signals. At 5:50 from flag "Take blockading stations _____ _____. - Harry Phelps, Lieutenant, U.S.N.

6 to 8 pm Fair and pleasant. _____ and light airs from N.N.E. Stood down to westward and at end of watch in position blockade formation. - F.J. Haeseler, Lieutenant, U.S.N.

8 pm to Midnight Generally fair. Light air and breeze from N.N.W. except first hour, when a heavy rain squall passed by moderate breeze from NNE _____ _____ to WSW. Breeze came out of the NW after squall. Moonlight at intervals. At 10:40 a vessel to the __'d signaled the approach of a torpedo boat, and firing was commenced by vessels of the western end of the line. Went to general quarters and at 11:20 secured. Lying to in assigned position. - S_____, Lieutenant.

Friday, July 1, 1898

Commences and to 4 A.M. Fair to clear. Pleasant weather. Light breeze from North. Off entrance, distance about 3000 yards. Moon set at 2.45. Bunker temperature normal. - H.A. Bispham, Lieutenant, U.S.N.

4 to 8 A.M. Clear. Light breezes from North. At 5.30 cleared ship for action. Steam in four boilers. On blockade station. Coal bunkers inspected and reported to in normal condition. At east of watch Morro Castle bore N.N.E. ½ E. distant 2 miles. - Mark L. Bristol, Lieutenant. U.S.N.

8 A.M. to Mer. Clear and warm. Light variable airs and breezes. At 10.20 in obedience to signals went to general quarters and closed in under the western battery hauling out again at 11.20. The New York and smaller craft shelling hills at other end of line. 4 regiments of land troops seen advancing westward along railroad track. Steam on four boilers. Coal bunkers normal. Magazine temperatures as per list. At 12:00 Morro Castle bore N by E 3/4 E. distant 4600 yards. - W.K. Gise, Ensign, U.S.N.

Mer. to 4 P.M. Clear and pleasant weather first half, cloudy latter part. Light breezes from East. Smooth sea. Lying stopped on blockading station. The New York, Oregon, Newark, and Gloucester continued firing at shore near Base Battery until 3.00. Coal bunkers in normal condition at end of watch. El Morro bore N.N.E. distant 5000 yards. At 4.00, Flagship made telegraphic signal "secure". - Harry Phelps, Lieutenant, U.S.N.

4 to 6 P.M. Cloudy but pleasant. Light breeze from North. At 5.00 mustered crew at quarters. At end of watch Morro Castle bore N.E. 3/4 E. distant 2 ½ miles. - F.J. Haeseler, Lieutenant, U.S.N.

6 to 8 P.M. Fair and Pleasant. Light breeze from North. Lightning to N'd and E'd. Moonlight after dark. At 7.00 moved in to two miles off Morro. At end of watch Morro bore N. by E 3/4 E. distant about 2 miles. Temperature of bunkers. Normal and of magazines as per list. (Highest 110 degrees). - H.A. Bispham, Lieutenant, U.S.N.

8 P.M. to Mid. Clear, bright moonlight. Gentle to light breezes from N.N.W. On guard at entrance to Harbor; all hands at quarters. At end of watch Morro bore N.E. by N. distant 2200 yards. Steam four boilers. Surgeon Clement Biddle U.S.N. reported for duty as relief of Surgeon W.R. DuBose, U.S.N. - Mark L. Bristol, Lieutenant, U.S.N.

Saturday, July 2, 1898

Commences and to 4 A.M. Clear and cool. Bright moonlight. Moon set at 3.45. Light to gentle N.N.W. breezes. Standing by ship losing search lights. Steam on four boilers. Coal bunkers normal. Flagship made signal "Be prepared to attack batteries at 5.00. After silencing East and West batteries, "S" and "A" will close in and fire on Punta Gorda. Same positions as last time." At end of watch Morro bore N.N.E. distant 2200 yards. - W.K. Gise, Ensign, U.S.N.

4 to 8 A.M. Clear and pleasant weather. Light breeze from N.N.W. Smooth sea. Lying at 3500 yards from Morro attending search light vessel. At 4.30 hauled off to blockading station and cleared for action. At 5.15 went to general quarters, and stood in to 3000 yards, by signal from flagship. Signal "Fire must be slow." At 5.30 opened fire on western batteries, the New York, Newark, Brooklyn, Oregon, Indiana, Iowa, Massachusetts and Vixen also opening fire east and west batteries. At 6.45 the flagstaff and colors were shot away from Morro. At 7.30 flagship signaled "Withdraw". Resumed blockading station. Expended ammunition as follows. 6 common shells 12", 2 S.A.P. shells 12", 2 A.P. shells 12", 7 ½ full charges 12", 104 common shells 6", 1 Shrapnel 6", 53 reduced charges 6", 55-6 pdr common shell, 50 electric and 70 Percussion primers. At end of watch El Morro bore N.N.E. distant 4500 yards. At 8.00 the west battery fired several shots which fell to seaward of this vessel. - Harry Phelps, Lieutenant, U.S.N.

8 A.M. to Mer. Clear and pleasant. Light to gentle breezes from S.E. At 11.00 U.S.S. Hornet came in from Westward followed by a U.S. tug, name unknown, towing a small schooner flying the English flag. Two large fires visible in the mountains, about three miles to the westward and near the shore. Signals as per record book. At end of watch Morro Castle bore N.N.E. 1/4 E., distant 2 ½ miles. - F.J. Haeseler, Lieutenant, U.S.N.

Mer. to 4 P.M. Fair and warm. Light breeze from S.E., shifting to North during last half hour, in a stiff squall, with rain in shore. At end of watch Morro bore N.N.E. ½ E. by steering compass, distant 4600 yards. Temperature of bunkers normal. Ship in position off entrance. - H.A. Bispham, Lieutenant, U.S.N.

4 to 6 P.M. Clear. Gentle breezes from N.E. to North. On blockade station, Morro bearing N.N.E. distant 2 ½ miles, at end of watch. Coal bunkers inspected. - Mark L. Bristol, Lieutenant, U.S.N.

6 to 8 P.M. Clear. Bright moonlight. Light N.N.W. breezes. In station close to search light ship. Steam in four boilers. At end of watch Morro bore N.E. distant 2200 yards. Fires on mountains to westward of entrance, and reflection of fire in city. Coal bunkers in normal condition. Magazine temperature as per list. - W.K. Gise, Ensign, U.S.N.

8 P.M. to Mid. Clear and pleasant weather. Bright moonlight. Light breeze from N.N.W. Lying at 3000 yards from Morro, attending search light vessel. at 11.50 the Indiana relieved this vessel. At end of watch proceeding to blockading station. Coal bunkers in normal condition. - Harry Phelps, Lieutenant U.S.N.

Sunday, July 3, 1898

Commences and to 4 A.M. Clear and pleasant. Bright moonlight. On blockade station. Large fires visible in Santiago and on neighboring hills. At of watch Morro Castle bore N.N.E. ½ E. distance about 2 miles. - F.J. Haeseler, Lieutenant, U.S.N.

4 to 8 A.M. Clear to fair, pleasant weather. Gentle breeze from North. At daylight stood out from entrance, taking day blockading position, about 3 miles from Morro. Temperatures of coal bunkers normal. The "Fern" came in at 6.30, towing a large lighter. At end of watch Morro bore N by E per steering compass, distant 5300 yards. Moon set at 4.50. - H.A. Bispham, Lieutenant, U.S.N.

8 A.M. to Mer. Cloudy to clear. Light breezes from north. At 9.55 (55 corrected over 45) the enemy's ships were sighted coming out; signaled "gen 250", went ahead full speed headed in, went to quarters and at one engaged the enemy, closing in. The ship leading was of the Vizcaya class and the flagship. Four ships came out, evidently the "Admirante Oquendo", "Viscaya", "Maria Theresa" and "Cristolbal Colon"; besides there were two torpedo-boat destroyers. These two latter were compelled to run ashore by this ship and the "Gloucester". This ship was warmly engaged with the third in the enemy's column until she ran ashore on fire, and about this time the fourth, engaged with the "Iowa", was run ashore on fire. Went ahead for the second which was engaged with the "Oregon". She steered in for shore at 11.10 and we opened at long range. A few minutes later she was on fire and struck her colors running in for the beach; at 11.30 she blew up. Remainder of watch chasing "Cristolbal Colon" to the westward, the "Brooklyn" and "Oregon" ahead and closing. Steam four boilers, forced draft. This ship was struck three times: by a 5.5 inch shell through the starboard forward superstructure, exploding and carrying away part of the ash hoist engine and blowing a large hole in uptake besides several small holes; one passing through pilot house; and the other striking starboard turret. D. S. Schwarm (Sea) was knocked over the concussion of the 12" gun, and falling down the ammunition hoist had right leg broken. Ammunition expended per list. - Mark L. Bristol, Lieutenant, U.S.N.

Mer. to 4 P.M. Clear and warm. In chase of "Cristolbal Colon"; steam in four boilers. Forced draft. At 1.20 the chase hauled in toward shore and ran bow on beach, hauling down colors. The "Brooklyn's ---- boarding officer, The "New York", "Resolute", and "Vixen" came up about 3.00. All ships lowered boats and transferred prisoners to "Resolute". Oregon sent prize crew on board. - W.K. Gise, Ensign, U.S.N.

4 to 6 P.M. Clear and pleasant weather. Light breeze from N.W. Smooth sea. Lying to. Boats transferring prisoners from prize to "Resolute". Signals as follows: At 4.30 from flagship, " Return with Brooklyn". Answered, "Shall we leave our boats." reply "No", At 5.30 to flagship "Chaplain Jones must be sent north. Had hemorrhage of lungs. Request that he can go by first steamer." Flagship answered, "Yes." The "Brooklyn" left for the Eastward at 4.30. - Harry Phelps, Lieutenant, U.S.N.

6 to 8 P.M. Fair and pleasant. Light breeze from N.W. Lying near wreck of "Colon" waiting for our boats to return. At 7.00 the "Vixen" came in and reported she had seen the enemy and flagship signaled to this ship. "Prepare to chase." - F.J. Haeseler, Lieutenant, U.S.N.

8 P.M. to Mid. Fair and pleasant. Bright moonlight. Light breeze from North. Remained by "Oregon" during entire watch by order from the "New York". The "New York" and the "Resolute" got underway and stood to Eastward at 10.30. Hoisted in cutter and steam launch, not being requested by "Oregon". Lost sight of "Colon" about 10.00 which vessel was later reported to be on her beam ends. - H.A. Bispham, Lieutenant, U.S.N.

Monday, July 4, 1898

Commences and to 4 A.M. Fair. Light breezes from north. Lying to off the wreck of the Cristobal Colon. Steam four boilers. - Mark L. Bristol, Lieutenant, U.S.N.

4 to 8 A.M. Partly cloudy and warm. Light and gentle northerly breezes. Hove to off wreck of Cristobal Colon, until 7.00, when headed eastward for Santiago. At daylight discovered the ship lying on starboard side, stem to beach, and low to seaward, with about one half of the midship section out of water. Guns of port battery still mounted. Port screw in view and apparently intact. Coal bunkers normal. Dressed ship with flags at masthead at 8.00. - W.K. Gise, Ensign, U.S.N.

8 A.M. to Mer. Fair and pleasant weather. Light air from N.E., shifting to East and banking to S.E. in stiff breeze at end of watch. Standing along South coast fo Cuba under steam, four boilers. At 10.15 passed wreck of "Vizcaya" on the beach. At 11.45 passed wrecks of "Admirante Oquendo" and "Infanta Maria Teresa" and two torpedo boats. Stopped engines to communicate with Press boat which offered 28 prisoners picked up on shore, but were not received. Board of Survey condemned and threw overboard 56 cans of sausage. Coal bunkers in normal condition. At meridian fired a salute of 21 guns. at end of watch about 3 miles west of Santiago. Magazine temperatures as per list. Found English ship "Indefatigueable" and Austrian "Infanta Maria Teresa" lying near entrance. Expended 42 lbs. Saluting powder, 21 cork plugs, 21 primers for 6 pdr cart cases. - Harry Phelps, Lieutenant, U.S.N.

Mer. to 4 P.M. Fair and pleasant. Gentle breeze from S.E. Standing to eastward until 12.30 when headed towards Santiago entrance and stopped engines. Lying still in water, using engines occasionally until end of watch. At end of watch Morro Castle bore north, distant 3 miles. Signals as per record book. Bunker temperature normal. - F.J. Haeseler, Lieutenant, U.S.N.

4 to 6 P.M. Cloudy. Rain squalls over land. Moderate breeze from E.S.E. Stood to Eastward to communicate with Flagship by signal. Signals as per signal record book. Surgeon W. R. Du Bose this day detached from this vessel and ordered to proceed to duty at Naval Hospital, N.Y. Chaplain H.W. Jones, U.S.N. was this day ordered to proceed to Naval Hospital, N.Y. for treatment. Coal bunkers in normal condition. - H.A. Bispham, Lieutenant, U.S.N.

6 to 8 P.M. Cloudy. Gentle to light breezes from E.S.E. On blockade station. Magazine temperature per list. - Mark L. Bristol, Lieutenant, U.S.N.

8 P.M to Mid. Clear. Bright moonlight. Gentle breezes from W.N.W. Lying off Santiago, Massachusetts playing search light on entrance. At 11.15 sighted steamer with two funnels and three masts heading out. Fired two red stars and went to general quarters. Opened fire with main battery on ship. Western battery answered. Coal bunkers normal. Steam four boilers. - W.K. Gise, Ensign, U.S.N.

Tuesday, July 5, 1898

Commences and to 4 A.M. Clear and pleasant weather. Gentle breeze from North. Bright moonlight. Lying off entrance to Santiago, firing at vessel in entrance, at range of 3500 yards, using port battery until 12.05, then starboard battery. The firing from the Western battery continued until about 12.20. At 12.45 the vessel sunk on eastern side of channel, of Estrella battery, heeling to port about 40 degrees, with lee rail about awash. At 1.00 secured, and returned to station on blockade line. Expended ammunition as follows, 4 common shell 12", 2 S.A.P. shell 12", 2 A.P. Shell 12", 3 common shell 6", 15 S.A.P. 6", 7 ½ Full charges 12", 18 Full charges 6", 16 Electric and 20 Percussion Primers. Coal bunkers in normal condition. At end of watch Morro Castle bore N. by E. and distant about 2 ½ miles. - Harry Phelps, Lieutenant, U.S.N.

4 to 8 A.M. Fair and pleasant. Gentle breeze from North. On blockade station abreast Santiago. At 6.30 located the vessel sunk in the channel as being a three masted vessel with two smoke-stacks, having the appearance of an old man of war. She was sunk a little inside Estrella battery, on the east side fo the channel, and apparently does not block the entrance. Bunker temperatures normal. - F.J. Haeseler, Lieutenant, U.S.N.

8 A.M to Mer. Fair and warm. Gentle breeze form East and E.S.E. Commanding officer went on board "New York" in obedience to signal. Other signals as per signal record. Received provisions from "Celtic" as follows, 1003 lbs. fresh beef, 879 lbs onions, 336 lbs tinned corn Beef. Off entrance to harbor, lying near "Celtic". Temperature of bunkers normal, and of magazines as per list. - H.A. Bispham, Lieutenant, U.S.N.

Mer. to 4 P.M. Fair. Gentle breezes from E.S.E. Lying to off Santiago. Coal bunkers inspected. Steam four boilers. - Mark L. Bristol, Lieutenant, U.S.N.

4 to 6 P.M. Cloudy but fine. Passing showers. Light S.E. breezes. Lying to off wrecks of Maria Theresa and Oquendo, and returning to station off Morro. Explosion on Oquendo. Steam in four boilers. Coal bunkers normal. - W.K. Gise, Ensign, U.S.N.

6 to 8 P.M. Fair and pleasant weather. Light Easterly airs. Smooth sea. Steamed to Eastward, and at 7.00 resumed station off Morro Castle. Temperatures of magazine taken as per list. Coal bunkers normal. - Harry Phelps, Lieutenant, U.S.N.
8 P.M. to Mid. Partly cloudy but pleasant. Light to gentle breeze from north. On blockade station. Bunkers normal. At end of watch Morro bore N.E. distant 2 ½ miles. - F.J. Haeseler, Lieutenant, U.S.N.

Wednesday, July 6 1898
Commences and to 4 A.M. Fair and pleasant. Gentle breeze from North. Bright moonlight. Lying to off entrance to harbor. Strong set to westward. Temperature of coal bunkers normal. - H.A. Bispham, Lieutenant, U.S.N.
4 to 8 A.M. Clear. Gentle to light breezes from North to N.N.W. Lying to off Santiago. Coal bunkers inspected. At 8.00 Morro bore North, distant 2 1/4 miles. - Mark L. Bristol, Lieutenant, U.S.N.
8 A.M to Mer. Fair and pleasant. Gentle breeze from E.N.E. Lying to off entrance. Temperature of coal bunkers normal. Steam in four boilers. Made routine reports at 10.00 and 12.00. - W.K. Gise, Ensign, U.S.N.
Mer. to 4 P.M. Clear and pleasant weather. Gentle breeze from E.S.E. Smooth sea. Lying on blockading station, engines stopped. At 1.00, the German gunboat "Geier" flying "G.R.M.N.", came in from S'd. Signaled to "Oregon" "Coming from Port Royal, Jamaica, as permission to enter Santiago de Cuba." "Oregon" answered, "Communication risky, we are likely to bombard at moment., to co-operate with Army." German answered "Thank you." and stood in towards harbor entrance, flying signal for pilot. None came out, and at 3.00 she left for westward. Coal bunkers reported in normal condition. At end of watch Morro bore N.N.E. distant 5100 yards. - Harry Phelps, Lieutenant, U.S.N.
4 to 6 P.M. Fair and pleasant. Light airs from South and West. Bunker temperature normal. At end of watch Morro Castle bore N.E. and N. distant 2 miles. - F.J. Haeseler, Lieutenant, U.S.N.
6 to 8 P.M. Fair and warm. Light westerly airs. Signals as per signal record. Temperature of coal bunkers normal, and of magazines per list, highest 112 degrees. At 6.01 a tug flying the British Jack and a flag of truce, came out from entrance, and communicated with this vessel regarding the whereabouts of the German man-of-war. The tug returned at 6.20. - H.A. Bispham, Lieutenant, U.S.N.
8 P.M. to Mid. Clear and moonlight. Light airs to light breezes from north. Coal bunkers inspected. At 12.00 Morro Castle bore N. by E. ½ E. distant 4 miles. - Mark L. Bristol, Lieutenant, U.S.N.

Thursday, July 7, 1898
Commences and to 4 A.M. Clear and fine. Bright moonlight. Gentle northerly breezes.. In position on blockade. Steam on four boilers. Coal bunkers normal. - W.K. Gise, Ensign, U.S.N.
4 to 8 A.M. Clear and pleasant weather. Gentle breeze from North. Smooth sea. Lying on blockading station., engines stopped. Coal bunkers in normal condition. At end of watch Morro Castle bore N.N.E. distant 5200 yards. - Harry Phelps, Lieutenant, U.S.N.
8 A.M. to Mer. Clear and fair. Warm weather. Light breeze to light airs from North shifting to S.E. last half of watch. Lieut. F.J. Haeseler, U.S.N., left ship on duty as member of a board to examine and report upon the wrecks of the Spanish vessels. Left station off entrance, following course of flagship to the westward. Temperatures of coal bunkers normal and of magazines as per list. Lieutenant H. Phelps inspected magazines and other compartments under his charge. Tested flood cocks. - H.A. Bispham, Lieutenant, U.S.N.
Mer. to 4 P.M. Fair. Gentle to light breezes from E.S.E. to S.E. Lying to off the wrecks of the "Admirante Oquendo" and "Infanta Maria Teresa". - Mark L. Bristol, Lieutenant, U.S.N.
4 to 6 P.M. Partly cloudy and fine. Gentle E.S.E. breezes. Proceeding to and lying in blockading position. Morro bore N by E, 6500 yards, at end of watch. Steam in four boilers. Bunkers normal. - W.K. Gise, Ensign, U.S.N.
6 to 8 P.M. Fair and pleasant weather. Gentle breeze from E.S.E. Smooth sea. Lying on blockade station, engines stopped. At 7.30 ship made general signal, "Until further orders, ports need not be closed at night if they add to the comfort of officers and men." Coal bunkers in normal condition. Temperatures of magazines taken as per list. At end of watch El Morro bore N by E. 3/4 E. distant 6000 yards. - Harry Phelps, Lieutenant, U.S.N.
8 P.M. to Mid. Fair to clear, warm weather. Lght breeze from North. Moon rose at 9.50. Signals as per signal record. Stood slowly to S'd and E'd at 9.00; when moon rose, returned to station off entrance. Temperature of coal bunkers normal. - H.A. Bispham, Lieutenant, U.S.N.

Friday, July 8, 1898
Commences and to 4 A.M. Clear. Bright moonlight. Gentle to moderate breezes from North to N.E. Coal bunkers inspected. At 4.00 Morro bore N. by E. distant 4 miles. - Mark L. Bristol, Lieutenant, U.S.N.
4 to 8 A.M. Clear and fine. Moderate to gentle breezes from N.E. and North. On blockade station. Steam on all boilers. Coal bunkers normal. The "Dixie" came in. - W.K. Gise, Ensign, U.S.N.
8 A.M. to Mer. Fair and pleasant weather. Gentle breeze form North first half, shifting to S.E. at 10.30. Lying on blockade station until 8.50, when steamed down to a position abreast wrecks of "Infanta Maria Teresa" and "Admirante Oquendo", lying there from 9.40 to end of watch. Lieut. Comdr. G. B. Harber and Asst. Surgeon H.H. Hase left the ship on board "Vesuvius" on duty. Signals at 8.35 from Flag. (Newark) "Board of survey meets on board this ship at 10.00 A.M." Temperatures of magazines taken as per list. Coal bunkers in normal condition. - Harry Phelps, Lieutenant, U.S.N.
Mer. to 4 P.M. Fair and pleasant. Gentle to stiff breeze from S.E., shifting to E.S.E. At 1.00 went ahead from wreck of "Infanta Maira Teresa" and resumed blockade station, having hoisted in both cutters. - H.A. Bispham, Lieutenant, U.S.N.
4 to 6 P.M. Fair. Stiff to moderate breezes from E.S.E. Coal bunkers inspected. At 6.00 Morro bore N.N.E. ½ E. distant 3 ½ miles. - Mark L. Bristol, Lieutenant, U.S.N.
6 to 8 P.M Cloudy and warm. Gentle E.S.E. breezes. Lying off entrance to Santiago. Steam on all boilers. Sent 8 -----; ammunition taken to Rough Rider Regiment. Coal bunkers normal. - W.K. Gise, Ensign, U.S.N.
8 P.M. to Mid. Clear and pleasant weather. Gentle breeze for North. Smooth sea. Lying on blockading station, engines stopped. Coal bunkers in normal condition. At 10.40 moon rose. - Harry Phelps, Lieutenant, U.S.N.

Saturday, July 9, 1898
Commences and 4 A.M. Clear and pleasant. Gentle breeze from North. Bright moonlight. Temperature of bunkers normal. Steam under three boilers. A.B. and C. - H.A. Bispham, Lieutenant, U.S.N.
4 to 8 A.M. Clear. Gentle breeze from North to N.N.E. Lying to off Santiago. At 8.00 Morro bore N.N.E. distant 3 ½ miles. Inspected coal bunkers. - Mark L. Bristol, Lieutenant, U.S.N.
8 A.M. to Mer. Clear and warm. Light breezes from North and S.E. Lying off Santiago. Steam on all boilers. Bunkers normal. Made routine reports at 10.00 and 12.00. Magazine temperatures as per list. Whitney, (O.S.) Reported expiration of enlistment. - W.K. Gise, Ensign, U.S.N.
Mer. to 4 P.M. Clear and pleasant. Moderate breeze from S.E. Smooth sea. Lying on blockading station. At 1.15 the Newark coaled from Altares. Brooklyn hoisted red pennant. Received mail from Vixen also stores as follows, 2000 electric primers, assembling rings for hydraulic rammers. Signals as per record book. Coal bunkers in normal condition. At 3.30 Newark left the fleet bound to Eastward. Sold contents of lucky bag, realizing $1.40. Received in S.E. Dept. 120lbs Tobin Bronze 1"; 106 lbs 1 ½", 64 iron screws (asstd) 36 Flex nuts (asstd), 5 9/16 lbs Condenser Tube packing, 12 Brass Reducers. - Harry Phelps, Lieutenant, U.S.N.

4 to 6 P.M. Fair and pleasant. Gentle breeze from S.E. Boiler "B" disconnected at 5.10. Steam under boilers A. + C. Signals as per record book. - H.A. Bispham, Lieutenant, U.S.N.
6 to 8 P.M. Fair. Gentle to light breezes from S.E. Lying to off Santiago. At 8.00 Morro bore N.E. by N. distant 3 ½ miles. Inspected coal bunkers. - Mark L. Bristol, Lieutenant, U.S.N.
8 P.M. to Mid. Clear and fine. Light to gentle breezes from N.E. to North. Lying off entrance. Steam on 2 boilers. Bunkers normal. - W.K. Gise, Ensign, U.S.N.

Sunday, July 10, 1898
Commences and to 4 A.M. Clear and pleasant weather. Bright moonlight. Lightning to E'd. Gentle breeze from North. Smooth sea. Lying blockading station, engines stopped. Coal bunkers reported in normal condition. - Harry Phelps, Lieutenant, U.S.N.
4 to 8 A.M. Fair and pleasant. Light to gentle breeze from North. At 6.00, U.S.S. St. Paul came in from New York with more troops. Bunker temperature normal. At end of watch Morro Castle bore N.E. by N. distant 3 miles. - F.J. Haeseler, Lieutenant, U.S.N.
8 A.M. to Mer. Clear and warm. Gentle to moderate breeze from N.E. to E.S.E. Stood down towards Aquadores at 9.30 and at --- headed to W'd to stand by launch which was sent from Brooklyn to inspect enemy's wrecked torpedo boats. At _____ went ahead again to the E'd to rejoin flagship. The Brooklyn was seen to stand to the S'd and board a Norwegian steamer supposed to be loaded with provisions for the enemy. Made continue signals at noon, which Brooklyn _____. Other signals as per signal record. At end of watch to W'd of Aquadores and three miles off shore. Held prelimin _____ quarters at 8.45. Bunker temperatures normal. - H.A. Bispham, Lieutenant, U.S.N.
Mer. to 4 P.M. Clear to fair, with squalls over the land. Moderate to gentle breezes from E.S.E to East. Lying to off Aquadores. Coal bunkers inspected. Steam three boilers. J. O. McCormick (A 2 Cl.) and W. DeForest (A 3 Cl.) were transferred to the Hornet with ------ and effects. - Mark L. Bristol, Lieutenant, U.S.N.
4 to 6 P.M. Cloudy and cool. Passing showers. Gentle to light easterly breezes. Hauled to position east of Morro and well inshore. B_____ opened fire on town at 4.45 ceased firing at 6.05. Texas opened with 12" at 5.27. Fired six 12" Common shell and three 6" common shell at about 10000 yards range. Coal bunkers normal. - W.K. Gise, Ensign, U.S.N.
6 to 8 P.M. Cloudy with light passing showers. Light breeze from East. Ceased firing at 6.05 and secured. Remainder of watch lying near "Brooklyn". At 7.55 "Brooklyn" signaled "Take blockading station 3 ½ miles S.E. of Morro. Asst. Surgeon H.H. Hass U.S.N. — on board from special duty on shore with army. Temperatures of magazines as per list. Coal bunkers in normal condition. - Harry Phelps, Lieutenant, U.S.N.
8 P.M. to Mid. Cloudy but pleasant. Light breeze from N.N.E. and N.E. At 8.05 flagship signaled "Annul last signal", and then made signal blockading station 3 ½ miles S.W. of Morro. "In obedience thereto proceeded to that station arriving there at 9.00. Morro bore at _____. At end of watch on blockading station, Morro Castle bearing N.E. ½ N distant about 3 miles. Bunker temperature normal. - F.J. Haeseler, Lieutenant, U.S.N.

Monday, July 11 – Tuesday, July 12, 1898
[omitted]

Wednesday, July 13, 1898
Commences and to 4 A.M. Clear and pleasant. Light airs and breezes from N.E. Moon rose at 2.20. Working engines to keep position three miles to S.E. of the wreck of the "Colon". Bunker temperatures normal. - F.J. Haeseler, Lieutenant, U.S.N.
4 to 8 A.M. Fair and pleasant. Light to gentle breeze from North. Stood in for beach at daylight. At 5.50 sent whale boat ashore to the wreck of the "Colon", with working party in charge of the Executive Officer. Whale boat was followed, with additional men in fourth cutter. At end of watch off Rio Taquino. Bunker temperatures normal. Inspected life buoys. - H.A. Bispham, Lieutenant, U.S.N.
8 A.M. to Mer. Fair. Gentle breezes from East. Boats at work securing "Christobal Colon". Boats returned at 11.30, and hoisted them in. Coal bunkers inspected. - Mark L. Bristol, Lieutenant, U.S.N.
Mer. to 4 P.M. Cloudy. Light breezes from S.S.E. and N.N.E. Lying about 3 miles Rio Taquino. At 2.30 the wrecking tug T. J. Merritt ran in, when steamed close to wreck, and sent armed boat to cover landing of wreckers to carry wire hawser ashore. Steam on three boilers. Bunkers normal. - W.K. Gise, Ensign, U.S.N.
4 to 6 P.M. Cloudy. Light breeze from N.W. Smooth sea. Lying about 3 miles off Rio Taquino all the watch. - Harry Phelps, Lieutenant, U.S.N.
6 to 8 P.M. Cloudy with passing showers. Light breeze from N.E. At 6.20, armed boat protecting wrecking tug came alongside. At 6.30 headed east, steaming at full speed. Put over patent log reading 0.0. At end of watch on course E by S. about 2 ½ miles off coast. Bunker temperature normal. - F.J. Haeseler, Lieutenant, U.S.N.
8 P.M. to Mid. Fair to clear, pleasant weather. Passing showers first hour. Light breeze from from N.E. Underway, standing to the E.d along the coast. Stopped at 10.40 and hauled in patent log. reading 35.3. Lying to remainder of watch. Bunker temperature normal. Average steam pressure 132 lbs. Av. revs. stbd. 61.6 port. 61.7. - H.A. Bispham, Lieutenant, U.S.N.

Thursday, July 14 – Friday, July 15, 1898
[omitted]

Saturday, July 16, 1898
Commences and to 4 A.M. Clear and pleasant. Light northerly airs. Moon rose at 3.20 Bunker temperatures normal. - H.A. Bispham, Lieutenant, U.S.N.
4 to 8 A.M. Clear light airs from North. Commenced coaling ship at 5.15. Took in 73 tons for watch. Received 18 [8?, 28?] barrels of oil from the "Lebanon" for the Engineers Dept. One transport and a Norwegian steamer left the harbor. - Mark L. Bristol, Lieutenant, U.S.N.
8 A.M. to Mer. Partly cloudy and hot. Light Northeasterly airs to light S.E. breezes. Coaling ship. Received on board for day to noon 200 tons. Received from "Vulcan" 19-12" Common Shell. Flag of truce boat with French flag at bow came down Bay from Caymanera. - W.K. Gise, Ensign, U.S.N.
Mer. to 4 P.M. Cloudy weather. Light breeze from East. Continued coaling ship until 2.30, when stopped, having received in all 519 ½ tons. Received from U.S.S. Vulcan 6-12" Common Shell. Coal bunkers in normal condition. The DuPont left the port at 3.30. - Harry Phelps, Lieutenant, U.S.N.
4 to 6 P.M. Fair and warm. Light breeze from East, falling calm during last hour of watch. At 5.30 the U.S.S. Annapolis came in and anchored further up the harbor. At 5.45 the Army Transport #22 came in. At 5.55 the Red Cross ship "State of Texas" came in. The Commanding Officer of the French man of war "Admiral Rigualt de Genonilly" paid and official call. Bunker temperature normal. - F.J. Haeseler, Lieutenant, U.S.N.
6 to 8 P.M. Clear and warm. Light airs from East. Bunker temperatures normal. The "Detroit" came in and anchored at 2.15. Signals as per signal record. Temperatures of magazines as per list. - H.A. Bispham, Lieutenant, U.S.N.
8 P.M. to Mid. Clear and cool. Light airs from North. Bunker temperature normal. Barometer slowly falling. - Mark L. Bristol, Lieutenant, U.S.N.

BIBLIOGRAPHY

Books:
Adler, Fred T and Green, Harry C. (1899) The Official Dewey Souvenir Programme. Mayor's Committee on Plan and Scope: New York.
Albertson, Robert Brooke. () Portsmouth Virginia. Arcadia: Chicago.
Alden, John D. (1989) American Steel Navy. Annapolis, MD: Naval Institute Press.
Allen & Ginter, Inc. (1886) Our Navy. Allen & Ginter: Richmond, Virginia.
Allen, Willis Boyd. (1899) Cleared for Action. E.P. Dutton & company: New York.
American Jewish Committee. (1901) The American Jewish Year Book. Jewish Publication Society of America: Philadelphia.
American Ordnance Company (1894) Artillery Catalogue. American Ordnance Company: Bridgeport, Connecticut.
Archibald, E.H.H. (1971) The Metal Fighting Ship in the Royal Navy, 1860-1970. ARCO Publishing: New York.
Armstrong, G.E. (1896) Torpedoed and Torpedo-Vessels. George Bell and Sons: London.
Armstrong, LeRoy. (1899) Pictorial Atlas Illustrating the Spanish American War, G.F. Cram: New York.
Andrews, H. Franklin. (1900) The Hamlin Family. H. Franklin Andrews: Exira, Iowa.
Attwood, Edward L. (1904) War-Ships: A Text-Book. Longmans Green and Co.: London.
Azoy, A.C.M. (1964) Signal 250! The Sea Fight Off Santiago. David McKay Company: NY
Bancroft, Hubert Howe. (1893) The Book of the Fair. Bancroft Company: Chicago.
Bannerman Company (various) Bannerman Catalog various.
Beeler, John. (2001) Birth of the Battleship. Chatham Publishing: London.
Benjamin, Park. (1892) Modern Mechanism. MacMillan and Co.: New York.
Bennet, Frank M. (1900) The Monitor and the Navy Under Steam. Houghton, Mifflin and Company: Cambridge.
Bertin, Louis Emile and Robertson, Leslie S. (1906) Marine Boilers Their Construction and Working. John Murray: London.
Bonner, Kit and Bonner, Carolyn. () Warship Boneyards. MBI Publishing Co.: Osceola, Wisconsin
Brown, D.K. (1997) Warrior to Dreadnought. Chatham Publishing: London.
Brownlee, James Henry. (1898) War-Time Echoes.
Bruff, Capt. Lawrence L. (1896) A Text-Book of Ordnance and Gunnery. John Wiley & Sons: London.
Buel, James William. () Hero Tales of the American Soldier and Sailor as Told by the Heroes Themselves.
Chadwick, French E., Kelley, J.D.J. et. al. (1891) Ocean Steamships. Charles Scribner's Sons: New York.
Chadwick, French E. (1911) Relations of the United States and Spain. Charles Scribner's Sons: New York.
Chisholm, Hugh ed. (1911) Encyclopedia Britannia. Encyclopedia Britannica Company: New York.
Clark, Arthur H. (1911) The Clipper Ship Era. G.P. Putnam's Sons: New York.
Clarke & Courts. () The Texas A Southern Built Battleship. Clarke & Courts, Manufacturing Stationers: Galveston, Texas.
Cochrane, Charles Henry. (1899) The Wonders of Modern Mechanism A resume of Progress in Mechanical, Physical, and Engineering.
Corthell, Elmer L. (1886) The Atlantic and Pacific Ship-railway Across the Isthmus of Tehuantepec in Mexico.
Cotter, Arundel. (1916) The Story of Bethlehem Steel. Moody Magazine and Book Company: New York.
Crabtree, J. B. (1898) The Passing of Spain and the Ascendency of America. King-Richardson Publishing Co.: Springfield, Massachusetts.
Davenport, Charles Benedict. (1919) Naval Officers, Their Heredity and Development. Carnegie Institution of Washington: Washington D.C.
Dodd, Meade & Company. New International Encyclopædia. Dodd, Meade & Co.: New York.
Doubleday, Russell et al (1898) A Gunner Aboard the "Yankee".
Doubleday, Russell. (1904) Stories of Inventors. Doubleday: New York.
Doubleday, Russell (1901) A Year in a Yawl A True Tale of the Adventures of Four Boys in a Thirty-foot Yawl
Draper, Andrew S. (1898) Battle of Santiago Land and Sea.
Edmonds, Franklin Spencer (1902) History of the Central High School of Philadelphia.
Ellis. (1900) History of Our Country from the Discovery of America.
Fanning, C.E. (1906) Selected Articles on the Enlargement of the United States Navy. H.W. Wilson Co.: Minneapolis, Minnesota.
Faulk, Edwin A. (1931) Fighting Bob Evans. Jonathan Cape & Harrison Smith: New York.
Fiske, Rear-Adm. Bradley A. (1919) From Midshipman to Rear Admiral. The Century Co.: New York.
Fostle, D.W. (1988) Speedboat. United States Historical Society & Mystic Seaport Museum Stores: Mystic Connecticut.
Freidel, Frank. (1958) The Splendid Little War. Bramhall House: New York.
Friedman, Norman. (1985) US Battleships. Naval Institute Press: Annapolis, Maryland.
Friedman, Norman. (1983) US Naval Weapons. Naval Institute Press: Annapolis, Maryland.
Gardiner, Robert ed. (1993) The Advent of Steam. Conway Maritime Press: London.
Gardiner, Robert ed. (1992) Steam Steel and Shellfire. Conway Maritime Press: London.
Garn, Andrew. () Bethlehem Steel.
Gibbons, Tony. (1983) The Complete Encyclopedia of Battleships. Salamander Books Ltd.: London.
Goldstein, Donald M.; Dillon, Katherine V.; Wenger, J. Michael; and Cressman, Robert J. (1998) The Spanish American War. Brassey's: Washington D.C.
Gould, Arthur Corbin. (1894) Modern American Pistols and Revolvers. B. Whidden: Boston.

Graham, George Edward. (1902) Schley and Santiago. The Home Publishing Company: Chicago.
Gunsaulus, Frank Wakeley. (1906) Modern Engineering Practice. American School of Correspondence: Chicago.
Halstead, Murat. (1899) Life and Achievements of Admiral Dewey from Montpelier to Manila. H.L. Barber: Chicago.
Halstead, Murat. (1898) The Story of the Philippines. H.L. Barber: Chicago.
Hamersly, Lewis R. (1898) The Records of Living Officers of the U.S. Navy and Marine Corps. L.R. Hamersly & Co.: New York.
Harris, Brayton. (1965) The Age of the Battleship: 1890-1922. Franklin Watts, Inc.: New York.
Harvey, Capt. Chas M. (1898) The Navy Our Heroes in Cuba.
Herrick, Walter R. Jr. (1966) The American Naval Revolution. Louisiana State University Press: Baton Rouge, Louisiana.
Hill, Richard. (2000) War at Sea in the Ironclad Age. Cassell, Wellington House: London.
Hobson. (1899) Sinking of the Merrimac.
Holbrook, Franklin F. (1923) Minnesota in the Spanish-American War and the Philippines. Minnesota War Records Commission: Saint Paul, Minnesota
Hore, Peter. (2005) The World Encyclopedia of Battleships. Hermes House: London.
Captain Howeth, Linwood S. (1963) History of Communications-Electronics in the United States Navy.
Illustrated Publishing Company. (1897) Illustrated Souvenir of the Naval Review: Grant Monument Inaugural. Illustrated Publishing Company.
International Textbook Company. (1906) Mariner's Pocketbook. International Textbook Company: Scranton, Pennsylvania.
Jane, Fred T. (1997) The British Battlefleet. Conway Maritime Press: London.
Jane, Fred T. ed. (1898) Jane's All the World's Fighting Ships 1898. Sampson Low Marston.
Jane, Fred T. ed. (1906) Jane's Fighting Ships 1906-7. Sampson Low Marston.
Jones, Chaplain Harry W. (1901) A Chaplain's Experience ashore and Afloat. A.G. Sherwood & Co.: New York.
Jordan, J. Murray. (1896) Warships of the United States Navy. J. Murray Jordan: Philadelphia.
Kelley, J.D.J. () The Navy of the United States.
Kelley, J.D.J. (1884) The Question of Ships. Charles Scribner's Sons: New York.
Kelley, J.D.J. (1897) The Ship's Company. Harper & Brothers Publishers: New York.
Kimberly, J.B. (1900) Souvenir of Fortress Monroe. Old Point Comfort, Virginia.
King, Howard, and Evans. (1899) The Story of the Spanish-American War and the Revolt in the Philippines. Collier: New York.
Kittelle, Sumner Ely Wetmore.(1946) The Ketel Family. Washington D.C.
Knight, Austin M. (1921) Modern Seamanship. Von Nostrand Company: New York.
Konstam, Angus. (1998) San Juan Hill 1898. Praeger: Westport, Connecticut.
La Follette, Robert Marion (1906) The Making of America.
Leask, A. Ritchie. (1894) Triple & Quadruple Expansion Engines & Boilers. Tower Publishing Company, Ltd.: London.
Leonard, John William. Who's Who in New York.
Lewis, Alfred Henry. (1906) Compilation of the Messages and Speeches of Theodore Roosevelt, 1901-1905. Bureau of National Literature and Art.
L.H. Nelson Company. (1908) On The Pacific with Our Navy. L. H. Nelson Co.: Portland, Maine.
Lodge, Henry Cabot. (1898) War With Spain. Harper & Brothers: New York.
Long, John Davis (1904) The New American Navy. Grant Richards: London.
L.R. Hamersly & Company. (1910) Men and Women of America. L.R. Hamersly & Company: New York.
McNamara, John. (1978) History in Asphalt: History of Bronx Street and Place Names. Harbor Hill Books: New York.
Maclay, Edgar Stanton. (1904) The Life and Adventures of Jack Philip. American Tract Society.
Markwick, W. F. and Smith, W. A. (1900) The True Citizen, How to Become One. American Book Company: New York.
Martin, Frederick. (1876) The History of Lloyd's and of Marine Insurance in Great Britain. MacMillan & Co.: London.
Mason, Herbert B. (1908) Encyclopaedia of Ships and Shipping.
Maver, William Jr. (1904) Maver's Wireless Telegraphy. Maver Publishing Company: New York.
Miles, Nelson A. (1899) Harper's Pictorial History of the War With Spain. Harper & Brothers Publishers: New York.
Miller, Nathan. (1977) The U. S. Navy: An Illustrated History. American Heritage Publishing Co., Inc.: New York.
Moore, Capt. John. (1991) Jane's American Fighting Ships of the 20th Century. Mallard Press: New York.
Morris, Charles. (1898) The Nation's Navy Our Ships and Their Achievements.
Muller, (1905) Book of the United States Navy.
Musicant, Ivan. (1998) Empire by Default : The Spanish-American War and the Dawn of the American Century. Henry Holt and Company.
Myszkowski, Eugene. (1999) The Winchester Lee Rifle. Excalibur Publications: Tucson, Arizona.
New Century Club of Utica, New York. (1900) Outline History of Utica and Vicinity. L.C. Childs & Son: Utica, New York.
Newhart, Max R. (1995) American Battleships. Pictorial Histories Publishing Co.: Missoula, Montana.
Nofi, Albert A. (1996) The Spanish American War, 1898. Combined Books: Pennsylvania.
O'Toole, G.J.A. (1984) The Spanish War: An American Epic. W.W. Norton & Co.: New York.
Padfield, Peter. (1972) The Battleship Era. David McKay Company, Inc.: New York.
Paine, Lincoln P. () Warships of the World to 1900.
Paine, Ralph Delahaye. (1922) Roads of Adventure. Houghton Mifflin Co.: New York.
Palmer, Mrs. Potter et. al. (1893) Rand, McNally and Co's Hand Book of the World's Columbian Exposition. Rand, McNally & Company: Chicago.
Peabody, Cecil Hobart. (1904) Naval Architecture. John Wiley & Sons: London.
Persons, Eleanor Alice. (1899) Our Country in Poem and Prose Arranged for Collateral and Supplementary Reading. American Book Company: New york.
Pearson Publishing Company. (1898) Pearson's War Pictures. Pearson Publishing Company: New York.
Phi Gamma Delta. (1899) The Phi Gamma Delta.
Plummer, Edward Clarence. () The Edward Clarence Plummer History of Bath Maine.
Pollock, David. (1884) Modern Shipbuilding and the Men Engaged in it. E.&F.N. Spon: London.
Poor Family Association. (1881) The Poor-Poore Family Gathering. S.W. Green's Sons: New York.
Powles, H.H.P. (1905) Steam Boilers Their History and Development. Archibald Constable & Co., Ltd: London.
Pratt, Fletcher. (1939) Sea Power and Today's War. Harrison-Hilton: New York.
Preston of New Hampshire. (1898) Two Historic Days. Preston of New Hampshire.
de Quesada. (1898) Americas Battle for Cuba's Freedom.
Rand McNally and Co. (1898) Our Modern Navy. Rand McNally and Co.: New York..
Reynolds, Francis Joseph. (1917) United States Navy From the Revolution to Date. P.F. Collier: New York.
Rickover, H.G. (1976) How the Battleship Maine was Destroyed. Naval History Division, Dept. of the Navy: Washington D.C.
Roberts, Michael. (1991) Illustrated Directory of the United States Navy. Brian Trodd: London.
Robinson, R.H.M. (1906) Naval Construction. United States Naval Institute: Annapolis, Maryland.
Roscoe, Theodore & Freeman, Fred. (1956) Picture History of the U. S. Navy. Charles Scribner's Sons: New York.
Sampson, William Thomas. (1899) With Sampson Through the War. Doubleday & McClure Co.: New York.
Sands, Robert W. () Glassboro. Arcadia: Chicago.

Schroeder, Seaton, Rear Admiral, ret'd. (1922) A Half Century of Naval Service. D. Appleton and Company: New York.
Scott, J.D. () Vickers: A History. Weidenfeld and Nicholson: London.
Shurter, Edwin Du Bois ed. (1910) American Oratory of To-day.
Sigsbee, Capt. Charles (1899) The Maine An Account of her Destruction in Havana Harbor. The Century Co.: New York.
Simpson, George. (1914) The Naval Constructor. D. Van Nostrand company: New York.
Sleeman, C. (1889) Torpedoes and Torpedo Warfare. Griffin & Co.: Portsmouth, England.
Sondhaus, Lawrence. () Naval Warfare 1814-1915.
(1901) Souvenir United States Training Station Newport, Rhode Island 1901.
Spears, John R. (1898) Our Navy in The War with Spain. New York: Charles Scribner's Sons: New York.
Spofford, Ainsworth Rand; Weitenkampf, Frank; and Lamberton, John Porter (1900) The Library of Historic Characters and Famous Events of all Nations and all Ages - Supplement. J.B. Millet: Boston.
Sterling, Christopher H. (2007) Military Communications.
Stewart, William H. (1902) History of Norfolk County Virginia and Representative Citizens. Biographical Publishing Co.: Chicago.
Taft, Helen Herron. (1914) Recollections of Full Years. Dodd, Mead & Co.: New York.
Taylor, Daniel W. (1907) Resistance of Ships and Screw Propulsion. Macmillan Company: New York.
Thearle, Samuel J.P. (1877) Theoretical Naval Architecture A Treatise on the Calculations Involved in Naval Design. G.P. Putnam's Sons: New York.
Thomas, J.J. (1905) Fifty Years on the Rail. Knickerbocker Press: New York.
Thurston, Robert Henry A History of the Growth of the Steam-engine.
Trask, David F. (1996) The War with Spain in 1898. Bison Books.
Tyler, John W. (1901) The Life of William McKinley.
Vivian, Thomas J. (1898) The Fall of Santiago. R.F. Fenno & Company: New York.
Wagner, Lt-Col. Arthur L. () The Army of the United States.
Washington Booker T. (1906) Tuskegee and Its People Their Ideals and Achievements. D. Appleton and Company: New York.
Watterson, Henry. (1898) History of the Spanish-American War. The Werner Company: New York.
White, Trumbull.(1898) Pictorial History of Our War with Spain for Cuba's Freedom. Freedom Publishing Company.
Who's Who in Pennsylvania.
Wilder, Marshall P.; Haley, Bart and Graham C. (1905) Sunny Side of the Street. Funk & Wagnalls Co.: New York.
Williamson, Joseph () History of the City of Belfast in the State of Maine.
Wilson, Herbert Wrigley. (1900) The Downfall of Spain. Sampson Low, Marston and Company: London
Wimmel, Kenneth. (1998) Theodore Roosevelt and the Great White Fleet. Brassey's: Washington D.C.
Wright. (1899) Wrights Official History of the Spanish American War.
Young, James Rankin. (1898) History of Our War with Spain.

Magazines and Journals:
American Engineer and Railroad Journal
The Century Magazine
Christian Advocate
Christian Index
Cinema Journal
Confederate Veteran
Congregationalist
Cosmopolitan
Economic History Review
The Electrical Engineer
Engineering
Engineering News
The Express
Frank Leslie's Popular Monthly
Guns & Ammo
Harper's New Monthly Magazine
Transactions of the Institute of Naval Architects
Journal of the American Irish Historical Society
Journal of Military History
McClure's Magazine
Medical Record
Military Affairs
El Mundo Naval
National Magazine
New York Evangelist
New York Observer
North American Review
Outlook
Overland Monthly
Popular Mechanics
Proceedings of the American Railway Master Mechanics Association
Proceedings of the Michigan Schoolmasters Club
Publishers Weekly
Scientific American
Technology Quarterly
Transactions of the American Society of Mechanical Engineers
United Service
United States Naval Institute Proceedings
Warship International
Youth's Companion

Newspapers:

Aberdeen Weekly Journal
Atchison Daily Globe
Bangor Daily Whig & Courier
Belfast News-Letter
Brisbane Courier
Birmingham Daily Post
Bismarck Daily Tribune
Boston Daily Advertiser
Brooklyn Eagle
Blumington Bulletin
Dallas Morning News
Denver Evening Post
Deseret Evening News
Deseret News
Freeman's Journal & Daily Commercial Advertiser
Friend of India &Statesman
Galveston Daily News
Glasgow Herald
Hampshire Telegraph & Sussex Chronicle
Hawaiian Gazette
Hopkinsville Kentuckian
Houston Daily Post
Irish World & American Industrial Liberator
Kansas City Journal
Los Angeles Times
Liverpool Mercury
London Daily News
London Times
Macon Telegraph
Memphis Commercial Appeal
Milwaukee Journal
Milwaukee Sentinel
Minneapolis Journal
Morning Oregonian
Washington National Tribune
New Orleans Daily Picayune
New York Times
New York Tribune
Philadelphia North American
Raleigh News & Observer
Richmond Times
Rocky Mountain News
Saint Paul Globe
Salt Lake Semi-Weekly Tribune
Stanford Semi-Weekly Interior Journal
The San Francisco Call
Vermont Watchman
Wall Street Journal
Washington Times
Washington Post

U.S. Government Publications and Serials:

Bowles, Francis T. (n.d.) Construction Notebook. – In the collections of the New York Public Library.
Cervera Y Topete, Rear-Admiral Pascual (Arranged by) [Office of Naval Intelligence] (1899) The Spanish American War, A Collection of Documents Relative to the Squadron Operations in the West Indies. Government Printing Office: Washington.
Concas Y Palau, Captain Victor M. [Office of Naval Intelligence] (1900) The Squadron of Admiral Cervera, Government Printing Office: Washington.
Fullam, Cmdr. William F. & Lt. Hart, Thomas C. (1905) Text-book of Ordnance and Gunnery. United States Naval Institute: Annapolis, Maryland.
Muller y Tejeiro, Lt. Jose [Office of Naval Intelligence] (1898) Battles and Capitulation of Santiago De Cuba. Government Printing Office: Washington.
U.S. Adjutant Generals Office () Correspondence Relating to the War with Spain.
U.S. Congress. (multiple dates) Congressional Serial Set. Government Printing Office: Washington D.C.
U.S. Executive Department. Executive Department Reports (multiple dates) – Includes numerous naval manuals and technical reports.
U.S. Naval Academy. (multiple dates) The Lucky Bag. Annapolis, Maryland.
U.S. Navy (1893) Catalogue of the Exhibit of the US Navy Department at the World's Columbian Exposition. Government Printing Office: Washington D.C.
U.S. Navy (1898) Handbook of Naval Gunnery. Government Printing Office: Washington D.C.
U.S. Navy (1906) Manual of Wireless Telegraphy for the Use of Naval Electricians. Government Printing Office: Washington D.C.
U.S. Navy (1898) Ship's Log of the U.S.S. Texas. Government Printing Office: Washington D.C.
U.S. Navy (1898) Signal Flags. Government Printing Office: Washington D.C.
U.S. Navy (1900) Standard Designs for Boats. Government Printing Office: Washington D.C.

U.S. Navy (1905) Text-book of Ordnance and Gunnery. Government Printing Office: Washington D.C.
U.S. Navy (multiple dates) *USS Texas Armaments Lists*. U.S. Navy.
War Department (multiple dates) Report of the Secretary of War. Government Printing Office: Washington D.C.
(1886) *Report of the Select Committee on Ordnance and War Ships*. Government Printing Office: Washington D.C.
(1905) Annual register of the United States Naval Academy 1904-05. Government Printing Office: Washington D.C.

U.S. Patents:
Browning, John M. – Patents related to the Colt Machine Gun.
Ehbets, Carl J. – Patents related to Colt's New Navy revolver.
Fiske, Bradley A. – Patents related to command and control on US warships.
Haesler, Francis J. – Patents related to hydraulic turning machinery.
Mosher, Charles D. – Patents related to machinery of torpedo boats.

Websites:
Library of Congress. http://www.loc.gov/index.html
Navweaps.com. http://www.navweaps.com/
Naval History & Heritage Command. http://www.history.navy.mil/
Navsource Online. http://www.navsource.org/
Spanish American War Centennial Website. http://www.spanamwar.com/
Wikipedia http://www.wikipedia.org/
Yonge Library, University of Florida. http://web.uflib.ufl.edu/spec/pkyonge/index.html.

About the Illustrations:
The photographs and illustrations used in this publication were collected over a period of more than a decade through the cooperation of a number of generous individuals and organizations. The images were selected for inclusion based on their historic significance and the information conveyed rather than their visual quality. Unless noted otherwise these images are public domain, having originated from United States government sources, historic publications now out of copyright, private and institutional collections made available to the public, and/or from the authors' own collections.

The photo on page 233 showing the Colt machine gun at Guantanamo is used under license from Getty Images. Drawings of the USS *Vixen*, USS *Gloucester*, and *Reina Mercedes* on page 254 are used with the kind permission of their creator, Jullio Pillet.

Cover	postcard	55	(t.) US Navy
Title	author's illustration	55	(b.l.) *American Engineer and Railroad Journal* (August 1894)
1	The Monitor and the New Navy Under Steam	55	(b.r.) *American Engineer and Railroad Journal* (August 1894)
2	(top left) *Scientific American* (April 15, 1893)	56	*American Engineer and Railroad Journal* (August 1894)
2	(top right) *Scientific American* (April 15, 1893)	57	US Navy/New York Public Library
2	(bottom) public domain	58-59	US Navy
3	(t.r.) public domain	60	(all) *American Engineer and Railroad Journal* (August 1894)
3	(middle right) public domain	61	(t) public domain
3	(left) US Navy	61	(b) *American Engineer and Railroad Journal* (August 1894)
3	(b.) The Monitor and the New Navy Under Steam	62	*American Engineer and Railroad Journal* (May 1894)
4	(top) US Navy	63	(t.l.) US Navy
4	(middle) US Navy	63	(top center) US Navy
4	(b.) US Navy	63	(t.r.) US Navy
5	(t.) The Monitor and the New Navy Under Steam	63	(b) War with Spain
5	(bottom right) The Monitor and the New Navy Under Steam	64-65	US Navy
5	(bottom left) US Navy	66-70	(all) Proceedings of the United States Naval Institute 1896
6	(all) US Navy	71	(all) Information from Abroad 1892
7	(t.) The Monitor and the New Navy Under Steam	72	(t.) stereoview card (ca. 1898)
7	(b.) *The Illustrated London News* (September 24, 1870)	72	(b.l.) US Navy
8	(t.) Brassey's Naval Annual 1888	72	(b.r.) US Navy
8	(b.) public domain	73	(l.) Information from Abroad 1891
9	(t.) Brassey's Naval Annual 1889	73	(r.) US Navy
9	(b.) public domain	74	(all) Information from Abroad 1891
10	(t.) Brassey's Naval Annual 1888	75	(all) Electrical Installations of the United States Navy
10	(b.) public domain	76	US Navy
11	(t.) Brassey's Naval Annual 1888	77	(t.) *American Engineer and Railroad Journal* (April 1894)
11	(b.) public domain	77	(b.) *American Engineer and Railroad Journal* (March 1894)
12	(t.) Brassey's Naval Annual 1888	78	(all) US Navy
12	(b.) public domain	79	(t.) Description of Modern Ordnance
13	(t.) Brassey's Naval Annual 1888	79	(m.l.) Description of Modern Ordnance
13	(b.) public domain	79	(m.r.) Description of Modern Ordnance
14	(all) Brassey's Naval Annual 1889	79	(b.) Catalogue of the Exhibit of the US Navy Department World's Columbian Exposition
15	(t.) Brassey's Naval Annual 1889	80	(all) *American Engineer and Railroad Journal* (April 1894)
15	(b.) public domain	81	(t.) Information from Abroad 1895
16	(t.) Brassey's Naval Annual 1888	81	(b.l.) Information from Abroad 1895
16	(b.) Brassey's Naval Annual 1888	81	(b.r.) *Scientific American Naval Supplement* (1898)
17	*Scientific American* (June 9, 1888)	82	(t.l.) US Navy
18-19	(all) Proceedings of the Institute of Naval Architects 1888	82	(t.r.) US Navy
20	(t.) Modern Shipbuilding and the Men Engaged in it	82	(m.l.) Information from Abroad 1895
20	(b.l.) Ocean Steam Ships	82	(m.r.) Information from Abroad 1895
20	(b.r.) postcard (ca 1905)	82	(b.l.) Information from Abroad 1892
21-23	(all) Proceedings of the Institute of Naval Architects 1888	82	(b.r.) Information from Abroad 1895
24	US Navy	83	(t.r.) Information from Abroad 1895
25	(all) US Navy	83	(b.l.) *American Engineer and Railroad Journal* (March 1894)
26	(t.) Brassey's Naval Annual 1888	84	(t.l.) US Navy
26	(b.l.) *Munsey's Magazine* (April-September 1898)	84	(t.r.) US Navy
26	(bottom center) The New American Navy	84	(b.) public domain
26	(b.r.) The New American Navy	85	(t.) 6 Inch Guns Mk. I II III IV VI
28-31	(all) US Navy/New York Public Library	85	(b.) Detroit Publishing Company/ Library of Congress
32	(all) *Scientific American* (January 16, 1892)	86	(all) US Navy
33-35	(all) US Navy/New York Public Library	87	(t.) Nomenclature and description Fletcher Rapid Fire Breech Mechanism
36	*Scientific American* (August 27, 1892)	87	(b.) US Navy
37	(all) US Navy/New York Public Library	88	(t.) Description of Modern Ordnance
38	(all) *American Engineer and Railroad Journal* (April 1894)	88	(b.) Catalogue of the Exhibit of the US Navy Department World's Columbian Exposition
39	(t.) US Navy	89	(all) Description of Modern Ordnance
39	(m.l.) US Navy/New York Public Library	90	(t.l.) Gunnery Drill Book of the New Armaments
39	(m.r.) US Navy/New York Public Library	90	(m.) Catalogue of the Exhibit of the US Navy Department World's Columbian Exposition
39	(b.) US Navy/New York Public Library		
40	(all) US Navy/New York Public Library	90	(b.) *Leslie's American Magazine* (3rd Quarter, 1898)
41-44	(all) US Navy	91	(all) Detroit Publishing Company/ Library of Congress
45	*American Engineer and Railroad Journal* (March 1894)	92	(all) Textbook of Ordnance and Gunnery
46	(t.) *Scientific American* (March 14, 1891)	93	stereoview card (ca. 1897)
46	(b.l.) *Scientific American* (February 28, 1891)	94	(all) Textbook of Ordnance and Gunnery
46	(b.r.) *Scientific American* (February 28, 1891)	95	(t.l.) Textbook of Ordnance and Gunnery
47	(t.) *Scientific American* (February 28, 1891)	95	(t.r.) *American Engineer and Railroad Journal* (March 1894)
47	(m.) *Scientific American* (March 14, 1891)	95	(bottom inset) American Ordnance Company Catalogue 1894
47	(b.l.) *Scientific American* (February 6, 1892)	95	(b.) Catalogue of the Exhibit of the US Navy Department World's Columbian Exposition
47	(b.c.) *Scientific American* (May 7, 1892)		
47	(b.r.) *Scientific American* (May 7, 1892)	96-97	(all) US Navy
48-49	(all) Catalogue of the Exhibit of the US Navy Department World's Columbian Exposition	98	(t.) 6 Pounder Guns
50	(l.) US Navy/New York Public Library	98	(b.) Description of Modern Ordnance
50	(r.) public domain	99	(t.) Textbook of Ordnance and Gunnery
51-52	(all) *American Engineer and Railroad Journal* (May 1894)		
53-54	US Navy		

Page	Credit
99	(top inset) US Navy
99	(b.) *American Engineer and Railroad Journal* (March 1894)
100	(t.) US Navy
100	(b.) Magic Lantern slide (ca. 1897)
101	(t.) *Scientific American* (September 3, 1898)
101	(b.) Nomenclature Steel Breech Loading Rifled Guns Carriage Mounts for Hotchkiss Guns
102	(t.) 1 Pounder Rapid Fire Guns
102	(m.) Information from Abroad 1887
102	(b.) Detroit Publishing Company/ Library of Congress
103-104	(all) Nomenclature Steel Breech Loading Rifled Guns Carriage Mounts for Hotchkiss Guns
105	(all) Detroit Publishing Company/ Library of Congress
106	(t.) Catalogue of the Exhibit of the US Navy Department World's Columbian Exposition
106	(m.) *American Engineer and Railroad Journal* (March 1894)
106	(b.) Catalogue of the Exhibit of the US Navy Department World's Columbian Exposition
107	(all) Description of Modern Ordnance
108	(t.) US Navy
108	(m.l.) *Scientific American Naval Supplement* (1898)
108	(m.r.) US Navy
108	(b.) US Navy
109	(t.) US Navy
109	(b.) Wright's Official History of the Spanish American War
110	(t.) Mariner's Pocketbook 1906
110	(b.l.) US Navy
110	(b.r.) Mariner's Pocketbook 1906
111	(all) Mariner's Pocketbook 1906
112	(t.) Proceedings of the United States Naval Institute 1888
112	(b.l.) US Navy
112	(b.r.) US Navy
113	(t.) Textbook of Ordnance and Gunnery
113	(b.l.) Textbook of Ordnance and Gunnery
113	(b.r.) Detroit Publishing Company/ Library of Congress
114	(all) The Navy of the United States
115	public domain
117	(t.) stereoview card (ca. 1895)
117	(m.) Textbook of Ordnance and Gunnery
117	(b.) Bain News Service / Library of Congress
118	(t.) Handbook on Naval Gunnery
118	(b.) Detroit Publishing Company/ Library of Congress
119	(t.) Colt Automatic Gun Caliber 30
119	(m.) *Scientific American Coastal Defense supplement* (1898)
119	(b.) The Lucky Bag 1904
120	(t.) public domain
120	(top inset) Bannerman Catalog
120	(m.) New International Encyclopedia 1902
120	(b.) Knight's American Mechanical Dictionary
121-122	(all) The United States Navy Rifle Caliber 6 Millimeters Model 1895 – Description and Nomenclature
123	(t.) Modern American Pistols and Revolvers
123	(top inset) Description of Colt's Revolver Caliber 38
123	(m.l.) US Patent #392,503
123	(m.r.) Modern American Pistols and Revolvers
123	(b.) The Maine: An Account of her Destruction in Havana Harbor
124	(t.) Bannerman Catalog
124	(top and bottom inset strips) The Petty Officer's Drillbook
124	(b.l.) Detroit Publishing Company/ Library of Congress
124	(b.r.) US Navy
125	*Dallas Morning News* (February 20, 1897)
126	(all) Bannerman Catalog
127	(all) Signal Flags US Navy
128	(t.l.) Wright's Official History of the Spanish American War
128	(t.r.) Wright's Official History of the Spanish American War
128	(b.) US Marine Corps
129	(t.l.) The Monitor and the Navy Under Steam
129	(t.r.) The Monitor and the Navy Under Steam
129	(b.) public domain
130	(all) US Navy
131	(all) Brassey's Naval Annual 1889
132	(t.) US Navy
132	(b.) *American Engineer and Railroad Journal* (March 1894)
133	(t.) stereoview card (ca. 1897)
133	(b.) Detroit Publishing Company/ Library of Congress
134	(t.) public domain
134	(b.) Detroit Publishing Company/ Library of Congress
135	(t.l.) Information from Abroad 1888
135	(t.r.) *The American Engineer* (April 1894)
135	(b.) American Ordnance Company Catalog 1894
136	(all) Catalogue of the Exhibit of the US Navy Department World's Columbian Exposition
137	(t.) Catalogue of the Exhibit of the US Navy Department World's Columbian Exposition
137	(b.) *American Engineer and Railroad Journal* (August 1894)
138	(t.) Catalogue of the Exhibit of the US Navy Department World's Columbian Exposition
138	(b.) *American Engineer and Railroad Journal* (May 1894)
139	(t.) American Photo Company / Library of Congress
139	(b.) postcard (ca 1912)
140	*Harper's Weekly* (January 1896)
141	*Scientific American* (October 10, 1894)
142	(t.) *American Engineer and Railroad Journal* (March 1894)
142	(b.) US Navy
143	US Navy
144	*Engineering News Supplement* (November 22, 1894)
145	(t.) Steam Boilers Their History and Development
145	(b.) *Engineering News Supplement* (November 22, 1894)
146	US Navy
147	Detroit Publishing Company/ Library of Congress
147	(inset) US Navy
148	(t.l.) Jane's Fighting Ships 1919
148	(t.r.) Jane's Fighting Ships 1919
148	(b.) Souvenir of Fortress Monroe
149	Magic Lantern slide (ca. 1895)
150	(t.) Detroit Publishing Company/ Library of Congress
150	(m.) Detroit Publishing Company/ Library of Congress
150	(b.) *El Mundo Naval Ilustrado* (May 1898)
151	(t.) Schley and Santiago
151	(m.) *El Mundo Naval Ilustrado* (July 1898)
151	(b.) Detroit Publishing Company/ Library of Congress
152	(t.) Annual Report of the Secretary of the Navy 1899
152	(b.) *Minneapolis Journal* (April 12, 1901)
153	(t.) Jane's Fighting Ships 1919
153	(b.) Wright's Official History of the Spanish American War
154	(t.) Magic Lantern slide (ca. 1895)
154	(b.) Detroit Publishing Company/ Library of Congress
155	public domain
156	US Navy
157	(t.) Detroit Publishing Company/ Library of Congress
157	(b.) Samuel H. Gottselo collection / Library of Congress
158	(t.) public domain
158	(m.) public domain
158	(b.) *Dallas Morning News* (March 21, 1900)
159	(t.) public domain
159	(m.) *Dallas Morning News* (November 10, 1896)
159	(b.) public domain
160	(t.) Detroit Publishing Company/ Library of Congress
160	(m.) stereoview card (1897)
160	(b.) Schley and Santiago
161	(t.) stereoview card (ca. 1896)
161	(b.) stereoview card (ca. 1896)
162-163	(all) Detroit Publishing Company/ Library of Congress
164	(t.) stereoview card (ca. 1898)
164	(b.) Detroit Publishing Company/ Library of Congress
165	(t.) Detroit Publishing Company/ Library of Congress
165	(b.) *National Tribune* (June 16, 1898)
166	(t.) postcard (ca 1900)
166	(b.) Detroit Publishing Company/ Library of Congress
167	(t.) stereoview card (ca. 1897)
167	(b.) *Munsey's Magazine* (September 1898)
168	*Harper's Weekly* (April 9, 1898)
169	US Navy
170	*Scientific American* (April 1, 1899)
171	(t.) stereoview card (ca. 1898)
171	(b.) stereoview card (ca. 1898)
172	US Navy
173	(t.) Detroit Publishing Company/ Library of Congress
173	(2) public domain
173	(3) *National Tribune* (June 16, 1898)
173	(4) US Navy

Page	Credit
174	(1) US Navy
174	(2) Detroit Publishing Company/ Library of Congress
174	(3) *National Tribune* (June 16, 1898)
174	(4) US Navy
174	(5) A Chaplain's Experiences Ashore and Afloat
175	(t.) stereoview card (1898)
175	(m.) postcard (ca 1907)
175	(b.) Wright's Official History of the Spanish American War
176	(t.) *The Times* (April 17, 1898)
176	(b.l.) stereoview card (1898)
176	(b.r.) stereoview card (1898)
177	stereoview card (1898)
178	(all) Detroit Publishing Company/ Library of Congress
179	(t.) *National Tribune* (April 21, 1898)
179	(b.) stereoview card (1898)
180	(t.) *Munsey's Magazine* (October 1898)
180	(b.) stereoview card (1898)
181	Harper's Pictorial History of the War with Spain
182	(t.) US Navy
182	(m.l.) *El Mundo Naval Ilustrado* (April 1898)
182	(m.r.) *El Mundo Naval Ilustrado* (April 1898)
182	(b.) *Scientific American* (August 6, 1898)
183	(t.) US Navy
183	(m.) Information from Abroad 1892
183	(b.) *Collier's* (1898)
184	(t.) US Navy
184	(m.) public domain
184	(b.) Wright's Official History of the Spanish American War
185	(t.) Photographic History of the Spanish American War
185	(m.) Wright's Official History of the Spanish American War
185	(b.l.) US Navy
185	(b.r.) *El Mundo Naval Ilustrado* (August 1897)
186-187	(all) Information from Abroad 1894
188	*El Mundo Naval Ilustrado* (August 1897)
189	(all) Wright's Official History of the Spanish American War
190	(t.) Information from Abroad 1892
190	(b.) *El Mundo Naval Ilustrado* (June 1897)
191	(t.) *El Mundo Naval Ilustrado* (June 1897)
191	(b.) Bannerman Catalog
192	(t.) US Navy
192	(m.l.) *El Mundo Naval Ilustrado* (March 1898)
192	(m.r.) *El Mundo Naval Ilustrado* (April 1898)
192	(b.) *Scientific American* (February 6, 1897)
193	(t.) US Navy
193	(b.) How Uncle Sam Fights
194-196	US Navy
197	(t.) *Harper's Weekly* (July 9, 1898)
197	(b.) Wright's Official History of the Spanish American War
198	(t.) US Navy
198	(b.) Brassey's Naval Annual 1889
199	(t.) *Scientific American* (July 16, 1898)
199	(m.) *Scientific American* (July 16, 1898)
199	(b.) US Navy
200	(t.) *Scientific American* (July 16, 1898)
200	(b.) *El Mundo Naval Ilustrado*
201	(t.) Photographic History of the Spanish American War
201	(b.) Brassey's Naval Annual 1906
202	(t.) *El Mundo Naval Ilustrado* (1897)
202	(b.) *El Mundo Naval Ilustrado* (March 1898)
203-205	(all) US Navy
206	Annual Report of the Secretary of the Navy 1898
207	(all) *The Century* (April 6, 1899)
208	(t.) Harper's Pictorial History of the War with Spain
208	(m.) The downfall of Spain
208	(b.) public domain
209	(t.) Harper's Pictorial History of the War with Spain
209	(m.) public domain
209	(b.) US Navy
210	(t.) US Navy
210	(b.) stereoview card (1898)
211	(t.) stereoview card (1898)
211	(b.) *The Times* (February 18, 1898)
212	(t.) stereoview card (1898)
212	(m.) stereoview card (1898)
212	(b.) US Navy
213	Harper's Pictorial History of the War with Spain
214	(l.) Proceedings of the United States Naval Institute 1898
214	(b.) *El Mundo Naval Ilustrado* (June 1897)
215	Proceedings of the United States Naval Institute 1898
215	(inset) *El Mundo Naval Ilustrado* (July 1898)
216	*The Century* (April 6, 1899)
217	(t.) Detroit Publishing Company/ Library of Congress
217	(m.) *El Mundo Naval Ilustrado* (June 1898)
217	(b.) stereoview card (ca. 1898)
218	(t.) postcard (ca 1900)
218	(m.) postcard (ca 1900)
218	(b.) Detroit Publishing Company/ Library of Congress
219	(t.) Wright's Official History of the Spanish American War
219	(m.l.) stereoview card (ca. 1898)
219	(m.r.) Schley and Santiago
219	(b.) Wright's Official History of the Spanish American War
220	(t.) postcard (ca 1900)
220	(b.) Wright's Official History of the Spanish American War
221	(t.l.) Harper's Pictorial History of the War with Spain
221	(t.r.) Wright's Official History of the Spanish American War
221	(m.) Wright's Official History of the Spanish American War
221	(b.) Proceedings of the United States Naval Institute 1898
222	(t.) Detroit Publishing Company/ Library of Congress
222	(m.) US Government – public domain / Yonge Library, University of Florida
222	(b.l.) US Government – public domain / Yonge Library, University of Florida
222	(b.r.) US Government – public domain / Yonge Library, University of Florida
223	(all) US Government – public domain / Yonge Library, University of Florida
224	(t.) Detroit Publishing Company/ Library of Congress
224	(m.) US Government – public domain / Yonge Library, University of Florida
224	(b.) US Government – public domain / Yonge Library, University of Florida
225	(all) US Government – public domain / Yonge Library, University of Florida
226	(1) US Government – public domain / Yonge Library, University of Florida
226	(2) The War the Spain
226	(3) US Government – public domain / Yonge Library, University of Florida
226	(4) Detroit Publishing Company/ Library of Congress
227	(all) US Government – public domain / Yonge Library, University of Florida
228	Wright's Official History of the Spanish American War
229	(t.) US Navy
229	(m.) The Sinking of the Merrimac
229	(b.l.) The Sinking of the Merrimac
229	(b.r.) The Sinking of the Merrimac
230	(t.) Schley and Santiago
230	(m.l.) The Sinking of the Merrimac
230	(m.r.) The Sinking of the Merrimac
230	(b.) stereoview card (ca. 1898)
231	(t.l.) *The Century* (May 1, 1899)
231	(m.r.) *The Century* (May 1, 1899)
231	(1) Exciting Experiences in our Wars with Spain and the Filipinos
231	(2) Exciting Experiences in our Wars with Spain and the Filipinos
231	(3) US Navy
231	(4) Detroit Publishing Company/ Library of Congress
231	(5) *The Century* (May 1, 1899)
232	(t.) Harper's Pictorial History of the War with Spain
232	(m.l.) public domain
232	(m.r.) Wright's Official History of the Spanish American War
232	(b.) US Navy
233	Getty Images
234	(t.) *El Mundo Naval Ilustrado* (July 1898)
234	(b.) Detroit Publishing Company/ Library of Congress
235	(t.) *The Times* (February 18, 1900)
235	(m.) The Navy of the United States
235	(b.) public domain
236	(all) Detroit Publishing Company/ Library of Congress
237	(t.l.) public domain
237	(t.r.) Detroit Publishing Company/ Library of Congress

Page	Credit
237	(m.) Detroit Publishing Company/ Library of Congress
237	(b.) Harper's Pictorial History of the War with Spain
238	(all) Detroit Publishing Company/ Library of Congress
239	(t.) US Marine Corps
239	(m.) US Marine Corps
239	(b.) *Collier's Weekly* (1898)
240	(t.) annotated excerpt from US Defense Mapping Agency Nautical Chart No. 26218
240	(b.) The Battle of Santiago on board the US Battleship "Texas"
241	(t.l.) *Blumington Bulletin* (August 19, 1898)
241	(t.r.) stereoview card (1898)
241	(b.) Harper's Pictorial History of the War with Spain
242	(t.) Detroit Publishing Company/ Library of Congress
242	(b.) public domain
243	Battles and Capitulation of Santiago
244	public domain
245	(all) Harper's Pictorial History of the War with Spain
246	(t.) Wisconsin Troops in the Spanish War
246	(m.) Harper's Pictorial History of the War with Spain
246	(b.) *The Graphic* (September 3, 1898)
247	(t.) Harper's Pictorial History of the War with Spain
247	(m.) Harper's Pictorial History of the War with Spain
247	(b.) public domain
248	(t.) Schley and Santiago
248	(b.l.) *Scientific American* (August 20, 1898)
248	(b.r.) *Scientific American* (August 20, 1898)
249	(t.) *Scientific American* (August 20, 1898)
249	(inset) US Navy
249	(b.r.) *Scientific American* (August 20, 1898)
250	(t.) Detroit Publishing Company/ Library of Congress
250	(b.) stereoview card (1898)
251	Harper's Pictorial History of the War with Spain
252	(all) Harper's Pictorial History of the War with Spain
253	Harper's Pictorial History of the War with Spain
254	Brassey's Naval Annual (various years 1880s-1900s)
254	Drawings of USS Vixen, USS Gloucester, and Reina Mercedes courtesy of Jullio Pillet
255	(t.) stereoview card (1898)
255	(b.) Annual Report of the Secretary of the Navy 1898
256	(t.) *Dallas Morning News* (July 4, 1898)
256	(m.) *Harper's Weekly* (January 1899)
256	(b.) Harper's Pictorial History of the War with Spain
257	(t.) *The Century* (April 6, 1899)
257	(b.) Harper's Pictorial History of the War with Spain
258	*Look Magazine* (1898)
259	(t.l.) The Downfall of Spain
259	(t.r.) *The Century* (April 6, 1899)
259	(b.) *The Century* (1898)
260	(t.) *The Century* (April 6, 1899)
260	(m.) US Navy
260	(b.) *The Century* (April 6, 1899)
261	(t.) Harper's Pictorial History of the War with Spain
261	(m.l.) *The Century* (May 1, 1899)
261	(m.r.) *The Century* (May 1, 1899)
261	(b.) *The Century* (April 6, 1899)
262	(t.) Detroit Publishing Company/ Library of Congress
262	(m.) Detroit Publishing Company/ Library of Congress
262	(b.l.) *Collier's* (1898)
262	(b.r.) *The Century* (May 1, 1899)
263	(t.) Detroit Publishing Company/ Library of Congress
263	(m.l.) *The Century* (May 1, 1899)
263	(m.r.) public domain
263	(b.) *The Century* (April 6, 1899)
264	(t.l.) Harper's Pictorial History of the War with Spain
264	(t.r.) public domain
264	(b.) *Engineering* (February 18, 1898)
265	(t.) *The Century* (April 6, 1899)
265	(m.) Detroit Publishing Company/ Library of Congress
265	(b.l.) *The Century* (May 1, 1899)
265	(b.r.) Detroit Publishing Company/ Library of Congress
266	(t.) Harper's Pictorial History of the War with Spain
266	(b.) *The Century* (May 1, 1899)
267	(t.l.) *The Century* (May 1, 1899)
267	(t.r.) Harper's Pictorial History of the War with Spain
267	(b.) *The Century* (May 1, 1899)
268	(t.) *The Century* (May 1, 1899)
268	(b.) public domain
269	(t.) Detroit Publishing Company/ Library of Congress
269	(m.) Detroit Publishing Company/ Library of Congress
269	(b.) US Navy
270	(all) Detroit Publishing Company/ Library of Congress
271	(t.) *The Century* (May 1, 1899)
271	(m.) postcard (ca 1905)
271	(b.l.) Brassey's Naval Annual 1897
271	(b.r.) Annual Report of the Secretary of the Navy 1878
272	Detroit Publishing Company/ Library of Congress
273	Schley and Santiago
274	The Downfall of Spain
275	(all) Schley and Santiago
276	US Navy
277	(b.l.) US Navy - with authors' notations
277	(b.r.) *National Tribune* (June 16, 1898)
278	(t.) *The Century* (May 1, 1899)
278	(upper left) *National Tribune* (June 16, 1898)
278	(upper right) *National Tribune* (June 16, 1898)
278	(m.) stereoview card (1898)
278	(b.) The Story of the War of 1898
279	(t.l.) *Scientific American* (August 20, 1898)
279	(t.r.) *Scientific American* (August 20, 1898)
279	(b.) *Blumington Bulletin* (August 19, 1898)
280	(t.l.) *Collier's Weekly* (July 23, 1898)
280	(t.r.) Detroit Publishing Company/ Library of Congress
280	(b.) *Scientific American* (August 20, 1898)
281	(t.) Detroit Publishing Company/ Library of Congress
281	(b.l.) *El Mundo Naval Ilustrado* (August 1897)
281	(b.r.) *Scientific American* (August 20, 1898)
282	(t.) Wright's Official History of the Spanish American War
282	(b.) public domain
283	(t.) Wright's Official History of the Spanish American War
283	(b.) Harper's Pictorial History of the War with Spain
284	(t.) US Government – public domain / Yonge Library, University of Florida
284	(m.l.) *El Mundo Naval Ilustrado* (June 1898)
284	(m.r.) Harper's Pictorial History of the War with Spain
284	(b.) US Government – public domain / Yonge Library, University of Florida
285	(t.) The Story of the Spanish American War
285	(b.) Wright's Official History of the Spanish American War
286	(t.) *The Century* (May 1, 1899)
286	(m.) Wright's Official History of the Spanish American War
286	(b.) public domain
287	(t.) The Story of the War of 1898
287	(m.) Detroit Publishing Company/ Library of Congress
287	(b.) The Downfall of Spain
288	(t.) Annual Report of the Secretary of the Navy 1898
288	(m.) *Munsey's Magazine* (October 1898)
288	(b.l.) Wright's Official History of the Spanish American War
288	(b.r.) Wright's Official History of the Spanish American War
289	(t.) stereoview card (ca. 1898)
289	(m.) *Collier's* (1898)
289	(b.) public domain
290	(t.) Schley and Santiago
290	(m.) stereoview card (ca. 1898)
290	(b.l.) US Navy form the Revolution to Date
290	(b.r.) Magic Lantern slide (ca. 1898)
291	(t.) US Navy form the Revolution to Date
291	(m.) Magic Lantern slide (ca. 1898)
291	(b.) Magic Lantern slide (ca. 1898)
292	(t.) Schley and Santiago
292	(m.l.) Magic Lantern slide (ca. 1898)
292	(m.r) Magic Lantern slide (ca. 1898)
292	(b.) public domain
293	(1) public domain
293	(2) Magic Lantern slide (ca. 1898)
293	(3) stereoview card (ca. 1898)
293	(4) stereoview card (ca. 1898)
294	(t.) Schley and Santiago
294	(b.) *Collier's* (July 30, 1898)
295	(1) stereoview card (ca. 1898)
295	(2) *Munsey's Magazine* (October 1898)
295	(3) postcard (ca 1907)

295	(4) US Navy	327	(b.) postcard (1907)
296	(t.l.) Wright's Official History of the Spanish American War	328	(all) postcards (1907)
296	(t.r.) Harper's Pictorial History of the War with Spain	329	(t.) postcard (1908)
296	(m.l.) public domain	329	(m.) Annual Report of the Secretary of the Navy 1899
296	(m.r.) Congressional Record 1898	329	(b.) postcard (1908)
296	(b.) public domain	330	(l.) Scientific American (April 1, 1911)
297	Naval History of the United States	330	(r.) US Navy
298	(t.) public domain	331	(t.) US Navy
298	(b.) US Navy	331	(b.) postcard (1911)
299	(t.) US Navy	332	(1) Scientific American (April 1, 1911)
299	(b.l.) stereoview card (1898)	332	(2) Scientific American (April 1, 1911)
299	(b.r.) stereoview card (1898)	332	(3) US Navy
300	(all) stereoview cards (1898)	332	(4) Battleships of the United States Navy
301	(t.) Scientific American (September 3, 1898)	333	(all) US Navy
301	(b.l.) Munsey's Magazine (1898)	334	(t.) US Navy
301	(b.r.) Detroit Publishing Company/ Library of Congress	334	(m.) US Navy
302	(t.) public domain	334	(b.) Youth's Companion Magazine (April 20, 1920)
302	(b.) Harper's Pictorial History of the War with Spain	335-338	(all) US Navy
303	(t.) Harper's Weekly (1898)	339	(t.) US Navy
303	(m.) Cosmopolitan Magazine (May 1898)	339	(m.l.) Scientific American (April 1, 1911)
303	(b.) Detroit Publishing Company/ Library of Congress	339	(m.r.) US Navy
304	(t.) stereoview card (1898)	339	(b.) US Navy
304	(b.) Cosmopolitan Magazine (May 1898)	340	(t.l.) US Navy
305	(t.l.) Harper's Pictorial History of the War with Spain	340	(t.r.) US Navy
305	(t.r.) Wright's Official History of the Spanish American War	340	(m.l.) Scientific American (April 1, 1911)
305	(m.) Man O'War Views	340	(m.r.) US Navy
305	(b.l.) stereoview card (1898)	340	(b.l.) US Navy
305	(b.r.) stereoview card (1898)	340	(b.r.) US Navy
306-308	(all) Detroit Publishing Company/ Library of Congress	341	(all) US Navy
309	(1) Detroit Publishing Company/ Library of Congress	342	(t.) postcard (ca. 1912)
309	(2) public domain	342	(m.) public domain
309	(3) stereoview card (1899)	343	(t.) Washington Times (August 23, 1912)
309	(4) Detroit Publishing Company/ Library of Congress	343	(b.) public domain
310	(t.) public domain	344	(t.) postcard (ca. 1912)
310	(m.) stereoview card (ca. 1899)	344	(b.) postcard (ca. 1912)
310	(b.) public domain	345	Library of Congress
311	(t.l.) postcard (ca 1900)	347-354	(all) US Navy
311	(t.r.) public domain	360-369	(all) Standard Designs for Boats of the United States Navy
311	(m.l.) public domain	370	US Navy
311	(m.r.) public domain	371-375	Journal of the United States Artillery (November-December 1912)
311	(b) Detroit Publishing Company/ Library of Congress		
312	Detroit Publishing Company/ Library of Congress		
313-314	(all) US Navy		
315	(t.) US Navy		
315	(b.) postcard (ca 1905)		
316	Detroit Publishing Company/ Library of Congress		
317	(t.) World Today (1903)		
317	(b.) stereoview card (1903)		
318	(t.l.) postcard (ca 1904)		
318	(t.r.) postcard (ca 1904)		
318	(m.) postcard (ca 1903)		
318	(b.) The Book of the United States Navy		
319	(t.) Detroit Publishing Company/ Library of Congress		
319	(b.l.) postcard (ca 1904)		
319	(b.r.) postcard (ca 1904)		
320	(t.l.) postcard (ca 1904)		
320	(t.r.) postcard (ca 1904)		
320	(m.l.) The Book of the United States Navy		
320	(m.r.) The Book of the United States Navy		
320	(b.) Hampton Roads Naval Museum		
321	(t.) postcard (ca 1904)		
321	(m.) Proceedings of the Michigan Schoolmaster's Club 1903		
321	(b.l.) Manual of Wireless Telegraphy for the use of Naval Electricians		
321	(b.r.) Cyclopedia of Applied Electricity		
322	(t.) The United States Navy from the Revolution to Date		
322	(b.) postcard (ca 1905)		
323	(t.) Detroit Publishing Company/ Library of Congress		
323	(m.) Detroit Publishing Company/ Library of Congress		
323	(b.) postcard (ca 1904)		
324	(all) The Lucky Bag (various from 1900's)		
325	postcard (ca 1905)		
326	postcard (ca 1905)		
326	(m.) Detroit Publishing Company/ Library of Congress		
326	(b.) US Navy		
327	(t.) postcard (1907)		

ABOUT THE AUTHORS

Mark David Cowan is a native Texan and has a Masters Degree in Architecture with a Certificate in Historic Preservation from Texas A&M University where, in addition to his architectural studies, he completed courses in engineering, nautical archeology, military, and naval history. He has worked both privately and for the State of Texas in the field of architectural preservation for over a decade and is currently a project reviewer for the Texas Historic Courthouse Preservation Program at the Texas Historical Commission.

Alan K. Sumrall is the author of the book Battle Flags of Texans in the Confederacy, published by Eakin Press, Austin, 1995. He is professionally an attorney at law in Austin, Texas and volunteers as the Antique Vehicle Coordinator at the Pioneer Flight Museum located at Kingsbury, Texas. He is a contributing author to the Spanish American War Centennial and the Flags of the Confederacy websites and is a member of the associated email-ring of Confederate vexillologists. His next literary project is anticipated to be "America's First Machine Gun - The Colt 1895 Automatic." He is also an active living history participant focusing on 1916 US Army Impression (border period).

Made in the USA
Charleston, SC
30 August 2012